CLAIR

The Complete Reference

Mac OS X

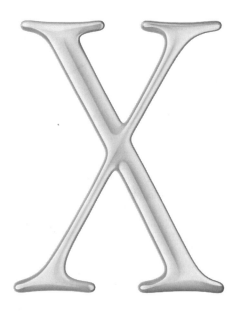

D1264923

Osborne **McGraw-Hill**

New York   Chicago   San Francisco
Lisbon   London   Madrid   Mexico City
Milan   New Delhi   San Juan
Seoul   Singapore   Sydney   Toronto

Jesse Feiler

Osborne/**McGraw-Hill**
2600 Tenth Street
Berkeley, California 94710
U.S.A.

To arrange bulk purchase discounts for sales promotions, premiums, or fund-raisers, please
contact Osborne/**McGraw-Hill** at the above address. For information on translations or book
distributors outside the U.S.A., please see the International Contact Information page
immediately following the index of this book.

Mac OS X: The Complete Reference

34567890 DOC DOC 01987654321

ISBN 0-07-212663-9

Publisher	Brandon A. Nordin
Vice President & Associate Publisher	Scott Rogers
Acquisitions Editor	Jane Brownlow
Project Editor	Jenn Tust
Acquisitions Coordinators	Emma Acker, Alissa Larson, and Cindy Wathen
Technical Editors	Scott Keith and Greg Titus
Copy Editors	Lunaea Weatherstone and Paul Medoff
Proofreaders	Paul and Linda Medoff
Indexer	Jack Lewis
Computer Designers	Carie Abrew, Melinda Moore Lytle, Dick Schwartz
Illustrators	Michael Mueller, Alex Putney, Lyssa Sieben-Wald
Series Design	Mickey Galicia
Cover Series Design	Dodie Shoemaker

This book was composed with Corel VENTURA™ Publisher.

About the Author

Jesse Feiler is Software Director of Philmont Software Mill; he has served as manager, software developer, consultant, author, and speaker for organizations such as Apple Computer, the Federal Reserve Bank of New York, Young & Rubicam, and Prodigy.

Jesse's books include end-user guides, such as *Database-Driven Web Sites* (AP Professional, 1999); *Managing the Web-Based Enterprise* (Morgan Kaufmann, 2000); *FileMaker Pro 4 and the World Wide Web* (FileMaker Press, 1999); *ClarisWorks: The Internet, New Media, and Paperless Documents* (Claris Press, 1997); *Cyberdog: The Complete Guide to Apple's Internet Productivity Technology* (AP Professional, 1996); and two books on the Y2K problem (AP Professional, 1998 and IDG Books, 1999). He also has written a variety of books geared toward developers, including *Mac OS X Developer's Guide* (Morgan Kaufmann, 2001), *Real World Apple Guide* (M&T Books, 1995); and *Perl 5 Programmers Notebook* (Prentice-Hall PTR, 1999).

Contents At A Glance

Contents

Acknowledgments

The sheep in Chapter 16 are Southdowns from Sauerkraut Hill Farm, Claverack, NY; Nancy Brousseau, shepherdess.

Anni is a rescued greyhound; she appears in Chapter 1. For further information, contact Greyhounds as Companions, http://www.albany.net/~greycomp/.

The cat in the iMovie in Chapter 16 is Blanche.

Scott Keith of OpenBase International helped not only in the technical review of the manuscript, but also in providing a variety of quick answers to questions and concerns that suddenly arose in mid-sentence now and then.

Greg Titus of Omni Group also provided invaluable input on the technical side for many chapters in the first version of this manuscript.

At Apple, the Apple Developer Relations group helped get answers to questions and was instrumental in reconciling the author's hieroglyphic notes from the World Wide Developers Conference in 2000 with the reality of Mac OS X as it emerged later in that year.

Perhaps most important of all, Jenn Tust and the production staff at Osborne/McGraw-Hill worked incredibly long and hard hours to make the book as complete as it is. The sheer logistics of producing a book of this size are quite daunting; they are even more so when you add in the complications that arise from incorporating illustrations of a new operating system in which the graphics are optimized for a computer screen and not for paper. Jenn has truly worked wonders. In addition, Lunaea Weatherstone and Paul Medoff provided thorough, helpful, and encouraging copy edits; and Paul and Linda Medoff caught many mistakes while proofreading. Jane Brownlow is a great acquisitions editor to work with.

Notwithstanding the assistance of so many people, any errors that remain are solely the handiwork of the author.

Jesse Feiler

Introduction

This book is complete: my checklists and FileMaker databases have cross-indexed features, preferences, and the applications that ship with Mac OS X, to make certain that everything shows up somewhere in the book. It has been revised against the second update—Mac OS X 10.0.2. We have tried to include screen shots of almost every feature, preference, and application, but sometimes for the sake of space we have omitted one or two. Fear not—the text walks you through anything that might be missing, and the Web site (http://www.philmontmill.com) has even more goodies and updates.

Q&A with Jesse Feiler

There is one thing that is missing from the book, and I've tried to provide it in this introduction. Before moving to the more formal body of the book, here are the questions I'm most often asked about Mac OS X—along with my answers.

How Did You Write This Book?

This book has been several years in the making—as has Mac OS X. Through early prototypes that didn't even run on Macintosh computers, through developer previews, a public beta, and the first releases of Mac OS X, I've watched its evolution and used it for most of my everyday work over the last year and a half. My perspective has constantly shifted from that of a user working with prepackaged applications to that of a software developer working within the new interface to that of an author trying to explain the operating system and its interface to a user—you.

Watching the changes has been a fascinating lesson in software and interface design. Some broad patterns emerge clearly: buttons, for example, have steadily grown smaller over the last year. Certain features have moved around from one set of System Preferences panes to another. In still other cases, such as for Software Update, an application became a preference. Graphical user interfaces of elegance and simplicity appeared on top of Unix and industry-standard features, such as Apache. Menus and their commands came and went; they were reorganized several times, because several very logical combinations of commands made sense at various times during the process.

Being able to observe these changes has made it possible to see more clearly, than in a static environment, how Apple's designers have worked to make the interface as powerful, yet as easy to use, as possible. Want to know why the Delete button is where it is in the Mail window? Well, it wasn't there a year ago, and it had a different name.

How Did You Learn Mac OS X?

I learned it the same way I suggest everyone learn it—by using it. Looking at it just doesn't cut the mustard. You can observe that a certain menu command you've used in Mac OS 9 is renamed or moved—but until you use it for a while, you won't understand why or what the significance of it is.

I was very lucky to be working with Mac OS X during a period of great transition in telecommunications and the Internet. When this book was started, I used a dial-up Internet connection; halfway through the project, I converted to an always-on cable connection. In fact, the conversion was not mine alone: the stalwart gang at Mid-Hudson Cablevision swept through Columbia County leaving always-on broadband Internet access in their wake. Friends and neighbors asked questions—and I learned a lot about networking Windows and older Macintosh computers from helping them out. I also learned that setting up a Mac OS X Internet connection is the easiest of them all, because with Mac OS X you have both an excellent setup assistant and a clear graphical interface to the TCP/IP settings. The frustrating search for where one particular value might be set—that is so common on other operating systems—is minimized on Mac OS X. In part, this is because TCP/IP has been part of the operating system since long before it became the basis for what is now Mac OS X.

What's a Complete Reference

I took the title literally. In my mind, an 800-page book that is a complete reference should include everything—either completely or in the form of a reference to other sources. The size of the book has allowed me to move beyond a road map of the menu bar to provide some background of how and why things are as they are in Mac OS X. This isn't window dressing: understanding the principle behind a variety of interface elements means that you need to remember only one thing (the principle) rather than a variety of seemingly unrelated details.

Mac OS X ships with extensive assistance as you will see in Chapter 9, "Getting Help." Each of the pieces of the assistance puzzle has its own part to play. When you are trying to accomplish something, online help may be just what you need. However, when you don't know what you can do with Mac OS X, a broader perspective (such as that in this book) might help. In a more extreme case, if you do not even have Mac OS X (or a computer) online help is of no use to you whatsoever.

Why Isn't This in an Apple Manual?

As I see it, Apple's job is to provide task-based help to get you up and running quickly. Its online help and variety of Web-based support products let you explore the possibilities. (In this regard, its advertising and publicity also play a key role.)

What a third-party book like this can do is provide suggestions and perspective. For example, in Chapter 19, "Using AppleWorks," I didn't feel the need to do more than skim over the basic word processing features that most people know. However, I did take time to look at some of the features, such as styles and databases, that most people don't explore. As one Apple developer said to me many years ago, I can play favorites among the commands and features.

And I do. You'll quickly see that I'm very intrigued with the possibilities of automating tasks with AppleScript, the command line, and basic programming. Let's get our computers to work and spend our days and nights in more interesting endeavors.

What's the Coolest Feature in Mac OS X?

If you ask me what feature of Mac OS X I think is most important, I always pick the *Build Web Page* feature in Image Capture. Here's how it works. You take a bunch of photos with a digital camera. Plug it into a Macintosh computer and turn it on—Image Capture automatically opens immediately. Select Build Web Page from a pop-up menu and click a button (Download All). The photos are downloaded, the Web page is built, and it opens in your default browser. (If you want to move it to a Web site, you do have to drag a folder to a Web server.)

I can show a neophyte how to do this in moments—plug in the camera, choose Build Web Page from the pop-up menu, click Download All. It's simple and natural—and rather unimpressive to a novice. It's what's expected: photos in a digital camera put onto a Web page. Experienced computer users, however, are confused. Where are the files? How do you edit the HTML? How does it work?

How it works is actually a great glory of Mac OS X: it brings together a host of hardware and software achievements that are part of the operating system and Apple's modern hardware. The plug-and-play feature of Universal Serial Bus (USB) makes it possible to plug in the camera; the computer recognizes it, and Mac OS X knows to launch Image Capture. AppleScript has long been used for extensive prepress automation: here it's used by Apple to build HTML and insert references to your automatically downloaded photos. A lot of effort has gone into making it "just work," and that effort reflects the design and flexibility of Mac OS X.

What's the Easiest Way to Learn Mac OS X?

Use it. I remember in the early days of the Web that when people showed up in public library classes wanting to "learn Internet," they always failed. People who showed up wanting to make a Web page of their kids for the grandparents to see, or people who showed up wanting to learn how to send and receive email learned.

Don't try to learn Mac OS X—try to do your work (or play). Use this book to help you understand the features that are there and the tools you can use, but then go about your business. True, there are some cases (noted in the book) where you should practice the techniques themselves (editing iMovie clips comes to mind), but in most cases, read about the features and capabilities and then just go to work.

You might want to come back periodically to the book. Learning to do your work is all well and good, but there may be shortcuts or new features that you have missed out on. It's amazing how many long-time computer users are less sophisticated than new users: the new users learn today's software, and the old-timers learn how to keep doing what they did back in the days of diskettes and dot-matrix printers.

What's the Biggest Mistake People Make in Learning Mac OS X?

The biggest mistake in learning Mac OS X or in using any application is customizing it too early. Some people sit down and start by playing with preferences and adding settings of dubious provenance (from the Internet or other back alleys). Before long, they've customized the software so that it looks like some other operating system—or, more often, like no other combination of settings that anyone has.

At that point, if the software is hard to use (or if it is unresponsive), you haven't a clue as to what the problem might be. Start by using the software (Mac OS X or an application) as it is. Give it some time: for an operating system, that might mean a day or two. There is logic behind each interface choice, so see if the interface doesn't grow on you. If, after that time, you find that you really need a non-standard customization, go ahead.

Trying out the interface as it ships is akin to successfully learning a foreign language; language teachers call it total immersion. If you attempt to learn a foreign language by painstakingly translating each word and phrase of your native tongue into the other language, you will never succeed. You have to jump in and use the language as best you can to get a feel for it and truly learn it.

Do You Have Tips for Writing Instructions for a Computer Lab or Office?

Be direct, to the point, and use terminology that your users will understand. This does not mean avoiding all technical terms. There is nothing worse than describing "the row of words across the top of your screen such as File, Help, Window, and Edit." That's a menu bar, and people should know that term.

Note, too, that the wishy-washy paraphrase of a menu bar presented here is all too common—and it's wrong. The "row of words" includes at least one icon (the Apple icon), and the order of the menus is different from that described here.

If you are in doubt as to whether a word or concept is generally understood, look in print advertising that your users might read (a daily newspaper, a law journal, or whatever they might encounter). If Apple and other computer vendors use a term without explaining it, you can rest assured that their market research indicates that the readers can understand it.

Use your users' terminology where possible. In a classroom lab, users may be teachers, teachers' aides, or students. Differentiate if necessary; explicitly group together if the distinctions don't matter.

Make sure your instructions work. Another flaw is something like, "When you turn on your computer, you will see a round globe…." Maybe your users won't. Describe what they definitely will see (use screen shots taken with Grab)—and only if it matters. Put an AppleScript script in the Dock if you want to avoid a lot of mousing around with windows and folders.

Test your instructions and try to break them. Users will not always do what you say. Finally, keep your instructions up to date.

What's the Biggest Change You've Seen in Computers?

Although more powerful processors, faster telecommunications, and the public use of the Web and email have had marked effects on computing since the dawn of the computer age, nothing has compared with the changes wrought by widespread availability of large, high-speed, relatively cheap disks and always-on Internet access.

Over time, you will discover the amount of disk space that your computer work (and play) takes up. In my case, it's about 12-15 gigabytes. That includes the operating system, current files, archived files (including projects going back about five years), and everything else that I use. With that amount of storage space, I don't have to archive anything; as a result, a 20-gigabyte drive is sufficient to store everything I need.

As I repeatedly point out in this book, it is essential to back up disks, and I do so regularly with Retrospect in the middle of the night (automatically). What I don't have to do with this amount of disk space is clear off space for a new project by archiving and removing an old one.

An enormous amount of effort has been devoted over the years to such archiving. Just as an always-on Internet connection provides a substantially different user experience than a dial-up one, an always-there disk provides a different experience than a partially archived one.

Depending on what you do with your computer, you may use more or less storage space; if you are working with video, you may use a great deal more, and you may need to offload completed projects (or even parts of incomplete ones).

But overall, the biggest change I've seen in computers is the always-on, always-there aspect of large disks and broadband Internet connections.

What Would You Like to See in Mac OS X That Isn't There Now?

Can't think of a thing. Sure, I can think of many features and capabilities of Mac OS X that aren't in the applications I want them in (although AppleScript is supported in many applications, not enough of them are recordable, for example). But that's not something that's missing from Mac OS X—it's just not adopted as widely as I would like it to be (yet).

The more critical question is what would I like to see in Mac OS X that can't be done. After several decades of working with mainframes, personal computers, and handheld devices, as well as the same amount of time dealing with operating systems and application programs from the likes of Control Data to Burroughs to IBM, Microsoft, Apple, and Adobe, I have a reasonably good sense of how you can modify applications and operating systems to fit new features in. In every case that I've seen or heard of, the question of adding a new feature to Mac OS X isn't so much whether it can be done but rather how best to do it and where to fit it in. Apple is convinced—along with a great many people including myself—that this framework will stand us in good stead for the next few decades.

If You Find a Typo...

Every attempt has been made to make this book as accurate as possible. It has been checked and double-checked and triple-checked, but in any work of this size some mistakes may get through. If you think you've found one, please let me know. Send email to macosxref@philmontmill.com with details of what you've caught. It will be investigated and corrected in future editions.

For general questions and queries, check out the Philmont Software Mill Web site (http://www.philmontmill.com), which has a Mac OS X section for this book as well as other Mac OS X information.

For More Information and Updates

Updates and more information about Mac OS X are on the author's Web site— http://www.philmontmill.com—under the Mac OS X navigation button at the left. Chapter 9, "Getting Help," summarizes a variety of other sources of information.

How This Book Is Organized

There are 5 parts, 26 chapters, and 3 appendixes in this book.

Part I: Welcome to Mac OS X

The chapters in this section provide a brief history of Mac OS X as well as a description of how it works.

Chapter 1: Mac OS X

This is the overall introduction to Mac OS X.

Chapter 2: Aqua

The Aqua interface is the most visible difference between Mac OS X and other operating systems. This chapter shows you how to use it all—the Dock, buttons, sliders, window controls, and the like. If you want a quick guide to how to use Mac OS X, here's where to start.

Chapter 3: How Mac OS X Works

This chapter describes the hardware and software underpinning Mac OS X. It helps you not only to understand how it works but also how to use USB and FireWire peripherals, what the role of OpenGL is, and more.

Part II: Using Mac OS X

Part II details using files, printing, getting help, and otherwise making your computer usable. It covers everything you need to know about your computer as a stand-alone device.

Chapter 4: Working with Files

The Finder is the application that you use to work with files and directories on the desktop; individual applications also work with files. This chapter explains the terminology and provides step-by-step guides to using the standard open, close, and save dialogs.

Chapter 5: Printing

Printing in Mac OS X is much simpler—yet more powerful—than printing in other operating systems. PDF formatting for electronic documents is built in, as are standard tools for managing printer queues and jobs.

Chapter 6: Setting Preferences

System Preferences let you set everything from your keyboard layout to the format of dates and times to network choices. This chapter provides a visual guide to each of the operating system preferences.

Chapter 7: Securing Your Computer

Security in the form of keychains and a variety of login options are described in this chapter, along with commonsense tips for protecting your computer investment.

Chapter 8: Managing Your Computer Environment

This chapter walks you through the processes involved in setting up your computer environment. It describes the Mac OS X disk utility applications along with what you need to know to set up your directory environment using LDAP or NetInfo.

Chapter 9: Getting Help

Here's where you'll find descriptions and examples of everything from online assistance to Apple's discussion boards. You also will see how to get additional support from Apple iServices and other groups.

Chapter 10: iTools: Apple's OS Tools on the Internet

Use iDisk, KidSafe, and HomePage to extend the reach of your computer to the Internet.

Part III: Networking

This part integrates your computer with the rest of the world—both a local area network (LAN) and the Internet. The first two chapters help you set up client computers on a LAN and the Internet; the next two help you set up server computers on a LAN and the Internet. The last chapter shows you how to set up the Apache Web server (included with Mac OS X): it can run in any of the four configurations described in this part of the book.

Chapter 11: Communicating Over a Local Area Network

Here you'll find how to configure your computer to communicate over a network. You'll also see how to connect to shared disks using Apple File Protocol.

Chapter 12: Communicating Over the Internet

This chapter includes the Internet settings you need to access file and mail servers.

Chapter 13: Setting Up a Network Server

Setting up a file server with Mac OS X is simple. This chapter shows you how to do so with both Mac OS X and Mac OS X Server (for larger environments). It includes tips on security and management.

Chapter 14: Setting Up an Internet Server

Chapter 14 provides a review of the issues you need to consider in setting up an Internet server. As you will see, the basic technology is covered primarily in Chapter 13; this chapter addresses the issues that opening your LAN to the world raises.

Chapter 15: Setting Up the Web Server

This chapter shows you how to set up the Web server (Apache) using Mac OS X as well as how to use Mac OS X Server and the Server Admin application.

Part IV: Using Applications on Mac OS X

From specific applications, such as Apple Mail and AppleWorks, to general features, such as Services, to the host of applications that ship with Mac OS X, Part IV helps you actually use your computer for productive work and play.

Chapter 16: Working with Applications

Here you'll find all the information you need about using standard application features. File manipulation is covered here (as well as in Chapter 4). You'll also find information on dialogs and windows, and detailed instructions for using the applications that ship with Mac OS X, including iTunes (for managing your music and MP3 files), iMovies (for creating movies), TextEdit, Chess, and more.

Chapter 17: Working with Services

One of the most forward-looking features of Mac OS X, services, lets you put pieces of programs together in a way that is convenient for you. This chapter covers the technology of services that you manipulate directly as well as of those that work behind the scenes, such as system-wide spell checking.

Chapter 18: Using Apple Mail

The Mail program handles multiple mail protocols (IMAP and POP), multiple mail accounts, scripting, automatic rule-based sorting, attachments, styled text, and more. This chapter shows you how to set up Apple Mail and use it to your best advantage.

Chapter 19: Using AppleWorks

Apple's premier productivity tool, AppleWorks, provides text, graphics, database, spreadsheet, and presentation tools. This chapter reviews the tools and details some of the more useful aspects that may be new to you.

Part V: Programming Mac OS X

Programming on Mac OS X ranges from AppleScript to the Unix command line to sophisticated development environments such as Cocoa. All are described here.

Chapter 20: Automating Your Work with AppleScript

AppleScript was introduced in Mac OS 7. Today, it is an integral part of the environment for all power users of the Macintosh computer. This chapter shows you how it is implemented in Mac OS X and helps you move beyond keystroke automation to powerful workflow management.

Chapter 21: Using the Command Line

The Unix command line is available in Mac OS X, but it's enhanced with Apple's typical interface improvements (such as drag-and-drop for complex file names). This chapter shows you how to use the Terminal application, and it lists some of the more important Unix tools and commands. It also offers step-by-step instructions on how to remove orphaned files on your system using the superuser password, which is normally not available to you.

Chapter 22: Programming Mac OS

This overview shows how programming works on the Macintosh. Whether you intend to start programming yourself or want to know how it happens under the hood, this chapter should answer your questions.

Chapter 23: Classic

This chapter guides you through the basics of programming for Mac OS 9 and earlier. You may need to write such programs, but more likely you will have to understand them well enough to read them so that you can rewrite or convert them to Mac OS X. This chapter's emphasis is on reading this ancient code.

Chapter 24: Carbon

This chapter describes the transitional environment, Carbon, and it shows how it differs from Classic programming.

Chapter 25: Cocoa

Cocoa is the new, totally object-oriented development framework that powers the most advanced Mac OS X applications.

Chapter 26: Creating a Nothing Program with Cocoa

Finally, a step-by-step tutorial walks you through the process of creating two basic programs with Program Builder and Interface Builder. The second program is designed not just to show you how these development tools work, but it's also a template that you can use to build sophisticated graphical user interfaces around legacy C, Fortran, or Basic code.

Appendixes

Appendix A: Installing Mac OS X

Whether you are reinstalling Mac OS X on a newly formatted hard drive or upgrading from a previous installation of Mac OS 9, Appendix A shows you how and explains the choices available.

Appendix B: Glossary of Terms

The Glossary of Terms explains some of the basic terminology that is referred to in the book. As is usually the case, the glossary focuses on material that is not fully described in the book: use the index to find full information of Mac OS X terms.

Appendix C: Visual Glossary

This glossary provides the name and a description of images that you'll find on your display.

About the Figures and Illustrations

Mac OS X is optimized for display on a computer: it takes full advantage not only of color but also animation. Both of these are hard to achieve on a black-and-white printed page. In order to show you as much as possible of Mac OS X, there are a lot of screen shots in this book. The author and the Osborne/McGraw-Hill production department have worked to make the black-and-white reproductions that you see here as clear as possible. Bear in mind the following points:

1. Because of the number of screen shots, figures may appear more than a page after their references. Have no fear: they are there—you just might have to turn an extra page or two.

2. You can customize windows in System Preferences as well as in Finder Preferences and View Options. The customizations shown in this book (such as very large icons in some cases) are set to make black-and-white reproduction on paper as good as possible. For day-to-day use, you will probably set Mac OS X preferences differently. (This is described in the book.)

3. Some of the Mac OS X visual effects (particularly translucency) are almost impossible to reproduce on paper. To see them in their full glory, visit the author's Web site— http://www.philmontmill.com. Click Mac OS X at the left and then Search at the top. Type in **Aqua Images**, and you'll find a list of full-size, full-color images that augment those in this book.

Code Snippets

Some samples of code from Apple's examples for Mac OS X are provided in this book. They are governed by Apple's license agreement, which follows:

"In consideration of your agreement to abide by the following terms, and subject to these terms, Apple grants you a personal, non-exclusive license, under Apple's copyrights in this original Apple software (the 'Apple Software'), to use, reproduce, modify and redistribute the Apple Software, with or without modifications, in source and/or binary forms; provided that if you redistribute the Apple Software in its entirety and without modifications, you must retain this notice and the following text and disclaimers in all such redistributions of the Apple Software. Neither the name, trademarks, service marks or logos of Apple Computer, Inc. may be used to endorse or promote products derived from the Apple Software without specific prior written permission from Apple. Except as expressly stated in this notice, no other rights or licenses, express or implied, are granted by Apple herein, including but not limited to any patent rights that may be infringed by your derivative works or by other works in which the Apple Software may be incorporated.

"The Apple Software is provided by Apple on an 'AS IS' basis. APPLE MAKES NO WARRANTIES, EXPRESS OR IMPLIED, INCLUDING WITHOUT LIMITATION THE IMPLIED WARRANTIES OF NON-INFRINGEMENT, MERCHANTABILITY AND FITNESS FOR A PARTICULAR PURPOSE, REGARDING THE APPLE SOFTWARE OR ITS USE AND OPERATION ALONE OR IN COMBINATION WITH YOUR PRODUCTS.

"IN NO EVENT SHALL APPLE BE LIABLE FOR ANY SPECIAL, INDIRECT, INCIDENTAL OR CONSEQUENTIAL DAMAGES (INCLUDING, BUT NOT LIMITED TO, PROCUREMENT OF SUBSTITUTE GOODS OR SERVICES; LOSS OF USE, DATA, OR PROFITS; OR BUSINESS INTERRUPTION) ARISING IN ANY WAY OUT OF THE USE, REPRODUCTION, MODIFICATION AND/OR DISTRIBUTION OF THE APPLE SOFTWARE, HOWEVER CAUSED AND WHETHER UNDER THEORY OF CONTRACT, TORT (INCLUDING NEGLIGENCE), STRICT LIABILITY OR OTHERWISE, EVEN IF APPLE HAS BEEN ADVISED OF THE POSSIBILITY OF SUCH DAMAGE."

Part I

Welcome to Mac OS X

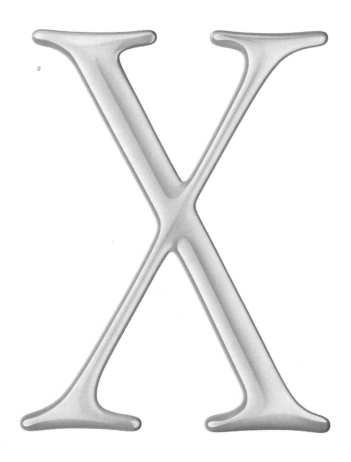

Chapter 1

Introducing Mac OS X

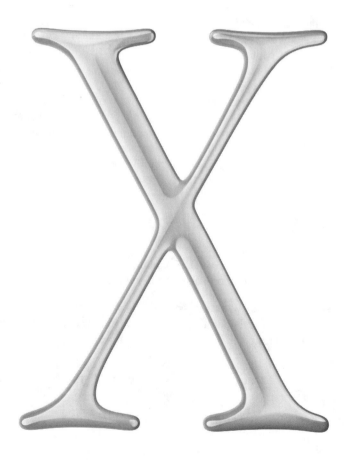

This chapter consists of three parts. In the first, you will see how Mac OS X evolved; in the second, there is a brief introduction to what Mac OS X looks like. In the third part, you will find an overview of what Mac OS X does. The next chapter provides you with an introduction to Aqua, the user interface of Mac OS X. Chapter 3 completes the first part of this book. In it you will find a description of how Mac OS X works—how the concepts described in this chapter are actually implemented.

The evolution of an operating system influences the product you have installed on your computer and the way it works. Operating system technology is almost half a century old now; it has not started from scratch each time a new one has been built. Learning from the successes and failures of other operating systems helps engineers work with hardware and software developers to provide you with the most powerful and useful operating system possible. The extensive roots that Mac OS X has in some of the most important operating systems—Unix, Mach, and Mac OS 9 and earlier—help make it strong, amazingly powerful, and as user friendly as you expect from a Macintosh operating system.

The preview of Mac OS X in action that you will find in the second part of this chapter introduces you to what your computer will look like as you run this new operating system. Many more details are provided in Chapter 2.

Some of the most important features of Mac OS X are discussed in this chapter. They work behind the scenes to improve the power and reliability of your Macintosh. Terms such as "symmetric multiprocessing" and "protected memory" are not marketing fluff or meaningless jargon. They describe aspects of Mac OS X that set it apart from previous operating systems on the Macintosh and on other personal computers and that make your computer and you more productive. This chapter helps you understand these terms and why they are important. Then, for most of the rest of the book, most of them will remain in the background—just as the concepts remain in the background of Mac OS X as you use your computer.

The Evolution of Mac OS X

In 1984, the original Macintosh personal computer had no hard disk drive (few computers did in those ancient days). When you wanted to run a program, you popped in a floppy disk, turned the computer on, and went to work. The floppy disk contained a minimum of three files:

- **System**   This was the basic operating system and was located in the System Folder. It interacted with additional operating system code that was loaded into read-only memory (ROM) each time you turned the computer on.

- **Finder**   This program managed the desktop; it was the software that let you drag folders around, rename them, and move them to the trash. It, too, was located in the System Folder.

- **Application program**   This was MacWrite, MacDraw, or early versions of Word, Excel, and other programs.

In those days, you ran one program at a time. The operating system helped the application program use the printer and optional add-on disk drives, but it did not have to worry about managing multiple programs. This made sense because the computers did not have enough resources to run more than one program at a time.

Resources on the early personal computers were expensive and scarce. For example, floppy disks on the Macintosh in 1984 held about 400 kilobytes (KB) of data. By contrast, the System 9 System file alone is over 13 megabytes (MB) in size and the Finder is over 2 MB. (A megabyte is 1,000 times the size of a kilobyte.) Those two files alone would take up nearly 40 old-style floppy disks. (Because of the change in architecture from System 9 to Mac OS X, a comparison of System 9, rather than Mac OS X, to the original file sizes is appropriate.) Today, in an era of multigigabyte-sized hard disks, concern over the file size of an operating system is much lower on the list of priorities for developers than it was fifteen years ago. Likewise, in an era in which 64 and 128 megabytes of memory are standard on most computers, the concerns about memory resources used by an operating system are less serious than they were in the past.

Original Macintosh Operating System Architecture

As described at the time, there were six components to the original Macintosh environment:

- **Hardware** This was the computer itself and the printer or modem that might have been attached to it.

- **Macintosh Operating System** This ROM-based code managed memory, input/output, and serial communications (such as to a modem or a network).

- **QuickDraw** This set of routines was used to manage graphics.

- **Pascal and Assembler** These were the programming tools available at the time.

- **User Interface Toolbox** These routines managed windows, menus, and other aspects of the interface.

- **Application programs** MacWrite and MacDraw—basic word processing and graphics programs—shipped with the first Macintosh computers. Other early programs were Excel (the spreadsheet) FileMaker, and later HyperCard.

The first two components were implemented in the hardware and memory, QuickDraw and the User Interface Toolbox were implemented in the System file and in memory, and application programs were implemented in their own files.

NOTE *Most of the routines in memory were implemented in ROM—customized chips that were installed in the computer. Some lesser-used functions were stored in the System file and loaded into RAM—standard memory—as needed. Over time, the customized ROM chips were replaced with an operating system that was loaded totally into RAM, but that did not happen until the late 1990s.*

Operating system architecture is frequently illustrated in layered drawings. Figure 1-1 shows the first Macintosh architecture. These drawings should be interpreted from the bottom up; each layer depends on the layers below it. Thus, the QuickDraw imaging routines are used in the User Interface Toolbox to create windows and menus. Windows and menus from the User Interface Toolbox are used in application programs. This is what gives a unified look and feel to Macintosh application programs.

The programming tools and User Interface Toolbox layers are highly interrelated. An argument can be made that those layers should be shown in reverse order—that is, with programming tools above the User Interface Toolbox. Apple's presentation of the Mac OS X architecture uses this layering sequence and for the sake of consistency, it is adopted here.

The original Macintosh architecture, which is implemented in Mac OS 9 and earlier, is referred to as the *Classic Mac OS environment*. Classic appears on Mac OS X so that applications written for Mac OS 9 and earlier can run under Mac OS X.

DOS Architecture

To understand why the Macintosh was so revolutionary in 1984, it is helpful to look at the architecture of DOS—the operating system that was first released in 1981. DOS (and CP/M, another operating system, which was used starting in 1975 on the very first personal computers) has a much simpler architecture, as shown in Figure 1-2.

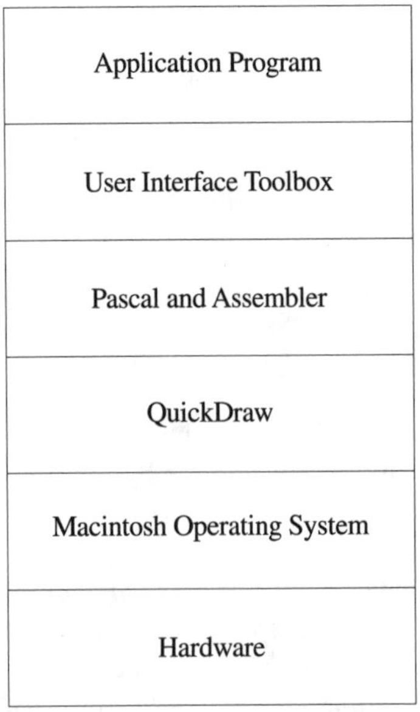

Application Program
User Interface Toolbox
Pascal and Assembler
QuickDraw
Macintosh Operating System
Hardware

FIGURE 1-1   First Macintosh operating system architecture

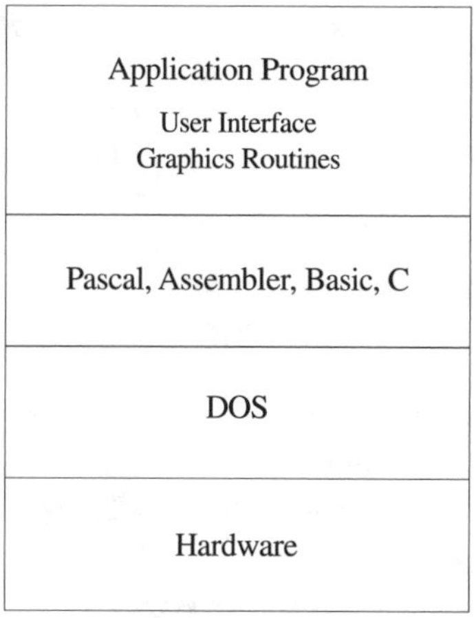

```
┌─────────────────────────────────┐
│      Application Program         │
│                                  │
│        User Interface            │
│       Graphics Routines          │
├─────────────────────────────────┤
│                                  │
│     Pascal, Assembler, Basic, C  │
│                                  │
├─────────────────────────────────┤
│                                  │
│              DOS                 │
│                                  │
├─────────────────────────────────┤
│                                  │
│            Hardware              │
│                                  │
└─────────────────────────────────┘
```

FIGURE 1-2   DOS architecture

In the world of DOS, the user interface and graphics routines are implemented in application programs (if at all). Even functionality provided in DOS itself was often reimplemented in application programs by programmers who wanted to customize or extend it. That is why DOS programs have a much wider range of interface elements and styles than do Macintosh programs. That diversity is what makes it hard to learn to use those programs: no two appear to work the same way. In addition, the cost of reimplementing interface and graphic elements is significant, and to add insult to injury, the quality of those implementations varies.

NOTE   *The tense in the previous paragraph is correct: the present. DOS remains the underpinning for consumer editions of Windows that are still in widespread use, such as Windows 95, Windows 98, and Windows ME.*

Programming languages for DOS include C and Basic. Those languages also were implemented on the Mac OS, but Pascal was a preferred language for the Macintosh at the beginning.

The Operating System Grows More Complex

In the late 1980s, more powerful processors, cheaper memory, and hard disks made it feasible to run more than one program at a time. The operating system needed not just to manage a single program's resources, but it also had to manage those resources among a number of programs that might be running at the same time. Meanwhile, more files began to accumulate in the System Folder: extensions, control panels, disk and printer drivers, and the like. Apple adopted a comprehensive version-control mechanism with System 6. Instead of specifying the individual versions of the Finder, System, and various other files, users (and programmers) could know that

System 6 meant a certain basic set of features would be available. Even so, programmers needed to check whether specific functionality was installed and available for use. A system called Gestalt was provided to let programmers do this.

The System file was enhanced to provide many new features, including the ability to handle very large amounts of memory, large disks, scripting, and color. (The original operating system allowed for color, but its implementation of color support was not appropriate for the advanced monitors that began to appear, and so a more sophisticated color system was implemented.) At the same time, the Finder was also enhanced to provide a more sophisticated desktop experience.

These enhancements kept the Macintosh up to date with new hardware products and new user expectations. They also began to weaken the foundations of the operating system. As people started to run several programs at a time, interactions among those programs were not always felicitous. Routine updates to the operating system were forced to focus not just on new features and compatibility with new hardware, but also on stability and reliability.

Meanwhile, Back on the Mainframe...

When the primitive operating systems for the first personal computers were designed in the late 1970s and early 1980s, operating systems for mainframe computers were already highly developed. Most of the mainframe operating systems were more than a decade old, and their precursors stretched back a quarter of a century to the early 1950s. Many lessons had been learned, and many improvements in operating systems had been made over time.

Unfortunately, it seemed clear that most of those lessons did not apply to personal computers. Perhaps the biggest challenge was the fact that mainframe operating systems required powerful processors. While early personal computers compared quite well with mainframes with regard to memory, their processors were not in the same league with those that powered corporate behemoths. Those powerful processors were able to devote a large amount of their resources to running the operating system; user programs often took up a relatively small amount of the computer's resources.

Over time, processors on personal computers became more powerful, and operating system designers began to cast covetous eyes at the features that were standard on mainframe computers, with their more plentiful resources. Starting in the mid-1970s, a new architecture was evolving. It involved breaking the operating system and application programs into several components each. Processes (or tasks or programs, depending on your terminology) were invoked, not to handle enormous jobs such as a corporate payroll, but to handle many small jobs such as a single employee's vacation schedule. If you looked at the control monitor of a mainframe computer in the 1970s and 1980s, you would see these small programs popping up and then disappearing rapidly. Operating systems, too, started to use this type of architecture. Instead of the operating system itself printing a document in response to a request from an application program, the operating system launched a separate process that did the printing and then went away.

"Task" and "process" are often treated as synonyms. Much of the standard operating system and Unix literature uses process rather than task. People in the field often use the terms interchangeably, but to many people a task is a smaller entity than a process is (a very fuzzy distinction). The issue is trivial except for the rather annoying fact that the mechanism for sharing a processor among several processes/tasks is called multitasking. Multiprocessing refers to the use of several processors in a single computer. Thus, you are perfectly correct to define multitasking as the sharing of a single processor among several tasks (or processes).

This architecture has many advantages over the previous monolithic architecture. Among the advantages are these:

- ■ **Development advantages**   Breaking an application program or operating system into smaller pieces can make development faster and simpler. Each component is easier to design and test. Furthermore, smaller components can frequently be reused from one application to another.

- ■ **Runtime advantages**   A computer's resources can be allocated to individual processes and the entire system can be tuned. Priorities can be associated with each process; for example, printing can proceed in the background at a low priority, while communications processes can run at a high priority to avoid missing messages. Furthermore, processes that are not needed at any given moment do not even need to run.

- ■ **Runtime damage control**   If one of the processes has a problem, that process crashes, leaving the rest of the computer's processes intact (usually).

On the other hand, this architecture poses a number of challenges, such as the following:

- ■ **Process management**   The operating system needs to manage multiple processes and to support prioritization and other management issues.

- ■ **Memory management**   Some way must be devised to move a process's data in and out of the processor's view. In today's operating system architectures, memory is not divided among the multiple processes. All of the memory is available to each process when it is running, and something must handle the mechanics of sharing memory. (Otherwise the memory demands of multiple processes would quickly exceed a computer's capacity.)

- ■ **Interprocess communication**   The architecture must support interprocess communication so the multitude of small processes can communicate with one another.

- ■ **Rewriting old code**   Existing application programs need to be redesigned to take advantage of this type of architecture.

Enter Mach

In 1984 (the same year the first Macintosh was sold), work began on a new operating system project called *Mach*. In 1989, Mach 3.0 was restructured into the architecture that today is at the

The Evolution of Mac OS X

very foundation of Mac OS X: Darwin. Its heart is a *microkernel*—a very basic and primitive underpinning to the operating system. The microkernel is concerned with three issues:

- **Managing multiple processes**   Processes consist of two elements: *processes* (the data, program instructions, and stacks—also known as an *address space*) and *threads* (program counters and memory registers). In a slight oversimplification, you can think of processes as nouns and threads as verbs. (The terminology here may be ambiguous, but fortunately it is only the concept that matters. In fact, what Unix calls a process is a combination of a Mach process and a Mach thread. With this tidbit of information, you may be able to win a bet in a very peculiar barroom.)

- **Implementing virtual memory**   Unique to Mach, *memory objects* are sophisticated ways of doing this.

- **Handling interprocess communication**   This is the ability for one process to send a message to or receive a message from another process. To implement interprocess communication, the Mach microkernel defines *ports* (the origins and destination of messages) and *messages*. Ports are stored inside the microkernel; they are created by the microkernel in response to a request from a given process.

How fortuitous that these three issues are precisely the challenges of the architecture described in the previous section! (The fourth challenge—renovating existing software and developing new application programs—is discussed in "Environments" in Chapter 3, "How It Works.")

The microkernel handles processes, memory management, and interprocess communication. That's all. This makes it extremely robust, since its code is limited just to these activities. This also makes the entire system very reliable, because all other processing is handled in what is called *user space*. The microkernel is allowed to execute very basic machine instructions: it can directly access memory, the processor, and devices in ways that processes running in user space cannot. These basic machine instructions are necessary to implement the microkernel, but they can wreak havoc when used inappropriately. Confining these instructions to the microkernel makes the entire system very sturdy.

> NOTE   *The routines in the original Macintosh Operating System—the routines that manage memory, input/output, and serial communications—can be accessed by application programs. In the more structured environment of kernel and user space, such routines cannot be accessed directly by programs running in user space. Typically, both on the original Macintosh and on DOS, programs that need very high performance (such as games) manipulate the hardware directly with these routines.*

Add Unix to Make Darwin

In fact, in the Mach architecture, Unix can run in user space—and it does. Darwin—the kernel at the heart of Mac OS X—is based on the Mach 3.0 microkernel and a version of Unix called FreeBSD 3.2 (derived from the University of California at Berkeley's BSD 4.4-Lite).

Unix is an operating system that was originally developed by Bell Labs starting in 1970. Its origins were on minicomputers with resources as constrained as those of the early personal computers. Everything about Unix is as small as possible: even commands and filenames are as short as they can be. Since these computers were so limited in terms of resources, Unix was designed with the philosophy of keeping each component of the system as small and simple as possible. Unix included techniques for combining programs with scripts; thus, very complicated tasks could be performed using the simple building blocks of the operating system.

With the advent of more powerful computers, it turned out that this characteristic of Unix was still more valuable. In fact, as the complexity of operations increased, having an operating system that easily allowed small processes to communicate and cooperate was instrumental in developing very robust systems. By the 1990s, many of the mission-critical systems in large corporations (particularly in the financial services sector) were powered by Unix.

Unix Architecture

This architecture is shown in Figure 1-3. Unix consists of three layers that are built upon one another:

- First, there is the *hardware* of the computer.

- Next, there is a *kernel* that performs the basic operations.

- On top of the kernel is a *shell*—a command-line interpreter. This is a simple program that accepts input from a user and converts it to the appropriate commands to be sent to the kernel or to programs.

User programs (or *tools* in Unix parlance) are launched in response to a user's command typed into the shell. The tools interact with the kernel (and through it, with the hardware). Tools can communicate with one another, with the user, with files, and with the shell.

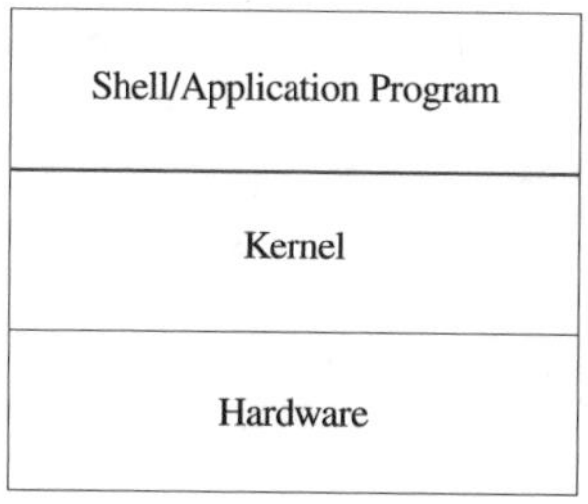

The Evolution of Mac OS X

```
+-----------------------------+
|  Shell/Application Program  |
+-----------------------------+
|           Kernel            |
+-----------------------------+
|          Hardware           |
+-----------------------------+
```

FIGURE 1-3   Unix architecture

Unix has clearly defined interface standards. You can use any of a variety of shell programs in many Unix environments. In fact, one of the criticisms of Unix has been the ease with which new shells and tools can be created. At one point in the 1980s, this threatened the very future of Unix because there were so many divergent software projects that some managers despaired of making sense of them.

You will notice that this architecture is very simple. That is one of the great strengths of Unix. You will also notice the absence of graphics routines and user interface. That, too, is part of the Unix user experience.

The Unix User Experience

In Unix, you can write a command such as:

```
$ lp -d PSMLaser chapter1
```

This command prints a file called chapter1 to a destination printer (-d) called PSMLaser. If you are used to the Macintosh, you will understand why "Unix" was a dirty word in the Mac community for many years. What could be farther from dragging an icon labeled "chapter1" to the printer icon labeled "PSMLaser"? The dreaded command-line interface that the Mac OS rebelled against in 1984 was the common interface for Unix and for primitive operating systems such as DOS.

Improving the Unix User Experience

Putting an intuitive graphical interface onto Unix was a challenge attempted by many people over the years. Unfortunately, that was easier said than done. The challenge of improving the Unix user experience was not fully met until Mac OS X.

> NOTE   *The predecessors of Mac OS X—NeXTSTEP and OpenStep—made significant strides in improving the UNIX user interface. This process culminated in Mac OS X.*

Only when Apple was able to combine all of the pieces into one project—Mac OS X—could the inner workings of the operating system (Darwin) be truly integrated with an intuitive user interface, and for those die-hard command-line folk, Mac OS X allows access to the shell via command-line entries.

It is important to point out that many Unix devotees think there is nothing wrong with the Unix user experience. There still are people who would rather type than manipulate a mouse, and there are people who believe that $ lp -d PSMLaser is more intuitive than dragging a document icon onto a printer icon.

Mac OS X Architecture

Mac OS X architecture is diagrammed in Figure 1-4.

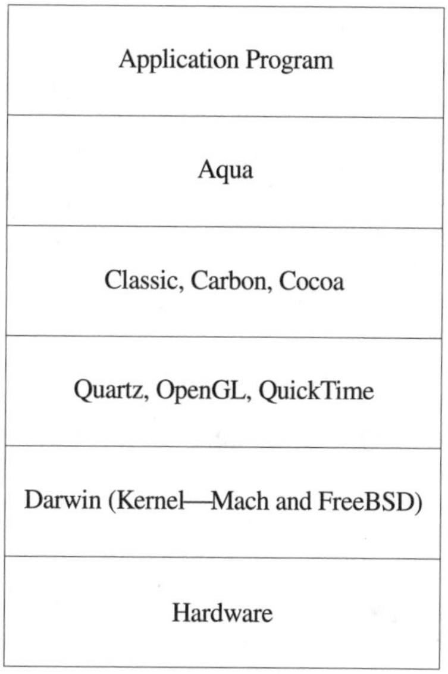

Application Program
Aqua
Classic, Carbon, Cocoa
Quartz, OpenGL, QuickTime
Darwin (Kernel—Mach and FreeBSD)
Hardware

FIGURE 1-4   Mac OS X architecture

The architecture is comparable to that of the original Mac OS (shown previously in Figure 1-1). Note the differences:

- Instead of the original Macintosh operating system (partly implemented in ROM and partly in the System file), there is now Darwin, the kernel built on Mach 3.0 and FreeBSD 3.2. This reflects the influence of modern operating system design, including many aspects of Unix.

- Instead of QuickDraw, there now are three technologies: Quartz (based on Adobe's Portable Document Format—PDF), OpenGL (an industry standard for 3-D graphics), and QuickTime (Apple's technology for multimedia). This change accommodates the increased needs of today's users. By implementing 3-D graphics and multimedia in the operating system, individual application programs do not have to provide their own implementations Together, these make up the Display layer of the Mac OS X architecture.

- The programming tools now consist of the Classic tools (primarily Pascal, C, and C++), along with Carbon (the same languages) and Cocoa (implementing Java and Objective-C). These tools are discussed in Chapter 3, "How It Works."

■ Aqua is the new User Interface Toolbox. It provides not just a visual makeover, but also substantially greater functionality than the old User Interface Toolbox. Remember that each layer in the architecture can build on the functionality implemented by lower layers. That means Aqua can take advantage of multimedia and 3-D graphics in its interface.

This, then, is the architecture of Mac OS X. It consists of the layers discussed here implemented in an environment of multiple processes (this will be described in more detail later). What does it look like in nonconceptual terms? The final section provides an answer.

Mac OS X in Action

Figure 1-5 shows Mac OS X in action. It shows how you can run Classic applications written for Mac OS 9 and earlier alongside Mac OS X applications and how you can share data.

FIGURE 1-5   Mac OS X in action

In the upper left, you see a Finder window. It lists a series of JPEG graphics files. Their unimaginative names were generated automatically by a digital camera; plugged into a Macintosh computer, its images are automatically transferred using the Image Capture application that is part of Mac OS X.

The display of files in the Finder window is different from that in the Finder of Mac OS X and earlier. You can use the other displays, but you now have a powerful display of files in *column view*, as well as the traditional icon view and list view. Note, too, that when a file is selected, a preview is often displayed, along with information about the file's size, creation date, and modification date.

In the upper right, the selected file has been opened in Preview, an application that is part of Mac OS X that lets you preview images.

There is a new look to windows in Mac OS X. Note the rounded corners at the top, as well as the round buttons in the upper left of the window. Scrollbars, too, are rounded.

In the lower right, the same file has been inserted into a FrameMaker document. This version of FrameMaker is a Classic Mac OS application—that is, one written for Mac OS 9 or earlier and not rewritten for Mac OS X. You do not have to worry, the Classic Mac OS environment starts up automatically in Mac OS X to let you run these programs. As demonstrated here, you can share files and cut and copy between applications of all sorts.

Finally, in the lower left, the ProcessViewer application is shown. It lists the various processes running on this computer. Some have been selected in this window. The Dock is the row of icons at the bottom of the screen: it is a process. The Finder itself is another process. Grab is a screen capture utility (also part of Mac OS X) that was used to create this screenshot. Preview and ProcessViewer have been described here. TruBlueEnvironment is the Classic Mac OS environment—the application program that runs Mac OS 9, in which Classic applications such as this version of FrameMaker run.

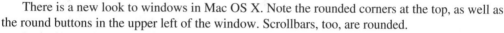

The microkernel provides an architecture that makes it possible to run many processes at the same time. This is daunting: 46 different processes running on the computer. There are even more processes than have been described here. All run together in an environment that is remarkably stable and productive.

What OS X Does

There is yet another way of looking at operating systems. You have seen the architectural layers, the concept of multiple processes, and a few other elements of Mac OS X. This section looks at Mac OS X in terms of what it does.

As operating systems have become more complex, talking about them has necessarily become a little more complicated. By looking at an operating system from these different points of view, you can gain a better understanding of it. On personal computers, operating systems have three primary functions today:

- ■ They provide *process control*.

- ■ They implement *user management tools and features*.

- ■ They furnish *application program support*.

Mac OS X in Action

Process Control

As you have seen, processes are the application programs—and parts of application programs—that run on your computer. Thanks to the Mac OS X microkernel, processes can communicate with one another via interprocess communication, and they can access memory as needed with virtual memory.

Much of the process control in Mac OS X is built into the Mach 3.0 microkernel that is at its heart. There are a number of critical features implemented in the microkernel and elsewhere in Mac OS X that help provide process control. As noted previously, process control is necessary for the computer to run efficiently and reliably. You normally do not interact directly with process control features of the operating system. Still, these are important aspects of Mac OS X, and they are features you will hear and read about. For most people, despite these features' importance to Mac OS X, there is no need to explore these topics in greater depth than that provided here.

There are six features for process control:

■ Mach 3.0 kernel and Darwin

■ Preemptive multitasking

■ Virtual memory

■ Protected memory

■ Symmetric multiprocessing

■ BSD networking stack

Some of these features have been implemented in recent versions of the Mac OS; some of them also have been implemented to one extent or another in other operating systems. The combination of them is unique to Mac OS X.

Mach 3.0 Kernel and Darwin

The kernel of Mac OS X—Darwin—is built on Mach 3.0 and FreeBSD 3.2. It is an open source project, which means that the source code can be seen and studied. This is critically important in the development of the still-young world of computer software development. Many companies keep their software source code proprietary. (Source code is the code that programmers write; special programs called *compilers* then generate low-level computer instructions from it.)

When software source code is proprietary, it is hard to learn from others. That's the point: vendors do not want others to profit from their own research and development. However, for the good of the industry—and computer users—it is important for students and developers to be able to study and compare different approaches to similar problems. In many ways, open source leads to the type of research and study that comparative linguistics students have conducted for years. It also allows interested third parties to extend the software and to build components that interact with it in new and innovative ways.

Preemptive Multitasking

Although a number of processes can run at the same time on a computer, only one can use the processor at any given moment. Multitasking is the mechanism by which the processor is shared among a variety of processes (or tasks—these terms are used synonymously, as previously mentioned).

Multitasking is one of the operating system functions that require significant computing resources to implement. If your computer is struggling to recompute a simple spreadsheet, it doesn't have the power to share its resources among that spreadsheet, a word processor, and a database. Multitasking also requires significant memory and disk resources, since inactive processes must be parked somewhere while other processes are serviced. This is why multitasking did not appear on the first personal computers, although it was commonly available on mainframes in the late 1960s. On mainframes, multitasking was often called time sharing or time slicing.

There are two types of multitasking: cooperative and preemptive. Cooperative multitasking relies on each process being a good citizen and periodically giving up control of the processor. In preemptive multitasking—the type implemented in Mac OS X—the operating system suspends each task when it (the operating system) deems it appropriate. In cooperative multitasking, the process can put itself into a neutral condition so it can continue to work when it is reawakened. In preemptive multitasking, the operating system must be able to store and restore the entire process environment quickly. Preemptive multitasking is harder to implement in the operating system; however, its advantage over cooperative multitasking is that it does not require the individual processes to be well behaved.

> **NOTE**   *On the original Mac OS, a program could gain control of the main event loop—the events generated by the keyboard, mouse, and other devices. If it did not release the event loop periodically, no other program—or the operating system—could process such events. You can see this type of behavior in modal dialog boxes that (if not dismissed with an OK or Cancel button) remain on the screen, preventing background activities from happening. This behavior is common, not only to the original Mac OS, but also to many other operating systems.*

Multitasking is not to be confused with multithreading. Multithreading refers to the use of a single program's code by several threads of the same process at more or less the same time. There is more on multithreading in the "Multiprocessing" section later in this chapter.

Virtual Memory

In order to implement preemptive multitasking, significant memory resources need to be available to park the inactive processes. For this reason (and for many others), virtual memory exists in Mac OS X. Virtual memory is the mechanism by which disk space is used to augment the computer's memory temporarily. Using the Mach memory object architecture, Mac OS X very efficiently blends disk and memory storage.

Originally, virtual memory (which debuted in System 7) was viewed simply as a way to turn a computer with 12 MB of memory into one that apparently had 24 MB of memory. It was considered slow, and in many cases it was. Many users felt that if they could afford to buy real memory, virtual memory was better turned off. (The slowness reflects the fact that it is much faster to access data in memory than data on disk.)

Virtual memory has been improved in the years since System 7. Its reimplementation in Mac OS X is its best yet. In fact, Virtual Memory is no longer an option: it is always on, and it does not degrade performance. If you wonder how that is possible, consider that while it does take a certain amount of processor time to move data between disk and memory, the throughput of the computer is enhanced through the use of virtual memory with preemptive multitasking, and that makes up for the cost of implementing virtual memory.

Protected Memory

With larger and larger amounts of memory available—both real and virtual—it has become increasingly necessary to keep each process's memory locations separate from those of other processes. In the old days, when only one application program ran at a time, all of the computer's memory other than that used for the operating system was available to that program. Later, memory was shared among several programs. There were cases in which one program accidentally wiped out another's data; commonly, this led to crashes of the operating system and all application programs running at the time. Furthermore, because these crashes were due to particular combinations of programs running together, they were hard to diagnose because that particular combination of programs (and of particular commands within programs) might not be readily reproduced by accident or even with careful analysis.

Mac OS 9 implemented guard pages, a limited form of protection for memory. Guard pages are barriers in memory between different processes' data. This is yet another feature that is made possible with more resources. When you have a lot of memory, you can erect these barriers, which themselves use up memory. The situation is akin to that of two people sharing a pantry closet. The boundary between their two sides cannot be delineated by a brick wall; not much of the closet would be left, but two people sharing a vegetable garden might well be able to afford the space to erect a brick wall.

NOTE   *The implementation of virtual memory and protected memory on Mac OS 9 involves application programs cooperating with the operating system. On Mac OS X, the implementation is automatic, and programs need have no special coding to use virtual and protected memory. In fact, part of the conversion process for programs is to remove memory management that they implemented for Mac OS 9 and earlier.*

Multiprocessing

Computers with more than one processor are now on the market. Apple was the first major computer manufacturer to ship multiprocessor desktop models for the consumer market; it started in the summer of 2000. Using multiple processors efficiently is a challenge. There are two general approaches:

- **Parallel processing**   In this scenario, both the operating system and the application program need to be aware of the multiple processors. The work to be done is broken up by the application program and distributed among the processors. Sometimes this is done by the compiler—the program that converts the programmer's codes into machine instructions. Parallel processing is often implemented on supercomputers for specialized tasks such as weather prediction and scientific research. It is implemented to a certain degree in advanced database systems. Parallel processing can successfully be implemented with large numbers of processors.

- **Symmetric multiprocessing**   In this case, the application program and compiler are essentially unaware of the multiprocessing environment: it is managed completely by the operating system. For symmetric multiprocessing to function efficiently, each process—on whatever processor it happens to be—must be able to access all system resources (including memory) at any time. Symmetric multiprocessing normally is implemented with fewer processors than parallel processing: two to eight is the usual number. Symmetric multiprocessing is the type of multiprocessing implemented on Apple Macintosh computers.

Multithreading is the capability of a process to do more than one operation or set of operations at a time. The operation or set of operations is called a thread. Programmers need to do some work to make their programs multithreaded, but that work can pay off when they run on a multiprocessor system. For example, a Web browser may create a number of threads to draw a single page image. Each thread may draw a different portion of the page. How the browser divides the work is its choice—it may be by media type, or it may be by location on the page. When the browser runs on a single processor system, each thread will be serviced in turn (this is multitasking). The page will ultimately be rendered, and—with a sufficiently fast processor and a sophisticated operating system such as Mac OS X—the overhead for the multitasking will not make the operation much longer than it would otherwise be. The fact that different portions of the page are being drawn more or less simultaneously may present a user experience that appears faster than a single-thread top-down rendering of the page. If this same threaded Web browser runs on a multiprocessor computer, Mac OS X can put each thread onto a separate processor, and the rendering of the page will be substantially faster because the threads automatically take advantage of preemptive multiprocessing, in addition to multitasking.

NOTE   *Symmetric multiprocessing is part of Mac OS X; it only comes into play if your computer has more than one processor. However, if it does have more than one processor, it is invoked automatically: you need do nothing, and you do not need special application programs.*

BSD Networking Stack

TCP/IP is the basis for all Internet communications today. It is the protocol that is used to transmit email, Web pages, files, and other communications over the Internet—whether via telephone or cable lines or using wireless technologies (such as AirPort). The networking stack runs in Darwin to manage TCP/IP as needed for any purpose.

Also built into Darwin is support for dial-up connections (using Point-to-Point Protocol—PPP) and the AppleTalk networking protocol that dates back to the original Macintosh in 1984. The point of having these technologies built into the operating system is that they are guaranteed to be available to all applications, and they can run in the most efficient way possible.

> NOTE
>
> *If you have used Macintosh computers (or others) for a while, you may have become used to installing applications such as FreePPP, MacPPP, or PPP in order to be able to dial into the Internet. You no longer need these separate helper applications. It is all in Mac OS X.*

User Management Tools and Features

User management tools and features encompass elements that let you manage your computer environment and the application programs you run there. They include the user interface used throughout the operating system (Aqua), the Finder, the Dock, and Advanced Device Support.

Aqua

Aqua is the new user interface in Mac OS X. It comprises all of the interface elements—buttons, scrollbars, windows, and the like—that you use to achieve your purposes in using the computer. It is described fully in Chapter 2, "Aqua."

Finder

The Finder lets you manipulate files—both application and data files. You can create and rename them from the Finder; you can view them; you can rearrange them in hierarchies within folders (which you also create in the Finder); and you can open them. You use the Finder to access files not only on your own computer but also on file servers on your network or on remote servers on the Internet.

The Finder has been part of the Macintosh operating system from the beginning. The behavior of the Finder has changed in response to the increased complexity of gigabyte-sized disks with scores of thousands of files on them. Its interface is more structured than before, but that allows the efficient management of these vast amounts of data. It is remarkably customizable and powerful.

The Finder is discussed more fully in Chapter 4, "Working with Files."

The Dock

Located at the bottom of the screen, the Dock contains icons for running applications and for open documents. It also contains icons you can drag there for any reason you choose. Its behavior is dynamic—the icons change size to accommodate the width of the screen, and they automatically enlarge themselves as you pass the mouse over them. Clicking an icon displays or opens applications and documents. Furthermore, relevant menu commands for each icon appear as you click the mouse over them.

The Dock is one of the most noticeable new features in Mac OS X. Like the Finder, it can respond to a variety of user preferences (you do not even need to use or see it if you do not want to). You will see how to use the Dock in Chapter 4, "Aqua."

Advanced Device Support

Advanced Device Support is a collection of technologies that support not just plug-and-play capabilities for devices using technologies such as FireWire and USB, but also very fast data transfer rates that allow a high degree of concurrency. This concurrency relies on the multitasking, multithreading, and multiprocessing capabilities described in the previous section; it also relies on the kernel-based architecture of Mac OS X.

Application Program Support

Finally, Mac OS X provides technologies to support application programs. These technologies are also used to support the user management tools. Thus, application programs and user management tools have similar interface and behavioral characteristics.

The Mac OS X features for application program support consist of four technologies involved in presenting information: Quartz, Portable Document Format (PDF), OpenGL, and QuickTime. Other technologies provide additional application program support. Many of them are not new in Mac OS X, but even those that are new are likely not to be visible to you.

Quartz

Quartz replaces the QuickDraw routines of the original Macintosh. When QuickDraw was developed, the big news was color. In fact, although QuickDraw supported color from the start, it was reimplemented in QuickDraw when color monitors came into widespread use.

Today, color is old hat on computer monitors and on many printers. Three-dimensional graphics and multimedia are in the forefront. Aqua relies on Quartz and its related technologies to implement these (including the translucent effects of the sheets for saving and printing documents).

Quartz itself is a two-dimensional graphics system; it relies heavily on PostScript and PDF. Perhaps its most significant step beyond previous two-dimensional graphics systems is its ability to make objects translucent. Technically speaking, an alpha channel is added to each color description; it defines the degree to which images behind the color can be seen through it.

Translucency and transparency are sometimes confused. Transparency is the ultimate step of translucency: you see right through something (opacity is the opposite of transparency). Translucency is the middle ground that you see in the translucent cases of many Macintosh computers, as well as in natural effects such as fog and manmade effects such as sheer curtains.

PDF

Three-dimensional graphics and multimedia share a common characteristic: they are hard to represent on paper. In fact, computer graphics have typically been hard to reproduce on paper and to move from one computer to another. Missing fonts are a nuisance to people who share documents; they are a serious business problem to font manufacturers, since the solution to the missing font problem frequently is the illegal copying and distribution of copyrighted fonts.

Portable Document Format (PDF) is a standard developed by Adobe that addresses these and other issues. It is tightly integrated into Mac OS X and is used as a basic file type so all applications can save documents to PDF. In turn, they can be shared with other users without concern about fonts, colors, and other appearance problems.

You may have used Adobe Distiller or other products to create PDF files in the past. With Mac OS X, any file that you can print can be saved as a PDF file using the standard Print dialog.

OpenGL

Introduced in 1992, OpenGL is an industry-standard graphics architecture. Among its key features are its reliability, portability, and scalability—features that allow Mac OS X to work well with other operating systems as well as to provide mind-boggling 3-D effects to its own application programs and interface.

QuickTime

Finally, QuickTime, one of Apple's most successful software innovations, is used for multimedia. QuickTime's strong cross-platform architecture and reliable implementation have made it a compelling industry standard. It supports a vast number of formats, including JPEG, GIF, TIFF, MP3, Flash, AVI and WAV files, text tracks, and others. Its architecture is highly modularized and its footprint is small—just the sort of software that integrates well with the highly structured architecture of Mac OS X.

Summary

Operating systems run computers. They manage the processes, implement user management tools, and support application programs. In 1984, the original Macintosh operating system was revolutionary. To users, it provided a graphical user interface and a way around text-based (and often gibberish-based) commands. To developers, it offered an integrated User Interface Toolbox and sophisticated graphics support. Now, in Mac OS X, Apple has provided an even more sophisticated user interface—Aqua—and more powerful support both for computer operations and for application programs.

This chapter introduced the basic architecture of Mac OS X: a layered approach that addresses hardware; a powerful kernel based on the Mach microkernel and FreeBSD; graphics support with Quartz, OpenGL, and QuickTime; a development environment of Classic, Carbon, and Cocoa; the Aqua user interface; and new, modern application programs and user management tools that can run alongside older Macintosh programs.

Many of the most important aspects of Mac OS X, such as preemptive multitasking and protected memory, are part of its process control. You see their results, but you do not interact with them directly. You do interact with the user interface, however. The next chapter focuses solely on Aqua. The final chapter in this part of the book addresses the part of Mac OS X that may or may not be visible to you: the environments in which application programs run.

Chapter 2

Aqua

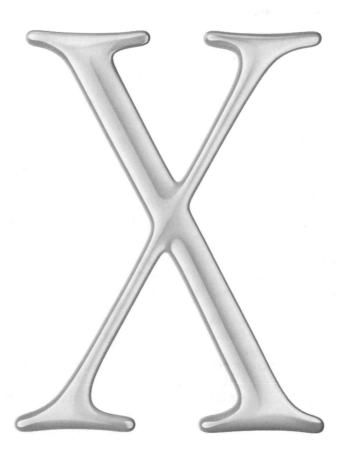

This chapter examines the new look of Mac OS X. It's called Aqua—the new way of using your computer that is the most visible aspect of Mac OS X. You'll find the basic information about how to use the interface, including how to handle features you may be familiar with, such as windows and menus, as well as new features such as the Dock, drawers, and sheets. The traditional Macintosh Finder and desktop are here, too; their appearance is changed in their use of Aqua, and their functions are streamlined and simplified (yet made more powerful).

Some of the features of Aqua are little tweaks that improve decades-old aspects of the graphical user interface, while others are revolutionary. Others reflect the changes in the inner workings of the operating system that are discussed in the next chapter, "How It Works."

The new way of using your computer is not hard to learn. In fact, if you are familiar with Mac OS 9 or earlier, you can use most of what you already know. If you have used another graphical user interface such as Windows, you also know much of what you will need to know. In both cases, you will find that you can forget some of the awkward tricks you may have needed in the past. In any event, you will find using your computer easier and more pleasant than ever before.

In this chapter, you'll find sections covering

- **The Aqua Story** How we got here and why

- **Windows and Controls** Everything from scrolling and resizing windows to push buttons, checkboxes, and all the other controls you find within them

- **Sheets** The replacement for dialogs in Mac OS X

- **The Dock** The new center for applications and documents that you are using or want to return to quickly

- **Menus** The menus and commands that are available in all Aqua applications, as well as in the Finder

- **Using Aqua** Tips on running a computer that behaves just a little differently from computers you have used before

- **Using the Classic Compatibility Environment** Running Mac OS 9 and earlier applications on Mac OS X. (Chapter 3, "How Mac OS X Works," describes how this legerdemain happens; this chapter shows you what it looks like.)

If you are just starting to use Mac OS X, reading this chapter will help you understand the features of the interface. This chapter starts with the operating system fully installed and with at least one user created (which happens during installation). If you want to experiment with Mac OS X, and you do not have Mac OS X installed on your computer (which is the case if you have an older Macintosh computer that did not ship with Mac OS X preinstalled), you will need to install Mac OS X. Appendix A, "Installing Mac OS," provides information on this subject.

This chapter describes your interactions with the graphical user interface using the keyboard and the mouse. Using the mouse involves a few very basic processes:

- **Pointer**   You move the mouse on your desktop or table; on the screen, a pointer moves in response to your moving of the mouse. On a laptop, you use a trackpad to move the pointer.

- **Dragging**   Position the pointer over the object you want to move; press and hold the mouse button down; then move the mouse until it is over the location where you want to position the moved object; then release the mouse button. If you get to the edge of the table on which you are moving the mouse, keep the mouse button down, pick up the mouse (still holding the button down), and reposition it to a spot where there is more room to continue moving. The pointer on the screen only moves when the mouse is in contact with a surface.

- **Clicking**   Position the pointer over the object you want to click, the press the mouse button, and release it. Clicking is used to refer to the objects on the display; pressing is used to refer to the mouse itself.

The Aqua Story

You do not see the sturdy and flexible design of the software in Mac OS X, but you do see the interface, Aqua. In fact, for many people, the look of a computer and its operating system is all they have to go on when they are evaluating hardware and software. The Aqua interface has been years in the making. This section examines the importance of design, the principles behind Aqua, and why Aqua has emerged now.

The Importance of Design

Every aspect of Apple's hardware and software reflects good design and the attention to detail for which Apple is famous. Aqua is no exception. Good design is not something superficial that is added on at the last minute. Good design reflects not only usability but also appearance—shape, color, and texture. It reflects the owner's personality, as well as pride of ownership. Good design matters as much (if not more) for everyday tools and objects as it does for the playthings of the rich. If you have banged your elbow on the taps of a poorly designed bathtub, you know this painfully well. Contrast such an ordeal to luxuriating in a well-designed tub, one with a pleasing shape and color, with a carefully crafted nook for your martini, and a cleverly engineered cranny for its toothpick and olives.

Whenever you pay attention to the tools you are using rather than the work (or play) you are doing, some aspect of the tool's design is faulty. You may know firsthand that if you watch the golf club you miss the ball and if you watch the hammer you will hit your finger rather than the nail. Apple's designers and engineers know as well as anyone that no one really wants to use an operating system (or even a program). People want to write letters or email, they want to make photo albums of their children or pets, and they want to create and edit videos for training or promotional purposes.

The Aqua Design Principles

Aqua did not just pop out of a box as a marketing ploy. It evolved from Apple's direct experience with Mac OS 9 and earlier, as well as from careful study and analysis of other operating systems and interfaces to various technologies. In one form or another, these design principles have been published by Apple since the first Macintosh in 1984. They have formed the basis for the interfaces of Macintosh operating systems and application programs. Indeed, developers have routinely been encouraged in the strongest terms possible to abide by these guidelines. The fact that they were published allowed reviewers of software products to criticize those products that reinvented the interface wheel (almost always for the worse).

The guidelines have served as the basis for many computer interfaces, not just those on the Macintosh. They are generally accepted as the basic goals of interface design. Of course, many of these principles and guidelines are scarcely new with Apple and the Macintosh. Renaissance artists would be perfectly at home with the notions of consistency and aesthetic integrity, among others of the principles.

The guidelines and principles are not a rigid framework; in some cases, they are inconsistent. Arguments can and do take place over their application to special cases, and the fact that such arguments take place indicates the seriousness with which designers and developers consider the entire interface and user experience. Application and operating system designers use them to create the best-designed interface they can.

Each of the basic dozen design principles is presented in this section. The following parts of this chapter show you how they have been transformed into the tools you use in Mac OS X.

If you want, you can purchase the book, *Inside Macintosh: Human Interface Guidelines*, published by Addison-Wesley in 1995. It is also available online at http://www.apple.com/. Specifically for Aqua, *Inside Mac OS X: Aqua Human Interface Guidelines* is also available online. This section is based on those sources.

Metaphors

The graphical user interface uses objects and images to convey information and to allow users to interact with their computers. The computer display itself is either a flat screen or a cathode ray tube, as blank a canvas as one could hope for. The designer can put words or images anywhere on that canvas.

The first design principle suggests that elements of the real world that the user already knows be used on the screen. The trash can, for example, is a metaphor for throwing things away or disposing of them. All of the basic elements of the original Macintosh interface were metaphors: a desktop, file folders, and documents.

As in literature, metaphors are not the objects themselves, they suggest objects and activities. For designers, choosing the right metaphors is one of the hardest parts of interface design. The metaphors must be familiar to users, and they must be appropriately suggestive.

Modelessness

One of the most maddening aspects of computers can be the presence of *modes*, situations in which commands are unavailable to the user for reasons that are obvious to the software designer, but not necessarily to the user. Some people have compared modes to the sense of being trapped on a freeway as you zoom past your destination with no off-ramp in site.

Apple suggests that if designers do use modes, they use them sparingly and in such a way that users can get out of them easily. A common case of modality in interface design has been Save dialogs that prompt you to save a document before closing it. Typically, these dialogs freeze the application, in some cases the entire machine, until you have clicked OK or Cancel. This freezing is a mode. In Mac OS X, sheets freeze only an individual window for a Save dialog. (Sheets are discussed later in this chapter.)

User Control

Perhaps because the first computers were designed for clerks to operate, the tendency has been for software designers to dictate to users what they should do. User-centered computers place the user in control. The software designer presents an array of tools and features for the user to use—when, how, and if the user chooses.

If you want to do something, it is the software developer's job to make that possible. You should not have to ask how you should do this task—you should do it the way you want to, and the developer should have facilitated that.

Direct Manipulation

You use the mouse to drag around items on the desktop and in windows. If you want to bring the left margin of a page in a little bit, you can drag the margin (or an icon in a ruler) to the place where the page looks right to you. This is contrasted with indirect manipulation in which you type something such as

```
move left margin +2
```

See-and-Point

Two versions of see-and-point exist. In the first, you select something (usually with the mouse), and then you choose a command (usually from a menu) to act on that object. For example, you select a word, and choose Italics from the menu. Or you may select an email message in the Mail application and click the Delete button in the toolbar. The sequence is always the same: select; then do.

The second version involves dragging one object onto another. For example, you can drag a document from one folder to another, or you can drag an email message from one mailbox to another in the Mail application.

Both versions can be provided for the same operation. In the Mail application, for example, you can drag a message from one mailbox to another. You also can select a message and then choose the mailbox to transfer it to from the Transfer submenu.

Consistency

Similar interface elements should have similar functions. Consistency makes it easier for you to use new programs, as they all work similarly. Perhaps the best reference on this subject is Donald A. Norman's book *The Design of Everyday Things*, published by Currency/Doubleday, 1990. Norman worked for Apple in the late 1990s.

Feedback and Dialog

Particularly when lengthy operations are involved, it is important for users to know what (if anything) is happening. You will note during the installation and setup processes of Mac OS X that you have a variety of types of feedback provided to you. A progress bar shows how the installation is proceeding; in addition, other parts of the screen move slightly to show you that something is going on.

An absence of feedback is tremendously frustrating, and it leads to all sorts of problems. People click OK buttons repeatedly, and thus they launch dozens of database queries or the like. The software designer's job is to identify those operations that may take time and to let users know the operations will be lengthy and that progress on the task is being made.

What You See Is What You Get (WYSIWYG)

Before the Macintosh in 1984, people used computers with dark screens on which light-colored text appeared. They then printed their documents on paper—usually white paper with black text. The notion of WYSIWYG was revolutionary then.

Today, WYSIWYG is no less challenging. The goal of having images on the screen look like images on output media is not easy to meet when the output medium is black-and-white printing and the screen image is a movie. Nevertheless, the goal of coming as close as possible remains at the core of the Aqua design principles.

Forgiveness

Before the days of word processors, typists were all too familiar with the anxiety that arose as they got to the bottom of a long page of important text. One mistake, and the entire page had to be retyped (corrections to typewritten text are always visible in one way or another).

One keystroke or inadvertent mouse click should not cause a disaster. If it will result in an action that could be regretted, it should be reversible or it should be confirmed with a dialog ("Are you sure you want to delete this?"). When programs are forgiving, people experiment with them. They learn new features and become more comfortable using them.

Perceived Stability

A user's computer environment should change in response to the user's actions, not in response to unsolicited behavior by the program or operating system. If the user chooses Clean Up from the View menu in the Finder, folders should be neatly arranged in a window or on the desktop, but the system should not automatically clean up those folders without the user's request.

The interface to a program or operating system lays down its own rules about what can be done in its own little world. Those rules should be clear and include what a user can control and what the program or operating system can control.

Aesthetic Integrity

The interface should look good. What that means varies from person to person and from time to time. It is also highly dependent on the display devices available. One of the most interesting aspects of interface design is how quickly it goes out of style. Experienced developers can look at interfaces and date them almost to the year—the year floating windoids came in (or out) of fashion, the year of smudgy buttons, and the like.

Aqua is made possible by the underlying operating system and today's hardware capabilities (see the next section for more on this). It is designed to be attractive in the mainstream of early 21st century design.

Additional Considerations

Finally, design should focus on users. Not all programs are designed for a mass audience; however, an operating system is. That means providing universal access—features that are convenient for people who may have difficulty manipulating a mouse or keyboard or seeing a monitor.

In addition, users of computers like the Macintosh are all over the world (and beyond it—at least one PowerBook has flown on the space shuttle). The detailed guidance for developers who are designing interface elements provides information about spacing buttons so that various languages can be accommodated.

Why Aqua Now

In 1984, the original Macintosh used floppy disks encased in a plastic shell. They were smaller and much easier to handle than the larger disks used in other personal computers. How radical a notion it was that instead of referring to the disk as A:\ or B:\, you could refer to it with the almost lifelike icon.

Today, floppy disks are gone from most users' computers. Multigigabyte hard drives are installed within almost every computer made today. Removable media in the form of CDs, DVDs, and Zip disks are used instead. For many people, offline data storage and data transfer are accomplished over networks and the Internet. They need no external disk dives. The next image shows today's typical internal hard disk.

This is the same icon that appears in Mac OS X to represent it. In a way, it sums up the Aqua interface. Three advances in computing make Aqua possible. They are

- A phenomenal increase in all aspects of computing power (storage, processor speed, and monitor size, resolution, and color).

- A decrease in symbolism, with icons giving way to images of the actual objects. This is as true of disk drives as it is of documents, where thumbnail views of contents of a document can replace generic icons. To a large degree it is made possible by the first element—the increase in computing power.

- A new context from which the metaphors of the interface are drawn. This is no longer the context of a paper-based office and desktop. Instead, it is the context of the world of personal computers as people have come to know and understand them. Basic concepts of a graphical user interface such as the folder/document metaphor, a trash can for deletion, and cut-copy-paste were new to people used to text-based computers (and typewriters). Today, however, those concepts—along with much more sophisticated concepts such as the World Wide Web—are old hat. Finding an icon to represent the Web is tricky if your repertoire consists of images of clerical procedures that were perfected over a century ago.

The icon you just saw is no longer a stylized representation, it is an image of the thing itself. The image could not have been displayed on the black-and-white monitor of the original Macintosh computer, and the size of the image's data would have been impractical to manipulate on that computer (which shipped with 64KB of memory—quite lavish at the time). It is not a stripped-down and symbolic representation of an object, and it is recognizable to people as an object from the context of the computer world.

These advances (along with the skills of Apple's designers) are what have made Aqua possible. What follows in this chapter is a roadmap to working with Aqua. If you have used other graphical user interfaces, you may have to unlearn some of what you have mastered over the years. While graphical user interfaces are significantly easier to use than text-based ones, they nevertheless do need to be learned. They have their own idiosyncrasies, styles, and features. Mac OS X removes a number of these and simplifies many of the ones that are left.

Using Windows

The heart of a graphical user interface is the window: a display of information that can be manipulated by the user. (There is even a previous-generation operating system that is named after this concept.) Windows can be moved around the screen, resized and reshaped, and layered with one appearing to be on top of another one. Each graphical user interface has slightly different window controls, and each interface has its own distinctive look to the window's frame.

You can have as many windows open at one time as you want, but only one window is active. That is the window into which your keystrokes and most mouse clicks are directed. The active window has a brighter title bar at the top than an inactive window.

You may take windows for granted, but since they are the heart of a graphical user interface, there is a lot to say about them. That information is divided into three categories:

- What windows look like

- What you can do with windows

- Working within windows

Many of the screen shots in this section use the Mail application that is part of Mac OS X. Chapter 18, "Using Apple Mail," is devoted to Mail and contains much more information about using it.

What Windows Look Like

Windows can contain user data: these are called *document windows*. *Utility windows* may contain messages from the program or they may contain tools that you can use to create and edit your document. Such tools include color palettes, drawing tools, and the like. This section focuses on document windows. For more on utility windows, see Part IV.

Aqua windows immediately look different from all the other windows you have seen on computers. Here are some of their unique characteristics.

Windows Are Not Rectangular

You can see that windows are not rectangular as soon as you launch the Mail application that ships with Mac OS X. It lets you send and receive email. It also serves as a demonstration of how Mac OS X application programs work and what they look like. Figure 2-1 shows the main window of the Mail application that ships with Mac OS X.

If you look at the top of the window, you will notice that the top left and right corners are rounded. This minor point is echoed throughout Aqua with its curved interface elements.

Windows Are *Really* Not Rectangular

Mail also demonstrates the degree to which windows are really not rectangular. If you want to view your mailboxes, you can click the Mailbox button in the toolbar at the top of the window. The Mailboxes drawer slides out from the side of the window as shown in Figure 2-2.

Although you cannot see the behavior on the printed page, rest assured that the pane does indeed slide out gradually. Its animated movement conveys the very convincing impression that it is contained within the main window. In addition, the entire assemblage of drawer and parent window moves as a single unit, further strengthening the impression that it is, in fact, one entity.

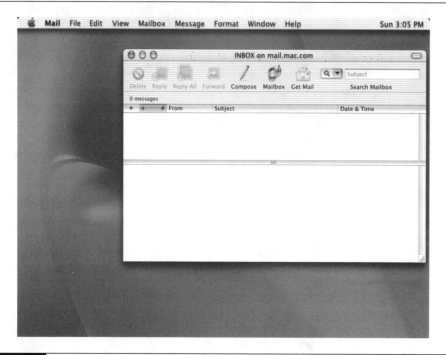

FIGURE 2-1   Mail application ships with Mac OS X.

The basic code for drawers is implemented in Aqua and its programming framework Cocoa, not in individual applications. That means that any programmer who wants to add drawers to an application can easily do so with Cocoa. Drawers appear on the side of a window that is most appropriate: if the window is close to the right edge of the monitor, the drawer slides out to the left. Moving the window close to the left edge of the monitor will cause the drawer to slide out to the right the next time it is opened.

Windows Cast Believable Shadows

On the subject of convincing impressions, the shadowing effects of windows on Mac OS X are quite impressive. Other operating systems either provide no shadowing or a simple heavy line to suggest a shadow. Of course, when windows are perfectly rectangular, a straight line is a reasonable approximation of a shadow.

The imaging capabilities of Mac OS X (implemented in Quartz, which is described in the next chapter) can be used not only by the operating system, but also by individual programs to achieve effects such as these. Figure 2-3 shows the same window as that shown in Figure 2-2 with a white desktop. The white desktop makes the shadowing of the window more noticeable.

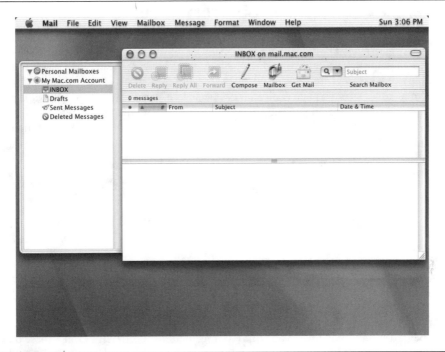

FIGURE 2-2   The Mailbox drawer slides out from the Mail viewer window.

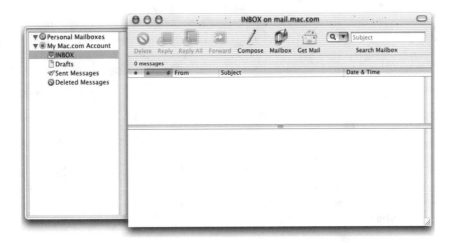

FIGURE 2-3   Windows and the menu bar cast shadows on the desktop.

Windows Show Through Other Interface Elements

In the next illustration, you can see a menu that is pulled down from the menu bar. Notice that the Clock application's round window behind the menu can be seen through the translucent menu items. Aqua is designed for the Macintosh running Mac OS X and the Quartz imaging engine. Many of its effects are minimized when they are printed on paper. What may seem slightly blurry on the printed page is elegant on the screen. If you want to see the next illustration in all of its colorful and translucent glory, it is available on the author's Web site (http://www.philmontmill.com) as Clock and Menu. Just click on Mac OS X and follow the link to Aqua screenshots.

Window Controls Are Usable in Inactive Windows

At the upper left of most windows, you will find three buttons. From left to right, these buttons let you close, minimize, or zoom the window. *Zooming* a window enlarges the window while leaving its contents the same size. In other words, you can see more of the information in a zoomed window. Zooming the contents of a window—an option available from within some applications—leaves the window's size unchanged, but enlarges its contents. The first type of zooming is handled by the operating system, which is why you click the Mac OS X-provided buttons at the upper left of the windows. The second type is handled from within application programs. On Mac OS X, the OS-type zooming that enlarges the window and leaves its contents the same size is called *maximizing*. When the window is active, they are colored (from left to right) red, yellow, and green. When you move the mouse over that area—even if the window is not active—the colors appear, as well as symbols inside each button.

Why This Matters

These features not only contribute to a pleasing appearance of the computer monitor, they also convey a variety of subtle cues as to a window's state and condition. The controls you use to manipulate a window are described in the next section. They need to be visible and stand out from the background of a window. Furthermore, the window frames and management tools need to be visible no matter where windows are on the screen. The combination of the distinctive frame and its shading help you distinguish windows from content. It's not just attractive design, it's very utilitarian.

Being able to click buttons on inactive windows is referred to as *click-through*. In Mac OS 9 and earlier, you had to click once on the window to activate it and then click a second time to click the button or other tool you wanted to use.

Window Terminology

Figure 2-4 shows the Mail window and its mailbox drawer again. Each part of the window is labeled with its name. Not all windows have all of these features; many windows of other standard elements such as scroll bars. All of the interface elements are discussed in this chapter and in Part IV, "Using Applications on Mac OS X," which focuses on using specific applications.

- **Close button**   Click this button to close the window. If its data is unsaved or if closing without saving will cause a problem, you will be asked if you want to take other actions to prevent problems.

- **Minimize button**   Click this button to move the window to the Dock.

- **Zoom button**   Click this button to enlarge the window as much as possible on the screen.

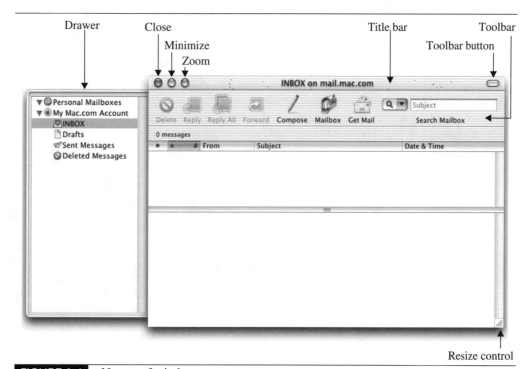

FIGURE 2-4   Names of window components

- ■ **Title bar**   The name of the document is displayed in the title bar. You can move the window by dragging the title bar. Double-clicking the title bar minimizes the window. When the window is active, the title bar is highlighted.

- ■ **Toolbar**   Many windows have a set of controls in a toolbar at the top of the window.

- ■ **Toolbar button**   Windows with toolbars let you show and hide the toolbar with this button.

- ■ **Resize control**   Drag this control to resize or reshape the window.

The toolbar and toolbar button are new in Mac OS X. Minimizing the window by moving it to the Dock is also a new behavior since the Dock did not exist in Mac OS 9 and earlier.

What You Can Do with Windows

Since windows are the basic units of the graphical user interface, it stands to reason that you should be able to do a lot of things with them, and you can. Windows have a variety of controls that are located in their frames. These controls are described in this section.

How to Move a Window

First of all, you may want to move a window around on the screen. The *title bar* is the bar along the top of the window. You can drag the window around by using the title bar. In the center of the title bar, the title of the window is displayed. Dragging a window activates it unless you hold down the COMMAND key while dragging it.

In Mac OS 9 and earlier, an outline of the window moved on the screen as you dragged a window. Now, the window and its content move.

How to Layer Windows (Activation)

Dragging a window lets you move it from side to side or up and down on the screen. If you have several windows open at the same time, you can move windows forward—that is, you can create the illusion of stacked windows with one window in front of another.

Only one window at a time is active. Windows that are inactive have a slightly different appearance; their title bar is subtly changed. Controls in inactive windows are often dimmed. Figure 2-5 shows two windows: one is in front of another, and the rear window is inactive.

You cannot send a window backward on the screen. What you can do is click another window to bring it forward. When you click a window, it becomes *active*. Windows that are inactive can still be updated. For example, if you have a mail application in the background, you will see incoming messages as they are displayed in its windows. Clicking on a message window will activate it so you can deal with it.

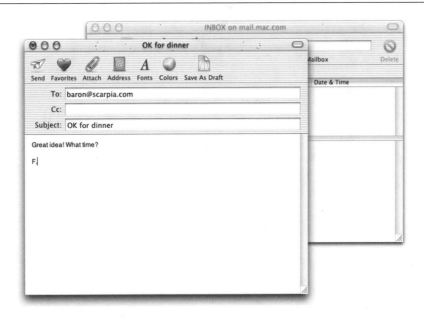

FIGURE 2-5   Active windows have colored Close, Minimize, and Zoom buttons, as well as a more prominent title bar.

Each window is layered separately from all other windows. On Mac OS 9 and earlier, clicking any of an application's windows activated the application and the window: all of the application's windows were brought forward. On Mac OS X, clicking a window activates it and the application, but only that window is brought forward. Other windows for the application may remain behind other applications' windows.

When an application is made active, it may have floating palettes that appear. Typically floating palettes with tools and the like are only shown for the currently active application.

Scrolling a Window's Content

Windows frequently contain more information than can be displayed in the area allotted to them. In such cases, scroll bars are provided to let you move the window's content into view. You may have horizontal or vertical scroll bars or both. Windows may have individually scrolling panes with their own scroll bars. As a result, a window can have multiple horizontal and vertical scroll bars.

If a window's contents fit entirely within its area, the scroll bars are not visible. However, when the contents expand beyond the window's area, one or both scroll bars come to life, as shown next. Scrollbars let you view window content that lies beyond the boundaries of the window.

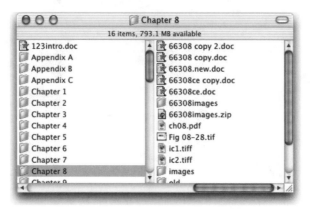

The *scroll arrows* at the top and bottom (or left and right) of the scroll bars let you move continuously through the content. If you hold the mouse down over one of the arrows, you will see the window's (or pane's) content move in the appropriate direction.

Within the *scroll track*, a *scroller* moves with the window's content. It shows you where within the document you are. In Mac OS X, the size of this scroller varies so that you can get an idea of how much of the content is visible: the more of the scroll track it takes up, the more of the document is visible.

In addition to clicking on the arrows at the ends of the scroll bar, you can drag the scroller up and down (or from side to side) to position the document's content appropriately. Furthermore, you can click in the scroll track next to the slider to cause the document to move. Depending on how you have set the General pane in your System Preferences, a click in the scroll track will either move the document by one page in the direction you have clicked or it will position the document to that relative position. In the latter case, clicking 90 percent of the way down a scroll bar track will position the document to 90 percent of the way to its end.

In the previous illustration, the horizontal scroll bar across the bottom of the window scrolls the entire display from left to right. The two vertical scroll bars control the two panes, each of which can be scrolled independently. This is the Finder's columns view, and it is new in Mac OS X. See Chapter 4, "Working with Files," for more information. Preferences—including General—are discussed in Chapter 6, "Setting Preferences."

How to Zoom a Window

Rather than scrolling around in a window, you can change its size so that more information can be displayed. The simplest way to do that is to zoom the window—automatically resize it to take up as much of the screen as possible. You do this by clicking the Zoom button on the title bar. It is the rightmost of the set of three buttons on the left side of the title bar. It is green and contains the + symbol when the mouse is moved near it.

Not all windows support zooming. If a window's content is always small, it may not be resizable. Note, too, that you can zoom inactive windows. If you move the pointer over the Zoom button of an inactive window and it turns green, feel free to click it. This will zoom the window and make it active.

How to Resize or Reshape a Window

A more precise way of resizing a window is to use its *resize control* (in the lower-right corner). Most windows with variable content are resizable; those that contain constant and small amounts of data usually are not. To resize a window, drag the resize control in whatever direction(s) you wish to resize or reshape the window.

How to Minimize a Window

Now that you have seen how to enlarge a window (with the Zoom button or by resizing it with the resize control), you might want to consider how to reduce a window to its smallest possible size. This has always been a problem with graphical user interfaces. Windows are spawned apace, and before you know it you have a screen full of windows that prevent you from doing what you wanted to do in the first place.

Mac OS X has a new feature—the Dock—located at the bottom of the screen. It is described later in this chapter. For now, suffice it to say that the middle of the trio of buttons at the upper left of the window (the yellow one sporting the – symbol when the pointer is over it) will minimize the window by moving it to the Dock. You can also minimize windows by using the Minimize Window command in the Window menu or by double-clicking its title bar.

How to Close a Window

The leftmost of the trio of buttons at the upper left of each window is its Close button. It is red and contains the × symbol when the pointer is over it. Click it to close the window. A document window containing unsaved changes will contain a dot in the center of the Close button.

In some cases, you may need to take further action before the window can be closed. For example, if you have unsaved data in the window, you must respond to a message asking you if you want to save the data. See "Using Sheets" later in this chapter.

How to Work in a Window

To work in a window, it must be active. You activate an inactive window by clicking anywhere in it. (Try to click the window's background rather than on a button or other control within the window. Some window controls can be used even in inactive windows, and you would not want to accidentally close a window instead of activating it.)

Working Within Windows: Using Controls

Within the window's frame is its content, which is what you usually care about. That content can be passive—an image, for example—or it can be a complex combination of buttons, checkboxes, and other items. These are all called controls, and they are the objects that appear similar across all Mac OS X applications. Their behavior is governed by interface guidelines promulgated by Apple (and

Using Windows

enforced by application development frameworks such as Cocoa). Since they work the same way in all cases, you should know what their names are, what they do, and how they do it.

Push Buttons

Push buttons are the simplest form of controls. They are round (or oval) and contain a simple image or text—such as OK or Cancel. They cause an immediate effect. This window from Mail shows the most commonly used buttons, Cancel and OK:

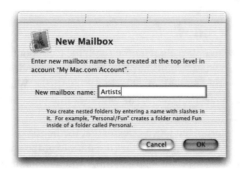

Bevel Buttons

Like push buttons, bevel buttons also cause an immediate effect. They may open a window, change a display's formatting, or otherwise help you on your way. They frequently contain both an image and some text. In the next dialog, bevel buttons let you choose the paper orientation for printing. Bevel buttons frequently are arranged in a row, either vertically or horizontally. Bevel buttons also sometimes change their appearance to reflect status information.

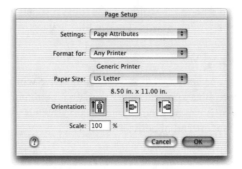

Toolbars

Toolbars are often placed at the top of a window. They group various controls together—buttons, text fields, and the like. If a toolbar is present, it can frequently be shown or hidden by using the

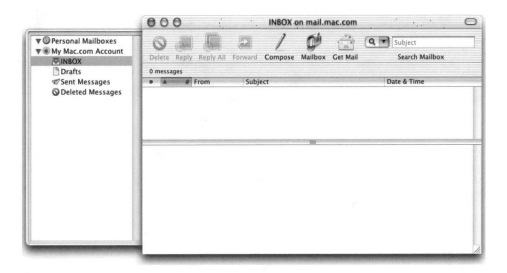

FIGURE 2-6   Use the toolbar buttons to manipulate the Mail Viewer window.

Toolbar button at the right side of the window's title bar. Figure 2-6 shows a toolbar in the Mail application; the toolbar contains buttons such as Compose and Get Mail. Inactive buttons in the toolbar such as Delete and Reply are dimmed. Windows with toolbars have a Hide Toolbar command in their View menu; you can use that, too.

If a window is too narrow to accommodate a toolbar, a double arrow appears at the right. You can see the missing toolbar commands that are outside the window's frame by holding the pointer over the double arrow, as shown here:

You can usually customize toolbars by choosing Customize Toolbar from the View menu. You can drag icons into the toolbar or rearrange them. Figure 2-7 shows the Forward button

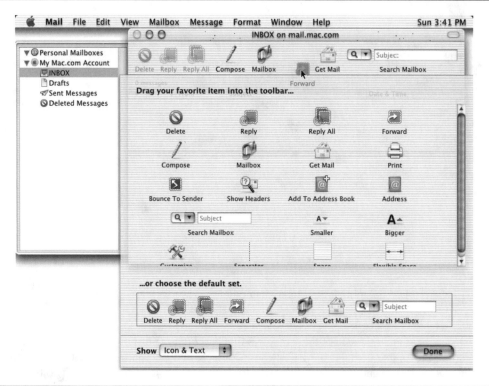

FIGURE 2-7 Add icons to the toolbar with the Customize Toolbar command.

being moved into the toolbar between the Mailbox and Get Messages icons. The icons in the toolbar automatically move aside to accommodate the new icon.

You can rearrange icons in the toolbar just by dragging them. For example, in the next illustration, the Delete button has been moved far away from the Reply button to prevent accidents. Within a toolbar, icons can be used as buttons. When an icon is placed in a toolbar, it generally needs to be placed within the frame of a bevel button to provide an indication that it can be clicked.

Pop-Up Menus

Pop-up menus let you choose from a list of items. The currently selected item is displayed within a button; when you click the button, the entire list is displayed until you release the mouse button. In some cases, the selection you make is not acted on until you click a push or bevel button, close the window, or otherwise start events in motion. Pop-up menus provide you with multiple choices in a small amount of space. A pop-up menu is shown here:

Radio Buttons

Radio buttons occur in clusters, and only one of the cluster can be selected. Clicking a radio button causes any other button in the cluster to be deselected. Accordingly, radio buttons have a very distinct on and off appearance. Radio buttons are used to select one of a number of options. Typically, they cause no immediate effect; the effect occurs when another button is clicked or the window is closed. The next illustration shows e-mail Internet preferences from System Preferences. You can choose between POP and IMAP account types with radio buttons.

Checkboxes

In the previous illustration, a checkbox lets you choose to use an iTools e-mail account. (The checkbox is not checked in the figure.) Checkboxes are used to select any of a number of choices or to select an option that can be either on or off. Whereas radio buttons appear in a cluster in which only one can be on, any number of checkboxes in a group can be on. They, too, do not cause an immediate effect.

Tabs

Tabs provide an efficient way to organize information within a window. The next illustration shows the iTools tab of Internet preferences. Compare it to the Email preferences shown in the previous illustration. The contents of the changeable area of a window that is controlled by tabs is called a *pane*. Use tabs to move from pane to pane within a window.

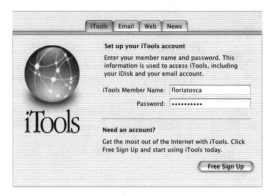

Sliders

Sliders let you set values along a sliding scale and are normally used to set relative values. Where specific values are involved (such as font sizes), pop-up buttons are normally used. Use sliders to set the volume and balance of your computer's sound, as shown here:

Resizable Panes

Some windows have multiple panes that can be resized. The small bar shown in Figure 2-8 with its distinctive set of lines is used to resize the panes. The overall size of the window remains unchanged. Note that sometimes the cursor will change to this distinctive multiline image as it moves over boundaries of resizable panes; the small bar does not always appear in the window itself. Note, too, that sometimes resizing a pane will cause scroll bars to appear or disappear as shown in the figure.

Using Sheets

One of the biggest changes in Mac OS X is the way in which alerts are handled. Alerts have typically been a problem. They are messages that pop up on the screen and require you to take some action to acknowledge a problem or to deal with a potentially troublesome situation (such as an unsaved file). The problem is that as originally implemented, these alerts often lock the computer

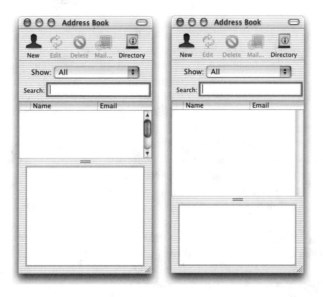

FIGURE 2-8   You can resize the panes of the Address Book application.

Using Sheets

until they are dismissed. If you are sitting at the computer this is not a problem, but many times alerts pop up at unforeseen times. For example, if you are going out to lunch, you might start a lengthy process—a backup of files, perhaps. You start the backup and race out the door, not noticing that a dialog saying "Are you sure?" has popped up on your screen. Rather than returning to a backed-up computer, you return to a computer that hasn't even started the work.

In Mac OS 9 and earlier, many of the system alerts were handled with small windows that could be closed. This reduced a number of these inadvertent lockups. However, the problem still remained with applications. For Mac OS X, alerts are attached to specific windows; they freeze that window, but no others. The next illustration shows such an alert. The sheet immobilizes the window until you act on it. The alert appears to roll down like a window shade from the window's title bar. These interface elements are called *sheets*. The effect is clever—not just because it is a new and attractive use of animation, but also because it draws your attention to the alert. When an alert pops up on a cluttered screen, it can easily be missed. This window shade action helps you see which window needs attention.

Until you dismiss the alert, that window cannot be closed. It can be moved aside (which you may need to do to find out what course of action to pursue), but otherwise it stays where it is. Since alerts are attached to individual windows, multiple alerts can be present at the same time. Alerts behave consistently across applications. If an alert requires you to do something or to accept (or reject) a course of action, it will have at least two buttons in the lower right. The rightmost one will be the most common choice such as OK, Yes, or Save, and to its left will be a Cancel button.

A third button may be present to the left of these. A common case is an Apply button that applies settings for your review before you actually accept them. In the case of an alert prompting you to save data, the third button is a Don't Save button. The Cancel button cancels the operation you just attempted to perform, such as closing the window. Use Don't Save (or a similar button) to respond negatively to the alert. In the case of unsaved data, clicking the Save button may open a sheet in which you can choose the name for a file. This is described fully in Chapter 4, "Working with Files."

The default button is highlighted and pulses; the keyboard's RETURN key has the same effect as clicking the default button. Default buttons are typically the rightmost button; however, if the action of the rightmost button could cause serious damage, another, less damaging button is the default. Thus, a dialog that asks if you really want to erase a disk might have Continue (i.e., No) as its default, and Reformat (i.e., Yes) as another button.

Using the Dock

One of the most striking new features of Mac OS X is the Dock. It is shown in the next illustration. The Dock provides functionality that is similar to some features on other operating systems, including Mac OS. However, much of its functionality is unique to Mac OS X. Try to avoid comparing it to other interface elements you may have encountered. If you do so, you are likely to miss some of its most useful features. Treat it as an entirely new part of the graphical user interface—which it is.

The Dock contains a variety of icons:

- An icon for each application that is running
- Icons for applications or documents that you place there by dragging them from Finder windows or the desktop
- Icons for applications that Apple preloads when you install Mac OS X
- Icons for minimized windows

Icons in the Dock can change to reflect information about their applications. For example, in the next illustration, you can see that the Mail application now has an unread message. The number of unread messages is constantly updated in the Dock, even if you do not have Mail windows open. Small triangles appear underneath the icons of applications that are running. In addition, if you hold the mouse button down over an icon in the Dock, you will see a pop-up window that lets you open a Finder window that is focused on that application or document.

If an application in the Dock is running, this pop-up window will also show you all of its open windows and will let you quit from the application. Individual applications may have other menu commands available—for example, you can change your monitor's resolution by dropping the Displays Dock Extra into the Dock. Look in the Dock Extras folder in your Applications folder for other items to add to your Dock. PowerBooks and iBooks normally have the Battery Monitor Dock extra installed automatically, but you can add it—and the AirPort Signal Strength extra—if you need to. The Dock grows and shrinks as you place icons into it. Since it contains an icon for every application that is running, it may grow and shrink as you launch or quit applications. You can also place an icon in the Dock by dragging it from a Finder window. (The Finder is discussed in Chapter 4, "Working with Files.")

If you have placed an application's icon in the Dock, it remains there, and launching or quitting applications has no effect on it. If you have not placed an application in the Dock, it will appear there while it is running and disappear when you quit the application. Icons for documents are not automatically placed in the Dock when you open them. The pop-up window for an application that is in the Dock while it is running, but which is not normally in the Dock, will include a Keep in Dock command: this will leave it there after it quits.

The Dock's behavior is quite dynamic. It expands from the center of the bottom of your screen in both directions. When it hits the edge of the screen, its icons are slightly reduced in size. This process continues so that the Dock is always one row of icons centered on—or filling—the bottom of the screen. Because of its dynamic behavior, it is difficult to present anything but a pale image of the Dock at a single point in time. It is one of the features of Mac OS X that you really have to experience for yourself.

What the Dock Does

The Dock provides a mechanism for you to collect documents, folders, and applications that you are working on or that you frequently need. (In addition to documents, folders containing a variety of documents can be placed in the Dock. For example, you can place a folder representing a project in the Dock.) Until now, you needed to keep track of where specific files, folders, and applications were located. Now you can keep track of them logically without worrying about their physical locations on your disk. This is very important to the new way of using your computer that Aqua provides.

Look at Figure 2-9, which shows part of a disk. In fact, it is the section of the author's hard disk that contains the files for this book. (This is not a retouched example, this is what it looks like!) The display of files is the Finder's new Columns view, a very efficient way of browsing files. It is described later in Chapter 4, "Working with Files." For now, all you need to know is that there is a folder called Current Projects (not shown) which contains, among other folders, one called Mac OS X; that folder is selected and highlighted in the first column. Within that folder, a number of subfolders contain research information, management and scheduling files, and the book itself. Within the Book folder (selected in the second column), each chapter has its own folder, and within each chapter, the actual files—in several versions—are stored.

In Figure 2-10, the Mac OS X folder itself has been placed in the Dock. In fact, several other folders from the Current Projects folder are there. When the mouse is clicked and held down over the Mac OS X folder, the file and folder hierarchy within that folder is displayed, as shown in the figure. It is very easy to then open an individual file. What is useful about this way of working with the Dock is that when a project is no longer on the front burner, its document or folder icon in the Dock can be removed: nothing on disk is affected by this. Thus, you can have

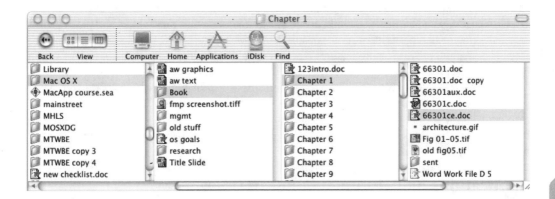

FIGURE 2-9   File and folder layout for the Mac OS X project in Finder columns view

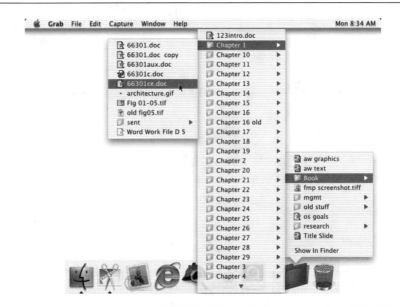

FIGURE 2-10   You can look at the document and folder structure within a folder that has been placed in the Dock.

your current items one mouse click away in the Dock and have different items there tomorrow or next year. You never have to move files around on your disk. (To remove an item from the Dock, simply drag it up above the Dock and release the mouse button. It will vanish.)

On Mac OS 9 and earlier, you could create aliases to documents and folders and place them on the desktop or in other folders. You can still do that with Mac OS X, but placing items in the Dock is easier and provides more features (such as the ability to look at contents of folders in pop-up windows).

By guaranteeing that icons for all running applications are visible in the Dock, Mac OS X provides you with a simple way to switch among those applications. The Dock also works together with the Minimize window button and menu command. When a window is minimized, it is placed into the Dock (with a rather impressive animated swish). Clicking its icon in the Dock reopens the window as it was.

Applications and Documents in the Dock

Application icons appear in the left side of the Dock; documents appear in the right side. A small space with a vertical white line differentiates between the two areas. You can resize the Dock by dragging this divider left and right.

Options for the Dock

You can set various options for the Dock. From the Apple menu, the Dock command lets you open Dock Preferences or turn hiding and magnification on or off. The Dock command is shown next. (A menu item with a triangle next to it is a hierarchical menu. Clicking the mouse in the menu item brings up a secondary menu to its right.)

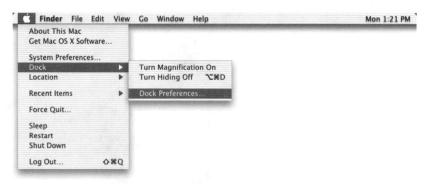

When you choose Dock Preferences, the window shown next is opened. See Chapter 6, "Setting Preferences," for complete coverage of Mac OS X preferences.

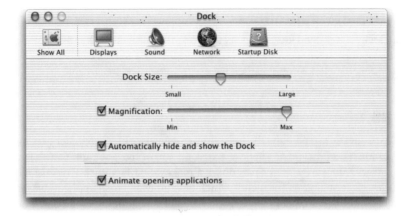

Dock Size

The Dock Size setting controls the size of the icons in the Dock. Making them smaller means that more of them can stretch across the bottom of the screen. Since the Dock grows and shrinks as necessary, you can wind up with a Dock that spans the entire monitor or just stays in the middle with very small icons.

Magnification

Magnification specifies the degree (if any) to which icons are enlarged as you move the mouse over them. The following illustration shows the Dock with magnification on.

Hiding and Showing the Dock Automatically

You can choose to have the Dock shown at all times (this is the default). If you choose Automatically hide and show the Dock, the Dock appears only if you move your mouse to the very bottom of the screen. It rises up from the black abyss at the bottom of the screen and remains in view until you move your mouse above its icons.

   The hot area for causing the Dock to display is all the way at the bottom of your computer display. If the Dock does not appear, move the mouse even lower on the screen than you have it. This choice may be necessary if you are using an application that normally places a status bar or toolbar across the bottom of the screen (several programs in Microsoft Office do this).

Animate Opening Applications

When you click an icon in the Dock, it opens the document or application that it represents. If you choose this option, the process includes a swirl as the icon moves to the center of the screen. Without this option, the click simply causes the appropriate windows to appear.

Using Menus

Next to windows, menus are perhaps the most important aspect of a graphical user interface. On Macintosh operating systems, menus appear across the top of the screen, rather than at the top of individual windows. They are a major part of what makes the Macintosh look like a Macintosh.

There are interface standards for menus which help all Macintosh applications behave consistently. The interface standards govern what menus appear in the menu bar, where certain standard menu commands appear, and how menu items should be worded. For example, a menu command that ends with ... always is associated with a menu item that will require more information before it can be performed.

Creating a new document is done by selecting a command called New. Opening an existing document or printing a document is done by selecting a command such as Open... or Print.... The ellipsis (...) is present in those cases because you will need to supply the name of the document to open or to specify the pages to be printed before the command can be carried out.

Standard Menus

Six menus are standard in most applications on Mac OS X. From the left of the menu bar, they are

- Apple
- Application
- File
- Edit
- Window
- Help

Application-specific menus may appear between the Edit and Window menus. (In other words, Apple, Application, File, and Edit are the start of the menu bar; Window and Help are the end of the menu bar.)

The Apple menu was present in Mac OS 9 and earlier. On Mac OS X, commands from that version of the Apple menu are split between the Apple menu and the new Application menu. Over time, the Apple menu grew to contain a variety of commands that had no other home. Many of those functions are now provided in a more elegant way by the Dock. Another menu in recent versions of the Mac OS is the process menu that has appeared at the right side of the menu bar. That menu contains an entry for each program running on the computer, letting you switch easily among them. It also lets you hide the active application or all applications except the active application. The Dock also provides many of these functions. Application hiding and showing is in the Application menu on Mac OS X.

Keyboard Equivalents

Some menu commands have a COMMAND-key equivalent. If you hold down the key with Apple logo/propeller/cloverleaf symbol (located next to the SPACEBAR on most keyboards), you press the other key and the menu command will be performed. COMMAND-key equivalents are very common in menus.

Some keyboard equivalents involve more than one modifier key. The SHIFT and OPTION keys frequently need to be pressed in addition to the COMMAND key. All of these are modifier keys, and you can hold them down first; when you press the final key (often a letter or number on the keyboard) the command is executed.

Apple

The Apple menu is crowned with the Apple logo. It contains commands that are general to your computer—that is, they are not related to an individual application.

About This Mac

This command opens a window that shows you the version of the operating system you are running, the amount of memory installed in your computer, and the processor that powers it.

Get Mac OS X Software

This command connects you via the Internet to Apple's Web site where you can get more software for Mac OS X.

System Preferences

System Preferences let you manage your computer environment, including your network connections, sound and display preferences, language choices, and the like. Chapter 6, "Setting Preferences," is devoted to System Preferences.

Dock

The Dock submenu was described in the previous section of this chapter.

Location

The Location command lets you set a group of network preferences together so you can collectively activate them. It is very useful when you are moving around with an iBook or PowerBook. For example, you can have one location described for your home with an always-on cable or DSL

Using Menus

connection. Another location can be defined for an office with a local area network, and a third location can be defined for when you are traveling and using a dial-up connection to the Internet.

The Automatic location that is the default lets you define a number of advanced settings in the Network pane in System Preferences; Mac OS X will automatically use the first group of settings that works at any given time. Thus, you can let the operating system switch from an Ethernet connection to a dial-up connection or vice versa if one or the other fails. There is more on this in Chapter 6, "Setting Preferences."

Recent Items

This is a submenu that keeps track of recent applications and documents you have used, as shown next. It is maintained automatically by Mac OS X, but as you can see from the figure, you can clear the submenu at any time you want.

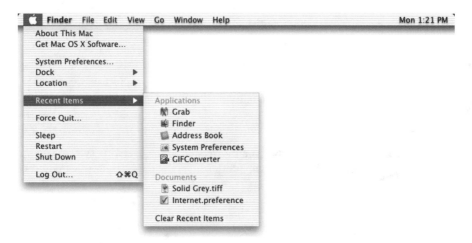

Force Quit

This command opens the window shown next. Under normal circumstances, you do not need to use Force Quit. However, if a program seems to be out of control or is not responding, you can use Force Quit to cause it to stop. It may lose some of your data, but if you have no other choice than turning off your computer, Force Quit is preferable.

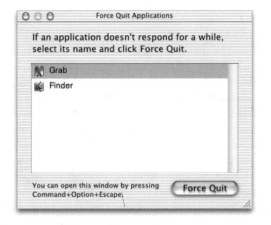

You can open the Force Quit window with the keyboard combination of COMMAND, CONTROL and ESC. Press all of the keys at the same time; it is deliberately a bit awkward so that you do not accidentally do it. Furthermore, holding down the OPTION key changes the Quit command in the Dock's pop-up windows to Force Quit for running applications.

TIP

Occasionally, programs in the Classic Compatibility Environment will hang and stop responding. If you force one of them to quit, it is possible that the entire Classic Compatibility Environment— including other programs—may quit as well.

Sleep

This command puts your computer into a low power mode with the disk and monitor powered down. The Energy Saver preference described in Chapter 6, "Setting Preferences," can do this automatically for you.

Restart

Restarting your computer causes it to completely restart its operations. You can use Restart if you are having serious problems. In most cases, however, Force Quit is preferable since you simply get rid of the offending application. You can also use the Classic preference to restart the Classic environment without touching the rest of the Mac OS X environment. (See Chapter 6.)

Restarting is the right approach to take if unexplained problems are occurring in a wide variety of applications. Problems occurring in a number of Classic Mac OS applications may

Using Menus

indicate a problem with the Classic Compatibility Environment, which you can restart from the Classic pane in System Preferences. In general, restart the smallest unit of work to avoid losing data. Quit from those applications that are responsive. That may solve your problem.

If it does not, examine what is not responding. If the problem seems to be confined to Classic Mac OS applications, force Classic to quit or restart (but manually quit from those applications in the Classic Compatibility Environment that you can). If the problem extends to applications other than those in the Classic Compatibility Environment, follow the same strategy: quit from those that you can so that they terminate normally without any loss of data. Then, restart the computer.

Under Mac OS X, this is a rare situation. Individual applications and the Classic Compatibility Environment occasionally do hang, but the computer as a whole usually remains stable. The one system-wide area that does sometimes have problems is the networking interface. This can be due to problems within your computer, as well as problems in the network (both the local network and the upstream—ISP—connections). Since networking is handled at a very basic level, it can cause a variety of applications to fail or hang. (If your computer is set up to support sharing, it does so as soon as it is started up: no one needs to be logged on.) You may need to restart your computer or even your network router to clear out such communications problems. Again, follow the same strategy: restart the smallest unit. Before restarting your router (and thus destroying all networked computers' internet and network access), try restarting each individual computer.

There is one significant exception to all of this careful trial-and-error work. If your computer (or your network) is not heavily loaded and very little work is currently underway, restarting may be the quickest way out of an unexplained problem. Restarting does, indeed, work: it just is usually overkill, and the consequences in terms of lost data can be severe. Restarting a router for a classroom of computers in the middle of a class probably ends all possibility of further class work using those computers. However, restarting a classroom of computers during a lunch break will frequently solve mysterious problems. It does not take much time, and you can lock the door, eat a sandwich, and get your computers, your mind, and your body ready for the next horde of bright-eyed scholars.

Shut Down

This completely powers down your computer.

Log Out

 Log Out lets you walk away from your computer without worrying about someone accessing your files. The computer continues to run, but you (or any new user) need to log in again before you can access it. When you have logged out, the computer is still running, though. Network services—such as file sharing—are still available to others over your network

Application

 The Application menu is new in Mac OS X. In Mac OS 9 and earlier, the first menu on the left was the Apple menu. The Application menu carries the name of the currently active application. The Application menu is now a coherent collection of commands that pertain to a given

application. Commands that pertain to individual windows or documents within the application are located elsewhere. Figure 2-35 shows the Application menu for Mail.

About

The first item in each Application menu opens the application's About box. This box provides information about the application and frequently includes its version number. A serial number or the name of a licensed user may also appear in this box. If you are having a problem with an application and are thinking of calling for technical support, opening the About box and copying down its information can save you time.

Preferences

One or more Preferences items appears next in the Application menu. Preferences are normally set using a window with a variety of controls in it.

Services

Services are an important feature of Mac OS X that let you combine functionality from a number of application programs. Hierarchical menus are typically used to display submenus with variable items. The Services menu is a good case in point. Services are described in Chapter 17, "Using Services."

Hide Application

Hiding an application causes all of its windows and menus to be removed from the screen. Since all applications that are running are shown in the Dock, you can unhide an application that you

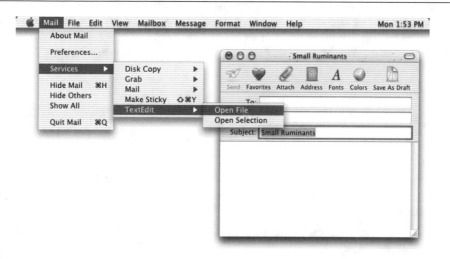

FIGURE 2-11   Mail program's Application menu provides program-related commands

have hidden by clicking on its Dock icon. Hiding an application is particularly useful when you have opened a variety of windows and positioned them in a way to let you work efficiently.

When you hide an application, only its application icon is visible in the Dock. If you minimize all of its windows, each of those windows' icons and the application icon are visible in the Dock.

Hide Others

The Hide Others is the reverse of Hide Application: everything except the application itself is hidden.

Show All

This command shows all hidden applications so that everything is visible on the screen. Note that windows that have been minimized and placed in the Dock remain there; only the applications that were hidden are shown.

Quit

Finally, the Quit command is the last item in the Application menu. You use it to end an application program.

Quit used to be the last command in the File menu on Mac OS 9 and earlier. The COMMAND-key equivalent (COMMAND-Q) is unchanged. For many users, the placement of the Quit command is completely immaterial, since they only use the COMMAND-key equivalent.

File

The File menu lets you create, open, save, close, and print files. Each application has its own File menu layout, but the sequence of items remains the same. If an application does not support commands, they may be omitted. If they are not available, the menu items are dimmed and you cannot click them. The File menu for TextEdit is shown in Figure 2-12. (Chapter 16, "Working with Applications," has more about TextEdit, the word processing application that is part of Mac OS X.)

New

This command creates a new document and opens it in its own window. Some applications have two types of documents; in such cases, two separate New commands exist.

Open

This command opens a dialog that lets you open a document that already exists.

Open Recent

This is frequently a hierarchical menu in which the most recent documents you have worked with are displayed.

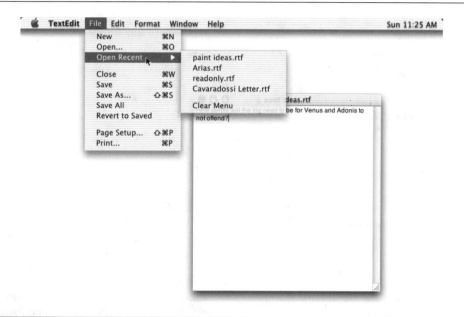

FIGURE 2-12   Use the File menu to open and close windows, as well as to print.

Using Menus

Close

This command closes the active window. If it contains unsaved data, you will be prompted to save it.

Save

This command saves the current document. If it has never been saved, you will be prompted to enter a name for the file. If it has been saved, it will be saved to the same location as it was previously saved; in other words, the previously saved version will be overwritten.

Save As

This command lets you save the current document either with another name or with another format. You can use it to keep copies of versions of your documents. All of the previous commands involve file manipulation. You will find more details in Chapter 4, "Working with Files."

Save All

This command saves all active windows. It is the same as choosing Save for each window in turn. It is not present in all File menus.

Revert to Saved

Many File menus include this command that applies to the active window if it has been saved in the past. It is equivalent to closing the window without saving it and reopening it from the last version on disk. Do this if you have made several unsaved changes that you want to remove. You normally cannot go back to a second prior (or earlier) version.

Page Setup

This command lets you specify the format for the pages of your document—their size and orientation (whether vertical or horizontal).

Print

This command opens a dialog that lets you specify what parts of the document should be printed and how many copies should be made. Page Setup and Print are discussed more fully in Chapter 5, "Printing."

Edit

The Edit menu contains the commands that let you cut, copy, and paste data within and among documents. Figure 2-13 shows the Mail edit menu. Note that the Edit menu typically contains commands related to finding or replacing text as well as for spelling (if the application supports them). Find/replace is discussed further in Chapter 16, "Working with Applications"; spell-checking is discussed in Chapter 17, "Working with Services."

The processes outlined here are basic to graphical user interfaces although they are implemented differently in different applications with different types of data. This is a cursory and general introduction. Two concepts are key to this process: selection and the insertion point.

Selection

Each application normally lets you select information to be cut or copied in a window. In text-based applications such as word processors, you often cut and copy text. In graphically oriented applications (and in the Finder), you cut and copy icons.

There are several ways of doing this:

- You can drag the mouse around the data to be selected. It either changes color or some outline will appear around it.

- You can double-click a word to select it. Triple-clicking will normally select the paragraph in which a word is contained. (Double-click and dragging selects a word and then adds additional words to extend the selection as you drag the mouse. Triple-click and dragging selects a paragraph and then adds additional paragraphs to extend the selection as you drag the mouse.)

- Many Edit menus contain a Select All command, which will select all editable objects in a document.

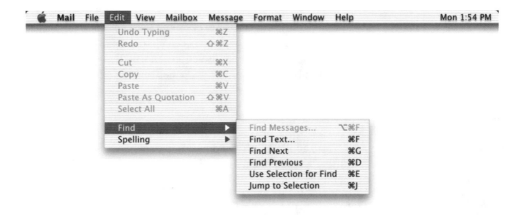

FIGURE 2-13   The Edit menu handles cut, copy, and paste, as well as finding and spell checking.

Some applications let you select multiple objects in a document. To do so, hold down the COMMAND key as you select the individual items. If you have selected several items, you can deselect one by holding down the COMMAND key and clicking the item. Thus, you can select all items except one by choosing Select All from the Edit menu and then COMMAND-clicking the one exception.

You can use the SHIFT key to select a range of items. Click the first item, press the SHIFT key, and then click the last item. All items between those two (as well as those two) will be selected. You can change the end of the selection if you continue to hold down the SHIFT key and click another item. Using SHIFT selecting requires that the items be ordered (as in a Finder window's list). If they are unordered, you must use COMMAND-click to select each one.

Once you have selected one or more items, you can then cut or copy them. In either case, the items are copied to an internal storage space (the *Clipboard*). If you choose Cut, the items are removed from the document and placed on the Clipboard. If you choose Copy, the items remain in the document and a copy is placed on the Clipboard as well.

Insertion Point

You need to have an insertion point in a document when you are editing it. In a text document, this is the place where the next character you type will appear or where the next item you draw will be placed. Graphics documents and those containing video have comparable interpretations of the insertion point. You need not have an insertion point when you are viewing a document.

If you have items on the Clipboard and you have an insertion point in your document, you can choose Paste from the Edit menu to insert those items at the insertion point. Any text field that is available for entry has a *focus ring* around it—a slightly darkened border that shows you can type in it.

Undo/Redo

All of this is quite simple, and it requires little courage to experiment with cut-copy-paste. That is because the first item in an Edit menu is Undo or Redo. You can choose Undo to reverse the action you have just taken. Thus, even the most horrendous action can usually be undone. However, once a document is saved, the Undo queue is often flushed and the changes are committed.

Window

The Window menu lets you manage an application's windows. It is new in Mac OS X, although a variety of such menus have proliferated in applications over the last several years. The next illustration shows the Window menu for Mail.

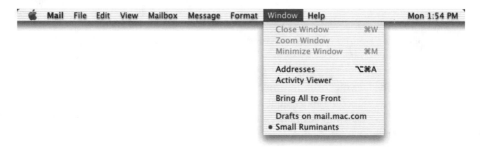

Actually, the Window menu debuted in Mac OS 9 as part of the transition to Mac OS X. The first three commands in the Window menu correspond to the three buttons at the left of the title bar.

Close Window

This closes the active window. If no window in the application is open or active, the command is dimmed.

Zoom Window

The Zoom Window menu command is the same as the Zoom button discussed previously. It alternately maximizes the window and returns it to whatever size you have set for it.

Minimize Window

Discussed previously in this chapter, the Minimize Window command moves the window to the Dock. It has the same effect as clicking the Minimize Window button.

Application Windows

For an application with special windows (such as Mail's Addresses and Activity Viewer windows), these are listed next. Choosing each one activates that window. Such special windows are always available in a given application.

Bring All to Front

In Mac OS 9 and earlier, clicking on a window brought that application and all of its windows to the forefront. On Mac OS X, windows are layered without regard to their applications. In other words, you may have a FileMaker Pro window in front of a FrameMaker window with yet another FileMaker Pro window behind the FrameMaker window. Bring All To Front brings all of that application's windows forward, eliminating any interleaving.

All of an application's windows moved together in Mac OS 9 and earlier. If the application was active, all of its windows were on top of all other applications' windows. With Mac OS X, windows from various applications are interleaved.

Window Names

The Window menu terminates with an item for each of the application's windows that the user creates. Choosing a window's name will move it to the front and activate it. This applies whether the window is layered behind other windows on the screen or if it has been placed in the Dock by minimizing it. Windows with unsaved changes are marked with a dot before the name.

Help

The Help menu contains one or more commands to let you find out more about the application you are using. Many Help menus have more than one item in them. For more on Help in Mac OS X, see Chapter 9, "Getting Help."

Using Aqua

In this chapter, you have seen many of the features of Aqua. Some are revolutionary and new, while others are variations on technologies with which you may already be familiar. However, the sum total of them (together with the underlying architecture and functionality of Mac OS X) is a new way of using your computer. Particularly if you are someone with years of experience, you should consider how to take advantage of these new ways of working. Here are some ideas.

Using Menus

Don't Turn Off Your Computer

Most computers today come with energy saving features for their processors, monitors, and disks. You can put all models of the Macintosh into Sleep mode manually or automatically after a certain period of inactivity. (See "Energy Saving" in Chapter 6, "Setting Preferences," for more information.)

Mac OS X is remarkably stable; its predecessor, the NeXTSTEP operating system, was famous (like all Unix-based systems) for running without interruption for months at a time. This stability means that your computer can indeed run for days—or weeks or months—without needing to be restarted. Even if individual processes or programs have problems, the computer itself will chug merrily along.

Use the energy saver features (see Energy Saver in System Preferences) to conserve energy. As with all energy use (including lights, automobiles, and appliances), finding out a bit about how the energy is used can help you make the best of it. For example, many devices use more power to start up than they do to keep running once the start-up cycle is finished. This may be because power is needed to spin up a disk drive, get an air conditioner compressor running, or the like. Turning a computer on and off several times a day may actually be more expensive in terms of power and wear and tear on the computer than leaving it on.

Certainly, if you will be away for a week, it makes sense to power down your computer, printer, and other peripherals. It is the intermediate time periods that require some thought.

Another aspect of power management that you should consider involves recharging batteries for portable devices. In locations where power is priced differently depending on the time of day (or even where the price is the same but certain time periods are more prone to shortages than others), you can charge batteries overnight so that your daytime power consumption is from the battery and not the overstressed power grid.

Leave Applications Running

Since your computer can run for extended periods of time, you should consider letting applications run for long periods of time, too. This not only reduces the amount of time you have to wait for an application to launch, but it also means that your recent work—even if it was several weeks ago—is right at hand. (Minimizing windows by placing them in the Dock can leave your monitor uncluttered.)

Because memory is managed in a new way in Mac OS X, an application that is running but not active takes almost no system resources. It's not going to harm you by being there.

Not all applications are ready to function in this long-running world, however. Applications that periodically make backup copies of data files may spawn scores of such copies over the course of a week. There may be other consequences of letting applications run for long periods of time. The best rule of thumb is that if you are running older applications, keep an eye out for unusual behavior until you are satisfied that you can work in this way. The good news is that most applications have been tested thoroughly with Mac OS X by now and such problems have been discovered, documented, and often fixed. And, of course, if you are a developer, you need to add long-term performance to your list of features to test!

What This Means

Putting this all together—not turning off your computer, and leaving applications running—you will find that you have a device that has everything ready for you at all times. The Dock is critical to this way of working, and that is why comparing it to favorites or start-up menus in other operating systems may prevent you from seeing the true power at your fingertips.

Using the Classic Compatibility Environment

Classic Mac OS applications run on Mac OS X with their traditional interfaces. Figure 2-14 shows Microsoft Word running on Mac OS X. It looks just like it does on Mac OS 9.

If you click the desktop or on a Mac OS X application or document, the Word and Classic Compatibility Environment interface elements disappear, but the window remains, as shown in Figure 2-15.

There are some minor difference in the ordering of windows on Mac OS 9 and earlier, but they are easy to get used to. Also, as you can see, window borders are different. The most

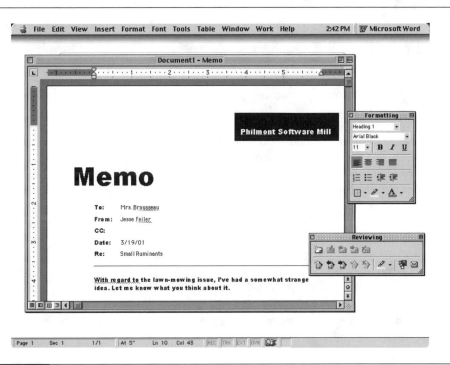

FIGURE 2-14   Microsoft Word running in the Classic Compatibility Environment on Mac OS X

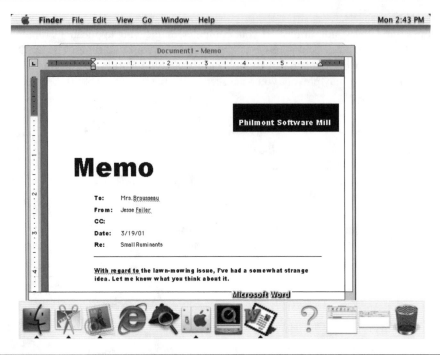

FIGURE 2-15   Microsoft Word running in the background on Mac OS X

significant difference you may find—and it is demonstrated here—is that some applications on Classic Mac OS use the bottom of the screen for a status bar. In such cases, use the Turn Hiding On command from the Dock submenu in the Apple menu. In that way, the application's status bar is visible, but when you move the mouse over it, the Dock will rise up.

Summary

Aqua is the heart of the new way of working that is implemented in Mac OS X. This chapter has provided an overview of the user interface: how windows work in Aqua, using the Dock, using menus, and the new way of working made possible by Aqua and the functionality and reliability of Mac OS X. There is more to Mac OS X than the interface. The next chapter completes this introduction to Mac OS X by delving into the various environments and technologies that make it all work.

Chapter 3

How Mac OS X Works

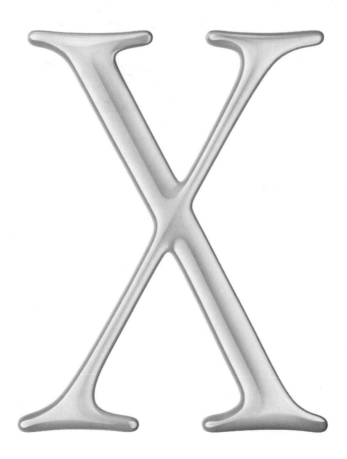

In Chapter 1, "Mac OS X," you explored the basics of Mac OS X: how it evolved, what it looks like, and what's new. In the course of that chapter many of the underlying technical concepts such as multiprocessing and multitasking, as well as protected and virtual memory were described. In Chapter 2, "Aqua," you saw what the interface looks like and why Aqua is such a revolutionary improvement in the way in which people use modern computers.

To wrap up Part I, this chapter focuses on how Mac OS X works. With an understanding of the concepts at the root of the operating system, as well as with a glimpse of what it looks like, you can delve into everything that lies in between. For the casual user, this may be an idle curiosity—or it may be of no interest whatsoever. (If that is the case, feel free to move on to the next part of the book.) For people who want to understand how Mac OS X works, for developers who need to write for the operating system, and for managers who need to plan for deployment of Mac OS X and for applications to run on it, this chapter should provide a guide, not only to the structure, but also to the terminology within that structure.

The major sections of this chapter encompass the seven layers of the Mac OS X architecture: hardware, Darwin, graphics, frameworks and environments, Aqua, application programs, scripting and messaging, and connecting the layers.

The Seven Layers of Mac OS X

Figure 3-1 shows the seven layers of Mac OS X, which were introduced in Chapter 1. As noted there, this diagram is an expanded version of diagrams used by Apple in describing Mac OS X.

The Programming Tools layer from Chapter 1, "Mac OS X," has been renamed Frameworks and Environments. This reflects the evolution of those tools in Mac OS X, and it will be discussed later in this chapter.

Some of these layers are more obvious to you than others. The hardware, for example, is sitting on your desk or your lap; the Aqua interface is what you interact with. Application programs are what you purchase or develop and what you (or others) run to accomplish work or play. Application programs include aspects of Darwin, the graphics layer, and the environments (some are used in development and others actually do the work of the application program). Accordingly, you don't often see Darwin, the graphics layer, or the environments on their own. Finally, scripting and messaging are features that not all application programs support and that not all people use.

> NOTE   *The separation of features into layers suggests some kind of hierarchy: certainly hardware does seem to be the most basic element of all. Do not become too enamored of the hierarchical view. Each layer does basically rely on the functionality provided by the layers beneath it, but when you get to the top, there is a chicken-and-egg situation that is really not worth worrying about. Application programs implement interfaces as well as scripting and messaging. If you want to reorder the top three layers, feel free to do so if it makes you more comfortable.*

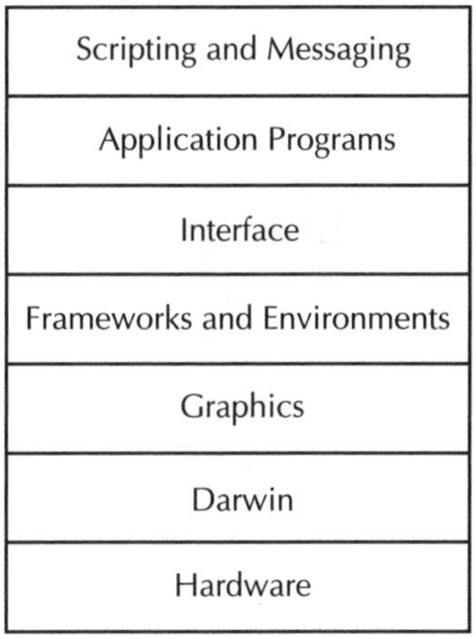

Scripting and Messaging
Application Programs
Interface
Frameworks and Environments
Graphics
Darwin
Hardware

FIGURE 3-1   The seven layers of Mac OS X

In Figure 3-2, you see the diagram again, but this time the technologies of each layer are identified. The architecture (shown in Figure 3-1) is extensible in many ways. In the simplest way, the application programs that you have on your computer will change over time as you install and remove them. Technologies implementing any of the other layers may also change over time. It is likely that there will not only be replacements, there will be additions as well. This chapter focuses on the technologies, shown in Figure 3-2, that comprise Mac OS X today.

Hardware

At the heart of it all is the hardware. A few decades ago, everyone knew what a computer looked like: it was a collection of big metal boxes in a specially air-conditioned room with a raised floor beneath which miles of cables snaked back and forth connecting the components. About one decade ago, most people started to think of computers as personal computers; generally located on desktops, they consisted of a processing unit, a monitor, a keyboard, and then a mouse.

Today computers are—or are in—everything from cellular phones to refrigerators and pocket organizers. The trend of miniaturizing components, increasing power, and decreasing price has continued apace, although the trend of improving graphics has not continued. Displays, particularly flat panel displays, are easier to view than ever. However, the graphics output on handheld devices, including cell phones, is sometimes a throwback to the quality of yore. (In a few years' time, it is likely that the issues regarding displays in small, portable devices will be resolved.)

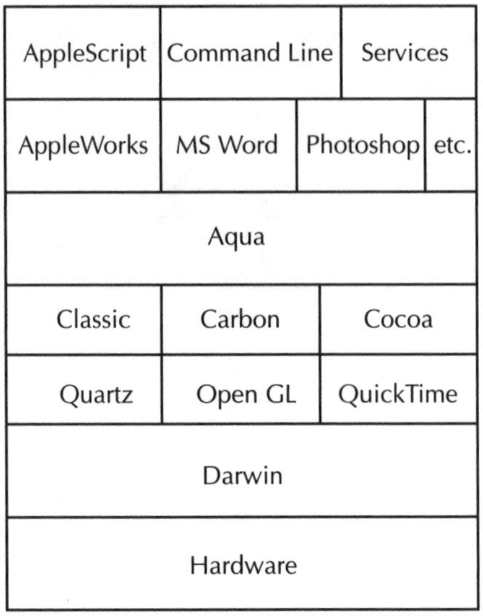

AppleScript	Command Line	Services	
AppleWorks	MS Word	Photoshop	etc.
Aqua			
Classic	Carbon	Cocoa	
Quartz	Open GL	QuickTime	
Darwin			
Hardware			

FIGURE 3-2   Technologies of the seven layers of Mac OS X

What this means to you and to Mac OS X is that the particular components of today's hardware are unlikely to be around very long. Yet, the basic elements of the hardware that the operating system deals with will. This section describes those basic elements and briefly discusses some of their implementations today.

Mac OS X supports hardware configurations on all Macintosh computers sold since 2000. It supports many of the hardware configurations on previous Macintosh computers, but for older machines you need to check to see exactly how (and if) Mac OS X deals with your hardware. Use Apple's Web site at http://www.apple.com/ for more information. You can also refer to the resources in Chapter 9, "Getting Help," and go to http://www.philmontmill.com/ for additional information on older computers.

The basic hardware elements are

■ Processors

■ Special-purpose processors

■ Internal bus connections

■ High-speed connections

■ Lower-speed connections

- Video connections
- Network connections
- Printers

Processors

Today, Mac OS X runs on the PowerPC processor. Based on the IBM Power chip, it was designed by the alliance of Apple, IBM, and Motorola. The kernel, Darwin, interacts directly with the hardware. Layers above the kernel interact with the hardware through Darwin. This means that if Darwin is reprogrammed to use another hardware design, the layers above it should not know that a change has occurred.

As noted in Chapter 1, "Mac OS X," computers with multiple processors are now shipping from Apple. The Darwin kernel is designed to handle such computers. In general, multiprocessing refers to computers that have more than one general processing chip. See the next section for another architecture.

Special-Purpose Processors

Many computers, including some Macintosh models, have additional processors that handle special tasks. The most common of these tasks involve graphics. Graphics processing units (GPUs), such as the NVIDIA or ATI RADEON GPUs included in the G4 and high-end PowerBook G3 models, are designed to accelerate graphics processing. Other special-purpose processors handle sound and special devices, such as instruments.

Typically, special-purpose processors (also called execution units) are used to handle time-dependent operations. You want the processing of speech or of video to continue unabated while the computer is opening files, sending data over the Internet, and calculating spreadsheets. Vendors such as Apple often incorporate special-purpose chips into some of their products. In other cases, users customize their computers to provide the special computing resources needed for specific situations.

Starting with Apple's G4 computers, the Altivec technology from Motorola—marketed as Velocity Engine—is included. These additional circuits and instructions provide very fast processing of large amounts of data using the same instruction: exactly what is required in manipulating graphics data, for example. Mac OS X is optimized to use Velocity Engine extensively in its operations.

Internal Bus Connections

Bus connections are connections within the computer that handle very large amounts of data very quickly. Typically, these are used to transfer data to and from memory and internal disks. Buses transfer data among several locations. They have separate channels for the data, status information, and addressing information. This is a different architecture from the point-to-point connections in which a single device, such as a modem, is attached to a single port. Very much

Hardware

like a mass transit bus for people, a computer bus transports information that is removed when it reaches its destination (its address). It bypasses other locations.

The speed of a computer is a function not only of the speed of its processor, but also of its bus speed. The processor needs to work with data, and if the data can't get there in time, the processor is idle. (This is one reason why upgrading a processor does not always result in overall speed improvements.) Older Macintosh computers used a bus technology called NuBus. Starting with the second generation of PowerPC Macintosh computers (such as the 8600), Apple switched to the PCI (Peripheral Component Interconnect) bus architecture. If you have bought a G3, iBook, or iMac computer, you almost certainly have a PCI bus. This matters because Mac OS X works only with the PCI bus architecture. If you have a G4 Macintosh, you have a PCI bus architecture.

High-Speed Connections

The buses described in the previous section connect internal devices in most cases. External devices, peripherals, are connected using other technologies. Two important ones for Macintosh users are FireWire and SCSI. They both allow you to connect a number of devices to a single connection, or port. They are used for the high-speed data transfers required of disk drives, CD-ROM and DVD drives, and often for video. FireWire is the newer technology, but many SCSI devices are still around.

The high-speed connections described here are built into the computer. If you want to attach peripherals to your computer, you must buy them with the appropriate type of connection. Note that these connections are not just a matter of plugs; you normally do not buy a converter to convert a SCSI disk drive to a FireWire disk drive—you buy a FireWire disk drive if that's what you want.

SCSI

The Small Computer System Interface originated on DEC minicomputers and was adopted by the Macintosh fairly early on in its development. Devices connected to a SCSI port each have a number, normally from 0 to 7. (Some SCSI implementations have a pair of channels, allowing up to 16 devices.) These devices are referred to as a SCSI chain. A SCSI chain is connected to a single computer, and it is limited in length to 6 meters (just under 20 feet).

SCSI ports have never existed on the iBook and iMac product lines. Starting with the PowerBook G3 (FireWire) in February, 2000, they were removed from that line. Currently, they are optional on the desktop product line.

You must set the ID number of each device, since no two devices on the SCSI chain can have the same device. Typically, a small dial or other mechanical device on the rear of the SCSI device enables you to select the ID number. Data is transferred along the chain and drops off the chain when it arrives at the numbered device it wants. Each SCSI device has two identical connectors on the rear. A cable from the computer goes to one connector on the first device, and a cable from the other connector goes to one connector on the next device, and so on. (It doesn't matter which connector you use on a SCSI device. One is connected in the direction of the computer, the other in the direction of the rest of the chain.) As a result of this architecture, the final device in the chain must be terminated—either by pressing a button on its back panel or by adding a special plug to one of its connectors; some terminate automatically.

SCSI devices are set up when the computer is powered on. You should never disconnect or reconnect SCSI devices while the computer is in use.

Speeds for SCSI devices typically range from 4 Mbps (megabytes per second) to 80 Mbps. Data transfer speeds—whether over modems, networks, or connections such as these—are highly variable. Speed is degraded by automatic error detection, noise on the line, and even external conditions such as the temperature (which can cause connections to waver as connectors expand and contract).

FireWire

FireWire is a newer standard, invented by Apple, which can easily be defined in comparison to SCSI. Unlike a SCSI chain, the FireWire connections are maintained dynamically. ID numbers and special terminators are not needed. Speed is presently at 400 Mbps. Most important, FireWire devices are hot-pluggable: you can connect and disconnect them without powering off your computer.

FireWire is typically used for disks and digital video—situations in which relatively large amounts of data need to be moved quickly. Although you can place several computers on a FireWire port, it is not really a substitute for networking (discussed later). A FireWire chain is limited in length to approximately 4 meters (14 feet) and can contain up to 63 devices.

FireWire is now an international standard (IEEE 1394) supported by a number of different vendors, each of which may have its own brand name for its implementation—Sony's version is i.LINK. Because the underlying standard is the same, you can safely connect different vendors' products together, for example, plugging an i.LINK camera into your Macintosh computer's FireWire port.

Lower-Speed Connections

Personal computers typically have lower-speed connections, often parallel and serial ports. On the original Macintosh, there were two serial ports; one was normally used for the printer and the other for the modem. You could only connect a single device to each port.

Today, a variety of technologies exist: some are on their way up, others are on their way down. The following lower-speed connections are discussed in this section:

- Universal Serial Bus—USB (on the way up)

- Wireless (on the way up)

- Serial ports (on the way down)

- Apple Desktop Bus—ADB (on the way down)

Hardware

USB

The Universal Serial Bus (USB) is like the SCSI or FireWire peripheral connections. It is a bus connection to which you can connect up to 127 devices. On Macintosh computers today, a USB port (or two) is provided. Into it, you plug the keyboard, mouse, and other peripherals, connecting them in a chain—mouse into keyboard into computer. If you have two USB ports, you can connect the devices to separate ports.

The USB cable includes the power for the needed device. You do not need a separate power cord in most cases; however, some USB devices need to be connected directly to an electrical outlet. USB hubs can be powered, and if so, you plug them into an electrical outlet to help power the devices plugged into them.

As of this writing, USB ports support data transfer speeds of up to 12 Mbps. Like FireWire, they are hot-pluggable: you can plug devices in and out while the computer is powered on. USB is used for the mouse and keyboard, some disks, and digital image capture (not digital video; USB is normally not fast enough for video).

There are two types of USB cables. Device cables have a USB A plug at one end and a USB B plug at the other. B plugs connect to devices such as printers or cameras; A plugs connect to USB hubs or computers. (Most Macintosh computers today have one or two USB A receptacles.) Extension cables with an A plug at one end and an A receptacle on the other connect USB hubs to other hubs or to computers. And some devices use A plugs rather than B plugs.

When purchasing USB peripherals, check to see that the appropriate cable is included. Frequently, you will need to purchase it separately. An extra USB cable may be left in the packaging that came with your Macintosh computer (if you can find it). Cables are not inexpensive, so keep track of them so that whenever you need USB cable, or a telephone cable, you know where to look. Coil cables loosely so as not to damage them.

Since your Macintosh will probably have only one or two USB plugs, you will probably need a USB hub to connect more than one device. Before setting out to buy a hub, check your keyboard and monitor: they may have extra USB receptacles on them. A four-port USB hub is not very expensive ($25–$50 is common).

Connecting a hub to your computer with a fairly long cable enables you to plug in a printer, digital camera, disk cartridge drive, and pocket organizer while keeping them off your desk or work surface. Place the hub on a side table along with these devices.

Because power flows over the USB cables, there are some idiosyncracies of USB devices and cables of which you should be aware. In particular, the USB plug on your computer keyboard may not have enough power coming through it to support your printer connection. As printer documentation will explain to you, if your printer does not work, plug it into your computer directly or into a hub that is connected directly to your computer (rather than into your keyboard or monitor).

USB hubs can be powered or unpowered. Powered hubs require connection to a power source. In general, it is a good idea to use a powered hub because if you have several USB devices, your computer may not be passing enough power along to them. A powered hub may be able to function either powered or unpowered. A switch can indicate which mode it is using. (Make certain that the switch is correctly set; a powered USB hub with the switch set to unpowered but that is plugged into a power source may not work properly.)

Wireless

Wireless connections are increasingly important. The cost of building and maintaining wired networks is beginning to be outweighed by the cost and convenience of maintaining wireless ones. Two important wireless technologies are used on the Macintosh today: IrDA and AirPort.

IrDA   The IrDA (Infrared Data Association) standard for high-speed, short-range, line-of-sight, point-to-point cordless data transfer is implemented on PowerBooks and many small devices, such as pocket organizers and digital assistants. IrDA connections run at speeds of up to 4 Mbps making them suitable for relatively small data transmissions. The line-of-sight constraint means that the connections can be unstable if they are moved or if structures intervene between the two communicating devices.

AirPort   AirPort uses radio waves (rather than infrared) for its transmissions. The AirPort system consists of a base station that serves as a hub for your wireless network. Computers installed with AirPort antennas and hardware can connect to the base station from distances of up to 45 meters (150 feet). Since the technology is based on radio, line-of-sight considerations do not apply.

The AirPort base station can be plugged into another network, and it can also have a modem attached to it. It functions exactly as a network hub does. Data transfer rates can reach 11 Mbps on an AirPort network. AirPort is based on the IEEE 802.11 Direct Sequence Spread Spectrum (DSSS) and can be used with other devices that support that standard. Many airports and other places where people spend a lot of time waiting are now being wired for AirPort technology.

Other Technologies   Wireless communication is one of the fastest-growing areas of computer technology; stay tuned for further developments. Mac OS X, TCP/IP, and modern networking standards all combine to insulate users and application programs from changes in the mechanisms of data transport. As a result, you should be able to avail yourself of new products without having to make major changes in your operating system or its configuration.

Serial Ports

Serial ports are still used to connect devices, particularly small ones with limited data transfer requirements, such as digital still cameras, pocket organizers and eBooks. Unlike disk drives where, in many cases, you have a choice of FireWire and SCSI models, some of these devices do not give you a choice. As a result, you may have to accommodate serial devices. Since the latest Macintosh computers do not have serial ports, and Mac OS X does not support serial ports, you need to work around this limitation if you have a serial device that you need to connect.

There are two ways you can do this. You can buy a converter to connect a serial device through a USB port. Or, if you only periodically use the serial port and there is one installed on your computer, you can restart in Mac OS 9 to use the serial port. Mac OS 9, unlike Mac OS X, recognizes serial devices. Serial ports on the Macintosh typically run at speeds between 0.2 and 2 Mbps.

Serial ports for modems and printers never existed on the iBook, and they were removed from the iMac starting in October 1999. They were eliminated from PowerBooks starting with the PowerBook G3 (FireWire) in early 2000, and they faded from the desktop product line starting with the G4 series.

Apple Desktop Bus (ADB)

This low-speed bus (10 Kbps) was used to connect the keyboard and mouse to the Macintosh. It has been replaced by USB on recent computers.

Video Connections

Video devices—monitors, projection devices, video cameras and recorders—can be connected to your computer in various ways. Until the advent of the high-speed FireWire connections, these were analog connections. Using FireWire means you do not need a special plug or port to connect a camcorder or video monitor. You use the same FireWire port and connectors that you use for disks and other devices.

On Macintosh computers, two common analog connections are VGA and S-Video. These connections are still available on many computers because the peripherals—the cameras and so forth—do not yet have FireWire connections. If you are using a PowerBook for presentations and you need to constantly plug in a variety of equipment at various locations, you may need several connections and converter plugs. Digital video cameras generally use FireWire, and all-digital computers, such as the Apple G4 Cube, no longer have specialized video connections. As of the release of Mac OS X, if your digital camera or camcorder does not have USB or FireWire connectors, it is now old enough that it should be replaced.

VGA

Video Graphics Array (VGA) is the technology used to connect monitors to many computers. Macintosh monitors used a different form of connection, but several years ago the industry-standard VGA port began to appear on PowerBooks. (This is important because many people take a PowerBook with them and plug it in to projection equipment in meeting and conference rooms.)

S-Video

Video is different from computer output. S-Video is a video-based technology that is used to connect video equipment. Some PowerBooks contain S-Video output ports so they can be connected to camcorders and video display devices. The S-Video ports on those devices can also be connected to other video equipment.

Network Connections

Mac OS X supports networking via both Ethernet and AppleTalk.

Ethernet

Ethernet is now the standard way of connecting computers over a local area network (LAN). It consists of cables, connectors, devices (such as computers), and network management devices (such as hubs and routers).

Today, many cables and connectors use Category 5 (Cat 5) standards for the cables and RJ-45 connectors to attach them to devices. Macintosh computers come with built-in RJ-45 receptacles.

There are many variations on Ethernet physical cabling; these involve the type of cabling and connectors. Rather than memorizing a whole set of specifications, you can remember one common point: the maximum length of cables from one device to another is 100 meters (about 300 feet). Some implementations make the maximum length much longer, but if you assume that 100 meters is your limit, you are unlikely to have problems.

The two common systems today are 10BaseT and 100BaseT. The first runs at speeds up to 10 megabits per second; the second at speeds up to 100 megabits per second. A computer's Ethernet connector is connected internally to an Ethernet card. Each card has its own unique ID number. A single computer can have several cards, with one connector for each. In that way, a computer can communicate either on several networks or by appearing as several devices on one network. Gigabit Internet—speeds of up to 1,000 megabits per second (or 1 gigabit)—now exists as well.

In mixing equipment on a network, you may not be able to use the highest speeds, since the various devices that are communicating may need to compromise on a low speed that both ends of the connection support. As you replace equipment, your network speeds may increase without you doing anything, as the lower-speed devices are removed. In any event, you usually do not have much say about the speed of your network connections. The most common bottleneck may be a hub or router that is old. Its replacement can sometimes speed up all of your network devices.

AppleTalk

AppleTalk is both a communications protocol and a cabling implementation. Original AppleTalk connectors and cables were designed strictly for that purpose; however, for more than a decade AppleTalk has been able to run over standard Ethernet cabling (although it does not do so in every installation).

Not only can AppleTalk run over standard Ethernet cabling, but it can also run over the TCP/IP protocol. TCP/IP is becoming the preferred way of connecting Macintosh computers and printers, since it does not require proprietary protocols. There is more on this in Part III: "Networking."

Printers

Printers can be attached to individual computers with serial connections, low-speed buses (USB), or high-speed buses (FireWire and, rarely, SCSI). These printers are usable only by the computer to which they are attached. If the computer is networked, it may be able to respond to network print requests. It is the computer, not the printer, which interacts with remote network users in these cases. Both Mac OS 9 and Mac OS X support the sharing of USB printers connected to an individual computer.

Hardware

Other printers are attached directly to a network. They can be shared among several network users. Printing is discussed in Chapter 5, "Printing."

Darwin

Darwin—the kernel of Mac OS X—is based on Mach and BSD (a variant of Unix).

Mach

Mach handles memory and processor resources on the computer. All of its major features are involved in one way or another with using and sharing these resources. Mach 3.0 is the version currently part of Darwin.

Resource sharing is very important because small independent processes run in order to handle printing, networking, and other tasks. An "idle" computer running Mac OS X can easily have 30 processes running at the same time.

Processor Resources Under Mach

Using and sharing processor resources is done primarily with preemptive multitasking, its message system, the scheduling features of Mach, and real-time support.

Preemptive Multitasking   In order to allow multiple processes to run on the same computer at more or less the same time, Mach implements *preemptive multitasking*. This architecture allows each task in turn to use all of the computer's resources. Individual tasks normally do not know when they have been swapped in or out: their processing is continuous from the task's perspective.

On Mac OS 9 and earlier, as well as on some other operating systems, cooperative multitasking is implemented: tasks can control when they relinquish the computer's resources. In such a case, one "poorly behaved" task can hijack the computer's resources and prevent other tasks from getting any time. A typical case in point is an application that on Mac OS 9 or earlier posts an alert that requires a user to click OK or Cancel. In some cases, that alert can prevent anything at all from happening on the computer until it is dismissed.

Preemptive multitasking means that your computer's environment is more stable and efficient. It is forgiving of design flaws in programs that might occur in cooperative multitasking. Programs can be simpler because they do not have to be concerned with sharing processor resources—it happens automatically.

Messaging   One of the particularly sophisticated aspects of Mach architecture is its messaging system. Messaging involves the use of ports in each thread that are resources owned and managed by the thread's task. Structured messages can be sent across this messaging system with ease. The system messaging architecture easily accommodates messaging within a single computer's tasks, as well as among tasks on a network.

The messaging system built into Darwin means that application programs (and their threads) need very little coding in order to implement messaging. This can allow applications to be written so that a number of cooperating threads can work together on a common task. Messaging lets the threads keep track of the task's data and status; preemptive multitasking lets the threads run almost simultaneously. This improves throughput and simplifies sophisticated application design, particularly in a multiprocessor environment.

Scheduling   Scheduling of tasks in Mach uses the messaging system to start and stop tasks and to keep programs running efficiently.

Real-Time Support   Time-sensitive and critical applications (including advanced media) often need direct access to the computer's hardware. Recognizing this, the Mach architecture provides a simple and direct route for applications to get to the low-level devices they need to keep video rolling, games playing, and so forth.

The absence of such support requires application programmers to write kludgy code to bypass the operating system. The formal inclusion of real-time support makes such hacks unnecessary which, in turn, contributes to the stability of well-behaved programs that do not break the rules.

Memory in Mach

Much of Mach is devoted to memory issues. In particular, protected memory and virtual memory.

Protected Memory   Protected memory is one of the most significant features that contributes to the stability of Mach applications. On Mac OS 9 and earlier (and other operating systems), an individual application could trespass on another application's memory or even on that of the operating system. In fact, some programs were designed deliberately to do so. The problem, of course, is that unwanted interactions could occur even in the best of cases. In the worst cases, bugs in application programs caused them to corrupt the memory spaces of other application programs or of the operating system, resulting in computer-wide failure.

In Mach, it is impossible for such cross-application memory corruption to occur. You may be able to see this for yourself. The Classic Mac OS environment actually is an application that runs under Mach. If a poorly behaved Classic Mac OS application accidentally corrupts the memory of another application, or of the Classic Mac OS environment itself, the Classic Mac OS environment will crash. However, none of the Mac OS X applications will crash.

Virtual Memory   Virtual memory in Mach essentially makes the computer's memory almost unlimited and relies on memory objects for its implementation. Rather than the degradation in performance that some original virtual memory schemes caused, virtual memory in Mach is fast and efficient. Because virtual memory relies on disk as temporary memory is needed, you should invest in the fastest disks you can for your computer.

BSD

BSD 4.4 is implemented in Darwin. It is a variant of Unix that was developed at the University of California at Berkeley (hence, Berkeley Standard Distribution). It is concerned with slightly higher-level features than is Mach. Specifically, it deals with files, networking, and processes. (Mach deals primarily with memory and processor resources.)

Two aspects of BSD, POSIX and the Darwin implementation of multiple file systems, are of particular importance in allowing you to take advantage of existing programs and files on other operating systems.

POSIX

BSD includes many Portable Operating System Interface (POSIX) APIs. In the 1980s, several of variants of Unix arose. Each was slightly different from the others, and as a result programs written for one Unix often could not be recompiled on another Unix without some errors. The POSIX APIs embody a standard set of APIs that programmers can employ to develop code that can be recompiled on any POSIX system.

Adopting many of the POSIX APIs means that programs written to POSIX standards can be recompiled on BSD, often with little if any modification. This is the primary mechanism by which Unix programs can be recompiled and run on Mac OS X. While you may not find a complex graphics program that you can recompile, the number of small programs that perform utility tasks is enormous. Mac OS X starts with a very large number of applications ready to run in this way. (Typically programs that perform computations and operations without having a graphical user interface built into them are the best candidates for this process.)

File Systems

File systems are implemented in BSD, and five major formats are supported in Mac OS X: Mac OS Extended Format (HFS+), Mac OS Standard Format (HFS), UFS, UDF for DVD, and ISO 9660 for CD-ROMs.

File systems determine how the raw media of a magnetic disk or optical disc is formatted. They also specify how individual files are stored. By supporting a file system, the operating system can read and write files using that format.

It is the incompatibility of Mac OS file systems and DOS- or Windows-based file systems that prevents you from using Macintosh-formatted disks on DOS or Windows computers. You can reformat the disks on the Macintosh into a DOS or Windows format.

HFS+: Mac OS Extended Format   This format is a modification and expansion of Apple's original format. Files consist of two forks: a data fork, which contains data in whatever format an application wants to use, and a resource fork, which contains semiformatted data—often icons or small graphics.

Files also contain some additional maintenance information, including codes for the application that created them and for the type of file they are. The operating system uses this information to select the icon used to display the file and to choose the default application to open the file when you double-click it.

Aliases—links to other files—are supported on HFS+, as are hard links. Aliases, hard links, and symbolic links are discussed in Chapter 4, "Working with Files." This format is well adapted to gigabyte-sized hard disks. It is used by default on Mac OS X, Mac OS 8 and Mac OS 9.

HFS: Mac OS Standard Format   An older Macintosh format, this was used in Mac OS and earlier operating systems. Named the Hierarchical File System (HFS), it differs from HFS+ in a variety of ways. Most noticeably, it is very inefficient on large (gigabyte-sized) disks. Disks formatted in HFS can be read on HFS+ systems; the reverse does not apply.

UFS   Based on BSD's Fast File System (FFS), this format is used on many Unix systems. Files have single forks, and they do not have type or creator codes. Aliases are not supported, but symbolic and hard links are. If you are transferring HFS or HFS+ files to Unix computers, you need to combine (or "flatten") the two forks into one. See Chapter 4, "Working with Files," for more information.

UDF for DVDs   This is the standard format used for DVDs.

ISO 9660 for CD-ROMs   CD-ROMs use ISO 9660, which is also supported in Mac OS X.

Networking File System Support   Over a network, Mac OS X supports three primary file server systems: AFP (Apple File Protocol), NFS (Network File System), and WebDAV. AFP is the file-sharing protocol that was implemented on Mac OS 8 and Mac OS 9. Its support in Mac OS X means you can share files over a network with computers running those operating systems. Computers running Unix, or that are compatible with Unix, frequently use NFS. It, too, is implemented in Mac OS X, allowing you to share files with those systems. Finally, WebDAV is a new, Internet-based protocol for sharing files.

Device Support

A framework based on a subset of C++ is provided with Darwin to implement device support. Called the I/O Kit, it enables drivers for printers and other devices to be written quickly. The I/O Kit itself implements most of the plug-and-play capabilities that users expect, as well as hot-plugging (that is, connecting and disconnecting without powering down) and power management.

As with messaging in Mach, this is a sophisticated framework, and it means that the actual writing and testing of code for drivers of new devices can be minimized.

Graphics

The graphics environment of Mac OS X consists of Quartz for 2-D graphics, OpenGL for 3-D graphics, and QuickTime for time-dependent graphics, such as audio and video.

Graphics

Quartz

Quartz provides all 2-D graphics support, which includes graphics themselves, as well as 2-D representations of 3-D or time-dependent graphics such as windows and printing. It uses PDF internally to render graphics.

Quartz separates graphics services from rendering. Core Graphics Services manages the graphics environment (color, layering, window management, and the like). Core Graphics Rendering actually draws on the screen and produces PDF. It relies on the Core Graphic Services.

Because PDF is provided in the operating system at such a basic level, it is available to all applications for print previews and as an alternative output format without special programming

On Mac OS 9 and earlier, QuickDraw was the primary 2-D graphics environment. Carbon applications can still use QuickDraw: Core Graphics Rendering provides a QuickDraw interface so that developers who are porting graphics code can use the Quartz imaging mechanism (including PDF) without rewriting their code. (This is a significant benefit, in view of the fact that so many Macintosh applications contain so much graphics code.)

Quartz is optimized for Velocity Engine.

OpenGL

OpenGL is an industry standard for 3-D graphics, with code that is fairly self-contained. However, when 3-D images must be drawn on the 2-D screen or a 2-D piece of paper, OpenGL interacts with Quartz, which does the necessary rendering.

QuickTime

QuickTime is Apple's technology for time-dependent media such as video, sound, animation, and music, as well as for other multimedia, such as virtual reality. As the industry-leading tool for creating and manipulating such media, it supports all of the major file formats in use today. These include PICT, BMP, GIF, JPEG, and PNG for still images; AVI, AVR, DV, M-JPEG, MPEG-1, and OpenDML for video; and HTTP, RTP, and RTSP for streaming video.

QuickTime runs on Mac OS 8 and Mac OS 9, as well as all flavors of Windows since Windows 95.

Frameworks and Environments

Originally, the programming tools of the Macintosh were Assembler and Pascal. Over time, other languages were added, including C, Object Pascal, and C++. Still more languages including Fortran, Cobol, Lisp, Smalltalk, and Dylan (among others) were implemented to a greater or lesser extent on the Macintosh.

The seven-layer diagram of Mac OS X includes a frameworks and environment layer. It consists of Classic Mac OS, Carbon, and Cocoa. Each is a way of writing and running programs; however, each is also actually a different type of technology. The Classic Mac OS environment is an application program, Carbon is a set of libraries, and Cocoa is an application framework. All three concepts are related.

Object-Oriented Programming and Frameworks

Object-oriented programming is a technique that provides for writing reusable sections of code. It is now used for almost all custom programming. Many application programs are either written using this technique or are being revised to incorporate it. Object-oriented programming is discussed in much more detail in the last part of the book.

The use of object-oriented programming has spurred two separate trends in writing reusable code:

- People sometimes write small, self-contained objects that can be used and reused in different environments. Some of these enhance the interface of programs and Web pages; others provide enterprise-specific database access and business operations. Some of the technologies used in this way include Visual Basic, Java Beans and Enterprise Java Beans, and ActiveX controls.

- People have written very large and extensible frameworks of code in which parts can be replaced or extended easily. Examples of these frameworks include MacApp (the ur-framework on the Macintosh), Cocoa (the Mac OS X native framework), Microsoft Foundation Classes (MFC), and PowerPlant from Metrowerks.

With the use of object-oriented programming, the programming languages used become somewhat less important than the framework and the objects. Just to make life more interesting, object-oriented designs can include traditional components—and they frequently do, particularly for low-level routines. Describing the development tools that go into an application program is now much more complicated than just mentioning a programming language. There may be several languages, one framework, and a variety of small objects.

From a user's point of view, knowing what programming languages and frameworks have been used in creating an application is irrelevant in almost all cases. For a developer—or for a manager hiring consultants or programmers—it can be critical. In the context of Mac OS X, there are three frameworks whose names you should know:

- **MacApp**   Originally developed in the 1980s using Object Pascal, this is perhaps the first widely used framework on any platform. Currently in its fifteenth major revision, it has served as the basis for products such as Photoshop, ObjectMaster, GIFConverter, and Tango 2000, many Apple software tools (such as Apple System Profiler), and a host of in-house customized solutions. Programs written in MacApp run on Mac OS X and on Classic Mac OS.

- **Cocoa**   This framework was derived from NeXTSTEP and OpenStep. It is the preferred framework for Mac OS X applications that do not need to run on Classic Mac OS.

- **PowerPlant**   This framework from Metrowerks is available for both Windows and Mac OS. As a result, it is a good choice if you want to write a single application to run on both platforms. However, its functionality is somewhat more limited than those of MacApp and Cocoa.

Frameworks and Environments

Libraries and Environments

The frameworks are the shells for new applications. They contain objects—not all of them used in each new application—and you can add customized objects to them. All of this is thoroughly object-oriented.

There is another concept that you need to know, that of code libraries. These, too, are reusable, but they are not object-oriented (or at least do not have to be). When a programmer writes a line of code, such as:

```
X = sin (Y);
```

the compiler and linker convert it to actual computer instructions. As part of those instructions, a section of code implementing the sine function may be inserted into the application program. In other cases, the application program is created with an instruction that causes the program to execute a stored routine at runtime.

To programmers, there is a very big difference between linking to libraries at compile/link time and linking to libraries dynamically at runtime. However, in both situations, the application program invokes code provided in a shared library that usually is not written by the programmer.

In either case, the external code becomes part of the application program either at compile/link time or at runtime. Apple provides the basic libraries, and there are several versions of them. Since libraries contain some of the actual computer instructions, they can include separate sets of code for different operating systems and architectures. Apple encourages programmers to link against the most recent and most general libraries; this allows the best versions of the code to execute.

When a well-written program is recompiled and relinked, the libraries to which it is attached can often be changed without further ado. By simply changing the libraries, a programmer can produce code that is designed for one environment or another. This is the primary mechanism by which the conversion from the Motorola 68xxx chips to the PowerPC chips was done. Programmers linked against 68xxx libraries and then linked against PowerPC libraries. The results were either separate applications or "fat binaries"—files containing both types of applications.

Classic Mac OS

The Classic Mac OS environment is a Mac OS X application that happens to be Mac OS 9. That application—the Classic Mac OS—can then run applications within it. Almost all Mac OS 9 or earlier applications can run in this way on Mac OS X, and these application programs aren't "aware" that they are running in Mac OS X.

The first release of Mac OS X actually used Mac OS 9.1, not the first release of Mac OS 9. For example, the windows that an application program opens in the Classic Mac OS environment look like Mac OS 9 or earlier windows—because they are. They are managed by the Mac OS 9 window manager, which is running as part of the Classic Mac OS environment on Mac OS X.

There are some links between the Classic Mac OS environment and Mac OS X that implement a number of user interface features—particularly those related to cutting and pasting between applications in the two environments. As always, the reality is a little more complex than the concept.

Carbon

The Carbon environment is essentially a set of libraries that contain code that runs on Mac OS X (if that is where it is launched) or on Mac OS 9 (if that is where it is launched). For many application programs—particularly if they are well written and not unduly complex—a programmer can relink the program using the Carbon libraries to produce a Carbon application.

Carbon applications when running on Mac OS X have the Mac OS X look and feel. Their windows look like (and are) Aqua windows. The programmer's definition of a Carbon application is the presence of a `carb` resource with an ID of zero.

Cocoa

The third environment that exists in Mac OS X is Cocoa. Cocoa is actually an object-oriented framework. It implements all of the features of Mac OS X. In fact, Cocoa is a set of frameworks including a foundation framework and an application framework. As a result of its implementation of all aspects of Mac OS X, Cocoa is not compatible with Mac OS 9.

As a user, it is hard to see the difference between an application program developed using Carbon and one using Cocoa (that's part of Apple's point in making the transition as smooth as possible for developers). However, there are many under-the-hood differences in how Carbon and Cocoa applications run.

Typically, a developer will write or modify an existing program to use Carbon. Over time, as the need for supporting Mac OS 9 and earlier users diminishes, the program will be rewritten to use Cocoa.

The conversion from Classic Mac OS to Carbon is typically less involved than that from Classic Mac OS or Carbon to Cocoa. For example, you can use MacApp to write applications that compile and link as Classic Mac OS or Carbon applications (depending on how you set certain parameters).

Aqua

Aqua, the user interface, was described in Chapter 2, "Aqua."

Application Programs

Application programs, the tools you use to do your work and play your games, are what you really care about on an operating system. Part IV, "Using Applications on Mac OS X," is devoted to them.

Scripting and Messaging

The top layer of the diagram may be new to you, or it may be something you know about but haven't considered much. You are probably used to sitting at your computer, clicking the mouse,

Scripting and Messaging

choosing menu commands, and typing. This is a very efficient way of working, particularly when compared to how old-style mainframe computers worked.

However, it can be very inefficient in some ways. If you're composing a letter or designing a flyer, your clicks, choices, and keystrokes are valuable. If you're moving files around, converting images from TIFFs to JPEGs, or otherwise performing routine tasks, that piece of hardware on your desk should be able to do those things for itself.

That's where scripting and messaging come in. Mac OS 7 implemented Apple events and AppleScript: sophisticated techniques for communicating between programs. On mainframe computers, interprogram communication (IPC) evolved in the late 1960s as a way not only to communicate between programs, but also to allow big problems to be broken up so they could be worked on by several relatively independent programs.

Mac OS X, following in the footsteps of Unix, implements a command-line on which text-based commands can be typed. It then goes further and uniquely implements services. All are discussed in this section, and all are designed to let you automate the running of application programs. This can make routine and repetitive operations easier and less subject to keystroke and mouse errors. It also can free up your time and make your computer productive during hours when you would otherwise not be using it.

Apple Events

Messaging between applications is implemented on Mac OS using *Apple events*. Events consist of commands, as well as attributes and optional parameters that contain data to be acted on or other information needed to carry out the task. Apple events are sent from one application to another. The sender is referred to as the client, and the receiver is the server.

Apple events are defined by Apple, as well as by developers. For example, an Apple-defined class of events is the class of required events. Its events are the open application (start), open document, print document, and quit events.

Events may be defined as having a direct object—an object on which the event acts. Thus, an open document event has a direct object that is a document or list of documents. An open application event has no direct object: it opens the application to which it is sent.

Suites of events can be defined for applications or sets of applications. They are particularly well implemented in the world of graphics and prepress. Apple events are defined by developers. They may be invoked through menu commands or other processing; they may also lie in wait for an end-user to write a script.

AppleScript

AppleScript is a scripting language with two bases:

- It rests on the highly structured semantics of Apple events, which define operations and data in a very precise way.

- It also rests on a natural language-like syntax that helps you write instructions that translate into Apple events.

AppleScript is implemented both on and in the Mac OS X environment. You can use it to tie applications together, construct repetitive tasks, and otherwise automate your work. For more information, see Chapter 20, "Automating Your Work with Apple Script."

Command Line

The command line (available through the Terminal application) lets you launch and provide data to applications. Typically, these are the applications that run in the shell without the Aqua interface, but you can also launch some other applications this way. Combining command-line commands into scripts enables you to automate your workflow into AppleScript-like jobs.

Services

Services are a very high-level form of communication on Mac OS X. Described more thoroughly in Chapter 17, "Working with Services," they require a degree of cooperation between two applications. However, that cooperation is minimal—in other words, each application can work with the other, provided that they both play by the rules.

A service is defined as some sort of functionality that accepts data of a particular type and returns data of another particular type. The functionality can be whatever the application wants to define. As part of that definition, the application specifies the type of data accepted or returned and weather data will be accepted or returned. For example, a spell-check service might accept data of type text and return data with a value of correct or not. An email sending service might accept data of type text and return nothing, but have an email program create a message with that text in its body, ready to send. Yet another service might accept nothing, but return text representing the current date in a specified format. Each of these exists. See Chapter 17 for more particulars.

Connecting the Layers

Many of the layers of the Mac OS X architecture can be connected. In common with most modern connectivity architectures, this architecture relies on peer-to-peer connectivity. In other words, the lines are horizontal, not diagonal, as shown in Figure 3-3.

Knowing which layers connect with one another and what means are used can help you in debugging problems. The four layers that commonly are connected are described in this section.

Hardware

Connecting computers is very common today. In fact, the stand-alone computer may not be long for this world.

The hardware layer is responsible for these connections. If you do not have an Ethernet card and port, you cannot connect an Ethernet cable. In a well designed system such as Mac OS X, the hardware is responsible for very little more than the physical connection.

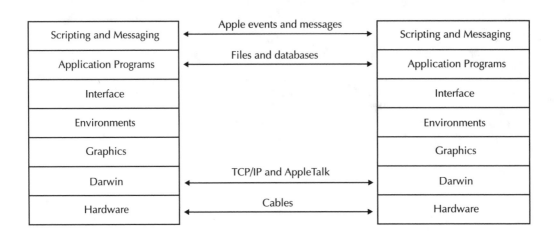

FIGURE 3-3 Connecting Mac OS X layers

With the advent of wireless connectivity, you should recognize that the means of connectivity is not only cables, but also infrared, radio waves, and other media.

As in all diagrams of this sort, each level of connectivity may rely on technologies below it, but it does not know about technologies above it. Thus, network connectivity at the hardware level can be implemented across operating system platforms: an Ethernet connection is an Ethernet connection.

Kernel

The kernel implements TCP/IP and AppleTalk features; you control them with System Preferences, which is how you normally set all kernel settings, unless you are an advanced user using the command line in Terminal.

The fact that these protocols are implemented in the kernel means that they should either work or not. If your email program works and your Web browser doesn't, it's probably not your TCP/IP connection. (It may be your host names, since the mail and Web hosts differ.)

In troubleshooting network connections, try to find out how many of your network applications do and don't work. This will help you determine whether you've got kernel problems, such as bad Preferences for your network, or application problems.

TCP/IP is a platform-neutral protocol; it is implemented on almost all types of computers today. As a result, you can establish a physical connection at the hardware level with most computers. You can also establish a TCP/IP connection with Macintosh, Windows, and Unix computers.

AppleTalk, on the other hand, is an Apple protocol. It is normally implemented only on Macintosh computers, although some limited implementations on Windows are available.

Application Programs

Application programs communicate with one another using files and databases. The formats and contents of these files and databases are defined by the application programs. Microsoft Word may read WordPerfect documents, but then again it may not.

Application programs typically read more data types than they export. Vendors are very happy for you to convert your data to their proprietary format; they're not so happy to see you leave. Consumers must start making it clear that this capturing of their data is unacceptable. In purchasing any software product, make certain that your data, which you own, can if necessary be exported in a standard format or in other vendors' formats. This is one reason for using SQL and ODBC in the database world.

File and database formats, defined by applications, may be implemented across platforms. For example, the same Microsoft Word file can be read and written on Windows and Macintosh operating systems.

Scripting and Messaging

Scripting and messaging rely on operating system-defined formats such as Apple events and Mac OS X messages and services. Communication at this layer is real-time, as opposed to the application program file- and database-based communication. It also is normally platform specific.

A lot of work today is going into cross-platform and cross-computer messaging. The Common Object Request Broker Architecture (CORBA) and Microsoft's Distributed Component Object Model (DCOM) are two such efforts. Enterprise Java Beans represents another type of cross-computer messaging. It relies on CORBA and can interact with DCOM.

For Mac OS X users today, scripting and messaging is normally limited to one computer or to other Mac OS X computers that are linked via a TCP/IP network, which includes the Internet. Real-time messaging connectivity to other platforms and types of devices (such as cell phones half a world away) is sure to come.

Summary

Summary

The first part of the book has presented Mac OS X. In the first chapter, you saw the concepts and technologies, in the second, the Aqua interface, and in this one an overview of the components of Mac OS X from the hardware to the most advanced messaging. The terms used in this chapter will recur in this book, as well as in other books and articles you may read. With this basis, it is time to move on to actually using Mac OS X. The next part of the book introduces you to those adventures.

Part II

Using Mac OS X

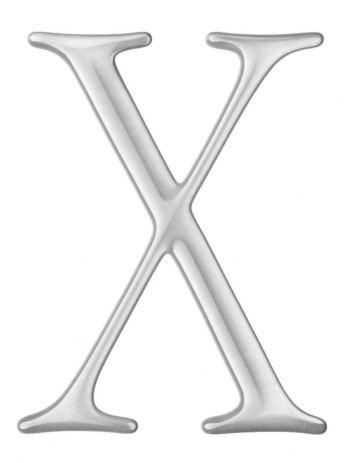

Chapter 4

Working with Files

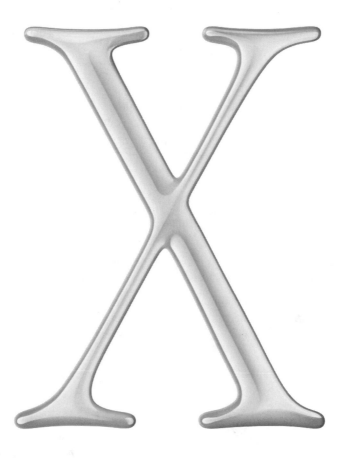

This part of the book shows you how to use your computer with Mac OS X. The focus is only on your own computer. Refer to Part III for coverage of networking; Part IV for applications; and Part V for information on automating your work with Mac OS X.

To start with, this chapter is devoted to files. Files store information on your computer's disk. They may contain text, graphics, video, sound, or even an application program. If it is stored on your computer's disk, it's in a file.

Critical as this is, there are some situations in which you can safely ignore just about everything related to files. In other words, you can skip this chapter in these cases:

- If you use your computer only on the Internet (that is, if you only use a browser and an email program, whether as one program or two), you can skip this chapter.

- If you use only custom-written software that has already been installed for you, you *may* be able to skip this chapter. In this case, ask the person who has written and/or installed the software if you need to worry about files.

- If you use a database program such as FileMaker that accesses a database located on a local area network (but not on your computer), someone else will worry about your database file.

In these cases, you almost certainly will still be using files, but your programs (the browser, the email program, the database, or the custom-written software) may take care of all of this behind your back. Most people do need to read this chapter, but if you are certain that you are in one of these categories of users, feel free to go on to the next chapter. You can always come back later.

The chapter is divided into seven sections:

- **Mac OS X File Concepts**   Offers a brief introduction to the architecture and terminology of the Mac OS X file system. It's what all users should know about files.

- **Notation, Identification, and Partitions**   These topics help you talk about files and understand how they are stored on your computer.

- **Using the Finder**   The Finder is the application that lets you manage your files. This section shows you what it looks like.

- **Opening a File**   In addition to managing files directly with the Finder, you can manipulate them with application programs. (In fact, that is the most common way of working with files.) This step-by-step guide shows you how to open a file from any Mac OS X application.

- **Saving a File**   You almost always save or create files with applications. Here is the companion to the previous section.

- **Menus**   All of the Finder's menus are described here.

- **Working with the Mouse and Keyboard**   The Finder's mouse and keyboard commands enable you to copy and move files and reorganize your desktop.

Mac OS X File Concepts

Four basic concepts are important for understanding how data is stored on Mac OS X:

- Files and documents

- Folders and directories

- Aliases and links

- Packages and bundles

Although the concepts are common, the terminology varies somewhat. Rest assured that there are only four concepts here, however, each has two commonly used names that are used interchangeably in this book. Most of these concepts are common to all operating systems, although there are some slight variations from platform to platform.

For example, DOS-based operating systems frequently restrict you to two-part filenames: the first part can be up to eight characters long and the second part can be three characters long. The Mac OS was the first mainstream operating system to allow much more flexibility in filenames: they could be longer, and the three-character suffixes (which allowed the operating system to determine the type of file) were no longer required. Mac OS X allows long filenames, and its file suffixes are frequently hidden (although they are there).

Files and Documents

All information on your computer's disks is stored in *files*. Part of the job of the operating system is to manage files and disks. Application programs treat files as contiguous chunks of data, and the programs format and organize their data according to their own standards. The actual data storage on disk is rarely contiguous. The operating system stores bits and pieces of file data all over the hard disk and assembles the data as needed for the program. This is the source of *disk fragmentation*: as files are created, enlarged, and reduced in size, their constituent parts are scattered over the disk. A file that is located in one actual location is usually more efficiently accessed than one that is scattered. Disk maintenance programs consolidate files for you.

Files and documents are usually the same thing on any Macintosh operating system. The desktop metaphor of the Macintosh uses the less technical term, *document*. Files may also be databases, supporting information, and even application programs. A distinction is made between files that contain executable code and all other files. This is in part because an operating system needs to know that opening a file containing executable code means launching a process, whereas opening a file containing data requires finding an application to manipulate the file's data. The operating system must launch the application, rather than the file itself.

Filenames

Each file has a distinct name. Files that you create can usually have any name you want. You must remember how you store your information, so it makes sense to assign names such as Guestlist or Chapter3. Files created by the operating system or by application programs for internal use generally have names that are known only to the operating system or program. (These files are usually kept out of your sight, but sometimes—particularly in the case of automatic backup files—they are visible. If you don't know what a file is and you're in the mood to clean up your hard disk, be careful and don't throw out something that might be important.)

From a practical point of view, shorter filenames are better than longer ones. You can organize documents into folders, so that instead of a file called AccountingInformationPersonal2002 you can place a file called 2002 in a folder called Personal, which is in a folder called Accounting Information. This makes it easier to keep track of files.

On Unix file systems, capitalization matters—myfile is not the same as MyFile. This is not true on HFS+. It may trip you up if you are transferring files to and from other computers, as is the case if you are setting up a Web site on a Web server. Try to set a standard for yourself to use.

Although you can use spaces within filenames, they often cause problems. One way of avoiding this is to use an underscore (_) to connect two words, as in my_file. Unfortunately, the underscore is not always visible to the careless observer. It is far better simply to run two words together (perhaps capitalizing the second, as in myFile). One useful rule of thumb is to use a logical file naming structure for your own files. If you need to share files with computers running other operating systems, you might want to consider making the rules stricter than they need to be on Mac OS X (in other words, no spaces).

Finally, you should know that two characters are automatically removed from filenames. On Mac OS 9 and earlier, the colon (:) character was automatically removed from filenames and replaced with a hyphen (–). On Mac OS X, the forward slash (/) character is not allowed within filenames.

File Headers

While the contents of a file are the responsibility of an application program, the operating system maintains the contents of a file header. The header stores the security information for the file (see Chapter 7, "Securing Your Computer" for more information), as well as its length, when it was created, and the last time it was modified. You can view this information in the Finder's Info window (described later in this chapter in the section on the File menu).

Folders and Directories

Files on a hard disk are assembled into *folders* or *directories*. The terms are interchangeable. The more technical terms, files and directories, were supplanted by terms that are more familiar from the world of paper, documents and folders, with the advent of graphical user interfaces.

Folders or directories can be established by users to organize their files, just as file folders in a filing cabinet do. You create folders in the Aqua interface; when using the command line, you create directories. Nevertheless, they are the same objects, and your command line-created directories show up as folders in the Finder windows of the Aqua interface.

Operating systems and application programs also use folders and directories; sometimes this is merely for organization. Other times, there are more sophisticated purposes afoot. For example, security can be set not just for individual files but also for directories. Consequently, the files in one directory may be visible to other users, while the files in another directory may be visible only to you.

Directories themselves can contain other directories. For example, this allows you to organize your personal documents into a general folder called Personal Matters and to create subfolders in it called Bank Statements, Tax Returns, and To Do. The structure of directories on your computer is a combination of the operating system's choices and your own.

There are two sets of basic directories on Mac OS X that you will be able to see on your computer. One set is created at the *root* of your hard disk. Root-level documents and directories are not in any other directories. You can see these folders by clicking Computer in the Finder's toolbar. You will see the disks available to you, and if you open the disk from which you start up your computer, you will see these folders. (The Finder toolbar and opening disks and folders are described later in this chapter in the section, "Using the Finder.")

The other is the set in your *home* directory or home folder, visible when you click Home in the Finder's toolbar. Each user who uses a computer has a separate home folder named with that user's name. Thus, the root-level folders are shared among all users, and the home-level folders are private to each user (unless the user allows access to others).

While early personal computer operating systems were designed for a single person's use, Mac OS X is designed from the ground up for multiple people to use a single computer. This is discussed further in Chapter 7, "Securing Your Computer." Even if you are the only user with access to your computer, it is configured so that other users can be set up at any time.

Each of the basic folders is described in this section. Some folders appear both at the root level and at the home level. For example, you can have fonts installed on your computer for all users to use, or you can have fonts installed for just your own use. Similarly, applications can be shared or not, depending on your choice. The names of these folders are set by Mac OS X, and you should not rename them. Their contents should be as described here—for instance, do not put documents in the Applications folder. If you put files in the wrong places, Mac OS X will function correctly most of the time, but some of its features may not work as well as they might.

For most people, all of these files are on your computer. However, either set of files can be located on another computer on a network. Mac OS X Server allows your network administrator to specify that your home folder is located on another computer.

In these folders, you can create any other folders you want. Documents, for example, typically contain a host of subfolders that each individual creates.

In addition to the folders listed here, you may find many others created by Mac OS X. If you install Mac OS X on a computer on which Mac OS 9 has already been installed, all your folders will be commingled. Gradually, you can move them into the Mac OS X Documents and Applications folders if you want.

When moving your files to another computer (perhaps a new computer in another location or that you have purchased as an upgrade), you can usually move all of the files in your home folder to the new computer. It is best to reinstall software on the new computer (rather than copy it), since software installations affect the root level Applications and Library folders, and installers properly handle these matters.

In addition to organizing information, this folder structure lets Mac OS X seamlessly customize applications for you. For example, when it is searching for a resource to be used in a program—a font, image, or sound, for example—it looks first in the Library folder of your home folder in the Users folder. If it does not find the file for which it is looking, it looks next in the Library folder inside the root level. This means that the skilled user (or network administrator or developer) can deploy alternative interface elements such as fonts that override standard features. These can be deployed for one user only (inside the Users folder) or for everyone using the software installed in the System folder.

Applications

This folder contains applications. There is an Applications folder at the root level, as well as one for each user. The files in the Applications folders are just the applications; they should not change over time except for updates to the software itself. Documents you create with these applications are stored elsewhere, as are application preferences and settings.

Library

In this folder you will find supporting files—fonts, graphics, preferences, and the like. Often, applications create and maintain these files without your having to worry about them. You may never open the Library folder at all. (In fact, that is probably a good idea for most people!) There is a Library folder for the root and each user. Among the folders in the root level Library folder is one called Printers folder. Inside, you will find drivers and utility programs for many printers. If you buy a new printer, its drivers (either from a CD-ROM or from the Web) will probably be installed in this folder automatically when you install the printer according to the manufacturer's instructions.

System

This is emphatically not the System Folder of Mac OS 9 and earlier. There are no user-serviceable parts inside. It is present only at the root level.

Users

In this folder, there is one folder for each of the computer's users. Each of those folders is a home folder for that user, and the user's folders reside there. In other words, in the Users folder, there might be a folder called ftosca, and in ftosca (a home folder) will be found an Applications folder, a Documents folder, a Library folder, and so forth.

Documents

This folder lets you store your documents. By default, most well-behaved applications attempt to store or read documents from this folder. You can create subfolders in Documents for various projects. The Documents folder is for text-based and other general documents. The following folders—Movies, Music and Pictures—are for specialized kinds of documents. This folder is present in each user's home folder.

Movies

Use the Movies folder for movies you create and share with friends. The iDVD and iMovie applications store files in this folder. This folder is present in each user's home folder.

Aliases allow you to apparently have files in two places at the same time. You can put your movie documentation and scripts in your Documents folder and place an alias to them in the Movies folder (and vice versa). See the section on aliases later in this section.

Music

Your music files (such as those you create with iTunes) are stored in the Music folder. This folder is present in each user's home folder.

Pictures

Digital images are stored here. The Image Capture application stores pictures from digital cameras in this folder automatically. This folder is present in each user's home folder.

Public

This folder is set up so that other users on the network can access some of your files. Place files (or aliases) in the Public folder if you want them seen by others.

A Drop Box subfolder is set up in the Public folder. It allows people to store files into it, but they cannot view its contents (although you can). This is a convenient way to let people send you files without compromising the security of each file since only you can view them. This folder is present in each user's home folder.

Desktop

The Desktop folder contains the files you place on your desktop. If you remove files from your desktop or from your Desktop folder, they disappear from both places. This folder is present in each user's home folder.

Since the Desktop folder is present in each user's home level, there is a separate desktop for each user.

MailAccounts

Subfolders in this folder correspond to each mail account that you have set up. A mail account has its own password and user ID; it is established by your Internet service provider. This folder is present in each user's home folder.

The MailAccounts folder is maintained by the Mail application or via System Preferences | Internet Preferences. It is set up initially during your setup and installation of Mac OS X.

Mailboxes

In the Mail application, you will set up these mailboxes. Mail comes in to your mail accounts (in the MailAccounts folder) and then is distributing among mailboxes by Mail. The distribution can be automatic, according to rules you set up in Mail, or you can do it manually. This folder is present in each user's home folder.

Aliases (Links)

In addition to files/documents and directories/folders, an important concept for Mac OS X is that of aliases (or links). Aliases are file headers that are not attached to a file, but rather, are linked to another file. The alias appears to be a file, but in fact, if you attempt to open it, you open the file to which it is linked. An alias can be used to make a file appear to be in two places.

Icons that represent aliases look just like the original items' icons except for the fact that they have a small arrow in the lower-left corner. Double-clicking an icon that is an alias opens the underlying item.

The icons in the Dock are aliases, although they do not have the small arrow. The documents, applications, and folders that you "place" in the Dock remain where they are on your computer; only an alias appears in the Dock. That is why removing an item (an alias) from the Dock leaves the item untouched on disk.

Aliases can be created for directories and folders, as well as for files. This allows for great flexibility in creating logical structures of folders and subfolders. Those subfolders can be aliases, and if they are aliases, a folder (and all of its contents) can appear in more than one place. This is impossible with paper-based objects, which cannot be in more than one place at a time (at least above the quantum level). This flexibility can also be a source of confusion and disorganization: if you are used to remembering where things are, you may be perturbed to find them in two or three places.

Since aliases behave very much as their underlying files do, you may not notice that you create them periodically. For example, if you drag a document or folder icon from a write-protected folder (such as the Computer folder) to your desktop, you create an alias on the desktop. This is because you cannot write to the Computer folder, and thus cannot remove its contents. But you can create an alias to that object on your desktop, which is just what you do. The fact that you never may notice that this is an alias shows how complete the mechanism is.

In Unix, links are similar to aliases, but they are more limited. You can move aliases around, and the operating system will normally be able to keep track of the original item. Unix links generally are less flexible.

In order to avoid confusion, leave the file/folder structure of Mac OS X alone until you have used it for some time. If you start your use of Mac OS X by designing a complicated structure of folders and subfolders, you may well confuse yourself (and others). Also, make sure to read the section later in this chapter on "Managing Your Files": you'll see that the physical locations of your files are less and less important in Mac OS X, compared to earlier operating systems.

Packages and Bundles

The last important file concept of Mac OS X is the concept of an application bundle. A bundle is a directory or folder that appears to be a single file—an application. The files in the package include the actual code, separate files with the application's graphics, its sounds, and even the text that appears in its menus and on its windows. These graphics, sounds, and text are those of the application, including its icons and text such as "OK" or "Paste Special." Your graphics, sounds, and text are stored separately, usually in your Documents, Pictures, Movies, or Music folders.

In previous operating systems, this information was all part of a single file—the application program. This made customizing the applications rather difficult. Separate versions needed to be shipped for each language and for any other customizations that were necessary. With a bundle, only the files that deal with button names or with icons need to be changed to localize an application program.

This substitution can occur when a developer creates a bundle (thereby creating a localized version). It also can occur when you run the application program—your localization preferences determine which resources are used. The decision of whether to ship multiple versions or a single version is more of a business decision than a technical one.

Notation, Identification, and Partitions

You see documents and folders displayed in windows and on your desktop: you just point and click to manipulate them. You also see disks in windows and on your desktop. The disk icons represent the disks connected to your computer (internally, externally, or over a network).

Sometimes it is necessary to refer to files by name; the section on file notation that follows shows you how to do that. In addition, sometimes the disk you see is not actually a disk, but a partition. That is explained in the following section, too.

File Notation

A naming convention for files and folders is used in Mac OS X and most other operating systems today. The filename is preceded by the folders in which it is contained. Thus, the Mail application—located in the Applications folder—can be described as follows:

```
/Applications/Mail.app
```

All the folders on a computer have a common enclosing folder: the root. That is why the full name of a file always starts with a forward slash (/) representing the root folder, followed by any directories and subdirectories and then the filename.

A user's files are located in a directory such as Documents. The file electionRules.doc can be identified as:

```
/Users/ftosca/Documents/electionRules.doc
```

Because so many files are located within a user's subdirectory, a common method of identifying a given subdirectory is used: the tilde (~). Thus, for a user logged in as ftosca, the two following filenames are identical:

```
/Users/ftosca/Documents/electionRules.doc
~/Documents/electionRules.doc
```

You can use this notation not only to specify a file, but also to specify a *path*—that is, the directory in which a file or directory is located. The path to your home level might be this (paths end with a slash: /).

```
/Users/ftosca/
```

There is much more on this in Chapters 7, "Securing Your Computer" and 21, "Using the Command Line." The Finder is the graphical user interface to the file system, and you don't need to worry about these details for most of your daily routines.

Identification

One of the most important aspects of a graphical user interface is that when you open a document the "right" application automatically is launched (if necessary) and displays the document's contents. Keeping track of the right application is no mean feat.

Mac OS X uses a database to keep track of applications. This information is used, not only to determine which application to launch when you open a document, but also which icon to display in the Finder.

Three pieces of information are used to identify an application to match a document:

- On HFS and HFS+ file systems, each file contains a document *type code* and a *creator code*. Each of these is four characters. The combination of codes allows a document type (such as TEXT) to be identified with a specific program that created it—Microsoft Word, for example, or AppleWorks. With this combination, text files created by Word are opened with Word, while text files created by AppleWorks are opened with AppleWorks. Nevertheless, since both programs can handle text documents, either can open such documents created by the other. Unfortunately, type and creator codes are not implemented on other file systems, and they are not even required to be used on HFS+ in Mac OS X.

- A *hint* can be provided in the first thousand bytes of a file. The operating system peeks into those bytes looking for a hint. It can be used to identify an application.

- A suffix of three or four characters can identify a document type. Text documents often sport a suffix of txt, JPEG files may have a jpg suffix, and so forth.

Mac OS X uses whatever information of this sort that it can find to select the document's icon in the Finder and the application to launch.

Changing a document's suffix in the Finder may change its icon immediately and may change its default application. This can work both for and against you. If you receive a file via email and you know it is a JPEG image, add .jpg to the filename and it will be displayed properly. Likewise, be aware that the Finder automatically strips .app suffixes from application files when they are displayed in the Finder. They are there, but you see Mail, not Mail.app in your Finder listing.

> TIP
>
> *Drag a document onto an application icon (either in a Finder window or in the Dock), and that application will be used to open the document. In the case where any of several applications can be used to open a standard file type, this allows you to control which application is invoked.*

Partitions

A disk can be divided into several *partitions*. A partition behaves exactly as a disk does. It is named as a disk would be, and it appears with a disk icon on the desktop or in Finder windows.

You set up partitions using Disk Utility in the Utilities subfolder of the Applications folder. (There is more on Disk Utility in Chapter 8, "Managing Your Computer Environment.") Once set up, you cannot change partitions without destroying the data in them.

Since Mac OS X handles multiple users very effectively, you do not need to set up partitions if several people use one computer. You can create multiple users even for yourself if you want to keep sets of data separate.

Developers and software testers find partitions very effective for installing multiple operating systems. You can have one operating system in each partition. During development of Mac OS X, many developers had two or three partitions on their hard disk. One partition contained a standard operating system such as Mac OS 9; this was used for daily work. Another partition contained the latest version of the developing Mac OS X operating system. Still another contained an earlier version of Mac OS X (such as Mac OS X Server 1.2).

Files cannot span partitions. That is one reason for minimizing your use of partitions. If you have an 80GB hard disk divided into 10 partitions of 8 gigabytes each, none of the partitions will be large enough to store a 9GB movie.

One strategy is to create a small partition—with a very stable set of software—on your hard disk. You do this with Disk Utility before you install any other software. On the small partition, install only the operating system that ships with the computer. For applications, install a backup program such as Retrospect and perhaps a file utility such as StuffIt Expander. That way, you can change your startup disk to the small partition at any time and reboot your computer even if your main partition is corrupted in one way or another. From the small partition, you can remove files in the main partition or even reinstall the operating system in the main partition if necessary.

Using the Finder

The Finder is the application that provides the graphical user interface to the file system. You do need to know the four concepts described previously (files/documents, directories/folders, aliases/links, and packages/bundles), but you don't need to worry about the details of file notation unless you are doing advanced work.

The Finder consists of its windows and menus. The background of your computer—the desktop—is not part of the Finder in the way it was in Mac OS 9 and earlier. You can place folders, documents, and disks on the desktop, but you are actually dragging them to a specific folder (the Desktop folder in your home level in the Users folder). The contents of the desktop display are the contents of the Desktop folder.

Using the Finder

The Finder is available from the Dock—click on the Finder icon; it is normally running on your Mac OS X computer, and you can activate it by clicking on the background of the desktop. It is also the leftmost item in the Dock at all times. If you can't see a Finder window, choose New Finder Window from the File menu of the Finder. If the command is not visible, the Finder is not active; click on the desktop or click the Finder icon in the Dock. (The rest of the menu commands will be described later in this section.)

This section walks you through the tasks you frequently do with the Finder: browsing files and folders. The Finder lets you view files graphically. It has three types of displays:

- Icons
- List
- Columns

When you first see the Finder, it may be configured in any of these three ways. In addition, a Finder window may have a toolbar at the top. The toolbar (which is customizable) contains icons for quick navigation, as well as for common tasks you want to perform.

You can see the same folder or document in several Finder windows at the same time. You can customize these displays so that you use different views (icons, list, or columns) to look at these objects from different perspectives. There is no single "Documents" window: there are as many views into the Documents folder as you want. This differs from Mac OS 9 and earlier where when you opened a window into a directory, you opened the same window.

View as Icons

Figure 4-1 shows the Finder window displayed as icons. The toolbar is visible at the top of the window. The Finder menus are shown at the top of the figure, and the Dock is shown at the bottom. The icons in Figure 4-1 represent two disks and a network to which the computer is connected.

> **NOTE** *The icons in your Finder window will vary depending on your computer's configuration; likewise, the icons in the Dock will vary. Even the buttons in the toolbar at the top of the window are variable.*

If an icon in the Finder's window represents a document or application, double-clicking it will open it, launching the appropriate application. If, however, it represents a folder (or disk drive), double-clicking it will change the Finder window's display to the contents of that folder (or disk drive).

The Finder window when viewed as icons changes its display as you navigate. New windows do not open. This is a difference from Mac OS 9 and earlier, but that behavior can be simulated if you double-click an icon while holding down the OPTION key. A new Finder window will open to display the contents of the folder or drive. Such subsidiary Finder windows do not have the row of buttons at the top.

FIGURE 4-1   Finder window viewed as icons

List View

If you switch the Finder to view its contents as a list, the List view appears.

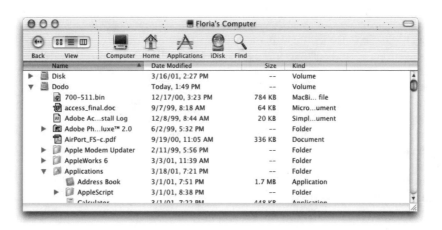

Using the Finder

This view is similar to views in Mac OS 9 and earlier Finder windows. The *disclosure triangles* to the left of entries let you expand or contract each item so you can see its contents. Note that the list view can show you two or more levels of the file structure, whereas the icons view shows you only a single level at a time.

As in icons view, double-clicking a folder while holding down OPTION will open that folder in its own Finder window. This window will contain the contents of that folder. As noted previously, subsidiary Finder windows will not have the buttons at the top to navigate to Home, Favorites, and so forth.

Columns View

The columns view shown here is new in Mac OS X:

This display is similar to the list view, but it is more structured and livelier. As you can see in the screens, there are several columns in the Finder window; the number varies as you resize the window. Compare the information in the icon, list, and columns views. You will see that the columns view contains the most information in the smallest amount of space.

Selecting an entry displays its contents in the column to the right, as shown in Figure 4-2. A folder or document on the desktop is also present in the Desktop folder.

As you click on folders and documents, the columns view scrolls automatically from left to right. Each pane also scrolls automatically up and down to display the currently selected folder or document.

Columns view is a very efficient way of looking at documents and folders; however, it does not show the contents of two folders at the same time. If you need to look at the contents of two folders simultaneously, you need to either need open two Finder windows or use a list view.

The highlighting of the containing folders for a document is slightly lighter than the highlighting of the currently selected document.

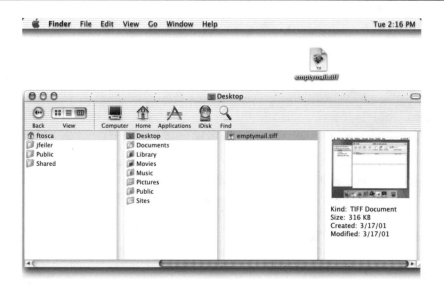

FIGURE 4-2   Finder window with preview

The Toolbar

At the top of the Finder window is a toolbar, as shown here. The toolbar helps you navigate through the Finder.

You can show and hide the toolbar using the Toolbar button at the right side of the window's title bar (or keyboard equivalent COMMAND-B). The contents of the toolbar vary, and you can control them. The most common items are described here. They appear in the toolbar starting at the left.

Back Button

The Back button lets you go to the previous display in the Finder window. It functions like a Web browser's Back button. It does not retrace the hierarchy of folders; you can scroll the columns browser to the left or hold the COMMAND key down while clicking on the Finder window's title to see the folder hierarchy menu:

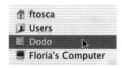

View Selection Buttons

The group of three buttons next to the Back button lets you select from icons, list, and columns views in the current Finder window. The next several buttons enable you to move quickly to special folders:

- **Computer**   This displays the disks connected to your computer as shown in Figure 4-1.

- **Home**   This is your home folder—the one in the Users folder with your name on it.

- **Applications**   The Applications folder is at the root level of your computer's startup disk.

- **iDisk**   Discussed in more detail in Chapter 10, "iTools: Apple's OS Tools on the Internet," iDisk is part of the iTools suite. It is located on computers at Apple, and you can use it as a disk on your own computer.

- **Find**   This button launches Sherlock, the disk and Internet search tool that is part of Mac OS X. It is discussed further in Chapter 16, "Working with Applications."

Renaming Documents and Folders

To rename a document or folder in the Finder, simply click its name once (double-clicking will open it). The name will be selected. You can wait a moment and click again at the place at which you would like to add characters (or delete them). You can also press RETURN to position the insertion point at the beginning of the name of the document or folder. Typing will replace whatever is there.

Be careful about renaming documents and folders that you did not create. The operating system or an application program may expect to find them in the same place and with the same name later.

Opening a File

The behavior of the Finder—particularly in columns view—reappears in Aqua as you open and save files. Here is an example of how you select a file to open. Choose Open from the File menu in almost any application. (A few, such as Mail, do not have this command because they handle data using their own file structure.)

You can also use the keyboard equivalent COMMAND-O to open a file. When you choose Open, the window shown in Figure 4-3 appears.

You can navigate through a miniature version of the Finder until you locate the file you want to open. This miniature version of the Finder is a *column browser*. The view in the Open dialog is always a columns view; list and icons are not available.

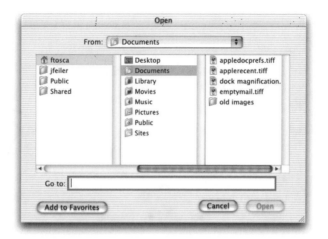

FIGURE 4-3   The Open command lets you browse files using an embedded Finder window.

This is the standard way to select a file to be opened in an application. Thus, even if you never use the Finder itself for your navigation, you will see it periodically in these windows.

You can type a filename or path in the Go To field; that will scroll the column browser to the appropriate location quickly.

The From pop-up menu at the top of the window also lets you navigate quickly to certain folders. It is shown in Figure 4-4. Your five most recent folders are shown, as well as the folders and documents you have identified as favorites. Other default folders or files may be shown in this list, too.

Finally, an Add To Favorites button lets you add documents or folders to Favorites from within this dialog. This is useful when you are starting to work on a project or set of data. You can bookmark your location for later use.

NOTE   *Some applications provide additional buttons and controls in their Open windows.*

You have three ways of selecting a file to open: from the pop-up menu, by typing in its name in the Go To field, or by navigating in the columns browser. There is no one right way of doing this; do what is easiest for you at the time.

Opening a File

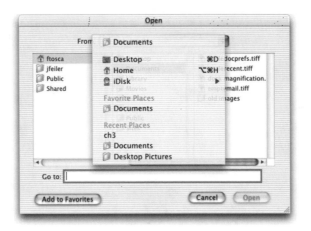

FIGURE 4-4   The From pop-up menu lets you move to folders in the Open dialog.

Saving a File

You will frequently need to save a file to disk. Doing so requires that you provide a name for the file and a location—a folder or directory—into which to place it. Here, again, you interact with elements of the Finder's interface.

Basic Saving

When you choose Save (or the keyboard equivalent COMMAND-S) from an application's file menu, you see a Save dialog like that shown in the next illustration. You can type in the name for your document and click Save. The file will be saved in whatever directory or folder you are currently working in.

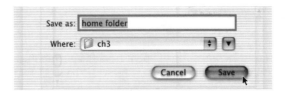

Saving to a Specific Folder or Directory

Normally, you want to save a file to a specific folder or directory. The Where pop-button, shown in Figure 4-5, will let you change the directory to a recent or Favorites directory.

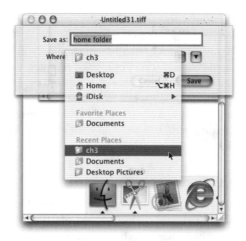

FIGURE 4-5   Use the Where list in the Save dialog to choose a folder quickly.

Navigating with a Save Dialog

If the directories shown in the Where list do not satisfy you, you can click the down arrow to open part of the Finder interface, as shown in Figure 4-6.

FIGURE 4-6   Select a directory in the Save dialog.

Saving a File

This panel lets you navigate around your computer (and the network) to find a directory you want to select. You can also use this panel to create new folders on the fly and to add items to Favorites.

Well-behaved Mac OS X applications normally will position you by default in the appropriate directory. Even applications written or revised recently will normally behave properly and you will not need to worry about choosing a directory. However, old applications (or those that are not written with rigid adherence to Macintosh standards) may let you wander all over the place. The first time you use a program, just check to make certain that you are saving files where you want to put them. It is very easy not to notice the name of the directory into which you are saving files.

A Real-Life Example

Figures 4-7, 4-8, and 4-9 demonstrate just a few of the ways of looking at documents and folders and working with them. Figure 4-7 shows a columns view of a part of the author's disk.

In Figure 4-8, a folder has been moved into the Dock; by holding the mouse button down over that icon, you can navigate through its subfolders. Note that this structure is identical to that displayed in Figure 4-7.

When saving a file, the Save dialog contains its own columns browser, as shown in Figure 4-9. This, too, shows the same information that was shown in Figures 4-7 and 4-8.

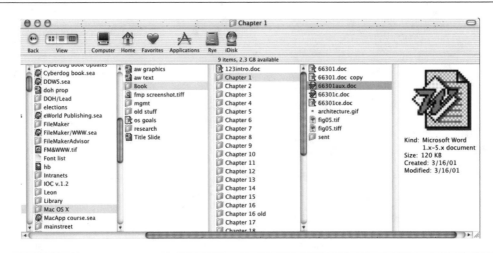

FIGURE 4-7   Columns view shows documents and folders efficiently.

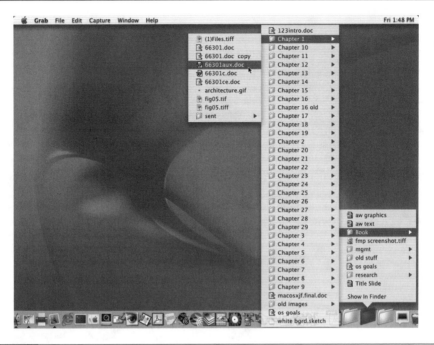

FIGURE 4-8   Use the Dock and the Finder to navigate through documents and folders.

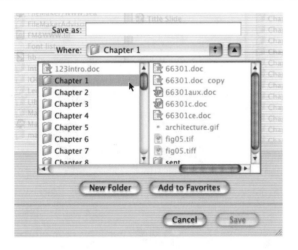

FIGURE 4-9   Columns browser in a Save panel shows the same information.

Menus

The Finder's menus let you customize Finder views and manipulate files and folders. They are described in this section. The Finder menus are the Finder's Application menu, File, Edit, View, Go, and Special.

Application

As with all applications, the Finder's Application menu (next to the Apple menu at the left of the menu bar) contains commands at the application level rather than at the level of individual documents and windows. As described in Chapter 2, "Aqua," the Finder Application menu commands include About the Finder, Preferences, and the commands to show or hide the Finder and other applications. In addition, here is where you empty the trash.

The Finder's application menu is shown here. Use the Finder's application menu to set preferences, as well as to show or hide applications.

Choose the Preferences option in this menu to set preferences with the dialog shown in Figure 4-10.

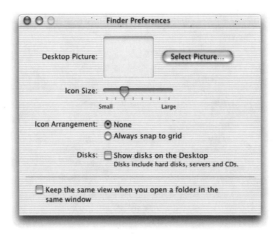

FIGURE 4-10   Use Finder preferences to control the way Finder windows look and behave.

Here you set the desktop image. A number of images are provided for you to choose from. You can also add a TIFF or JPEG file to the Desktop Pictures folder inside Library at the root level of your computer. You can use this dialog also to select any TIFF or JPEG file to which you have access no matter where it is. (Images in the Desktop Pictures folder can be used by all users of your computer; those within your home folder can only be used by you unless you mark them as public.) If the image is smaller than your screen, it will be repeated until it fills the screen.

This is also the place where you can determine whether disks and removable drives appear on the desktop as they did in Mac OS 9 and earlier.

File

The File menu lets you manipulate the files and windows of the Finder.

File	
New Finder Window	⌘N
New Folder	⇧⌘N
Open	⌘O
Close Window	⌘W
Show Info	⌘I
Duplicate	⌘D
Make Alias	⌘L
Show Original	⌘R
Add To Favorites	⌘T
Move To Trash	⌘⌫
Eject	⌘E
Find...	⌘F

Menus

- ■ **New Finder Window**   Creates a new Finder window. You may want to open a second Finder window if you are comparing two directories, copying or moving documents between two folders, or working with documents or folders in two locations. It is also useful to have two Finder windows open using different views (icons, lists, and columns). Note that the New Finder Window command opens a full-fledged Finder window. Subsidiary windows opened with OPTION-double-click (or double-click in columns view) do not have the toolbar across the top, but you can show the toolbar in any Finder window by clicking the Toolbar button at the right of the title bar.

- ■ **New Folder**   Creates a new folder in the currently selected directory in the active Finder window. Although the currently selected window is used to determine the directory in which the folder is created, it is visible in all windows. New Folder is not undoable. You can always move a folder to the Trash if you did not mean to create it.

- ■ **Open**   Opens the currently selected item in the active Finder window. If that is a document or application, the document is opened or the application is launched. If the currently selected item is a folder, it is opened in its own window.

- ■ **Close Window**   Closes the currently selected window.

■ **Show Info**   Opens the Info window, which lets you see a variety of attributes of an item. It is used more extensively than in Mac OS 9 and earlier. An Info window for a document is shown in Figure 4-11 next to the Finder window in which the selected file is shown.

The pop-up menu in the window lets you choose the types of information you can see. General Information is available in all cases, as is Privileges. Privileges and file sharing are discussed in more detail in Part III, "Networking."

In the Privileges pane for a document, shown in Figure 4-12, you control who can view or use your documents.

You can set privileges for a folder in a similar way.

A Drop Box folder (located inside your Public folder) has privileges that allow others only to add documents to it. In Figure 4-14, you can see that except for the owner, everyone has write-only access (in other words, they cannot view the contents of the Drop Box Folder.

For documents, the Application choice in the pop-up menu opens another Info window, in which you can select an application to use when opening this document. Normally, this is set automatically for you. If you wish to change the default, you can use this approach.

Finally, for many documents you can set a preview for the document. This is used in the Dock and in the Finder windows.

The Application Files choice in the pop-up menu is available for applications; it is shown in Figure 4-14.

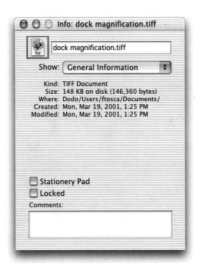

FIGURE 4-11   Info window: General information for a file

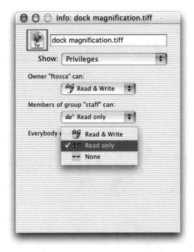

FIGURE 4-12   Info window privileges for a document

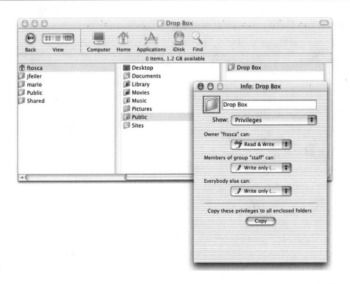

FIGURE 4-13   Drop Box folder Info window

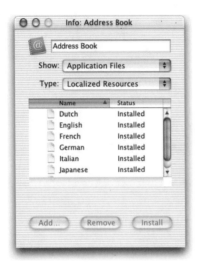

FIGURE 4-14 Info window: Application Files

This window lets you peer inside an application package (see "Packages and Bundles" earlier in this chapter). You can see the localized resources within an application package.

- **Duplicate**   The Duplicate command duplicates whatever item is selected in the active Finder window. The word "copy" is inserted into the file (or directory) name. If nothing is selected, this command is not available.

- **Make Alias**   Aliases (or links) are placeholder files that stand in for other files. You can place the aliases in various locations on your disk so that files or directories are available in other than their normal locations. Mac OS X uses aliases throughout its internal operations; for example, the icons in the Dock are all aliases.

- **Show Original**   If an alias is selected in a Finder window, Show Original will locate the original icon and show its information in the Information window. If an alias is not selected, this command is not available.

- **Add to Favorites**   The Favorites list is a collection of aliases for items you choose to place there. You can put applications, documents, or directories into your Favorites list. Each user has a Favorites list, so you need not worry about creating confusion with people who share your computer. The standard file open and save dialogs contain a button for Favorites. You can use it to locate files or directories you want to use quickly.

- **Move to Trash**   When you use this command, the currently selected items in the active Finder window are moved to the Trash. This does not yet delete them; Use Empty Trash from the Finder's Application menu to erase them from disk. Until you do so, they remain in the trash. You can click the trash icon in the dock to open a Finder window and drag them back to another location where you can work on them.

■ **Eject**   This command ejects a removable disk such as a CD-ROM. It is only available if you have selected such a disk in the Finder. Eject devices, such as digital cameras, before turning them off or unplugging them. This will avoid data loss.

Edit

The Edit menu provides the standard items that you expect in a graphical user interface. It includes undo/redo as well as standard editing commands, which were described in Chapter 2, "Aqua." The Edit menu is shown here.

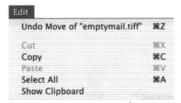

Use Show Clipboard to see what you have copied from one application before you paste it into another. It is always available in the Finder en route from one application to another.

View

The View menu lets you control how information is displayed in the active Finder window. It is shown here.

The first three items let you toggle among the three types of views—columns, icons, and list. You can achieve the same effect with the View button in Finder windows with a toolbar at the top. (Remember that subsidiary windows do not have a toolbar; you need to control the display using the menu commands or use the Toolbar button to display the toolbar.)

■ **Clean Up**   In the case of icons view, the icons in a Finder window can be moved around. The Clean Up command lets you have Mac OS X automatically arrange them in a neat way. The Show View Options command lets you set an option for an icons view so that icons are always aligned to a grid. That is another way of achieving the same effect. If the active Finder window is not currently shown in icons view, this command is not available.

- **Arrange By Name**   In icons view, you can have Mac OS X automatically arrange the icons by name. This command is only available in icons view.

- **Show/Hide Toolbar**   This command has the same effect as the Toolbar button at the right side of the title bar.

- **Customize Toolbar**   You can customize the toolbar with this command. when Desktop window opens, you can drag items to or from (or around in) the toolbar. You can also drag documents or folders from Finder windows into the customized toolbar. The customized toolbar appears in all Finder windows. You can only have one customization for all of your Finder windows.

- **Show/Hide Status Ba**r   The Status Bar appears below the toolbar in Finder windows. It describes the amount of space on the disk displayed in a Finder window, as well as the number of items in the current Finder view. The following status bar shows 8 items and 1.2 gigabytes of available disk space.

> 8 items, 1.2 GB available

- **Show View Options**   If you choose Show View Options, a window opens to let you set icon size, icon arrangement, and folder background, which lets you select a background picture for icon views; it will appear in the Finder windows displaying icons. The window's Global tab lets you set options globally—that is for all icon view windows unless you specify otherwise.

You can also set global options for list views in this tab, as shown here.

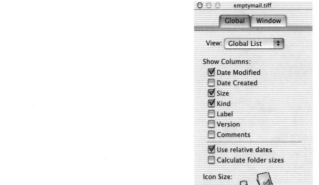

The Relative Dates option lets you set the modification dates of files to use the terms Yesterday and Today (as appropriate). If it is unchecked, the actual date will be displayed. When it is checked, dates are displayed except for Yesterday and Today.

The Calculate Folder Sizes option tells the Finder windows to show you the size of a folder and all of its contents. This is normally turned off because calculating this value can take a significant amount of computer processing time. Furthermore, when a folder is located on a remote computer, the network can be adversely impacted.

Use the Window tab to set options for the currently selected Finder window. In this way, you can override the global settings for an individual window.

Go

The Go menu lets you go quickly to Favorites, recent folders, and other places. These locations can be placed in your toolbar if you want.

Go	
Computer	⌥⌘C
Home	⌥⌘H
iDisk	⌥⌘I
Favorites	▶
Applications	⌥⌘A
Recent Folders	▶
Go To Folder...	⌘~
Connect To Server...	⌘K

One of the most important items in the Go menu is Connect to Server. This is the command you use to log on to other computers in your local area network (or even over the Internet). Choosing Connect to Server opens the window shown in Figure 4-15. This window replaces the Chooser from Mac OS 9 and earlier.

You can use the pop-up menu at the top to choose a recently used server. You can also type in a server's TCP/IP address in the bottom. (The afp prefix stands for Apple File Protocol; you can only open afp servers from this window.)

You can use the browser in the center of the window to select from servers on your network. When you have selected a server, click Connect. You will be asked to log in with the dialog shown here. If you are already logged in to a server, you will bypass this screen.

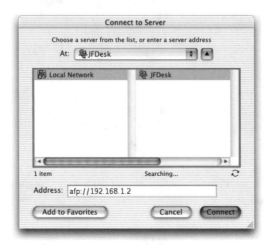

FIGURE 4-15   Connect to a server using the Go menu.

Many servers allow you to log in as a guest; you may have limited privileges in such a case. If you have a user ID and password, you can enter them here. Note that this user ID and password should be valid on the server you are logging in to, not the computer from which you are working. The security options are discussed further in Chapter 7, "Securing Your Computer."

Once you are logged in, you can select the disks you want to open from the dialog shown in Figure 4-16. If a disk is dimmed, you either already are logged in or you do not have access to it. (Hold down the SHIFT or COMMAND key to select multiple disks at once.) The remote disk will then appear in your Finder window.

NOTE   *Network access takes more time than access on your own computer. There may be pauses between your mouse clicks and responses in this sequence. Be patient.*

Using the Mouse and Keyboard

You use the mouse to navigate through the Finder, select documents and folders, move them, and open them. Generally, the behavior is intuitive, but sometimes copying files confuses people. Here are the rules:

- When you are moving a file from one location on a disk to another, dragging it with the mouse *moves* it.

- When you are moving a file from one disk to another, dragging it with the mouse *copies* it.

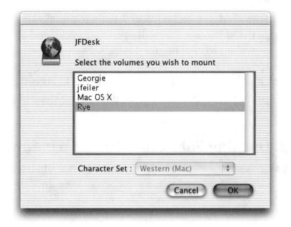

FIGURE 4-16   Select the remote disks you want to use.

Shortcuts

A number of shortcuts apply to mouse and keyboard behavior in the Finder.

Copying a File

Hold down OPTION while dragging a file to a new location and you will create a copy of the file with exactly the same name in the new location. This is contrasted with the Copy command, which creates a file with the word "copy" in the name—myfile copy.doc from myfile.doc, for example.

Creating an Alias

To create an alias of a file, hold down COMMAND and OPTION while you drag the file. An alias will be created in the new location, and the original file will remain unchanged where it is.

Opening and Closing Folders in List View

When using a list view in the Finder, select a folder, hold down the COMMAND key and press the right arrow on your keyboard; that will open that folder in the Finder window. This is equivalent to clicking the folder's disclosure triangle. Holding down COMMAND while pressing the left arrow on the keyboard will close the selected folder. This is equivalent to clicking the open disclosure triangles to "fold up" the contents of the folder.

Opening and Closing All Folders in List View

When using a list view in the Finder, select a folder and then hold down the OPTION key while pressing the right arrow on the keyboard; that will open that folder and all subfolders in it in the Finder window. This is equivalent to clicking the folder's disclosure triangle and the disclosure triangles of all its subfolders.

Holding down OPTION while pressing the left arrow on the keyboard closes all subfolders and the folder which is selected. This is equivalent to clicking all open disclosure triangles to "fold up" the list.

The Toolbar and Opening Subsidiary Finder Windows

When you double-click a folder in a Finder window, the presence or absence of a toolbar helps determine whether that folder is displayed in the same window or another one.

■ If the toolbar is displayed, opening a folder in a Finder window displays its contents in the same window.

■ If the toolbar is not displayed, opening a folder in a Finder window displays its contents in a different window.

Holding down the COMMAND key while you do this action reverses the behavior.

Modifier Keys in the Finder

The behavior of the SHIFT and COMMAND modifier keys in the Finder in Mac OS 9 and earlier was different from their behavior in applications. It has now been made consistent. Thus, SHIFT lets you select a first and last item in a list and everything between those two items. COMMAND lets you hold it down while you click items in any order (and with intervening unselected items).

In Mac OS 9 and earlier, the SHIFT key in Finder windows let you select individual items (rather than those between a first and last item).

Contextual Menus

If you hold down the CONTROL key while clicking the mouse on a Finder icon, a *contextual menu* will appear as shown here.

A contextual menu contains various commands from menus that are enabled for that selection. Contextual menus normally do not contain disabled items—everything you see should be usable.

Contextual menus are also frequently implemented in applications. Hold down the CONTROL key while clicking the mouse on an interface element to see what you can do with it.

Summary

This chapter has provided an introduction to the file system in Mac OS X. In the first section, the four basic concepts were introduced: files/documents, directories/folders, aliases/links, and packages/bundles. The second section provided a thorough look at the Finder with its three types of views: icons, lists, and columns.

Opening a file from within an application uses standard system tools. Refer back to the section on opening a file for more information. Likewise, saving a file may require you to use Finder types of navigation to locate the directory in which you want to save a file.

The Finder is the basic tool you use to manage your computer's files. Each of its menus and menu commands has been described.

Chapter 5

Printing

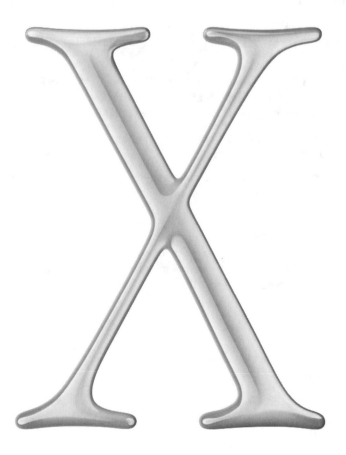

Like so much else in Mac OS X, printing has been rethought. In fact, "printing" is scarcely the right word to use for the set of technologies that involve transferring images from a window drawn and managed by an application program to a platform- and program-neutral medium, such as paper or the Internet. (If you just want to print a birthday card, don't worry: plain, ordinary printing is the first topic in this chapter.)

This chapter is divided into seven sections:

- **Printing** The first section shows you how to print a document. If your needs are basic, you may be able to stop here.

- **Page Setup** This section shows you how to print on various sizes and shapes of paper.

- **Choosing and Connecting Printers** A printer is often the first peripheral device that is attached to your computer. This section provides a brief overview of printer hardware and how to connect it.

- **How Printing Works** This section provides an overview of what goes on in the background: how printing works on Mac OS X.

- **Preview: Print Previews and Printing to Disk** Mac OS X makes it easy to see what will be printed in advance. It also makes it simple to produce disk versions of the documents that will be printed. The disk versions are often suitable for posting to the Web.

- **Print Center: Setting Up Printers and Managing Print Jobs** This section helps you manage your printing environment.

- **Printing in the Classic Mac OS Environment** For applications running in the Classic Mac OS environment, the commands are slightly different.

Once your computer is set up for printing, all you normally need to worry about is printing and previewing—the two sections of this chapter. If your computer is not yet set up for printing, you will need to configure it using Print Center before you can print or preview. In that case, you may want to skip to the section, "Print Center: Setting Up Printers and Managing Print Jobs," and then come back to the beginning of the chapter.

Printing

Once your computer is properly configured, printing is very simple. Choose Print from the File menu, and the dialog shown here appears.

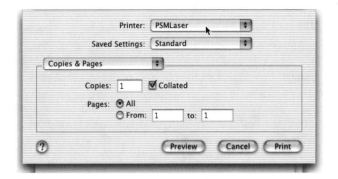

To print one copy of the entire document on your default printer, just click Print (or press RETURN, since Print is the default button).

That's it! If all you ever want to do is print single copies of complete documents on your default printer, you can skip the rest of the chapter. However, there are many additional features and options you can use. Remember that in many cases these features are not necessary, but you will need them for specialized print jobs.

Changing the Printer

You use the Printer pop-up menu in the Print dialog to choose among the printers that are installed on your computer. (For installation instructions, see "Print Center" later in this chapter.)

Installed printers are not necessarily powered on, filled with paper, or free from jams. Only when a print job is sent to the printer will such messages come back to you. If you are planning to print a lengthy document while you go to lunch, wait a moment before you run out the door to make certain that printing has started successfully.

Using Saved Settings

If you have saved settings for the printer you have chosen, you can select them from the second pop-up menu. This lets you avoid having to reconfigure settings repeatedly if you are not using the defaults but are using a repetitive setting. ("Save Custom Settings," later in this chapter, shows you how to create those settings.)

Copies & Pages

The pop-up menu in the center of the Print dialog lets you control a variety of choices. The first one is Copies & Pages.

Setting the Number of Copies

By default, Max OS X prints one copy. If you want more than one copy to be printed, you can enter that number in the Copies box.

Setting the Pages to Print

Normally the entire document is printed. However, you can set a specific range of pages to be printed by entering the first and last page number. The first page in the document is numbered 1, no matter what page number may appear on the document. Thus, even if your first page is iv or 17, you still type **1** into this box to print it.

If you want to print from a certain page number to the end of the document, you can type in a large number, such as **999**, for the final page number if you don't know how many pages are in your document or you can leave the To: box blank.

Layout

The Layout choices are shown in Figure 5-1. While you will most often print one image on one piece of paper, that will not always be the case. For example, in the United States, pages are normally 8.5 × 11 inches. If you are printing a tabloid newsletter, you can purchase paper that is 11 × 17. It allows you to print two pages on each side, which actually gives you four pages per sheet. You can see those options here, as well as the direction in which pages are to be printed. In addition, you can choose a border to be placed around each page image.

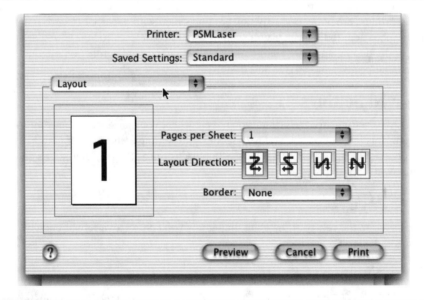

FIGURE 5-1   Printing layout choices

Output Options

Here is the output options pane. This is where you can save the print job to a PDF file. A PDF file contains an electronic image of your printed document.

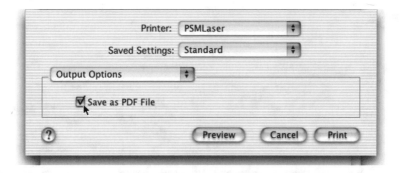

PDF is discussed later in this chapter in the section, "How Printing Works." In short, PDF files are platform-neutral files that contain the image to be printed. They can be read by any program that reads PDF files, including the widely available (and free) Acrobat Reader, available on the Web at http://www.adobe.com/.

PDF files preserve your document's formatting and fonts, no matter where they are printed or displayed. Send PDF files or post them to a Web site when you want to maintain document formatting in this way.

If you have selected the PDF output option, when you click Print, you will need to provide a name for the output file, as shown here:

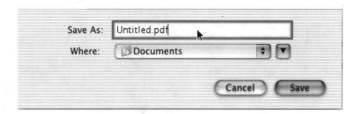

Paper Feed

The following illustration shows the Paper Feed pane of the Print dialog. Use it to select paper sources for printers with multiple trays. As you can see from the figure, you can select a default paper source for all pages. You can also select a separate tray (perhaps containing your company's letterhead) for a first page and another tray for subsequent pages. Select manual feed if you want to insert paper into the printer by hand.

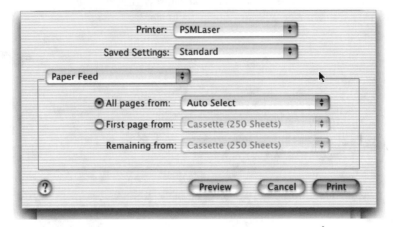

Not all printers support multiple paper trays. Desktop ink jet printers, for example, often have only one paper feed bin.

Error Handling

The Error Handling pane, shown in Figure 5-2, lets you select actions to take when errors occur.

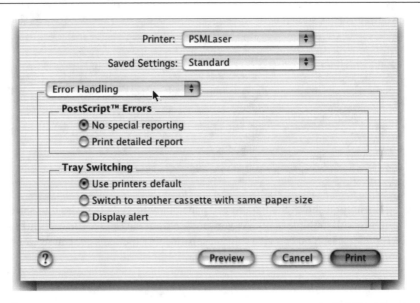

FIGURE 5-2   You can choose error handling options in advance in case of printing problems.

Summary Pane

The Summary pane shows you the choices you have made, as shown in Figure 5-3.

Save Custom Setting

The Save Custom Setting command in the pop-up menu saves the choices you have made. Thereafter, you can return to the settings by choosing Custom (rather than Standard) in the Print dialog's Saved Settings pop-up menu. Custom settings are stored with the document and apply only to the document you are printing.

More Settings

Other settings may be available in this pop-up menu. Many programs have special printing needs based on the type of data they print. Web browsers may have options regarding printing URLs in headers. High-end graphics programs may have options to print preview-quality images, and word processors may have options to print normally invisible editing symbols.

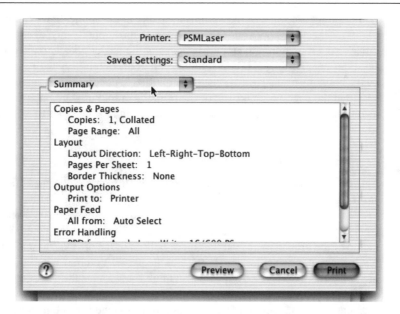

FIGURE 5-3   You can see a summary of your printing options before proceeding.

Depending on the program you are using, a variety of such printing options may be available. In addition to options such as those previously listed, common printing options can include

- Printing pages in reverse order.

- Printing only even- or odd-numbered pages.

- Collating copies. If not, the number of copies you enter in the Print dialog is applied to each page in turn. That is, you get three copies of page 1, then three copies of page 2, and so forth.

- Printing data or field descriptions for programs such as databases and spreadsheets.

If you want to use options that are not implemented in your application program, see the discussion of Preview in the section on print previews later in this chapter. You may be able to use Preview to provide the options that are lacking in your application.

Managing Paper

If you are doing anything more complex than handling one-sided simple documents, you may want to explore the tips and techniques in this section.

Printing Face Up (Ink Jet Printers)

For more efficient printing, use some of the options available in the application Printing dialog's pop-up menus. Start by checking how your printer generates its output. If the pages feed directly through (as for many ink jet printers), the top of the page in the feeder goes into the printer, is printed, and then slides out. The pages accumulate face up in the output tray with each page sliding on top of the previous page. This means that a multipage document is printed sequentially from start to finish, but the pages you take out of the printer's output tray are back to front (that is, reversed). If you are using a printer of this sort, print pages in reverse order to avoid having to manually re-sort them.

Printing Face Down (Laser Printers)

For many laser printers, the page is turned upside down during processing because the paper feeding paths are more complex. You can quickly check how your printer generates output by marking an arrow in pencil on the top side of the top page in the paper tray. Print a one-page document and check to see if it is printed on the side with the arrow or on the other side. Note also whether the top of the printed page is at the top or bottom of the arrow. For many printers, you will find that the output is printed on the bottom of the paper. You may also find that the top of the page is not at the end of the paper tray that you think it is.

In many of these printers, the pages accumulate in the output tray face down. This means that a multipage document is printed sequentially from start to finish, and the output is in the right order. You don't need to use reverse printing to get pages correctly sorted with these printers.

Printing Two-Sided Documents

You can save a tree or two by printing your documents on both sides of the paper. The following steps work for face-up printers, such as ink jets, as well as for lasers that print on the bottom of the pages as they are fed from the paper tray. If you are using another type of printer, or if you are printing the pages on two different printers, see the next set of instructions.

1. Print the odd-numbered pages in forward order.

2. Remove the printed pages and reload them. For a printer with a simple printer path, the top of the pages in the paper tray is the side that will be printed. When you reload the pages, simply turn the entire stack over so that the blank sides are face up. The top page should be the back of page 1. You may also need to turn the paper around; make certain that the top of the pages is facing the right way.

3. Print the even-numbered pages in forward order.

Sometimes you may print one side of the pages on one printer and the other side on another printer. You might do this if one side needs to be printed on a color ink jet and the other side can be printed on a much faster laser printer. You also may find yourself in this situation if you print one side of the pages from a laser printer's normal paper tray and the other side from a secondary paper tray that allows manual feeding. This situation may occur if you find the paper jamming as you print the second side—a common problem with some types of paper when they go through the printer for a second time.

1. Print the even-numbered pages in reverse order.

2. Remove the printed pages and reload them. If necessary, turn the stack of paper over so that the blank sides are face up (or down). In addition, check whether you need to turn the stack of paper around so that the top of the pages is at the correct side of the paper tray.

3. Print the odd-numbered pages in forward order.

You should never have to manually collate or re-sort the pages for double-sided printing. If your printer can handle two-sided printing automatically, you should be able to find the feature on the Print dialog pop-up.

Paper

The results you get from your printer are highly dependent on the paper you use. You can now buy paper that is specifically designed for various types of printers and for special purposes. Color ink jet printers typically have a broad range of papers available for them; the results are startlingly different with different papers.

Expensive paper designed for typing or handwriting often fails abysmally in a computer printer. Likewise, the very cheapest paper frequently gives substandard results and can even jam laser printers.

Because of their high speeds, laser printers are prone to jams from poor quality paper, or from paper that has absorbed water from a humid atmosphere. If you are having problems, consider moving your printer from a poorly ventilated closet to an air conditioned room (or at least one with good ventilation). Also, if you do a lot of printing, note the brand and specific product number of the paper that works best with your printer.

Print One Copy Menu Command

Some application programs have a menu command to print one copy. This command accepts the default values, default printer, all pages, and one copy, and it bypasses the Print dialog. After you choose the Print One Copy menu command, printing commences automatically. This is implemented, if at all, in individual application programs. It is not available in all of them.

Canceling the Print Dialog

If you have decided that you do not want to proceed with printing, click the Cancel button. Cancel cancels the Print dialog itself; it is not used to cancel a print job that has already started. Once you have started printing, you need to use the Print Center to remove jobs from queues. (Print Center is discussed later in this chapter.) While your print job is being sent to the printer, a progress dialog appears. You can cancel printing from there, but it only briefly appears unless the print job is quite large.

Page Setup

The Page Setup menu command is available in the File menu for all programs that print. Use the Page Setup dialog to set the orientation of the paper—landscape (horizontal) or portrait (vertical). You also can use it to set the percentage by which the page image is magnified or reduced. Once chosen, the window, shown in Figure 5-4, opens. You only need to set these options once for each document, and most of the time you do not need to adjust them at all.

The pop-up menu at the top lets you select the Page Setup attributes to set. Mac OS X supports Page Attributes, which are described here. Other applications may have other attributes in the pop-up.

Next, choose the printer you want to use. This matters because it controls some of your other options. (You can select a generic printer, which is the default, but you may find additional options for specific printers you select.) You can add printers to this pop-up menu using the Print Center application.

A pop-up menu enables you to choose the paper size. This option is dependent on the printer you select, since not all printers support all sizes of paper. Figure 5-5 shows the generic printer page sizes on Mac OS X. If you selected a printer that has been configured as an Apple LaserWriter (see Figure 5-6), you'll have a wider range of paper size choices than those available for a generic printer. Next, choose whether you want the paper oriented vertically or horizontally. The small outlines of people indicate which way the paper will print.

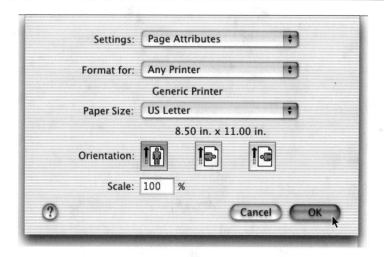

FIGURE 5-4   Use Page Layout to adjust paper size and orientation.

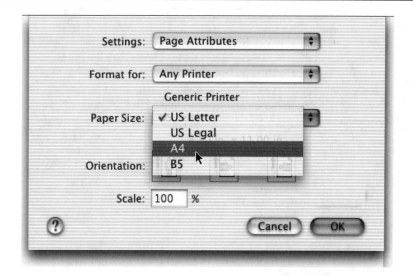

FIGURE 5-5   Several printer sizes are available, depending on the printer you have selected.

Page Setup

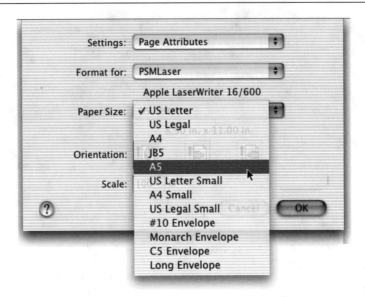

FIGURE 5-6 The Apple LaserWriter offers more page sizes than a generic printer does.

If you are printing envelopes, you may need to experiment on plain paper—which is cheaper than envelopes—to set the parameters, such as orientation and margins, correctly. Finally, you can set the scale of the output. Normally, you'll print at 100% size, which is the default. Adjusting the output scale is very useful when you have an image that is bigger than the paper you are printing on. You can use a combination of scaling and the Print dialog's layout choices to place a number of images on a single printed page. As with the Print dialog, additional choices may be provided in this dialog by your application program. This illustration shows the summary you can display of your setup choices. You can review your Page Setup choices before continuing.

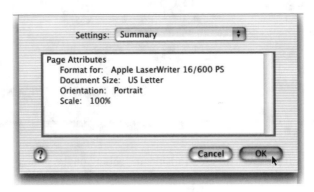

In Mac OS 9 and earlier, there was no standard keyboard equivalent for Page Setup. Now, the combination COMMAND-SHIFT-P brings up Page Setup.

Choosing and Connecting Printers

A printer is frequently the first device that you connect to your computer other than a monitor and keyboard. Consequently, some of the adventures involved in wiring and connections often hit people first when they deal with printers.

Types of Printers

Today, there are two commonly used printing technologies: ink jet and laser. A number of other technologies are used, particularly for special types of output, but for individuals, small or home offices, schools, and most other organizations, laser and ink jet printers are the standards.

The printer market is very competitive. At any given price, you are likely to get almost exactly the same printer from any manufacturer. Printers are mechanical devices; as such, they may need service and repair. Before buying a printer, you'll need to decide what you'll use the printer for and how much money you'd like to spend. A lower-priced printer (most likely an inkjet) may give you a few years of service before it has to be recycled. A higher-priced printer (probably a laser) will give you a decade of service but will need regular (annual) cleanings and maintenance.

Laser Printers

Laser printers are relatively fast, and they produce excellent black-and-white output. They commonly are used in offices and other places where high volumes of printouts are produced. They use cartridges of a fine dust (toner) that fuses onto the paper in the same way in which a photocopy machine produces copies. Depending on the model, cartridges for black-and-white printing typically last for thousands of pages. When they begin to produce light copies, it is time to replace them. Color laser printers produce very good quality output at relatively high speeds, but slower than for black and white.

Laser printers often have multiple paper trays. You can put envelopes in one, letterhead in another, and plain paper in a third (if you have three). Paper trays often hold large amounts of paper—250 to 500 pages is not uncommon.

Ink Jet Printers

Ink jet printers are slower than lasers and are normally used for smaller tasks. Instead of a toner, ink jet printers use ink that comes sealed in small containers. Ink jet printers typically have two sets of ink cartridges—one for black and white and another for color. Each can be replaced separately.

Ink jet printers often have a variety of settings that can produce very high-quality output. Even the lowest priced ink jet printers today can produce photographic quality images (when the appropriate paper is used).

CAUTION   *Ink jet printer inks are not always stable. They fade very quickly—sometimes in a matter of months. For archival projects, look at your printer manufacturer's Web site for tips on papers to use, storage techniques, and the like. For now, the best advice if you have a color document that you need to keep is to save the electronic version so that it can be reprinted on demand.*

The ink cartridges for ink jet printers do not gradually get lighter with use: they simply stop working. Therefore, you should always have a spare on hand. Ink jet printers are designed for lower volumes than laser printers. Their paper trays typically hold 50 to 100 pages.

Ink jet printers are significantly cheaper than laser printers. Excellent results can be obtained from even the lowest priced ink jet printers, which cost about $100. In terms of value for money, the next tier of printers (priced at about $150) is probably the best.

It is not uncommon for individuals to have ink jet printers connected to their own computers for small-scale work and also have access to a networked laser printer for high-volume print jobs. (A black-and-white laser printer in this scenario represents a good choice, since color can be printed on the ink jet printer.)

USB Connections

Except for networked printers, most printers today use USB connections. Since USB is a platform-neutral industry standard, you can buy printers that are compatible with Macintosh and Windows computers. Indeed, a stroll through the aisles of an office supply store reveals a host of USB peripherals that work in any environment. Among these platform-neutral devices are printers, scanners, removable disk drives (such as Zip drives), memory card readers, and digital cameras. Unlike the situation a few years ago, there are not Macintosh or Windows versions of these products in most cases.

NOTE   Home Office Handbook *by Barbara Butler (Hungry Minds, 2000) provides a very detailed treatment of printers, scanners, and other such devices. The book was written in cooperation with Hewlett-Packard, and it contains extensive information about printers and scanners. Jesse Feiler, the author of this book, contributed the sections on Mac OS X.*

How Printing Works

In most cases, you view a document in a window and then print the contents of that window. This was one of the revolutionary aspects of graphical users interfaces: What You See Is What You Get (WYSIWYG). In other cases, an application program can produce output that is sent directly to the printer. This may be a modified version of what you see on the screen, or it may be something that is printed and not shown at all.

Software design has changed drastically over the last two decades. Printing a document to the printer and not showing a screen version used to be standard procedure. Today, most output is shown in a window, and printing is optional.

This section provided information about printing that applies to all operating systems. In the following sections, you will see how Mac OS X implements this functionality.

Print Jobs

When a program has an image to print—whether it is displayed in a window or not—it creates a *print job*. That job has a *name* (assigned by the operating system), a *destination* (the printer to which it will be sent), a *priority*, and the *time* at which it is to be printed. The print job is created by the application program and is then passed on to the operating system, where it is actually sent to the printer and printed.

In Mac OS 9 and earlier, an option in the Chooser let you select background printing. In Mac OS X, all printing occurs in the background as described here. Note, too, that the Chooser no longer exists; its functions have been distributed to the Print dialog and other logical places in the operating system.

Queues and Spooling

The job is normally sent to a print spooler (on Mac OS 9 and earlier, this was referred to as *background printing*). The print spooler keeps track of the jobs and sends them to the appropriate printer at the appropriate time. You can examine the print queue to change priorities, reset the times for printing, or delete print jobs.

This is an example of the need for an operating system to multitask. Typically, the process of printing a document is slower than the process of generating its printable content because printers function at slower speeds than computers. If the computer had to wait for the printer to finish its work, you would have plenty of idle time. (Turning off background printing in Mac OS 9 and earlier demonstrates this.)

PostScript

The image to be printed is converted to PostScript, which is a *page description language*—a programming language that uses vector graphics to describe a page. (Vector graphics are commands such as "draw a line from here to there," "draw a curve at this location with these dimensions," and so forth.) PostScript is in turn converted into the actual image that will be put on paper (or film or printing plates). Mac OS X provides the routines programs use to generate PostScript. The PostScript is processed by a Raster Image Processor (RIP). (Printers talk about "ripping files.") The RIP rasterizes the image: it produces the tiny colored dots that make up an image. Raster images are often referred to as *bitmapped* images. The point of rasterizing an image is to produce the individual colors or shades of gray that need to be applied to a piece of paper by a printer's ink jet nozzles or the guts of a laser printer.

How Printing Works

The RIP may be a microchip inside a laser printer. In such cases, the PostScript file is transmitted to the printer and the imaging—ripping—is done by the printer's hardware and software.

Printers without processing capabilities are much cheaper. They may rely on your computer's processing to RIP the file. In that case, what is sent from your computer to your printer is a set of printer-specific instructions.

PostScript was developed by Adobe and is widely used in the computer industry. Therefore, PostScript output can be printed on a variety of different devices. Once a PostScript file has been ripped, it is normally prepared only for a specific device. (If it is ripped inside a printer, it is ripped just for that printer.)

Since PostScript files can be output on so many different devices, it is common to send PostScript files to printers and service bureaus for printing. This makes it easy to print output in another location, whether or not the application program is installed at the other site. (You will see how Mac OS X takes this concept much further with the use of PDF.)

Printing to disk is the term used for generating a PostScript file independently of a print job. Whereas the normal processing of a print request creates the print job and the PostScript file, printing to disk generates only the PostScript file—and you can name it what you want. You can then email or otherwise transmit that file to a printer.

PDF

WYSIWYG was one of the great achievements of the Classic Macintosh. However, the process of converting a screen image to PostScript and then ripping it to another image does sometimes involve some changes. Since the capabilities of a printer are different from those of a monitor, some of these are inescapable; in other cases, the inconsistencies arise from the conversion process itself. Consequently, there is sometimes a need to RIP images on your computer so that you can view the ripped image, the PostScript output. Adobe's Portable Document Format (PDF) does just this.

The Adobe Distiller application program takes PostScript files as input, rips them to objects (not bitmaps), and produces PDF files. Many people use Distiller to create PDF files for their Web sites. Using the Adobe Reader application (downloadable for free from Adobe's Web site), users can then view documents in all their glory.

Like PostScript, PDF is a way of describing a page. It uses the same image model as PostScript does, but only a small subset of the PostScript commands. Because of its use of the subset, PDF files can be smaller than PostScript files. In addition, there are often fewer differences between the screen and print images. PDF files can be viewed on the screen or printed on an output device. They are portable—once the image has been converted into PostScript by your application program, it is in the realm of standard formats that can be used on a multitude of devices and operating systems.

PDF files also can include a variety of additional features. With Adobe Acrobat, users can annotate the files, indexes and cross-references can be created, and the documents can be searched. The PDF specification permits this, but it does not require it. A basic PDF file is just the ripped output.

PDF files are similar to Encapsulated PostScript (EPS) files. However, PDF files are normally substantially smaller than EPS files—often by an order or two of magnitude. This is because EPS files normally contain a bitmapped image of the page as a thumbnail; PDF files contain only the vector description of the page.

For all of these reasons, many commercial printers today now prefer to accept PDF rather than PostScript files when material is transmitted to them electronically.

TIFF, GIF, and JPEG Formats

PostScript and PDF files provide cross-platform and application-neutral formats for the display of print images. There also are standard cross-platform and application-neutral formats that can be used for graphics images. Their function is much the same: an image is saved to one of the standard formats and can be imaged onto another device using standard software. In the case of images, the output device is normally another computer display; often it is a Web page that will be viewed on a variety of displays.

The most common platform-independent graphics formats are TIFF, GIF, and JPEG. Most graphics software (even the most basic programs) can read and write each of these formats. Once you have an image in one of the formats, converting it to one of the others is not difficult. Here are the main characteristics of each format.

TIFF

TIFF (Tagged Image File Format) is widely used to store images that will need to be printed. It handles all of the concerns of printing (including color) very well. The format can contain a variety of information about the image. Consequently, TIFF files can be imaged with great accuracy on many devices. However, TIFF files are not always the smallest versions of images, due in large part to the data they contain that may not be needed for display on a particular device. TIFF files are normally not the first choice for graphics on Web pages, although they are for printers.

GIF and PNG

GIF (Graphical Image Format) is designed for images that are generated by computers. GIF files compress their contents efficiently. In the case of artificially created images such as computer graphics, there are normally large blocks of color that respond very well to the type of compression used in GIF files. As a result, GIF is used extensively for images on the Internet.

PNG (Portable Network Graphics) is a newer version of GIF that addresses the one serious problem with GIF, the fact that it relies on a compression algorithm (LZW) that is proprietary. Indeed, at one point the then-owner of the copyright threatened to charge for all uses of that algorithm in images, sending a bit of a panic through the then-smaller world of the Web. PNG has no proprietary algorithms contained within it, so you can use it without fear of copyright infringement.

JPEG

JPEG (developed by the Joint Photographic Experts Group) compresses images, as does GIF. JPEG works best with images created by photography; in such images, even apparently large blocks of a single color turn out on closer examination to have a variety of different colors blended together. JPEG is a *lossy* format: when the image is converted to JPEG, some of its detail is lost. Repeatedly converting a JPEG file degrades the image quality due to repeated loss of data, just as photocopying photocopies degrades the quality of the image. For that reason, people using JPEG compression typically save the original version of the image in a safe place and make their various modifications over time to copies of it, saving those modifications as JPEG files. Since JPEG incorporates compression, it, too, is widely used for images on the Internet.

WYSIWYG

WYSIWYG can never be fully achieved if you are comparing images on the screen to images on paper. You can get very close, but you cannot avoid the fact that paper is a *reflective* medium—light bounces off it and onto your retina—and a computer monitor is a *transmissive* medium—light comes through it from behind. Colors in particular appear different in the two types of media. As you may have noticed from your own experience, images on a computer monitor will appear to change color as the ambient light in the room changes. Apple's ColorSync technology and the use of standard colors, such as Pantone colors, can help deal with these issues; however, the underlying optics and perceptual issues cannot be avoided.

This means that if you are working on very critical output, you must do your final proofreading and checking on the medium that will be used for the output. In the case of printed output, check printed copy; if you are designing a Web page, do your final check on the screen, not on a printed copy.

Networked and Non-Networked Printers

The last topic of general concern for printing is the distinction between networked and non-networked (or personal) printers. A networked printer is attached directly to a network. Like all network devices, it must have an identifying address and a name. In order to function, it needs network hardware and software built into it. A networked printer is accessible to all of the computers attached to the network. When a print job is sent to a networked printer, the computer that sends the job transmits a PostScript file to the printer. The printer RIPs the file and prints it.

A non-networked printer is connected directly to a computer with a USB or serial connector and is available only to that computer, although other computers on the network can often communicate with the computer and through it to the printer. Non-networked printers are normally cheaper than networked printers are because they do not need the networking hardware and software. In addition, frequently the ripping is done on the computer, and the raster file (rather than a PostScript file) is sent to the printer.

Mac OS X Server provides print server management that goes far beyond what is available in Mac OS X. See Chapter 13, "Setting Up a Network Server" for more on the print server features in Mac OS X.

Preview: Print Previews and Printing to Disk

In Mac OS 9 and earlier, as well as in other operating systems, applications frequently implemented print preview functionality. This was done as an additional menu command that appeared near the Print command. Typically, it caused a window to open in which you could see what the printed output would look like—sort of. Each application program implemented its own print previews if it wanted them.

In Mac OS X, print previews are part of the standard Print dialog. Located next to the Print and Cancel buttons, Preview lets the operating system create your print preview. While some legacy applications may still have their own idiosyncratic print preview commands, all applications created today have print preview capabilities that don't need to be implemented anew each time.

The Print Preview menu command in many applications is replaced by the Preview button in the standard Print dialog. The Preview button works very simply. It creates a PDF file. Then it launches an application that is part of Mac OS X called Preview, and voilà—you have a preview of what will be printed. Since a PDF file is also created internally when you print a document, the preview and final images are as close as possible.

Preview is a separate application and has its own menus. While your print preview is open, you can manipulate it with these commands. You can also go back to your original application to continue working while leaving the print preview open. This addresses a very annoying aspect of most print preview implementations. In many cases, the preview window was modal—until you closed it, you could not do anything else in that application.

Preview can open various types of graphics files and export several formats (see the Export command later in this section). You can use it as a utility to convert graphics files of all sorts, not just print previews (PDF files). The following paragraphs discuss the Preview menu commands, arranged by menu. Standard commands, such as Quit, are omitted.

File

The three most frequently used commands, Save As PDF, Export, and Print, are in the File menu.

Save as PDF

If you save the preview as a PDF file, you can post it on a Web site for downloading or viewing with the Acrobat Reader plug-in (available from Adobe). The PDF file can be viewed and printed by people without the application that you used to create it.

In addition, the PDF file is an image of the file itself. If someone has a utility program, such as the full version of Acrobat Reader, they can mark it up and make changes. Those changes are made only to the page images, not to the underlying document.The Output Options in the Print dialog (discussed previously in this chapter) lets you create and save a PDF file more easily.

Export

Use the Export command to create a file in any of the industry-standard formats:

- **TIFF**   This format is frequently used for printing.

- **JPEG**   JPEG files are compressed files that are frequently used on Web sites for photographic images.

- **PICT**   The PICT format was created on the original Macintosh. It is a useful format for graphics to be shared on Macintosh computers. While supported on other platforms, it is not universally used. PICT is based on QuickDraw, the graphics engine of Mac OS 9 and earlier. It is a bit-mapped format: everything—including text—is preserved as a bit-map and, consequently, images that need to be resized often do poorly in PICT format.

- **QuickTime Image**   These images can be opened by the QuickTime plug-in and application.

- **Photoshop**   Photoshop is one of the most popular graphics programs among designers.

- **Silicon Graphics**   Silicon Graphics workstations use this format.

- **MacPaint**   One of the oldest formats for the Macintosh, MacPaint format is similar to PICT, but is limited to black and white and no larger than 8 × 10 inches.

- **Targ**   The Truevision (Targa) format is a bitmapped format that is used for 24- and 32-bit color images.

- **BMP**   Windows bitmap format is used on this platform. Like all bitmapped images, they do not scale particularly well.

- **PNG**   PNG (Portable Network Graphics) is a format that replaces GIF. It is widely used on Web sites to display computer-generated images. It differs from GIF primarily in that it uses no proprietary algorithms.

When you choose Export, a sheet is displayed that enables you to select the format you want. An Options button lets you select options specific to that particular format. You can also use this sheet to name the exported file.

Print

Printing the preview is the same as clicking the Print button on the Print dialog. If you have gone to the trouble of creating a print preview, it's slightly faster to print the preview, rather than closing it and going back to the Print dialog.

Display

The Display menu lets you view the pages of the document. These settings control how the document is shown and how you move through it. The settings are stored when you save the document. They do not affect the content of the document, only the way in which you view it in Preview.

Page Forward

This command moves you one page further into the document. It is the same as clicking the forward arrow on the preview window.

Page Backward

This moves you back one page. It is the same as clicking the back arrow on the preview window.

Zooming

These commands let you zoom in or out on the page image, show it at actual size, or resize it to fit the window.

Rotation

Use these commands to rotate the image 90 degrees (a quarter of a circle) at a time. You can also flip images horizontally or vertically: flipping involves 180-degree changes (half a circle).

Antialiasing

Antialiasing makes it easier to read text and view graphics on displays with relatively low resolutions, such as the common 72 dot-per-inch displays on many Macintosh computers. The boundaries between one color and another (for example, between a black letter and a white background) are manipulated with intermediate shades of color (gray in this case) so that the jagged boundary that is inherent in the low resolution display becomes slightly blurred. Together with the eye's natural tendency to improve the images that it perceives, antialiasing makes reading type on a computer screen much easier.

Preview: Print Previews and Printing to Disk

Continuous Scrolling

Instead of showing one page at a time, you can choose to view the content of your print preview as if it were one long continuous page through which you scroll.

Print Center: Setting Up Printers and Managing Print Jobs

Print Center is the application you use to set up printers and manage their operation. If your computer is properly installed, all this may have been done for you and you can skip this section. If you are adding another printer to your computer (or your network), you may need to revisit this section. In addition, if you want to manage your print queues, you need to use Print Center.

In Mac OS 9 and earlier, Print Monitor fulfilled the roles that Print Center now handles. Refer to "Printing in the Classic Mac OS Environment" in the next section for more information.

Print Center is found in the Applications Utilities folder. It can also be opened automatically from the Print dialog. Figure 5-7 shows the Print dialog as it appears when no printer is selected. In that case (or any other case in which the printer you want is not visible), you can edit the printer list as shown in Figure 5-8. That command launches Print Center, and you can manage your printers from there.

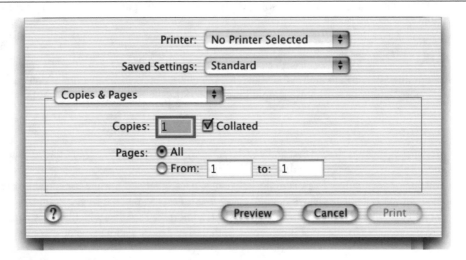

FIGURE 5-7   At first, no printer is selected.

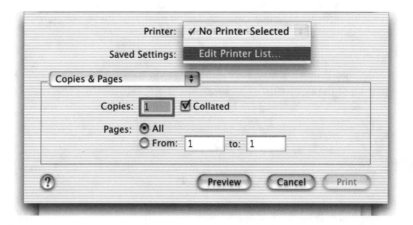

Managing Printers with the Printers Menu

You select and set up printers to use in the Printers List window with the Printers menu.

View Printer List

You open the Printers List window from the View Printer List command in the Printers menu or from the Print dialog. The Printer list is shown here.

You'll see a list of your printers, identified by name and type. The printers in this window are the printers that are available in the pop-up menu of the Print and Page Setup dialogs.

Add Printer

To add a printer to your Print Center, choose Add Printer in the Printers menu or click Add Printer at the bottom of the Printer list. This opens the sheet shown here.

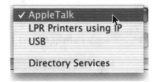

In this window, the pop-up menu enables you to choose from at least three types of connection: AppleTalk, LPR, and USB. AppleTalk and LPR are protocols used to connect to network printers; USB is a protocol used to connect to a non-networked printer on your own computer.

Choose the type of connection and you will see the available printers. These are the printers available on the network (or connected to your computer's USB port); you can choose from these printers.

Macintosh networks frequently use AppleTalk. In order to connect to an AppleTalk printer, AppleTalk must be active on your computer. If it is not, you will get the message shown here:

Click Open System Preferences to immediately turn on AppleTalk, if necessary. The AppleTalk tab of the Network preference pane will open in the System Preferences application. Turn AppleTalk on by clicking Make AppleTalk Active, as shown in Figure 5-9. You will need an administrator password to turn on AppleTalk unless you are logged in as an administrator.

With AppleTalk now on, you can browse the printers on your AppleTalk network, as shown in Figure 5-10. Highlight the one you want and click Add.

AppleTalk networks can be divided into zones. For large networks, this improves efficiency and helps the manager run the network. If you have an AppleTalk network, when you choose the AppleTalk connection you will see a second pop-up menu that lets you choose from the various zones, if they exist. If you are connected to such a network, you may have access to only some of the zones. You'll need to ask your network administrator which zones are appropriate for you to use.

FIGURE 5-9   Turn on AppleTalk from the Network preferences pane in System Preferences.

FIGURE 5-10   Select your AppleTalk printer from those available.

The process for selecting a USB printer is similar. For LPR printers, you need to type in the IP address of the printer, as shown in Figure 5-11. This is because Print Center cannot display the universe of possible printers available to you on the Internet.

Show Queue

This command opens the printer queue display, which is discussed in the following section. You can also open the queue by double-clicking any printer in the Printers window.

Make Default

If you have more than one printer in your Print Center, you can make one the default. That will be the printer to which you print and for which page setup commands are set by default, although you can switch printers in both the Print and Page Setup dialogs. You should have a default printer. You can always change it for individual print jobs and documents. Select a printer in the

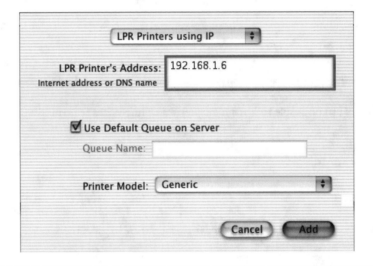

FIGURE 5-11   Enter the address of an LPR printer.

Printer list and choose Make Default from the Printers menu. A default printer has a dot to the left of its name in the Printer list.

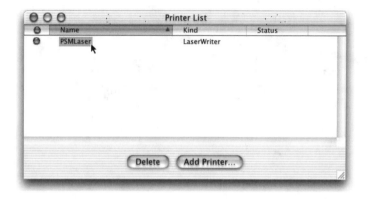

Delete

To remove a printer, select it in the Printer list and choose Delete. This removes it from your Print Center; it does nothing to the printer itself. Adding and removing printers is something you do not do on a regular basis. Normally, you have at least one printer in your Print Center. If you choose not to use one of your printers for days—or years—at a time, it does no harm to leave it there. Do not add and remove printers each time you print something.

Managing the Print Queue with the Queue Menu

The print queue contains a list of all of the active print jobs. Once a job has been printed, it is removed from the queue. Each printer has its own queue. You can open the Queue window by double-clicking a printer in the Printer list or by selecting a printer in the Printer list and choosing the Show Queue command in the Printers menu. The Queue window for a printer is shown in Figure 5-12.

A job is removed from the queue when it is completed in the computer's terms. Some computers, particularly laser printers with their own memory, can store several pages of output. Thus, the computer may have sent all of a job to a printer, but it may still have one or two pages to process.

Start Print Queue/Stop Print Queue

You can start and stop the entire print queue. While the queue is stopped, you can print in the sense that the Print command works and PostScript files are produced, however, they are not sent to the printer. When the print queue is restarted, the PostScript files are sent to the printer.

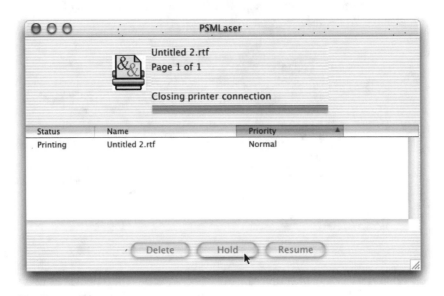

FIGURE 5-12   Printer queues show the jobs that are printing and waiting.

One reason to stop a print queue is if you are traveling with a laptop and have no printer attached to your computer. Instead of accumulating files to print later, you can stop the queue and continue working normally, printing jobs to the stopped queue. When you return to your home or office, you can connect to the printer or the network, restart the queue, and the print jobs will come out.

Another reason to stop the queue is to rearrange print jobs in it; this is described in the next section. Still another reason is to continue working if a printer is not usable for one reason or another. It may be jammed or out of paper, and you may want to continue your work before solving the problem. Stopping the print queue lets you do what you want to do when you want to do it.

Hold Job

Rather than stopping the entire queue, sometimes you want to hold a specific print job. This might be the case when that job needs special paper or envelopes. You can hold such a job until you have a chance to reload the printer with the appropriate paper. Another reason to hold a job is to delay a lengthy job until your lunch hour or the end of the day.

To hold a job, select the job in the queue window, then choose Hold Job from the Queue menu. If you know you are going to hold a job (for example, if you need to load the printer with envelopes), you may want to open the Print Center's Queue window before you print so that as soon as the job appears you can hold it.

Resume Job

If you have held a job, select the job in the Queue window and then choose the Resume Job command to start it up again. You can also click the Resume button in the Queue window, as shown in Figure 5-13.

Delete Job

Finally, you can select a print job in the Queue window and delete it with the Delete Job command. Do this if you printed something in error. If you want to delay the job, use Hold Job.

Print Center: Setting Up Printers and Managing Print Jobs

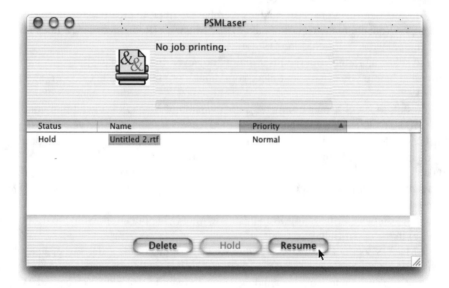

FIGURE 5-13   You can hold a job until you are ready to print it.

Printing Problems

Error messages for print jobs appear in sheets, as shown here. They also may appear in dialogs on your display if the Print Center Queue window is not open. You can deal with them by stopping the queue, stopping the print job, or deleting the print job—or perhaps by simply reloading a depleted paper tray.

Printing in the Classic Mac OS Environment

Printing in the Classic Mac OS environment is similar to how it is in Mac OS X because Print and Page Setup are much the same. In Mac OS 9 and earlier, however, PDF files are not created during the print or print preview process. Instead, if you want to generate a PDF file, choose to print to a file and then run a program, such as Acrobat Distiller, to create the PDF file. The Page Setup dialog is available in the Classic Mac OS environment. (Remember that it does not have a keyboard equivalent as it does in Mac OS X.)

You can select a printer from the Print dialog; however you must have the printer you want to use installed before you can do so. Select your default printer using the Chooser, as shown in Figure 5-14.

If you install Mac OS X on a computer with a version of Mac OS 9.1 on it that you have used, you probably do not have to worry about this. However, the first time you need to print from the Classic Mac OS environment, you may need to use the Chooser to select a printer even though you have done so in the Mac OS X Print Center.

You access the Chooser from the Apple menu of Classic Mac OS environment applications. It is not available unless the Classic Mac OS environment is running and a Classic Mac OS application is active.

Figure 5-15 shows a Print dialog from a Classic Mac OS application. Note the destination (Printer/File) in the upper right of the dialog.

Classic Mac OS does not use the Print Center's queues. When printing starts from an application in the Classic Mac OS environment, the PrintMonitor [Classic] application starts up—you can see it in the Dock. If you click on its icon, the window shown in Figure 5-16 opens. You can select a print job from the queue and use the buttons to cancel it or set it to print at a specific time. PrintMonitor jobs do not show up in Print Center queues although they may go to the same printers.

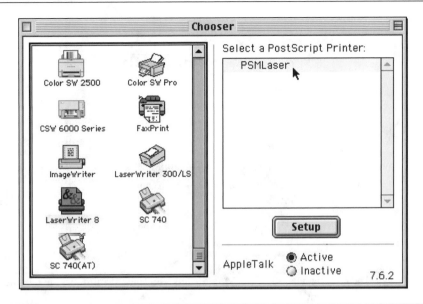

FIGURE 5-14   The Chooser lets you select printers to use.

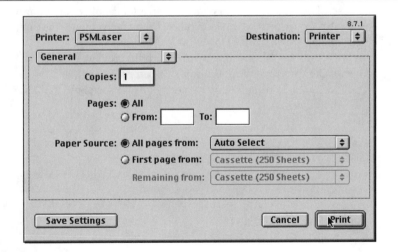

FIGURE 5-15   A Classic Mac OS application's Print dialog is similar to that in Mac OS X.

Printing in the Classic Mac OS
Environment

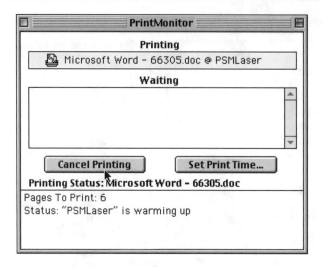

FIGURE 5-16   The Classic Mac OS PrintMonitor lets you track printing in the Classic environment.

Summary

This chapter has provided an overview of printing in Mac OS X. Printing is not just a matter of putting images on paper. It includes all processes that convert an application's image of data to a format that is transferable from one medium to another, from one computer to another, or from one application to another.

You have seen how to print a document, how to get a print preview (and transfer files from one format to another using the Preview application's Export command), and how to use Print Center to control your computer's print functions. You have also seen how to manage printing in the Classic Mac OS environment.

Chapter 6

Setting Preferences

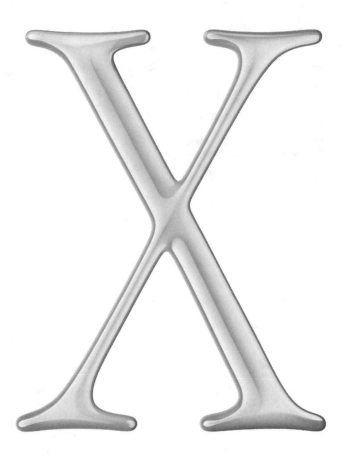

This chapter shows you how to set your preferences for various options on your computer. They include such features as the date and time, the sound to be used to alert you to problems, and how you are connected to a network, as well as interface choices.

Additional preferences are covered in other chapters of this book, as well as in this one. Printing is handled by the Print Center application; it is covered in Chapter 5, "Printing." Networking and security are also covered in their own chapters; however, the basic preferences that apply to them are described here. Also, preferences for individual applications are described in discussions of those applications or in their documentation.

The preferences discussed in this chapter can apply to the computer as a whole or just to your own preferences that are active when you log in under your ID. (If you have two IDs, you can have two sets of preferences for this latter type.) Here are the preferences described in this chapter; those marked with an asterisk (*) apply to the computer as a whole.

- **Classic**   This lets you run Mac OS 9 and earlier applications under Mac OS X.

- **ColorSync**   You can adjust the ways in which colors are displayed on your monitor and printer.

- **Date & Time***   These are the settings for date, time, and time zones.

- **Displays**   Use this preference to set the resolution of your monitor.

- **Dock**   You can control the behavior and appearance of the Dock.

- **Energy Saver***   This is where you set sleep parameters and control how your monitor, computer, and hard disk behave when you are not using them.

- **General**   This set of preferences controls the appearance of your computer's windows and the behavior of scroll bars.

- **International**   Set your language and type preferences here.

- **Internet**   This is where you control what applications you will use for email, the Web, and so forth. You also set passwords and user IDs here.

- **Keyboard**   If you switch between character sets, you may need to switch your keyboard mappings.

- **Login***   You can control the login process, including automatic logins and hints for forgotten passwords.

- **Mouse**   The mouse tracking speed and click speed are set here.

- **Network***   This is the pane to set dialup or always-on Internet parameters.

- **QuickTime**   You can control how QuickTime plays back movies and how it downloads data from the Internet.

- **Screen Saver**   Not only can you specify an image to be displayed on the screen when it is not in use, but you also can cause the computer to automatically prevent other people from using it.

- **Sharing***   Here is the place to specify whether other people can connect to your computer and its files.

- **Software Update***   Use this to check for updates to the operating system from Apple.

- **Sound**   Select the sounds to use for alerts; also use this pane to set volume and stereo balance.

- **Speech**   Speech synthesis is controlled from this pane.

- **Startup Disk***   You can decide which disk to start up from. Use this pane to alternate between starting up in Mac OS X and in Mac OS 9.

- **Users***   You can manage the user IDs on your computer.

If you have used Mac OS 9 and earlier, you may be familiar with a variety of other ways of setting preferences. The unified System Preferences application in Mac OS X provides a common interface; in doing so, a number of other interface elements have been removed. The Chooser, Control Panels, and Extensions handled many of the features that are now handled by System Preferences.

Using System Preferences

System Preferences can be opened by choosing the System Preferences command in the Apple menu. You can also launch it easily by clicking the System Preferences icon in the Dock.

When the Preferences application is launched, the Preferences window is opened, as shown in Figure 6-1. Your Preferences window may differ depending on which Preferences button is selected at the top of the window. Furthermore, there may be additional (or fewer) preferences in your version of the operating system.

At the top of the window is a row of preferences that you can customize. Drag any of the preferences icons from the center of the window to this area so that you can access them quickly. (This will copy the icons for handy access; all system preferences icons always remain in the body of the window.)

A single click on any icon opens those preferences options for viewing and setting. The preferences appear in the System Preferences window. System Preferences will roll up or roll down the bottom of the window to allow sufficient space for the preferences that you are viewing. (System Preferences does not automatically resize the width of the window.)

While you are working with one set of preferences, the top row of icons remains visible. Clicking the Show All icon in the upper left of the window will replace individual preference settings—for your monitor, as an example—with the display of all available preferences, as shown in Figure 6-1.

Using System Preferences

System Preferences consolidates most settings for your computer environment.

The preferences are presented in the System Preferences window and, in this chapter, in alphabetical order.

Hierarchies of Preferences

In addition to your computer preferences, preferences can be set for individual applications, as well as for specific documents. For example, you can set a sound for a mail application to use to alert you to incoming email; it can be different from the system's alert sound. Within a word processing document, you can set default values for each document, determining whether it is to be printed vertically or horizontally. The preferences in this chapter are defaults, and (if not overridden by individual applications and documents) apply uniformly. Some preferences, such as alert sounds, are logically overridden by individual applications that may want to have distinctive alert sounds.

Preferences are sometimes set for individual users: whenever that user logs in, the preferences for sounds, login items, and so forth, apply. Other preferences—such as network connections—apply to all users on the computer. In order to set them, you need to have an administrator password. Typically, you can view these preferences even if you do not have an administrator password.

Preferences and Settings on Mac OS 9 and Earlier

If you use Mac OS 9 and earlier applications in the Classic environment on Mac OS X, you will often find that the settings you make for System Preferences in Mac OS X carry through properly. However, if you restart your computer to start up from Classic Mac OS (that is, you reset the startup disk to be a Mac OS 9 disk—see "Startup Disk," later in this chapter), you may need to adjust the settings in Mac OS 9 using the Chooser, Control Panels, and Extensions.

There are two situations in which you may need to be concerned about Mac OS 9 preferences: the case in which you have previously used Mac OS 9 on your computer and the case in which you have not (but need to do so in addition to using Mac OS X).

If You Have Already Been Using Mac OS 9 on Your Computer

If you have Mac OS 9.1 or later installed on your computer and if you have been using it, it should be configured properly. Many of the configuration choices such as networking will be reset when you install Mac OS X. However, other configuration choices, such as the fonts in your Mac OS 9 System Folder and the preferences for your applications running in the Classic environment, will be used by Classic applications running under Mac OS X.

If you will be using Classic applications under Mac OS X, verify that they work properly before attempting to use them from Mac OS X. For the programs that you use on a regular basis, this will not be difficult. For others, you may want to restart your computer using Mac OS 9 to verify that they work as you come to them. See "Startup Disk," later in this chapter.

If You Have Not Been Using Mac OS 9 on Your Computer

If you have not been using Mac OS 9, you can install it together with Mac OS X (if it is not already installed). To use applications in the Classic environment, you should install them from their original media (CD-ROM, downloaded files, and so on) in Mac OS 9. Verify that they run properly.

These are transitional issues. Depending on the applications you use, you may not need to use the Classic environment. On the first day of the release of Mac OS X, you could use native email, Web, and productivity applications on Mac OS X without using the Classic environment at all. In fact, if you want to ignore the Classic environment, you can probably do so until such time (if ever) that you need to address it. Classic is one of the things that "just works" about Mac OS X.

Classic

You set parameters for the Classic environment by clicking the Classic button to open the pane shown in Figure 6-2.

If you already are using Mac OS 9, choose the startup disk from the scrolling list at the left of the preferences window. If you are still using a lot of Classic Mac OS programs, you may want to have the Classic environment launched when you log in. The checkbox lets you do so. This can save time since it does take a little while for Classic to be launched. Of course, once it is launched, it remains running—even if not being used—until you shut it down.

You can have a Mac OS 9 startup disk for your Classic environment that is separate from the one you use when you start up from Mac OS 9 itself.

You also use this pane to restart the Classic environment or to force it to quit. Remember that all applications within Classic will be terminated if you force it to quit or shut it down.

Classic

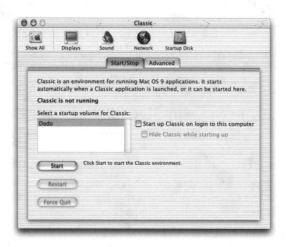

FIGURE 6-2   Classic preferences let you manage the Mac OS 9 environment on Mac OS X.

If you do not see your current startup disk in that list, restart using Mac OS 9, and use the Startup Disk control panel to select your startup disk. If you cannot do this, you may need to reinstall Mac OS 9; it will replace any missing files without removing your preferences, fonts, and so forth. There is more information on this in Appendix A, "Installing Mac OS X."

If you have more than one existing Mac OS 9 environment, make certain that you set the Classic preferences for a startup disk before you do anything that might cause a Classic application to be launched.

Extensions

Extensions in Mac OS 9 and earlier are loaded when the operating system starts up. They can provide additional or changed functionality to the basic system. Extensions have long been a source of some difficulty. They often need to be loaded in a precise order, and sometimes they interfere with one another. If you have problems launching the Classic environment, set the pop-up menu here to Turn Off Extensions. You can then use the Extensions Manager in Mac OS 9 to gradually add one extension after another back into the mix until you find the one that is causing a problem.

When the Classic environment is starting up, a window is displayed. You can use the disclosure triangle to see a full-screen image of the startup screen. The extensions that are loaded will appear across the bottom of the startup screen. The last extension that appears may be the one that causes problems; alternatively, the one that follows the last extension may cause the problem. Restart in Mac OS 9 to see the full series of extensions and note the one that you see starting up in Mac OS 9 and that you do not see when Classic starts up in Mac OS X. Note, too, that if you cannot start up from the Mac OS 9 startup disk, you will not be able to start up from the Classic environment that uses it. If you are having startup problems, diagnose and fix them first in Mac OS 9. Running the Classic environment in Mac OS X is not going to magically fix problems that you already have in Mac OS 9.

Rebuilding the Desktop

The button that lets you rebuild the desktop can also be handy in repairing problems with the desktop file. As noted in Chapter 4, "Working with Files," it is not a simple matter to keep track of icons for documents, the applications to launch when they are opened, and the like. In Mac OS X, each of these items is managed separately (in the Info window). In Mac OS 9 and earlier, the structure was somewhat more complex as components were pressed into duty to handle more than one task.

Rebuilding the desktop reestablishes the links to icons and applications. Some people routinely do it as often as once a week. Others never do. If you have peculiar behavior of icons or applications that launch documents, try rebuilding the desktop.

ColorSync

Color is one of the most complex issues that computers (and people) deal with. Everything from the type and angle of illumination in the room to the age of a CRT can affect how color is displayed. In addition, color on reflective media—paper, for example—is very different from color on media that transmit light—video monitors, for example. And, not to make things too simple, the interaction of colors among themselves means that the same color can look different in different environments and that two colors can appear the same under other circumstances. (See Josef Albers's *The Interaction of Color* for more on this topic.)

ColorSync is Apple's technology to match and manage colors in various environments. If you use your computer for graphic production, you may need to adjust your ColorSync settings. Most users do not need to worry about ColorSync, but it is there if you need it.

The ColorSync preferences consist of profiles describing devices and documents. You can create profiles, but they are normally created and distributed by hardware vendors. You can assemble a collection of profiles into workflows, which are named collections of them. One workflow, for example, might encompass the monitor you have on your desk, the printer that is used for printing in-house documents, and a scanner that you regularly use. Another workflow might be calibrated for a high-end printer used for running large jobs at a printer; it might also include the profile for a digital camera.

In addition to profiles, a workflow contains a color matching method that is used to convert and match colors. It also can contain notes (so you can specify which printers it applies to and so forth).

Setting Profiles

Profiles come from vendors, you create workflows from the profiles, and ColorSync helps you assemble workflows and choose among them. Application programs that support ColorSync (and most graphics programs do) use the current workflow settings to adjust their input and output accordingly. The basic ColorSync pane is shown in Figure 6-3.

ColorSync

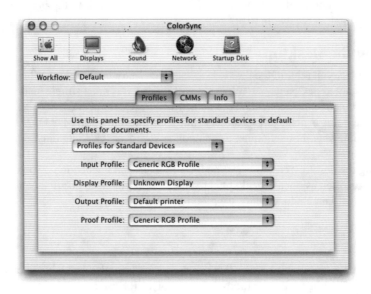

FIGURE 6-3
The ColorSync pane lets you control your computer's color management.

The pop-up menu in the Profiles tab lets you select the profiles for standard devices, as well as for documents. There are four types of profiles for standard devices:

- Input profiles are used for devices that send color images to your computer. These include digital cameras, scanners, and the like.

- Display profiles are used for your computer's display.

- Output profiles are used for the devices that produce final output, such as printers.

- Proofer profiles are used for the devices you use for producing proof materials. If you use a commercial printer, for example, the proofing device may be your own printer; the output device could be the printer's press.

Documents need color profiles to be specified if their color quality needs to be carefully controlled. There are several underlying color models—systems of describing colors in numeric terms. RGB (red, green, blue) consists of three numbers indicating the values of red, green, and blue in a specific color. It is typically used for monitors.

CMYK (cyan, magenta, yellow, black) consists of four numbers indicating the amounts of those four colors that are combined in a particular color. CMYK has typically been used for printing processes. By adjusting the ColorSync profiles, you can control how the system converts a color from one representation to another.

Setting Color Matching Methods (CMMs)

The profiles provide the data for ColorSync to do its work. In the CMMs tab (shown in Figure 6-4), you select the type of method used to match colors based on the profiles you have selected.

Documenting a Workflow

Use the Info tab to provide a meaningful name for your workflow and to provide comments. What seems clear today may be confusing next year—particularly when some of the devices for which you set up a workflow have been replaced. The Info pane is shown in Figure 6-5.

Saving a Workflow

If you have made any changes to the workflow, you will be prompted to save them. The workflows that you create are specific to your login ID: one user's workflows are independent of another user's, even on the same computer. You can select or edit workflows by clicking the scrollbox next to the Workflow field. For more information, visit Apple's ColorSync Web site at http://www.apple.com/colorsync/.

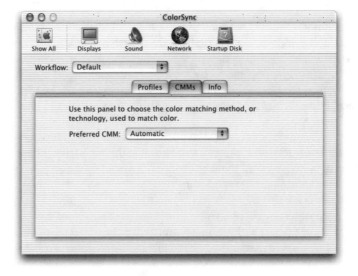

FIGURE 6-4   Color Matching Methods (CMMs) refer to the technology used to describe color.

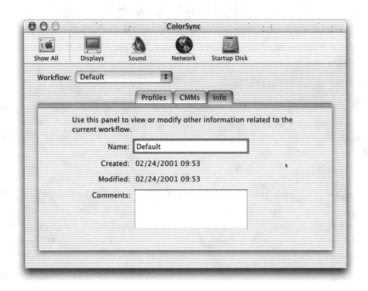

FIGURE 6-5   You can document your ColorSync workflows in the ColorSync Info pane.

Date & Time (Requires Administrator Password)

Your computer requires the correct date and time for many of its tasks. Not the least is the automatic time-stamping of documents when they are created and modified. Other important purposes include automatically setting the date on documents (including checks and other transactions). In the early days of personal computers, it did not matter if the date and time were wrong; today, they are essential, and they must be correct. Date & Time preferences let you set the date and time. To set the formatting and display of the date and time, use the International preferences.

Click the Date & Time preferences icon to open the pane shown in Figure 6-6.

The icon in the lower left of the window indicates that these preferences are locked and require the administrator's password to make changes. If you click the lock, you will see a dialog asking you to provide an administrator password.

The administrator is the first user that you create when you install Mac OS X. If your computer is used by a variety of people, you may not have the password and may be unable to change the date and time (as you will see, many preferences that affect the computer as a whole require the administrator's password). If you have that password, enter it, click OK, and you will return to the Date & Time pane.

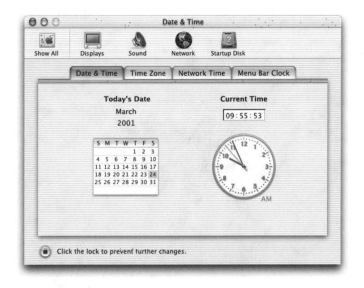

FIGURE 6-6	Set the date and time so that your computer can properly manage communications and files.

Setting the Date and Time

Simply click the date you want in the calendar at the left. To set the time, you can either type in the time in the digital display at the right, or you can drag the clock's hands to the correct time.

Be careful about setting the time back. You may cause documents to be stored out of sequence, with later documents actually dated as if they were earlier. This can cause problems with backups and can confuse you when you look at them. If you need to set the time back, the best way to do it is the first time you use your computer on a day. If you set the time from 3:00 P.M. to 2:00 P.M. and have not used your computer at all, there is no possibility of confusing documents from (old) 2:00 P.M. with those from (new) 2:00 P.M.

Setting the Time Zone

The Time Zone tab is shown in Figure 6-7.

You click the map in the approximate location of your time zone. Then, from the pop-up menu below the map, choose the specific time zone you are in, as shown in the figure.

FIGURE 6-7   Time zones allow the computer to interact with networked computers elsewhere in the world.

Using Network Time Synchronization

Finally, the Network Time tab lets you synchronize your computer's clock with another computer using the Network Time Protocol—one of the Internet's standards. Synchronization of this sort is often necessary when transactions are processed over a network and it is necessary to know which transactions precede or follow other transactions. If each computer's time is slightly different, the actual sequence of events may not be the apparent sequence of events as determined from the times at which documents or transactions are created.

Network Time Synchronization makes a great deal of sense if you have an always-on Internet connection such as DSL or cable. If you use dialup connections or if you normally are not connected to the Internet, it is not a good choice.

Time synchronization is also used in a variety of circumstances other than transactions. It can make maintenance of a network of computers easier (since the time needs to be set only once), and it can make real-time network events more accurate. For example, if you are producing a Webcast—or participating in one—you need to know exactly when it will start. In practice, Webcasts and satellite transmissions typically "start" some time before the scheduled time so that all participants can be ready. When time is synchronized, this preparatory time can be reduced.

The Network Time Protocol (NTP) deals with Universal Time (formerly known as Greenwich Mean Time); as a result, you do not have to worry about time zones. If your computer's time zone is set properly (as described in the previous section), all will be well. NTP relies on Network Time Servers—computers that provide reliable time to their clients. Time servers get their accurate time from outside sources—satellites, highly accurate clocks, and so forth. Many time servers actually rely on a variety of outside time sources, averaging their times to provide an accurate consensus.

If you want to synchronize your computer with a network time server, click the Network Time tab in the Date & Time preferences to open the pane shown in Figure 6-8.

If you want to use network time synchronization, you need to specify the server that you want to use. You can use the NetInfo network settings (described in Chapter 8, "Managing Your Computer Environment") or you can specify an NTP server's IP address or name manually.

If you are using network time synchronization, it is because you need to keep your computer consistent with a standard time. Normally, that is so that your computer and another one—usually not the time server—have the same time. As a result, both computers should use the same network time server. You and the other computer user (or your network administrator) must select that time server. You can use Apple's time server (http://time.apple.com/) or one of the public time servers on the Internet, which you can locate with a search engine.

Once you have specified your network time server, click Start to begin synchronization. Be careful about turning network time synchronization on and off. The warning about setting your computer's clock back in time applies here. Network time synchronization may have the effect of turning your clock back when it is turned on (since the network time may be slightly

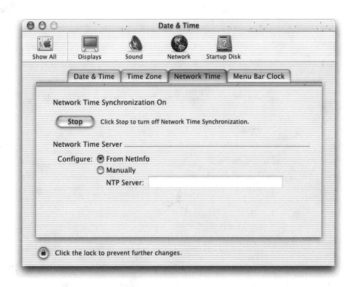

FIGURE 6-8   Use network time synchronization to keep your computer's clock accurate.

Date & Time (Requires Administrator Password)

behind your computer's time). As a result, documents and transactions on your computer may appear to be out of sequence. If you are going to use network time synchronization, leave it on or off. If you are using a portable computer such as a laptop, turn it on when you are connected to a network and off otherwise. In such a case, turn it on or off when you start up your computer; do not turn it on or off in the middle of your work.

Menu Bar Clock

The Menu Bar clock appears at the right of the menu bar. You use the last tab in the Date & Time preferences to set its options.

Display

The Display preferences are set using the pane shown in Figure 6-9.

This pane lets you set the resolution for your display; it also shows you details of the settings (at the right). If you are using Apple monitors, the recommended resolutions will almost certainly include appropriate ones. If you are using other monitors, you may need to use the Customize button to add other settings.

The display resolution is expressed in the number of pixels horizontally and vertically that are shown. The fewer pixels, the larger the image. (The screen's size is a given.) The Hz value that follows the pixel resolution is determined by your display. Consult the instruction manual (or look on the back of the monitor) for the appropriate setting. Not all monitors support all settings.

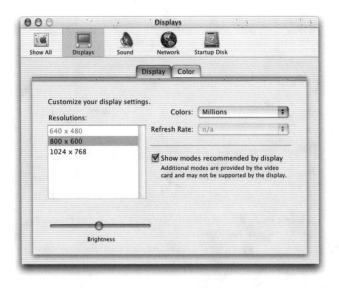

FIGURE 6-9   Display preferences control the color and resolution of the image you see.

At the right, you can select how colors are displayed on your monitors. The greater the number of colors, the more accurately images will be displayed; however, greater color depths require more memory to display them. Since Mac OS X manages memory efficiently, and since many models of the Macintosh now provide separate video memory, using the highest setting usually does not impose major performance problems. However, if you experience peculiar problems and strange error messages, try setting the color depth to a lower value (thousands instead of millions, for example).

If your display requires you to set a resolution or refresh rate that was not provided in the default settings, you can do so here.

If your monitor does not change after you have reset the Monitors preferences, try turning it off and back on again. You usually do not have to reboot your computer; you merely need to have the monitor and the computer reestablish communications.

The Color tab lets you use previously configured settings for common displays; you can also create your own.

| FIGURE 6-10 | Dock preferences control appearance and behavior of Dock icons. |

Dock

Dock preferences are shown in Figure 6-10.

You will note that as you adjust the slider for icon size and as you click the checkbox to automatically show and hide the Dock, these effects take place immediately. You can thus see how your settings will look before accepting them.

Dock preferences are also available from the Apple menu.

Energy Saver (Requires Administrator Password)

As shown in Figure 6-11, you can adjust energy saving preferences using the Energy Saver preferences.

All Macintosh computers today have a variety of energy saving settings. The most basic settings involve the processor, the display, and the disk. Each of these components uses electricity to function, and you can set each one to save power when you are not using your computer but it is still turned on. These settings are called *sleep* modes.

Energy saving is particularly important for battery-powered computers such as laptops. It is also important for desktop computers that are left on for long periods of time. Since Mac OS X is very stable and in view of the fact that leaving your computer powered on is easy and useful, you can save a significant amount of energy by using these settings appropriately. Remember that it

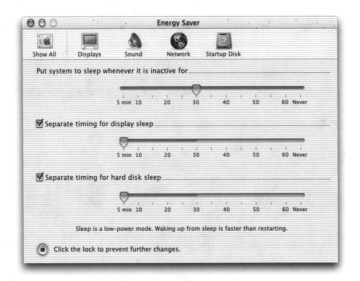

FIGURE 6-11   Use Energy Saver preference to avoid wasting energy.

is not just your computer's electrical demands that use energy; heat is generated by the computer, and that in turn can increase air conditioning demands.

Processor Sleep Mode

The most basic sleep mode is for the processor—the system itself. This is not the biggest consumer of power in your computer (the disk is), but it is almost always the single largest source of heat. Sleep mode is essential for most laptops to achieve long battery life.

Use the slider to select the period of time after which you want the computer to enter sleep mode. This time starts from the last time that you do something—type or move the mouse, for example.

To wake your computer, press any key or move the mouse. When your computer is asleep, any such movement will wake it: a cleaning person may be startled when a flick of a dust cloth brings the screen to life. A cat may be annoyed that its stretching on your desk casts an unflattering glare on its slumbers when the screen brightens.

When waking up your computer, move the mouse or press the SHIFT, CONTROL, or OPTION keys on the keyboard. Since the screen will be dimmed, you generally cannot tell where a keystroke will land. Pressing RETURN is the worst way to wake up your computer since you might inadvertently dismiss an unseen dialog. The SHIFT, CONTROL, or OPTION keys and the mouse will not affect any documents or applications that you have open except in very unusual cases.

When the processor is asleep, the display and hard disk will also be asleep since they cannot function without the processor. Network connections will also be shut down for the same reason. However, you can set display and disk sleep times separately so that they sleep before the processor does.

Display Sleep

You can use the Energy Saver preferences to set a shorter time for display sleep. You might want to do this in a situation in which you do not want the processor to cycle off, but you do want the screen to dim. If you are leaving your computer to do some intense calculations, backups, or database updates, you may not need to look at the monitor for some time, perhaps even overnight. If a computer is used as a file server, the monitor can be allowed to go to sleep while the processor and disk remain awake at all times. Monitors use electricity and can be a significant source of heat if they include video cathode ray tubes (flat panel monitors do not generate much heat).

Hard Disk Sleep

Like the monitor, the hard disk can be set to go to sleep before your processor. If your computer is used as a file server, other people may need to access the disk on a periodic but unpredictable basis. Since bringing a disk to full speed is probably the lengthiest awakening of any of the three components, keeping it spinning can improve performance of your file server.

General Preferences

General preferences control scrolling behavior and the appearance of Aqua, the interface to Mac OS X. They concern its appearance and behavior. The General preferences pane is shown here.

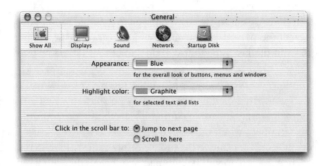

Setting Appearance

Use the Appearance pop-up menu to set an overall look for your computer. The default appearance—which may change as Apple revises the operating system—is now called Blue. It uses the translucent colors that you normally see. In some cases—particularly for graphic artists who are working with colored images—the colors of the standard interface may interfere with their work. For them (as well as anyone else who wishes to use it), there are other appearance settings. Platinum uses shades of gray so that the colors in your work are seen without interaction of other colors. Experiment with them to see what you like best. They have no effect on how the computer operates.

Setting the Highlighting Color

When you select text in a window, it is highlighted. You can select the highlight color from the pop-up menu shown in this figure. This highlighting color is used for all selected text in all applications for the user who is logged in. The Aqua interface is very different from that of the Classic Mac OS (as well as from other graphical user interfaces). One of its differences is in the colors that it uses—its palette. While you can select any color that you want from the pop-up menu, you will note that the colors available (other than a custom color) tend toward the blue-green part of the palette. If you are used to another color (yellow, for example), try one of the Aqua colors before reverting to what you are used to.

Setting Scrolling

Mac OS 9 and earlier scrolling behavior is the first choice (Jump To Next Page) in the scrolling section. When that choice is made, each click above or below the scroll box moves the document forward or back by an equal amount, usually one page. The other choice (Scroll To Here) presents the scroll bar track as a map of the document. Clicking 25 percent of the way down the track moves you to (approximately) 25 percent of the way into the document.

International

The International preferences let you set formatting of dates, time, and numbers. You also can adjust to various keyboards and to the language used in system alerts and dialogs.

These preferences affect the operating system itself, as well as application programs. Some application programs do not respect these settings; they allow you—and sometimes force you—to enter this information again for their own use. Start by making certain that this information is correct so that the programs that do pick it up will be able to do so. Note, also, that this preference is for each login ID on the computer. Different people—or you at different times—can have different international preferences.

Setting the Language

The first tab in the International preferences is shown in Figure 6-12.

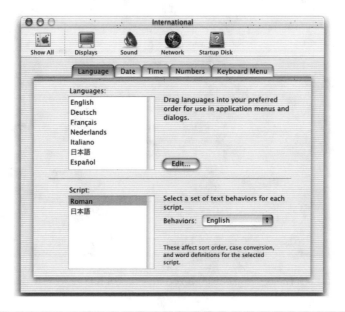

FIGURE 6-12   Mac OS X supports a variety of languages and scripts.

You can set the language and script (character sets) in this pane. Note that the languages can be ordered; most advanced Mac OS X applications (those that use Cocoa) can use that order to find the resources that are needed for window titles, error messages, and the like. Not all resources will be available in all languages.

Do not neglect to set the appropriate behavior in the lower right so that features such as sorting characters with accents (like è) are done properly.

These settings are normally configured automatically for you during installation. You may need to change them if you move your computer to another country or if you sell it to someone else.

Setting the Date Format

Figure 6-13 shows the preferences you can set for date formats.

The operating system uses two types of data formats; many programs pick up their own formatting from these preferences. Samples of the date formats are shown at the bottom of the window as you adjust the preferences.

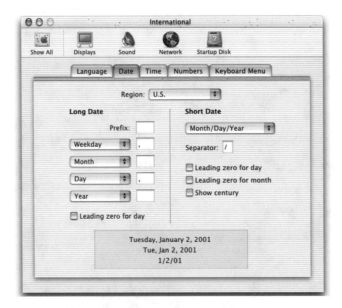

FIGURE 6-13   Date formats can be customized in Mac OS X.

The Region pop-up menu provides default settings. You can always override them, but they may be sufficient.

Long Dates

Long dates consist of up to four components: the day of the week, the month, the date, and the year. They can appear in any order, and various separators—commas, spaces, and so forth—can be used between them. (You can use combinations, such as a comma followed by a space.) Use the pop-up menus to select the items you want to appear in the date, and type the separator characters into the fields that follow them. You can even add a prefix, such as "Date:." Remember, though, that these will be the default settings; a prefix such as "Date of Birth" will show up all over the system.

The long date can also appear in abbreviated form; the second line of the example shows what this looks like. The abbreviated format is automatically constructed from the long date.

Short Dates

Short date formats are set on the right of the preferences. You can use the pop-up menu to specify the sequence of elements. You also can choose the separator and whether or not to show leading zeros.

These are default formats. You can override them in individual programs in most cases. Have no fear that these settings will confound your spreadsheets.

Setting the Time Format

In the Time tab, you can set the formatting preferences for the time display. You set the time according to the region you're working in, and the type of clock—24-hour or 12-hour—you want to tell time by.

Setting the Numbers Format

The numbers formats in the Numbers tab let you set preferences for numbers and currency. You can use the Region pop-up menu to set defaults. You also can see the result of your choices in the display at the bottom of the pane.

Setting the Keyboard Layout

Finally, keyboard layouts are shown in Figure 6-14. You can use multiple keyboard layouts just by clicking more than one checkbox in the list provided. If you do so, a Keyboard menu appears in the menu bar allowing you to switch easily among keyboards.

International

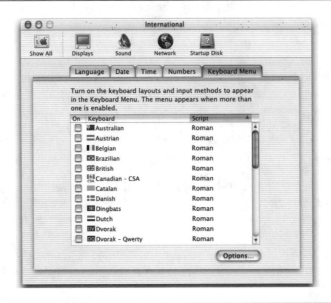

FIGURE 6-14   Keyboard Layout preferences let you use one keyboard for several languages or scripts.

Internet

The Internet Preferences icon opens the panes shown in this section. This information was stored in Internet Config in Mac OS 9 and earlier. As you will see, it also is often stored in preferences for browsers and email programs. By setting it here, you can often avoid having to repeat it: many programs automatically pick up this information. If you enter it for a specific program, such as a browser, it may be used there but not for other purposes. Use the system-wide preference if at all possible.

This information is set up by the Installation assistant when you install Mac OS X. However, if it changes—and Internet addresses frequently do—you need to adjust it.

iTools

The iTools pane is shown in Figure 6-15. You can login to your iTools account from here. For more information about iTools, see Chapter 10, "iTools: Apple's OS Tools on the Internet."

Setting Email Preferences

Email preferences are set in the pane shown in Figure 6-16.

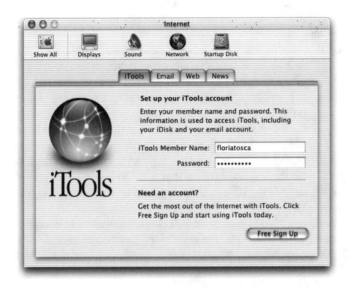

FIGURE 6-15   Set iTools login information in Internet preferences.

FIGURE 6-16   Email preferences set in Internet preferences can then be used by Apple Mail or other email programs.

You can choose your default email application (Mail is the Mac OS X application program that ships with the operating system, but you can choose products such as Microsoft Outlook and Eudora if you have them installed).

As you can see, this set of preferences lets you describe one incoming and one outgoing mail server. Many people have more than one; you can describe the others in your email application. (See Chapter 18, "Using Apple Mail.")

For your email address, use the return address you want on your outgoing emails. People should send you email to this address.

Your network coordinator or Internet service provider (ISP) will provide you with the names of the incoming and outgoing mail servers, as well as whether your account is a POP or IMAP account. (If you do not know, use POP—it is still more widespread than the newer IMAP.)

The user account ID is the account name that you use to log into the mail server system. This may or may not be the same as the ID you use to log into an Internet dialup connection. Your ISP or network coordinator should provide you with this information.

As you can see in Figure 6-15, your password is often stored in an encrypted format. More than one person has used an email password for years and been unable to reconstruct it after a disk crash. Keep your account ID and password in a very safe place on paper in case of such problems.

Setting Web Preferences

The Web preferences shown in Figure 6-17 can be set in a browser's preferences. However, the default Web browser needs to be set here so that when you double-click a URL, the correct browser can be opened.

FIGURE 6-17   Web preferences can be used by your Web browsers.

Sometimes, your default Web browser preference is overridden. Some products automatically default to—or require—a certain browser regardless of your preferences. If you have several browsers installed, make certain that the correct one is selected here. If you do not want to use other browsers (or other versions of your default browser), make certain that they are removed from your system. However, make copies of them so that if you encounter a software product that requires one of the other browsers, you will be able to restore it.

Setting News Preferences

Finally, you can set news preferences. Internet news is a protocol that was very important in the early days of the public Internet. News groups—discussion groups with threaded conversations—are being supplanted by purely Web-based technologies. However, the news infrastructure still exists.

Keyboard

Keyboard preferences are set using the pane shown here:

You can set the repeat delay and rate in this window. If you are used to holding down a key to have it repeat, this is a setting that you may want to adjust precisely. Individuals get used to very specific repeat delays and rates. You can test the settings in the text box in this window.

  The International preferences—described previously—are used to adjust the layout of the keyboard to various languages.

Login

There are two sets of preferences for the Login pane: Login Items and the Login Window.

Setting Login Items

When a user first logs into Mac OS X, any items in the Login Items preferences are automatically opened. The pane is shown in Figure 6-18.

FIGURE 6-18   Login items are opened automatically when you log in to your computer.

Use the buttons at the bottom of the window to add applications or documents to the pane. Select items and then click Remove to remove them.

Remember that Mac OS X is very stable and that its memory management imposes a minimal burden on the system for running inactive applications. If you choose to have half a dozen or more login items, it may take a while to reboot your system; but once that cycle is complete, everything will be just a mouse click away.

You can hide items that are opened at login time. The reason for doing this is to have a document (or application) prepared for use and one click away in the Dock.

On Mac OS 9 and earlier, login items were files or aliases placed in the Startup Items folder within the System Folder.

Setting the Login Window (Requires Administrator Password)

Figure 6-19 shows how you can set the Login Window.

The two sets of options are complementary. The first set, Automatically Log In, is appropriate if your computer is used in a secure environment or if other people are not around. You turn it on, and you are automatically logged in.

The second option, Disable Restart And Shut Down Buttons, means that users can log out, but cannot leave the computer in any state other than on. (Of course, if they can interrupt its power, they can turn it off.) This is a secure setting for computer labs, public kiosks, and the like.

It would be a very unusual situation to use both automatic login and the disabling option. One is for a secure environment; the other is not.

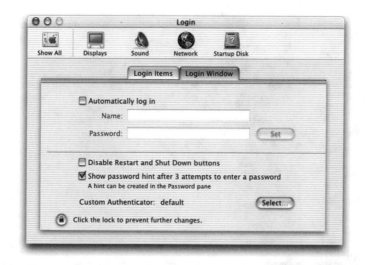

FIGURE 6-19   You can set preferences to totally bypass login when you restart your computer.

By default, Mac OS X uses its own authentication scheme to authenticate a password. You can modify this using the Select button. Kerberos is a popular cross-platform authenticator that you can use.

Finally, note that you can display a hint after three unsuccessful login attempts. You set user password hints in "Users," later in this chapter.

Mouse

You use the Mouse preferences, shown in Figure 6-20, to adjust how the mouse behaves.

The Tracking Speed adjustment controls how quickly the mouse moves on the screen in relation to its actual movement on your desktop or trackpad. If you have a limited space in which to move your mouse, try setting the speed to a faster level. You will be able to move it further on the screen without moving it very far on your desk.

Double-Click Speed lets you set the system's sensitivity to double-clicks: whether it distinguishes two separate clicks or one double-click. You can experiment on this pane to see what feels right to you.

New computer users often have more trouble with double-clicking than with almost any other aspect of the computer. Very determined mouse clickers will go slowly and heavily into a double-click, thereby generating two separate mouse clicks. You can adjust this parameter to suit them (or yourself). However, after a day of using a mouse, most first-time mouse users master the digital rodent.

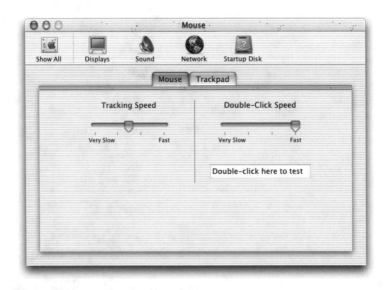

FIGURE 6-20   Mouse preferences control mouse movement and click speed.

If you are using a desktop computer, there may be no Trackpad tab in your Mouse preferences. However, with a laptop, you may have a trackpad and you will see a different set of preferences.

Some people prefer to use the buttons next to the trackpad for clicking; others prefer to tap the trackpad. If your trackpad is sensitive, you may find that setting it to respond to clicks can cause stray finger movements to be interpreted as clicks. If your pointer jumps around the screen, turn off Clicking in the trackpad preferences as a test.

Network (Requires Administrator Password)

You can change your computer's network settings if you have an administrator password. If you do not, you can browse those settings but not change them. Network settings control your local network environment, including how you connect to the Internet if you connect through a network.

Chapter 11, "Communicating Over a Local Area Network," and Chapter 12, "Communicating Over the Internet," contain far more details on networking along with definitions of many of the terms used in this section. Also, note that the setup process steps you through the entry of this information. However, if you change your configuration—as is the case if you use a new Internet service provider—you must update your settings.

Setting TCP/IP Preferences

TCP/IP is the protocol that is used on the Internet; it is also used on many local area networks. Each device on a TCP/IP network has an IP address. This includes networked printers, computers, routers, and all other addressable network components.

The Network preferences TCP/IP pane is shown in Figure 6-21.

At the top of the pane is a Location pop-up menu. You can use it to switch quickly among various sets of networking preferences that you define. You can also use it to create a new location.

Locations are particularly important for computers that move from one network environment to another; PowerBook and iBook computers are most commonly in this category. Instead of resetting each network preference individually, you can group them into a location. A location can be physical, such as your office, your dorm, your home, or a cybercafé. It can also be a composite—you might have dialup access from your home, as well as an always-on Internet connection. Having alternate connections available can come in handy both for troubleshooting and for handling problems with one network or another.

These choices described in this section must be made in conjunction with your network administrator or ISP. If you are on a local area network, make certain that you have your settings written down before you start.

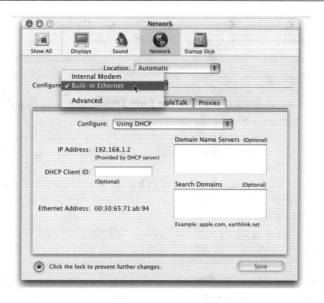

| FIGURE 6-21 | TCP/IP lets you control basic settings for modems and other connections. |

Network (Requires Administrator Password)

Setting the Port

First, you set the communications port you are going to be using. The pop-up menu to do so is shown previously in Figure 6-21. The items in this list will vary depending on your computer and its configuration. You probably have a built-in Ethernet connection, and many computers have a modem built in. A combined modem/printer port is available on some PowerBook models. A second Ethernet card may be installed. In addition, you may have an AirPort (wireless) card to use for communications. Select the port to configure in the rest of this pane and then continue.

The settings for each port remain in place when you switch to another port. You can also store several sets of settings for each port with the Location pop-up menu.

Setting the Address

There are two parts to this pane. At the left, you configure your computer's address. You have four choices for configuration in the pop-up menu: manually, BootP, DHCP, and no connection. Also, if you have specified manual configurations, each one of them will be added to the pop-up menu so that you can switch among them if needed.

If you connect through a cable or DSL modem, it is likely that the DHCP setting will be the best one to use. Check with your Internet service provider. The terms DHCP and BootP are standard Internet terms, so you need not get specific advice for a Macintosh from your ISP.

Your network administrator or Internet service provider will tell you how to configure your computer if there are any specific settings you need to use.

Setting the Domain Name Servers

At the right of this pane, you set your DNS addresses. These are the addresses of domain name servers (at least one is required), which are used to convert domain names (such as apple.com) to IP addresses (the quartet of numbers such as 192.168.1.251). Typically, your domain name server is located at your Internet service provider. The address of one or two domain name servers is part of the information that your ISP provides you when you sign up.

If you forget this information and have not written it down, most ISPs have all of the information on their Web site. You can use someone else's computer—or a computer in a public library—to access the information.

DNS settings can be configured automatically or manually. Even if you use an automated technique for getting the addresses in the left part of the window, you may need to manually set the DNS settings in the right.

If you cannot access any Web site and your email connection cannot be made, your DNS settings may be wrong or missing. In general, failure of both your browser and email program means either that the entire connection to the Internet has failed (or does not exist) or that you need to reset your DNS settings. It may appear that you have many problems, but it is probably only the one.

Checking the Address Settings

Use the TCP/IP tab of the Network preferences as a diagnostic tool. If there is something wrong with your network or the router, your DHCP settings may be incorrect. You can talk to your network administrator or ISP about this if you are having a problem, and they will probably want to know what DHCP settings have been generated. Read out the information from this pane.

Your computer's Ethernet networking card address is shown at the bottom of the pane. It consists of a 12-digit hexadecimal number (that is, a number in base 16, rather than the traditional base 10). Since your Ethernet address uniquely identifies a port on your computer, it can by inference identify your computer. As a result, you may need to register this number with a network administrator. For example, some university networks require incoming students to identify their computers with Ethernet addresses. The network support staff then enters this information, and unregistered computers cannot be attached to the network. If you are asked for your Ethernet address, always confirm that it is an Ethernet address and not an IP address.

AppleTalk

AppleTalk is a protocol used for local area networks that primarily contain Macintosh computers and printers. IBM-compatible PCs may appear on AppleTalk networks, but heterogeneous networks and newer networks generally use TCP/IP. You can configure your computer to use both AppleTalk and TCP/IP; this helps you communicate with the Internet and with legacy networks to which you may be attached.

The AppleTalk settings were shown in Chapter 5, "Printing."

QuickTime

QuickTime is Apple's technology for handling video, sound, animation, graphics, text, music, and virtual reality (360-degree scenes that you can navigate with a mouse). It provides support for rich media, including images, music, MIDI, MP3, and more. QuickTime comes installed on all Macintosh computers (as well as on many PCs). You can set QuickTime preferences from the QuickTime icon.

Only one preference—Connection Speed—is essential. If it is not set, you will be prompted to do so the first time you use QuickTime.

QuickTime Plug-In Settings

Figure 6-22 shows the plug-in settings for QuickTime.

For most people, the configuration shown in the figure is appropriate. If you are managing a public access computer (in a computer lab, a public library, or the like), you may want to check Enable Kiosk Mode so that well-intentioned people do not cause problems.

QuickTime plug-in settings control how downloaded media files are handled.

The button at the bottom lets you access MIME settings. In this dialog, you can specify which MIME types QuickTime should handle. This matters because some media types can be handled by a variety of products, and each MIME type needs to be associated with only one handler (so that Mac OS X knows which one to use). (iTunes, described in Chapter 16, "Working with Applications," can handle some of the media types that QuickTime can also handle.)

QuickTime Connection Speed Settings

Figure 6-23 shows the Connection Speed tab. This is one setting that you do want to adjust.

QuickTime is very effective at optimizing your connection, but you need to help it by providing information about your connection speed. Do not be wishful in your thinking here: if your connection is of poor quality, consider using the next lowest setting. Also, note that this connection speed refers to the connection to the Internet. If you are on a local area network, its speed (10 or 100 Base T, in most cases) is generally faster than the connection from the local area network to the Internet. It is that connection speed—such as the speed of the DSL or cable modem—that matters here.

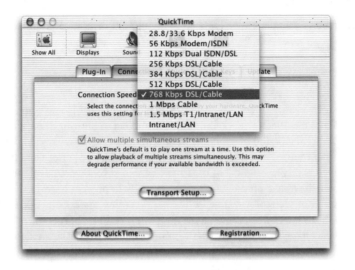

FIGURE 6-23 Make certain that your Connection Speed settings are correctly set for optimal QuickTime performance.

Music

QuickTime can use its own synthesizer for music or you can install another one. Normally, the default synthesizer from QuickTime is fine.

QuickTime Media Keys

Media keys are used to unlock secured (encrypted) media files. You may need to pay or otherwise be authorized to open these files. If you are given a media key, enter it in the dialog shown here:

Click the Add button at the bottom of the pane to open the data entry sheet.

Updating QuickTime

Finally, you can specify that the QuickTime software should be updated regularly in the Update tab.

Screen Saver

Mac OS X comes with several screen savers, and you can add others if you want. Screen savers were very important in the 1980s when monitors were subject to burn-in: if the same image was left on the screen for a long period of time, it would burn into the phosphors and appear ghost-like, even if the monitor was turned off. (Many automatic teller machines suffer from this problem, since their Welcome screen is displayed most of the time.) Screen savers were developed as a way to automatically change the image on the monitor periodically to prevent burn-in.

Advances in monitor technology along with energy saving features helped eliminate this problem (if the monitor is not displaying anything, nothing can be burned into it). However, many people like the changing images on their monitors, and they serve a useful purpose in some cases by reminding people that their computer is turned on (or, in the case of kiosks and public access computers, that the computer is ready for use by anyone).

If you want to use the screen saver, select the Screen Saver preference icon, as shown in Figure 6-24.

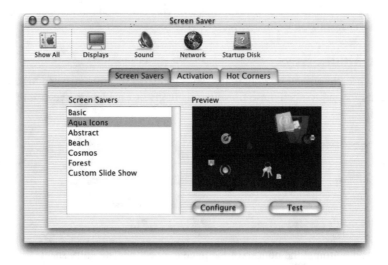

FIGURE 6-24   A variety of screen savers is built into Mac OS X.

Any screen saver modules that are installed will be shown here along with a preview image. You can click the Test button to see what the image looks like full size.

Some screen savers (including Aqua Icons) can be configured in this dialog:

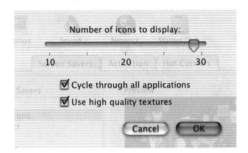

Here, the screen saver pulls icons from files that you specify and sends them floating over your screen.

Click the Activation tab to specify when the screen saver starts. You also can specify that your password needs to be reentered when the screen saver is dismissed. This means that if you leave your computer unattended, no one will be able to use it without your password. You will not be logged out, and applications can continue running, but the computer will be secure.

You can also make corners of your display hot, as shown in Figure 6-25. When you move a mouse into a hot corner, the screen saver either starts automatically at that moment or is

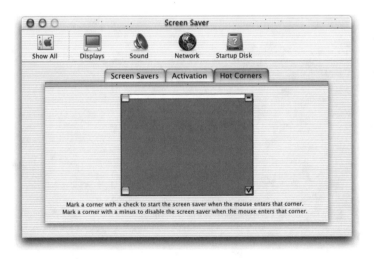

FIGURE 6-25   Hot Corners provides even more control over screen savers.

prevented from starting. Click in each corner to cycle through the choices—none, activate (+), or prevent activation (–).

If you are giving a presentation using your computer, you might want to either turn off your screen saver or position the pointer in a corner where the screen saver will not be activated.

Sharing (Requires Administrator Password)

Use the Sharing preferences to turn file sharing on and off, as well as to turn FTP and remote access on and off. The Sharing preference pane is shown in Figure 6-26.

If file sharing is on, people who can connect to your computer over a local area network, AppleTalk, or the Internet can access folders that are public. FTP is the Internet standard File Transfer Protocol that allows people to retrieve files and folders from your computer or to place

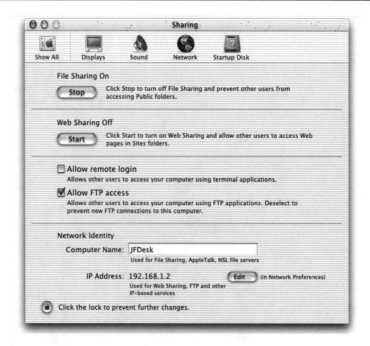

FIGURE 6-26   Sharing controls file and Web sharing.

them onto your computer (again, with appropriate security constraints). File sharing allows remote users to actually open files; FTP merely allows transfer of files.

Your computer's name may appear in the Chooser for other network users who are running Mac OS 9 and earlier.

Telnet is an Internet protocol that allows people to connect to your computer and to run applications on it. These are command-line applications that can be controlled by the text interface (as in the Terminal application).

If you have an always-on Internet connection such as cable or DSL, think twice—or more— about enabling Telnet or FTP access. You can become the prey of hackers who misuse your computer and cause damage. If you do have such a connection, make certain that you study Chapter 7, "Securing Your Computer," for appropriate security measures to take.

Software Updates

You can control when (and if) Mac OS X checks automatically for updates from Apple as shown in Figure 6-27. More on Software Updater is provided in Chapter 16, "Working with Applications."

FIGURE 6-27   Software updates lets you get the latest software from Apple automatically.

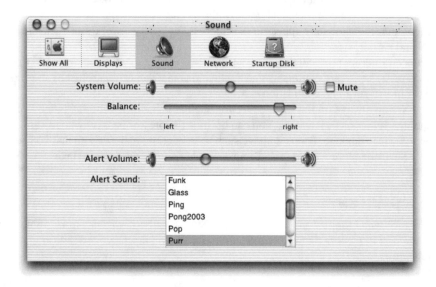

FIGURE 6-28   Sound preferences control volume as well as the type of sounds you hear.

Sound

Use the Sound preferences shown in Figure 6-28 to adjust the volume level and stereo balance of your computer's speakers.

You use the scrolling list at the bottom to choose the alert sound that you want to hear when the computer needs to get your attention.

Speech

Speech synthesis and recognition are built into the Macintosh operating system. You can choose a default voice that will be used when text is spoken. Use the Speech preferences option to do so, as shown in Figure 6-29.

Speech synthesis is a very useful aspect of Mac OS X (as it has been in Mac OS 9 and earlier). The synthesis is very sophisticated, and pronunciation is quite good. It can be helpful for not only people who have trouble reading the screen, but also in cases in which you may not be looking at the screen when your attention is required.

When speech recognition is on, a small microphone appears, as shown in the following illustration. In the center is an indication of how recognition will proceed. If you must hold down the ESCAPE key, Esc appears, as shown in the illustration. If you must use the word "Computer" in speaking, that word appears rather than Esc.

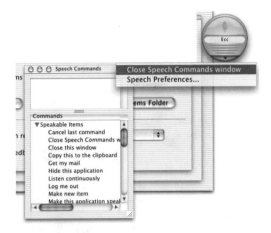

The small triangle at the bottom opens a window that shows you the speakable items. The Listening tab shown in Figure 6-30 lets you set further speech options. A variety of voices are available to generate speech in those applications that support it. Click the Text-to-Speech tab for additional preferences that you can set.

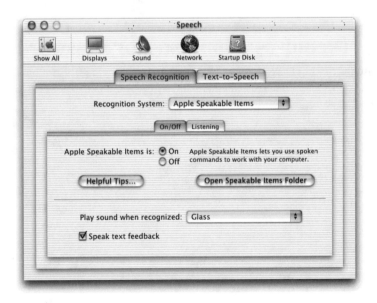

FIGURE 6-29   You can select the conditions under which your computer attempts to recognize speech.

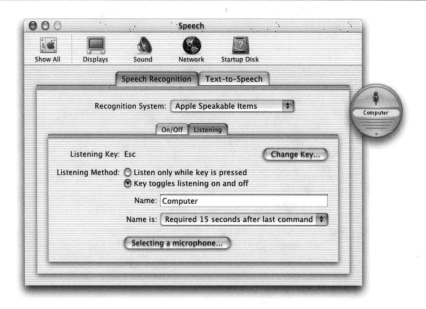

FIGURE 6-30   Further listening options control how your computer listens.

Startup Disk (Requires Administrator Password)

Finally, you use the Startup Disk preferences shown in the following illustration to determine from what disk you will start up. This can make it easy to switch between Mac OS X and Mac OS 9 if you need to do so.

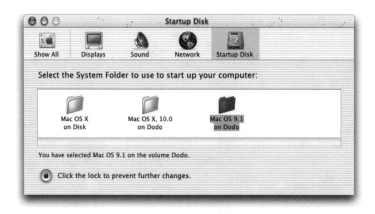

On Mac OS 9, use the Startup Disk control pane to set the startup disk to Mac OS X, as shown here.

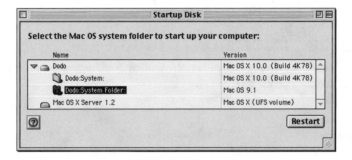

Users (Requires Administrator Password)

Users preferences let you add or delete users from your computer. You can also specify their password and whether they have administrator privileges. The basic Users preferences are shown in Figure 6-31.

Editing or adding a user opens another window in which users can log in with either their short or long names, as well as their passwords. If you have set the hint option in login preferences, the hint you type here will be displayed after three unsuccessful login attempts.

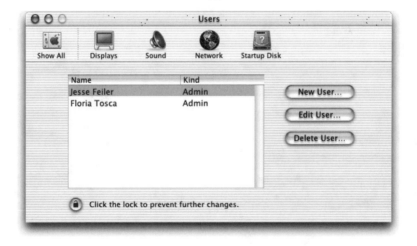

FIGURE 6-31 Users preferences lets you create, edit, or delete users.

See Chapter 13, "Setting Up a Network Server," for more sophisticated user management available with Mac OS X Server.

Customizing the Preferences Window

You can drag any of the preferences icons into the toolbar at the top of the Preferences window, as shown here. If you do this, the icon remains in the body of the window; however, a duplicate appears in the toolbar.

Summary

In this chapter, you have seen how to set the various preferences that you can apply to your computer and to individual users. By creating several different user IDs and setting preferences accordingly, you can create customized versions of your computer that are suitable for different individuals or different types of work that you do.

Other customizations include your network configuration, as well as preferences for the desktop and individual applications. These are described elsewhere in the book.

Chapter 7

Securing Your Computer

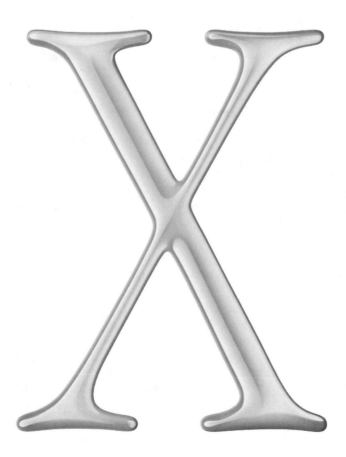

T his chapter provides you with the information you need to know to secure your computer. As people put more and more of their lives on computers, the need for security grows. Mac OS X provides a variety of security features that you can use to implement the degree of security you need.

In this chapter, you will find:

■ An introductory survey of security issues

■ Managing security and multiple users on Mac OS X

■ File access security

■ An overview of the keychain technology that can make your life easier in a world of multiple passwords and user IDs

For security aspects of network operations, see the chapters in Part III of the book, "Networking." This chapter deals only with the issues of security involving a single computer and the user or users who have access to it.

Computer Security

People who use computers grow increasingly reliant on them. They use them for word processing, financial management, email, and games. Data and applications that they need for their daily lives are located on computers. Despite this increasing reliance on computers, it is remarkable how lightly many people take the security of their computers and data.

Computer security boils down to two issues: your need to keep your property from being stolen or misused and your need to keep your property from being damaged. Similar measures may be taken to achieve both goals, but they are fundamentally different.

Protection from Theft

Mac OS X is not going to protect your computer from being stolen. In fact, it can increase the risk of theft. Laptop computers are among the most commonly stolen items in airports and other public spaces. If you were a thief, you would probably choose the newest model to steal. Mac OS X and the distinctive Apple designs are as attractive to thieves as they are to users.

How often have you seen someone in a public space using a laptop and then putting it away in a bag or briefcase—which is then left on a chair while the owner goes for a cup of coffee or to make a telephone call? If you don't protect your property at the most basic level, all the passwords in the world won't help you.

The most disturbing aspect of computer theft is that well-protected computers, that is, those with appropriate password protection, may be useless to a thief. The stolen computer may wind up discarded and of no use to anyone at all.

There is no security measure better than a lock and key. Do not leave your computer—laptop or desktop machine—unattended in a public place. Even in a private place such as an office, remember that your computer contains the means of accessing all sorts of data. If you are logged on to a network when you go out to lunch, anyone passing by can continue to work under your login ID. The difference between this type of theft and the physical theft of a computer is that you may not know what has been stolen. In the mildest case, it is merely access to the network, but in the most severe case, it can be copies of important data. Next to a lock and key, the best security measures are preparation—for theft of both hardware and software. In additional to physical security measures that you should take for any valuable equipment, make certain that you can identify your computer if it is stolen. Every computer has a serial number; locate it and write it down.

Many people tape a piece of paper with the serial number to the back or bottom of their computer. That may help for internal inventory management, but it doesn't help if it's stolen. Make certain that you know what peripherals you have; it's amazing how easy it is to forget external disk drives and the like. If your computer is stolen in a robbery, you will be upset over its loss and the loss of other valuables and may find it easy to forget the other items that have also disappeared.

Preparing for the theft of software and data is a little more complicated. In the case of the theft of hardware, it's gone. When software or data is stolen, you may not know that it's gone—there may now be extra copies of it floating around. It is just as critical to have a list of serial numbers for your software as it is for your hardware. If you have the serial numbers of your software products, as well as the vendors from which you bought them, you can often get replacements for a minimal fee. In the case of data, an inventory is even more critical; no one else may know what you have.

TIP

Particularly when it comes to laptop computers, make certain that your insurance policy covers theft and damage as you travel. You may need to register the serial number of the computer with your insurer before a problem occurs. You may also want to investigate specialized coverage for your hardware, software, and data.

Protection from Damage

Hardware and software can be damaged either deliberately or inadvertently. You need to prepare equally for damage as for theft. Sometimes damage to hardware and software is similar to theft: the item is unusable. In other cases, however, it continues to function. In the case of your data, know how it should function so that you can catch errors.

Preventive Steps to Take

In each of these cases, it is important to take preventive steps. Not surprisingly, those steps have a great deal of commonality.

Computer Security

Inventories

Maintain a good listing of your hardware, software, and data. Make certain that serial numbers are stored in an accessible place. In addition, make sure that all critical information you need to run your software is stored (securely) somewhere outside your computer. Many people have had to reinstall network software only to discover that their network password or login ID is stored on a corrupted disk. Worse, the password is shown only in a secure manner (•••••) and what those dots hide is a mystery.

Backups

Keep backups of everything important. Relying on manual backups is almost always fruitless. Use automated backup products (such as Retrospect from Dantz) to back up your computer reliably at regular intervals. You can add manual backups (such as to your iDisk on Apple's iTools site) to augment routine backups with off-site storage.

Access Control

Finally, you can use software controls to limit access to your computer and its resources. Mac OS X provides a wide variety of tools that you can use in this way: chief among them are the users that you set up and Keychain Access. Both are described later in this chapter.

You can also encrypt files on your computer so that no one can read them without a password. That way, even if the files are stolen, no one can use them. In addition, you can set passwords for many software products and for the documents you create in them so that only you can use them.

Passwords

When passwords were first introduced for computer login accounts and other security purposes, people were advised never to write them down. Over time, however, the proliferation of passwords has left many people at a loss. Some people use a single password for all of their accounts; others just make a list and put it in their wallet. Both strategies are dangerous.

If you use a single password for several accounts, be sure you keep a list of the accounts for which it is used. (It's not too dangerous to write them down; writing the password down is what's dangerous.) The reason for keeping this list is so that if the password is discovered, you will know which accounts need to have their password changed.

The recommendation that passwords be routinely changed seems to be falling into disuse. The problem is that frequently changing a multitude of passwords simply encourages people to write them down. Furthermore, some passwords (such as those required for access to always-on Internet services such as DSL and cable) may be provided by a third party and not easily changeable.

Managing passwords requires that you have a list of all your user IDs and the passwords for them. Obviously, this is a dangerous list to leave lying around. Use Keychain Access (described later in this chapter) to handle your passwords in a secure way. Keychain Access even handles non-computer passwords and access codes such as the combination to the lock on your supply cupboard at the community art studio, your personal identification number (PIN) for your bank account, and the like.

Automatic Passwording

If you use the Screen Saver preference to enable a screen saver, you can use the Activation panel to set when the screen saver starts; that panel also allows you to specify whether a password is needed to wake from the screen saver. This allows you to lock your computer automatically (while leaving it running). The Activation panel of Screen Saver preferences in shown in Figure 7-1.

Mac OS X Security and Multiple Users

Mac OS X security consists primarily of the principle that each user of the system needs to log in with a known ID.

Unlike Mac OS 9 or earlier, all users of Mac OS X must have a user ID. In Mac OS 9, you can use the Multiple Users control panel to implement this; in Mac OS X, multiple users is not optional.

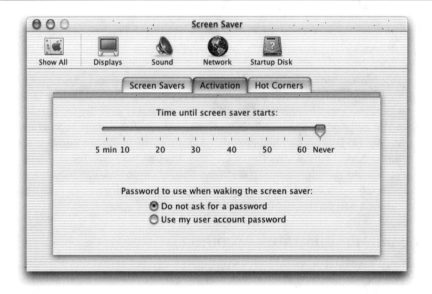

FIGURE 7-1   You can require a password to wake your screen saver.

Once the user is logged in, the system controls access to its resources. Each user has a separate set of files to work with; another set of files applies to the computer as a whole. Users are sometimes referred to as accounts. You can designate one or more users as an administrator of the computer. An administrator user can change settings on the computer (such as its network address).

Why Set Up Multiple Users?

It is clear to most people how valuable it can be to create two or more accounts on a computer that is used by a variety of people. One user—the administrator—can set up the computer; all others can access limited resources on the computer. This can prevent damage due to inadvertent modification or deletion of files.

Each account has its own set of files and its own preferences; these are stored in the Users folder in a subfolder with each user's name, as described in Chapter 4, "Working with Files." After the accounts are set up, users can set their preferences for displays, sounds, and other system services. (As noted in Chapter 6, "Setting System Preferences," some preferences, such as network connections as well as the date and time, are set only with an administrator's password, and they affect all users. Interface preferences and other choices are set by individual users.)

It is not always so clear why a single-user computer should also be installed with at least two accounts. Even the most experienced user is sometimes tired or careless. For that reason, set up an administrator account and use it only when you are doing system maintenance. Use a second account for your normal operations. This will help prevent accidents.

NOTE   *User accounts can be assigned to individuals or to the functions they perform. You can also use a combination of the two. The account called jfeiler belongs to an individual; the account called teacher belongs to whoever may be fulfilling that role.*

In addition to people who will use the computer directly, you need to create user accounts for people who will access the computer over a local area network (or over the Internet if you enable FTP or Telnet). Not all such users need such accounts: you can allow guest access (as with AppleShare on Mac OS 9 or earlier) and provide certain security levels for guests as a group.

Beware of going overboard with security. Creating separate accounts for you to use when you do word processing or online banking is almost certainly going too far. You can limit access to files and folders, but you can also create completely separate environments with duplicate preferences and other settings by setting up multiple users.

Creating an Administrator Account

This account will have total access to your computer. It is created automatically when you install Mac OS X. You must assign a password for it, and if you forget the password, you must follow the procedure in the next section.

You must confirm the password by typing it twice when you enter it. When you do, look carefully at the keyboard; if the CAPS LOCK key is down, you may enter it twice—in capital letters—and be unable to use it again. If you cannot log in with a password that you know is correct, try it with CAPS LOCK down in case you did this. In addition, write down the password and place it in a very secure place (such as a safe deposit box). Without it, you're sunk.

Handling a Missing Administrator Password

This section shows you how to handle a missing administrator password and still gain access to your computer. In other words, it shows you how to bypass security. There are two ways of handling the problem. If you have a second administrator user and you know that password, you can log in and use the procedures described in the next section to change the password for the user account in question. If you do not have a second administrator user account and password, and if you do have a Mac OS X installation disk, you can proceed as follows. Boot from your Mac OS X installation disk. You do this by inserting the CD, holding down the C key and powering your computer on. From the first screen, choose Reset Password... from the Installer menu. This will launch the Reset Password utility. You must then select the disk and the user on that disk that you want to reset. Type the password twice and click Save. You will get confirmation of the password change in a dialog; you dismiss it by clicking OK. You can change other passwords if you wish. When you are done, choose Quit (COMMAND-Q) from the Installer menu. You can then restart back into Mac OS X.

NOTE   *As you can see from this procedure, your Mac OS X installation CD-ROM is a very valuable (and potentially dangerous) key to your computer. With issues of security such as this, there is always a balance to be struck between the absolute needs of security and the legitimate needs of users who may have (horrors!) merely forgotten their password. This balance, consisting of the Reset Password utility application that is distributed on the installation CD-ROM, seems to be a reasonable choice. However, since it is a compromise, be aware of it, and lock up your installation CD-ROM. This is so that you are protected from someone using it to change your administrator password as well as from someone "borrowing" it to unlock another computer.*

Employing Users Preferences to Add, Edit, and Delete Users

You can create other accounts, edit existing ones, and delete accounts using the Users preferences, either when you install Mac OS X or later on. Figure 7-2 shows the basic Users pane. You can add, delete, or modify users from this window.

You may need to unlock the pane by clicking the lock in the lower left and entering an administrator user password. After you have done so, you can select a user and click the Edit User button to open the pane shown in 7-3.

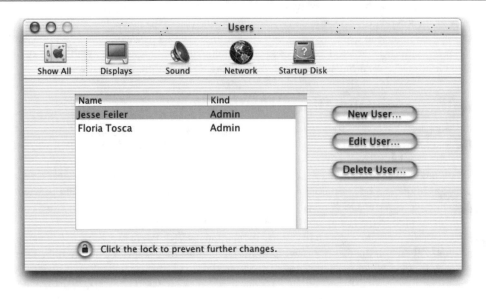

FIGURE 7-2   Add, edit, or delete users with the Users preferences.

Simply type the revised information. Note that you can allow individual users to serve as administrators. You must have at least one administrator user at all times. If someone has forgotten his or her password, you (as an administrator user) can change it in this way. You can add a user by clicking the Add User button to open the same pane shown in Figure 7-3. Both the name and the short name will be seen by others at various times; the password is stored in encrypted form. The short name can contain letters and numbers, but it cannot contain spaces. The full name can contain spaces and is normally the name the person uses. When logging in, you can use either the name or the short name.

In setting up user accounts, try to use a standard naming convention such as first initial and last name, first name and last initial, and so on. While this scarcely matters on an individual computer, in a computer lab or office network, it can help to be able to guess the login IDs of others. Obviously, the passwords should be protected and should not be easily guessed, but it can save time for the publicly visible information, the login IDs, to be consistent.

When you quit Multiple Users, Mac OS X will automatically set up the environment for the new user. You can see this in Figure 7-4.

FIGURE 7-3   Updating user information

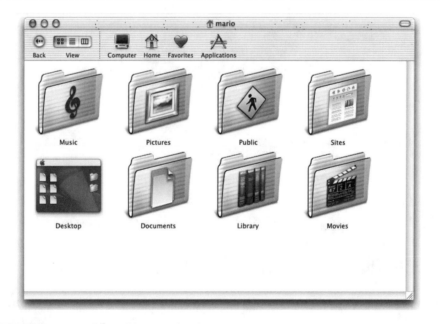

FIGURE 7-4   New user environment in the Finder

Mac OS X Security
and Multiple Users

Each user starts with a directory inside the Users folder that is named with the short name, in this case mario. Within that, a Documents folder is created. A Library folder is created, and inside it, preferences are stored. They can later be updated by the new user. Folders for pictures, movies, and music are also created.

The Public folder is accessible to anyone who has access to the computer, and users can place files they want to share there. The Site folder is also accessible to others: it is used to store files for the Web server you can run.

Automatic Login

You can set a preference for a specific user to automatically be logged in at startup. You do this in the Login Window pane of Login preferences, as shown in Figure 7-5.

Groups of Users

Users can be consolidated into groups; an individual user may be in several groups. You can set access privileges for groups which apply to all members of that group. In Mac OS X, the operating system takes care of assigning users to groups automatically. For finer conrol, use Mac OS X Server and select Users & Groups in Server Admin.

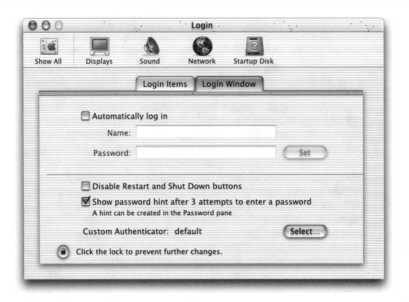

| FIGURE 7-5 | When you turn on the computer with automatic log in, it automatically does everything, and you can start to work immediately (with no apparent login). |

Maintaining Security

Your security setup will collapse if you do not maintain it. If new people have access to your computer, either directly or over a network, give them new login IDs, don't reuse an old login ID for someone else. Make sure that new documents are created with appropriate security, and don't tape your password to the front of your monitor.

File Access Privileges

Each file and folder on the computer has a set of privileges which determine who can access it and in what way. Unix traditionally uses the word *permission*. The Macintosh interface traditionally uses the word *privilege*. You can set privileges for a file or folder you own by selecting it in the Finder and opening the Info window (COMMAND-I). Use the pop-up button to select the Privileges options, as shown in Figure 7-6. For each file and folder, you can set three sets of privileges: for the owner, for a specified user or group, and for everyone else. You must be the owner of the file or folder to set these privileges. You can change the ownership of the file or folder by typing in a new name for the owner or user/group.

FIGURE 7-6   Setting privileges in the Info window

This does not affect the location of files on disk. You can wind up with files owned by user X located inside user Y's Documents folder. If you have selected a folder to set privileges, you can copy those privileges to all subfolders and documents, as shown here:

The Copy button at the bottom of the window lets you change privileges for a folder and copy those privileges to all files within that folder. If you change the privileges for a user's root folder, such as mario in the previous section, you can copy them to the Document, Application, and other folders for that user. By doing so, you can prevent the user from executing any programs. This is almost always a bad idea (or a mistake).

You normally need read and write access for your own files—that is what you do with them. You typically allow others either full access (read and write) or read-only access. In the latter case, they cannot make changes to your files. Of course, you can also allow no access to others, or to specific individuals or groups.

Privileges for folders are similar to those for individual files. If someone has read access to a folder (either read only or read and write), they can see the files and folders within it. If they have write access, they can create files and folders within it.

Write-only access for folders allows people to create files and folders inside a folder, but not to see other files and folders. This can be useful for collecting documents from a variety of people who should not see what else is there. These are called *drop folders*, and they are frequently used on local area networks.

Figure 7-7 shows the various users on a typical Mac OS X installation. Note that the current user's folder (mario) has a different icon (a home).

FIGURE 7-7   Users' home folders contain their files.

If you open a user's folder other than your own, you will see the folders within it, as shown in Figure 7-8. There are indications of the privileges associated with each one and the type of access (if any) that you have.

For example, you are barred from folders such as Movies and Music. You can update (that is, write to) the Documents folder, but you cannot open it (that is, read it). The Public and Sites folders have no access icons; you have both read and write access to them. If you try to access a folder that you cannot, an error message like the one shown in Figure 7-9 is displayed.

Keychains

Mac OS X handles the variety of passwords that you encounter using the Keychain Access application. It is located in the Utilities folder inside Applications.

Keychains consist of entries that contain an account or user ID and a password. The password is stored in an encrypted form, but it can be decrypted. The keychain itself is protected by a password. If you know the keychain password, you can see the password for each individual item on that keychain.

Because passwords are stored securely, and in view of the fact that you can unlock the keychain and see them, you can use a keychain to store any password for any account.

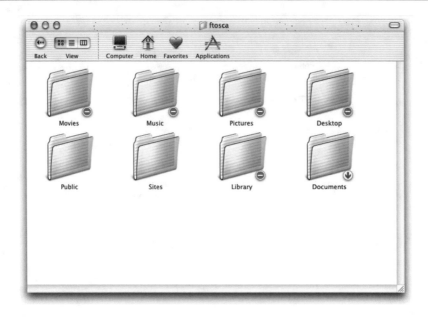

FIGURE 7-8 Icons indicate your access to folders.

FIGURE 7-9 Mac OS X warns you if you attempt unauthorized access.

You can store the combination to a lock, your bank account PIN number, or any other secure information. Programs can access your keychains automatically, but you can take advantage of the secure storage to keep track of other confidential information of this sort. (Keychains are appropriate for storing passwords and short codes, not large amounts of data.)

You can have any number of keychains; many people have one for business and one for personal use. Keychains can be moved from computer to computer. They are stored in each user's Library folder, and you can move them from their other computers. (See "Managing Keychains" later in this chapter.) In order to be used, a keychain needs to be unlocked with its password. You can do so explicitly or wait to be prompted when an application needs a password.

If a keychain-aware application needs access to a password, it can check in all of the unlocked keychains to see if any of them have a password for the account in question. An account can be a user account, an Internet URL (such as an FTP site), or any other item for which a password is required.

Unlocking a Keychain

When you launch Keychain Access, you will be asked to unlock a keychain the first time you use it, as shown here:

A default keychain is created automatically for each user. You will see later in this section how to create additional keychains. Once the keychain is unlocked, you can see all its password items:

You can lock a keychain by clicking the Lock button or using the Lock command from the Keychain Access File menu. A locked keychain is shown here:

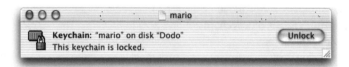

Adding a New Password Item

There are two ways of adding items to a keychain. For a keychain-aware application, when you log into a site or access a passworded account, you can be given the opportunity to store the password on a keychain. In addition, you can add password items manually.

You can also add a password item from Keychain Access. Click the Add button at the lower left of a keychain window to add a new password item. When you click the button, the dialog shown in Figure 7-10 will open.

You can name the password item anything you want, as the dialog suggests. However, if the password is for an Internet site (such as an FTP site), it should be the URL of that site. Enter the account or user ID and the password. When you finish, click Add.

FIGURE 7-10 Adding a new password item

The format of the user or account ID, as well as of the password is determined by the account itself. In other words, if your account identifier must contain numbers (not letters), Keychain Access will not enforce that. However, when items are added automatically to your keychain, they are added only after a successful access to an account. In that way, Keychain Access is assured of having a valid ID.

Editing a Password Item

If you already have a password item, you can select it in the keychain window and click Get Info to open the dialog shown in Figure 7-11. The dialog shows the account or user ID. It also provides a button for you to view the decrypted password. If you click View Password, you may get a standard keychain access dialog, as shown in Figure 7-12. This is the same dialog you get whenever an application wants to use a password. You can avoid it by granting permission to a given application to access a given password. You do so with the check box at the bottom of this dialog. If you do so, you will see the decrypted password.

FIGURE 7-11   Getting info for a password item

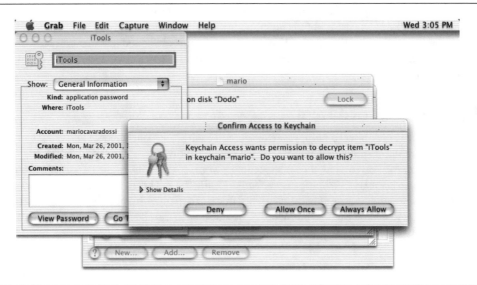

FIGURE 7-12   Allowing access to a keychain request

Access controls let you determine how the password item is used. For example, Figure 7-13 shows the setting for any application to use the password item without warning; this is the loosest setting. Use this setting if you are using Keychain Access simply to store your passwords and if you are not worried about anyone else using your computer to access your private files or accounts.

Figure 7-14 shows a more restrictive type of access—no warning, but limited to certain applications (in this case, Mail). If you do not allow access without warning, you will see the dialog that was shown previously in Figure 7-12.

Adding a Keychain

You can have more than one keychain. You can create a new one by using New Keychain from the File menu. You can also show the Keychain List using Keychain List from the Edit menu. That will open the window shown next, and you can then use the New button to add a keychain.

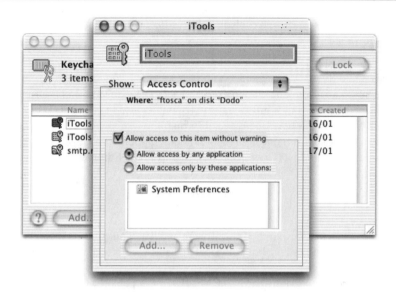

FIGURE 7-13   No warning keychain setting is the least secure.

FIGURE 7-14   You can limit keychain access to individual applications.

You name the new keychain as shown in Figure 7-15, and in Figure 7-16 you must provide a password for your new keychain. Keychain access will force you to use a reasonably secure password, as shown in Figure 7-17.

Managing Keychains

You can move keychains from one computer to another. They are stored in the Keychains folder within the Library folder at your home directory. (Being located in each user's home directory means that each keychain has only one user's information.)

If you copy a keychain from one computer to another, you still need to add it using Keychain Access. Open the Keychain List (Open Keychain List from the Edit menu) and click Add at the bottom of the window.

Summary

Your computer is a valuable resource. The software and data you store on it can be even more so. This chapter has outlined the steps, both physical and software-based, that you can take to protect your property.

Mac OS X security is based primarily on user IDs. Each person who uses your computer has an account complete with a set of files. Individual files can be set for varying types of access by different individuals. This relies on the identity of each user being determined at login time. Finally, security is made much easier for you by consolidating information into keychains, which are managed by the Keychain Access application.

FIGURE 7-15   Name a new keychain...

FIGURE 7-16   …and give it a password

FIGURE 7-17   Do not use very short passwords.

Chapter 8

Managing Your
Computer Environment

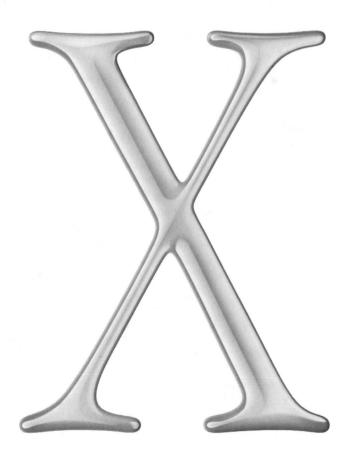

This chapter offers a variety of information on how to customize your computer environment. All of the topics discussed may or may not apply to you. Most likely, some will matter a great deal, and others you can safely ignore.

The chapter is divided into eight main sections:

- **Directory Environment**   Here you'll see how to use Directory Setup.

- **Disk Environment**   Disk Utility and Disk Copy are described here.

- **Displays**   Color Sync Utility, DigitalColor Meter, and DisplayCalibrator help you control what you see.

- **Processor Environment**   Apple System Profiler, Console, and CPU Monitor allow you to see and manage what your computer's processor is doing.

- **Using the Clock**   You can manipulate the menubar clock display.

- **Keyboard Environment**   Learn how to use Key Caps.

- **Battery Monitor**   For laptops, you need to manage your own power supply.

- **Travelling with Your Computer**   Here are tips on travelling with your computer.

Directory Environment

This application helps you manage the directories that are used for directory services, authentication, and contacts. If you run your computer yourself, connecting to a LAN only for networking and Internet access (or not connecting at all to a network, using dial-up Internet access for any Internet access you may do), you do not need to worry about this application and its settings. However, if you are part of a campus or enterprise network, these settings may be required.

Mac OS X makes it very easy to substitute network-based services and directories for those it can provide itself. In the most dramatic example of this, it can use a NetInfo server to manage user IDs. In this scenario, users (and groups of users) are established and managed on the NetInfo server. Your computer automatically connects to it and uses the information it finds there to verify your login. When you have logged in to your computer, your computer provides the processing power as always, but your home directory may very well lie elsewhere. Rather than having your name on it and being located in the Users folder on your own computer, it may have your name on it and be located far away—perhaps halfway around the world.

The concept of a self-contained user environment is built into Mac OS X so thoroughly that changing the location of that environment from your Users folder to a folder on another computer is a trivial task for the operating system. This architecture makes it possible for you to log into your desktop from any Macintosh computer. Your user files are wherever they happen to be, and you access them from wherever you happen to be. Obviously, if your connection is over the Internet and your connection is not high speed, things will be sluggish. But with today's high-speed connections, performance is quite acceptable.

The concept of a stationary user environment that is accessed from wherever you happen to be is in contrast to older architectures in which you had to carry your environment around with you on a laptop. In that case, you need to be careful to synchronize your files, since they are located on two (or more) computers. Neither architecture is clearly better than the other; each has different advantages and drawbacks.

Setting Preferences and Parameters for NetInfo and LDAP

In Directory Setup, use the Services tab to set NetInfo and LDAP preferences, as shown in Figure 8-1.

TIP *If you are using NetInfo, LDAP or the other technologies discussed in this section, your network manager will provide you with the information you must use. If you are connecting to a non-Macintosh network, you can show this chapter and its figures to your network manager, who will be able to tell you easily what values go where. That is why every step of the process is illustrated here.*

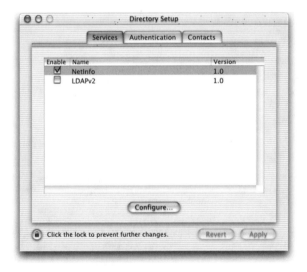

FIGURE 8-1   NetInfo and LDAP services let you share directory and user information from a network.

Directory Environment

You enable NetInfo and/or LDAP by clicking the appropriate checkboxes. Highlight either one and click Configure to provide the settings. Figure 8-2 shows the NetInfo configuration settings.

These settings are given to you by your network manager. Note that if you are connecting to a NetInfo server that is not on your local area network, you must provide an IP address.

LDAP configuration opens the list of LDAP servers shown in the upper-left background of Figure 8-3. The name of the server can be whatever you want. The Address entry must be either a domain name or IP address that is provided by your network manager. Each server can be added, deleted, or configured, as shown in the front window in Figure 8-3. There are four tabs on the window. The first one lets you set the identity of the LDAP server. The second tab, Records, lets you map LDAP record identifiers to Mac OS X constructs. Again, your network manager will provide you with the mapping you need.

The point of LDAP is that it's a very simple protocol that in its simplicity becomes quite powerful. Not everyone has to name a record referring to users as "Users"—some people can name such a record "Clients." The mapping lets you take the identifiers on the LDAP server you are connecting to as they are.

Note that you can add additional mappings, delete default mappings, and otherwise set up anything that you (and your network manager) desire.

Beneath the record level are individual data fields that are mapped using the Data tab shown in Figure 8-4. The process is the same as for record mappings.

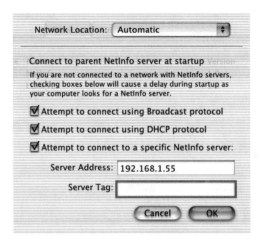

FIGURE 8-2   You control how you connect to NetInfo.

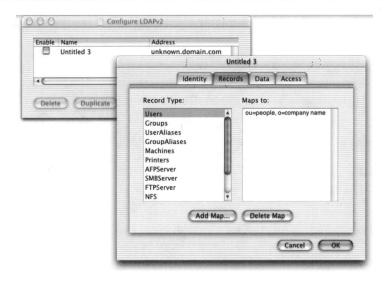

FIGURE 8-3   LDAP configuration lets you name each server.

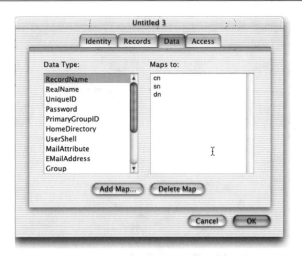

FIGURE 8-4   You can also map data items for LDAP.

Directory Environment

Finally, you may need to provide a name and password for access to the LDAP server. You do so with the Access tab. When you are finished, you are reminded that you will have to restart your computer.

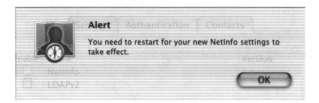

Setting Authentication Directories

Use the Authentication tab in the Directory Setup window, as shown in Figure 8-5, to set the directory in which Mac OS X will look for authentication.

Setting Contacts Directories

Likewise, you can set the directories to look for contact information. Note that you can rearrange the sequence in which directories are searched. Applications such as Mail and Address Book use LDAP directories. You can set them separately for those applications.

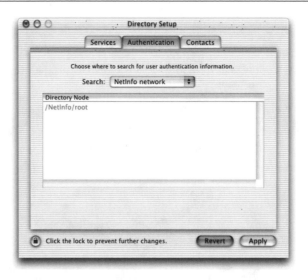

FIGURE 8-5   Authentication can rely on a NetInfo server or a directory on your own computer.

Disk Environment

Use Disk Utility to check, repair, format, and partition disks. Use Disk Copy to manage self-mounting disk images (.smi files).

Using Disk Utility

Disk Utility helps you manage and troubleshoot your disks. When you think of the size of today's disks and the amount of valuable data that is on your own disk, you can easily appreciate how important it is to keep your disks in top-notch shape. Of course, the best disk utility is not this application—it's regular backups of all of your important data to a safe location, including periodic backups that are stored off-site, away from your computer. See "Retrospect" later in this section.

The minimum safe backup is your home directory. That contains your documents, movies, pictures, and individual settings. Applications can be backed up, but it is usually better to back up their installers (or to keep installation disks). It is better to reinstall an application than to copy an installed application's files. The difference is that one works in all cases and the other does not. Remember to keep any installation passwords that you need for a reinstall.

 Disk Utility combines two functions that were provided in separate applications on Mac OS 9 and earlier: Disk First Aid and Drive Setup. You choose which one you want from the buttons on the panel.

Drive Setup

Use the Drive Setup window's Info tab to check your disk drive's information and to format or partition it. The Info tab and its contents are shown in Figure 8-6.

 Formatting or partitioning a hard disk destroys all of the data on that disk. It is a step that you do not take very often (if ever).

All preinstalled disks today come formatted; even external disk drives usually come formatted for you. Formatting a disk erases everything on it and sets it up for use. You can then install Mac OS X, your backed-up files, and your applications. The reason for reformatting a disk is generally to handle some very serious problem on the disk. Before doing so, try First Aid, which is described in the next section.

Reformatting a hard disk is an extreme step, and in most cases, it is a remnant of an age gone by. There are many more diagnostic tools today, and the drastic step of reformatting is not nearly so necessary. (See "Norton Utilities" later in this section.) With other operating systems, such as Windows, this is not always the case, but it still is often true. The fact is that reformatting the hard disk and reinstalling your operating system, applications, and data files will usually fix any problem you have unless it involves mechanical aspects of the computer. The fact that it will do so makes it attractive, but less severe remedies may do the trick and cause fewer side effects.

Partitioning a hard disk formats it into several sections, each of which can behave as if it were a separate disk. Thus, you can partition a 20-gigabyte hard disk into two 10-gigabyte

Disk Environment

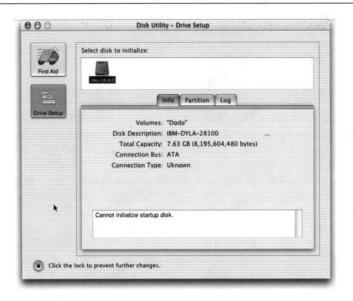

FIGURE 8-6 Drive Setup Info tab shows you the drive's hardware information.

partitions. Each partition shows up as a disk in your Finder windows. This behavior has positive and negative consequences. On the positive side, you can use one partition to back up another, or you can use one partition as a test environment and another for production. On the negative side, if you have two 10-gigabyte partitions on your hard disk, there is nowhere you can store a 12-gigabyte video presentation—each disk is separate.

The partitions do function as one disk in a single case, and that is when you partition or format the disk itself. Reformatting or partitioning the disk will erase all partitions and their data. Formatting a disk is the same as partitioning it with one partition. Thus, formatting and partitioning are the same operation. If you click the partition tab, you will see the pane shown in Figure 8-7.

Use the icons at the top of the window to select the disk you will initialize. (It cannot be the startup disk; to reformat or partition it, you must start up from another disk or from the installation CD-ROM.)

Use the pop-up button to select the number of partitions you want. Remember that the more partitions you have, the smaller each one will be. Remember, too, that you can use separate user IDs to keep sets of files separate on your computer. Doing so will allow you to use vary the amount of size in each user's home directory as needed. This is much better than having separate partitions for separate people.

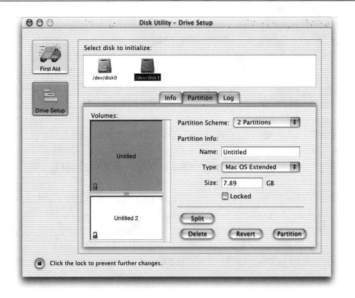

FIGURE 8-7   The Drive Setup Partition tab lets you partition and format a disk.

You name each partition, and the name will show up as a disk name in the Finder. The Type pop-up button lets you select the formatting method for each partition. Your choices are

- **Mac OS Extended**   This is normally the choice you make.
- **Mac OS Standard**   This is the older format.
- **Unix File System**   UFS is used for many Unix systems.
- **Free Space**   This simply blocks off space.

To set a partition's size, you can select it in the diagram at the left of the pane and type in its size to the right. You can also adjust partition sizes by dragging the boundary between two adjacent partitions. This will give you good approximations; for very accurate sizing, you must type in the number.

If you do not specify a partition size, the disk is evenly divided among the number of partitions you have selected.

First Aid

Disk drives occasionally have mechanical failures. To make certain that these inevitable failures cause as little damage as possible, you should always back up your files to a safe copy.

Make certain that you not only back up your files, but that you also periodically restore them. If you haven't practiced restoring files, or if you do not test your backups, you may find yourself one day with a damaged disk and a pile of useless backup cartridges or tapes.

More common than hardware failures are miscellaneous problems with the disk directories that track where files are. Disk First Aid can scan a hard disk and perform basic repairs.

Running First Aid periodically can help to catch errors before they become severe. What "periodically" means depends on how valuable your data is, how frequently you back it up, and how often you modify the data on your computer. For many people once every week or two is fine. When you launch First Aid, you will see the window shown in Figure 8-8.

Select one or more of the disks shown at the top of the window (to select more than one, hold down the COMMAND key while you click the disk icons). First Aid will issue a report as to what it has found and what it has fixed.

The Verify button simply checks the disk; the Repair button checks and repairs—if possible.

You cannot repair a disk to which you cannot write: that includes CDs, DVDs, and other locked media. You also cannot repair the startup disk. If you run Verify and discover problems on the startup disk, restart from the system software CD-ROM that came with your computer or from a Mac OS X installation disc. Hold down the C key as you start up with the CD-ROM in the

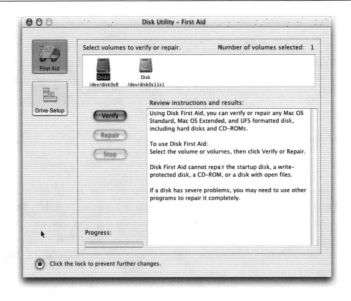

FIGURE 8-8   First Aid often lets you repair disks before their problems become insurmountable.

drive. Even if this is an earlier version of your operating system, it will contain Disk Utility, and you can repair the normal startup disk.

You will see results of the diagnostics in a window such as that shown in Figure 8-8. Note that over time it is common for some small problems to appear on any disk. Running Disk Utility periodically will prevent them from growing large.

Disk Copy

Disk images are files ending with .img, .dmg, or .smi that can be sent via email or included on CD-ROMs. When opened, they expand to images of disks: they appear on the desktop or in the Finder as disk icons, rather than file icons, and within them are documents and folders. Self-mounting image files (.smi) expand themselves to disk images when you double-click them. .img and .dmg image files are expanded by Disk Copy. (You can also manually open .smi files with Disk Copy, but it is not necessary.)

Disk Copy is a utility application that is automatically launched when you double-click a file with the .img or .dmg suffix. Disk Copy is shown here:

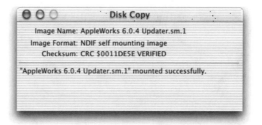

You can set preferences for Disk Copy by launching the application and choosing Preferences from the application menu as shown here:

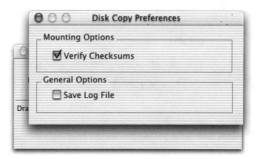

The Checksum is a mathematical computation applied to the data that comprises the disk image. The result of the computation is stored as part of the disk image, and it is recomputed—if you check the Verify Checksums box—when you open a disk image file. If the two checksums—computed and stored—do not match, it is likely that something has been corrupted. Verifying checksums helps guard against corrupted files, and it takes very little time.

Once your file has been extracted, it appears as a disk icon in the Finder, as shown here—an .smi file (AppleWorks 6.0.4 Updater) in the Finder.

Retrospect

The applications described in this chapter are all from Apple and are distributed as part of Mac OS X. Retrospect is different. Developed by Dantz (http://www.dantz.com), it is the most widely used backup software for the Macintosh. The basic window is shown in Figure 8-9.

Retrospect uses the concept of *backup sets* to keep track of your files. You define a backup set, and Retrospect will create and maintain it according to your commands. The most common approach is to create a backup set that consists of an entire disk; when you create it, everything is copied to the backup set. Thereafter—perhaps automatically at 2 AM each day, Retrospect automatically runs and updates the backup set with the files that have changed that day.

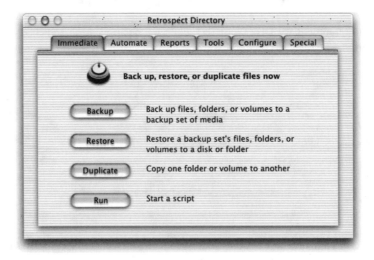

FIGURE 8-9   Retrospect lets you backup and restore files.

You can specifically exclude certain files from the backup, and this is a good idea if you are constantly working with very large media files that are backed up elsewhere. For most people, daily backups are remarkably small, since most of the files on your disk are not updated each day.

In addition to routine backups, you can create special backup sets containing an image of your disk at critical times, such as the end of a project. If you have one (or more) such backups, you can then delete the files you have worked on for months and years and reuse the disk space.

As noted previously, make certain that you have periodic "fire drills" with your backups. Make certain that you can restore the files if you need to. Also, if you are using media that can degrade over time (such as tape for backups), be certain to store it safely and to periodically test that it is still readable. Of course, in such cases, duplicate backups are a good idea.

Backups can be done to FireWire disks, CD-RW disks, and over a network.

Displays

ColorSync Utility, DigitalColor Meter, and DisplayCalibrator help you manage your display environment.

ColorSync Utility

This program functions very much as does First Aid in Disk Utility. You click Verify for it to search out all ColorSync profiles on your computer; it reports if any are damaged. If they are, you can then click a Repair button to fix them.

DigitalColor Meter

DigitalColor Meter is shown next. It allows you to move the pointer over any area on the screen and see it enlarged. You can find out the color of the pixels underneath the pointer. You can change the measurement scales as you wish.

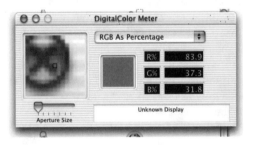

Remember that the color on the screen is a representation of the color specified by a programmer or designer. There is no guarantee that it is accurate (whatever that means when it comes to color).

Displays

DisplayCalibrator

Finally, DisplayCalibrator is an assistant that walks you through the process of setting up your display's settings. Use DisplayCalibrator in the place where you will use your computer and with the light that you will usually use. It consists of a sequence of panes in which you are to adjust colors and brightness until objects appear most distinct or most similar. Because it is designed to adjust color in a subjective manner, none of the screens is shown here. Rest assured that it is simple to use. Perhaps the most difficult part of DisplayCalibrator to understand is how you can wind up setting your display to such wildly different settings—each of which looks "natural."

Processor Environment

To find out what is going on in your computer, you can use the processor environment tools: Apple System Profiler, Console, CPUMonitor, and ProcessViewer.

Apple System Profiler

This program examines the hardware and software on your system. It can be very useful for troubleshooting. If you need to contact a technical support center, saving the output of Apple System Profiler (with the Save command from its File menu) will produce a file that you can attach to an email message to help in diagnostics.

The System Profile tab (shown in Figure 8-10) shows an overview of hardware and software. Some of this information is displayed in various System Preferences panels, but Apple System Profiler brings it together in one place.

The Devices and Volumes tab is shown in Figure 8-11. It shows graphics cards (such as the PCI card powering the display on this computer), as well as disks and PC cards. You can see the details on each of the devices on your computer.

For manufacturing purposes, the same model number of computer may have different components inside when it comes to disk drives. If you are having problems, this information is invaluable. Note, however, that if you have purchased your computer with disk drives installed, you should contact Apple first if you have questions.

Figure 8-12 shows the Frameworks tab. The architecture of Mac OS X provides a variety of independent software objects that work together to provide the functionality and user experience you expect. As you can see from this list, there is a large number of these shared objects. Sometimes, being able to let a troubleshooter know what versions are installed may help in tracking down obscure problems.

The extensions shown in Figure 8-13 are not the extensions of Mac OS 9 and earlier. Rather, they are kernel extensions—other software components that can be updated and replaced as needed (but not by you!). They may even be stopped and started automatically in response to changing needs.

Finally, the Applications tab (shown in Figure 8-14) provides a list of the applications. You can use the disclosure triangles to see version control information about each one.

FIGURE 8-10 System Profile tab provides an overview of your computer environment.

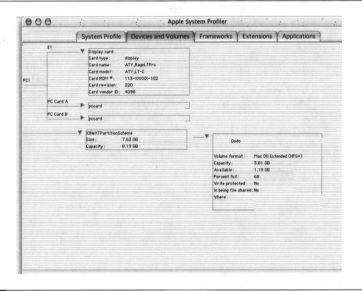

FIGURE 8-11 Devices and Volumes shows disk hardware information

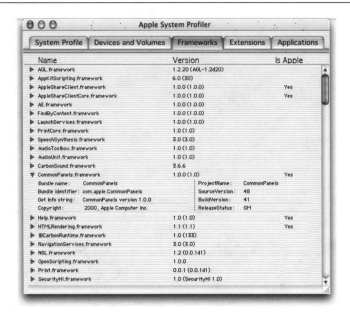

FIGURE 8-12   Frameworks lets you see versions of installed frameworks.

FIGURE 8-13   Extensions shows kernel extensions.

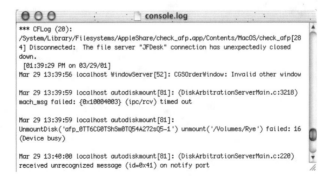

FIGURE 8-14   Applications identifies all your applications.

Troubleshooting with the Console

The Console application lets you see the messages that applications write to the console—the window representing the control console on the computer. (This terminology is a remnant of the old days of mainframe computers.) The console is only for output. The Terminal application (discussed in Chapter 21, "Using the Command Line") provides interactive text-based communication with your computer.

As shown in the following illustration, the messages in the console window may not be particularly meaningful to you. However, they can be critical in helping to debug an application.

Each message is marked with the date and time at which it was generated. If you are encountering problems with an application and you contact technical support, they may want to know what messages you have seen in this window. (You can save the output to a disk file and send it away for further analysis.)

Do not worry if you see error messages: programs running normally often generate messages to the Console window. Some of them may even be alarming. If you are not having other problems, ignore them.

Troubleshooting with CPUMonitor

A further troubleshooting tool is CPUMonitor. It lets you see a graphical version of how your computer is being used, as shown in Figure 8-15. Two types of views are shown in their own windows: in the upper left, the Standard view is shown; in the lower left, the Extended view is shown.

The displays are updated continuously. You can set the colors for the displays in the Preferences window shown at the right of the window. You can choose to display either the Standard or Extended view in an icon in the Dock; if you do, it is constantly refreshed. If you do not choose to show either view in a Dock icon, a small monitor at the lower left of the display shows CPU usage. It is shown in this and the following CPUMonitor figures.

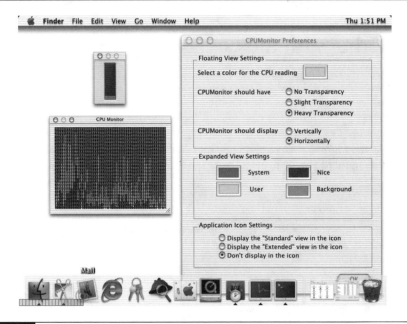

FIGURE 8-15   CPUMonitor shows processor usage.

The Open Top command from the Processes menu opens the shell top command, as shown in Figure 8-16.

This provides numeric information about the most active processes on your computer. The Open Process Viewer command in the Processes menu opens the ProcessViewer application; you can also launch it directly. The display is updated continuously.

ProcessViewer

ProcessViewer lets you examine each of the processes running on your computer, as shown in Figure 8-17.

At the top, you will find a scrolling display of the processes on your computer. You can use the pop-up menu at the upper right to limit the display to user processes or all of them. Each column's title can be clicked to sort that column: click Name to alphabetize the list; click on %CPU to view by the amount of processor time each process is taking up, and so forth. (Click the triangular icon at the right to sort in ascending or descending order.)

The Process ID information is shown at the bottom; that information is specific to the process at that time. It may have another ID number the next time it runs. If you click on the Statistics tab, as shown in Figure 8-18, you will see additional information with regard to processor usage and memory, as shown in the figure.

This information, too, varies over time; however, for debugging and troubleshooting, it can be important. The process cannot control its process number, but it can control its memory usage. If you are helping to debug software, you may be asked to provide this information periodically.

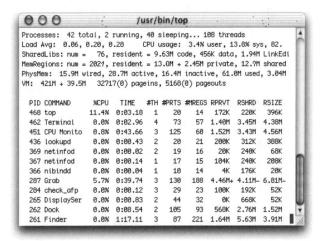

FIGURE 8-16   top listing reports on active processes.

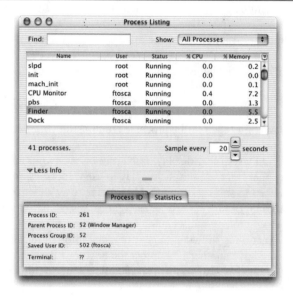

FIGURE 8-17   ProcessViewer shows you what is running.

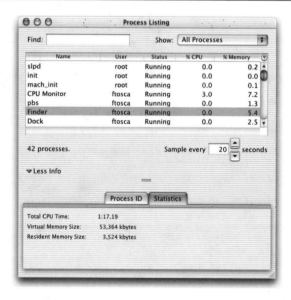

FIGURE 8-18   Statistics lets you see how much memory a process is using.

Using the Clock

The Clock application shows a digital or traditional clock. You can customize it (with its Preferences) to show seconds. The Clock can appear as an icon in the Dock; in that case, it shows the time. You can also set a preference for it to appear in its own small window on the desktop. The preferences are shown here:

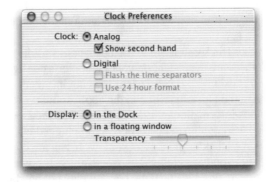

Many people include the clock in their login items so that it is always visible. You can use the Date & Time pane in System Preferences to turn the standard menu bar clock on and off; thus, you can replace the menu bar clock with a Dock clock if you are so inclined.

Key Caps: Using Special Symbols on the Keyboard

The Key Caps application displays the keyboard, as shown in the following illustration. As you depress a key on the keyboard, it is highlighted on the Key Caps display. If you depress a key such as CONTROL or OPTION, the symbols on the keyboard represent the characters that would be generated if you pressed that key while holding down the CONTROL or OPTION key. The illustration shows OPTION depressed; as you can see, a variety of special symbols is available.

Note that some keys have a white outline. If you hold down the OPTION key and press one of those keys, the symbol—an accent or diacritical mark—is placed over the next character you type. Thus, holding down OPTION and pressing ˆ causes that symbol to be placed over the next key—such as î.

Power Supply

If you use a PowerBook or iBook, it has a battery that needs to be recharged periodically. The Battery Monitor Dock extra shows you the state of the battery's charge. Drag it to the Dock, and its icon shows the portion of the charge remaining in the battery. As you use it, it will decrease visibly.

Battery Monitor and other Dock extras are in the Dock extras folder inside Applications. The Dock extras you find there are dependent on your computer's configuration. On a desktop computer with no battery, for example, Battery Monitor is not installed.

You can click the icon in the Dock to switch to the application; you then can use Preferences to display a window with this information in it. Most people find the Dock display sufficient.

If you are traveling and are not able to keep your laptop plugged in, make sure Battery Monitor is visible either in the Dock or in its own window. If you are concentrating on your work, you may not notice that you are running down the battery. If power is low, the computer will automatically shut down to avoid losing data, but you may not be able to do the one little task that is essential—like checking the address of your hotel before you get there.

Traveling with Your Computer

If you are traveling with a PowerBook or iBook, you need to keep track of the settings for various locations. When it comes to networking, an easy way to do that is with locations that you can define in the Network System Preferences. Just select a new location from the Apple menu, and your settings for modem versus local area network connection are changed.

If you will need to access a network or the Internet, make certain that you have at least one way of doing so. If you normally dial in to a network or the Internet, have an appropriate telephone number for your destination—before you leave. If you normally log in by connecting directly to a LAN, make sure you will be able to do so on the road. Many security systems are implemented based on the physical addresses of computers; you may discover the hard way that you no longer have access to databases when you log in from another location.

Many Internet service providers have relatively inexpensive access accounts with a very limited number of hours of usage. You may want to purchase one of these before you travel. That way, for a small fee (perhaps five dollars a month for two hours' usage), you will be guaranteed some form of access. Of course, be sure you have a modem in your PowerBook if you need to do this. (And always travel with spare Ethernet and/or telephone cables—put distinctive labels or tape on them so you will know which cables are yours and which to leave at your destination.)

Remember that traveling is dangerous for computers. They can get lost, dropped, or stolen. Make certain that your computer's data is backed up before you travel. Even more important, make certain that you know what is on it.

Of course, you keep track of the serial numbers and versions of all software that you have installed on your computer. And if you keep track of them in an FileMaker database or AppleWorks spreadsheet, you do have a current hard copy printed out, don't you? (No one's watching: do it now.)

Summary

This chapter has presented an assortment of tools you can use to handle specific issues, including traveling with your computer, managing color, and troubleshooting. This concludes the summary of the basics of Mac OS X. You have seen everything it can do, and you should be ready to go out and conquer the world.

Except…maybe you have a few questions. Or maybe everything seems clear now, but in the midst of a real-life project, it's not quite so clear. The next chapter shows you how to use the variety of help and assistance tools that are built into Mac OS X.

Summary

Chapter 9

Getting Help

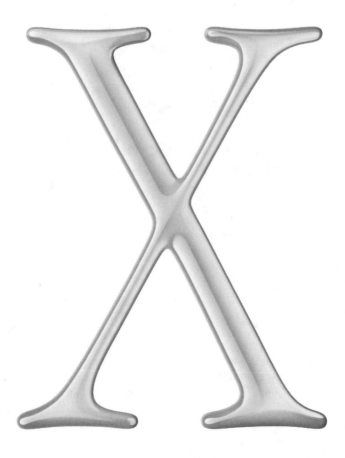

Although the Macintosh has always been very easy to use, there are times when you need help. Sometimes that's because you don't know how to do something; other times, it's because you aren't aware of the variety of tools you have at your disposal. In either case, you can benefit from knowing just what this combination of hardware and software can do.

This chapter introduces you to the full range of help and assistance available to you on Mac OS X. The array of resources is impressive; you just have to know what is available and where to find it. This chapter groups those resources as follows:

- Manuals and other printed materials

- Mac Help and Help Tags—the electronic assistance that is part of Mac OS X

- Online help from Apple available over the Internet

- In-person assistance available through Apple and third parties

- The Web site for this book

- Apple Developer Connection (ADC) for support of programmers and developers

In using all of the resources described in this chapter, keep an eye out for terminology—particularly if it is different from your own. Knowing how features and functions are correctly described helps you make the most of the search tools.

Manuals and Other Printed Materials

Computers used to come with enough books and other documentation to deforest several acres for each product shipped. Many customers never opened the manuals: the sheer size and number of them was daunting. Companies that purchased several computers at a time wound up with multiple copies of (unopened) manuals. Furthermore, the need to keep the documentation up to date meant that computer manufacturers were constantly updating various aspects of their manuals in a never-ending process of reprinting and revising.

Today, printed documentation from manufacturers is kept to a bare minimum. You will receive documents that help you set up your computer. From there on, you're on your own with the electronic resources that come preinstalled with your Macintosh and its operating system. This not only saves trees, but it also allows changes to be made very quickly to keep the documentation up to date.

However, you have to do your part in this world of electronic documentation. There is not much of it, but you must know where it is. Make certain that your computer's model and serial number are written on the inside cover of the installation guide (you will probably have to do this yourself). Further, keep all hardcopy documentation of your computer (such as its invoice) in one place, and keep duplicate copies in a secure location away from your home or office. Remember that if your computer has a catastrophic failure or is stolen, everything stored on it will be unavailable.

Decide how you will store documentation and the distribution media (such as CD-ROMs) that come with hardware and software products. Some people keep them all together in the original cartons. Others store manuals and documentation in one place, media in another, and serial numbers in a third. Take a moment to decide what you will do and then organize things.

Using Apple Help and Help Tags

Electronic help now consists of two elements:

- Apple Help provides online assistance using text, graphics, and QuickTime content. It is searchable, and it often provides AppleScript automations to help you carry out tasks. Apple Help often answers the question, "How do I do something?"

- Help Tags (similar to Balloon Help in earlier versions of Mac OS and to Tool Tips on Windows) let you identify and understand elements of the interface. Help tags often answer the question, "What does this do?"

Apple Help

You can open Apple Help in one of three ways:

- **Help menu**   The Help menu is located at the right of the menu bar for each application, including Mac OS X itself. It may contain a variety of commands for the various types of help and assistance that an application can provide. In the Finder, you will find Mac Help; other applications insert their own help items. The Apple Help system merges all available and relevant help for you.

- **Help buttons**   These are available in many windows or dialogs (often in the lower left, and often using a ? icon). Clicking them opens Apple Help with information relevant to that window or dialog.

- **Contextual Help menu**   When you place the pointer over an interface element (including icons in the Dock) and press the CONTROL key, the cursor changes to a small menu. Clicking the mouse button opens a contextual menu with relevant commands. If help is available for the item you are over, it will be the first item in the contextual menu.

Help Center consolidates information about the operating system, applications, and your computer itself. You can open it by choosing Mac Help from the Help menu in the Desktop, shown next. You can also use the keyboard equivalent COMMAND-?; remember that the ? requires the SHIFT key, so you must hold down all three keys: COMMAND, SHIFT, and / (which becomes a ? when SHIFT is pressed.)

Help for Mac OS X—and help for other applications—is displayed using the Help Viewer application. You can type a question or keyword in the space at the top of the window and click Ask. You also can navigate using the forward and back arrows in the lower-right corner of the window. You can click underlined links, just as in a Web browser, to navigate from topic to topic. Finally, the question mark icon shown next on the left opens Help Viewer's own help, as shown next on the right.

Using Help Viewer

From here, you can use the Quick Clicks at the left to go to prepared topics. You can also type in a question or keywords at the top and click the Ask button. At the right, you usually find links to news and to a Web page. This page varies from application to application; it also varies depending on the version of Mac OS X that you have installed. Opening help from within Mac OS X or an application may open the Help Viewer to a section that is relevant to what you are working on.

Using Quick Clicks

If you click on a topic such as "How do I change computer settings?" you will see the page of answers presented in the Help Viewer, shown on the upper left corner of the next page. There may be more than one page of answers; if there is, click More, and you can go from page to page of your answers, as shown on the right on the following page.

Click the answer you want to see detailed explanations of what to do, as shown in the illustration on the bottom of the following page. Often, you will see an underlined link at the bottom left that will do something for you—in this case, clicking it will open System Preferences.

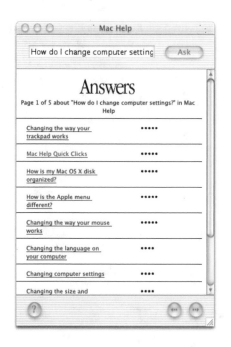

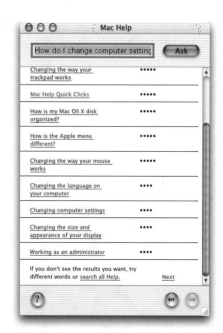

In the lower right, you will frequently see a Tell Me More link; clicking it launches a new search that tells you more about the topic, as shown here:

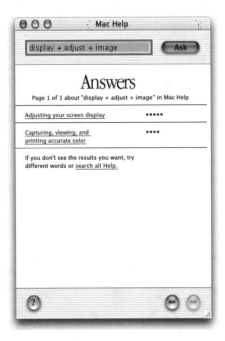

Searching Help

You can type in a question or keywords and click the Ask button to search the contents of the help system. You can formulate simple logical combinations when you type in the field at the top of the window:

- ■ Place a plus sign (+) between two words to search for pages with both of them. If you do not place the + between them, the search will retrieve pages with either word on them.

- ■ Place an exclamation point (!) before a word to exclude it from a search.

- ■ To form more complex combinations, use parentheses to group words and operators. A grouping surrounded by parentheses is evaluated before other parts of the expression.

Before formulating a complex search query, try just typing the keywords. If the broadest search returns only a few references, it will be much easier for you to simply look at them to find out what you want to see. Only if the results are too numerous do you need to limit the query.

How It Works

In case you're wondering how it's done, the two essential components of the Mac OS X help system are HTML and the Apple Information Access Toolkit (AIAT). Much of the information provided in Help Center is coded using HTML; this lets the hyperlinks be implemented very easily.

Searching is implemented using AIAT, which is an object-oriented information access engine. AIAT provides sophisticated indexing, searching, and analysis tools to manage large volumes of documents. It was first known as V-Twin when Apple developed it in the mid-1990s. Its technology is now used in Sherlock. If you've ever wondered what that indexing in Sherlock is all about, it's AIAT doing its work.

NOTE   *AIAT is available to developers as a licensable product from Apple. If you want to add help or sophisticated document searching to an application, you can use it.*

Help Viewer can update the information you see by integrating online content from Apple's Web site as you use Help Viewer. If you have an Internet connection, you will often see brief status messages showing these updates.

Online Help from Apple

There is a vast amount of help and assistance on Apple's Web site. Sometimes, this is more up to date than the information installed on your computer. In addition, if you need help with a problem that renders your computer inoperable (such as "How do I finish installing memory if I forgot to print out the instructions before taking the machine apart?"), you can get information from the Web site by using another computer.

To use online help, you need an Internet connection and a Web browser. You can use online help from any computer with a Web browser and an Internet connection, even one that runs another operating system. You do need a Macintosh to access parts of the iTools part of the Apple site, but the rest is available with any computer.

Apple's home page—http://www.apple.com/—is shown in Figure 9-1. (This image is of the home page on March 24, 2001, the date of release of Mac OS X. This page changes periodically as Apple's products and news stories change.)

From the home page, click the Support tab at the top. This will open a Web page like that shown in Figure 9-2. It is the AppleCare home page.

As you move your mouse over the various products illustrated on this page, you will see a variety of support options. Some of them are specific to individual products; others are relevant to a variety of products, described in this section.

Information on the Web site is as up to date as it gets. Because this information changes in order to reflect new products, regional issues, and the like, the pages that you see are likely to be quite different from these. If in doubt, click on Support on the main Apple page—that button should always be there—and then carefully read the instructions that follow.

FIGURE 9-1   Apple's home page at http://www.apple.com/

In general, you will find the following types of items available for hardware and software support:

- Knowledge Base provides sophisticated searching on content and keywords.

- Tech Info Library provides official documentation of issues, problems, and solutions for Apple hardware and software. It is often geared toward developers.

- Apple Support Discussions are bulletin boards in which users can ask and answer questions.

- Apple Mailing Lists are similar to Apple Support Discussions, but you can receive (and post) messages via email as well as via the Web.

- Software Updates are downloadable modifications to software. (Software Update— discussed in Chapter 8, "Managing Your Computer Environment,"—automatically checks for these updates.)

- Manuals in PDF are available online for downloading and viewing.

- AppleSpec is the database of specifications for Apple products, including discontinued products from the past.

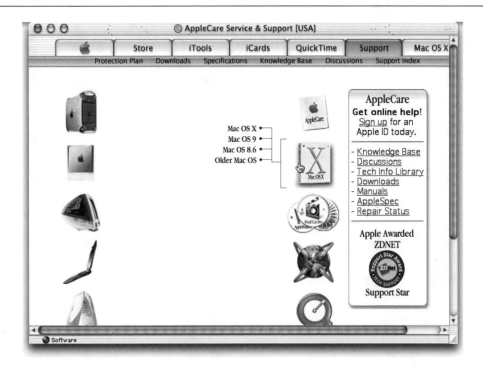

FIGURE 9-2   Apple support on the Web

Knowledge Base

The AppleCare Knowledge Base is a compendium of articles and information to help you use your Macintosh and troubleshoot problems. The Knowledge Base has a very powerful way of searching for information. You click on Knowledge Base from any of the pages in the AppleCare Support area; it is available as a link on many pages and is also available at the top of the page. You must log in and have cookies enabled in your browser to use AppleCare. Knowledge Base queries start from a window that looks like that shown in Figure 9-3.

Start by selecting the topic from the pop-up button at the top. The choices in the second pop-up (More Specifically) will change based on your choice of topic. Provide as much information as you can with additional details and by clicking the image of the computer you are using. When you click Continue in the lower right, you will see a display such as that shown in Figure 9-4.

From this screen, you can start a new search or examine the results. As you can see, 11 possible solutions were found. Clicking that link will display them. However, you can use the pop-up menu to refine your search.

Online Help from Apple

FIGURE 9-3   Knowledge Base query window lets you pose your question.

When you are finished with the Tell Us More page, you see a list of the articles that may help, as shown in Figure 9-5. You can click on one that looks promising. Using your browser's back button, you can return to this page to click on another one if you need additional help.

The results are displayed as shown a few pages away in Figure 9-6. These AppleCare articles follow a standard format.

At the bottom of each AppleCare articles, you will find links for further information as shown in Figure 9-7. These links are to other articles (under Learn), links to software updates that are related to the topic (under Update), and a link to discussions that may help (under Discuss).

This procedure is called *assisted* search. You can repeat it as necessary; in addition, Knowledge Base will continue providing additional pages to help you refine your search when too many responses are presented. Advanced search lets you type in a query all at once. You switch between assisted and advanced search using the button at the upper right (it says *advanced* in these figures; when you are in advanced search, it says *assisted*).

Apple Support Discussions

You can get information (or contribute information) to Apple Support Discussions. The Discussions button at the top of each AppleCare Support page gives you access. Apple Support

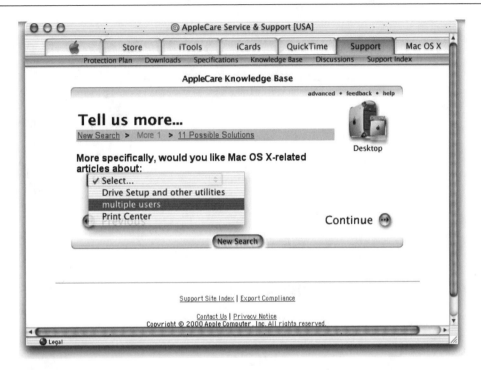

FIGURE 9-4   Knowledge Base Tell us more

Discussions are an open discussion board on which people can share problems and solutions. Turn ahead a few pages, the main page is shown in Figure 9-8.

You can click on any of the links to go to a summary of threaded conversations as shown ahead in Figure 9-9. (There are other discussion groups on the Internet about Apple products; however, Apple Support Discussions is monitored by Apple, and you will frequently find more reliable information here than on other sites.)

You can look for your problem or post your questions here. A common use for Apple Support Discussions is searching on a third-party product name. For example, to see how people use the Canon Elura digital video camcorder, you could search the iMovie discussion for "Elura." Some responses—marked with an apple icon—are official responses from Apple. Apple employees will also sometimes respond on their own in an individual, unofficial way.

Apple Mailing Lists

A number of mailing lists are available for additional discussions about Apple products and technologies. The complete list is shown at http://www.lists.apple.com/, and you can register for one or more mailing lists there.

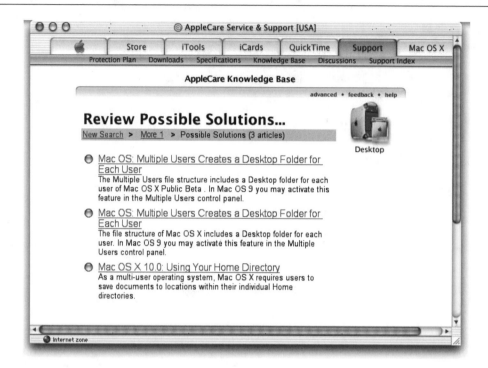

FIGURE 9-5   Possible solutions are presented.

These lists are email-based—that is, messages are sent back and forth as email messages to all members of the list. You can choose to receive messages individually or in consolidated digests (several messages at a time). You also can review messages on the Web rather than or in addition to receiving them via email. The main difference that most people find between Web-based discussions and mailing lists is that in Web-based discussions, you must choose (and remember!) to go look for new messages. In mailing lists, those messages arrive in your in-box at the sender's convenience.

Software Updates

From the Apple Support home page (and other pages in the Support area), you can find links that let you download software. Software Update (discussed in Chapter 6, "Setting System Preferences") will notify you of updates to software you have installed already. Remember always to check the Read Me associated with the software to know if you

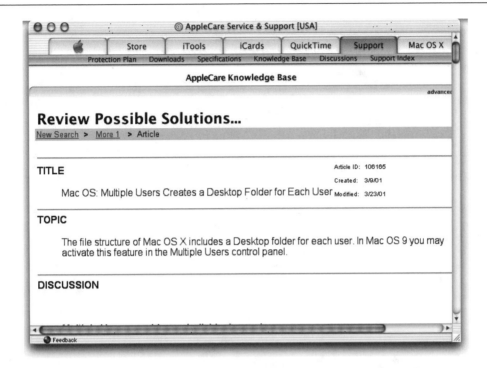

FIGURE 9-6 AppleCare articles answer your question.

should install it or not. Not all updates are needed (or desirable) for everyone. The Downloads button in the toolbar at the top of each AppleCare Support page takes you to the Download page.

Apple Manuals

You can also download PDF versions of Apple manuals for most of its products. This will help if you have misplaced your manuals. It also is useful if you are considering purchasing Apple hardware or software products and you want to learn more about them.

AppleSpec

AppleSpec is a database of specifications for all Apple products. These specifications can be helpful to you in comparing products when you are considering purchasing or upgrading them. Even more useful can be the information about operating systems for older computers. When

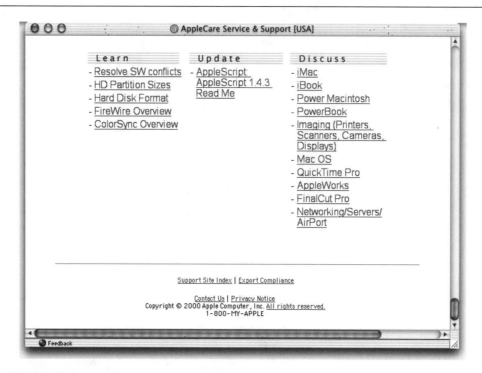

FIGURE 9-7   Links help you find more information.

you are considering purchasing a used computer or upgrading your software, look here to see what you options are. You can get to the AppleSpec database by clicking Specifications on the toolbar at the top of an AppleCare Support page.

Tech Info Library

The Tech Info Library (TIL) is a collection of articles written by Apple on a variety of technical topics. Some of them describe how to do things; others describe how to handle bugs. If you click Tech Info Library in the main Apple Support page or TIL on other pages, you will go to the basic Tech Info Library page, shown in Figure 9-10 found a few pages ahead.

A changing list of new TIL articles on various topics is shown at the right. You can also search using the features at the left. Note that you can search both the contents of articles and their titles. Searching the full text of the articles is often the better approach.

Many people try to make their search request too specific. Don't worry about getting too much information back; the search engine at Apple will not inundate you with thousands of articles automatically. Try the most general description of your problem. If the number of

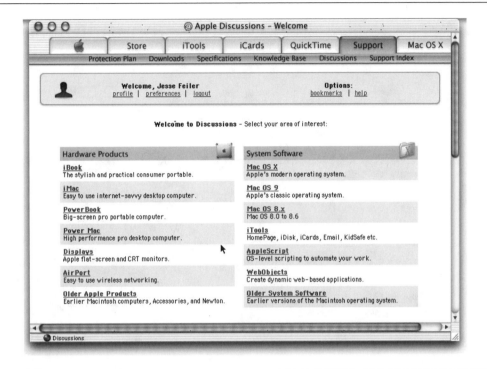

FIGURE 9-8   Apple Support Discussions home

articles returned is unmanageable, you can refine your search. If your broad area of interest returns only a dozen or so articles, reviewing their titles can be helpful.

Each article has a title of its own, and each article is also part of a topic, which may have several articles in it. In addition, each article has a unique identifier. You can also see the dates on which it was created and modified. If you have looked up something in the TIL archive and need to refer to it again, search by article ID to see if the article has been updated.

This range of online assistance from Apple provides a vast amount of information to help you troubleshoot problems and learn about your hardware and software. The Support section of the Apple Web site is periodically revised and reorganized. Still, you should be able to find the major components: the Knowledge Base, Apple Support Discussions, software updates, manuals, AppleSpec, and the Tech Info Library with links as shown here, or with slightly different names or icons.

You may want to sign up for Apple's eNews; there are links to it from several areas of the Support site. If there are particular areas in which you are interested, you might want to receive periodic e-mails with information. Rather than waiting until you have a problem, you can see what new features are available and what new choices you may have.

Online Help from Apple

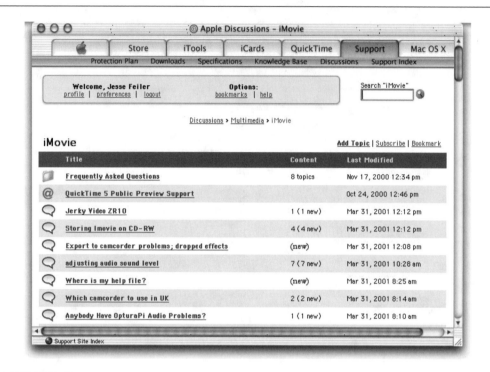

FIGURE 9-9   Apple Discussions for iMovie

In-Person Assistance

Despite the riches of Apple's online support, sometimes you really need to speak to a human being. Three types of in-person assistance are available:

- Telephone support (SOS-APPL)
- Apple iServices
- Apple Solution Experts (ASE)

SOS-APPL

Apple offers a variety of additional support plans as part of its warranties and after-sale support. In the United States, a toll-free number, (800) SOS-APPL, is available; other numbers are available in other locations. Find out what support options are available when you purchase your computer, and consider what protection plans you feel comfortable purchasing. Remember, when a problem occurs, it is usually too late to purchase insurance or a protection plan.

FIGURE 9-10   Tech Info Library home page

Make sure that you have all of the information you need to contact Apple written down. That includes model and serial numbers, the exact name of the computer's owner, and the telephone number to call. Having them on a dead computer isn't going to help you.

iServices

iServices is Apple's professional services organization. Specializing in support for customers and developers in creative, education, and business markets, iServices provides support for WebObjects, Mac OS X, and QuickTime.

Typically, iServices is contacted through Apple's regional offices. You can get information through a toll-free number, (800) 879-6398. Their Web site is http://www.apple.com/iservices/. iServices normally provides assistance to fairly large-scale installations. They are not the right people to call to help you set up a single computer. You can find iServices at http://www.apple.com/iservices/, as shown in Figure 9-11.

FIGURE 9-11   iServices can provide consulting and training for you.

ASE

Apple Solution Experts (ASE) are not Apple employees: they are consultants, trainers, and resellers who provide custom solutions to end-users. The program is administered by Apple, and you can find more information on the Web site at http://aspn.apple.com/, as shown in Figure 9-12.

The site lets you locate Apple Solution Experts by areas of expertise, as well as geographic location. These are the people who can provide onsite support and training, as well as solutions involving Apple equipment and third-party products.

The Web Site for this Book

Moreover, there's still more support available. Readers of this book can visit the author's Web site at http://www.philmontmill.com/, as shown in Figure 9-13. The navigation buttons at the left send you to specific areas of the site. In each one, you will see the navigation buttons at the top.

FIGURE 9-12   Apple Solution Experts

Search provides further links, updates (including late-breaking news about Mac OS X and changes to the book), and news about the subject. If you come across interesting links or information, you can add them yourself.

Q&A is a discussion area like the Apple Support Discussions. You can post questions or provide answers here. Like the Apple Support Discussions, this area is monitored; questions of general interest are answered by the author. The other buttons, Books, Sign In, and Help, let you find out more about books on the topic, sign in for optional email updates, and get assistance with using the site.

Apple Developer Connection

Apple Developer Connection (ADC) is the resource for developers—programmers and others who create software for the Macintosh. Much of that information is available for free on the Web site. Click the Developer tab on Apple's home page to go to the ADC site.

The materials on the ADC site are geared toward programmers rather than end-users. However, you might not be daunted by their technical approach. Furthermore, just by reviewing the titles

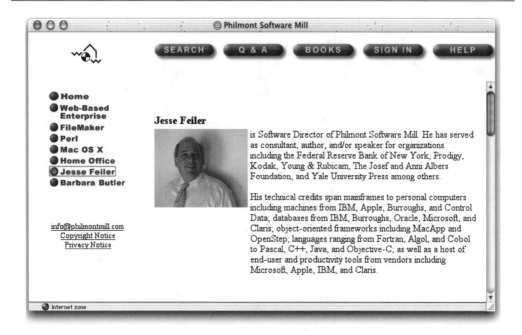

FIGURE 9-13   Web site for this book provides the latest updates.

you can get some sense of what Apple's plans for the future are. Of course, if you are a developer, you should definitely join ADC.

Industry-Related Pages

From Apple's home page, you can find major areas of interest in the toolbar at the top. Education, Small Business, and Creative tabs lead to pages that can be of help or interest. Other areas may not make it onto the main toolbar, but they provide support. For example, the Science and Technology page shown in Figure 9-14 is an important resource.

Summary

Apple provides a wide range of support for its hardware and software. This chapter has provided an overview of the printed documentation, Help Center, Web-based help, developer support, and other Apple assistance.

If you have a problem, remember that the first thing to do is to stop and think. Many problems are made worse—or even created—by hasty actions. When you have come up with a potential course of action or a diagnosis, sit back and think through whether that really can solve the problem or explain the difficulty. Only when you're certain you're on the right track should you proceed.

Apple integrates the Web thoroughly in its support of Mac OS X. It also extends the functionality of its operating systems with the Web—as you will see in the next chapter, which deals with iTools.

FIGURE 9-14   Use the Sci-Tech page to find out about Apple support and products for the science and technology community.

Summary

iTools: Apple's OS Tools on the Internet

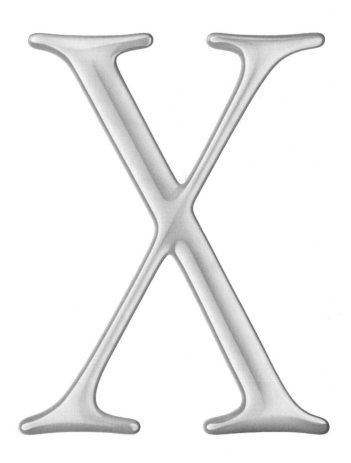

J ust as help and assistance are implemented in conjunction with Apple's Web site, so too, important features of the operating system and its tools are found on the Web site. This chapter provides an overview of those tools and how to use them.

These tools were first implemented in Mac OS 9; the download of software that was needed for Mac OS 9 is not needed in Mac OS X.

The tools evolve over time, and so the exact features you find may not be those shown in this chapter. Furthermore, additional tools may be available when you connect to the Apple Web site. Not all tools are useful to all people; however, some of them—particularly the remote disk storage— can be a critical part of your computer environment.

iTools enables you to put your own files on one of Apple's servers and to specify that they can be downloaded by anyone with a Web browser. This is the simplest way to share files with colleagues, students, and friends. Using standard file formats (GIF, JPEG, and TIFF for images, TEXT or RTF for documents, and so forth), you can let people share your files regardless of the software or operating system you use. Movies and music can also be shared with common formats such as QuickTime and MP3.

Exploring iTools is often the first time new users work with their Web browser. For that reason, this chapter details each of the steps involved.

The six online tools (called iTools) fall into three categories:

- **iCards**   A tool for creating and sending electronic greeting cards.

- **KidSafe**   Links to appropriate places on the Web, as well as filtering software you can install.

- **iTools**   A collection of advanced tools, including free email, free home pages you can design yourself, and disk space. This last collection of tools requires registration and special software that is automatically downloaded, but there is no charge.

    - **Email**   Your own email account at mac.com

    - **iDisk**   Storage space at Apple that you access just like a disk on your computer

    - **HomePage**   Your own Web site

Getting Started

If you connect to Apple's Web site—http://www.apple.com/—you will see a home page that is more or less like that shown in Figure 10-1.

Tabs across the top of the page let you connect to major parts of the Apple site. These tabs may vary over time and on different countries' Apple home pages. Some of them will take you to the online tools, such as iTools. When you select one of those tabs, the choices in the bar just

FIGURE 10-1   Apple's home page

below the tabs change. In Figure 10-1, for example, the lower choices (Hot News, Hardware, Software, and so forth) are for the selected tab—the Apple icon. Compare those buttons to those visible in Figure 10-2 when iTools is clicked.

iCards

Greeting cards on the Net have become very popular, and Apple provides its own facility for creating and mailing these cards. You can send them to anyone, whether they use a Macintosh or not. (They must, however, be able to view graphics on their computer. If they have Web access, they can usually do so.)

These cards are sent via email. They combine the efficiency of email with the attractiveness of cards or stationery. Use them for greetings, invitations, and other informal notes.

FIGURE 10-2   Exploring Apple's iTools

Start by clicking the iCards tab to open the window shown in Figure 10-3. (You can use either the iCards tab at the top of the window or the toolbar below the iTools tab.)

Click on the type of card you want to send. You may be given a choice of variations from which you can choose, such as the Fine Art choices shown in Figure 10-4. Click the image you want to use.

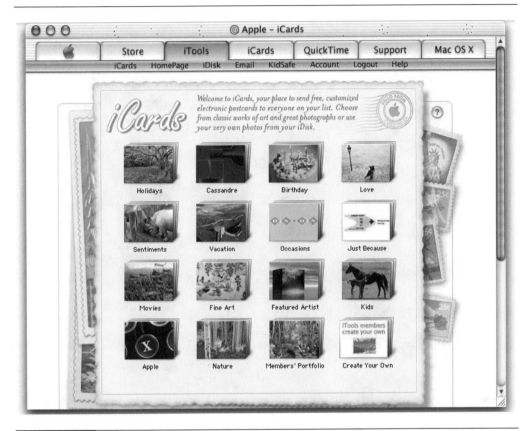

FIGURE 10-3   The iCards home lets you start to create your card.

The four numbers at the right of Figure 10-4 labeled More Cards are a common way of navigating on many Web pages. You can go to any of four pages by clicking the numbers; you can also use the left and right arrows to move forward or back one page.

If this is your first time using your Web browser, you may see a notice like the one shown next. It warns you that you are sending some information back to a Web server. You can click

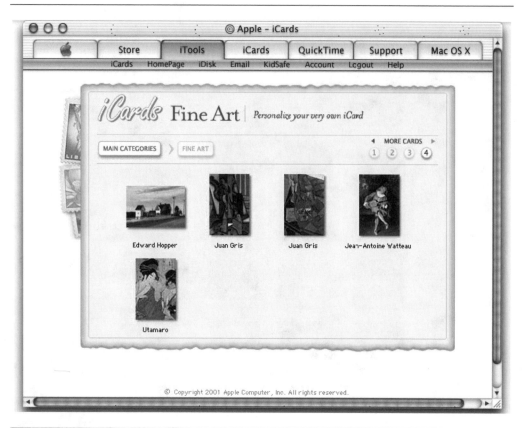

FIGURE 10-4   A variety of choices and subchoices let you find the perfect card.

the checkbox to turn off the alert in the future. Of course, you can also click Cancel so that no data is sent back:

Next, you will be shown a data entry screen (see Figure 10-5) in which you need to select the typeface you want and type in your text. The card image is shown at the bottom of the screen. The area for text varies—in this case, there is enough space for a few words, but not for a lengthy missive. When you click Continue (at the upper right of the screen), you move on to the next screen, where you can enter your recipients.

Type in an email address and click Add Recipient; the address will appear in the Recipient List at the right. You do not type directly into the Recipient List. If you want to remove someone, click on the address in the Recipient List and click Remove Recipient.

Hiding the distribution list is often a good idea when you are sending any email message to several people who do not necessarily know one another. If the distribution list appears on all messages, you may be publicizing email address that their owners would prefer to keep private.

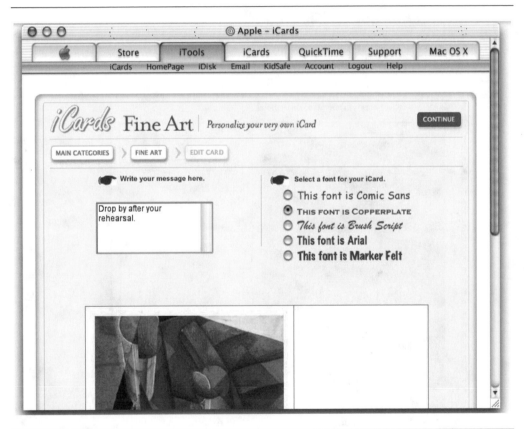

FIGURE 10-5 Address your iCard.

On email messages, use the BCC (blind carbon copy) header to do this; for iCards, click Hide distribution list here.

You can change the return email address. If you have registered with iTools (see the next section), you may have an address at mac.com which will be used as the default, but you can use your regular email address instead.

When you are finished, click Send Your Card (in the upper right). The cards will be sent via email. Depending on the email software your friends have, they may see the card completely in an email window or they may see it in its own window. A received iCard is shown in the Apple Mail application under Mac OS X in Figure 10-6.

You can also create custom iCards; this is discussed in the section on iDisk, later in this chapter.

FIGURE 10-6   Your friends can view their iCards in any email program.

KidSafe

KidSafe is a set of tools that help you limit access to appropriate sites for kids on the Internet. It relies on the multiple users feature of Mac OS 9 and on the login IDs that you assign on Mac OS X. It also puts a variety of appropriate links at your disposal. The KidSafe home page is shown in Figure 10-7.

Shortly after the Web was developed and opened for public use, sites with disturbing contents appeared. (This is what happened when the first VCRs were invented, too.) Pornography, fraud, and violence seemed to run wild on the Web. Today, they are still there—and still easy to find—but other material has swamped them. Still, many people want to find a way to keep their kids out of these dangerous neighborhoods.

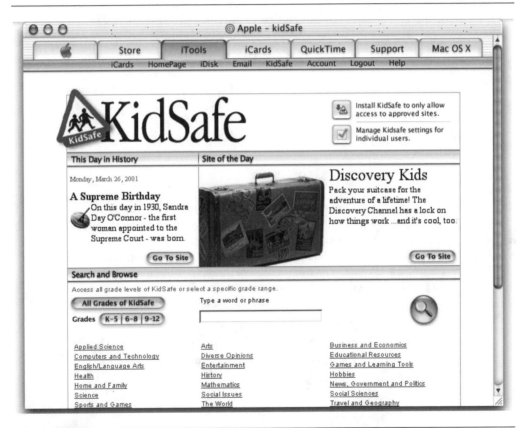

FIGURE 10-7   KidSafe lets you find useful and appropriate links for kids.

There are two ways to address this issue. You can use filtering programs—programs that check for undesirable sites either by name or by examining the words (and sometimes images) on them. Most Web browsers today implement a ratings system that helps with filtering. Filtering can be used to screen sites in or screen them out—in other words, only allowing access to specified sites or denying access to others. Filtering based on site names requires a review of the site's content by a rater. Automatic filtering (looking for specific words on a site) is much faster, but it can be less accurate.

In addition to using filtering programs to handle individual sites, you can lock out certain types of services—file transfer, email, chat, and games, for example. Such restrictions apply to any location; you simply remove the functionality from that user.

You can use KidSafe to implement either type of control on your computer. You must install this software as the administrator user on Mac OS X. You must then create other user(s) for whom you set up the KidSafe settings. The instructions for doing this are downloaded with KidSafe.

If you are setting up a school environment, look for specific tips on the KidSafe site for educators.

iTools

The iTools tab takes you to an area to which you need to log in. When you do, you will have access to a variety of additional tools that can be quite valuable to you. These include free email, free disk space at Apple, a free home page, and advanced features of KidSafe. Accessing any of these additional services from anywhere in the Apple Web site may also take you to the sign-in pages you see here.

Signing Up

Start by clicking the iTools tab at the top of any of the Apple Web site windows.

You may see a security notice, like the one shown next, that alerts you to the fact that the connection from your computer to this particular Web page is secure and that the information transmitted is encrypted. This is the reverse situation from the security alert (already shown) in which the data was not encrypted. You can use the checkbox to determine if this alert is shown in the future. As for the secure status of any particular Web page, that is under the control of the Web site and its proprietors; you can't make a Web site secure or nonsecure.

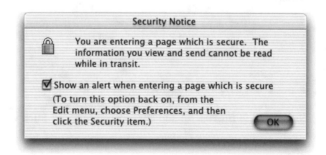

Next, you will go to a new account or sign-in screen. If you are already a member, sign in and click Enter (at the right of the window). If you are not a member, click the Sign Up button (at the left of the screen) to sign up for iTools. To register, you provide the information shown in Figures 10-8 and 10-9, shown a few pages ahead.

When you click Continue, you may see a dialog like the one shown next, which lets you know that AutoFill can store your frequently used form information. Some browsers (such as Microsoft Internet Explorer) can keep track of form data to use in the future. Items such as name and address can be automatically filled in for you. You can choose to save this data or not as you wish.

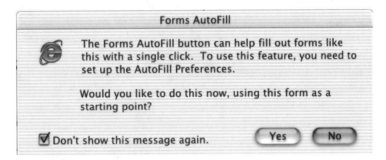

To complete the registration process, you will see a page that summarizes your account information, as shown next. Although the password is obscured in the figure, it will be legible on your version. Print and save this document in a safe place.

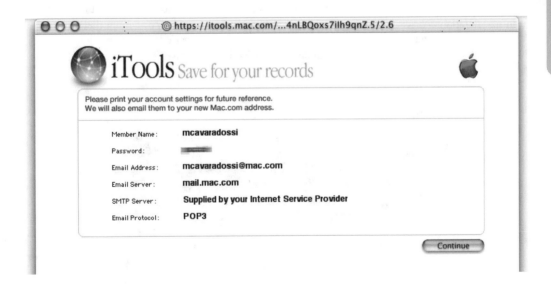

iTools

As a final step, to let your friends or acquaintances know about your new email address, iTools will offer to send an iCard, as shown here:

Before flooding your friends' in-boxes with cards announcing your new address, make certain you will actually use it. See Chapter 18, "Using Apple Mail," for more about using multiple email addresses. Your iTools email account may be a secondary account that you do not want to publicize widely. By the same token, it may be a secondary account that you want only your friends (as opposed to colleagues or coworkers) to use. This completes your registration for iTools.

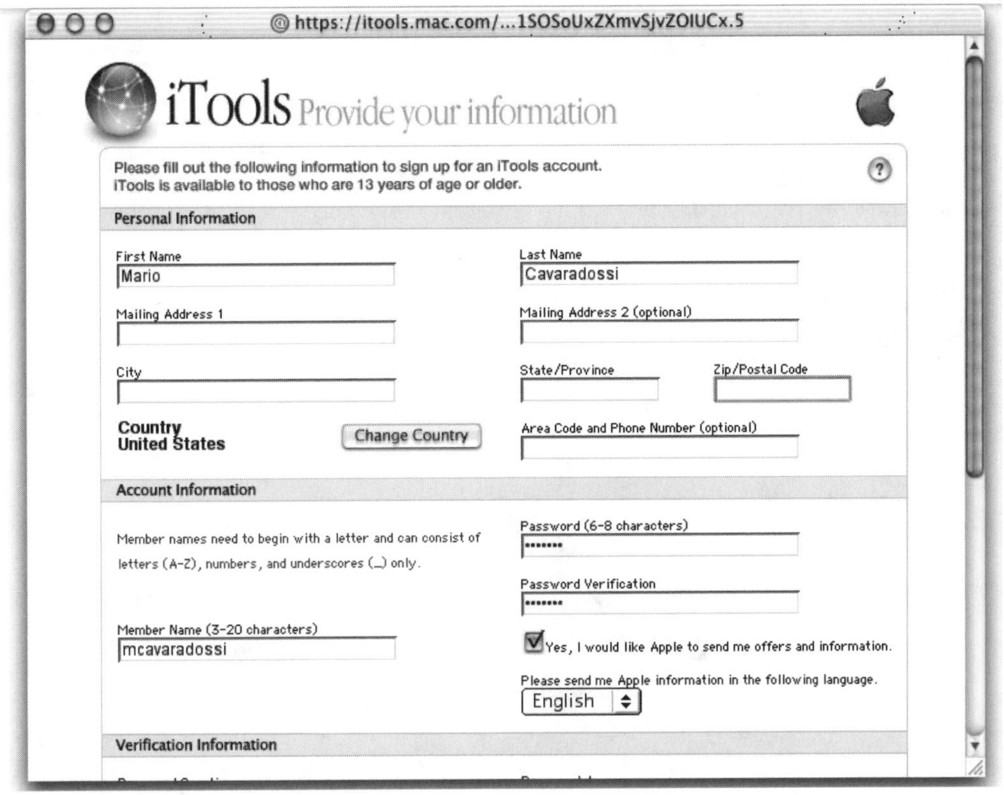
https://itools.mac.com/...1SOSoUxZXmvSjvZOIUCx.5
iTools Provide your information
Please fill out the following information to sign up for an iTools account.
iTools is available to those who are 13 years of age or older.
Personal Information
First Name
Mario
Last Name
Cavaradossi
Mailing Address 1
Mailing Address 2 (optional)
City
State/Province
Zip/Postal Code
Country
United States
Change Country
Area Code and Phone Number (optional)
Account Information
Member names need to begin with a letter and can consist of letters (A-Z), numbers, and underscores (_) only.
Password (6-8 characters)
Password Verification
Member Name (3-20 characters)
mcavaradossi
Yes, I would like Apple to send me offers and information.
Please send me Apple information in the following language.
English
Verification Information

FIGURE 10-8 You need to provide registration information to open an iTools account.

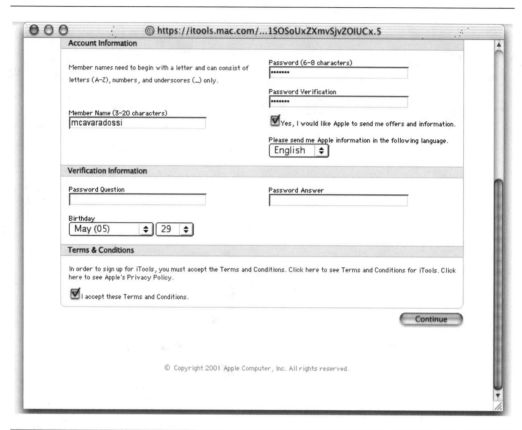

FIGURE 10-9   If necessary, scroll to the bottom of the page to complete all registration information.

Logging on to iTools

When you have logged on to iTools—either for the first time or as a returning user, you see the screen shown in Figure 10-10. From here, you can go to any of the areas of iTools. Each of them is described in the sections that follow.

Email

Apple offers a free email account to registered iTools users. You set the email account up through the Web site and then use your regular email software to retrieve your mail.

FIGURE 10-10   Registered users log in to iTools on this page.

Even if you already have an email account, an additional account can be very useful. You may need one account for work and one for personal use, or you may be tired of sharing your email account with your spouse, parents, or children. In addition, you may want to have an email account that you use for special projects. You can even link your Apple email account to your regular email account.

Your iTools email account is set up at the domain name mac.com. This means your address will be something like yourname@mac.com. You set up the email account by clicking Email at the top of an iTools window to open the window shown in Figure 10-11. Two features can be particularly useful in using this account: email forwarding and auto replies.

FIGURE 10-11
    Click the Email tab on iTools to manage your email account.

Email Forwarding

Set up mail forwarding to use another email account together with your mac.com account, as shown next. Email sent to your mac.com address will automatically be sent to another address—your regular email account or another one (even someone else's). The sender does not know if the mail is being forwarded. If you expect a small volume of incoming mail, this can save you time, since you don't have to remember to check the account.

Setting an Auto Reply

You can also set up an auto reply—a message that is sent automatically to people who send you mail. This can be helpful if you are on vacation. It also can be helpful if you want to provide people with other addresses they can use and information about how to contact you. For example, you can set up an auto reply message with names and phone numbers of your colleagues when you are on vacation. You set up auto reply messages using the screen shown in Figure 10-12. Remember that auto reply is set up only for your mac.com email account.

Email

FIGURE 10-12   An auto reply will let people know you won't respond right away.

iDisk

One of the most valuable iTools services is free disk space at Apple. You can use this in three ways:

- You can use it to safely back up files so that if your computer disk fails or your computeris stolen you can still access them.

- You can use it to share files with others (regardless of the operating system they are using).

- You can use files you store on your iDisk in iCards and on your iTools home page.

Accessing Your iDisk

Click the iDisk tab on iTools to open the window shown in Figure 10-13.

You can open your own iDisk by clicking the button at the top (Open your iDisk). You can access someone else's by clicking the button below that one (Open Public Folder). Remember that no one can get to this screen without having logged in to iDisk with your password, so your iDisk is secure.

FIGURE 10-13   Manage your iDisk from the iDisk area under the iTools tab.

When you open an iDisk—your own or someone else's—it will appear as a networked disk in the Finder alongside your other disks, as shown next. Here two iDisk icons are shown: floriatosca is a public folder; mcavaradossi is a private iDisk.

The folders at the top level of your iDisk—Documents, Movies, Pictures, Public, and Sites—are set up automatically on your iDisk. You can open them and manipulate their contents, but you cannot rename or remove them, nor can you create new folders within the top level of your iDisk (you can do so within the folders provided for you).

If you place anything in the folder marked Public, it will be visible to people who log in to your iDisk. This is how you share files: drag them to your Public folder and then let your friends and colleagues log in to your iDisk, open your Public folder, and remove them.

You can open someone else's Public folder if you have their member name. You use the iDisk page shown previously. You can also publish your own Public folder on the Web—click Publish Public Folder on that same page. This creates a page on your iTools home page; the process is described in the following section.

You can place movies in the Movies folder, graphics in the Pictures folder, and anything you want in the Documents folder. None of these are visible to other users, although you can use them on your Web site. Figure 10-14 shows an image (newyear2000.jpg) being dragged from a Finder window on the desktop to the Pictures folder on an iDisk.

Getting More Space

Your free iDisk has limited space—20MB in most cases. That is a large amount of space for documents, pictures, and the like. However, if you want to place movies on your iDisk or if you want to use it to back up important files from your hard disk, you may need more space. Apple lets you purchase additional iDisk space on an annual basis: this is not for temporary storage you might need for a day or two.

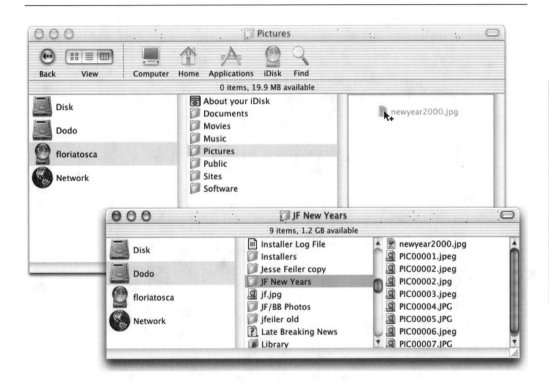

iDisk

FIGURE 10-14   You can drag files from the Finder into your iDisk folders.

Using Your iDisk Graphics on an iCard

If you have graphics in the Pictures folder, you can create your own iCards. From the iCards window, click Create Your Own in the lower right of the iCards window. That will open the page shown in Figure 10-15.

The pictures in your Pictures folder are shown in this window. Click the one you want to use and then click Open. You can click Preview to see a preview of the image at the right. Finish up by clicking Select This Image. All that is left is to add text to your card.

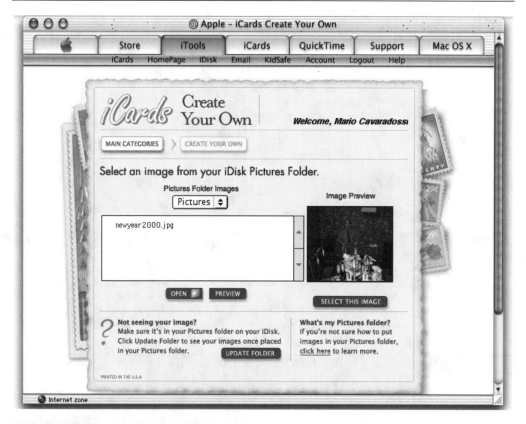

FIGURE 10-15   Select an image from your iDisk to use on the iCard.

HomePage

You can also create a home page for yourself on the iTools site. This may be your only home page, or it may be a special home page for friends, a project, or any other purpose you can think of. You don't have to design much of anything: the templates are all prepared for you.

Creating a Page

Click the HomePage tab under iTools to open the basic window shown in Figure 10-16.

To add a new page, click the type of page you want to add from the list at the left. If you click Personal, for example, you will open the window shown in Figure 10-17.

FIGURE 10-16   Click the HomePage tab to get started on your Web site.

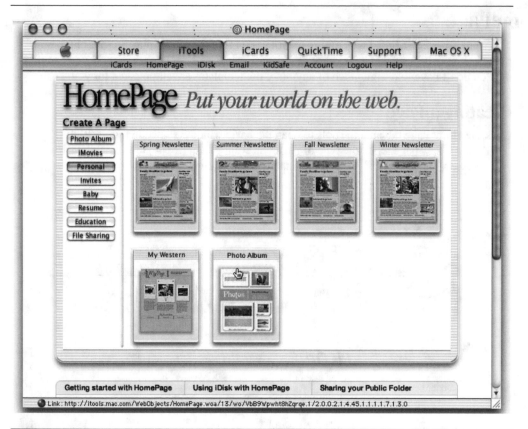

FIGURE 10-17   Select a template for your page.

You will see a variety of themes for the type of page you are creating. Click the one you want. This will open a window like that shown in Figure 10-18.

FIGURE 10-18	Plan your page's text and pictures.

You can see the basic layout of the page. Click Edit Text to continue to the page where you can enter text. Some pages—such as the Photo Album—let you add pictures from your iDisk Pictures folder. Others—such as iMovies—let you add movies from you iDisk Movies folder.

Click Apply Text to see exactly what your page will look like, as shown in Figure 10-19. If you are not happy, you can still change the theme or edit the text again.

FIGURE 10-19 Review the page before publishing it.

When you are done, click Publish (at the top right), and iTools confirms that your page is on the Web, as shown here:

You can organize your pages—add and remove them—by returning to the HomePage tab of iTools. Figure 10-20 shows that page once you have created a Web page. As you can see, you can delete or edit your home pages.

Your iTools HomePage site is useful for sharing photos with friends and providing relatively small amounts of information. It's perfect for kids who want to put up their own Web sites, and it's ideal for anyone who wants to share information without becoming a Web expert.

File Sharing with Your Home Page

When you select iDisk from the iTools tab, one of your choices is to publish your public folder. This is done by creating a page automatically for you. Click the File Sharing button in the Create A Page section, shown previously in Figure 10-20. Then select the page style you want and click it.

The files in your iTools Public folder are available to anyone who has your member name and who can run iTools (that means a Macintosh user). Publishing your files on a Web page allows anyone with a browser—any browser on any operating system—to view and download your Public folder files.

FIGURE 10-20   Manage all your iTools pages with the HomePage tab.

Clicking the File Sharing template lets you open the window shown in Figure 10-21. This page may be fine for you, or you may want to customize it. Click Edit Text (in the upper right) to modify the page. When you are happy with your changes, click Publish—just as you did for the Web page you created previously—and you will receive a confirmation with the URL. Now you—or your friends, students, or colleagues—can browse your Public folder and download files using any browser or operating system.

Sharing files in this way can be better than sending them as email attachments, particularly if they are large. Many email systems refuse to transmit files over a certain size (10MB is a common limit). Browsers do not have such limits. Also, remember that posting a file in this way makes it downloadable at the user's convenience. If you send a large attachment, your correspondent must wait until it has downloaded before reading other mail.

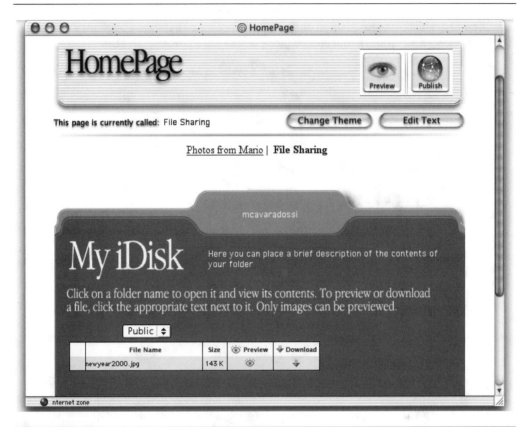

FIGURE 10-21   You can share files on your iTools Web site.

For example, here is how someone using Windows 2000 and Microsoft Internet Explorer can download a file from your Web site. They start by going to your mac.com URL. It is http://homepage.mac.com/yourmembername/, and it is in the confirmation of every page that you post.

A page like that shown previously in Figure 10-21 appears in any browser that someone uses. If they click the Download button on any file, Windows asks if they want to download the file, as shown next. They should choose the option to Save This File To Disk.

Next, they are asked to choose the location to store the downloaded file, as shown next. Finally, the progress bar shows the downloading of the file. Remember that the format of your downloadable files should be compatible with other users' software. Standard formats—TEXT, JPEG, QuickTime movies, and so forth—work best.

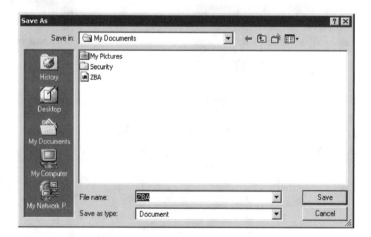

Summary

Apple's iTools suite provides basic Internet functionality to you with a minimum of fuss. You can create and send greeting cards (iCards), use iTools software to set up KidSafe browsing, use a free mac.com email account, and create your own Web page.

Part III

Networking

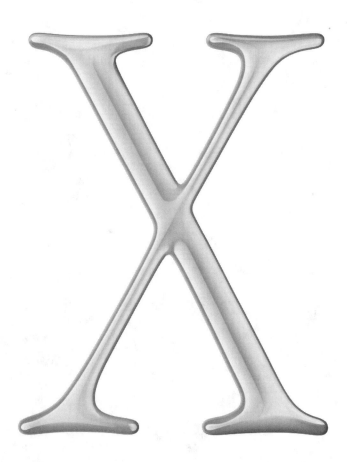

Chapter 11

Communicating Over a Local Area Network

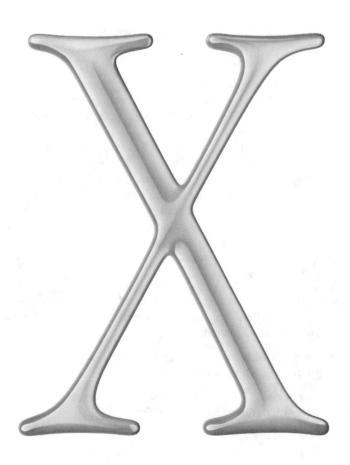

Networking has been built into Macintosh computers since the beginning, in both hardware and software. For a decade, it has been impossible to buy a standard Macintosh without built-in support for Ethernet, the primary technology used in local area networks (LANs) today. (This stands in stark contrast to many other brands of computers; it contributes in part to the perception that Macintosh computers are more expensive.)

The chapters in this part of the book address the issues involved in networking your computer:

■ Accessing computers and other resources on a local area network (that is, using it as a client on a LAN)

■ Accessing computers and other resources on the Internet (a client on the Internet)

■ Allowing others on your local area network to access your computer's resources (server on the LAN)

■ Allowing people on the Internet to access your computer (server on the Internet)

■ Running a Web server

Mac OS X allows you to do all of these things. Mac OS X Server, Apple's server platform is built on Mac OS X, and it allows you to accomplish the last three items in this list on a larger and more powerful scale than does Mac OS X by itself. Both products are discussed in this part of the book.

The nice symmetry of these chapters is marred somewhat by the fact that in reality the distinctions between clients and servers are not nearly so clear as they appear here. Even the largest Web servers frequently (and temporarily) become clients of other servers—sometimes very small ones. Likewise, the nice distinction between a local area network and the Internet is not so firm and fast as it was long ago—five years ago, for example. You should not try to find your situation once and for all in these chapters. Recognize that you will move from client to server to client as you use your computer and that you will probably integrate your LAN with the Internet so much that you cannot tell them apart.

This chapter consists of three sections:

■ **Understanding the Concepts**   This section introduces basic terminology and concepts including the difference between clients and servers, as well as between local area networks, intranets, and the Internet.

■ **Understanding the Realities**   Routers, hubs, wiring, and the details of addressing computers are covered in this section.

■ **Connecting to a Server**   Finally, you will see how to connect to a file server using Apple File Protocol and how to log on to an FTP site using Mac OS X.

Understanding the Concepts of Networking

There are two underlying pairs of concepts intrinsic to networking today:

■ Clients and servers

■ Local area networks and the Internet

Clients

Originally, computers each stood alone without communicating with one another. Gradually, technologies were implemented to allow computers to send messages back and forth. These communications could be between computers, and they also could be between computers and dumb terminals—monitors with keyboards attached, but with no local processing power or storage to speak of.

Over time, system architectures evolved so that the messages were more and more complex. By the late 1980s, an architecture known as client/server came into widespread use. It involved the use of smart terminals—and later, personal computers—to communicate with the computers (often mainframes) on which applications were running. The two communications models—computer-to-computer (peer-to-peer) and client/server—were conceptually and practically quite different.

Today, *client* is used to refer to the subsidiary device. It frequently is a personal computer connected to a larger computer, but it need not be. A powerful personal computer can connect to a router that in effect is a small and not very powerful server.

Servers

Servers traditionally were the powerful mainframe computers to which smart terminals (clients) and dumb terminals (CRTs or teletypes) were attached. Today, size and power are not determinants of clients and servers. The distinction between client and server does not always matter, but there are some areas in which it is useful to apply it:

■ The client makes the connection to the server. You dial in to an Internet service provider, or your computer connects to a cable or DSL modem, not vice versa.

■ User IDs, passwords, and so on, are provided by the manager of the server, not the client.

■ Security is implemented primarily on the server.

■ Since a variety of clients need to connect to it at their convenience, the server must be available at all (or most) times.

■ The server and its network are administered by a network administrator; clients typically do not administer the network.

Local Area Networks (LANs)

LANs initially were networks in a single building connecting computers and other devices within it. They were characterized by being relatively self-contained. (In the United States before telecommunications deregulation, a network that crossed property lines needed to use a telecommunications carrier, such as a telephone company, for that part of the network.)

LANs are typically created and managed by a single organization, such as your own home, an office, a school, or a business. There is frequently a central administrator. LANs can be as simple as two computers with a serial cable between them (the classic AppleTalk configuration), or they can involve very complex topologies. LANs today use TCP/IP more and more as their communications protocol. This involves using IP addresses and frequently involves using a router or gateway to the Internet. Other protocols used on LANs include AppleTalk and IPX.

AppleTalk has evolved to the Apple File Protocol (AFP). It runs over an AppleTalk network or over TCP/IP. For Mac OS X, you must use TCP/IP; on Mac OS 9 and earlier, you can use either AppleTalk or TCP/IP.

Internet

The Internet differs from LANs in much more than its sheer size. Whereas LANs are typically owned and managed by a single entity, the Internet is remarkably decentralized. Although there are centralized bodies setting policy, its operations are thoroughly decentralized. LANs often use Ethernet and TCP/IP, but they need not do so. Today, TCP/IP is the standard for communications on the Internet.

Understanding the Realities of Networking

The four concepts of the previous section are not so distinct as they once were. Clients and servers assume their roles dynamically: the same pair of computers can be clients and servers in different contexts and almost at the same time, although at any given moment and for any single transaction, you can usually determine which is the client and which the server.

LANs and the Internet are rapidly merging, as you will see later in this section. Other realities that need to be dealt with are the variety of telecommunications media, hubs and routers, virtual private networks and intranets, and the issue of LAN addressing.

Types of LANS (Wired, Wireless, AirPort, IRDA)

The rise of wireless technologies for telecommunications has had a big impact on LANs in particular. The cost of wiring a home or office (much less a college campus or business park) can be significant. Not only that, but changes to the network can be so expensive as to make it necessary to arrange office furniture around the network connection. (This is not new—many rooms are already arranged around power outlets and telephone connections.)

Reliable, high-speed wireless communications can make LANs much more affordable to create and maintain. Apple pioneered this concept with the use of AirPort technology for its iBooks and PowerBooks. Today, any Apple computer can be connected to an AirPort base station. (AirPort is based on the industry standard IEEE 802.11; other vendors implement 802.11 under other names.) The base station itself can be connected either to a LAN using an Ethernet (RJ-45) connector or to a modem. Either way, the base station can connect to the Internet using a wired connection. The wireless devices that communicate with the AirPort base station thus can log onto the Internet.

AirPort technology has received a hearty welcome from people who need to move around with their computers in a constrained area—it is widely used in schools, for example. It also is being deployed rapidly in airport terminals where business travelers can connect easily to a base station and thence to the Internet.

Hub, Routers, and Switches

The AirPort base station is an example of a router or a hub. Hubs are simple devices into which you can plug several computers. They communicate with one another by sending messages through the hub. (This arrangement is often called a hub-and-spoke topology.)

The alternative to hub-and-spoke topology is daisy-chaining devices together: each is connected to the one next to it and so forth. Daisy-chaining may appear simpler, and it frequently uses less cable; however, it is often harder to manage than a hub-and-spoke topology. In the hub-and-spoke topology, cabling is very simple: each computer (or printer) is connected to a hub. When you add or subtract a device from the network, only the connection from it to the hub needs to be modified. With a daisy-chain topology, you need to reconnect the devices on each side of the new or removed device.

Hubs can be very inexpensive—well under $50 for a small four-port hub. Hubs can be connected together on a network, so it is feasible, and often desirable, to have a small, four-port hub in an individual workspace or office. You can plug a computer, networked printer, and optional laptop into the hub, and use the fourth plug to connect it in turn to another hub.

If a hub connects to the Internet (or other larger network) either with a modem or via another connection, it is more complex and becomes a router. There are a variety of differences, including the fact that routers are capable of managing the addresses of devices on their part of the network. This is discussed in Chapter 13, "Setting Up a Network Server."

Hubs and routers pass messages along their networks. Each message has a device's address attached to it, and that device takes the message off as it comes by. Switches direct messages to specific devices (or to hubs and routers on the network). Switches can make networks run more efficiently, since they quickly distribute messages to subnetworks. You will often hear of network performance improvements that are quite dramatic when hubs are replaced by switches. For small-scale networks, such as those found in small businesses and homes, hubs are very cost-effective since the volume of traffic is not particularly high.

Virtual Private Networks (VPNs) and Intranets

Some of the ambiguity today over LANs arises from the fact that in addition to being carried over cables that are strung around an individual building or office, they can be implemented over the Internet. A virtual private network (VPN) uses Internet technology and the Internet's

Understanding the Realities of Networking

telecommunications to connect LANs and individual computers to one another with a very high degree of security. While using the public Internet, they are not really part of it in the way that public Web pages and email are.

Intranets are LANs that use Internet technologies—TCP/IP, POP/IMAP for mail, HTTP and HTML for Web, Telnet, and the like. A few years ago, they were something special; today, LANs that do not use Internet technologies are becoming less and less common.

Although non-Internet technologies on LANs are decreasing in use, they still are very important, and this should not be taken as suggesting that they do not exist at all. However, the standardization of Internet technologies has massive savings for everyone.

Setting LAN Addresses

Each device connected to the Internet or to a network using Internet protocols has its own IP address—the quartet of numbers that uniquely identifies it. On the Internet, the routing tables of the domain name system (DNS) link IP addresses to domain names so that you can type in www.apple.com, for example, rather than having to use its IP address.

The next chapter, "Communicating Over the Internet," explains how IP addresses are generated and assigned to your computer. For now, you just need to know a little about what they are so that you can fill in the information needed to connect to your LAN.

Many IP addresses are dynamic and vary with each connection. Other IP addresses must be static, so the DNS computers can reliably route traffic to the right IP address for a domain name. In general, if you have a Web server, you need a static IP address.

Dialup (PPP) Addresses

If you dial into an Internet service provider (ISP), you almost always have a dynamic IP address. When the connection is established, the ISP assigns you an IP address from a range of addresses it is allowed to give out. Thus, for the time you are connected, you have a unique IP address, but it varies with each connection.

You can sometimes arrange for a static IP address. In most cases, this means that you must dial a special number at your ISP to connect to a preconfigured modem that will give you the same IP address each time. This type of account typically is more expensive than a standard account.

LAN Addressees

If your LAN has a router on it, that router can assign you an IP address when you connect to the LAN. Two standard protocols exist: DHCP and BOOTP. In each case, your IP address is assigned from the router's pool of IP addresses. For most common routers, the pool of addresses ranges from 192.168.1.1 to 192.168.1.255. The router itself typically is configured as 192.168.1.1 or 192.168.1.255 (the exact number does not matter). These are the internal IP addresses.

The router has an IP address that is assigned by the ISP. If your computer is on a LAN and has been assigned 192.168.1.3, its actual address might be something like 205.32.14.5/192.168.1.3, where 205.32.14.5 is the router's address.

In the case of always-on Internet connections such as cable or DSL, the IP address is typically assigned for a period of 24 hours. If you have a router connected to such a connection, you can see in its log that once a day the router requests a new IP address. Often, the same IP address is returned, but that need not be the case.

Connecting to a Server

The purpose of connecting to a server is to mount its disks or shared folders on your desktop; you see them in a Finder window just as you see the disks connected to your own computer. You can open them, move and rename files, delete them, or create them—subject to security constraints, of course.

Connecting to an AFP or AppleShare Server

Use the Connect To Server command in the Go menu of the Finder as shown in Figure 11-1 to connect to any server running AppleShare or the Apple File Protocol (AFP). (The distinction between AppleShare and AFP is not important in this context; technically, Apple File Protocol is used to implement AppleShare. The AppleShare product is being subsumed into Mac OS X Server.)

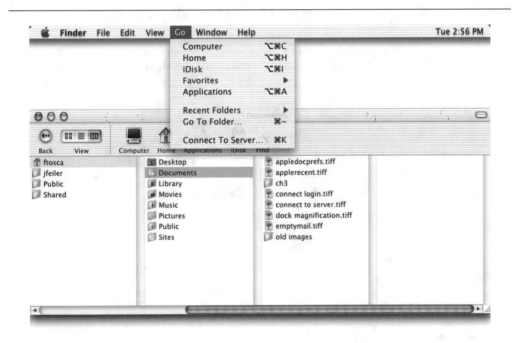

FIGURE 11-1   Use the Go menu to connect to a server.

Connecting to a Server

This server can be a Macintosh configured as a file server (that is, one equipped with large, fast disks to serve a workgroup), or it can be any Macintosh with file sharing enabled. You will see how to do this in Chapter 13, "Setting Up a Network Server."

Here you can see the next step, the Connect To Server window, which you use to select a server:

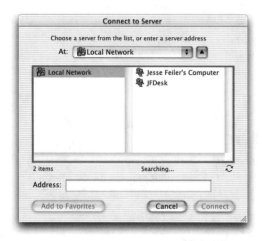

There are three ways in which you can select a server to which you connect. You can use the pop-up menu at the top of the window to select from recently used servers, as shown here:

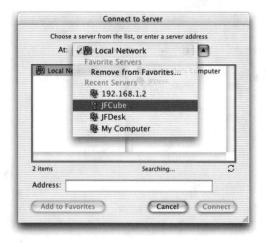

The browser in the center of the window lets you see any networks to which you are connected; you can select from the AppleTalk computers on those networks. The next illustration shows a selected computer (Jesse Feiler's Computer).

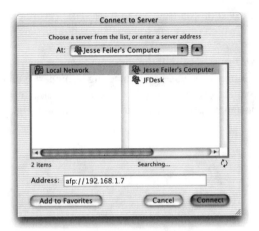

You can also type in the network address of the computer you want to use. Type it in the Address field at the bottom, and prefix it with afp (Apple File Protocol) as shown in the previous illustration. Note that when you select a computer in the browser, the AFP address is automatically filled in.

When you have selected a computer from the pop-up menu, in the browser or by typing in an AFP address, click Connect to open the login dialog:

If you do not see the server you want, check to see if it is available. (See Chapter 13, "Setting Up a Network Server," for more on setting up the server.) If no servers at all are visible, your local network connection may be broken. Use Print Center to connect to printers on the local network—if you can see network printers, your network connection is okay. If you use a router to connect to the Internet via a cable or DSL modem, see if you can send mail or browse a Web page. If you can do so, your local network connection is okay since you need it to connect to the router and thence to the Internet. (This is not a valid test if you use a dialup PPP connection.) If your local network connection is okay, investigate the server itself to which you want to log in.

Connecting to a Server

You can connect as a Guest or as a Registered User. The server administrator determines if guest access is allowed and which users can log on. The radio buttons may be dimmed if access is not allowed.

Type your login ID *for the server*—not the login ID for your own computer. Type the password, too, and click Connect. (If you are connecting as a guest, you do not need a login ID or password, just click Connect.) A number of options are available by clicking the Options button, shown next. For instance, you can set options for your password and change it.

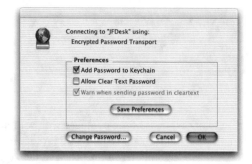

If you want to change your password on the remote server, you can do so here. You can also add this information to a keychain. Checking the Clear Text Password option means that your password will be sent in unencrypted form across the network and it can be intercepted. In general, you should not use this option unless you are working to debug a network connection.

If the server has more than one disk that can be shared, you will be able to choose the volumes you want to connect to in the dialog shown here:

If you want to select more than one, hold down the COMMAND key while you click the volumes you want. If the volumes are next to one another, you can hold down the SHIFT key while you click the first and last ones in the list.

When you have logged on, each volume (disk) that you have selected is available in the Finder. The next illustration shows two mounted server disks in the Finder window—jfeiler and Rye—along with two local disk drives —Disk and Dodo. You use these disks exactly as you would use local disks.

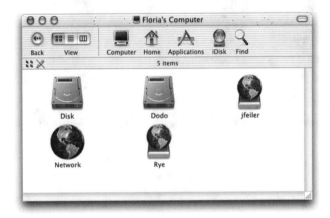

Connecting to an FTP Server

Using Apple File Protocol (AppleShare) lets you connect to computers through Aqua. You see folders and documents in your Finder windows just as you do on your own computer. The computer to which you connect must be running AFP or AppleShare. It need not be running Mac OS X; you can connect from Mac OS X to a Mac OS 8 computer.

You can use the Internet standard FTP (File Transfer Protocol) to connect at a much more basic level to another computer on your network. To do so, you can use a third-party product such as Fetch. When you launch Fetch, you can create a new connection using the IP address of the computer to which you are connecting as well as your user ID and password. Use Fetch to open an FTP connection via the New Connection window, as shown here:

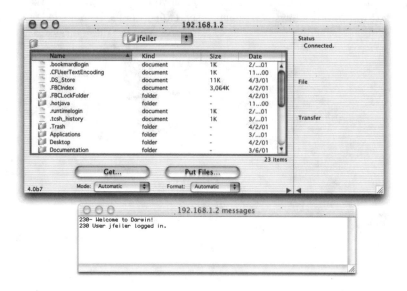

230- Welcome to Darwin!
230 User jfeiler logged in.

FIGURE 11-2   The Fetch directory listing differs from the Aqua Finder listing.

When you are connected, you will see the files and directories as shown in Figure 11-2. Note how different this is from the Finder. For starters, file and folder names starting with a period are shown; in the Finder, they are invisible. (Needless to say, that is true for a reason: leave them alone!)

Using the buttons at the bottom of the window, you can get files and directories from the remote computer. You can also put your files and directories onto it (providing, of course, that you have the appropriate privileges both for the files you are transmitting and for the destination disk and folder). Pop-up menus let you specify the format and mode of the transfer. Normally, the Automatic choice is appropriate; however, sometimes you want to force the transfer to use a particular format such as BinHex or Text. (Whoever you are sharing files with will tell you if there is a special requirement.)

FTP transfer occurs at the Darwin (kernel) level, not at Aqua. That is why the invisible files are not hidden, and that is why you cannot display an FTP connection in a Finder window. However, this means that you can connect to any computer on your LAN that is supporting FTP whether it is a Macintosh or not. Thus can be a very important advantage in heterogeneous networks.

By working at such a basic level, FTP transfer is not aware that there can be two forks to a Macintosh file. As a result, transferring files with resource forks can cause corruption in the transferred file (it is incomplete). Before transferring a file with a resource fork over FTP, it is necessary to flatten it into one unit. You can do this by transferring it as a MacBinary or BinHex file (these are among the Put pop-up menu choices). The recipient must have software (like

StuffIt Expander) to expand the file. Fortunately, StuffIt Expander ships with Mac OS X and can be found in the Applications folder inside the Utilities subfolder.

Summary

This chapter has provided some of the basic networking concepts, and it has shown you how to connect to servers on your local area network. Once you have connected to such servers, you can use their disks as if they were your own (subject to security constraints, of course). Connecting to the Internet is a somewhat more complicated procedure. That is the subject of the next chapter.

Chapter 12

Communicating Over the Internet

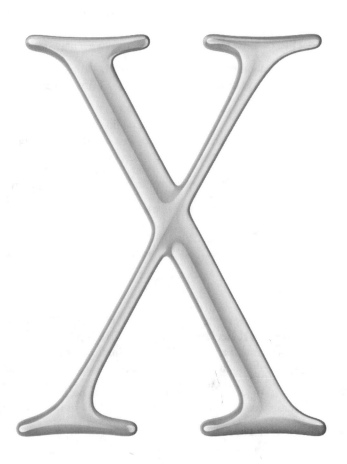

This chapter describes what you need to know to connect your computer to the Internet using Mac OS X. The process can be very simple—everything may have been done for you by someone else or by the vendor who sells you the computer. In other cases, you may need to get involved in the settings of various preferences and controls. Even if your computer comes configured for Internet access (or you use the Mac OS X installer to do so), you may need to modify settings if you move or change Internet service providers later on. Here's what you will find in this chapter:

- First, you will find a quick checklist of what you need to get started. This may be sufficient to get you up and running in many cases.

- The next section describes the process of connecting to the Internet. This will not only help you understand what is going on, but it also may be useful in helping you communicate with network managers and others who may not be familiar with Mac OS X terminology.

- The third section describes setting up network connections, both with a telephone line and modem, and over a local area network (the local area network route is what you use with a cable or DSL connection, even if you do not have a network).

- Not everything runs smoothly when it comes to Internet connections. A section on troubleshooting shows you how to use the Network Utility for services such as Ping, Traceroute, and so forth.

- Finally, you will find advice on collecting information you need from existing setups on Mac OS 9 and earlier or Windows. In this way, you can transfer the information from an already functioning Internet connection into Mac OS X.

Note that many of the settings in this chapter require an administrator password.

What You Need to Get Going

The next section describes Internet connectivity in detail; but for now, think of it as consisting of four elements:

- Your computer.

- Something that connects to an Internet service provider (ISP). This can be a modem (phone, cable, or DSL), a router, a proxy server, an AirPort wireless hub, or any of a number of other devices with all sorts of names. (Some of them may have proprietary, code, or brand names, although your company's connection might be called George.)

- Your Internet service provider. This could be America Online, EarthLink, or an in-house operation. You typically pay for this service on a monthly basis and sometimes by the hour.

- The Internet, its data, and its services.

In order to get going, you need to identify these four elements and the links between them. The first and last—your computer and the Internet—are easy to identify. One sits on your lap or your desk; the other is out there surrounding everyone these days. It's numbers 2 and 3—and the link between them—that are sometimes problematic.

Connecting to an ISP

If you are in an organization such as a school or enterprise, the second element may be part of your local area network. Ask your network coordinator for its name or address. If you don't get an immediate response, ask to see a successful setup for another computer. (Use the section later in this chapter called "Moving from Installed Connections" to interpret what you see.)

If you are on your own or in an organization that does not use a network to connect to the Internet, your connection may be via a modem connected to your computer. That modem may be inside your computer or it may be external.

Gathering the Cables

Having identified what it is that will connect you to an Internet service provider, you will need a cable. In the case of a modem, it is a telephone cable with RJ11 connectors at both ends (for the modem and the computer). In the case of a network connection, it is an Ethernet cable with RJ45 connectors at both ends (for the computer and the network connection). In the case of wireless access, you need no connectors.

Over time, you will accumulate extra telephone and Ethernet cables, as well as various other pieces of equipment. Instead of stashing them in desk drawers and closets, take a box—such as reams of paper are shipped in—and label it "Computer Equipment." Just throw these extra cables, power cords, and the like in there. When you need one, you'll know where to look. Furthermore, when you are setting up a new computer, automatically take the box with you. You may not need anything, but it will be there if you do need a cable. Good cables are not cheap!

Checklist for Connecting to an ISP

Here's a quick checklist you should go through before you proceed:

- How will you connect to an ISP? Modem, AirPort, router, proxy server, and so on.

- If not a modem, what is the address of the connecting device? (Just write it down; it will be explained later.)

- Have you been assigned an address for your computer? (This, too, will be explained later.)

- If you will use a dialup modem, do you have it (or is it built into your computer)?

- For a telephone modem, do you have an RJ11 cord; for other wired devices, do you have an RJ45 cord?

- If necessary, do you have a power cord and connection for an external modem?

What You Need to Get Going

Making the Connection

The connection between your modem or other device and your Internet service provider can be via POTS (plain old telephone service), a digital telephone line (ISDN, or more likely DSL), cable television, or even satellite. Not all connections are available in all areas. Some, such as DSL and ISDN, are useful only within a certain distance from a telephone switch. Others, such as cable television, are available only where the service exists. Your neighbor may be able to have DSL, and you may not. You have to check.

Dialup Connections

Dialup connections run at 55 kilobits per second (Kbps) as a maximum; practically, such connections are often around 40 Kbps. The other connections are faster and, most important, they are always on. You do not dial up or connect each time you want to use the service. When you consider that you may want to keep your computer on at all times, such an always-on service is valuable.

Always-On Connections

Many people have noted that DSL and cable create a very different experience in using the Internet when compared with dialup connections, and that experience differs not so much in speed but in the fact that it is always on. Features such as network time (which you can use with Mac OS X—see the section on setting date and time in Chapter 6, "Setting Preferences") are available to you. The integrated help that Mac OS X has works best with always-on connections: a mouse click brings the latest information, not the beeps of a modem dialing up. Of course, the speed matters, too. Video over the Internet actually works with higher speeds. It is basically a prototype on dialup connections, but on high-speed connections it is real. Internet telephony also relies on always-on connections. They are clearly the way to go. The pricing for telecommunications is changing every day—more than one person has discovered that high-speed always-on Internet connectivity is cheaper than having a second phone line to dial into an ISP.

In investigating connectivity, always ask whether a service is bidirectional. High-speed connections using cable and satellites sometimes are unidirectional: they are high speed for downloads from the Internet, but low speed—sometimes even requiring a telephone connection—for uploading to the Internet (that is, for sending email and requesting Web pages).

Finding and Using an ISP

If you are connecting through a network, the Internet service provider has been obtained by the network coordinator in most cases. If not, you will need to open an account for yourself. Your computer may ship with one or more ISPs' setup programs preinstalled. Alternatively, you may have a disk or a special offer from America Online, EarthLink, or another provider.

The basic Mac OS X installation will help you locate an ISP and open an account if you want. You will be walked through each step of the process described in this section.

Checking the Access

The ISP you use needs to be accessible from your computer using the connection that you choose. For most individuals, that means a modem and telephone line or cable connection. If it is a telephone line, choose an ISP whose telephone access number is cheapest for your calls. If you travel and need to access your account from several places, consider whether you know what those places will be—home and work, for example—or whether you need broader coverage, such as home, work, and on the road.

The services provided by ISPs are basically very similar for individuals; the issue of the cost of telephone calls is usually paramount. Check out ISPs with toll-free numbers, as well as the possibility of using several ISPs. You will see how to set up multiple ISP connections in the later section "Multihoming." Likewise, if you have a cable connection, you may have no choice of ISP. Your cable may be connected to one ISP that the cable company has selected.

Opening Your Internet Account

You typically set up your Internet account online; you will need a credit card to do so. Many ISPs also accept purchase orders and other forms of payment. It is usually easiest to set up an account using a credit card and then use the ISP's online assistance screens to modify the billing method.

To find an ISP, talk to other people in your area. You can do research online as well, using a friend's computer or a library's public access Internet terminals. The library may be a very fruitful adventure because you will typically find local people there who have experience with their own Internet connections, and you will often find them willing to share their experiences with you.

The connection between the device that connects you to your ISP (modem, router, AirPort, proxy server, and so on) and your ISP is normally over a wire. This can be a telephone cable, a television cable, a frame relay connection, ISDN, DSL, T-1, or other means. If you are using a dialup modem, it is over a telephone line. You may need an extra line or an extra connection to accommodate this. In the other cases, your network administrator (which may be you) will need to coordinate with the ISP as to what types of connections are available. That coordination has nothing to do with Mac OS X.

In order to use the ISP, you will normally need a user ID and password. These will be associated with an account that is set up in your name (or your organization's name). Make certain that you keep this information safe and secure. If you are converting from another operating system or computer, you may have your password stored in an encrypted form. It will do you no good to know that your password is ●●●●●●●●; you must know the unencrypted form to reenter it.

Types of Accounts

There may be restrictions placed on your account. Sometimes these are based on the type of service you have ordered (it may be off-hours or limited in other ways). Other times, these restrictions are based on other criteria. Internet accounts may be designated for individual use in residences; other accounts may be oriented toward businesses.

In the United States, telephone companies make a distinction between residential and business users. This distinction tends to apply to Internet access, too. Thus, home-based businesses may find substantial differences in the prices they pay depending on whether their Internet access is designated as residential or business.

Cable companies and other vendors often distinguish between residential and small business as opposed to commercial clients. One of the important distinctions between commercial and residential/small business accounts may be whether you can run a Web server on your computer. Most ISPs offer a Web hosting service: your Web site runs on their computers. However, if you want to run your own Web site that is accessible to people who are not connected directly to your computer, you may need to open a commercial account.

A Web site that is accessible to people on your local area network is invisible to the outside world and, therefore, is not subject to these rules.

Checklist for Finding and Using an ISP

Here's a quick checklist you should go through before you proceed:

- ■ If you are connecting through a network, does that network provide Internet access? Do you need to register to enable your access?

- ■ Do you have an ISP account?

- ■ If not, and if you are connecting through a modem, do you have an ISP you want to use? If not, do you want to use the default ISP that Apple's installer will connect you to?

- ■ If you need to set up an ISP account, do you have a credit card ready?

- ■ Once you have an ISP account, do you have your user ID and password?

How Internet Connections Work

For all its capabilities, the Internet is remarkably simple in its design. In fact, that is one of the main reasons for its success. Three basic aspects of the Internet's design matter to you in managing your Internet setup.

Connections and Communications

When you place a typical telephone call, a connection is made between you and the other party. If you traced through the telephone switches, you would find a path of copper wire and fiber-optic cable that went all the way from your telephone to the other party's, even if it is halfway around the world. For the period of your call, that physical connection would be maintained.

The Internet is a packet-switched network. That means that rather than establishing a direct connection and maintaining it for the duration of the call (or data transfer), the messages are split up into small packets. Each packet is addressed to the recipient and transferred independently over the Internet. When they arrive at their destination, the packets are reassembled into the message as a whole.

This mechanism, called TCP/IP (Transmission Control Protocol/Internet Protocol), allows the Internet to function very efficiently. Its network resources process many, many packets, but they are rarely tied up for long periods of time by long messages, because the long messages are all broken up. The packets are routed around the Internet from computer to computer until they arrive at their destinations. Each Internet computer (or node) receives packets and sends them on along the best route currently available. It is in this way that packets are routed around problems on the Internet—they may actually go far out of their way, but they almost always get where they're going.

What You Need to Know

The basis of the Internet's communications is TCP/IP. It runs on your computer (people refer to it as a TCP/IP stack). It also is implemented through the computers all over the network. TCP/IP is an Internet concept; it is not specific to Mac OS X.

IP Addresses

In order for TCP/IP to work, each device connected to the Internet requires a unique address. These are called IP addresses. IP addresses consist of a quartet of numbers separated by dots, such as 1.2.3.4, 192.168.1.3, and so forth. There are two kinds of IP addresses, static and dynamic.

Static IP Addresses

In order to send a message to a device connected to the Internet, you need to know its IP address. Many devices that are connected all the time to the Internet have static IP addresses—they never change. Although it is awkward and you wouldn't normally use this format, you can send a message to a device using its IP address.

If you are in an enterprise or organization with its own network, you may be assigned an IP address. You will need to know that as you proceed with the setup of your Internet connection.

The IP address may be written on the plate of your network connection where you connect your cable. If you are replacing another computer, you may find it written or taped to the case of the previous computer or one of its cables.

Dynamic IP Addresses

In many cases, IP addresses are assigned dynamically when you connect to the Internet or to a local area network. For example, when you dial in to an Internet service provider, you normally are provided automatically with a dynamic IP address until you log out. You generally don't have to worry about this. Likewise, some local area networks use a protocol called DHCP or BootP to dynamically assign addresses. There are many reasons for doing this, including the fact that it can make network administration easier.

Although it is frequently the case that dialup connections use dynamic IP addresses and network connections may or may not, that is not always the case. Sometimes it is necessary to have a known IP address at all times. This may happen for security reasons; it also is necessary if you are running a Web site or other Internet service to which people need to reliably connect at all times. Many dialup ISPs will provide you with a static IP address for an extra fee. In

How Internet Connections Work

addition, many DSL or cable connections use DHCP so that each time you connect, you receive a different IP address from your ISP. If your computer is always on and connected to the Internet, you, in effect, have a static IP address for days or weeks at a time.

What You Need to Know

When you are connected to the Internet, you always have an IP address. Whether it is the same as yesterday's (as in static) or a new one (dynamic) doesn't matter. Dynamic IP addresses are generated by ISPs (for dialup users) and by routers and other elements of local area networks.

Domain Name System

Using IP addresses for communicating over the Internet can be awkward. Not only can they be confusing (132.22.5.2), but they also can change, as in the case of dynamic IP addresses. The Domain Name System handles these problems.

The Domain Name System (DNS) is implemented throughout the Internet by many of its component computers. It serves two basic functions:

■ Given a domain name such as yourcompany.com, it converts it to an IP address.

■ When a message is received at an IP address that is assigned to a domain name, the system routes it accordingly.

Both of these functions are implemented using name servers. A name server is a computer with a known IP address that is associated with a domain name. Internet routing tables are maintained throughout the Internet to translate yourcompany.com to the IP address of its nameserver. (There actually are two—a primary and a secondary name server—so that the system works even if one computer is down.) These routing tables with the link between the domain name and the name servers' addresses are duplicated all over the Internet so that they are widely available.

When you register a domain name, you provide the IP address of the primary and secondary name server. If your ISP registers your domain name, that will be done for you. In setting up your domain, you specify various contacts—billing, administrative, and technical. Make certain that you or someone in your organization is listed as one of the contacts. That will allow you to make modifications, such as updating your name server IP addresses, that you will need to do if you switch ISPs, for instance. If you are leaving an ISP (particularly if there are hard feelings), you may encounter reluctance on their part to changing your name server addresses to your new ISP. If you can do it yourself, you eliminate that potential problem.

The second function is performed by the name server identified with a domain name. When traffic arrives at that name server, it is distributed to a mail server, a Web server, and so forth.

The domain name is something like yourcompany.com. The name server differentiates between www.yourcompany.com and ftp.yourcompany.com, and any other variation.

What You Need to Know

You need to know the IP address of the primary and secondary name server for your outgoing messages. That is the IP address of name servers at your ISP or on your internal network. Ask your network coordinator or ISP for the IP address of the name servers to use. These are not the IP addresses for your domain's name servers; they are the name servers to use to resolve other domain names.

Internet Connections

There are two common types of connections to the Internet: dialup (switched) and direct connections via cable, DSL, ISDN, leased lines, frame relay, or other technologies. You may use either one or both. It is common for PowerBook and iBook users to use a modem connection when traveling, and a network connection at home or the office.

Your connection to a network hub, router, or proxy server can be dialup, via a LAN, or wireless. It is the connection from that device to the Internet (or from your modem to your ISP) that is being discussed here. You can have a wireless connection to an AirPort that, in turn, has a dialup or direct connection to the Internet.

This section addresses the four standard types of Internet connections:

- Dialup connections (PPP)

- Always-on connections (DSL and cable modems) directly to your computer

- Always-on connections through a network router

- Hybrid (PPPoE)

After examining the four types of Internet connections, this section concludes with information on configuring proxy servers, routers, and firewalls, as well as multihoming.

The first step in each case is to configure your TCP/IP connection using the TCP/IP pane of the Network preference panel in System Preferences. You can use the Location pop-up menu to select from among existing locations; you can also save a configuration as a location. That is useful in configuring alternate setups for connecting to a local area network at work or school, via a modem to a local Internet service provider at home and via a modem to a toll-free Internet service provider number when you are traveling.

Using Dialup Connections (PPP)

PPP (Point-to-Point Protocol) is the protocol that is used to connect via a modem and a dialup line. To connect this way, you need a modem (internal or external) that is connected to a telephone.

TIP

In arranging your work area, remember that external modems usually require a power supply, too.

Getting Ready

Before starting, be sure you have the following information:

- **The phone number to dial**   This is not your ISP's help desk or billing office. It is the number of a modem (part of a modem bank) at your ISP. If you dial the number, you should hear the high-pitched squeals of a modem at the other end. (If you are having problems with your connection, try dialing this number from a regular phone. If you hear a busy signal, a human voice, or silence, your number is wrong or there is a problem at the ISP's end.)

- **Your Internet account name or login ID**   This may or may not be the same as your email name. It is your overall account name. (It normally appears on your bill from your ISP.)

- **Your Internet account password**   This was given to you when you established your account. Some ISPs allow you to change it; others do not. Capitalization always matters in passwords, so be careful.

- **Domain name server address**   You should have one or two DNS addresses given to you when you open your ISP account. If you do not have them, call customer support or look on your ISP's Web site—they usually list these settings. (You may not be able to connect without them; so if you need to look at your ISP's Web site, you will have to do so from another computer.)

- **Your domain name**   This is optional.

- **Your computer's IP address**   This is also optional and you usually do not provide it.

- **The type of modem you are using**   If you have an internal modem and do not know anything more than that, don't worry, that will be sufficient.

Write this information down and put it securely away. You can store it—encrypted—in your login settings; but if you need to retype it, you need the original password. Once this information is entered, you do not have to re-enter it unless it changes over time, and it usually doesn't unless you change ISPs or are notified of a new phone number to call.

Setting Network Preferences for Dialup Access

Your Network preferences may have been configured during installation. If not—or if you need to change them—here is what you do.

Using System Preferences, open the Network pane, as shown in Figure 12-1.

In the TCP/IP pane, select Using PPP from the Configure pop-up menu. Note that when you do so, the tabs across the top of the pane may change; they are different for each type of configuration.

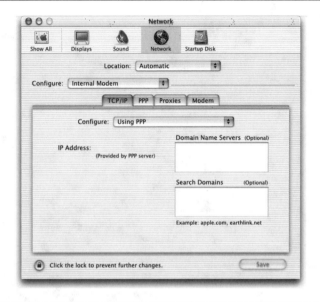

FIGURE 12-1   Set your PPP as your TCP/IP configuration.

You can select the modem that you want to configure. Many Macintosh computers today come with an internal modem installed. If yours is external, you may need to select it from this pop-up menu.

If you have the addresses of domain name servers or the name of a search domain, you can enter them here. Domain name servers are IP addresses—the familiar quartet of numbers, such as 192.168.1.2. Search domains are normally two-part domains, such as myserver.net or myisp.com. Click the PPP tab in Network preferences to enter the information shown in Figure 12-2.

You can name your service provider in the first field. This is optional, but it can help you keep track of multiple configurations. The telephone number to dial is required; an alternate number (for when the first is busy or otherwise unreachable) is desirable. Use a comma in a telephone number to insert a one-second pause. For example, if you need to dial a special number such as 9 before the call, enter **9,555-1212** so that the telephone system can have time to switch you to an outside line. You can put several commas together if your telephone system is slow: **9,,,,,555-1212** will insert a five-second pause.

You need to enter your account name and password. You can save your password by clicking the checkbox. If it is saved, anyone can log in from your computer. It is more secure (but somewhat of a nuisance) to have to retype your password each time you log in. Depending on whether your computer is in a secure environment or in a relatively public area, you can make the appropriate choice.

As noted previously, this account may or may not be the same as your email account. This is your connection account or your PPP account—those terms or others like them are what your

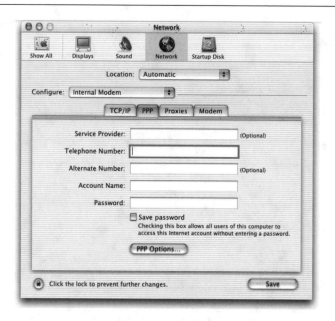

FIGURE 12-2   Account and telephone number information is entered in the PPP pane.

ISP will use when referring to it. PPP options can be set with the button at the bottom of the pane; it opens the sheet shown in the following illustration.

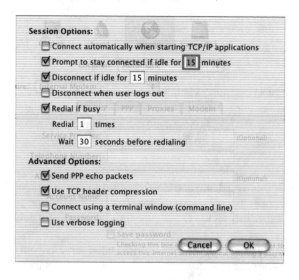

PPP options are divided into Session and Advanced options. The Session options affect your dialing and connection options:

- **Connect automatically**   When an application such as a Web browser or an email program wants to connect to the Internet, this option will control whether that happens automatically or not. You might want to turn this off if you are disconnected from a telephone line temporarily. It will save a delay followed by a message that no dial tone can be found. Once the connection is established, it can be used by other applications—you do not need to reconnect for email, Web, and other services.

- **Prompt to stay connected**   You can specify the number of minutes to which this option applies. If you pay by the minute for your connection (either the telephone call or the Internet connection, or both), you may want to have a prompt to remind you that your connection is open but idle.

- **Disconnect if idle**   This is a more drastic approach. The connection is simply dropped if you are idle for a specified period of time. (You can combine this and the previous option so that you are prompted if the connection is idle for 10 minutes and disconnected if it is idle for 15 minutes; of course, you should use your own values.)

- **Redial**   Finally, the redialing options let you specify how many times to redial and how long to wait between tries. If your ISP routinely is busy when you call, you may want to set redial to a large number—or use another ISP.

The issue of staying connected to an ISP has many aspects to it. Depending on how your telephone calls are charged, it may make sense to stay connected for long periods of idleness. Some telephone rate plans have a high charge for the first minute or two followed by lower charges for subsequent minutes. As a result, frequent but short dialup sessions can cost you more than a long session.

Advanced options should normally be left as they are unless you are having problems with your connection. If you are, your network manager or Internet service provider may ask you to check or uncheck these options. Finally, you need to configure your modem. Use the Modem tab to open the pane shown in Figure 12-3.

You can select the type of modem you are using from the pop-up menu. If Sound is on, you will hear the characteristic beeps of the modem as it connects, as well as the dialing tones. Turning Sound on can be helpful if you are having difficulties connecting. If, for example, the telephone number is incorrect, you may hear someone answer the telephone. You can also set tone or pulse dialing here.

Connecting

If you have set the option to connect automatically, you open your connection to the Internet by sending email, checking for it, using a browser to look at a Web page, or otherwise

Internet Connections

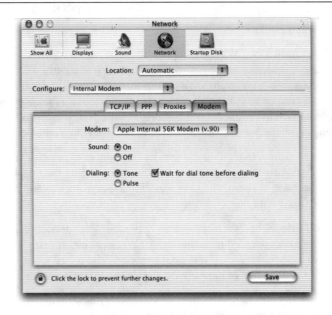

FIGURE 12-3   Select your modem before connecting.

requesting an Internet connection. To manually connect, you can run the Internet Connect application, which is located inside the Applications folder. Select the configuration with which you want to connect from the pop-up menu, as shown in the following illustration, and then click Connect.

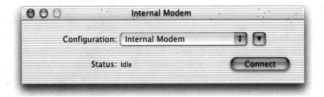

If you need to temporarily modify a telephone number or password, you can use the disclose triangle to expand this window, as shown in the following illustration. Note that other changes (such as to the account name) must be made in the Network pane of System Preferences as described in the earlier section, "Setting Network Preferences for Dialup Access."

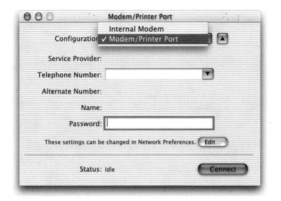

Troubleshooting

If you suspect problems setting the modem type, contact the modem manufacturer or your dealer for more information. You can try the ISP, but they may not be able to help if the problem is with your modem; however, some ISPs have a "hot list" of modems that are currently causing problems with their service.

If you manage to connect but the line drops, contact your ISP. Depending on how the line drop occurs, that could be a modem problem on your end, a modem problem at the ISP, or a combination. The ISP support staff may be able to provide step-by-step assistance to narrow down the problem.

A foolproof way of troubleshooting involves using another computer and/or another login ID. Go to a computer that does connect properly over a dialup connection. Reset the login ID password and other information to what you have typed in. (Of course, write down the settings you have changed so you can restore them.) If you can log in, the information is correct and it is your modem configuration and/or connection that is wrong.

Likewise, you can use another valid account name and password on your own computer. If you can log in, your configuration and connection are correct, but your account information (or phone number) is wrong.

Using DSL or Cable Modems Connected Directly to Your Computer

If you have a DSL telephone or cable television connection to the Internet, this section shows you how to connect. Physically, you need a cable (called a *patch cable*) that connects your cable or DSL modem, which has an RJ45 socket to your computer's Ethernet port that has another RJ45 socket. If your Ethernet port is already connected to a network or hub, you do not need an additional connection (provided, of course, that the network or hub is connected to the Internet).

Note that a cable or DSL modem can be connected to a router, and thence via a network to your computer; in that case, skip to the next section. Note, too, that if your provider uses PPPoE, you need to also follow the steps in the section "PPPoE" later in this chapter.

Internet Connections

Getting Ready

Before starting, be sure you have the following information:

- Does your provider use DHCP or BootP, or are you provided with a static IP address?

- If you have a static IP address, you need it.

- If you have a static IP address, you need a subnet mask.

- If you have a static IP address, you need a router address.

- Does your ISP automatically supply DNS addresses?

- If your ISP does not automatically supply DNS addresses, you need at least one. One or two DNS addresses should have been given to you when you open your ISP account. If you do not have them, call customer support or look on your ISP's Web site—they usually list these settings. (You cannot connect without them; so if you look at your ISP's Web site, you will need to do so from another computer.)

- Your domain name. This is optional.

You can ask for this information from customer support if it is not provided in the information you are given when you open your account. It is standard information—it has nothing to do with Macintosh computers.

BootP or DHCP can configure the IP address automatically; otherwise, you enter it manually. Likewise, DNS information can be configured automatically or entered manually. The following sections show you how to do both. Note that you can mix and match—you can use DHCP to automatically set your IP address, but you can manually set your DNS address, and vice versa. Thus, you can combine parts of each of the two sections that follow.

Your BootP, DHCP, and DNS choices are determined by your ISP and the equipment that it operates, as well as the type of account you have. You must enter the values for your specific account at your ISP.

DHCP or BootP

Open System Preferences and click Network. Choose BootP or DHCP from the pop-up button, as shown in Figure 12-4.

The Ethernet address in the lower left of this pane is the address of your Ethernet card. If you have more than one, you will have more than one entry in the Configure pop-up menu, and you can select which card you want to configure.

Cable modems often use DHCP. The DHCP and BootP panes are identical except for the fact that you can enter an optional DHCP Client ID on the DHCP pane. Note, however, that the protocols are not identical: you must choose the appropriate one. Your ISP will tell you which to use.

For many cable or DSL providers, once you have selected DHCP or BootP, your job is done: all other numbers are assigned automatically as soon as you connect. If you do need to enter domain name servers' IP addresses or search domains, your ISP will tell you so and provide the

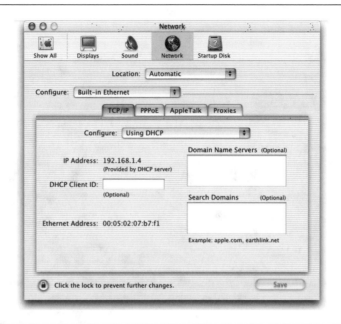

FIGURE 12-4 Setting preferences for BootP or DHCP

information. Remember that ISPs like self-configuring protocols such as DHCP just as much as you do—it means less customer support for them!

DHCP with Fixed IP Addressing

If you need to use fixed or static IP addresses, choose Using DHCP With Fixed IP Address, as shown in Figure 12-5.

To use a fixed IP address, you need to have one provided by your ISP. You might have a fixed IP address if you are running a Web server on your computer. You might also have a fixed IP address for security reasons; access to a database or to proprietary systems may be limited to known IP addresses. Enter the IP address and the optional domain name servers and search domains.

Manual Configuration

Configure your TCP/IP settings manually, as shown in Figure 12-6, if you are asked to do so.

The entries on this window will be provided by your ISP or your network administrator. These terms are general network terms; they are not specific to Macintosh computers.

Using DSL or Cable Modems Through a Network or Router

If you are connecting through a network or router to a cable or DSL modem, the process is very similar. What you need to know is that in most cases the router itself is configured as a DHCP client

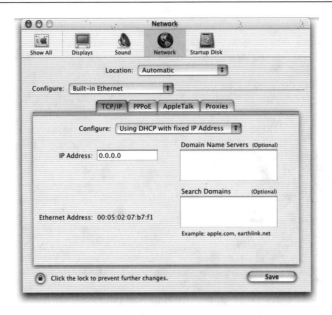

FIGURE 12-5   You can use fixed IP addresses with DHCP.

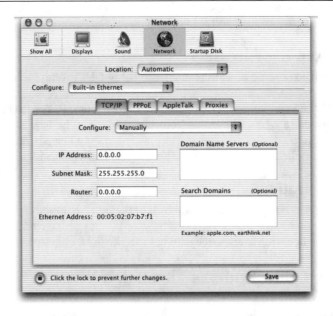

FIGURE 12-6   Manual configurations let you adjust everything to specific needs.

of the ISP, and your computer is a DHCP client of the router. In the previous section, you merely had to deal with your computer and the ISP; now you have to deal with the intervening router.

If the router and network function properly—that is, if other computers on the network can connect to the Internet—all you need to do is configure your own computer. If the other computers cannot connect (or if there are no other computers), you have more variables to consider.

If you have problems, you must make it very clear when talking to the ISP whether you are referring to the router as a client (the ISP's point of view) or the router as your server (your point of view). This matters most in manual configurations, such as that shown previously in Figure 12-6. If you are connecting directly to an ISP, the router address is the address of the ISP's router. If you are connecting via a network and router, the router address is your network router, not that of the ISP.

PPPoE

As you may have noticed in the preceding sections, PPP connections require a user ID and password; always-on connections do not. In general, always-on connections are installed by the cable or telephone company, and they know where their cables go. Thus, they may not know who is accessing their Internet services, but they know what customer premises are being used. That is sufficient security for many purposes.

PPPoE introduces the concept of sessions to always-on Internet connections. Although the physical connection may always be there, the connectivity lapses periodically and must be restarted with a password.

PPPoE—PPP over Ethernet—combines the password security of PPP with always-on connectivity. If you have installed a DSL or cable connection, you may also need to configure PPPoE over that connection. If you do, your ISP will tell you. (Telephone companies offering DSL services tend to use PPPoE more frequently than do cable companies.) Click the PPPoE tab on the Network preferences pane, as shown in Figure 12-7.

Your account name must be entered here. You may identify the service provider or service name for your own purposes, and you may enter your password here. If you do not, you will be prompted for it each time a PPPoE session is initiated. PPPoE options can be set with the button at the bottom of this pane, as shown here:

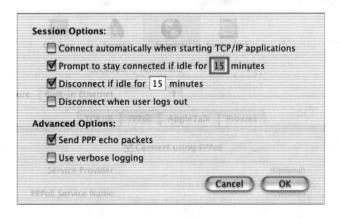

Session Options:
- Connect automatically when starting TCP/IP applications
- ☑ Prompt to stay connected if idle for 15 minutes
- ☑ Disconnect if idle for 15 minutes
- Disconnect when user logs out

Advanced Options:
- ☑ Send PPP echo packets
- Use verbose logging

Cancel   OK

FIGURE 12-7   PPPoE provides password security over always-on connections.

The Session options affect connection options:

- **Connect automatically**   When an application such as a Web browser or an email program wants to connect to the Internet, this option will control whether that happens automatically or not. You might want to turn this off if you are disconnected from a telephone line temporarily. It will save a delay followed by a message that no dial tone can be found. Once the connection is established, it can be used by other applications—you do not need to reconnect for email, Web, and other services.

- **Prompt to stay connected**   You can specify the number of minutes to which this option applies. If you pay by the minute for your connection (either the telephone call or the Internet connection), you may want to have a prompt to remind you that your connection is open but idle.

- **Disconnect if idle**   This is a more drastic approach. The connection is simply dropped if you are idle for a specified period of time. (You can combine this and the previous option so that you are prompted if the connection is idle for 10 minutes and disconnected if it is idle for 15 minutes; of course, you should use your own values.)

- **Disconnect when user logs out**   Finally, you can choose to disconnect when a Mac OS X user logs out. This is a security feature that is useful in many cases.

Using Proxy Servers and Firewalls

Proxy servers have two basic purposes:

- They can be used to control Web access.

- They can be used to improve performance.

In each case, the same basic procedure is followed. When a request is made for an Internet service, it is directed to a proxy server rather than directly to the specified address. Thus, if you have a proxy server for the Web configured at IP address 192.168.1.55, a request to http:// www.apple.com/ would be sent not to Apple's site but instead to the proxy server, which would then pass the request on to http://www.apple.com/. Responses are routed back to the proxy server and from there to the original requestor.

Proxy servers can be configured not to pass certain requests on. Requests to known sites may be passed on automatically; alternatively, requests to known undesirable sites may be dropped. Proxy servers can also cache information. Just as a Web browser caches pages, the proxy server can cache pages at the network level.

Proxy servers can be configured for any Internet service, and they need to be configured for each computer on the network. You use the Proxies tab in Network preferences to do so, as shown in Figure 12-8. Note that the entry field at the bottom allows you to bypass the proxy server for specified domains and hosts. Proxy servers can be hardware or software, or both.

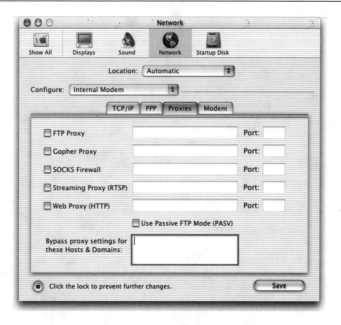

FIGURE 12-8   Use proxy servers to control access and improve efficiency.

Internet Connections

Firewalls can also be hardware or software; today's routers often include firewall capabilities. Firewalls block types of access into and out of the router. Thus, you can configure your router's firewall not to allow access to Web sites; a more common configuration is not to allow access from the Internet to your internal network.

Proxy server configuration is done with the Network preferences Proxies pane, as well as on the proxy server or router. Firewall configuration is done entirely on the router or firewall; no computer on the network is aware that a firewall exists.

CAUTION   *When using an always-on connection, you should always have some type of firewall protection. Software firewalls for individual computers are not expensive; as noted previously, routers provide this capability. It is not just that someone could access your computer's data. More serious is the threat that a hacker (or automated hacking tool) could use your computer's processor to send out millions of copies of junk email or to cause other damage. This could result in you losing your Internet access.*

Multihoming

Use the Advanced configuration, as shown in Figure 12-9, to set up multiple configurations. (Most people need not worry about this.)

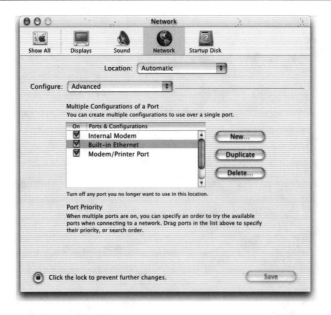

FIGURE 12-9   Advanced networking options allow multiple connections.

If you have configured multiple ports or connections, you can use this pane to prioritize them, as well as to turn them on and off easily. Mac OS X attempts to make TCP/IP connections as necessary. It uses these ports and configurations in the order that you specify. If one becomes unavailable, it automatically will try the next one.

This means you can set up all of your possible connections—wireless, dialup, networked, and so forth—and Mac OS X will automatically use whatever it can (hence "Automatic" in the location pop-up menu). Of course, if you specify one location, only it will be used.

This automatic port use also handles the case in which one type of communication fails and another one needs to take over the connection without interruption. If you have a high-speed connection that is unreliable, you can specify it as your first choice, and a slower but more reliable connection as your second.

Troubleshooting Internet Connections

Network Utility, located in the Utilities folder inside Applications, provides a host of diagnostics that you can use in troubleshooting connection problems. It provides a graphical user interface to standard Unix network tools. Each is shown here along with a brief description. Since these are standard debugging tools, network administrators should be familiar with them.

If you are trying to work to resolve a problem, be aware that the central pane of the Network Utility window can easily be sent to a help desk or technical support area. You can follow these steps to paste the output from one of these commands into an email message:

1. Click in the central pane where the report information is displayed.

2. Choose Select All from the Edit menu.

3. Choose Copy.

4. Go into an email program, create a new message, and then choose Paste from the Edit menu to paste the report into the message.

Alternatively, you can use Mac OS X services to do the same thing:

1. Click in the central pane.

2. Choose Select All.

3. From the Services submenu of the Network Utility application menu, choose Mail and then Mail Text. The selected text will be placed in a new email message.

Of course, you can manually select part of the report. In most cases, though, a troubleshooter would like to see everything. The reports are plain text, so formatting and indentation are achieved with spaces. This means they can be sent and read by any email program.

Troubleshooting Internet Connections

Info

The first pane is shown in the next illustration. You can view information for any of the Ethernet cards installed on your computer. (For most people, there is one Ethernet card.)

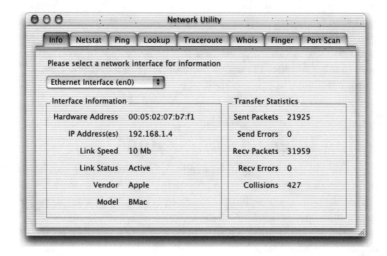

One of the most valuable items of information on this report is the Link Speed. In 10/100Base-T networks, computers and routers can run either at 10 or 100 Mbps (megabits per second). This report will tell you which speed is in use on your computer.

Netstat

Netstat shows the status of your network connection, including what has recently been received and sent, as shown in Figure 12-10. (The information about data sent and received is presented at the packet level; the content of those packets is not part of the report.)

Ping

Ping helps you determine whether another computer is communicating and how long it takes messages to get there and back. Figure 12-11 shows Ping output.

Ping sends a certain number of requests to the designated computer. When each returns, you see how long it took. As you can see from Figure 12-11, the roundtrip time for a ping to a given IP address varies somewhat, but it is normally within a fairly small range. If it is not, there may be network difficulties.

Lookup

Lookup provides domain name information, as shown in Figure 12-12. The pop-up menu shows the various items that you can check with Lookup. These items include domain names and IP addresses for various servers supporting that domain.

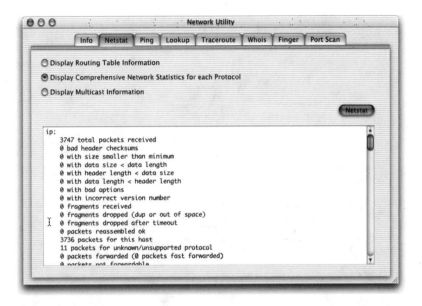

FIGURE 12-10   Netstat shows you the status of your network connection and information about recent packets.

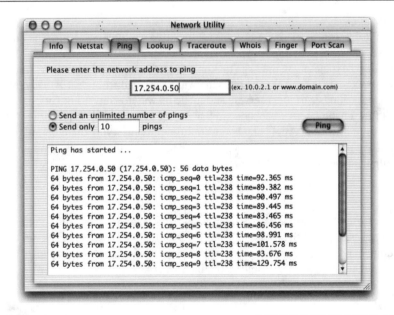

FIGURE 12-11   Ping lets you see the status of other computers.

Troubleshooting Internet
Connections

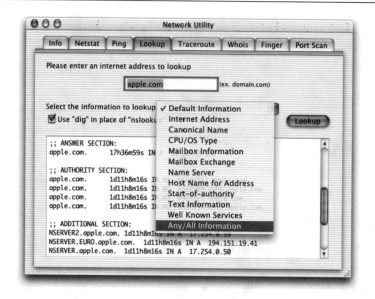

FIGURE 12-12 Lookup information shows you who owns a domain and where it is hosted.

Traceroute

The traceroute utility can be extremely useful when network problems occur. The output shown in Figure 12-13 shows a traceroute to Apple.

You can infer the route of the message to Apple from the names of the servers through which it passes. This traceroute is typical. The message was originated from near Albany, New York. It wandered around a number of local servers and made its way to New York City (steps 7 and 8). From there, it flew on the Internet backbone to San Jose, California (10, 11, and 12). After a couple of local bounces, it arrived at Apple and bounced through two servers there before reaching its destination. When problems arise in network routing tables, administrators sometimes ask for traceroute output so they can see where messages go astray.

Whois

The Whois command lets you look up domain name information, as shown in Figure 12-14. The default whois server has the root-level Internet information: you can check out the registered owner of a domain here. You can use other whois servers (including those on a local area network) to see private domains that are not visible on the Internet at large.

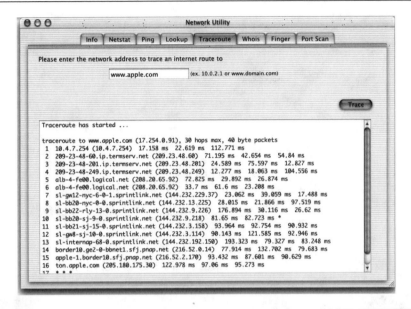

FIGURE 12-13   Traceroute for Apple shows the Internet's backbone.

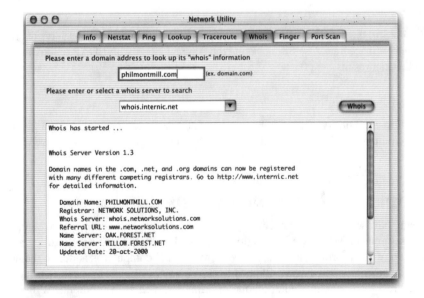

FIGURE 12-14   Whois provides domain registration information.

Troubleshooting Internet
Connections

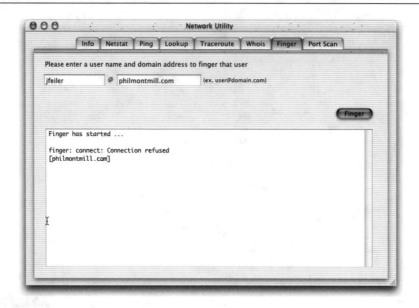

FIGURE 12-15   Finger does not always provide results.

Finger

Finger is a protocol that lets you look up a user name. As shown in Figure 12-15, results frequently are incomplete or inaccurate. Use Sherlock and the Address Book with LDAP to look up names, as they provide better results.

Port Scan

Finally, the Port Scan utility, shown in Figure 12-16, lets you scan open ports on a given IP address or domain name. This is normally used for diagnostic purposes. If you need it, you know how to use it.

Moving from Installed Connections

If you already have an Internet connection, you can use the information from that connection to help you set up your Mac OS X connection. If your Mac OS X computer is using the same connection, copy the information exactly. If your Mac OS X computer is added to the network in addition to the other computer, you will need to copy some information—such as router address and DNS address—and possibly enter unique information, such as the computer's IP address if it is not generated automatically.

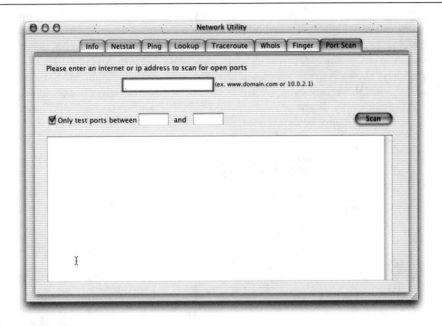

FIGURE 12-16   Port Scan provides advanced diagnostics.

Mac OS 9

On Mac OS, open the TCP/IP control panel, as shown here:

If you are connecting via a network, choose the Ethernet item from the Connect pop-up menu. Here you will find information about your Ethernet connection—the Name Server addresses (DNS), local computer address, form of connection, and so forth. Write down all of the information in this window to use in configuring your Mac OS X connection.

The IP address shown is the IP address in effect for this computer at the time you look at the TCP/IP control panel. If you are using DHCP or BootP, that address may change, so do not enter it. It is for information only. If you are connecting via PPP (dialup), choose the PPP item from the Connect via pop-up menu, as shown here:

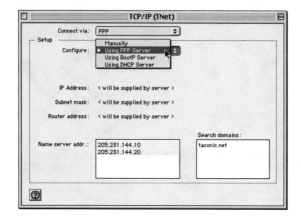

This will enable you to find the DNS addresses. Everything else is supplied automatically when the connection is made.

Windows

In Windows, open the Network control panel, as shown here:

You need to examine the properties for a TCP/IP adapter. Click the one you believe you are using, and then select Properties, as shown here:

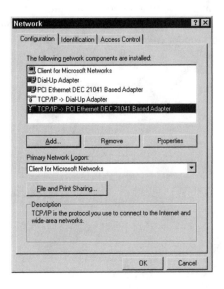

You will see the DNS addresses, as shown in the next illustration (you may need to click the DNS Configuration tab if it is not already selected).

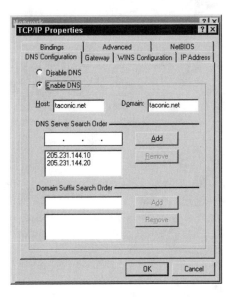

Click the other tabs to find other settings that may matter to you.

Moving from Installed
Connections

Summary

This chapter has provided details on setting up your computer for the Internet. Setup Assistant runs automatically when you install Mac OS X, so this all may be done for you. If it is not—or if your Internet connection environment changes—you will need to go through these steps.

Chapter 13

Setting Up a Network Server

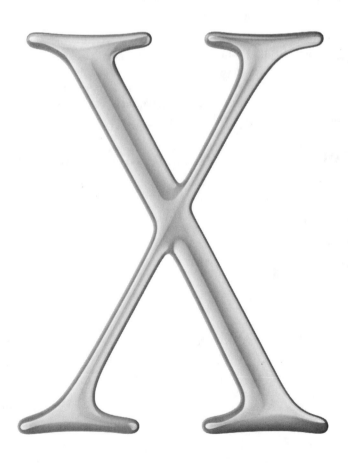

As is the case with most computers and operating systems today, networking is built into Mac OS X. Unlike some other systems (such as Windows 2000), the distinction between the client or workstation software and the network administrator software is not large—mostly a matter of packaging, in fact.

This chapter helps you set up a server on a local area network.

■ First, it describes the three models of networking and sharing you will encounter.

■ It then shows you how to configure your computer as a server on your LAN.

■ The most frequent use of a network server is to share files, and the next section of this chapter focuses on file sharing.

■ The last part of this chapter describes some of the tools available in Mac OS X Server. Basic networking and file sharing are built into Mac OS X; Mac OS X Server provides additional tools for resource sharing, hosting Internet services, and customizing the desktop environments of networked users.

Note that this chapter focuses on a local area network server; Internet servers are discussed in the next chapter. The distinction between the two is not nearly as great as you might expect since you can run a mail or a Web server on a local area network and never have it interact with the Internet. The Mac OS X mail server (Sendmail) is described in the "Using Mac OS X Server" section, later in this chapter, and the Web server in Mac OS X (Apache) is described in Chapter 15, "Setting Up the Web Server."

The Three Models of Networking and Sharing

Three different models of networking and sharing come into play today when you use your computer on a network:

■ Client/server sharing over a network

■ Multiple users on a single computer

■ Multiple computers on a network

NOTE   *These models interact with one another. Sometimes hybrid models occur, as is the case with NetInfo: the second model, multiple users on a single computer, can actually be implemented using the third case, multiple users on a network. To start with, however, the basic models are described here.*

Client/Server Sharing Over a Network

You use your computer as a client of a remote server when you use a browser to access a Web site or when you click Send in your email program, and it communicates with an SMTP mail server at your ISP. In these cases, you are assigned a user name (or allowed to choose it) by the administrator of the remote server. In some cases—such as most public Web sites—you do not even need a user name: anonymous access is allowed.

A client can also be a server in the world of the Internet. If you are a client of an ISP, it, too, is a client—of an even bigger ISP, which is its server. In almost all cases, every computer connected to the Internet is both a client and a server. In Mac OS X, the computer is identified, and so is each user running on the computer—as the next section describes.

Multiple Users on a Single Computer

Mac OS 9 introduced the concept of multiple users on a single Macintosh computer. In that OS it was an option; in Mac OS X it is required. There is at least one user who is designated as having administrative privileges on each computer running Mac OS X. (This is enforced during initial setup.) There may be several users with such privileges, and they may go by various names or types of names: superuser, root user, or owner. A user with administrative privileges can create and remove other users, as well as change their privileges to read, write, and execute files.

Multiple Computers on a Network

A local area network can contain various computers, all of which interact according to the rules that are set up. If a single computer is the server for the network, that computer's administrator winds up controlling all access. However, in most environments (particularly smaller ones) more than one computer, and possibly all, play a server role.

NOTE   *There is a special case in which one computer on a network does indeed have a special role to play. That is the case of the router, which may connect a local area network to another network (such as the Internet). Today, routers are not full-scale computers as they were a few years ago. Instead, they are hubs with built-in firewall and proxy server capabilities; a four-port router sells for under $200. It is, however, in many ways just another computer on the network.*

The Three Models of Networking and Sharing

Configuring Your Computer as a LAN Server

Each of these models of networking comes into play as you configure your computer as a LAN server. You may be using your computer to administer an entire network: other computers can access your computer and its resources subject to the rules that you set. In the extreme case, you set up and control all users on all computers from your computer: the section on NetInfo later in this chapter shows you how.

The first steps are described in this section:

■   Setting or confirming your IP address

■   Turning on AppleTalk

These two steps set up the communications environment in which your computer can become a server.

Setting or Confirming Your IP Address

Mac OS X uses TCP/IP for its communications—either over a local area network or over the Internet. In order to use TCP/IP, you must have an IP address for your computer. If you are not using a network at all, you do not need to worry about a TCP/IP address.

If you are connected to a local area network with a router that provides you Internet access, you will have an IP address when you connect to the Internet. It may be assigned automatically using DHCP or BootP; it also may be assigned manually by your network administrator or Internet service provider.

If you are on a local area network that is not connected to the Internet, you need to provide an IP address for your computer. You can do so using Network system preferences. Click the Network pane in System Preferences and then the TCP/IP tab, as shown in Figure 13-1.

Set the Configure pop-up menu to Manually. Enter a valid address in the first field. For a small network, the appropriate IP address is in the range 192.168.1.1 to 192.168.1.255. Each computer must have a unique IP address. If you use an address in this range, enter a subnet mask of 255.255.255.0. If you are not connecting to the Internet, you do not need to supply a router IP address or any DNS addresses.

Some devices on a local area network may have specific addresses assigned to them. Most commonly, addresses at the low end of the range may be taken; 192.168.1.251 to 192.168.1.255 also frequently are spoken for. If this is the case, number the devices that you control with numbers in the middle, such as 192.168.1.100 to 192.168.1.200.

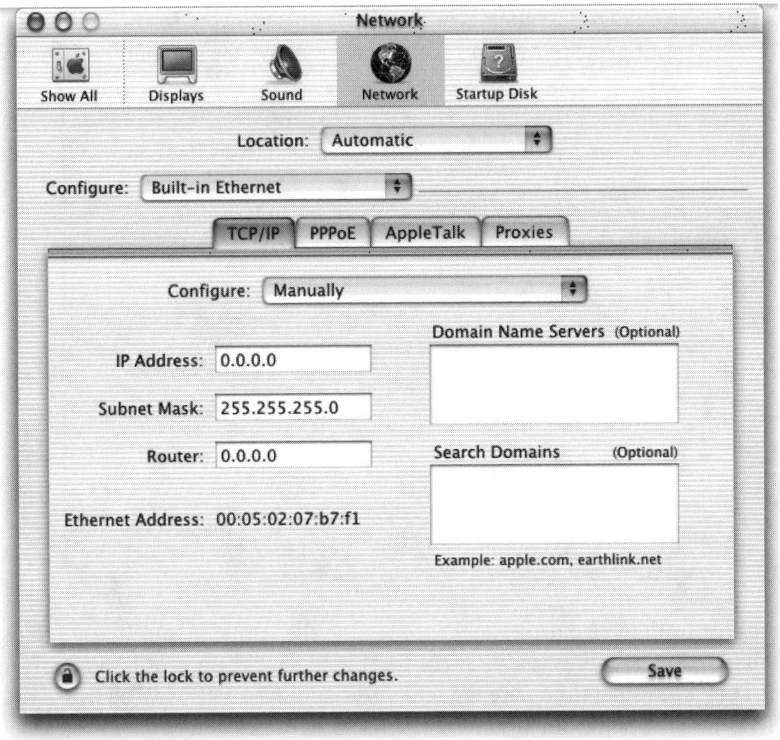

FIGURE 13-1   Set your IP address with the TCP/IP tab of Network preferences.

Setting or Confirming Your IP Address in Mac OS 9

Chapter 11, "Communicating Over a Local Area Network," showed you how to connect as a client to a Mac OS X server if you are running Mac OS X. However, if you are setting up a Mac OS X server, you may have people connecting to it using Mac OS 8 or Mac OS 9 (or Windows). Connections are discussed in the section on file sharing, later in this chapter, but you should know how to check the IP address in these other computers so that you can set a unique IP address in your Mac OS X server.

Remember that if your network is connected to the Internet, DHCP or BootP can be used with most routers to set unique IP addresses automatically, and you do not have to worry about this. The TCP/IP control panel in Mac OS 9 and earlier shows the computer's IP address:

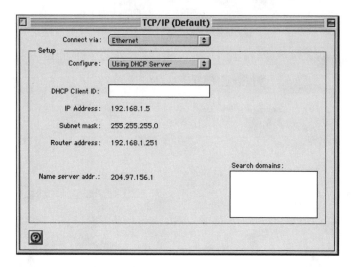

You open this from the Control Panel submenu in the Apple menu. If you are using BootP or DHCP to set IP addresses, you will be able to see the current IP address, in this case, 192.168.1.5. This means that if you are manually setting your server's IP address, you cannot use 192.168.1.5 because some other computer is using it.

Turning On AppleTalk

AppleTalk refers both to a communications protocol (such as TCP/IP) and a messaging system (similar to the higher-level Internet protocols such as FTP). Originally, the two were indistinguishable; today, they are separate. AppleTalk-over-IP refers to the use of the messaging system over TCP/IP (rather than over the traditional AppleTalk protocol). This technology is also now known as Apple File Protocol (AFP).

AFP can run over TCP/IP on a local area network, as well as over the Internet. If you are going to be serving computers that run AppleTalk, you will need to enable AppleTalk. You do so using the AppleTalk tab of the Network preference, as shown in Figure 13-2. Click the Make AppleTalk Active checkbox.

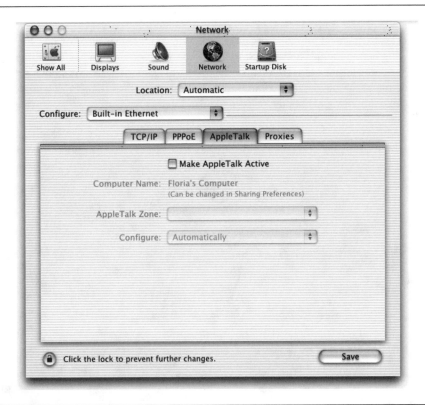

FIGURE 13-2   Turn AppleTalk on from the Network preferences AppleTalk tab.

Setting Up File Sharing

Once you have established your TCP/IP connection with a unique IP address and turned AppleTalk on, you need to allow people to connect to your server to share your files. There are two aspects to this: turning on file sharing and specifying privileges for files and folders.

Turning On File Sharing

You turn on file sharing using the Sharing pane in System Preferences, as shown in Figure 13-3. The File Sharing button toggles between Start and Stop to let you turn on basic file sharing. Web Sharing, remote login, and FTP are also shown on this pane. These are Internet protocols that let people run programs on your computer (Telnet) or move files to or from your computer. They are discussed in the next chapter, "Setting Up an Internet Server."

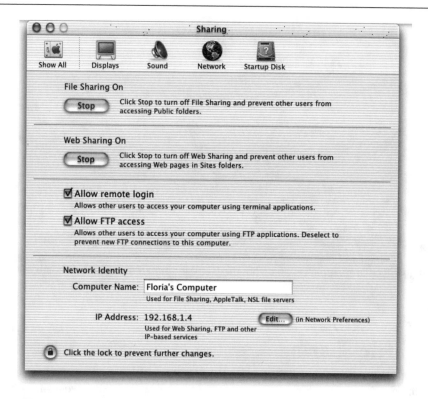

FIGURE 13-3   Setting File Sharing preferences

You can name your computer at the bottom of this pane. This name will appear in the Chooser (on System 9 or earlier) and in the Connect To dialog from the Go menu on Mac OS X. You should use a reasonably descriptive name and you should not change it. You may think that Beige is an interesting computer name; but if you are in a classroom with 20 students, each of who thinks that a color is a good computer name, your teacher may not be amused. (Of course, that might be the point!)

Connecting to File Sharing on Mac OS 9 (or Earlier)

Chapter 11, "Communicating Over a Local Area Network," showed you how to connect to a server when you are running Mac OS X. However, you need to show people who are running Mac OS 8 or Mac OS 9 how to connect to the AppleShare file server you have just set up.

First, on Mac OS 9 or earlier, open the Chooser (located in the Apple menu). The window shown next opens. The panel at the left may appear different; it reflects the types of printers and network you happen to have installed. Click the AppleShare icon at the left to see a list of the file servers in the pane at the right. The names of the file servers are the names of the computers; the individual disks can be selected later in the login process.

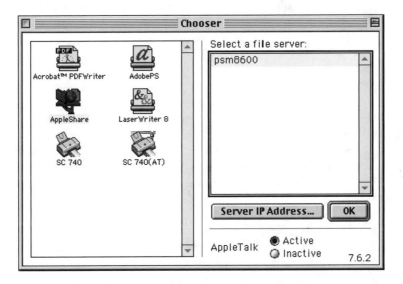

If no file servers are visible, you may not be connected to a network. If network printers (such as a laser) are installed, click the LaserWriter icon to see if any of them show up. If they do not, it is likely that there is a problem with your connection to the network. If printers show up and your file server does not, or if other file servers show up but your Mac OS X server does not, check that file sharing is turned on in the server's Sharing system preferences. Check cable connections as well if this does not work.

Click the name of the Mac OS X server and click OK (or just double-click). The panel shown next will appear. Enter the name and password you will use to connect. This should be the name of a user that was set up on the Mac OS X server; it is not a user name for the Mac OS 8 or Mac OS 9 computer from which you are connecting. If Guest access has been enabled on the Mac OS X server, you can click that radio button and not enter your name.

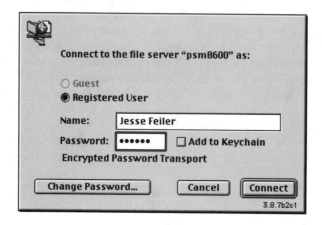

Setting up users is done with the Users pane in System Preferences in Mac OS X. On Mac OS X Server, you set up users with Server Admin for Mac OS X users and with Macintosh Manager for Mac OS 9 users; you use those applications to set up guest access, too.

In addition to connecting to a named file server, you can click Server IP Address (shown in the previous illustration) to open the window shown next. Here, you can type in the IP address of the server to which you wish to connect. After that, you log in the same way as to a named server.

Setting Privileges for Files and Folders

With file sharing turned on, people can access files and folders on your computer—but only if you provide them the appropriate privileges. Without file sharing, no one can access them (unless FTP is turned on); however, if file sharing is on and no access privileges are set, your files and folders are still secure. To set privileges, select a file or folder in a Finder window and choose Info (COMMAND-I). From the pop-up menu, show the sharing privileges as in Figure 13-4.

You can set privileges on three levels:

- For the owner of the file or folder

- For people in a group

- For everyone else

FIGURE 13-4   Viewing and setting sharing privileges

In general, permissions are progressively more restrictive: you normally want to read and write your files. You may allow another person or people in a specified group to read (but not write) them, and you may want others to have no access. As you can see in Figure 13-4, you can select from four privileges for each of these categories:

- **Read & Write**   This allows all access including renaming documents and folders, as well as deleting them.

- **Read only**

- **None**

- **Write only**   This is used for folders rather than for individual files. It means that someone can put a file into that folder, but that people cannot see the contents of the folder. This provides a mailbox or drop box for people to give you their documents, but not to scrounge around in other documents or see what other documents might exist.

You assign users to groups in Mac OS X Server.

Using Mac OS X Server

Mac OS X Server is a separate product from Mac OS X. It provides a powerful server platform for resource sharing, hosting Internet services, and managing the desktop environments of networked users. It includes WebObjects, Apple's premier Web authoring tool and application server. It comes with sophisticated management and monitoring tools that take advantage of the Aqua interface and traditional Macintosh ease of use.

What Apple has done with Mac OS X Server is to combine the strengths of the Mac OS X operating system with industry-standard networking and Internet tools (Sendmail, Apache, and the like), and to wrap everything in an easy-to-use interface. If you are familiar with hands-on running of a network or Internet server, you will find all of the familiar tools here: you can access them from Terminal if you want, but Server Admin makes it easier to manipulate them graphically. If you are familiar with networking and Internet concepts (but not with the hands-on nuts-and-bolts), Server Admin is perfect for you. The configuration files and commands of the Unix command line controls are banished in the graphical user interface.

If you are new to networking (perhaps you have experimented with file sharing on a local area network), you may want to read the Mac OS X Server documentation carefully and perhaps read one of the many books on setting up network and Internet services. On the author's Web site (http://www.philmontmill.com), there is additional information, more references, and some samples are provided. Click Mac OS X from the main page, and then use the Search and Q&A buttons at the top of the Mac OS X page. Searching on Server will find most of the references.

What Is Mac OS X Server?

Mac OS X Server provides support for groups of users from a dozen to hundreds or even thousands. On a small scale, it is used in many classrooms, publishing and content authoring environments, and small- to medium-size businesses and enterprises—any place where people need to share files, printers, and an Internet connection. The boundary between Mac OS X Server and the networking features of Mac OS X depends on the environment, and particularly on the sophistication of the network administrator. Sharing a few folders on a local area network is easy enough using the techniques described previously in this chapter. For a more complex environment, perhaps one in which students have their own individual desktop environments, share a classroom environment, and have limited access to a third environment shared by their teachers, Mac OS X Server provides more sophisticated tools for management and operations.

Mac OS X Server comes with excellent documentation in the form of *Mac OS X Server Administrator's Guide*, 350 pages of step-by-step guidance for setting up and managing all of the Mac OS X features. It also includes a worksheet to help you get started with your network, as well as concrete examples of various Mac OS X configurations. This section of the book shows you some of the features that are available in Mac OS X Server; consult *Mac OS X Server Administrator's Guide* for more details on these and other Mac OS X Server features. The specific aspects of Mac OS X Server that are briefly described in this section are

- Server Admin (including user management, as well as file and printer sharing)

- Macintosh Manager (for Mac OS 8 and Mac OS 9 clients)

- FTP

- Mail

Mac OS X Server and Server Admin

When you install Mac OS X Server, you are prompted to set up an administrator, just as you are with Mac OS X. This administrator has access to the primary configuration and management tool: Server Admin. When properly configured, remote computers on the network can use Server Admin (and an administrator password) to manage Mac OS X Server.

Mac OS X Server and its services (file and printer sharing, mail, Web, and so forth) starts up when the Mac OS X Server computer starts up. (This is also true of the sharing services on individual Macintosh computers running Mac OS X.) These services are available as soon as the computer has completed its startup routines—that is, they are in place and running when the login window appears. No one has to be logged into a server for it to provide its services.

In fact, it is frequently a good idea for no one to be logged into a server of this sort. Since it can be managed over a network using Server Admin, you can place your Mac OS X Server computer anywhere you want. If you are providing Internet services, you can even colocate the server—place it at an ISP's site where it can be connected directly to a very high-speed Internet connection.

Servers typically are located at such sites; those sites (*server farms*) not only have high-speed Internet connections, but they also have reliable and redundant power supplies. Since the servers are administered over a network (or over the Internet), there is no need for them to have keyboards or monitors attached.

Using Server Admin

To manage Mac OS X Server, launch Server Admin either from the Mac OS X Server computer or from another computer on the network. You will need to log into Mac OS X Server as shown next. The name and password that you use are the name and password that you created during installation of Mac OS X Server; if you are logging in from another computer on the network, do not use your login ID and password for that computer.

Once you have successfully logged in, the toolbar window, shown here, opens.

Each tab in the window lets you manage a different set of services that is shown in the toolbar. Click and hold the mouse over an icon to see the menu of commands available, as shown next. Menus for each module are available if you click and hold the mouse button down.

Managing Users and Groups

Much of your ongoing server management involves users and groups. In Mac OS X, you create and manage users using the Users pane of System Preferences. Groups (which appear in the Privileges pane of the Info window for documents and folders) are really not managed directly in Mac OS X: they are integral to Mac OS X Server, however. The menu for Users & Groups is shown next. You will use the Users & Groups menu frequently as you add and remove users from the network.

The list of users and groups is shown next. The Users & Groups list shows all registered users and lets you edit, delete, and create new ones.

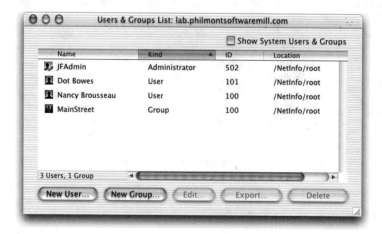

If you add or edit a user, the window shown next opens. As you can see, you provide a password for the user initially; you also can use this window to reset the password for a user who has forgotten it. The user should change the password quickly in either case.

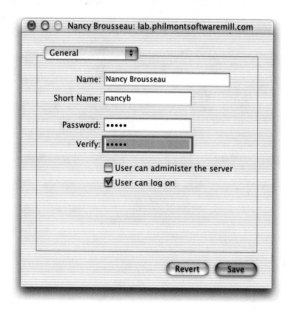

Do not use a default password (like *password*) for these cases; during the period in which it remains unchanged, unscrupulous people can experiment with it and cause damage. A temporary password should be as secure as the final password.

Advanced settings for a user are shown next. These settings allow people to log into a remote directory (that is, a directory on your Mac OS X Server—it is remote to them and local to the server) and to access the command line shell that you select. You also can set (and change) the user and group ID, but normally you do this using Macintosh Manager.

You create groups with the New Group button at the bottom of the Users & Groups window or with the New Group command from the pop-up menu in the sharing module. To add users to a group, drag them from the Users & Groups window, as shown in Figure 13-5.

Managing Logs

Use the commands shown in Figure 13-6 to view logs for the various services your server is providing. Because Mac OS X Server relies on industry-standard and open source products such as Apache and Sendmail, many network administrators are already familiar with these logs, their formats, and their terms.

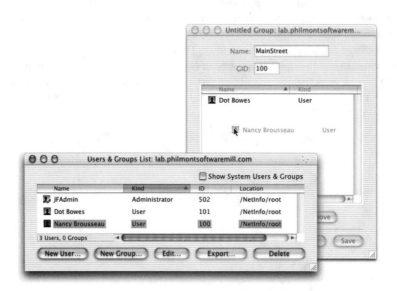

Drag users into a group from the Users & Groups window.

Logs help in debugging.

Managing Sharing

If you are running a server, you will need to set up sharing using the commands in the Sharing module as shown here:

If you choose the first command, Set Sharing Attributes, a standard open dialog appears so that you can select the disk or folder that you want to adjust. When you have selected it, the window shown next appears.

The most critical item on this window is the checkbox: make certain it is checked if you want to share the item. Next, you can specify the privileges for the owner, group, and everyone else; but if you do not check the sharing checkbox, none of that will matter.

This window is where you change ownership of documents and folders. Open Users & Groups, and then drag the appropriate user or group from there into the owner or group field on this window. Many people are perplexed that they cannot just type in a new owner or group name; requiring that you drag a user or group from Users & Groups means that there is no possibility of mistyping a name and winding up with an invalid group. Use the interface once, and you'll be hooked on it.

Most administrators of local area networks spend most of their time adding and removing users; the second most time-consuming task is managing shared resources like these. You can minimize your management tasks by creating shared folders inside which your users can play to their hearts' content: in other words, you should normally not be setting sharing attributes for small collections of documents. Create a Class 4-A folder and let all the students do whatever they want inside it.

A shared resource (that is, one with the sharing checkbox checked) is called a *share point*; share points can be seen in the window shown next. Share points can be disks, CD-ROMs, or folders. In most cases, share points are entire CD-ROMs or folders within a disk.

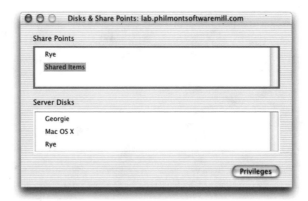

Managing Apple File Service

Click the File & Print tab to manage these services. Apple File Service (using Apple File Protocol, AFP) is an outgrowth of the older AppleShare technology. AFP runs over TCP/IP networks using AppleTalk. The menu of commands is shown here:

When you configure Apple File Services, the window with four tabs, shown next, opens. General Apple File settings include the server name.

You can control the number of users accessing your server over Apple File Service using the Access tab, as shown here:

When the limits are reached, users will not be allowed to log in. Of course, this can mean that idle users will hobble your network. You handle that with the Idle Users tab, shown next, which will disconnect users according to the parameters you set; thus, new users can log in.

Note that you can avoid this situation by not setting limits on the number of users. If your network is relatively small (a classroom or an office, for example), it is probably sufficient to leave the default settings; after all, with a maximum of 20 or 30 users, who cares if some of them are idle? However, if you are running a corporate network or a campus-wide network that includes remote users and Internet access, you may need to adjust these parameters. Also, you may need to disconnect users forcefully if you are sharing resources that are licensed to a certain number of people (such as databases).

You can set the parameters for your access log, as shown next. When you are running a server, you need to track security violations, as well as problems with the network and server.

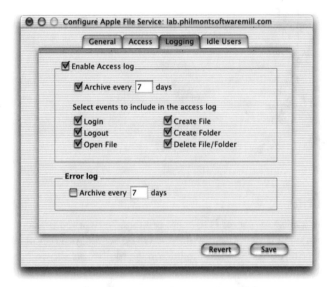

Finally, you can see who is logged in by looking at the status window shown next. You can send messages to users that you select in this window; you can also disconnect users from here. One use of the Disconnect button is to handle those mysterious cases in which people think they are logged out but are not. There are many reasons for this; one of the most common is that someone is sitting at a computer and knows it is not logged in (a blank login screen is visible), but they forget that they have remained logged in at another computer in another room. If you are providing technical support, don't argue: if the user claims to be disconnected, make it happen. As soon as the beep of the disconnect dialog wafts through the open doorway, the user will realize what has happened, stop shouting at you, and (possibly) apologize to you.

Managing Printing

One reason for using a network server is to share printers. Networked printers can be accessed by everyone on a local area network; but with Mac OS X Server, you can manage print jobs and queues more directly. Start with the Print module on the toolbar, as shown here:

The basic configuration of printing services is shown here:

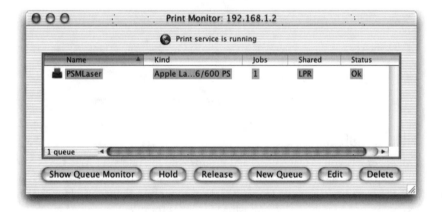

Just as you can look at the status of Apple File Service users, you can keep track of print queues with Print Monitor, as shown here:

Note that this window lets you manage each print queue (printer) separately. You can hold a queue: that means that people can print to it, but the print jobs will simply wait until you release the queue.

The Show Queue Monitor button at the bottom lets you examine an individual queue (select the queue in the window, and then click Show Queue Monitor). The following illustration shows an individual queue window. By clicking the Priority button, you can open the window shown at the bottom of the next illustration and reorder or reprioritize jobs within the queue. You can also hold or release jobs from the main queue monitor window. This gives you the ability to turn queues on or off, as well as to turn individual jobs on or off (or postpone or prioritize them) within each queue.

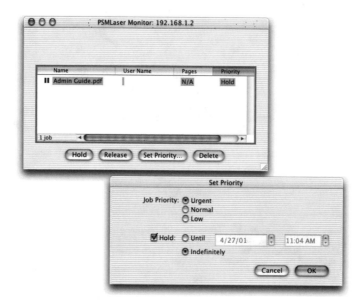

Using Macintosh Manager

Macintosh Manager lets you manage users and groups who log into your Mac OS X Server computer. It provides the most sophisticated management of all. The Users pane in System Preferences is the most basic, and the Users & Groups module in Setup Admin is the middle ground of complexity and power. (Macintosh Manager is for clients using Mac OS 8 or Mac OS 9; Server Admin manages these issues for Mac OS X clients.)

Logging into Macintosh Manager

You can launch Macintosh Manager by itself. By default, it is in the Dock on Mac OS X Server; or you can launch it from the Setup Admin toolbar, as shown here:

Just as you had to connect to the Mac OS X Server computer, you need to connect to an individual Macintosh Management Server, as shown next. You will need to log in with your Mac OS X Server user ID and password.

Managing Users in Macintosh Manager

The Users tab of Macintosh Manager is where you do most of your work. The users in italics in the list at the left are special users; in this case, All Other Users is the default setting. As you can see in Figure 13-7, unless otherwise specified, All Other Users can log in. As Figure 13-8 shows, you can drag users from the Users & Groups list in Setup Admin into Macintosh Manager.

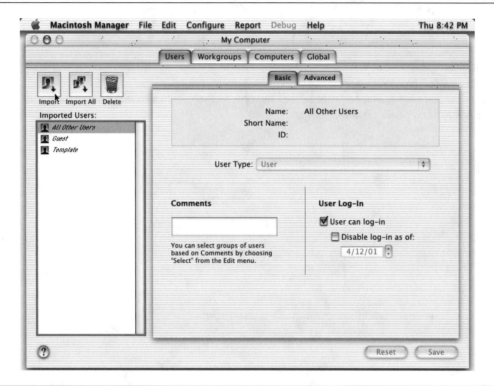

Using All Other Users to set default values

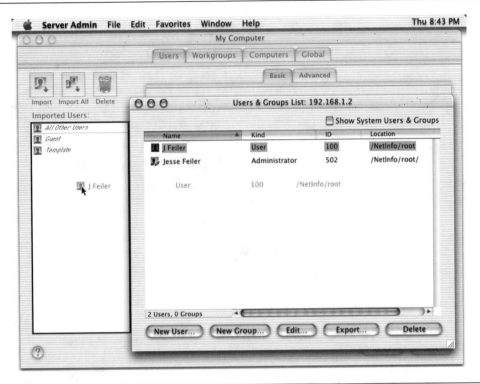

FIGURE 13-8 Dragging users from the Setup Admin Users & Groups list into Macintosh Manager

A dialog will pop up and you'll have a chance to OK your work. Two tabs let you set parameters for each user. The Basic tab, shown in Figure 13-9, lets you specify login privileges and the type of user. Advanced parameters are shown in Figure 13-10.

Perhaps the most important parameter in this window is the first one. Allowing a user to only use one computer at a time may be a good security measure for an ISP; however, in a more controlled environment, you might want to allow some people to use a laptop next to their desktop computer.

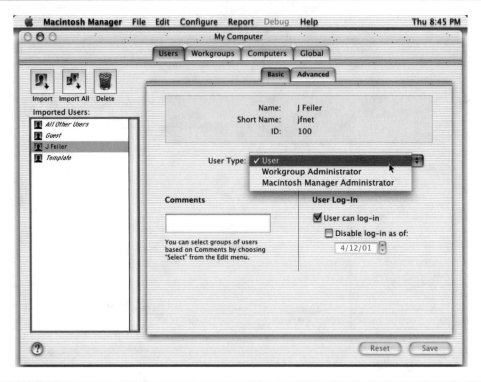

Basic privileges for users may be all you need to set.

Managing Groups in Macintosh Manager

Finally, you can manage workgroups as shown in Figure 13-11. You can set access privileges for the workgroup (and all of its users) as you can see from the tabs in this window. Each of the tabs and options is described in *Mac OS X Server Administrator's Guide*, included with Mac OS X Server.

FTP

FTP is one of the oldest and simplest Internet services. (In fact, FTP not only preceded Internet mail, but also it was actually the first protocol used to send mail messages back and forth.)

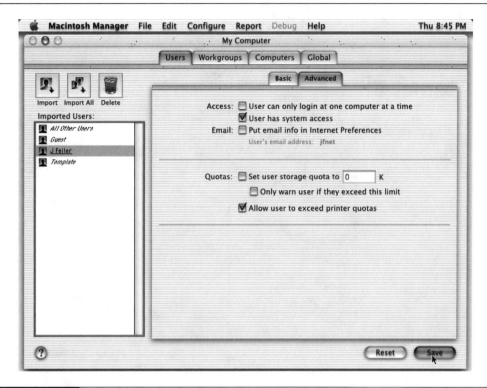

FIGURE 13-10   Advanced privileges can help you manage your network more precisely.

Whereas file sharing as described in the previous section relates primarily to Macintosh computers, FTP is an Internet standard that almost all computers today support. Configure FTP from the FTP module in the Files & Print tab of Server Admin as shown here:

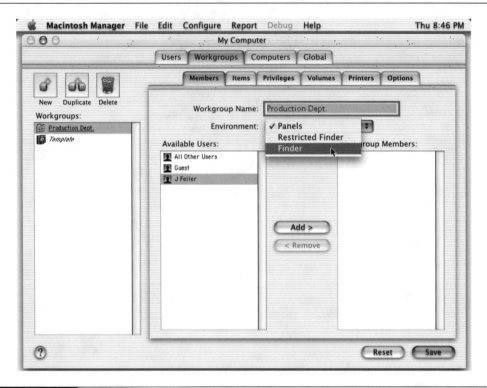

FIGURE 13-11   Adding and removing users from workgroups

The Configure FTP Service dialog shows the settings you can control for FTP. Allowing anonymous access (like Guest access for file sharing) means that anyone can use your server. This is appropriate if you are allowing downloads of promotional material, class assignments, and the like. However, for a public server, this may invite mayhem—particularly if anonymous users are allowed to upload to the server.

Mail

Apple has provided a graphical user interface to the industry-standard Sendmail application that is part of Mac OS X Server. Access it from the Configure Mail Server module of the Internet tab in Server Admin.

There are many resources, including entire books for working with the Sendmail program, which is what Mac OS X Server uses. You may find that they are helpful; you may also discover that the basic concepts of Sendmail (which can be expressed in a page or two) are sufficient. The graphical user interface that Mac OS X Server provides takes care of many of the details.

When you set up users, you set up their mail service. The General and Advanced settings were discussed previously in the section "Managing Users and Groups." Another setting is shown next: it lets you set up mail for a user. (Note that this is the user dialog that you access from the Users & Groups module in the General tab of Server Admin.)

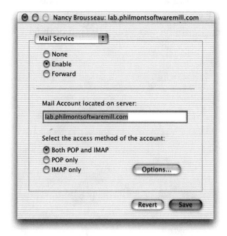

The Options button lets you further refine a user's mail service, as shown next. Options allow notification and control over both POP and IMAP incoming mail.

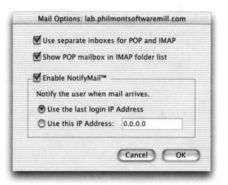

One choice for setting up mail is to allow mail to automatically be forwarded to another account. This allows you to provide an account on your mail server (and with your domain name as part of the email address) and to automatically forward the mail to other accounts in other domains. Users often like this: they can get all of their email on one account while still maintaining email addresses at their school, office, or various other domains.

Summary

This chapter has shown you how to set up a server using Mac OS X on your local area network. You have seen how to configure your computer and the client computers that will access it, as well as how to turn on file sharing and set privileges. In addition, Mac OS X Server has been described. This is the product you use for larger networks and for Internet services. The next chapter examines Internet servers; there, too, you will find both Mac OS X and Mac OS X features.

Chapter 14

Setting Up an Internet Server

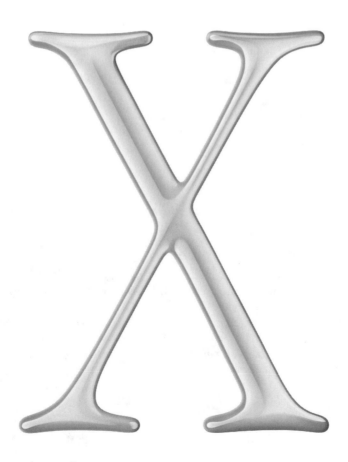

The first two chapters in this part of the book focused on client computers over networks—local area networks and the Internet. The previous chapter dealt with the issues associated with a local area network server. This chapter hones in on Internet servers. Thus, you will see the client/server paradigm examined both in the local area network context and in the context of the Internet. (The final chapter in this part of the book deals with the Apache Web server that comes with Mac OS X.)

Setting up an Internet server can be as simple as turning on some options in System Preferences to launch the built-in Web server of Mac OS X. It can be as complex as building an international network of high-speed channels to provide services to a range of clients. This chapter focuses on the general issues that apply in all cases. If you are setting up a large-scale Internet server, additional references are available both on the Internet and in bookstores.

In addition, if you are setting up an Internet server for more than experimentation or very small-scale use, consider investing in Mac OS X Server. Based on Mac OS X, this collection of software helps you deploy and manage an Internet server that can scale up to very large needs.

There are five sections in this chapter:

- First, you will find a description of what Internet servers are.

- Then, what may be one of the most important issues of Internet servers—the law—is discussed.

- Connecting your server to the Internet is not always as simple as connecting a client device (such as a computer with a browser or email software); the next part of the chapter focuses on connectivity.

- Running a Web server entails a lot more than dealing with technical concerns: a few of the most important points to consider are provided next.

- Finally, there is a section with tips to help you create and maintain your Web server and your Web sites.

NOTE   *Strictly speaking, a Web server is an HTTP server. It responds to HTTP requests such as http://www.yoursite.com/index.html. (Although you may consider that an address, it's actually a request to send a page of HTML code.) The Web is a combination of the HTTP request protocol and the HTML standard that specifies the format of the data that is most often produced in response to the request. "Web server" is the most frequently used term; "HTTP server" is technically more accurate. "HTML server" is wrong, since HTTP requests can ask for data other than HTML, such as files, video, graphics, and so forth.*

What Is an Internet Server?

Internet servers provide Internet services to people on the Internet. That seems simple enough. If you decide that you're going to set up an Internet server—or worse, if your boss decides that you're going to set up an Internet server—you'd better make certain that you know what you're providing and for whom you're doing it.

What Internet Services Are You Providing?

Internet services include some or all of the standard Internet protocols: email (incoming and outgoing), file transfer (FTP), the Web (HTTP), Usenet news (NNTP), Telnet, Gopher, and others less well known. Internet services can include additional protocols that work on their own or in conjunction with other protocols. These additional protocols include LDAP (Lightweight Directory Access Protocol), SSL (Secure Sockets Layer), and PICS (Platform for Internet Content Selection).

In addition to these services, there is a host of services and functionalities that Internet servers may provide. These include scripting and scripting languages (such as Perl); media streaming; credit card processing (for e-commerce); and a variety of operational services such as backups, logs, and even order fulfillment for shipping products bought online.

So, if you decide to set up an Internet server, make certain that you know what will be included. While there is no standard package, some general parameters can be given.

Setting up an Internet server is easy with Mac OS X. It is also quite exciting: there is nothing like being totally in charge of your Internet presence. A decade or more from now, everyone may have a Web site and Internet server. Alternatively, everyone may have a Web site, but very few people may actually run Internet servers. There are many issues of law, telecommunications, and technology involved here. Some of these are pointed out in the sections that follow. Do not take these warnings as an indication that you should not set up your own Internet servers. Take them as points to consider before taking a very public—and exciting—plunge into the Internet.

Web Servers

For a Web server, you obviously need a Web server product. Apache is one of the leading Web servers, and it comes with Mac OS X. The Web server sends HTML files out in response to requests. Those files are sometimes constructed dynamically, but often they simply reside on the Web server until they are needed.

You need a way to get those files onto the Web server. There are three ways to do so:

■ You can create them there with an authoring or editing tool. As you will see later on, doing anything on a Web server computer that is heavily used other than running a Web server is generally not a good idea. Therefore, for most people, this is not a reasonable choice unless their server demands are modest.

■ You can move the files to the Web server using removable media (CDs, zip drives, and so forth), or you can move them over a local area network to the server. In either case, this will probably involve you sitting at the Web server and bringing the files to its disk.

■ You can move the files to the Web server remotely using an FTP product such as Fetch. This is the safest way to move files, since you do not touch the keyboard and cannot accidentally disrupt Web services. It also means that you can access the Web server for the purpose of placing files there from anywhere in the world. Compared to the previous method, you will not be sitting at the Web server. Rather than bringing files to the server's disk, you will be sending them to it from another computer.

If you are using Mac OS X, all you need to do is run Apache, as described in the next chapter. Fetch runs on client computers. This basic configuration is sufficient to host Web sites with basic pages including text, graphics, and multimedia files. It is not sufficient for e-commerce and Webcasting, but you may not need to provide those services.

Mail Servers

Internet servers often provide email sending and receiving services. Except for the smallest Internet servers, those services are usually provided on separate computers. (In fact, it is common that Web serving, incoming email, and outgoing email be served on at least three separate computers.)

Who Are You Serving?

You need to determine who you are serving, both from the standpoint of who is creating and maintaining the Web sites you are serving and who will be connecting to them. You can describe those two groups as server users and server clients, respectively.

Server Users

You may have one server user—perhaps yourself—or you may be running a business of hosting Web sites. (You also may be somewhere in between, of course.) Mac OS X provides the power and stability to do both. However, you may have constraints that are far removed from the operating system.

While technically anyone with a computer, Internet connection, and Web server can run a Web site, the reality is quite different. Your connection to the Internet may explicitly prevent you from running a Web server. Even if it does let you do so, it may limit your ability to let others use your Web server.

Your server users need access to your computer or at least to their own directories on the computer. They need to be able to log in (preferably remotely with Fetch or Anarchie) and transfer files to their own directories. Use the procedures in the previous chapter to set up these user accounts.

> ## Investigate Your Internet Connection Terms of Service
>
> If your Internet access is provided as a personal or residential account, you may find out that you cannot run a Web server. Often, the way you will find out is when your service is cancelled or when you are upgraded to a more expensive account. Broadband (high-speed) Internet connections are particularly useful for running Web servers, and vendors promoting such services as ISDN, DSL, and cable have not always figured out how to price Web servers. You may find that your broadband connection does not allow you to run a Web server—at any price. If you have experience dealing with an Internet service provider, you may have developed an expectation that the people you deal with understand computers and the Internet. That may not be the case when dealing with telephone or cable companies. (You may have to patiently explain the difference between a Web server and call forwarding or the Home Shopping Network.) Do this early and leave plenty of time for it!

Server Clients

Server clients—people who log on to your Web server in order to download HTML (and other) files—typically have access to everything in the Web server's file directory. Apache and other Web servers provide mechanisms for limiting this access to a single directory (in which files and aliases reside). However, you can further limit access to subdirectories.

Realms are directories that require user IDs and passwords to be accessed via the Web server. (Web servers other than Apache use other terms for these passworded directories.) The authentication rules for realms can be set up in files—typically called .htaccess—located in the directories in question. These files can be created and modified by the client users. They can be uploaded just as HTML and other Web site files are.

The user IDs and passwords for authentication of realm access are created and modified by the server user, not by the system administrator. Someone who can access a directory with FTP or by logging on to the computer can modify the site's security mechanism. In fact, the system administrator may not even know that authentication rules have been placed on a realm.

The Law

As if it weren't enough to worry about whether setting up a server is allowed under the terms of your Internet access account, you need to bear in mind several critical legal issues. Two of the most important of these are copyright and the two-headed beast of pornography and treason.

Copyright

The material that is on your Web server is usually protected by copyright. Sometimes there are explicit copyright notices; other times, copyright is not explicitly noted. If you own the copyright (or if your server users own the copyright), there is no problem so long as they are using that copyrighted material in accordance with their license (or implied license).

If you or your server users do not own the copyright or a license to it for the material that is placed on their sites and that is hosted on your server, they—or you—can be liable for substantial damages.

There are some precedents in which an Internet service provider has not been liable for harm done by the posting of copyrighted material to its Web server when that has been done by server users without the knowledge of the Internet service provider. Do not rely on this as an excuse; although Mac OS X is very stable and scalable, chances are that if you do have users maintaining their own Web sites, they will number in no more than the hundreds, making it very hard for you to prove that you didn't know what was going on.

Distributing copyrighted material without a license to do so is illegal. The illegality of the act isn't mitigated by the fact that "everybody does it" or that "no one will know."

Make certain that all of the pages on your Web server contain copyright notices. This not only identifies the copyright owner and alerts downloaders to the fact that the material is copyrighted, but it also allows server clients to contact the copyright owner to secure permission to republish or reuse the copyrighted information. Making it difficult for people to do so may encourage people who would like to comply with copyright law to evade it for the sake of getting their work done. (This is no excuse, but it is very frustrating to be unable to discover how to abide by copyright law in licensing material.)

Pornography and Treason

By maintaining a Web server, you are distributing information to anyone in the world with a Web browser (subject to the authentication and access controls noted previously). Your responsibility for the information distributed is not limited to copyright issues; some information is subject to restrictions. Note that those restrictions may be in effect in the location to which the information is downloaded—you may be breaking one nation's laws while running your Web server in another nation.

In some countries, you need to obtain a license of one sort or another before publishing, either on paper or electronically. In other nations, this is not the case. Even in the (supposedly) most free and liberal environments, the reckless publication of inappropriate material may ultimately lead to calls for the regulation of all publication.

In other words, if you're going to publish inappropriate material, understand the consequences and know what you're doing. Accidentally doing so is inexcusable.

Some of the most serious problems arise in those areas of life that raise the greatest passions: religion, sex, and patriotism. The nature of Web publishing is such that unless you take precautions, you do not know who—or what type of person—is viewing your Web pages. What is innocuous or obvious to you may not be to the anonymous viewer of your site. (You may note that USB connectors are officially called "plugs" and "receptacles"; the long-standing reliance on "male" and "female" connectors has been supplanted because smarmy children of all ages and genders sniggered too much.)

You may provide a certain measure of protection by stating clearly on your site what its intended audience is. Be aware, however, that automated filters are increasingly used to block (or ferret out) sites using keywords. Your disclaimer may come to naught.

Jokes and sarcasm in life often rely on a raised eyebrow or changed tone of voice; on a Web page, these do not exist. "Drop dead" may get a laugh in a TV sitcom from the 1950s; on a Web site, it can lead to serious consequences.

Your site may contain information and images that are posted there by other people as comments, feedback, or in discussions. In many cases, you are responsible to a greater or lesser extent for these postings.

In short, temper your enthusiasm with some concern for what can go wrong and for what you can and should do to keep your site the kind of site you want it to be. In fact, being clear about your site's objectives and the audience for which it is designed will only increase the site's efficacy.

Connecting a Web Server to the Internet

The connection you use to connect to the Internet for your own purposes may very well not be satisfactory for your Web server's connection. You need to consider the physical connection (primarily its capacity), the IP address so that people can locate your site, its domain name, and where the connection is made—from your home, office, or school, or remotely from an access provider. This section gives you tips on how to proceed. It also provides some information for the special issues affecting Web servers set up in computer labs and on private networks.

Physical Connection

Web servers need sufficient bandwidth (network capacity) to provide responses to all of their server clients in a timely manner. Your Web server may be the next hot Internet start-up company; it may also be a vital part of your life or business that receives one or two visitors a week. (The latter situation may well be more profitable than the former!)

You need to know what your network performance needs will be in order to determine the capacity of your connection. If you have always used a dial-up connection, the advent of high-speed technologies such as ISDN, DSL, and cable may encourage you to use them to host your own site. Be forewarned, though, that even if your agreement with your ISP allows it, those technologies are not sufficient to host Web sites with more than a minimal amount of traffic.

The nature of network traffic and of shared resources means that you cannot rely on averages in planning your capacity. You must rely on estimates (or actual numbers) of peak periods. Having excess capacity at three in the morning is no good if you have a spate of users who log on at a quarter to five each day to fill in an electronic time card. If it takes them 45 minutes to do so, they will not be happy.

IP Address

People get to your Web site by using its IP address. Even if they type in a domain name (as described in the next section), they will be connecting via the IP address associated with that domain name. For that reason, your Web server must have a constant IP address. This normally eliminates dialup connections for Web sites, since most dialup connections have different IP addresses for each connection. Some Internet service providers will provide static IP address for dialup users. This solves the problem of not knowing an IP address, but it does not addresses the problem that a dialup connection is normally not sufficient to carry a Web server's traffic.

Dynamic IP addresses are generated on local area networks using the BootP or DHCP protocols, as described in the previous chapters. If you connect to the Internet through a local area network in that way, you also will have problems identifying your IP address to people who want to connect to your Web server.

DNS

The Internet's address directory is its domain name system: a distributed database that maps domain names (such as yourcompany.com) to IP addresses. These IP addresses are in fact the addresses of domain name servers that can further direct the traffic. Thus, an HTTP request to www.yourcompany.com goes to the domain name server for yourcompany.com; it is routed to www.yourcompany.com by the domain name server. Likewise, email to someone@yourcompany.com goes to the same domain name server; it is routed to the incoming mail server by the domain name server.

If your Web server is to be part of a named domain, it must be identified in the domain name server. This is done by whoever maintains the domain name server, usually your network administrator or your Internet service provider. It is not done as part of the domain registration.

You may discover that you are not allowed to set up a Web server when you contact your Internet service provider or administrator to ask that your computer be added to the domain name server. If there is any possibility of this happening, contact those people before you have invested time and effort in creating a Web server.

Location and Colocation

A Web server should run as little as possible besides the Web server application. Anything else may degrade performance.

As a result, a well-behaved Web server normally sits around running Apache or another Web server and its own operating system, through which server users can log on to use Fetch to upload and maintain the files on their Web sites.

In other words, a Web server doesn't really need a keyboard, mouse, or monitor. Since server users and clients access it over the Internet, you can set up what is called a *headless server*: a server without a monitor.

You can take this one step further and colocate the server. This means that your Web server computer is placed on the premises of an Internet service provider (or of your own organization's network connection). You can access it over the Internet, just as you would if it were under your own desk. Colocation is a common service provided by Internet service providers. It may come with support services such as backups, or you may get nothing more than a power outlet and a connection to the Internet. Colocation can involve your own computer at a remote site; it also can involve the Internet service provider providing a computer to you (by sale or lease). This can be a very effective way of implementing a Web server. Since Mac OS X is so stable, it can run for very long periods of time—weeks or months, in many cases—and having it far away can actually be useful to you.

If you have not administered a remote server before, practice with a server as if it were remote. Using either the computer you will ultimately ship away or another, configure it as you believe it will need to be configured for remote administration. Then, turn off the monitor and attempt to log on to it from another computer as you would. Continue doing so with normal maintenance for several days until you feel confident that you have worked out all the kinks. During this period, you can always turn the monitor back on or even sit down at the keyboard. Once the computer is a thousand miles away, it's not that easy.

Computer Lab and Internal Web Servers

If you are creating a Web server for a computer lab or internal network, you may be able to simplify several steps and deal with some additional considerations.

If the Web server is being set up as an experiment or project, it really doesn't matter what the IP address is. You need to be able to locate it at any given time so that you, your colleagues, or your teacher can log on, but there is no need to know what it is at any other time. For these purposes, a dialup connection or a BootP or DHCP connection with varying IP addresses is just fine.

On a local area network—even one with BootP or with DHCP—you may be able to assign a static IP address. Mac OS X supports this; you just need your network administrator to understand your reason for doing so, and you need to agree on what address will be used.

If a domain name server is running on your local area network to support internal users, you can name the Web server (again, with the cooperation of the network administrator).

When Apache starts up, it starts up under the supervisory/root user ID; it subsequently changes its ID. However, this means that if you are running a Web server, it normally runs at the computer's security level, not at the level of individual users on the computer. In a computer lab, this means you cannot easily use user IDs to let individual students set up their own Web servers. It's one Web server per computer in most cases.

Once the server is set up, however, you can modify its default directory so that the maintenance of the server and its files can be assigned to different people. In other words, if the class is in setting up the Web server, the computers can't easily be shared. If the class is in managing Web sites, it generally can.

You can get around these complications; but at a certain point, you wind up teaching people how to handle situations that only occur in the computer lab environment, not in real life.

Running a Web Server

Having decided what services you will offer and to whom, as well as how to connect your Web server to the Internet, you are ready to go. In most cases, that means that you are now open for business (or at least Web surfing) 24 hours a day, 7 days a week. Problems only occur on weekends or holidays; corrupted pages only appear when supervisors, the press, or teachers log on.

There are many strategies for running services that need to function 24/7. The most successful of these center on prevention of problems. Restrict server users to the smallest number possible, and restrict physical access to the server even more. (It is appalling how many Internet servers are not behind locked doors. Not a few are placed under receptionists' desks for some strange reason. This may provide security for much of the day, but lunch hours and evenings can leave the server unprotected.)

In addition to trying to prevent problems, make certain that you are prepared to deal with the inevitable problems that will arise. Again, the simplest preparations are often ignored. Backing up the server is common sense; storing backups off-site is good judgment. Interestingly, many people forget to keep track of what is on the server. In addition to the backups of files and folders, keep separate documents with listings of directories and users.

It cannot be stressed enough that anything running on the Web server that does not need to do so can be a serious impediment to successful operations. Probably the worst thing you can do on a Web server (or any production machine) is software development and testing. After that, a range of potentially troublesome applications stretches before you: anything that might hang or crash the machine (unlikely on Mac OS X, but still possible); anything that might monopolize communications channels; and anything that allows access directly or indirectly to the operation of the computer.

Creating and Maintaining a Web Server and Web Sites

Notwithstanding the previous cautions, running your own Web server on Mac OS X can be useful and productive, particularly for small organizations with their own access to the Internet and their own domain name servers. For smaller and larger organizations, running Mac OS X for a Web server that is colocated at an Internet service provider or at your own network center can be efficient and easy.

Obtaining a Domain Name

If you do this in the real world, the only thing you need is a domain name. The procedure for obtaining domain names has changed in recent years. In the United States, Network Solutions (InterNIC) used to be responsible for registering all names in the .com, .net, and .org domains. In those olden times, .com was reserved for commercial uses (in the United States), .net for network providers, and .org for non-profit and non-governmental organizations. Today, all of those restrictions have been eliminated.

In order to register a domain name, you must contact a registrar. Look at the website http://www.icann.org/registrars/accredited-list.html, which is the site of the Internet Corporation for Assigned Names and Numbers. This is the non-profit organization that manages registration today. You can find more information about them at http://www.icann.org. (You will also find a link to the registrars from that page.)

Security and File Layouts

Along with your domain name, plan for how your server will be used and how your domain will be managed—not just now but in the future. There is nothing worse than renaming servers and causing users' stored links to break. Set up directory structures that you can live with.

Innovation is not always a great idea here. Many Web servers use similar directory structures (often based on Apache defaults). This can help in maintaining that site and in training new people to maintain and use it. Remember that not every Webmaster knows as much as you do. The distinction between a filename specified in an official Internet protocol and one dreamed up by an administrator may be a subtlety.

Along with your file/directory names and layouts, implement the kind of security that you need for a publicly accessed Web server. Do this even if your Web server is now located on an internal local area network. Once access has been granted, it is hard to take it back. (In particular, once your Webmasters are used to certain types of access, they may balk at having it taken away from them.)

Summary

Mac OS X is an ideal operating system for a Web server. Its stability recommends it over less stable choices. The fact that it comes with Apache and with a very simple installation process makes it all the better a choice for a Web server.

In this chapter, you have seen how to define your Internet server, its services, and its users. After a brief review of some of the legal issues involved, the issues involved in connectivity have been presented. Finally, the issues involved in maintaining a Web server and in creating the site have been explored.

The mechanics of setting up the server are precisely those described in the previous chapter. The mechanics of the Apache Web Server are described in the next one.

Summary

Chapter 15

Setting Up the Web Server

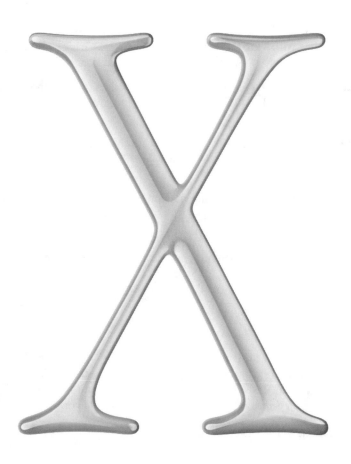

This chapter focuses on setting up the Web server (Apache) that is part of Mac OS X. You can set it up in the context of your individual computer when you run Mac OS X or you can set it up for a larger environment when you run Mac OS X Server.

People use Apache to power Web sites large and small. Most people using Mac OS X will use it to power small Web sites, such as personal Web sites or Web sites on intranets that are designed for workgroups and other small groups. This chapter focuses on such uses; it shows you how to get a basic Web site up and how to maintain it. It does not cover issues involving domain name services, hosting Web sites for others, and the like.

The sections of this chapter are

- **About Apache**   Background about the Web server itself.

- **Turning On the Web Server**   How to get started.

- **Out-of-the-Box Apache**   What you can do by simply placing HTML files in the right place on your computer.

- **Setting Up Sites with Mac OS X Server**   Handling the basics of setting up multiple sites on one Web server.

- **Extending Apache with cgi-bin**   Incorporating scripts (such as those written in Perl) into your Web pages. This allows you to process forms and to interact with databases and other applications.

- **Using Other Web Servers**   Apache is not the only Web server you can use with OS X. This section shows you how to use the FileMaker Web Companion to serve up FileMaker databases over the Web.

- **Moving Up...WebObjects**   An introduction to Apple's application server, the next step in power and productivity.

If you've set up a Web server before—particularly if you've set up Apache before—stop. Don't download the latest source code, don't compile anything, don't configure the config file, and just don't do anything you normally do. Stop. Relax. You'll need to click the mouse half a dozen times to set up your Web server. (And that will be that.)

About Apache

Apache runs many of the largest and most sophisticated sites on the Internet. It also runs many of the smallest sites. Apache itself is based on the first Web servers: the original one built at CERN (European Center for Nuclear Research) and then its successor built in the United States at NCSA (National Center for Supercomputing Applications). Written originally in C for Unix, Apache has been developed through the work of highly skilled volunteers. It is available for free, and its support site at http://www.apache.org/ contains source code and other information.

Apache, like all Web servers, is a very simple program. It receives incoming HTTP requests that arrive via TCP/IP, and it responds to them by sending out responses that are HTML documents. In the simplest case, that document is present on disk and is simply transmitted (with appropriate headers) back to the user who requested it. In more complex cases, Apache calls a script or plug-in to generate the HTML that will be returned. This chapter shows you how to handle both cases.

> **NOTE** *By default, Apache (and other Web servers) listens to port 80 for incoming messages. That means that any HTTP request addressed to your computer's IP address is normally sent to port 80—and to Apache. See the section "Using Other Web Servers," later in this chapter, for more information.*

Turning On the Web Server (and Turning Off Unwanted Access)

Your first step in using Apache is to turn on the Web server and turn off unwanted access. For Mac OS X, begin by opening the Sharing pane in System Preferences as shown in Figure 15-1.

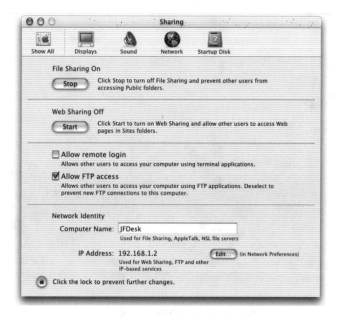

FIGURE 15-1   Turning on the Web server in Mac OS X

Turning On the Web Server

You will need an administrator password to complete this task. Just click Start for the Web Sharing item.

For Mac OS X Server, use Server Admin to configure the Web server. From the Internet tab, use the Web Server module to open the configuration window shown in Figure 15-2. You can set a variety of startup options here. You customize your Web server as you see fit; many other options are available in Server Admin and in the standard Apache configuration files. (If you are used to using Apache, you can administer Apache on Mac OS X or Mac OS X Server using Terminal exactly as you always have done on other platforms.)

NOTE *You can turn on the Web server during installation of Mac OS X or Mac OS X Server.*

Once the Web server is on, an HTTP request addressed to your computer—that is, an HTTP request such as http://192.168.1.9 (if that is your IP address)—will be sent to it. That is all very well and good if you are on an intranet or local area network. If you are connected to the Internet, you may not want everyone to be able to connect to your Web site. (For example, it may contain confidential information or information that simply is irrelevant to the world at large.)

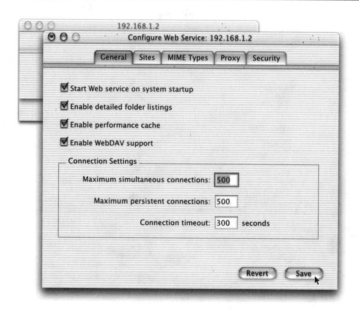

FIGURE 15-2   Turning on the Web server in Mac OS X Server

If your computer is connected to a firewall, you can adjust this access; indeed, you must do so in many cases. You can run a Web server—or a hundred Web servers—on your local area network. However, to run a Web server accessible to Internet users requires a contract with your Internet service provider that allows that. Because Web sites can generate a great deal of traffic, many Internet service providers, particularly ones providing DSL or cable modem access, limit or even prohibit running public Web sites.

With most routers and firewalls, you can create a variety of access rules that govern what people within the LAN can do on the Internet and what people on the Internet can access on the LAN.

Different products have different interfaces, but each will have some variation on the following formula.

- Access is allowed or denied (action)

- To a particular server (such as HTTP)

- When coming from a source on the LAN or outside the LAN

- When going to a resource on the LAN or outside the LAN

Rules can overlap, and they are normally applied in sequence.

CAUTION   *Do not skip this step if your Internet service provider does not let you run a Web server. Although you are just testing and no one from the outside accesses your Web site, ISPs have port sniffers—they scan the ports on their clients' always-on connections looking for the presence of Web servers. While they investigate whether you are actually running a Web server, you may lose your Internet access. Setting up your router or firewall is beyond the scope of this book, but that does not mean you are not responsible for doing so. If you want to experiment with a Web server on your local area network, one sure way to avoid possible problems is simply to unplug your router's Internet connection (the cable to a DSL or cable modem, for example). Then you can play to your heart's content, and you don't have to worry about setting up your firewall. Physical security trumps software security every time.*

Out-of-the-Box Apache

Once you have turned on the Web server, you can start to serve Web pages to anyone who has access to your computer via its IP address. You can do this using two computers on your local area network. You can also access your own computer via its IP address. Documents for the Web site are stored in the Documents folder of the WebServer folder, which is inside the Library folder, as shown in Figure 15-3.

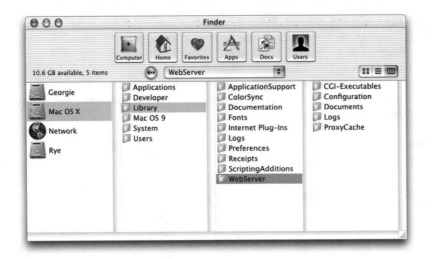

FIGURE 15-3 WebServer Documents folder contains the HTML pages for your site.

As it ships, you will find a variety of files in this directory already. A user requests a page by typing in your computer's IP address and the name of the file:

```
http://192.168.1.9/test.html
```

If the name of a file is omitted, the default file in the directory—index.html—is returned (if it exists).

Setting Up with Sites in Mac OS X Server

The Site tab in the Web Server configuration window lets you create a number of sites. Use a checkbox to enable or disable each site; in that way you can set up sites for later use or temporarily disable (but not remove) sites. Figure 15-4 shows the main site configuration pane. Use it to set the default page for the site and the other options shown there.

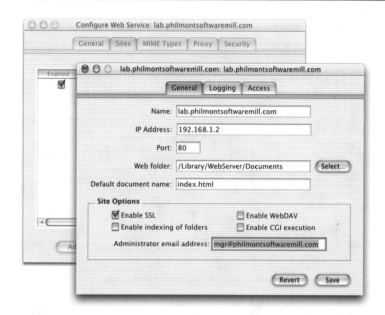

FIGURE 15-4 Configure each Web site with Mac OS X Server if you run a Web server for multiple sites.

Extending Apache with cgi-bin

You can create Web pages on-the-fly or process data from an HTML form using plug-ins and scripts. You place these inside the CGI-Executables folder inside WebServer. Use subfolders for security and safety rather than the top level of the CGI-Executables folder.

As shipped, Apache is configured appropriately to handle CGI scripts. You simply place the scripts within the CGI-Executables folder and Apache will automatically route requests to them if the URL ends with .cgi or if a form action is POST and the appropriate URL is provided.

You can change the behavior of Apache with regard to suffixes by using the MIME type configuration tab, as shown in Figure 15-5. Before you go on a MIME-type-suffix spree, remember that the shipping settings are probably just fine for you.

Many, many books have been written about the use of cgi-bin and scripts (including Perl). This section provides the high-level overview that can get you started. The author of this book is also the author of *Perl 5 Programmer's Notebook* (Prentice Hall PTR, 2000), which provides a number of useful ready-to-use Perl scripts for Web sites. (Perl is shipped as part of Mac OS X and Mac OS X Server.) Before moving on to other types of Web servers you can use, look at the Security tab available to you in Mac OS X Server; it is shown in Figure 15-6.

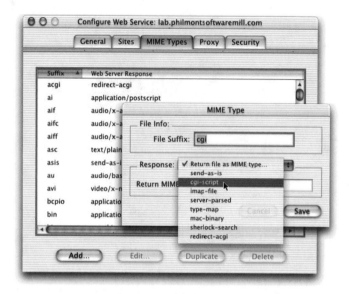

FIGURE 15-5   Configure MIME-type behavior in Apache.

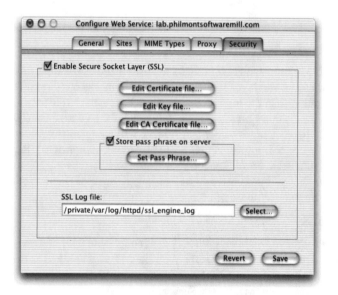

FIGURE 15-6   Security settings in Mac OS X Server

All of the major security features of Web servers are available in Apache; in Mac OS X Server, they can be configured with Server Admin. Opening your computer or server to other uses—particularly in the public world of the Internet—requires careful consideration of security issues. Fortunately, the world of the Web is now mature enough that very sophisticated security tools such as these are standard.

Using Other Web Servers

Apache is not the only Web server you can use with Mac OS X. If it is enabled, it will normally listen at port 80 for incoming HTTP requests, but you can have another Web server listening at another port.

The most common case for a second Web server is to use something like FileMaker's automatic Web publishing of its databases. FileMaker—like a number of other products—has a built-in Web server. Designed for limited use (10 users on the standard FileMaker product), it can be run on a local area network in conjunction with another Web server: you merely need to assign unique port numbers to each server. Users connect to the various servers by adding port numbers to URLs, as in http://192.168.1.2:591 (for port 591) and http://192.168.1.2:380 (for port 380). If a port is omitted from a Web address, it is assumed to be 80. In setting up your Web server on Mac OS X Server, you can set its port number for each site as shown previously in Figure 15-4.

Moving Up…WebObjects

With Apache, cgi-bin scripts, and products like FileMaker Pro, you can set up and manage a very powerful Web site. However, you can go much further. WebObjects—another Apple product—extends the functionality you have seen here in many directions. WebObjects is both a development environment and an application program that runs alongside Apache (or another Web server) to handle dynamic requests in a more sophisticated manner than scripting with Perl or other scripting languages. Starting with WebObjects 5 for Java, it is written totally in Java and is transportable to any computer running Java.

| NOTE | *WebObjects 5 for Java Developer's Guide, by Jesse Feiler, published by Osborne/ McGraw-Hill, provides all the information you need to use WebObjects effectively.* |

Summary

This chapter offered an overview of how to use the Apache Web server provided with Mac OS X. Placing a simple site on the Web, or on your LAN, merely requires turning on the Web server feature and moving files into the appropriate location. The chapter has also shown you how to extend Apache with cgi-bin scripts and how to use other Web servers.

Part IV

Using Applications on Mac OS X

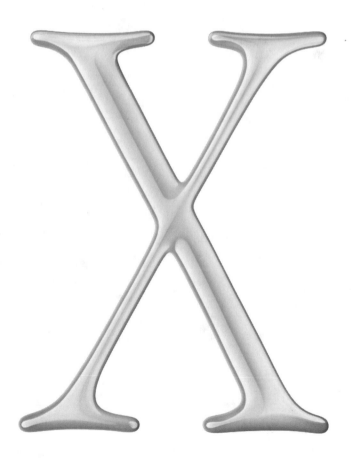

Chapter 16

Working with Applications

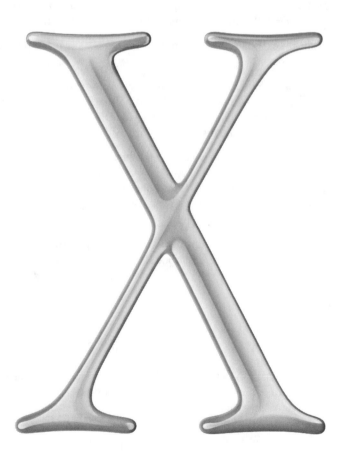

This part of the book is about applications and how to use them on Mac OS X. In this chapter, you will find an introduction to the applications and utility programs that ship with Mac OS X. The next chapter, Chapter 17, "Working with Services," explores services—a feature of Mac OS X that can revolutionize the way you work (truly!). In Chapter 18, "Using Apple Mail," you'll discover an email program that is part of Mac OS X, which may become your primary email tool. The final chapter in this part of the book, Chapter 19, "Using AppleWorks" explores Apple's suite of tools for word processing, spreadsheets, graphics, databases, and presentations. AppleWorks is included with some Macintosh computers; it is available on both Mac OS 9 and earlier, as well as on Mac OS X (and on Windows).

This chapter is organized into five sections:

■ **Application Support**   This section shows you some of the basics of opening and saving files, using standard system functions such as the Color Picker, as well as Find and Replace. These are the basic elements—together with the specific Aqua features described in Chapter 2, "Aqua,"—that make Mac OS X so easy to use.

■ **Using TextEdit**   TextEdit is a basic word processor, but for many people it is enough for most of their tasks.

■ **Media Tools**   QuickTime Player is used to play digital media in a variety of formats. iTunes lets you listen to and manage digital audio. Image Capture is a program that easily moves images from digital cameras to a Mac OS X computer, and iMovie lets you work with digital video. All are discussed in this section.

■ **Desktop Tools**   Sherlock helps you search the Internet and your local disks. Address Book is integrated with Mail and lets you keep track of individuals and groups. Stickies is a popular note-keeping program first introduced in Mac OS 7. Grab lets you capture screenshots of your computer's display. Calculator provides a desktop calculator for simple (and not-so-simple) calculations.

■ **Other Tools**   The Java Applet Launcher, Chess (an Apple front-end to the famous GNU chess game), and others are described in the final section.

Application Support

Mac OS X provides a host of support for applications—for their designers and implementers, as well as for users. This support ranges from the guidelines for the human interface to a variety of code samples for developers and application frameworks that actually implement code for developers to reuse. Not all of this support is used. As a result, you may well encounter application programs that violate the interface guidelines or that implement common functionality in idiosyncratic ways. In some cases, this is the result of ignorance or carelessness on the part of the developer; fortunately, such cases are rare. In other cases, this is the result of a developer attempting to reconcile conflicting guidelines from different environments. A developer implementing an application program for Windows, Classic Mac OS, and Mac OS X may forego the services feature of Mac OS X, as it does not exist in the other environments.

Even more common is the case of application programs that were written years ago. At the dawn of the personal computer era, each programmer had to implement basic functionality such as the manipulation of color. As that functionality was added to operating systems, programmers did not always remove their idiosyncratic (and formerly necessary) code. Periodically, good software developers do a wholesale cleanup of their code. This accounts for occasional new releases of products in which you cannot discern many new features.

Users, too, sometimes present difficulties in developers adopting new technologies. They can be comfortable with what they know. Users often say they'd rather settle for that than for a new feature they don't know how to use.

Put together, this suggests that the most innovative and easiest-to-use Mac OS X products are likely to be those written directly for it—and the software that ships with it. Older products will run on Mac OS X (either in the Classic Compatibility Environment or as Carbonized applications); however, they do not use many of the new and most useful features.

This section covers six basic application support features of Mac OS X:

- **Dialogs**   Changed from Mac OS 9 and earlier, these are windows that require a response from the user—often immediately.

- **Alerts**   These are messages that inform you about conditions that require immediate attention.

- **Working with Files**   You manipulate documents and folders in the Finder, but also in applications. The Open and Save dialogs help you do so.

- **Color Picker**   A common dialog that is used in many applications, the Color Picker is a powerful (and potentially complex) way of managing color.

- **Find/Replace**   Another common dialog helps you work with text.

You may want to refer to Chapter 2, "Aqua," which covers other common application interface elements such as the standard menus, buttons, and other controls.

Dialogs

Dialogs require you to respond to a question from the system. It may be "Where should this document be stored?" or it may be "How many copies should be printed?" Sometimes the response is needed before any other work can be done. Other times, it is needed before you do a specific task.

System Modal Dialogs

System modal dialogs no longer exist in Mac OS X. These were dialogs that brought the entire computer to a standstill until you responded to the dialog. Fortunately, they are outdated.

Application Modal Dialogs

Application modal dialogs require your attention before anything else can be done with that application. You can click on the desktop or on another application in the Dock or in a Finder window and continue your work in another application, but you cannot continue with the first application until you dispose of its application modal dialog.

   You often cause application modal dialogs to be presented if you quit from an application in which there are unsaved changes that are not associated with an individual document. You also cause an application modal dialog to be presented if you attempt to create something (such as a mailbox in Mail) that needs to be named before it can be created. An application modal dialog is shown next. You cannot continue working in Mail until you dismiss it.

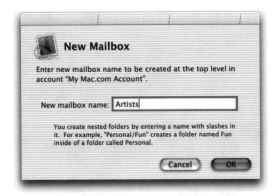

   Dialogs usually have at least two buttons. The default button, is highlighted and throbs slightly in the Aqua interface. It is generally at the lower right of a dialog and is the button you most frequently use. The RETURN key on the keyboard is equivalent to clicking the default button. Default buttons may be Save (in a Save dialog) or OK (in other dialogs). To the left of the default button, there is usually a Cancel button. This cancels the dialog. It does not cancel an underlying action, as you will see in the discussion of the Save dialog, next.

Document Modal Dialogs

Document modal dialogs are the most common sort. They prevent you from working in an individual document until you deal with them, but you can continue working in other

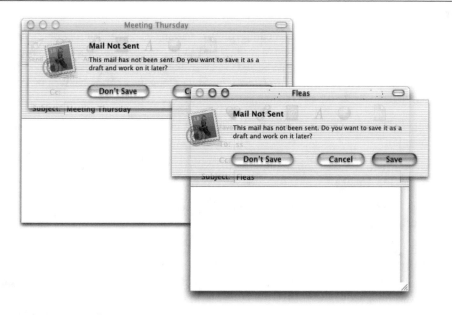

FIGURE 16-1   A Save dialog lets you name and save an unsaved document.

applications and in other documents within that application. Closing an unsaved document causes a document modal dialog to appear as shown in Figure 16-1.

The default (Save) button is in the lower right and is highlighted; the Cancel button is next to it. To the left, a third button, Don't Save, appears. This cancels the save operation. The Cancel button cancel the dialog and returns you to the unsaved document, while Don't Save closes the unsaved document. Document modal dialogs are typically implemented as sheets on Mac OS X. Sheets are clearly associated with an individual document.

Modeless Dialogs

Modeless dialogs include palettes, pickers, and Find/Replace dialogs. They allow you to choose a new tool (or color or word) easily just before you need to use it. They are dialogs in the sense that they require a response from you. They differ from the modal dialogs in that the response is required when you want to do something, not when the computer needs input from you.

Alerts

Alerts are dialogs that inform you of something, often a warning. (Dialogs ask for your input; alerts only ask that you notice them.) On Mac OS 9 and earlier, alerts featured icons of progressively graver countenance suggesting notes, alerts, and stop warnings. Their meanings are demonstrated by the sample text provided in *Macintosh Human Interface Guidelines* (Addison-Wesley Publishing Corporation, Boston, 1992):

- ■ **Note**   "The color 'mauve' is not very attractive in this context. Some people may complain."

- ■ **Alert**   "Are you sure you want to use the color 'Mauve' here? Your picture may suffer irreparable damage."

- ■ **Stop**   "You cannot use the color 'Mauve' in this context. Try using a more attractive color such as 'Teal.'"

For all the support of these alerts, most people did not distinguish between the levels. That, together with the fact that alerts can be associated with any of the many applications that are running on Mac OS X has resulted in a standard in which alerts contain the application icon rather than a warning icon.

Alerts contain at least one button. If there is only one, it is normally an OK button that you click (or use the RETURN key to accept) indicating that you have read the warning. A Cancel button may be available to stop the action; further buttons (Save or Erase, for example) may appear. Of course, if the Alert is cautionary and indicates that serious problems could occur, both an OK and Cancel button should appear so that you can prevent the dire consequences. An alert that says, "Your hard disk has just been erased" is not of much use.

Alerts that are specific to one document can be implemented as sheets. You will note that there are fewer and fewer alerts in the interfaces of Mac OS X applications. This is because good user interface design emphasizes prevention. You will not find menu commands enabled that allow you to do things that could cause problems (and generate alerts).

Working with Files

Many applications on personal computers are document-centric. You create or open a document, work on its contents, then close it—usually saving it so you or someone else can open it another time. The New command in the File menu is available in most applications (it was discussed in Chapter 2, "Aqua"). The commands to open and save files are discussed here.

Opening Files

The Open command in the File menu lets you open existing files. Most applications allow you to do so. An Open dialog is shown here:

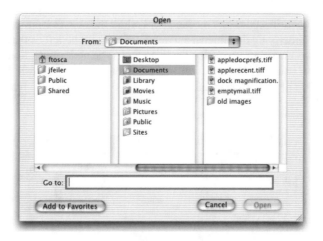

You can navigate through the files in your directories just as you do in a Finder window that is set to column view. If you want to go to a particular directory or folder, type its name in the Go To field toward the bottom of the window. You also can navigate from the current directory to enclosing directories using the From pop-up menu at the top of the window as shown here:

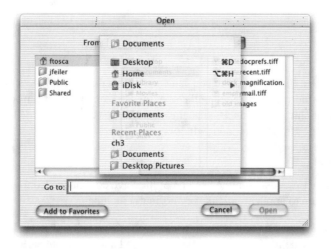

Note the Add to Favorites button here. Use it to add a directory or folder in which you're working to your favorites so you can quickly come back to it. Favorites can come and go; you don't need to make a major commitment to them. If you're going to be spending an hour working on one set of documents, use the Add To Favorites button. You can always remove files and folders from your Favorites folder later. (They are usually aliases created in response to clicking the Add to Favorites button. You can simply drag the aliases from the Favorites folder to the trash, and the underlying documents and applications will be left as they were on the disk.)

Some applications have more complex Open dialogs. The next illustration shows the Open dialog from TextEdit; you can select the way in which you want plain text to be encoded from the pop-up button. Other types of Open dialogs may let you choose specific types of files to open.

As you can with a Finder window, you can enlarge this dialog with the Resize control at the lower right of the window. By expanding the window horizontally, you can see more of your files and their hierarchies. You can also use the scroll bar to scroll from side to side in the column view of files, just as in a Finder window.

Saving Files

When it comes time to save a file, you use one of the Save commands from the File menu. These vary from application to application, but they normally include

- **Save**   Saves the data to the file in which it already resides; if it needs a name, you are asked to provide it. If you have already provided a name (in an earlier save) or if the file was opened by you (as opposed to having been created with a New command), there is no need to ask you for a name and no dialog is presented to you.

- **Save As**   Saves the data to a new file and prompts you for a name. That name becomes the name of the document.

When you choose a Save command and a name is required, a sheet rolls down from the top of the window as shown here:

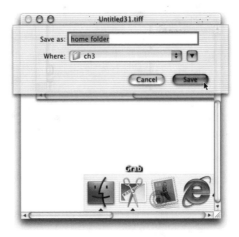

A default document name may be filled in for you, such as the name of the window—untitled for the first document you create in an application. You can use the Where pop-up button to select from recent folders, favorites, and other locations as shown here:

Depending on the application, you may also see a pop-up menu that lets you choose the file format to be used. Clicking the disclosure triangle will expand the dialog as shown here:

In the enlarged view, you can browse folders on your disks and across the network to determine where to place your file. (Note that you can also add files or folders to your Favorites from this dialog.)

You can also drag the Resize control at the lower-right corner of the Save dialog to see more columns, as shown in Figure 16-2.

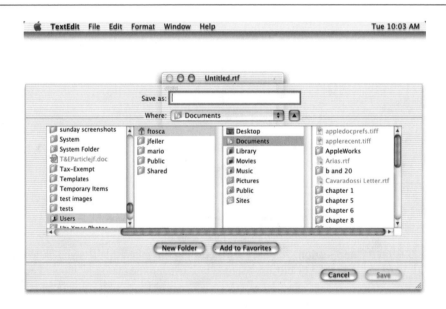

FIGURE 16-2   Enlarged and expanded Save dialog

Quitting an Application

When you quit an application and you have unsaved files, you are prompted to save them with an application modal dialog. Quit Anyway will jettison your unsaved documents. Cancel is used to cancel your Quit command—it has no effect on the files. You are returned to the application.

If you click Review Unsaved, each unsaved document will be presented to you in turn with a Save dialog. If only one unsaved document is open, a standard save dialog is presented. When the last Close dialog has been handled by you, the application quits.

Sheets are displayed within an individual window, and they relate only to that document. The dialog warning you about unsaved files is related to the application as a whole, not an individual document, and for that reason the dialog is shown on its own, rather than in a sheet attached to a document.

Color Picker

The Color Picker is available to all Mac OS X applications that let you select colors. You use it to select colors, just as you do in Mac OS 9 and other operating systems. What is different about the Mac OS X Color Picker is that you can easily store a palette of selected colors in it, and that palette is available to all applications. In this way, you can use standard colors for logos, fonts, and other graphical elements.

 Remember that color looks different in various contexts. Don't stomp your feet and say "It's the same color" when the burnt umber on your custom-designed t-shirt doesn't match the "identical" burnt umber on your Web site which in turn looks radically different from the "same" color printed on a high-quality paper.

To set a color, use the Color Picker, shown next. In TextEdit, you use it to set the color of text. It is located in the Format menu under the Font submenu; its command is Colors. In other applications, it appears in other places to set colors of other objects.

The Colors dialog has a variety of ways of showing colors. They are determined by the four buttons in the top row of the panel. The buttons select from a color wheel, four common color models, a spectrum, and selected palettes.

Representing color in a scientific or numerical form has intrigued thinkers for centuries. The color wheel and spectrum in the Color Picker attempt to show all colors in their gradations from one to another. Of course, not every color can be shown—only a rainbow does that (or so it seems). The color models approximate colors using numbers. These are good approximations, but they, too, miss colors. For example, a red value of 125 1/3 cannot be represented: it must be 125 or 126. Such tiny adjustments are the bane of graphic designers and printers.

By default, the Colors dialog opens to the color wheel shown in the previous illustration. The vertical slider at the right controls brightness, the colors are shown in a circle. To use the color wheel, you may want to enlarge the Colors dialog using the Resize control at the lower right. To choose a color, click on it. It will appear in the swatch rectangle at the lower left of the dialog.

If you click the second button, you can select from four popular color models. The next illustration shows the first model—grayscale. Here you can select from any of several standard shades of gray.

The second model is called RGB. It consists of three integers ranging in value from 0 to 255; each represents the relative value of red, green, or blue in the color. RGB is typically used to describe colors on computer monitors. As you can see in the next dialog on the left, you can specify exact values or use the sliders to adjust the color values. (The sample color at the lower left of the Colors dialog changes as you do so.) In the image on the right you see the third color model, CMYK. This is a set of four integers (not three, as in RGB), specifying values from 0 to 100 for each of cyan, magenta, yellow, and black. CMYK is typically used by printers.

Finally, the fourth color model is HSV—hue, saturation, and value. Used in television set calibration, the values are 0–360 for hue (it is an angle), and percentages (0–100) for saturation and value. It is shown here:

As noted previously, these models generally represent all colors. As you switch from one model to another in the Colors dialog, you will see the same color in your sample represented in

Application Support

the different systems. Because only integer values are used, there are often slight rounding errors that normally do not make much of a difference. For very intense graphics work, they must be taken into account.

The third button in the top row lets you use several predefined palettes of colors. These are most often used for setting the colors of interface elements such as buttons. This display is shown next on the left. Finally, rather than looking at color models, you can use the fourth button in the second row to select a spectrum display as shown next on the right.

Like the color wheel, this display attempts to show all colors. You can click one, and it will be shown in the swatch at the lower left; you can then switch to one of the color models to see its parameters. In any event, you can click Apply and the color will be applied to whatever object has been selected.

As with the color wheel, if you resize the Colors dialog, you can work more accurately with the spectrum in a larger version. In addition to applying colors to objects, you can store colors in the small palette at the bottom of the Colors dialog. Simply drag the color you want from the swatch to an unused cell in the palette.

Also at the bottom, you will find a tool (a magnifying glass) to examine the color of an object anywhere on the screen. Click it, then move it over the color you like—anywhere on the screen, in any application. When you click, that color will be placed in the swatch at the lower left of the Colors panel and the display you have selected will be adjusted to show it.

The button at the right—Apply—places the color you have chosen in the appropriate part of the selected object. Instead of clicking Apply, you can also drag the color from the Color Picker or from the sample at the lower left to the object to be colored. You simply click the mouse in the appropriate swatch of color and drag it.

Find/Replace

A standard Find/Replace dialog and standard menu commands in the Edit menu are used in Mac OS X. (Of course, Find/Replace is not implemented in all applications. It is text-oriented and is not germane to many graphics programs.)

Find and Replace are standard word processing functions that let you search for—and optionally replace—text. This can be individual letters, words, or even whole sentences. A computer's power comes into its own here, but you can work with it to make your documents easier to search.

For example, use consistent words or phrases—even notes to yourself. Searching for CheckThis in a document can find all the places where you have made notes to yourself—something that is impossible to do if you mingle CheckThis with Really?, Not Sure, and the like.

A TextEdit document is shown in Figure 16-3, along with the Find/Replace dialog and the Find command's submenu. This functionality is common to many application programs that you may have used. An added feature is the ability to automatically place selected text from your document into the search field with the Use Selection For Find menu command.

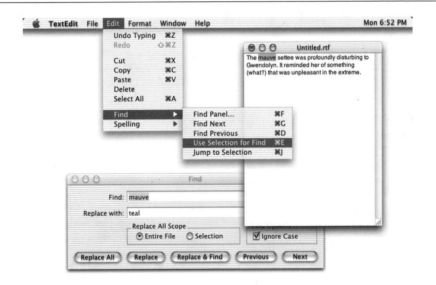

FIGURE 16-3   Find/Replace and Edit menu

Using TextEdit

TextEdit is a word processor that handles many of the tasks you need for creating basic documents. (What it does not focus on are the complexities of multipage documents: automatic numbering, headers and footers, and columnar layouts.) Everything that you would expect from a basic word processor is here: fonts, styles (such as bold and italics), find and replace, spell-checking, and even links to email.

If you have used small-scale text editors such as SimpleText and SimpleSound in Mac OS 9 and earlier, you may have noticed that they have a limit to the length of their documents. If you have attempted to open lengthy Read Me files, you may have seen the message, "This document is too long to be opened by SimpleText." This limit does not exist in TextEdit. The basics of TextEdit (and of word processing in general) are described in this section:

- Creating text documents

- Formatting text

- Setting preferences

- Integrating text from elsewhere

Use these basic techniques for other word processing applications such as AppleWorks and Microsoft Word. Use them also in other applications that handle text, such as PowerPoint, FileMaker, and even for entering titles into iMovie.

Creating Text Documents

When you create a new document (using the New command from the File menu), a blank window opens. Simply type the text that you want.

Word Processing Terminology   If you are new to word processing, some of the terminology may be new. Here are the basic words and concepts:

- **Font**   In general terms, a font is the set of characters used to display the alphabet in your document. (Both the computer and typographical definitions are more complicated and precise.) On manual typewriters, a font consisted of the actual typebars that struck the paper to produce images. You could buy typewriters with different fonts. In 1960, IBM produced the Selectric typewriter with a little replaceable ball so that one typewriter could produce different fonts, depending on which ball you placed in it.

- **Electronic fonts**   Today, fonts are created and used electronically. Fonts are installed on your computer and you can choose among them. You can also add to them.

- **Serifs**   These are the small lines at the top and bottom of font characters, as well as the small variations in size within them. Fonts are classified as serif or sans serif. Serif fonts (such as the font used in the body of this book) are easier to read than sans serif fonts when the text is lengthy. Sans serif fonts are often used in headlines—such as the word Figure that appears in captions beneath figures in this book.

■ **Non-proportional fonts**   Some fonts (such as Courier, a typewriter-like font) are characterized by using the same width for each character. Others, such as the font used in the body of this book, use different widths for different characters (an i, for example, is narrower than a w). Proportional fonts are generally easier to read than non-proportional fonts, at least for long passages of text.

■ **Style**   A font can be varied by making it bold (heavier), italicized, or underlined. This is achieved behind the scenes either by electronically manipulating the basic font or by using a variation of the font.

■ **Size**   You can change the size of a font. This is done electronically by scaling the font for you.

■ **Plain text/rich text**   Plain text consists of the text you type without any font or formatting information; it is only the keystrokes (letters, numbers, and spaces). Rich text (sometimes called styled text) includes font and formatting information—italics, different-sized characters, colors, and the like. Rich text files have a suffix of .rtf, and they can normally be opened by most word processing applications such as Microsoft Word or Corel WordPerfect. (Plain text is sometimes also called ASCII text—pronounced "askee.")

Experiment with fonts, styles, and sizes. Find the right balance for your documents between plain and boring text and annoying experiments. Pay particular attention to the relationship of the color of text to the color of its background (paper or monitor). Some combinations are much more legible than others. Also, pay attention to font sizes: not everyone has the same eyesight. In testing fonts, make sure that you test large enough sections of text—at least a paragraph. Showing someone the word "cat" by itself on a page and asking if the type is legible is not going to help you too much.

Word Processing Tips   Here are some tips for typing a document in TextEdit (or in any other word processor):

■ The text will automatically move to the next line when you reach the right margin. If you are used to pressing RETURN at the end of a typewritten line, do not do so. Use RETURN only at the end of a paragraph.

■ Text formatted on a computer looks best with a single space at the end of a sentence (after the period). Typists typically put two spaces after a period.

■ You can change fonts, styles, and font sizes at any time. Some people like to set everything up before they start. Others just type away and then go back to adjust the look of the text. Neither way is right: do what you prefer.

Using TextEdit

■ Tabs are set automatically in TextEdit. Use TAB to align columns of text, rather than spaces. Aligning columns with spaces only works if you use non-proportional fonts.

Formatting Text with TextEdit

As noted in Chapter 2, "Aqua," as you get further into the menu bar (that is, further to the right for Roman alphabet-based systems), the menus get increasingly specific to the application. Whereas the File menu is quite standard across applications, the Edit menu varies, reflecting the different needs of different applications. The Edit menu shown next enables you to cut and copy text, manage undo/redo, and use Find/Replace, as well as check spelling:

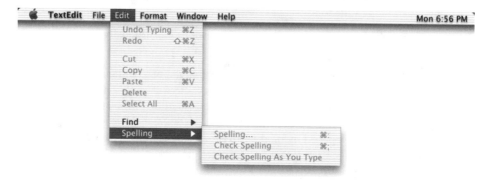

The next menu varies more from application to application. Its name is not always the same, and its purpose varies. The following shows the Format menu in the TextEdit application with the Font submenu visible.

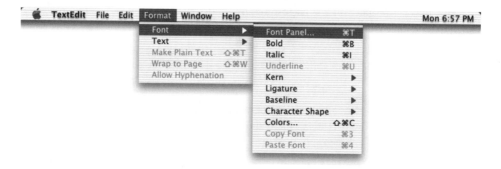

Many of these concepts are familiar to typographers, but they are normally implemented only in high-end graphics programs. They are implemented in the operating system itself, so they are available to any program that is written to use Mac OS X. (In other words, they are not normally implemented in the Classic Compatibility Environment or in Carbonized applications unless they have been implemented specifically by the developer.)

Font Panel   The Font panel is used in many Mac OS X applications. It provides a single place in which to set fonts, their sizes, and their typefaces or styles (italics, for example). A font panel is shown next. You open it with the Font Panel command in the Font submenu of the Format menu.

When you close the Font panel, its settings are applied either to the selected text in your document or to the text that you type from the insertion point forward. In font terminology, sometimes Black is used instead of Bold. Likewise, Oblique and Italics may be used interchangeably.

The leftmost column of the font panel may not be seen if the window is not wide enough. You can use it to display specific collections of fonts that you use. By creating your own collections, you can limit the fonts in documents to a relatively small number. The button at the bottom of the window lets you move fonts into and out of collections (including the special collection called Favorites). The window shown in Figure 16-4 lets you do this.

In addition to Favorites, you may find other collections installed on Mac OS X. The PDF collection is the standard fonts that are used for PDF documents; the Web collection is a set of fonts that most Web browsers can display on most computers. On the design front, Classic and Modern are collections of fonts that loosely fit into those categories.

Kerning   Kerning is the technical term for the horizontal spacing between characters. (Some word processors refer to it as spreading.) You can adjust it in TextEdit. Vertical spacing is referred to as leading (pronounced "ledding"), since in the days of lead type extra lead was inserted between lines of text to increase the space. Leading is not adjustable in TextEdit.

Using TextEdit

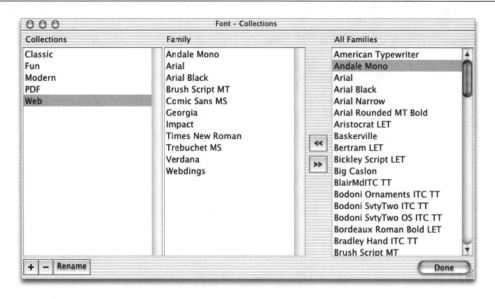

FIGURE 16-4   Managing font collections with the Font panel

Ligatures   Ligatures are two characters in a font that were originally cast as a single piece of type. They are set close together and handled as one character. The combinations ae and oe are frequently set as ligatures. In TextEdit, you can control the degree to which ligatures are closed up (spaced together).

Baselines   You can adjust the baselines of text to create superscripts and subscripts. You can use default values for these or you can specify your own values using these commands.

Font Colors   If you choose Colors from the Font submenu of the Format menu, you will open the Color Picker that was described earlier.

Copying and Pasting Fonts   A very useful feature of TextEdit is the ability to copy and paste fonts, not text. (This is sometimes implemented as a Copy Special or Paste Special command in other applications.) You simply select the text that has the font style, size, and other characteristics that you like and then select other text, and paste the font over it. Remember that copying and pasting fonts are in the Format menu, not the Edit menu with the other Copy/Paste commands.

The Text submenu lets you align text left, right, or centered. It, too, is a standard word processing command. It is shown in Figure 16-5. The alignment items (left, center, justify, and

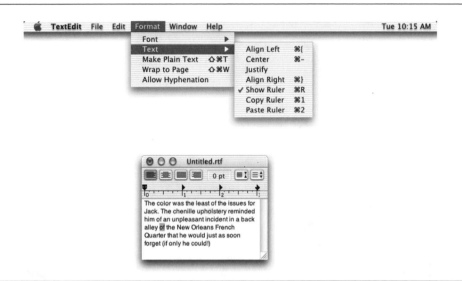

FIGURE 16-5   Format menu for TextEdit with Text submenu

right) let you set how the margins on the page appear. Left-aligned text has a straight left margin; characters are then placed on the line until there is no more room and then they are moved to the next line. (Left-justified text is also known as ragged-right: the left margin is straight, the right is not.)

Right-aligned text (also known as ragged-left) is the reverse of left-aligned text. Centered text is ragged on both sides, and the lines are centered on the page. Finally, justified text has straight vertical margins on both sides: spaces are inserted to make the text appear as a rectangular block.

Justified text when the lines of text are short has a tendency to look peculiar. The computer tries to justify the text, but without a sufficient number of characters on a line, the inserted blank spaces can look strange.

A ruler is shown in the next illustration's window; its commands are also in the Text submenu. Rulers let you set margins and tabs; they are used in many applications. At the top of the ruler is a variety of controls for the text that follows the ruler. A ruler applies to all text beneath it until another ruler is encountered. Note that you can copy and paste rulers with the commands from the Format menu. This lets you set a document style, insert a new ruler for a table or indented paragraph, and then return to the original formatting by copying and pasting the initial ruler below the table or indented paragraph.

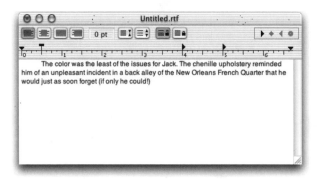

At the left are four buttons that set justification: left, centered, justified, and right. The data entry field lets you set the additional height of each line that you want. For a 12-point font, you may want to set 15 to spread the lines apart and make a more pleasing appearance. The two buttons to the right of this field do the same: the first decreases line height and the second increases it (the values that they produce are displayed in the data entry field).

Another pair of buttons let you control if line height is flexible or not. If you are using sub- or superscripts or inserting characters of various fonts and sizes, you may want to allow variation in line heights. Alternatively, you may want to set them large enough that all variations are accommodated and everything is consistent.

In the measured scale below these buttons, you can set margins and tab stops. You drag margin icons to the positions you want them. You can drag tab stops back and forth; you remove them by dragging them slightly above the measured scale (they will disappear). You create tab stops by dragging the appropriate tab from the box of four tabs at the upper right. These tabs specify alignment within the tabbed text. From left within the box, the produce the following alignments:

- **Left-aligned tabs** This is the familiar tab behavior.

- **Center-aligned tabs** The text that you type following the tab is aligned in the space between the tab and the next tab or the end of the line.

- **Right-aligned tabs** The text that you type following the tabs is right-aligned to the next tab or the end of the line.

- **Decimal-aligned tabs** Particularly useful in creating tables, this tab alignment places the decimal point of a number at the tab location you set. Other digits are placed before or after the decimal point. Thus, a column of decimal-aligned tabs looks the way you expect it to in a ledger or statistical table.

The two margins are represented by the down-pointing triangles. In the illustration shown above, the left margin is at 0, and the right margin is just beyond 6.5 You can separately set the first line indentation: here it is set at 0.5. As you can see from the typed text, the first line is indented. Note that you can create hanging indents—the first line indentation can be at 0 and the left margin (for subsequent lines) can be further to the right. The toggled menu command—Make Rich Text/Make Plain Text—lets you choose which type of text you type.

Normally in TextEdit, the text is placed in the window you have open. When your typing approaches the end of a line, it is wrapped to the next line. Reshaping the window can cause the text to wrap differently. The Wrap To Page command wraps text to the paper size that you have chosen in Page Setup. As a result, reshaping the window does not cause the text to reflow; changing the paper size in Page Setup does. Turn Wrap To Page on if your printouts are too small. This is not always the problem, but it frequently is.

Setting Preferences for TextEdit

The Preferences for TextEdit are shown in Figure 16-6. You can use the default settings or change them for all documents. You can also use the menu commands to override preferences and change them in individual documents.

Typing Away

You can type whatever you want in your TextEdit document. You don't have to worry about running over the limits of the program, and the editing tools at your command are extensive. Everyone occasionally makes mistakes. Either your fingers slip on the keyboard or you truly can't remember if it's wierd or weird.

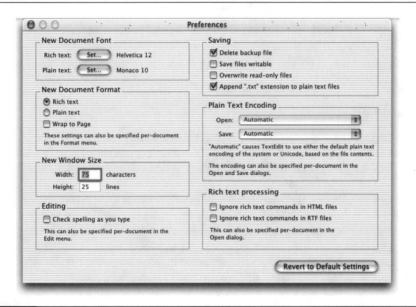

| FIGURE 16-6 | TextEdit Preferences |

The Spelling submenu in the Edit command lets you check spelling all at once or as you type. Both Check Spelling commands highlight misspelled words. The Spelling window, which you can open with the first spelling command, lets you check words, add unfamiliar words to your dictionary, and view a list of suggested replacement words. Spelling is discussed in the next chapter as well. It is a Mac OS X service, and it is available—with the same menu commands and the same dictionary—to any Mac OS X application that wishes to use it.

Media Tools

The first Macintosh computers came with two application programs that let you do everything you wanted to do: MacWrite handled word processing and MacDraw handled graphics. In the nearly two decades since then, a lot has changed. Perhaps the biggest change is that no longer is a personal computer seen as a tool to help people create documents that will be printed. The Internet and a wide assortment of digital media tools (sometimes lumped together in the phrase "new media") have made the days of paper as the primary medium seems quaint.

Four media tools are part of Mac OS X:

- **QuickTime Player**   Lets you view multimedia over the Internet or from CDs.

- **iTunes**   Lets you manage audio tracks; you can listen to them over the Internet, copy them to your own library, and play CDs.

- **iMovie**   The video authoring tool you use to combine video, audio, and text into your own movies that you can play, burn onto a DVD, convert to a QuickTime movie, or save as a live-action scrapbook.

- **Image Capture**   Lets you download still images from digital cameras and manipulate them on your Macintosh.

QuickTime Player

QuickTime Player is in your Applications folder; it also may be preinstalled in the Dock. You can use QuickTime Player to watch QuickTime TV—a variety of QuickTime TV channels sent out over the Internet with a wide selection of content. When you launch QuickTime Player, you see the channel list, as shown in Figure 16-7.

The two tabs at the top of the window let you switch between QuickTime TV (shown in Figure 16-7) and your favorites. To add a movie to your favorites, click on it to start it playing, then choose Add Movie As Favorite from the Favorites submenu of the QTV menu. Note that in QuickTime terminology, a movie refers to a stream of audio and video. It can be a great classic film like *Casque d'Or* or a live television broadcast of the latest weather report—both are streams of audio and video and thus both are considered movies.

FIGURE 16-7   Select the channel you want to play from the QuickTime player channels.

When you click a QuickTime TV channel or choose one of your favorites, the player turns into the controller shown next. (Use the round TV button in the lower right of both windows to toggle between the two displays.)

At the bottom, standard playback controls appear in the center. These five buttons are (from the left):

- You can jump to the beginning of the movie.

- You can rewind. Hold down this button until you get to the point you want to start playing from. Visual feedback is provided not only in the movie window itself, but also in the small bar above the buttons that shows the relative position in the movie.

- In the center, the largest button lets you play the movie from whatever location it is at. When you click it, it starts playing; if you click it again, it pauses at that location.

- Next, a fast-forward button lets you move ahead.

- Finally, a jump-to-end button lets you move to the end of the movie.

At the lower left of the controller, a slider lets you adjust the playback volume. Note that if you have muted sound output in System Preferences, you will not be able to hear any sound here. If there is a problem, check both the QuickTime Player control and the Sound preference in System Preferences.

Show/Hide Sound Controls from the Movie menu lets you use sound controls to adjust the quality of the playback audio. In the Window menu, the Show Movie Info command lets you see information about what you are watching, as shown here:

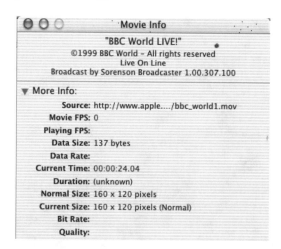

QuickTime preferences are shown in the next illustration. These control all displays of movies in QuickTime Player. In addition to launching movies from the QuickTime TV channels, you can also launch them by double-clicking movies on your disk, dragging movies onto the QuickTime Player icon, or entering a URL using the Open URL command in the File menu. These preferences affect all of the movies you open in all of these ways. Additional preferences are set in System Preferences in the QuickTime pane. These include your connection speed and a variety of lower-level preferences.

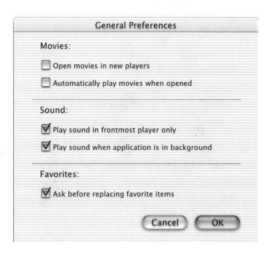

TIP   *Apple has authoring tools available for QuickTime. You can upgrade to QuickTime Pro in order to create your own movies. QuickTime Streaming Server provides a tool for sending movies out over the Internet. More information about both of these is available on Apple's Web site.*

Media Tools

iTunes

iTunes lets you play music CDs on your computer; in that role, it replaces Apple CD Audio Player, which shipped in Mac OS 9 and earlier. More than just a playback tool, iTunes let you assemble tracks from various sources and merge them into libraries on your disk or burn them onto your own CDs.

MP3

The big news in iTunes is MP3. The Motion Picture Experts Group (MPEG) is a working group of ISO/IEC devoted to developing "bit-efficient representation of audio-visual data." In other words, an international standards body has set standards for CDs, DVDs, set-top boxes, and the like. MP3 is one of their standards. It allows for a very efficient means of storing audio files. They are compressed using perceptual compression—frequencies that you cannot hear are removed from the original signal. Of course, at what point perceptual compression becomes distortion is a matter of debate. For all practical purposes (and for much casual listening), MP3 provides distortion-free sound reproduction in very little space.

The actual amount of storage space needed is typically 32 megabytes for one hour's worth of high-quality sound. Even a few years ago, that amount of storage space was beyond the realm of desktop computing capabilities. Today, when storage space and memory are both relatively inexpensive, those clumsy CDs can quickly be copied to disk and stored in MP3 format. From there, it is extraordinarily easy to attach them to email messages, post them on Web sites, and trade them with others.

You can connect an MP3 player to your computer using a USB cable. Once you have collected MP3 music and organized it, you can download it to your player where you can listen to several hours' worth of music before having to repeat a song (or recharge or replace a battery).

With many of today's MP3 devices, you can also record speech. Stored in MP3 format on the MP3 device, it can travel the same USB connection for you to store it on your computer, put it in a database, post it on a Web site, or otherwise distribute it. Because the recording capabilities of these devices are limited, they are best for recording meetings, speeches, and those dinner parties at which indiscreet guests tend to tell more than is appropriate about their betters.

Thou Shalt Not Steal

Unauthorized copying and redistributing copyright material (including music performances and—sometimes—classroom lectures) is illegal. The technology to support digitization and trading of music moved steadily forward during the 1980s and 1990s. With the advent of cheaper memory and disk storage in the late 1990s as well as the MP3 format that reduced demands on these already cheap resources, the business and societal aspects of the technology jumped into the forefront. Long-established laws do not always seem to apply today, and yet they are still on the books. See Andrew L. Shapiro's excellent book, *The Control Revolution: How the Internet is Putting Individuals in Charge and Changing the World We Know* (Public Affairs, New York, 2000) for more on these issues. See your daily newspaper or news broadcast for the latest on the legal front. In short, follow the steps in this chapter in order to legally use the copyrighted material to which you have access. Enjoy it, revel in it, and make certain that the creators and performers can continue doing what they love to do (and you appreciate).

Running iTunes for the First Time

When you first run iTunes, its Setup Assistant walks you through a few basic settings. In the first option, you can choose whether iTunes will be used to play MP3 audio streams in all cases. You may have other MP3 players on your computer (including QuickTime). It is up to you which one to choose. Note that iTunes is often a better choice for MP3 than QuickTime if you want to reassemble tracks and save them. QuickTime reads MP3 formats (and plays them), but iTunes both reads and writes MP3.

The second set of options determines whether iTunes can connect to the Internet to check the CD database (CDDB) at http://www.gracenote.com/ in order to provide information about the CDs you play. If you have an always-on connection such as cable or DSL, this connection is no big deal. For a dial-up connection, it may be an annoyance (or expensive!) to have the computer constantly connecting just to tell you the name of the artist whose song you are listening to. (If you do not like it, the extra cost of the phone call is likely just to add insult to injury.)

Using iTunes

iTunes maintains a library of your MP3 files. It can scan your disk to collect these files, or you can add them manually later. The Setup Assistant window lets you choose. Note that the disk scan can take some time for a large disk with many files. During the scanning process, you will see a progress bar.

iTunes scans all files. This is why you will see it checking files that are clearly not MP3 files. The source files will be left where they are on disk, but references to them will be placed in your iTunes library. If you move or delete those files, the library references will break. Other references will be okay.

Once iTunes completes its scan, you will see a display like the one shown in Figure 16-8. To start with, you will have only your Library and a Radio Tuner as sources (in the pane at the left). Clicking on either one will show its contents. (If you have not scanned your disk for MP3 files, the Library will be empty.) If you insert a CD, it, too, will be shown.

Internet Radio

The Radio Tuner source shows you Internet radio stations. You can click on one of them to play it, as shown in Figure 16-9. The stations are grouped into categories; clicking the disclosure triangles next to any category will open it.

The prebuffering referred to in the previous figure consists of iTunes downloading part of the audio stream before it begins to play. The strategy is to preload enough of the stream so while that preloaded data plays more data can be downloaded. Because of vagaries in connections, it is necessary to always have a bit of preloaded sound available to play so that if there is a brief interruption, that buffer will be used and you will not have an interruption in playing. (This is why setting your QuickTime preferences in System Preferences is important: knowing the type of connection you have will help all time-dependent media play.)

Media Tools

FIGURE 16-8 Adding files to iTunes

FIGURE 16-9 When you click a radio station, iTunes prebuffers the track.

CDs on iTunes

If you insert a CD, the CD itself is shown in the Source listing. Its tracks are shown in the main panel. You can enable or disable each track by clicking in the checkbox to the left of its title.

Start a track playing by double-clicking it. iTunes will continue to play each track in order until it reaches the end of the CD. The track that is playing will be identified in the pane at the top of the window and it will have a small icon next to it. The Source pane includes your Library and the Internet Radio Tuner; it also can include playlists that you create. The button in the lower left adds a new playlist. It controls the order in which items from your Library are played. Open the Library and then drag the tracks you want in your playlist onto the playlist icon in the Source pane. Next, click the playlist to open it. You can then rearrange these tracks. Note that the tracks must be in your Library before you can add them to a playlist.

If you connect an MP3 player with a USB connector, the player will appear in the Source pane; you can move tracks among the various sources (including the player). There are three buttons in the lower left of the window. The first adds a new playlist item to the Source panel. The next shuffles the tracks in the main window. Click it once and they will be randomized. Click it again, and they will return to their original order. Unselected tracks will be shuffled, but they will not be played.

The third button lets you repeat tracks. Click it once and you will see a small number 1 in the icon. This will repeat the current track over and over. Click it again, and it will be highlighted but without the 1. This will repeat the entire CD over and over. Finally, you can use the Turn Visual On command from the Visuals menu to create a dynamic light show.

iTunes Preferences

You can set preferences including those from the Setup Assistant in the iTunes preferences. The first tab is shown here:

The CD Insert pop-up menu lets you choose what happens when a CD is inserted. The choice shown here simply displays all of the tracks. Other choices are

■ Begin Playing

■ Import Songs

■ Import Songs and Eject

The importing options let you automatically convert all of the tracks on a CD to a different format. (Import Songs And Eject is useful if you are converting a collection of CDs one after the next.)

Importing preferences are shown in the next illustration. This is the preference for the format in which songs that are imported are stored. In other words, if you select AIFF, the Import Songs preference from the preceding panel will convert all songs on a CD to AIFF. The choices are MP3, AIFF, and WAV. You can also select the quality that is used. The higher the quality, the more disk space is used.

Finally, the next image shows the preferences you can set for the location of iTunes files and for burning CDs.

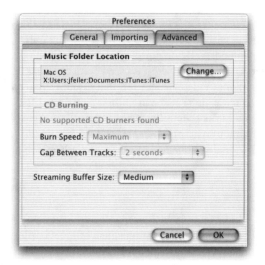

iMovie

iMovie is the authoring tool that ships with many Macintosh computers; you may also be able to download it from your iTools Software folder. iMovie helps you assemble movies from digitized video, audio, text titles, and transitions. Most often, the digitized video enters iMovie from a digital video camcorder such as the Canon Elura. You connect digital video camcorders via FireWire.

Output from iMovie can be an iMovie that you play in iMovie. It can also be a QuickTime movie that you post on the Web or send to others. You can also copy a completed movie to Apple's iDVD program to be written onto a DVD. (Other programs can do this as well.) You can also send the completed movie back to a digital video camcorder where it can be recorded on a DV cartridge.

Where Digitization Happens

Digital video has changed over the last few years. A decade ago, video devices such as VCRs and camcorders were analog. You could connect them to computers like the first Power Macintosh AV computers and later to the Power Macintosh 8600. Inside those computers, digitizing hardware and software converted the analog signal to digital video which can be stored on disk, transmitted, and otherwise handled like computer data. Today, digitization has moved out of the computer and into the peripherals. Digital cameras and video camcorders do their own digitization and communicate with the computer via USB or FireWire.

In the other direction, you normally do not play video as an analog signal from your computer. You export it to DVD or to the digital video camcorder's DV tape once it is digitized. From a DVD player or the digital video camcorder, that digital signal can be converted to an analog signal for display on television sets or monitors. And now, digital television is increasingly common; the monitors themselves can frequently receive digital input.

One exception to this paradigm is found on PowerBook computers. Because many presentation devices still use analog connectors, many PowerBook computers still produce analog output for that purpose.

iMovie Tips

The range of possibilities with iMovie is vast; you will find a number of suggestions and examples on Apple's Web site. Perhaps the simplest use of iMovie is to import a clip from your digital video camcorder and save it as a QuickTime movie. One step up in the sophistication chain is to do the same thing but add a title to the movie. You can continue progressively adding titles, transitions, and sound effects (included in iMovie) until the result is quite complex.

You can also approach iMovie as a tool for creating video in much the same way that a filmmaker creates a film. The chief difference in this approach from the simple conversion of video clips is that filmmakers shoot a great deal more footage than is ever used. When traditional film is used, that is expensive (both for the film and for developing costs). With digital video, the cost is much lower.

If you want to work in this way, start by recognizing that you will be shooting much more footage than you will ever use. You may shoot the same scene several times and use only the best one. (If you use every one, you will induce tedium or violence in your viewers.) This approach takes some of the pressure off your subjects and the camera operator (who may be you): you get more than one chance, and you make your decisions in iMovie.

iMovie makes editing easy—not just the editing that assembles clips, but the editing that trims the beginning and end of clips. One useful tip is to shoot just a little bit more footage at the beginning and end of each scene than you need. Shoot the doorway before someone walks through it; when someone leaves a room, shoot a second or two of the doorway after it is empty. This extra footage will help you in assembling a movie. It will be invaluable in preventing the amateurish movies in which people suddenly pop into a frame and then disappear.

Finally, remember that the wide variety of tools, audio clips, and effects that iMovie provides can help you create great videos when used appropriately. Experiment with them all, but for each video that you make, use only a subset. If you throw all the effects into every movie, no one will see your video. You do not have to use the same ones each time, but decide in advance what are the appropriate effects and use them for emphasis (not for distraction).

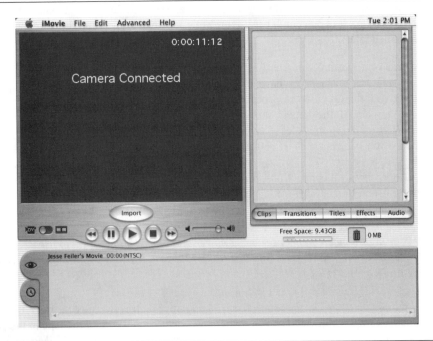

FIGURE 16-10   The iMovie desktop provides a monitor, two timelines, and a shelf.

Working with iMovie

When you launch iMovie, you see the environment shown in Figure 16-10. There are three major areas of the workspace:

- **Monitor**   In the upper left, the large window lets you view video. It has two modes that are controlled by the Mode Switch button in the lower left of this window. The DV/camera icon on the left is used to connect to the camera and view the images from its DV cartridge. The icon on the right representing two frames of film is used to view your iMovie.

- **Shelf**   In the upper right, a shelf contains items that you can insert into your movies. You use the buttons at the bottom of this window to select what appears in your shelf—clips, transitions, titles, effects, and audio.

■ **Viewer**   At the bottom, two viewers let you see your movie in a schematic version. The tabs on the left let you switch between the clip viewer (shown) and the timeline viewer (described later).

The process of importing video is simple. Step 1 is to shoot the video you want using your digital video camcorder. When you have shot the video, turn the camera off. Next, to import the video, connect your digital video camcorder to your computer via the FireWire port. (The computer can stay on, but the camera should be off while you connect it.) Turn the camera on in playback or VCR mode. If you select Camera mode in the Mode Switch at the lower left of the monitor, the iMovie controls such as play, rewind, and fast-forward will control the camera. Test this to make sure it works.

If it does not, check all connections, make certain that the camera is powered on (and has adequate power), and try again. If the camera is not recognized, sometimes quitting iMovie and restarting it will help.

NOTE   *If your digital video camcorder has a power adapter, you may want to use it for this process. Playing, rewinding, and fast-forwarding the DV tape in the camera can be a big drain on batteries.*

With a digital video camcorder connected, you can import clips from its cartridge by clicking the Import button. Importing will start from wherever you have positioned the tape in the camera (either with the camera's controls or with the iMovie controls as just described). iMovie will automatically break the video into clips and place them in the shelf. Clips are broken each time you stop the camera during shooting. Figure 16-11 shows two clips imported from a digital video camcorder.

You can drag clips into the clip viewer at the bottom of the window, as shown in Figure 16-12. You can move clips back to the shelf; you can also move them back and forth in the clip viewer (clips and transitions move aside automatically). With a clip selected, you can drag a transition from the Transitions tab of the shelf.

The Titles pane in the shelf lets you enter the text of titles and select how they are displayed, as you can see in Figure 16-13. Note the title is added to the clip that you have selected in the clip viewer. You can add titles at the beginning, end, or middle of your movie. The two lines of the title in this figure are Barn and Jesse Feiler; enter the title at the right and choose the font and effect there.

By default, clips are titled Clip 01, Clip 02, and so forth. You can rename them, check the length, and control the audio fade-in and fade-out from the Info panel. Show it by double-clicking a clip either in the clip viewer or in the shelf, as shown in Figure 16-14. You can apply a variety of effects using the Effects tab in the shelf, as shown in Figure 16-15. Experiment to see how different effects can be used.

Figure 16-16 shows the Audio tab of the shelf. You can select from a variety of audio clips or you can record your own (if a microphone is connected to your computer). Click the clock icon at the left of the viewer to show the timeline viewer. Whereas the clip viewer shows each clip in sequence, the time viewer shows clips and two audio channels with the proportionate amount of time each take. You can drag audio clips back and forth (and extend them).

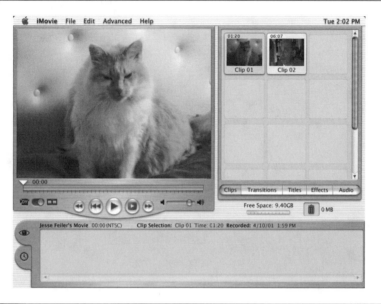

FIGURE 16-11   Import clips to the shelf.

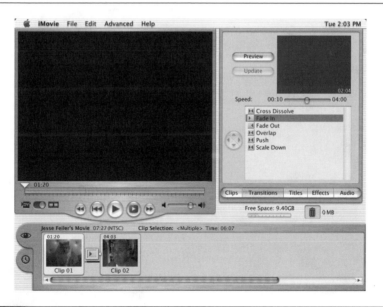

FIGURE 16-12   Rearrange clips and add transitions in the clip viewer.

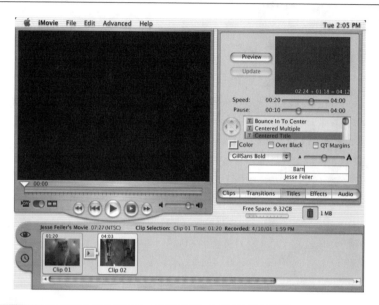

FIGURE 16-13   Add titles to your movie.

FIGURE 16-14   Rename and check clip info by double-clicking the clip.

FIGURE 16-15   Effects can be used for emphasis.

FIGURE 16-16   Audio effects can be chosen from the shelf.

When you have an audio effect in the timeline viewer, you can double-click it to open the Info window shown next. This lets you control the time length of fade-in and fade-out for the audio.

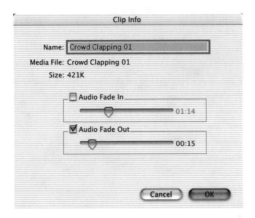

When you save your iMovie, it will be saved on disk, as shown in Figure 16-17. The clips are saved separately from the iMovie file; you an export the movie into other formats, as you will see later. If you have shot more video than you need, at some point you can destroy or archive the unneeded clips.

As you can see from the following illustration, you can set iMovie preferences for how imported clips are handled. Import preferences let you control how video from your digital video camcorder is imported. Most people like the default settings shown here.

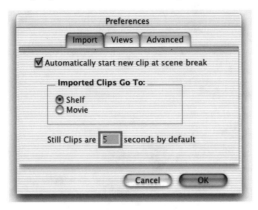

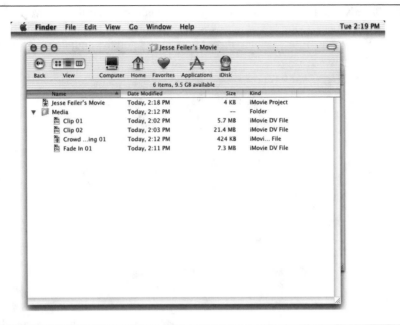

FIGURE 16-17   iMovie files are stored on disk clip by clip.

The Views preferences, which can show more or less information, let you customize the displays in the viewers, as shown here:

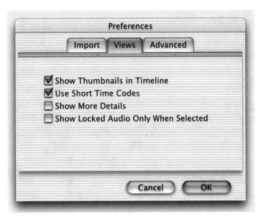

Finally, the Advanced preferences shown next lets you further customize iMovie. The Video Play Through To Camera option lets playback appear in your monitor window and be sent to the video camera. You do this if you want to record your iMovie on the digital video camcorder DV cartridge while you view it.

If you choose Export Movie from the File menu, you can export your movie in a variety of formats. The following image shows the first option: exporting back to the camera and recording on its DV cartridge. You want to do this if you want to use your digital video camcorder to play your iMovie. Some digital video camcorders have connectors for VCRs; if so, you can play back to the DV cartridge and from there create a standard VCR tape.

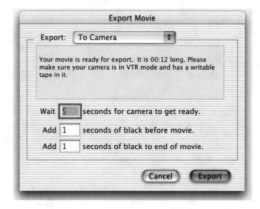

The QuickTime export options are shown in the next illustration. You can select the type of QuickTime movie you want to create. The biggest consequence of your choice here is the size of the playback window and the amount of disk space your movie will take up. Smaller windows take less disk space.

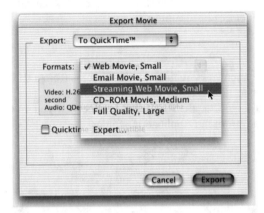

Finally, you can export your iMovie to iDVD for burning onto a DVD as shown here:

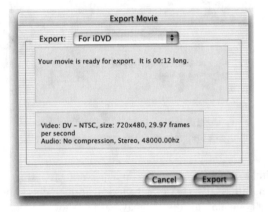

Experiment with your digital video camcorder and with iMovie. The worst thing you can do is to get started shooting a high-stakes event such as a wedding or graduation without a hands-on sense of what you are working with. It is not hard to use a digital video camcorder or iMovie, but it does take a little bit of experience to be comfortable with it.

Some people experiment on inanimate objects. It may not be profoundly interesting to have a video of a chair or a table, but you can shoot (and reshoot and reshoot) that chair or table until you are satisfied that you have mastered the skills involved. People get bored and cease cooperating faster than do pieces of furniture.

Image Capture

The Image Capture application lets you move digital images from a still camera into your computer over a USB connection. Start by turning the camera off. Then connect it via a USB cable and turn it on. You should see the window shown next. If you do not, manually launch the Image Capture application (from the Applications folder).

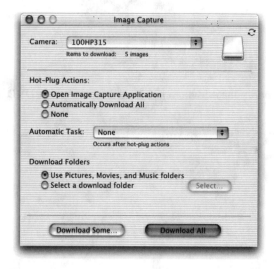

Your camera should be displayed in the pop-up menu at the top. If it is not, check that it is connected and turned on. If that fails, check the batteries. Further, check the camera's display: when it is connected to a computer, the display may flash or show a code, such as PC. In any event, it will most likely not show the normal display of the number of images remaining to be taken. If it does not show the computer connection display, consult your camera's operating guide.

You can download photos to your Pictures folder by clicking Download All. However, the Automatic Task pop-up menu in the middle provides a variety of even more useful features, as shown next.

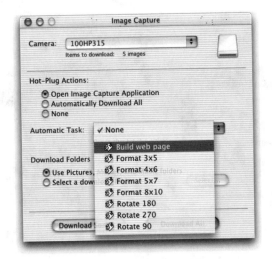

AppleScript is used to modify the images that are downloaded. The script that builds a Web page is one of the more interesting ones. It will build the HTML for a Web page with thumbnails of your photos. Clicking on each photo will open it in its own browser page. Try it! Figure 16-18 shows a Web page built by Image Capture.

Desktop Tools

There's more to the world than the Internet, and Mac OS X provides a variety of tools that help you manage your desktop. Four of them are discussed in this section: Sherlock, Address Book, Stickies, and Grab.

Sherlock

Sherlock has evolved from a number of other Apple software products and experiments. It provides a powerful way of searching files on your computer, as well as sites on the Web. When you launch Sherlock, you see the window shown in Figure 16-19.

Across the top, buttons indicate channels that you can search. Channels are types of information (names and addresses, shopping, news), locations (your disks), or the Internet itself. By default, several are provided. You can add new channels. Each channel has one or more locations that are searched.

If you click on the Internet channel as shown in this figure, you can search for a word or phrase in a number of Internet locations. You can turn the default locations on or off by clicking the checkboxes to the left of their names.

FIGURE 16-18   This Web page was built automatically by Image Capture with a single mouse click.

FIGURE 16-19   Sherlock Internet channel

The Files channel contains the disks on your computer. You can type in a word or phrase and click the magnifying glass icon at the right to start the search. You can search by file names or by content.

To search for a file, select File Names or Contents and type the word or phrase you are looking for, as shown in Figure 16-20. Only the disks or directories that are checked will be searched; note that for a Content search, the items must have been indexed. Sherlock indexes your disks to make searching faster. Because Sherlock runs in each user's Home directory, it cannot access certain files that are outside that directory. Thus, as you can see in this figure, the Home directory (ftosca) is being indexed automatically. The two disks (which contain other users' files as well as those for ftosca) cannot be indexed.

You can double-click files or folders in the list of items found to open them. You can also use the commands in the File menu to open them or their enclosing folders. You can create custom searches by choosing from the Custom pop-up menu, as shown in Figure 16-21. (The Edit command opens an even wider array of search options.) As you can see, you can search on a very wide variety of file characteristics.

The People channel searches LDAP directories for names and addresses. LDAP is discussed more extensively in the next section on Address Book. Another useful channel is the Apple channel. It lets you easily search the major Apple information resources for help with problems and technical information.

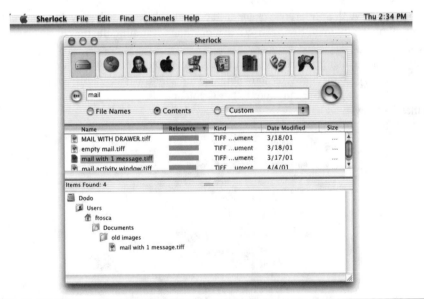

FIGURE 16-20   Sherlock Files channel lets you search the content of files.

FIGURE 16-21   Editing custom Sherlock searches

Sherlock comes with a Reference channel. It contains a dictionary, encyclopedia, and thesaurus—all on the Internet. Figure 16-22 demonstrates searching the thesaurus for a synonym of "search."

Finally, if you are using a local area connection to the Internet, you may need to set the maximum number of connections, as shown next. This window is available with the Preferences menu command. Most people can ignore it, but if you need it, you may be unable to use Sherlock without these settings.

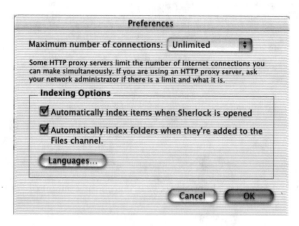

FIGURE 16-22   Reference channel (thesaurus)

Address Book

The Address Book application lets you collect addresses and contact information in one place and make it available to other applications. When you launch Address Book, the window shown next appears.

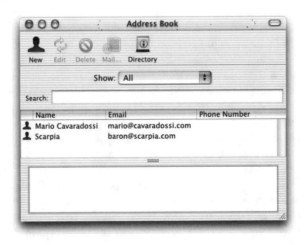

You can create new entries, but one of the most powerful tools is its integration with the Internet's Lightweight Directory Access Protocol (LDAP), as well as with Mail. In the case of Mail, incoming addresses are automatically stored in Address Book. Furthermore, mail that is received with vcf tags can be automatically added to Address Book: just drag the vcf tag from Mail into Address Book. Click on Find in the main Address Book window to open the LDAP directory search window shown here:

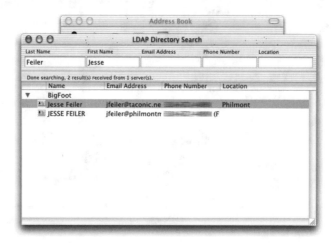

Type in whatever information you have, and press RETURN. Address Book will search LDAP servers for the name you entered. You can drag the little address file icon to the left of the name into the Address Book window, as shown in Figure 16-23.

When you have an entry in Address Book, you can select it and then edit it or delete it using the buttons at the top of the window. Often, the information provided through LDAP or in an email message is incomplete or not formatted in the way you like. You can edit it so that your formats and categories (such as Work or Buddy) are used. You can customize your LDAP searches by clicking on Preferences to open the window shown in Figure 16-24.

This figure shows a listing of some LDAP servers on the Internet. You can add or remove servers with the buttons at the bottom, and you can enable or disable them with checkmarks to the left of their names. If you add a new server, you type its address next to its name. You can also change its default name (such as New Server 2) to a meaningful name by clicking it and typing over the default name.

Organizations you are associated with—a business or school, for example—may have their own LDAP servers. You can enter their names here. Some LDAP servers are only accessible from within a local area network.

LDAP servers provide information about individuals and organizations. Whereas the Internet's domain name system provides information about domain names and IP addresses, LDAP information is typically the sort of information that you find in a telephone directory. There is no single LDAP format; each LDAP directory can contain varying types of information.

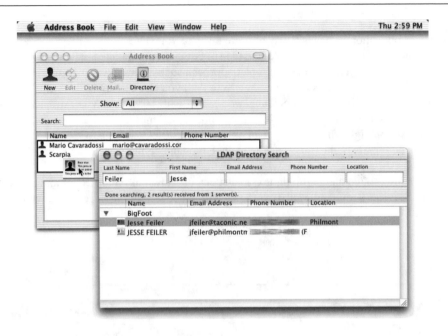

FIGURE 16-23   You can drag LDAP address cards into Address Book.

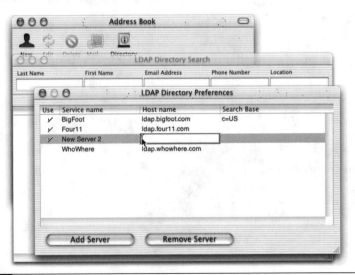

FIGURE 16-24   Customizing LDAP servers

Desktop Tools

Stickies

The Stickies application provides a way to write notes to yourself and have them appear to stick to your computer monitor. Some people like the structure of an organized database or personal digital assistant. Other people prefer a simpler approach such as is shown in Figure 16-25.

If you are used to the Mac OS 9 or earlier Note Pad, you can use Stickies instead of it to keep track of small items of information. Stickies works well with services as you can see in the following two examples. In Figure 16-26, an incoming email message contains the words Mario Cavaradossi. If you highlight them, you can use the Make Sticky service to create a sticky. (This figure shows both parts of the process—the menu command being chosen and its result, the created sticky.)

You can turn around and highlight text in a sticky as shown in Figure 16-71 and choose the Stickies Services command Mail Text to place it in a new Mail message, as shown in Figure 16-27.

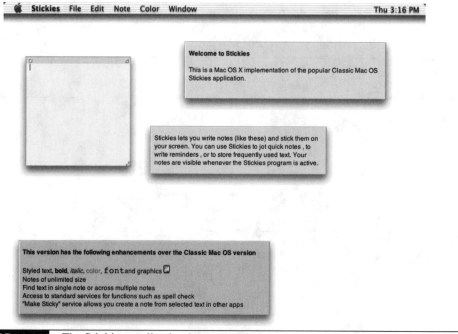

FIGURE 16-25   The Stickies application lets you write notes.

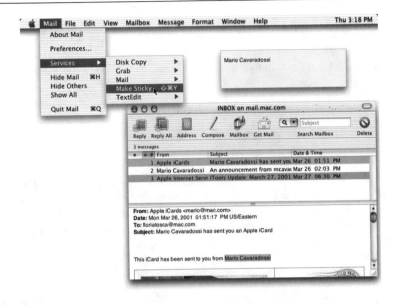

FIGURE 16-26   Creating a sticky from highlighted text

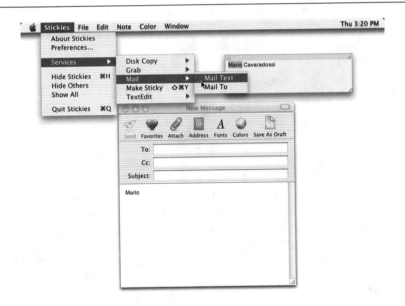

FIGURE 16-27   Stickies supports the Mail Text service.

Grab

The Grab application is essential to any documentation about Mac OS X or applications running on it. (All of the Mac OS X screenshots in this book were created with Grab.) Grab captures all or part of the screen. Its basic commands are shown here:

The Timed Screen command is one of the most useful. After you choose it, you have ten seconds to pull down a menu, click on a window, or otherwise set up the image that you want captured. When Grab runs as an application, the screenshots are stored in files that you can save.

You can also run Grab as a service from other applications. If you do so, the grabbed screenshot will be placed in the document you are working in at the insertion point.

Calculator

Calculator, shown next, lets you do quick math using either the mouse or the keypad keys on your keyboard. You can copy the results of calculations from the Calculator and paste them into other applications.

Chess

Finally, chess is provided, as shown in Figure 16-28. It comes with a variety of options as you can see in the preferences. Playing chess can be a break from your routine (and, since the computer can play against you, it can boost your spirits or depress you profoundly).

This is an Apple front-end to the GNU chess program available on many Unix platforms. Note in particular the speech recognition feature that allows hands-off playing. (This can be a good way to see how speech works on Mac OS X.)

| FIGURE 16-28 | Chess hones your game-playing skills. |

Summary

The software included with Mac OS X not only demonstrates the features of the operating system, it also provides important tools that help you create and edit documents, use the Internet, and manage your desktop. Applications are at the core of your work (and play) with the computer. However, in Mac OS X, you will find a new way of using applications: they can be incorporated into one another easily using the Services menu. That is the topic of the next chapter.

Summary

Chapter 17

Working with Services

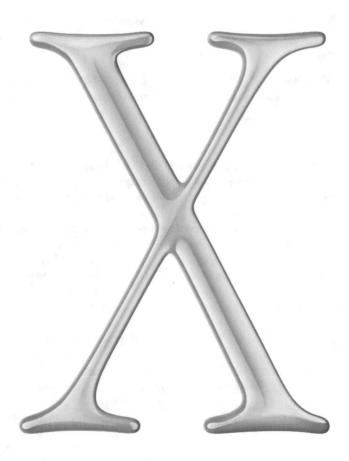

The Mac OS X services architecture allows applications to use functionality from other applications as if it were their own. It allows users to pick and choose from among features of various applications to create a productive environment they like and that works best for them. Services are an integral part of the operating system, but each application program must be programmed to take advantage of them, either by using services from other sources or by exporting its own functionality as services to others. This functionality is available in the Cocoa environment; over time, more and more applications will rely on services.

This chapter contains three sections:

- **Why Services?**   This section provides the background of services. They are one of many approaches to solving the problem of the high cost of software today.

- **What are Services?**   Services are not just a smarter version of cut-and-paste. This section provides the details.

- **How Services Work**   The Services menu provides the gateway to services that you see; others are programmed deep inside applications. This section shows you how both types of services are used.

Services are new in Mac OS X. They were part of the NeXTSTEP and OpenStep environments, but if you are a long-time Macintosh user, you have never seen them before.

Why Services?

If you take an inventory of the software you own and the functionality it contains, you will be amazed at the embarrassment of riches just beyond your fingertips. Not at—beyond. Inside Product A is a great printing routine that automatically sizes images to whatever paper is in the printer. Lurking in Product B is the most flexible paragraph automatic numbering and outlining code you've ever seen. And within Product C is automatic email sorting and management code that, if it could be combined with the email formatting logic in Product D, would fulfill all your dreams.

There it sits: a slew of software features that together would make your life easier. In reality, people tend to do one of two things about this situation: they either sigh and use the product that comes closest to providing the features they want, or they use the various features of assorted products, copying data to and fro with files, import/export routines, and the Clipboard (cut/copy/paste).

For example, the production of this book is a complex process. Nevertheless, it is probably not so complex that it requires as much software as has gone into it. Among the products used by the author are AppleWorks, Microsoft Word, Preview, PictureViewer, GIFConverter, Flash-It, Preview, Grab, Photoshop, FreeHand, FileMaker, BBEdit, Debabelizer, StuffIt, and Virtual PC.

The ability to combine features from within a variety of software products is something that consumers have been requesting for many years. Further, people have wondered why they need to purchase a $400 software product to get the $25 functionality they truly want. Attempts to address this in the past have been largely unsuccessful. Among the problems has been the fact that combining functionality from a variety of products and vendors requires very strict standards for data interchange. In addition, a reluctance in the software industry to change the way in which products are made and marketed surely has had some effect.

Services in Mac OS X offer an opportunity to finally provide consumers with this functionality they have been yearning for. The services architecture allows applications to export key parts of their functionality in a structured way. The operating system allows users to import that functionality into their own work environment—again in a structured way. Additionally, since the services architecture can coexist with traditional application programs, it does not require software developers to invent new business models or to threaten their installed base of products.

What Are Services?

Services are sometimes described as a more powerful or smarter form of the traditional cut/copy/paste functionality that lets you move data from one application to another. But cut/copy/paste focuses on data: you cut or copy it from one application, it is placed on the Clipboard, and then you paste it into another application that processes it. With services, an operation is usually performed on the data by the service. Thus, cut/copy/paste can be seen as a way of sharing data that does not change during its transfer; services usually do change the data.

Services are operations an application can perform on specified types of data. These operations are atomic in the sense that given an input of that data type, the operation can be performed—and a result generated—without the need for further inputs in most cases. Services do not necessarily have input data; if they do, its type is clearly specified. Services may have output, but they need not do so. Here are some examples of each type of service.

Services with Input and Output

A graphics conversion service may take as its input a color image and return as its output a copy of that image in grayscale. In this case, the input is sent to the service, processed, and returned in a different form.

A spell-checking service may take as its input a word of text. Its output may be an indication that the word is or isn't spelled correctly. Note that in this case, the output is not a processed version of the input (that is, another version of the word). Instead, it is a description of that input—is it spelled correctly.

A spell-checking service can also put up a dialog for the user to indicate whether the misspelled word should be replaced or if the "misspelling" is actually a new word that should be learned. In this case, the output of the service is the result of the interaction with the user: the word—corrected or not—that should replace the word flagged initially. The Spelling service in Mac OS X works with input only or with output only.

Service with Input Only

A service can be integrated with a database. Data sent to it is then passed on to the database and stored there. You can also send text to an email service and ask it to create an email message from the text. You will still have to address it and click Send (in most cases), so you might argue that there is some output (the email message to be sent). However, from the originating application's point of view, there is no output. The window that is created is an email window in the Mail application. The Mail application in Mac OS X supports a service like this.

Service with Output Only

Conversely, a service may be output only. The Grab program, for example, exports services. Thus, if you are in Mail or TextEdit, you can use the Grab service to capture a screenshot and place it in an open document.

How Services Work

A service is declared within a bundle: an application bundle or a service bundle. Each service has a list of properties, including its name, the type of data it accepts, what its command should be in the Services submenu, the application that will provide the service, and several other data elements.

The Services submenu is built automatically in the Application menu for each application. The specific commands are enabled when the appropriate data type for those commands is selected or active. It is very important to note that the application normally does not know what services are available. The application is responsible for alerting the services architecture as to the type of data selected or active. The operating system takes care of enabling the command in the submenu based on the active or selected data as reported to it by the application.

The application is also responsible for handling what is returned from the service, if anything. Again, the application normally does not know what the service is or what it has done; it receives data of a certain type (which it has specified that it accepts), and it acts on it.

In the case of output-only services; it doesn't matter what data type is selected. Likewise, input-only services (including those that use the data to open a new window in another application) do not worry about the data type returned. While the data type may not matter, other factors may. For example, an output-only service generally requires that you have a window open (where else could the output go?).

Working with Services

Services are used in two ways: through the Services menu (part of the Application menu) and as part of an application's own functionality, buttons, and menus. This section describes both mechanisms.

Services Menu

The services available in a given application—that is, the commands listed in its Services submenu in the Application menu—are placed there as a result of negotiation between the operating system and the application when the application is launched. The services that are enabled, the ones that are listed and that you can click at any given time, normally depend on what is selected in the current document. Some services are listed but disabled if the appropriate data type is not currently selected.

To use the Services menu, simply select any of the enabled commands. Many services rely on input; if they do, you must have selected data of the appropriate kind for the command to be enabled. Sometimes, selection is not necessary. You may merely need to have an active window containing the type of data (an image, for example).

Here is an example of using the Address Book and Mail applications, together with their services. In Figure 17-1, you can see an address book entry. Note that the email address at the bottom of the window is selected (mario@cavaradossi.com). If you try this yourself, remember to highlight the email address in the pane at the bottom of the window. Highlighting the entry in the list in the middle of the window is not sufficient. When text is selected, you can use the Services menu to instruct the Mail application to use that as an address—the Mail To command. Figure 17-2 shows the result of that service.

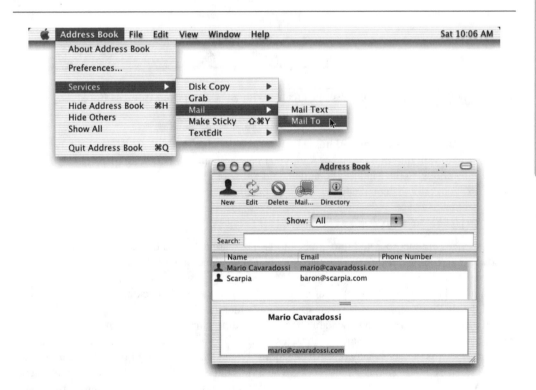

FIGURE 17-1   Use services to create an email message.

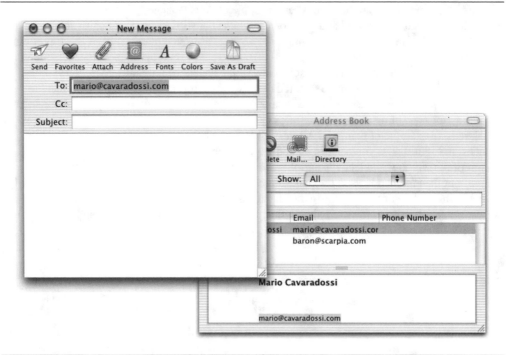

FIGURE 17-2 A new email message created with an address from Address Book

Mail creates a new message addressed to the address from Address Book. You can type whatever you want into that message. And, you can insert an email address into the body of a message by choosing the Mail Text command, as shown in Figure 17-3. The selected text is used as the text body, not the email address in a new email message.

Embedded Services

Some services are incorporated into applications. They are activated through the application's interface, rather than through the Services menu. This is the case with spell checking, for example. A spell-checking service is part of Mac OS X. It is used by the Mail and TextEdit programs and can be used by any other program. You use the spell-checking service by choosing one of the spelling commands from an application's menus.

Remember that services are available only to programs using the Cocoa framework. As a result, application programs that run in the Classic Mac OS environment or under Carbon do not use services. This includes many older applications. Even Cocoa versions of these applications may not use services. For example, AppleWorks, which runs either in the Classic Mac OS environment (AppleWorks 5 and earlier) or in Carbon (AppleWorks 6), has its own spell-checking software.

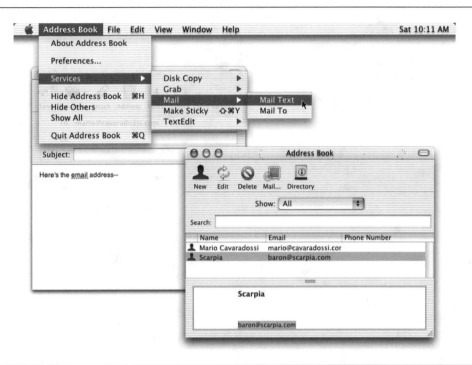

FIGURE 17-3   Inserting text into an email message uses the Mail Text command from the Services menu.

Even a Cocoa version of AppleWorks might continue to use its own spell-checking software for reasons of backward compatibility.

Using Spelling

Perhaps the most widely used service on Mac OS X, the unified spelling dictionary allows all of your Cocoa applications to share your idiosyncratic tastes in spelling. You can see it in use in the Mail and TextEdit applications. One of the great benefits of using a service is that it can consolidate functionality and data that would otherwise be spread around among various applications. In this case, customized dictionaries can be managed very effectively.

The Spelling service has the three menu commands located in the Edit menu. Spelling opens the Spelling window, Check Spelling initiates spell checking, and Check Spelling As You Type turns on dynamic checking. You cannot tell from these menu commands that you are dealing with a service. Applications that are implemented with a common interface might have identical commands but separate implementations. The fact that accepting a word in one context accepts it in another is a clue, but not a certainty, that a service is being used.

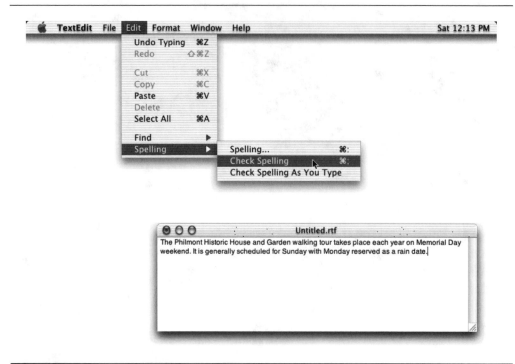

FIGURE 17-4   Check Spelling command in TextEdit

Check Spelling   Figure 17-4 shows a TextEdit document. From its Edit menu, the Check Spelling command is available. If you select Check Spelling, the result is shown in the next illustration: the word Philmont is highlighted, since it is not in the dictionary.

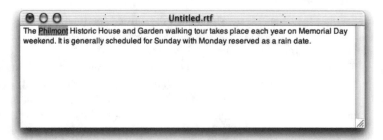

Check Spelling As You Type   Now, look as the next illustration. In the Mail program, a message is being typed. The spelling command Check Spelling As You Type has been enabled. Although you cannot tell from the figure, the word Philmont was highlighted as soon as it was typed. The same service and same dictionary are used by TextEdit and Mail.

Spelling   You can add the word to the dictionary using the Spelling command. In Figure 17-5, you can see the Spelling command in use. It opens the Spelling window shown at the right of the screen. The highlighted word, Philmont, is shown, together with any suggested alternatives. In this case, the word is correctly spelled, and the Learn button is clicked.

If you return to the TextEdit application and choose Check Spelling, the document is rechecked. This time, Philmont is not highlighted, as shown in Figure 17-6. The Spelling service used by both Mail and TextEdit uses a single dictionary. Thus, clicking Learn in the context of the Mail application updates that dictionary for all users of the service, including TextEdit. This can be an invaluable way of keeping track of your own additions to standard dictionaries.

Obtaining and Installing Services

Today, services are installed primarily as part of applications written for Cocoa. Although it is possible to write and distribute services on their own, there is not much of a market for them at the moment. Over time, it is likely that such a market will develop as people decide that they want to buy specific functional operations for their work and play.

Self-contained services are far more likely to exist in custom-written software and in-house applications. If you are developing or designing such software, investigate services as a solution to the problem of bridging gaps between products. A services-savvy piece of software does not know what services it uses, so you can extend applications very successfully. In addition, note that among the items in a service's property list can be the name of a host on a network on which the service is to run. You can implement very sophisticated distributed systems in this way.

FIGURE 17-5   Using the Spelling window

FIGURE 17-6   Checking documents with the same dictionary

Summary

Services are a powerful feature of Mac OS X. They implement the type of functionality that computer users and software integrators have wanted to have for years. Available at first only to Cocoa applications, services nevertheless promise to be one of the most useful parts of Mac OS X.

In this part of the book, you have seen how to work with basic applications: the examples shipping with Mac OS X. This chapter has explored services. These are powerful tools for you to use. Mail (which ships with Mac OS X) and AppleWorks (which ships with many Macintosh computers and is available for purchase separately) put it all together. They are the subjects of the next chapters.

Summary

Chapter 18

Using Apple Mail

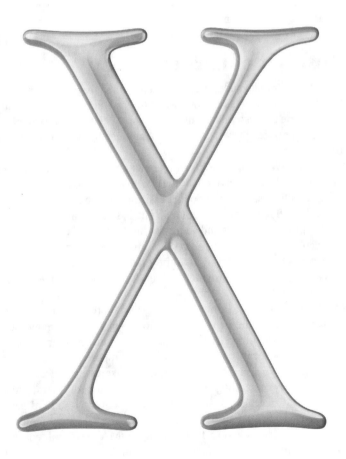

This chapter helps you use Apple Mail, the email application that is part of Mac OS X. If you have used the Mac OS X installer, you may have already set up your email account—either one you already have, a new one at an Internet service provider you have located during the installation process, or your iTools email account at mac.com. More than one person installing Mac OS X for the first time has been pleasantly surprised to receive email without having done anything except go through the installation process.

This chapter is divided into five sections:

- Getting the Most Out of Email
- What You Need to Set Up Email
- Using Apple Mail
- Setting Mail Preferences
- Customizing the Mail Toolbar

Getting the Most Out of Email

Perhaps no software products today are more varied than email programs. You can find long-time stand-alone email applications such as Eudora, Microsoft's Outlook Express, and the Mac OS X Apple Mail application. You can also find email applications within Web browsers such as Netscape Navigator. Some Internet service providers such as America Online provide email as part of their bundled software.

You can send and receive email from Web pages without the use of a special email program, and, of course, you can send and receive email with Web appliances such as WebTV and AOLTV, with some cell phones, and with pocket assistants (such as the Palm)

Email software fulfills three roles. The obvious one is sending and receiving email messages. The second role is that of storing names and addresses, and the third is that of saving and indexing messages. It is not uncommon for individuals to send or receive a dozen or more messages a day, and many people keep almost all of them. Email programs provide fast means of searching these messages in various ways. The email program and its storage thus become a combination diary, contact file, and to-do list.

It is easy to switch back and forth among different email programs on different computers to send and receive mail. However, the two other functions—maintaining names and addresses and storing messages—are best performed by using one program on one computer.

If you are going to use several programs or several computers, consider exporting email messages to a database for storage. Consider, too, using a separate address book so that your email program can focus only on sending and receiving, and your archival information is available separately with FileMaker, OpenBase, or another program. You can find third-party utilities that convert email messages to various database formats. In a corporate environment, mail may be automatically archived for you as it is sent. In addition, the IMAP protocol—discussed later—can help you manage your email messages without storing them on your own computer.

The Mac OS X Apple Mail program provides excellent email support. Its elegant and intuitive interface (along with some rather nifty Mac OS X features) make it a favorite for many people.

> NOTE   *Email is not confidential. The only way to make it so is to encrypt the messages in a way that only you and the other party can decipher. Copies of email messages reside in many locations on the Internet; even deleted and unsent messages can be recovered from a hard disk with enough effort by law enforcement authorities or others.*

What You Need to Set Up Email

To get started with email, you need a connection to the Internet and an email account. These are frequently provided by a single vendor, but they often are not. For example, your connection to the Internet may be provided by Earthlink, and you may use America Online or mac.com (iTools) for your email. Conversely, you may use America Online for your connection, and you may have an Earthlink account for email, or you may have any combination of these and other providers' options.

Internet Connection

Your Internet connection can be over a phone line, through a local area network, via the cable television system, by satellite, or wireless. (Setting up such a connection is described in Chapter 12, "Communicating Over the Internet.") You usually have an account with a user ID and a password. The account is charged in some manner—perhaps by the hour or with unlimited usage by the month. Your user ID is assigned to you, and your password is either assigned to you or selected by you. With this information you can connect to the Internet.

If your connection is through a campus or corporate network, you also have a user ID and password; however, the charges (if any) are often billed to your department or included in overall fees and rent.

An Email Account

Your email account also has an account name, a user ID, and a password. The account name may be the same as your Internet connection account, but it may be different. For example, if you use America Online over the Internet (rather than using AOL's dial-up software), your connection may be through an Internet service provider (not AOL), but your email account is at AOL.

Make certain that you maintain your email account name, user ID, and password separately from your Internet account information. All of this information is likely to be stored on your computer for automatic login procedures. It is not uncommon to not know what these accounts and passwords are until you desperately need the information and your computer has crashed or been stolen. It is like speed-dial buttons on a telephone: you may no longer know your best friend's telephone number, since you only press one button to dial the call. Be sure you have copies of all this information safely stored—on paper and under lock and key.

Most email accounts allow you to send and receive messages. Two protocols and two separate computers are involved in this process. Make sure you have your email user ID and password in order to continue. When you set up an email account, you will be given them.

Incoming Mail

In most cases, incoming mail is handled either by the Post Office Protocol (POP) or by the Internet Message Access Protocol (IMAP). POP, the earlier protocol, collects email messages addressed to you and downloads them to your computer when you check your mail. IMAP also collects messages; however, when you connect to your IMAP mail server, you can review messages by subject, sender, and so forth, downloading those you want in any order you want. You can use the IMAP mail server as a repository for messages both read and unread.

Not all email providers support IMAP. When they do, there may be a charge for the storage of large numbers of messages. Some email providers support both IMAP and POP; others support only POP. (Email through iTools at mac.com provides both POP and IMAP support.) You can connect to an incoming mail server from anywhere on the Internet if you have your mail password, user ID, and an Internet connection. As a result, if you have an Internet connection from a hotel room in the Silicon Valley or from a friend's computer in Milan, you can connect to your account at a mail server in Sydney. However, you have to have your mail account user ID, password, and mail server information to do so.

Make certain you know if your email account supports IMAP or POP or both. Get the name of your incoming mail server. It will typically be something like mail.*yourserver*.net or pop.*yourserver*.net. There may be a different name for an IMAP mail server than for a POP mail server. If you need to contact your Internet service provider about email, stress incoming when asking for the name of your server.

Outgoing Mail

Outgoing Internet mail is normally sent using the Simple Mail Transfer Protocol (SMTP). SMTP is an Internet standard, though its implementation frequently is somewhat more restrictive than the basic standard. Whereas you need a user ID to receive mail, normally, you do not need a user ID to send mail. The basic standard does not impose security on outgoing messages; in fact, there are no requirements that messages be correctly signed. You can send a message from president@ whitehouse.gov, even if you have never set foot in the United States. This led in the 1990s to spam—unsolicited email sent in quantities of millions of messages.

While the SMTP standard has not been changed, its implementation has been modified by many organizations. Many servers limit access to people who are connected directly to their network. In other words, your Internet connection user ID and password become your key to sending mail. Furthermore, many organizations require that your return address actually exists as an account on their system. In other words, if you send a message with a return address of someone@aol.com, many Internet service providers will not allow you to send it. (AOL will, of course—if you have paid your bill.) If you are connected to attglobal.net, your return address must be an attglobal.net address, or one that is recognized by attglobal.net. All of this is done to prevent spam.

Not all of this is widely publicized—security measures rarely are. If you are having trouble sending messages from an Internet connection that is different from your email account, this may be the problem. The solution is usually to change your return address to an acceptable address and to provide a reply-to address that is your preferred address. You will see how to do this with Apple Mail later in this section.

When you set up your email account, you will be given your SMTP server's name. Write it down. Stress outgoing when calling to get your SMTP server's name if you do not have it written down. It may be something such as smtp.*yourserver*.com or mail.*yourserver*.com.

Using Apple Mail

Apple Mail has a simple and intuitive interface. Its preferences are described in the next section. You may need to set them before being able to use Apple Mail. If you have performed an installation of Mac OS X and provided your email account, that information is picked up by Apple Mail the first time you run it.

Reading Mail

Here is how Apple Mail itself works once it has been set up. When you launch the application, you see the window shown next. The buttons in the toolbar at the top of the window let you perform the basic Apple Mail operations. The Search field lets you search the active pane for text that you type in. When you press RETURN, Apple Mail finds all messages with the text you have typed. They are ranked in the degree to which they match what you typed. These buttons can be customized, as you will see later in this chapter.

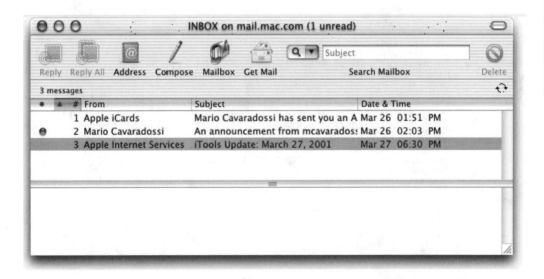

There are two panes in the window itself. At the top, you will find a list of messages in the mailbox. At the bottom, a currently selected message (if any) is displayed. If messages are in the mailbox, they are listed by sender, subject, or date/time. You can click any of the column headings in order to sort messages by the column. The little arrow at the right of each column heading indicates if it is sorted in ascending or descending order. Clicking it again reverses the order.

Messages contain a great deal of header information. Normally, you do not need to see it. If you do, you can choose Show All Headers from the Mailbox menu to display header information such as that shown in Figure 18-1.

If you are trying to solve problems with email, viewing all of the headers can be helpful. (Your ISP or incoming mail manager may ask for some of the information.): If you receive unsolicited junk email (spam), you may think that you can trace it back to its source with this information. You can in some cases, but most spam covers its tracks very well. Just sigh and delete the messages.

Apple Mail handles mail that uses MIME encoding. That means that it can display text in a variety of fonts and colors (as specified by the sender). It can also display graphics, as shown in these figures. Click Get Mail in the toolbar at the top of the window to collect new incoming mail.

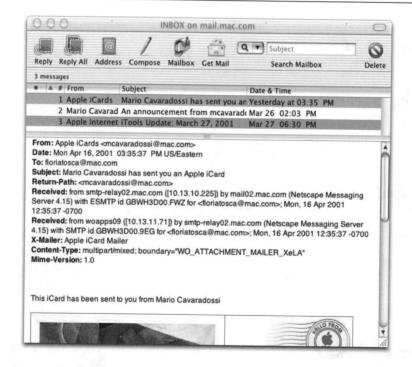

FIGURE 18-1   This Apple Mail message with all headers shows you how it has been routed over the Internet.

Sending Mail

You can send mail in a variety of ways:

- Click Compose to open a window into which you can type a new mail message.

- With a message selected, click Reply to open a window addressed to the sender of the selected message.

- With a message selected, click Reply All to open a window addressed to the sender and all other recipients of the selected message.

- With a message selected, click Forward to send the message on to someone else. You can type the new email address in the new window; you can also add a brief note at the top. (Do not add notes at the bottom of the message. People will likely not see them.)

In each case, the Compose window looks like the one shown in Figure 18-2. You can type addressees manually. You can also choose the Addresses command from the Window menu to

FIGURE 18-2   Write email messages in the Compose window.

open the Address Book application, from which you can drag addresses. (You can add an Address button to the toolbar as well). You can attach one or more files to an email message. Either drag the file to the body of the message or use the Attach button, which will open a Finder Open file dialog for you to locate the file.

Large attachments may not be properly processed by your ISP (or by the recipient's). By preference, use FTP for transferring large files. An arbitrary limit of 10MB is commonly implemented by many ISPs for the attachments to email messages.

Files that can be displayed in MIME messages (typically graphics) will be opened and displayed in the message. Others will appear as a document icon. When you are finished, click Send to send the email. If you are finished, but do not want to send the mail (perhaps you need to check something), choose Save from the File menu. The message will be saved in the Drafts mailbox.

Managing Mail

Mail is stored in mailboxes. The Mailbox button opens a list of your various mailboxes, as shown next. The mailboxes drawer slides out from the side of the window. You can create a number of mailboxes based on different subjects, different types of email accounts, and so forth. You can also create a mailbox in which you store copies of your outgoing mail.

A mailbox for incoming mail is associated with one email account. Other mailboxes are used for filing incoming and outgoing messages. You can manually move mail from your incoming mailbox to other mailboxes. You can also set up automatic rules for moving mail—see "Rules for Sorting Messages" later in this chapter.

Other Apple Mail Features

There are a number of other mail management features in Apple Mail. They are described in this section.

Restoring Drafts

If you save an unsent message as a draft, you can select it by clicking the Drafts mailbox and selecting the message in question. The Restore from Draft command in the File menu will reopen the message in a Compose window for you to continue working on and to save or send it when you are done.

Using Mailboxes

Mailboxes are a useful way of keeping track of messages. You can transfer messages to mailboxes by dragging them from the Mail Viewer window into a mailbox in the Mailboxes drawer. The Transfer command in the Message menu lets you do the same thing. (As you will see, the Sorting preference can make this automatic.) Mailboxes are individual files in each user's Library folder. You can copy them from one computer to another so that your old mail follows you around if you want.

BCC and Reply-To Headers

Using Add BCC Header or Add Reply-To Header from the Message menu, you can add either of these headers to a message you are composing. A BCC (blind carbon copy) header lets you send copies of the message to people without having their email addresses broadcast to all recipients of the message. A reply-to header lets you specify the address to which the Reply button on your correspondent's computer will automatically address mail. Use BCC headers for mailing lists.

Focusing on Messages

When you search for messages using the Search field at the top of the Mail Viewer window, the messages that match are listed. Other messages are not shown; the Mail Viewer is said to be *focused* on the listed messages. If you want to see others, use the Show All Messages command from the Mailbox menu.

Compacting Messages

This command (from the Mailbox menu) will permanently remove deleted and transferred messages. Until you have done so, you can choose the Show Deleted Messages from the Mailbox menu to see messages you have deleted or transferred.

Rebuilding Mailboxes

This command (from the Mailbox menu) rebuilds the table of contents of a mailbox. The table of contents is a separate file that is used by Apple Mail. You should not have to do this, but if your mailbox is corrupted, this may fix it. If you have transferred a mailbox from another computer, you can rebuild its table of contents with this command.

Setting Mail Preferences

To set this all up and start Apple Mail working for you, choose the Preferences command in the Application menu. It will open the Preferences window. When you install Mac OS X, you are asked for the name of your incoming and outgoing mail servers. In addition, the Internet pane in System Preferences lets you specify a mail account. Apple Mail—like many other programs— can pick up this information. You will need to set the preferences manually if you have changed email providers since you installed the software or if you have made modifications in another email program that are not reflected in System Preferences. Also, if you have more than one email account, you need to set up all but the first one manually, following the instructions here. The buttons at the top let you adjust various preferences. This section walks you through them all.

Preferences are set up for an individual user, not for the computer. You can create several different user accounts each with its own set of email accounts and preferences. If you do so, you may want to avoid setting up any email accounts for the administrator account. That way, if you attempt to run Apple Mail when logged in as the administrator, you will get a warning that there are no accounts set up, and it may remind you to run Apple Mail when logged in as another user.

Accounts Preferences

You need to set up at least one incoming account so that Apple Mail can receive messages for you. Click the Accounts button to open the window shown in Figure 18-3. There may be one or more accounts set up for you as a result of your computer's installation process. Check, too, that you have indicated in the lower part of the window whether you want Apple Mail to check automatically at an interval you specify.

If you use a dial-up Internet connection, checking mail automatically may force the connection to remain open. This can be a good way of keeping the connection active—or of running up a large telephone bill. Always-on connections (such as DSL and cable) allow you to check your email without worrying about expense at all times, day and night.

If you have Apple Mail check for incoming mail periodically, you may want an alert sound to let you know when mail has arrived. You can specify it on this screen. You can also specify the columns to be shown in the Mail Viewer window.

Setting Account Information

If your account is not there—or if the information appears wrong—click Create Account or Edit Account to open the window shown in Figure 18-3. Choose from the pop-up menu at the top whether your account is a mac.com, POP, IMAP, or Unix account. (Unix mail accounts are typically used on

FIGURE 18-3   Accounts preferences lets you create, edit, and delete email accounts.

Unix local area networks.) The account type is set when you create a new account; to change it, you must create a new account, transfer the information from the old account to the new one, and then delete the old one. Account types rarely change unless you have made a mistake in entering the information in the first place.

You can name the account anything you want (Business, School, Personal, and so on.). Type in your email return address for this account, as well as your full name. You next need to enter the incoming mail host information: the name of the incoming mail server, your user name, and your password. All three of these items should have been provided to you when you opened your email account with your Internet service provider.

Pay attention to the distinction between your account name, which usually includes the domain (the part after @), and the user name (which does not). The user name may appear in both. Apple Mail will accept incorrect entries here—it cannot determine what your ISP wants.

The SMTP host section provides outgoing mail information. Your SMTP user name and password frequently are the same as your incoming user name and password. The checkbox that lets you use authentication when sending mail lets you work with outgoing mail servers that enforce security. The original SMTP standards assumed that once you were connected to a mail server you had been authenticated to the mainframe or network to which you were logged in.

This is one of the ways in which spam was able to be sent: people connected to networks either legally or illegally and then had total access to the outgoing mail server. Forcing authentication on outgoing messages means that the SMTP server requires your password to be sent each time you attempt to send a message. This is done automatically if you check this box.

Setting Account Options

The Account Options tab on Mail preferences has different options, depending on whether you have selected a mac.com or IMAP account, a POP account, or a Unix account on the Account Information pane. Note that the type of account is determined by your Internet service provider. It is an option in your Mail preferences only in the sense that you have the option to configure Mail to work with the particular type of email account your ISP provides (your other option being to choose an incompatible option that will not work).

mac.com and IMAP Account Options   mac.com and IMAP account options are shown in Figure 18-4. The first checkbox lets you enable this account—that is, allow it to be used for incoming and outgoing mail. If you move around, you may want to leave accounts set up on your computer and merely enable or disable them as you wish, rather than reentering all of the information.

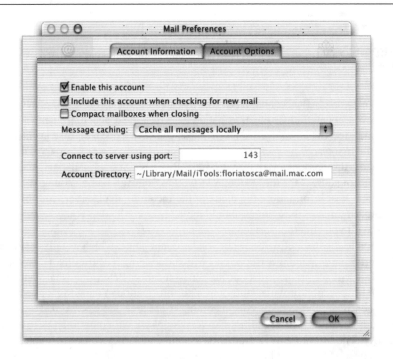

FIGURE 18-4   Set mac.com and IMAP account options including where messages are cached.

The second checkbox determines whether this account is searched when you click Get Mail. You can turn this off if you want to skip work-related messages (or personal messages) at various times.

The final checkbox, compact mailboxes on close, removes deleted messages permanently and otherwise tidies up your mailboxes. You are able to control whether messages are cached locally on your computer or only downloaded when you want to read them. The IMAP protocol that is also available on mac.com, can make your email management very efficient by not downloaded messages until you actually want to read them. This allows you to temporarily bypass certain messages (including those with large attachments).

The remaining options at the bottom of the pane are usually correct as is—that is, port 143, and the default account directory (blank). If the port number is to be changed, your ISP will tell you what it is.

POP Account Options   POP account options are shown in Figure 18-5. Unlike IMAP, which downloads messages when you read them, POP downloads all messages when you check your mail. As a result, there are some additional options.

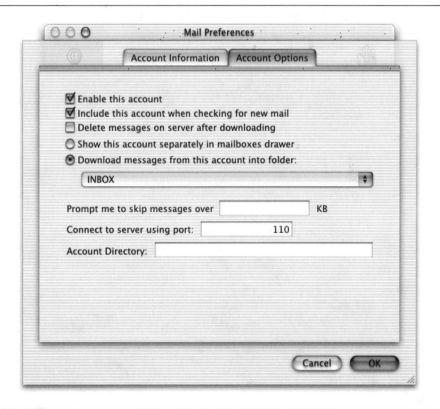

FIGURE 18-5   POP options are more extensive than IMAP options.

The option to delete messages on the server after download means that once they are downloaded to your computer, the messages will be erased. When first setting up your email account, you may want to leave this option unchecked. Your messages will remain on the server and may be downloaded a second (or third) time by other email programs. When you are satisfied that you have correctly installed Apple Mail, uncheck this option to avoid this duplication. In the meantime, however, you want to prevent the possibility of accidentally losing incoming email while you are configuring your system.

Since all messages will be downloaded when you check your mail (even if duplicates are left on the server), you need to select the mailbox into which they will be placed.

Unix Account Options   Unix Account Options are shown in Figure 18-6. On a campus or corporate network, you may have Unix mail for internal mail. If so, select the Unix mail account type in Account Information and set up the options shown in Figure 18-6. You can either leave those options as they are or reconfigure them according to your network manager's requests.

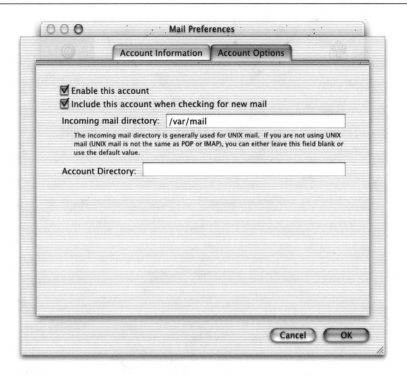

FIGURE 18-6   Unix account options are separate from Internet POP and IMAP mail options.

Setting Fonts & Colors

The following illustration shows the preferences for fonts and colors in the display of messages. Fonts & Colors preferences can make messages easier to read. These fonts and colors do not affect the fonts and colors in the transmitted messages themselves.

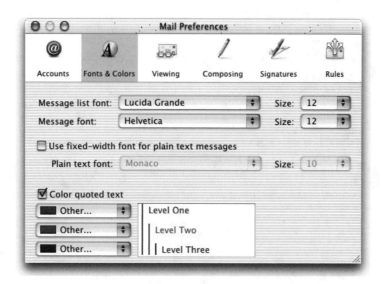

Setting Viewing Preferences

These preferences let you control the management of deleted mail, whether or not attachments are downloaded, and how much header detail is provided. The next illustration shows your choices.

Setting Mail Preferences

It is important to note that when you delete a message from a mailbox in Mail, you actually only mark it as to be deleted. You can use the Show Deleted Messages command in the View menu to see these messages, and you can then use the Undelete command in the Message menu to restore them. Messages marked for deletion are actually deleted when you compact the mailbox (from the Mailbox menu) or according to the time lapse you specify here.

You might want to uncheck the download check box to prevent attachments being downloaded. Some people are worried about computer viruses; if you back up your computer routinely, even damage that is done can be undone fairly quickly.

If you are on a low-speed connection (for example, dialing in to your mail account from a laptop in a hotel room), do not download attachments and do not check Delete Messages On Server (in Account preferences, described previously). This will enable you to read the messages— without potentially lengthy attachments—and then to download them again with attachments later.

Composing Preferences

The Compose preferences control how your outgoing messages are formatted and stored, as shown next. Use the two pop-up buttons to select the mailboxes for your sent and unsent mail. Saving copies of sent mail is useful if you use your mailboxes as a filing system.

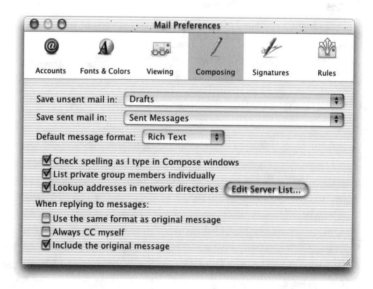

The most important option here is Use the same format as original message in the final set of checkboxes. You may receive plain text mail, as well as MIME mail (mail that includes font styles, underlining, colors, and the like). Instead of keeping track of who uses what type of email program, you can automatically respond in whatever manner the sender has communicated with you.

Signature Preferences

You can prepare a signature—a block of text or a graphic—that is appended to email messages. Signature preferences automatically add return address and contact information to your email messages, as shown here:

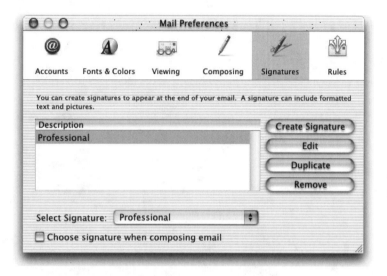

You create and edit signatures by clicking the appropriate buttons. Your signature can be plain text or it can include boldface type, italics, and the like. A typical signature is shown here:

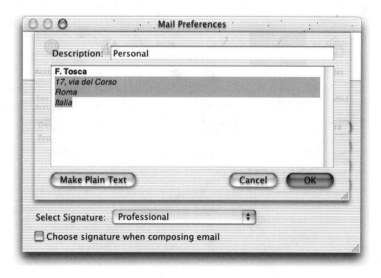

Setting Mail Preferences

A signature can be useful to provide the information that is normally found on letterhead stationery (name, address, logo, and the like). Some people like to add trenchant thoughts, which is why you might choose to rotate signatures in the Signatures preference (randomly or sequentially). Furthermore, if you have two or more different signatures—such as one for business and one for personal use—use Choose On Compose Window so you can make the choice there.

Signatures can save a lot of typing. One trick many people use is to place the closing—Best wishes, Hope that helps, and so forth—in the signature above the address information.

Rules for Sorting Messages

Rules preferences (shown next) let you automatically route messages to various mailboxes.

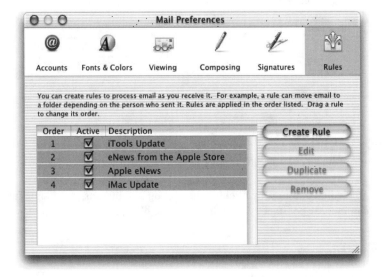

Figure 18-7 shows a typical sorting rule. You name it whatever you want and then you provide the criterion, which activates it. This involves one of the header fields in the message—From, To, Subject, and the like. You can select a variety of actions for each rule, including distinctive sounds, automatic forwarding, and storing in specific mailboxes.

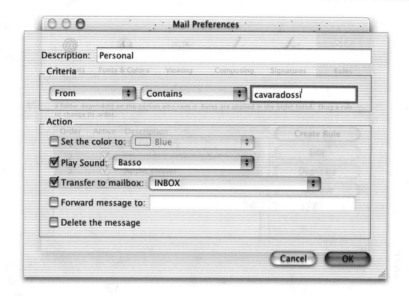

FIGURE 18-7 Rules can help you organize incoming and outgoing email.

Customizing the Mail Toolbar

The Mail toolbar allows the customization described in Chapter 2, "Aqua." On the next page, Figure 18-8 shows the buttons you can place in the toolbar; remember that you can also move them from side to side in order to rearrange them.

Summary

Email has become indispensable for most people both at home and at work. The Apple Mail application in Mac OS X provides all the functionality you need to manage multiple accounts, as well as to read and send email.

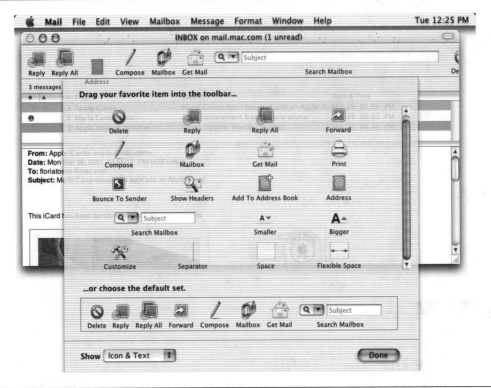

FIGURE 18-8 Customizing the toolbar makes Mail work exactly as you want it to.

Chapter 19

Using AppleWorks

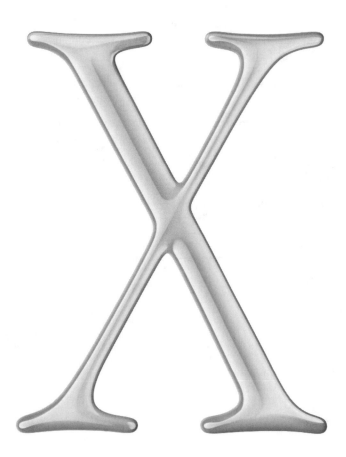

AppleWorks is an integrated suite of tools that you can use to create documents of all types—everything from novels and memoranda to flyers and slide show presentations. AppleWorks comes preinstalled on some computers (typically the iBook and iMac lines), and it may be part of a preinstalled package of software on other computers. It is also available as a separate product (both for Macintosh and Windows computers); you can buy it from the Apple store (http://www.apple.com) if you don't have it already.

Since AppleWorks is so widely available (and so useful!), this chapter focuses on its capabilities and provides some tips on what you can do with it and how to use it most productively. On the Macintosh, AppleWorks serves not only as one of Apple's most important software products, it's also a tool for demonstrating to users and developers how the operating system can be used to the best advantage and how human interface design can be implemented.

This chapter does not provide the basics of word processing, spreadsheets, or graphics. If you are unfamiliar with those personal computer applications, there are many resources available. Your dealer or vendor may provide hands-on training or demonstrations, and there are self-guided tutorials and many books available, too. The basics are the same for all types of computers and all types of programs, so you can inquire of anyone you know who uses a computer.

This chapter provides the following:

- **AppleWorks Overview**   How to work with documents and frames as well as how to use the Tools palette, set up links, and work with properties.

- **Word Processing**   How to create basic word processing documents; how to use advanced features such as styles, sections, outlines, and numbering.

- **Drawing**   How to work with vector-based graphics. You can create and scale to any appropriate size.

- **Painting**   How to work with bitmapped graphics. You can create using images from other applications.

- **Spreadsheets**   How to use spreadsheets. One of the archetypal personal computer applications, to display and manage large amounts of (mostly) statistical data.

- **Databases**   How to create databases, design layouts, sort and find data, and create reports.

- **Presentations**   How to prepare presentations for slides or computer-based shows.

- **Clippings and Accents**   How to liven up your AppleWorks documents.

- **Scripting**   How to automate your work.

AppleWorks Overview

AppleWorks has its roots in MacWrite and MacDraw, two simple programs that shipped along with the first Macintosh computers. Over time, Apple consolidated those programs along with others into a suite of tools. Still later, Claris Corporation—a subsidiary of Apple—was formed to market the product then called ClarisWorks along with Apple operating system software, FileMaker, Claris Organizer, Claris Impact (presentation software), and Claris Emailer. In the course of time, those products (with the exception of FileMaker) migrated back to Apple itself; Claris was renamed FileMaker International, and ClarisWorks became AppleWorks. Claris Organizer was subsequently sold to Palm: it is now the Macintosh software you use to update and display the information on your Palm handheld device.

From early on, AppleWorks has been compared with Microsoft's suite of applications that are marketed under the name Microsoft Office. Those applications (Microsoft Word, Microsoft Excel, PowerPoint, and—sometimes—Access) provide similar functionality to the tools in AppleWorks. However, there is one overriding difference: when it comes to new features and functionality, it seems to some that Microsoft Office errs on the side of including everything that is suggested, while AppleWorks carefully considers each new function. AppleWorks is smaller and simpler than Microsoft Office. For advanced users and very complex tasks, more sophisticated and specialized tools are often preferable to those found in either Microsoft Office or AppleWorks. Among these tools are such as FrameMaker; Quark XPress and InDesign; Freehand and Illustrator; Photoshop; and FileMaker, OpenBase, and Oracle. However, for the bulk of most peoples' work, AppleWorks is just right in its size, complexity, and sophistication.

The most noticeable difference between AppleWorks and Microsoft Office is that AppleWorks is a thoroughly integrated program: there is only one AppleWorks program. Microsoft Office is a suite of programs: you can purchase each component separately, and the integration among them is not so complete as can be obtained with a single application.

This brief overview of AppleWorks covers the following topics:

- **Documents and Frames**   This is the basic interface of AppleWorks. You work in documents, and you can also work in frames within documents.

- **Starting Points**   When you launch AppleWorks, you can start from any number of existing documents and templates.

- **Button Bar**   Use the Button bar for context-sensitive buttons that help you create and format documents.

- **Tools**   The Tools palette lets you edit documents.

- **Links**   You can create links (just like Web links) from one document to another or to the Web.

- **Properties**   You can always examine a document's properties using the Properties command.

Documents and Frames

As is the case with most personal computer programs, you work with documents in which you store data, write and draw, and otherwise do your work (and play). Each document in AppleWorks is of a specific type:

- Word processing documents are used for basic typing and text.

- Spreadsheets let you create documents with rows and columns of text or numbers. You can enter formulas to sum sets of cells, and you can use a host of other mathematical, statistical, and financial calculations to compute mortgages, interest, and so forth.

- Drawing documents let you create vector graphics. These are graphics that can contain line, rectangles, squares, and even text. Although you draw them with a mouse, the document stores the graphics as objects. This means they can be resized easily without losing fidelity.

- Painting documents let you work with bitmapped graphics. These are images that appear as dots—the same type of dots that you see if you look closely at a newspaper photograph. A line, rectangle, square, or text is translated into these dots as they are drawn. As soon as the object has been drawn, it exists only as the dots. Resizing the document can product peculiar effects, since the sense that a set of dots represents a square, for example, is lost. Bitmapped graphics of this sort often are derived from scanned-in graphics. While the human eye can convert the minuscule dots of a photographic image into a tree or a face, they are still only tiny dots.

- Databases are simple (but powerful) collections of data in which the data and its organizing information are both present. You can manipulate either one.

- Presentations consist of slides that are designed to be projected or handed out on paper as part of an oral presentation or speech.

Where AppleWorks differs from other programs is in its ability to create frames in any document. A frame is like a document within a document, and it can be any one of the six document types listed here. You can place a spreadsheet within a word processing document, and you can place a spreadsheet within a presentation. You can also place a fully editable graphics document within a word processing document that in turn is within another graphics document.

Frames can be placed at specific locations within a document's data or float over the document. In the first case, adding (or removing) other elements of the document will cause the frame to move. In the second, the frame will stay where you place it while the document's data flows behind (or around) it.

In Microsoft Office, this type of functionality is implemented with COM and DCOM (the Component Object Model and Distributed Component Object Model). However, as noted previously, Microsoft Office is a suite of separate programs. This means that when you click in a frame to try to edit an embedded graphic, you may be unable to do so if the supporting program is not available or cannot be run. Since all of the AppleWorks frames are supported by AppleWorks itself, there is never a question of not having the software to manage the embedded data.

Starting Points

When you first launch AppleWorks, you will probably see a Button bar at the top of the screen. This is a collection of buttons that create documents and perform a number of common tasks. You can customize the button bar, as you will see later in this section. In addition, the Button bar changes, depending on the type of document you are working on.

The Button bar, which makes commands available, is shown here:

The next illustration shows Starting Points—departures for documents you may want to create. It, too, can be customized.

The tabs at the bottom of the Starting Points window let you move from panel to panel. If the Starting Points window isn't visible, use the Show Starting Points command from the File menu.

Basic

The Basic tab, shown in the previous illustration, lets you create new documents with a single click.

Assistants

The Assistants tab launches interactive assistants that create documents, format them, and fill in data or document values for you. These can be very useful, both directly and indirectly. If you want to learn more about AppleWorks, trying using some of the assistants and then looking at the documents that have been created. See how AppleWorks uses the various features to create useful (and reusable) documents.

Recent Items

AppleWorks keeps track of your recently used documents. Use the Recent Items tab as shown in Figure 19-1 to see them.

Templates

A variety of templates are available as shown in Figure 19-2. Browse through these templates to see how the designers of AppleWorks envision the software being used. Pay particular attention to the types of documents the templates represent. Many people unthinkingly start with a word processing document, and many of these templates use other types of documents very successfully.

NOTE   *Templates differ from assistants in that they are documents that are all ready to go. Assistants walk you through the process of creating the document.*

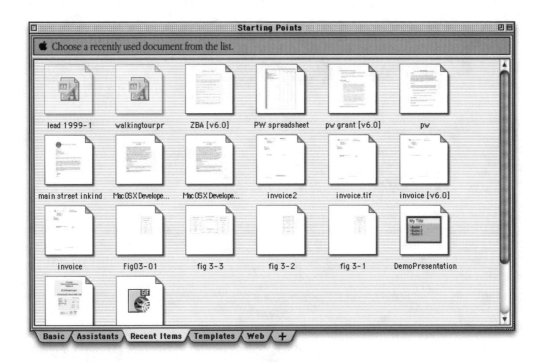

FIGURE 19-1   Recent Items Starting Points let you quickly move among documents.

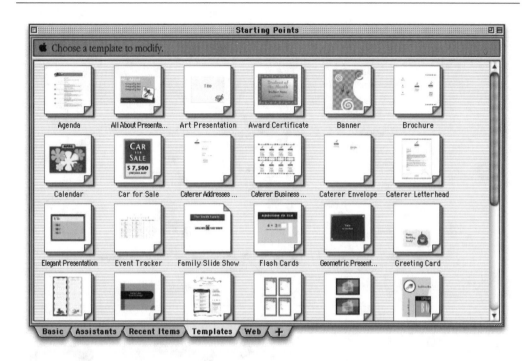

FIGURE 19-2   Templates Starting Points

Web

The Web tab in Starting Points, shown in Figure 19-3, lets you use your Internet connection to get new Starting Points from the AppleWorks site automatically. You need to be connected to the Internet for this to work.

Adding Your Own Tab

As with so much of AppleWorks, you can customize the Starting Points with your own tab using the + tab. This tab can contain any documents that you wish to place there. If you are responsible for a computer lab or for a number of computers in an organization, for instance, you might want to create a custom tab with documents for your students or colleagues to use.

Button Bar

You can customize the Button bar using the Button Bar command from Preferences in the Edit menu to open the window shown next.

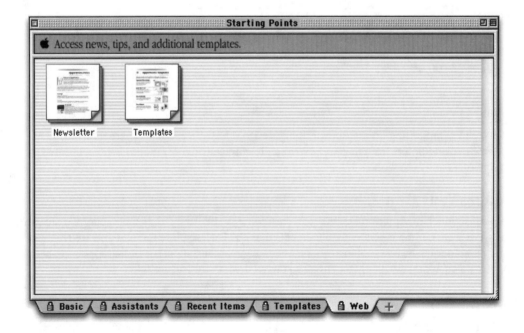

FIGURE 19-3   Use Web Starting Points to get new templates and ideas from Apple.

You simply drag the button that you want from the list of button commands to the place in the Button bar where you want it. You can add dividing lines and remove buttons by using contextual menus. Holding down the CONTROL key, click and hold on a button in the Button bar to see the available commands. But you're not limited to the prepared buttons. Click the New button shown in the previous illustration, and the window shown next will open allowing you to define new buttons.

Tools

The Tools floating palette is shown next. You can show or hide it by using the Show Tools or Hide Tools command from the Windows menu. You can also click the Toolbox icon at the lower left of all AppleWorks document windows to show it. There are two tabs at the bottom of Tools. The frame tab of the floating Tools palette is clicked. (The other tab is the tool tab.) You use Tools as you are creating or editing a document. It determines what is drawn as you use the mouse.

Frame Tab

The frame tab provides access to five tools. The arrow (at the top) is the tool that you use to select objects in a document. Below it are tools to insert text, spreadsheets, graphics, and tables.

To insert a frame into a document, click the tool you want and just draw the outline in the document. If you have an insertion point, the new frame is placed right there. As you add or remove data from the underlying document, the frame you have just created will flow with the remaining data. If you do not have an insertion point, the frame will float over the document; it will remain in the same place with regard to the margins of the document no matter how much data is added or removed.

To create a floating frame, make certain that you do not have an insertion point before drawing the frame. Click the arrow (the topmost tool) to eliminate the insertion point. Then click the spreadsheet, table, or graphics tool and draw the frame. When the arrow is selected, you are editing the document's frames, not its content. In the Options menu, you will find commands such as Object Size and Text Wrap that help you manage these embedded frames. The Options menu is only available when you click the arrow tool in a document in which one or more frames exist.

The tools are also used to help you enter data. For example, when you are in a spreadsheet frame, clicking the spreadsheet tool will let you click on spreadsheet cells and enter data as you do in any spreadsheet. Most of the time, you don't have to worry about this. When you click in a spreadsheet cell, the spreadsheet tool will automatically be selected for you.

There is one ambiguous case, however. If you want to place a spreadsheet in a spreadsheet, a word processing document in a word processing document, and so forth, you need to be able to draw with the tool that is also used for data entry. To do so, hold down the OPTION key while clicking the appropriate tool, and it will now draw a frame in the frame (or document). This is only the case in which a like-kind frame is placed in a frame or document of the same kind. If you are placing a word processing document within a graphics frame, for example, there is no ambiguity.

TIP   *Use floating frames—frames that retain their position with regard to the document's margins—to create documents that need to fit into window envelopes and other highly structured documents.*

In view of the fact that you can place frames in documents, the type of document that you start with is much less important than you might imagine. Your choice of the basic document is probably best determined by its pagination requirements than by its content. If your document is intended to flow from page to page as needed—as is the case with most typed documents—start with a word processing document, but if your document is intended to be a certain number of pages in length—as is the case with a flyer or other front-and-back mailing piece—use a graphics document because you can specify its size directly. For a drawing document, you specify its size in a number of pages across and down. For a painting document, you specify its size in a dimensions of pixels across and down.

Tool Tab

The tool tab at the bottom of the Tools floating palette gives you access to painting and drawing tools. In the next illustration, the tool tab has been clicked.

You use these tools to draw lines and shapes, as well as to select items (with the arrow) and areas (with the dotted-line tool). The paintbrush and spray can let you add color to your graphics. You can also add color by selecting objects (in drawing documents, not in painting documents) and then using the Colors palette described later in this chapter.

Links

You can place links in AppleWorks documents. These links consist of two parts: something that can be clicked on to send you to a link destination and the destination to which you go. Destinations can be in the same or other AppleWorks documents; they can also be on the Internet. Figure 19-4 shows a graphic object selected in a document window at the right and the Links window open to create a link destination (an anchor).

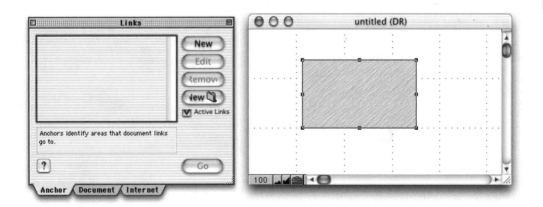

FIGURE 19-4   Creating a link destination is the first step of creating a link.

AppleWorks Overview

In Figure 19-5, you see a line of text highlighted. Select the text or other object that you want to be "hot." Then choose Create Link from the Format menu, and the subcommand Document from beneath that. You can select the graphics-containing document and its anchor. Once you have created a link, clicking on the text will open the graphics document and highlight the selected object.

TIP *Links work across documents and the Internet. You can link from text to graphics, and vice versa.*

This is the normal sequence: you create the destination and then create the link. Anything that is selectable in AppleWorks can be either end of a link—the destination or the active link on which you click.

Properties

You can set properties for any AppleWorks document using the Properties command in the File menu. Properties of a document include a title, the author, keywords, and an optional password.

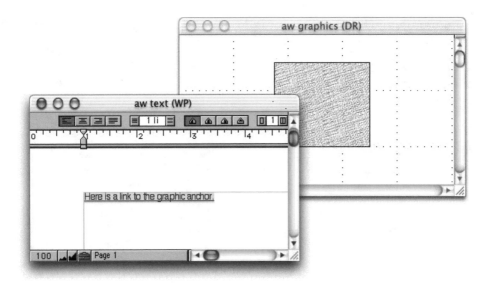

FIGURE 19-5   Creating a link requires selecting the destination and then creating a link from the "hot" object.

Word Processing

The word processing features of AppleWorks provide basic and advanced features that you will find in many word processing products. AppleWorks word processing documents differ from other products in that you can insert graphics, spreadsheets, and even other word processing frames into the flow of text. (You can also make them float about the word processing document, as noted previously.)

A typical word processing document is shown here:

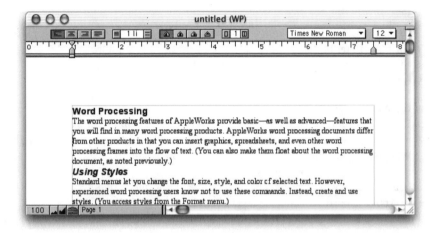

As shown, you can vary the fonts and sizes of text in the window. At the top, a ruler lets you adjust margins (including a separate indent for the first line of a paragraph). At the top of the window are six major controls:

- Four buttons let you set the alignment for the currently selected paragraph. From left to right, they make the paragraph flush left (with a ragged right margin), centered (with ragged left and right margins), flush right (with a ragged left margin), and justified (with even left and right margins). Justified text is managed by inserted small spaces to make both margins even. Note that short lines of text or lines with lengthy words (that is, few spaces between them), do not justify properly in most cases. This is a difficulty that is inherent in the text itself: all word processing applications have the same difficulty.

- The next controls let you adjust line spacing. You can explicitly set the spacing between lines by typing in the number. You also can use the buttons on either side to tighten up or loosen vertical line spacing.

■ Four tabs appear next. You simply drag the one you want to the location in the ruler where it should be set. You can move tabs back and forth in the ruler just by dragging them. The four tabs (from left to right) set text flush left at the tab, center text on the tab, set the text flush right on the tab, and—most useful to budget-makers—aligns the tabbed text on a decimal point. Use this to create neat columns of numbers with decimal points in them. Columns of numbers look best aligned on the decimal point.

■ The next controls let you add or subtract columns from your paragraph. You also can type in the number of columns you want.

■ A pop-up button lets you select the font for the selection. If nothing is selected, the font is applied to the insertion point and will be used for the new text that you type.

■ The final pop-up button lets you select the font size for the selection. As with fonts, if nothing is selected, it is applied to the insertion point and is used for the new text that you type.

All of these commands apply to the current selection. The first four apply only to paragraphs; if you need two types of alignment or two sets of tabs, you must have two paragraphs. To apply the new formatting to the entire document, select all (either using the command from the Edit menu or the keyboard equivalent COMMAND-A) before proceeding.

The remainder of this section covers three of the most useful word processing features in AppleWorks that tend to be overlooked by many people. If you are not familiar with word processing at all, use the AppleWorks documentation and tutorial to get started. For novices, the single most important point to remember is not to use the RETURN key at the end of each line (as you would do with a typewriter). Just keep typing, and AppleWorks will automatically adjust the line endings.

Using Styles

Standard menus let you change the font, size, style, and color of selected text. However, experienced word processing users know not to use these commands. Instead, create and use styles. (You access styles from the Format menu.) The Styles window is shown in Figure 19-6.

A style is a combination of text attributes—font, size, style, and color, for example—that you group into a named style. For example, you might create a style called Emphasis that consists of bold (or italicized) text. The advantage of using styles is that you can change the representation of the style by modifying the style rather than the document.

For example, if you have access to a color printer or are creating a document to be seen online, your Emphasis style might consist of red text. On some black and white printers, red text may be unclear or even not appear. Thus, you would need to change the style to bold, italics, or underlined. If you change the style, all of its uses in the document will change. You can create basic styles that can be assigned to any selected text. Other styles can only be assigned to paragraphs or outlines; these involve attributes such as line spacing.

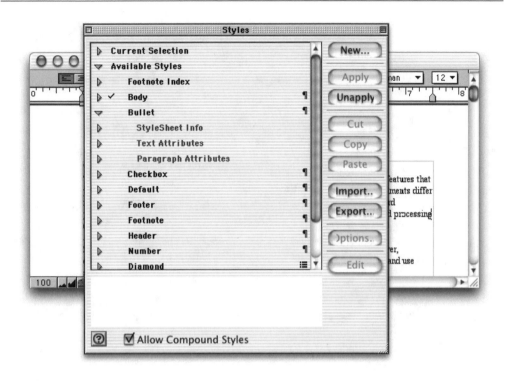

FIGURE 19-6   Styles window

Document Sections

You are probably familiar with the basic components of documents—words, paragraphs, and pages. However, there is another type of component—sections—which can be useful to you. A section can have its own formatting for headers and footers, as well as its own pagination. Choose Section from the Format menu to open the window shown in Figure 19-7.

You can specify that the first page of a section is a title page. In that case, headers and footers do not appear. Even if your document consists only of one section (the default), you may want to customize that section using the Format menu.

Using Sections to Create Letterhead

To create letterhead for your correspondence, you can use the following technique. Format your document's section with a title page. This will eliminate headers and footers from page 1. On

FIGURE 19-7   Section window

page 1, use the frame tab in the Tools floating palette to insert one or more frames. Typically, a graphics frame will be inserted with your logo, and a word processing frame will be inserted with your mailing address. These frames should both float—that is, they will be positioned at constant places on the document. (If necessary, turn on Text Wrap from the Options menu to keep your document's text away from them.) Then create headers and footers with the page number, your address, and so forth; these will appear on continuation pages (pages 2 and up). Your header or footer may in fact duplicate the data from your floating frames on page 1. Typically, continuation pages have some—not all—of the page 1 information.

Creating your own letterhead in this way means that you can print your correspondence on plain paper and have your logo, address, and other letterhead information printed out automatically. This saves money on custom printing and reduces the amount of time you need to spend loading and reloading your printer.

Outline and Numbering

You can use the AppleWorks outlining features to automatically number and outline paragraphs using various standards from the Outline menu. Be aware that the numbering (and bullets or other paragraph indicators) is internal to AppleWorks. If you copy an outline that has been carefully prepared with AppleWorks, all of the numbers will disappear if you paste it into another application's word processor.

Drawing

Drawing documents let you create vector-based graphics. These are graphics that maintain an awareness of their elements as lines, rectangles, and so forth (as opposed to simply collections of pixels). Vector graphics can be resized very easily and with a high degree of fidelity. They are perfect for creating graphics that use basic shapes. You can use them to advantage in flyers and mailing pieces that you want to catch people's attention.

> **TIP** *You can place bitmapped graphics frames (paintings in AppleWorks terminology) into documents; however, you cannot insert drawing frames. Thus, if you need the accuracy of vector graphics anywhere in your document, create a drawing document as the base and insert other frames into it.*

An AppleWorks drawing document is shown in Figure 19-8. To the left of the document are the Tool window and the Accents window; the latter lets you select colors and patterns for graphical objects. Note that the drawing document has the grid turned on—the dotted lines are not part of the document itself. You can use a grid to align objects as you draw them.

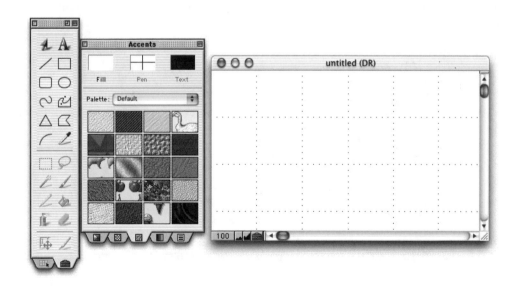

FIGURE 19-8   Drawing document

Painting

Bitmapped graphics don't scale well, but they do represent natural images very well with their absence of straight lines and intricate color variations. If you are using a scanned graphic from a photograph, it will be a bitmapped graphic. You can modify it on a pixel-by-pixel basis using the paint tools in AppleWorks. You can insert painting frames into any type of document.

Spreadsheets

Spreadsheets let you enter data—often numerical—into rows and columns of an organized document. Each cell of the document contains two sets of information: a data value and a formula used to derive it. (The formula may be blank.)

Thus, a cell can be created that contains the sum of several other cells; its value will change as those values change. Spreadsheets provide many formatting tools, and the AppleWorks spreadsheet is no exception.

AppleWorks spreadsheets are self-contained—that is, they cannot contain information from another spreadsheet. This limits the complexity of the spreadsheet—and that is very often a good thing. If you have more complex data needs, consider using databases, which are described next.

The next illustration is of an AppleWorks spreadsheet. When you click in a cell, it is selected. To enter data, you type in the entry field at the top; when you press RETURN, your entry is displayed in the selected cell. Cells are identified by their row numbers and column letters. In this case, cell A1 contains the word "Date." Cell B1 is highlighted (a small border surrounds it), and the date 5/29/2001 has been typed in the entry field. When you press RETURN, the data will be moved into the cell.

To use your own row and column headings, place them in the first column and first row. Enter your data below and to the right. You can set the print area of the spreadsheet to include the standard row and column numbers and letters or just to use your own. Spreadsheets allow you to enter data and have it formatted in a variety of ways. Double-clicking a cell opens the Format window shown here:

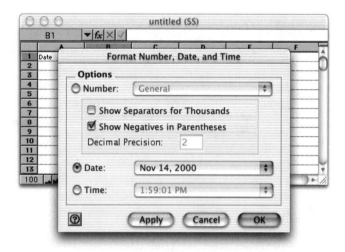

Format your cells appropriately; this will let AppleWorks guarantee that data is correctly entered. In a Date field, for example, the entry **dachshund** would be rejected.

Databases

Databases are one of the most important tools on computers; for some reason, many people fear them or think they are too complicated to use easily. On the contrary, databases—particularly in AppleWorks—are easy to use and can make your life much easier.

The reason for this is that a database not only contains data, it also contains information about the data. In a spreadsheet, for example, you may specify that a certain cell is a number or a date; however, only you know whether it represents an employment date or a birth date. Knowing the meaning of a data element can make it easier for people to understand the data. It also allows you to do many types of automatic error checking.

Since databases are one of the most powerful parts of AppleWorks, and in view of the fact that so many people are afraid to use them, this section walks you through the steps involved in creating and using a database.

NOTE   *AppleWorks databases are very powerful. If you need greater power, you should consider using FileMaker. It uses a very similar interface and terminology to AppleWorks. For devotees, the most important feature that is implemented in FileMaker that is not implemented in AppleWorks is relational technology. An another important FileMaker feature is ODBC, which lets you communicate with all sorts of other databases and applications.*

Database Terminology

A database is a collection of data. It contains records and fields. Each record represents one observation, individual, or item. Each field represents a type of data—name, address, age, and so forth. Each record in a database has the same fields; however, each record has different values for those fields. Many databases refer to these concepts in a tabular form, using the terms "rows" and "columns." Rows are equivalent to records, and columns are equivalent to fields.

Creating a Database

A database contains data and information about that data (often called metadata). The data is stored in fields; each field has a name and certain characteristics that you specify. When you first create a database, you are prompted to enter at least one field, as shown here:

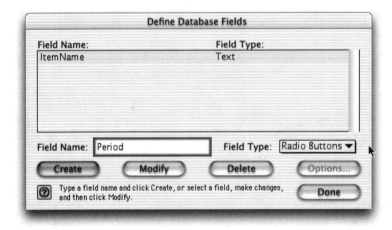

Name the field with a meaningful name. That name will appear by default on the database documents, but you can always change it. Therefore, its meaning should be clear to you.

TIP   *Although names can contain spaces, avoid them. There are circumstances in which the space will be confusing. Instead, use capitalization to combine two words, such as DateCreated.*

Using the pop-up menu in the lower right, you can specify the type of field it is—text, date, time, number, and so forth. Several other field types are particularly useful. Calculation fields present the results of calculations involving other fields in the record (much like spreadsheet calculations). Summary fields present summaries of data from many records in the database. You can also create fields that contain unique serial numbers, multimedia, and a variety of interface elements.

Make your field types as specific as possible. You can place dates in text fields, for example, but if you make them fields of type Date, you can avail yourself of many AppleWorks functions that only work on dates.

The Field Types pop-up button is shown next. Click Create to create each field. You can define as many as you want, and you can come back later and choose the Define Fields command from the Layout menu to modify your fields.

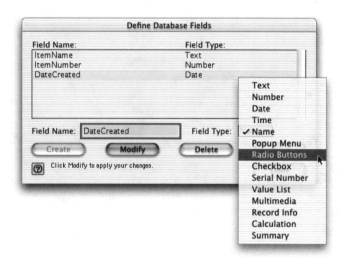

You can highlight any fields in this list in order to specify options. You do this by clicking the Options button. By setting options, you can let AppleWorks guarantee the integrity of data fields either by automatically entering values or by checking for certain conditions that you specify here. Options are different for each field type. The options for a date field are shown here:

The next illustration shows options for radio buttons. You can specify values for them, and you can choose a default as shown in the window. Using radio buttons or checkboxes can really clean up your interface. It also limits choices for entries and makes searching much easier to do, since users cannot enter new values: they must choose from the values you have placed in radio button or checkbox.

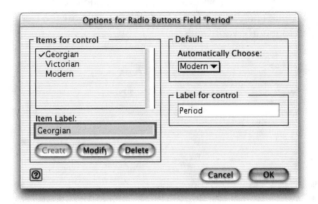

When you click Done, the database will appear as shown next. AppleWorks automatically inserts the name of the field and creates a data entry field into which you can type data. This collection of fields, labels, and optional graphics that you can add is called a *layout*.

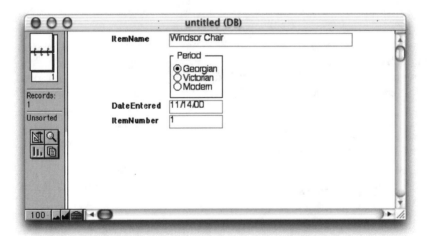

You can enter new records into the database by using the New Record command from the Edit menu. The following illustration reveals that two records have been entered. At the left of the database window are tools and information to help you maneuver through the database. The book icon shows you the record in the database you are currently viewing. You can use the bookmark to move forward and backward in the database.

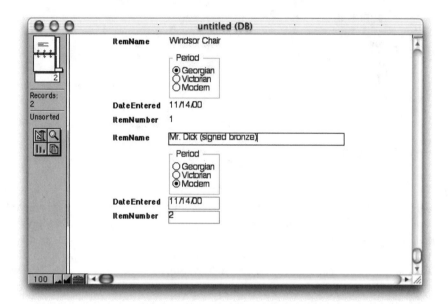

Below the book icon is status information about the number of records in the database and whether or not the database is sorted. Four tools appear next that let you work with layouts, find data, sort data, and produce reports. (They are described in the next sections.) You can view the data in the database in a number of different types of formats. The List format is somewhat similar to a spreadsheet view of rows and columns.

Using Layouts

You can choose Layout from the Layout menu to modify the look of this layout. When you do, the view will change to something like that shown in Figure 19-9. All of the commands in this section require you to be in Layout mode; you do that with the Layout command in the Layout menu.

You can click on the default name for a field and type in something else. This does not affect the name of the field in the database. When you are in layout mode, you can use the painting and drawing tools in the tool tab of the floating Tools palette to add additional text, provide graphics, and otherwise make the layout look better.

In Layout mode, you can create and modify parts of a layout. By default, you have one part—the body of a layout. As shown next, you can have headers and footers, as well as summaries.

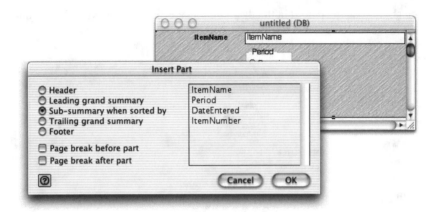

If you have Summary type fields, they will be filled with the appropriate data if you have a summary part. (For sub-summaries, the database must be sorted as you specify in this dialog.)

Summaries let you create very elegant database designs. For example, you don't have to store the total of outstanding invoices for each customer. You can create a database with invoices in it, sort it by customer ID, and create a sub-summary to represent each customer's current balance. Sub-summaries and summaries can contain data other than summary fields. However, the data in those fields is meaningless unless it has a single value for all records included in the

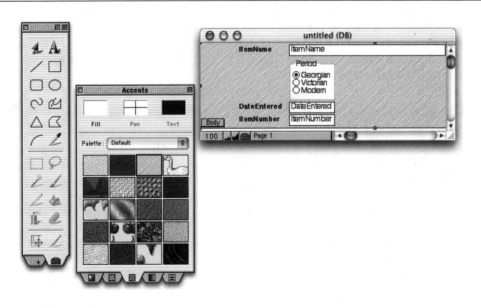

FIGURE 19-9   Modifying a layout

summary or sub-summary. An example of such a case would be a field with the customer name or ID. When sorted, each sub-summary could contain the customer name (which is constant for that sub-summary) and the current balance. Summary fields and summary parts are an important feature of AppleWorks.

You can have any number of layouts for a database. These might include layouts that are convenient for data entry (perhaps with length descriptions of the data) and other layouts that provide the data in ways that are useful to people who are browsing. Much of the design of AppleWorks databases consists of designing layouts rather than databases.

The following illustration shows the New Layout window. You will see the various types of default layouts from which you can choose. Notable is the collection of label layouts. As you can see here, AppleWorks ships with a variety of preformatted layouts that you can use for mailing labels and the like.

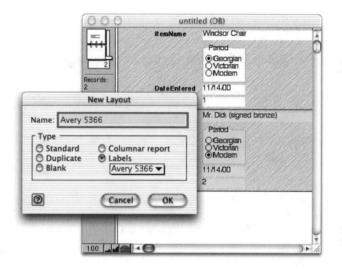

The layout is separate from the database design. You can have fields that are not on a layout, you just cannot enter them or see them in that layout. Typically, mailing list databases will have many more fields than appear on their label layouts.

Sorting

A very attractive feature of the AppleWorks database is the ease with which you can sort it. Sorting a database is helpful in preparing a report, and it is necessary in using sub-summary fields that require a certain sorted order. You must be in Browse mode—not Layout mode—to sort records. Choose Browse from the Layout menu.

You can sort your database using the Sort command from the menu. That will open a dialog. You can also use the Sort tool in the status area to create a new, named sort. (The Sort tool is the icon with three bars of decreasing height; it is the lower left of the four tools.)

You can choose any fields in the database that you want to sort, and the sort will be done in the order you specify. Click on the icons at the right to indicate if that field should be sorted in ascending or descending order. You can also specify a name for the sort at the bottom. This will let you repeat the sort. The following illustration shows what happens when you have saved a sort: it is available as a tool in the status panel at the left of the database window.

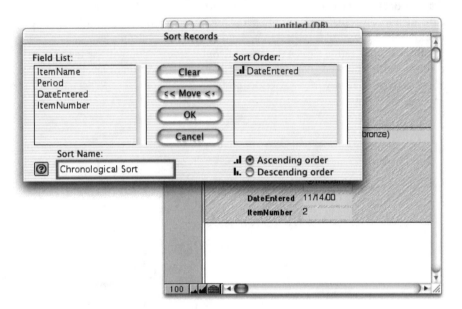

Most people sort databases too often. It is necessary for printed reports, but it is not the best way to find data. Remember that that is what the database does best. You don't have to alphabetize a database in order to find all the names beginning with J: let the database do it. (You'll see how next.) Every time you feel inclined to sort a database, ask yourself if you really just want to find data.

Finding Data

To Find data, you can choose Match Records from the Organize menu or use the Find tool. You must be in Browse mode; choose Browse from the Layout menu. When you click the Search icon (the magnifying glass at the upper right of the tools), you first are asked to name the search.

Next, you specify the search. A blank record opens; it is similar to a data entry record, but you use it to enter the data for which you want to search. It is common to search for only part of a field, such as **chair**, which matches Windsor chair, Eames chair, dining chair, and the like. A named search is added to the Search tool as shown next. This is a very easy way to create custom solutions for other people to use.

Reports

The fourth tool lets you create reports. Reports bring together each of the three previous tools: layouts, searching, and sorting. You create a report as shown next by clicking on the New Report feature of the Report tool (the lower-right tool, with the image of a printed page).

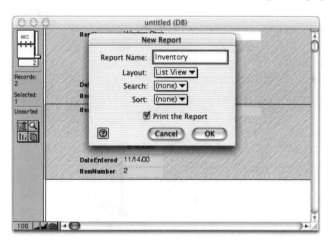

Presentations

Using AppleWorks, you can create presentations that are suitable for printing or presenting in front of an audience. The presentation document type lets you do this. When you have a presentation document open, the Presentation controls window is available as shown next.

The first tab at the bottom of the window lets you create master slides. The elements on these slides will be repeated on all slides you create until you create a new master. Add a new master by clicking the + button; delete one by selecting it and clicking the – button.

The next tab lets you create and delete individual slides based on the master slide currently selected. The slide tab is shown next. You create and delete individual slides in the same way you do master slides. In addition, you can specify whether a slide can be printed and whether it is viewable. This allows you to temporarily remove slides from a presentation (for example, if you have to shorten it) without disrupting the presentation as a whole. In addition, a pop-up button lets you control any visual effect applied to the slide.

The visual effect is applied as the slide is shown. When it is replaced by the next slide, the visual effect of the following slide is used.

Experienced presenters know that a variety of visual effects is distracting. Use one or (at most) two. If you use two, make certain that there is a substantive reason for using one or the other. One effect might be used to display slides summarizing a portion of the presentation; another could be used for the detailed slides within each portion.

The organization tab, lets you view the presentation as a whole; you can also name each slide here. Finally, the running controls shown next let you actually present the presentation.

Clippings and Accents

AppleWorks provides clippings and accents to help you improve your documents. Clippings are images—either on the Web or on your local computer—which you can insert into documents. Accents are graphical elements that can improve the look of your documents. The Accents window is shown next.

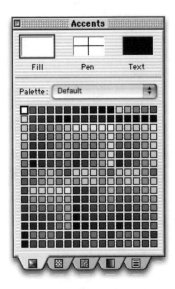

You can apply accents to lines (pens), the interior of graphic objects (fills), and text. Three basic types of accents are available. When you set an accent, it is used for drawing lines, objects, and text within that document. If you set another accent, it will be used for new drawing, but the existing elements remain with whatever accents they have. You can select text and objects and apply accents to them as well. Accents can be colors, patterns, or gradients. The best way to learn about them is to experiment with them.

Scripting

AppleWorks has defined four suites of Apple events that you can use to script the text, graphics, database, and spreadsheet features. If you open the scripts that ship with AppleWorks, you will see some of these commands in use. You can also use the Open Dictionary command in Script Editor to open AppleWorks and view its scripting commands. (See Chapter 20, "Automating Your Work with AppleScript," for more about AppleScript.)

Summary

AppleWorks is a powerful tool that can do many of the routine tasks you expect to do on a personal computer. Some of its features—particularly the spreadsheet and database—are likely to be all that you need in those categories. Its text editing is thorough, and its graphics tools are fine for many of the tasks you'll need to perform. In short, it is powerful, intuitive, and easy to use—just like the rest of Macintosh.

This part of the book has showed you how to work with applications—the applications that ship as part of Mac OS X, Apple Mail and AppleWorks, as well as the services you can create or use from the Services menu.

The final part of the book explores how to make everything even easier to use. It shows you how to program Mac OS X and its applications so that work can go on when you aren't even around. It starts with scripting and continues with advanced programming techniques so that you can write your own AppleWorks some day.

Summary

Part V

Programming Mac OS X

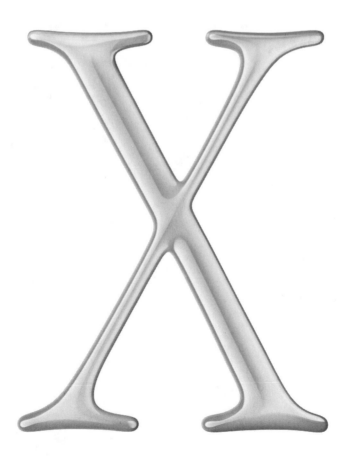

Chapter 20

Automating Your Work with AppleScript

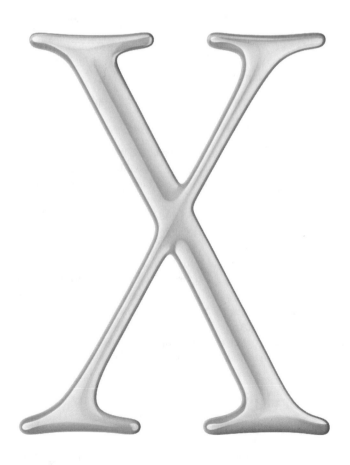

This part of the book covers programming for Mac OS X. *Programming* means any of the following:

- Creating a script to automate some tasks

- Writing shell scripts that work in the Unix-like environment of the Terminal application

- Developing your own programs using Carbon or Cocoa

This chapter is about AppleScript: the scripting language that lets you control your Macintosh with text commands, rather than with the keyboard and the mouse. The sections of this chapter provide you with the following:

- A programming overview, where you will find a capsule introduction to the different types of programming and who can do them

- Introduction to AppleScript, what it is and when to use it

- A guide to using Script Editor, the application program that lets you create AppleScript scripts

- The basic AppleScript language components

- An overview of Apple events, the underpinnings of AppleScript

- An introduction to using dialogs with AppleScript

When you consider the cost of your computer and the value of your own time, doesn't it make sense to have your computer work as much as possible and you work as little as possible? Why shouldn't it be chugging away while you're out chugging down lemonade on the veranda? Why should you be chained to the keyboard when you could be fingering the passages of a Bach fugue on a far different keyboard? This chapter, and the others in this part of the book, show you how to maximize your computer's productivity using programming techniques and tools that are part of Mac OS X.

This chapter provides an overview and introduction to AppleScript. For more information, look at the samples that come as part of the operating system: you normally find them in a folder called AppleScript inside Applications. Two documents from Apple are also of great use to users, scripters, and programmers. "AppleScript Language Guide" and "Apple Event Registry: Standard Suites" may be found on Apple's Web site. Search for them by title or search for AppleScript. In addition, the AppleScript section of Apple's Web site has a lot of examples, tips, tutorials, and other links; find it at http://www.apple.com/applescript/.

Programming Overview

Programming has evolved over the last half century; however, it remains what it was at the dawn of the computer age: a way to instruct a computer to carry out useful tasks. As computers and programming have evolved, the nature of programming has changed. With Mac OS X, there are few changes to this paradigm; but Mac OS X does offer a remarkably easier transition from one programming style to another.

This section describes the types of programs, types of programmers, and aspects of programming that are important for understanding where AppleScript fits into the picture.

Types of Programs

There are three general types of programs: scripts, byte-code, and compiled code. All three are part of Mac OS X.

Scripts

Scripts, also sometimes known as *macros,* can be the most basic type of programming. Some are simply recorded commands; on early teletype terminals, perforated tape recorded keyboard commands, and it was fed into the computer on demand. On personal computers (including the Macintosh), early macro languages let you record mouse movements, keystrokes, and menu commands. These primitive scripts were quite fragile: if you specified where the mouse was to be clicked, that is where it was clicked. A minor change to the program's interface could mean the difference between clicking the OK button and clicking in another application's windows.

In the 1980s, more sophisticated scripting languages evolved on personal computers. Probably the most sophisticated is AppleScript, which made its debut in Mac OS 7 in 1990. Visual Basic, developed by Microsoft, is used extensively in the Microsoft Office suite of products. It can also be used by independent programmers and end-users to extend those products (and others). Other scripting languages, including Perl, were developed to run primarily on Unix-based operating systems. Although AppleScript, Visual Basic, and Perl now all run on both Mac OS 9 and earlier, as well as on Mac OS X, their origins are still reflected in their features.

Modern scripts use a programming language that is based on semantic elements, not keystrokes or mouse positions. Their languages differ, but they all strive for a natural language look and feel (that is, they try to be like English, Japanese, or other human languages).

A script processor normally processes scripts. In the case of AppleScript, it is the AppleScript engine, which is part of the operating system. The script processor reads the script commands and converts them into computer commands. Scripts can be stored for reuse; however, they need to be reprocessed by the script processor each time they are executed. With AppleScript, you can store scripts in a partially processed state, as well as in basic textual representation.

Compiled Code

Traditional programming languages (such as Fortran, Cobol, the various C languages, and Pascal) are *compiled*. The conversion of programmers' commands to computer commands is performed not when the program is run, but in advance. The output of the compiler is the set of computer instructions. (Because these instructions are in binary code, sometimes compiled programs are called *binaries*; the output files are also sometimes called *executables* or *executable code.*)

For a program that is to be used repeatedly, it is more efficient to compile it once and run the executable code as needed. Not only is it more efficient, but compilers have built-in error checking. Some problems are caught during the compilation process, rather than during the execution of the program.

Compiled code is specific to a given operating system. For example, a C program can be compiled to run on Unix, Windows, or Mac OS; but while the *source code* (the input to the compiler) may be the same, the *executable* code (the output) cannot be moved at will from one operating system to another. When you save a script in AppleScript's run-only format, you are saving it in what is basically a compiled version.

Byte-Code

Some languages, such as Java, take an intermediate route. Java is compiled into *byte-code*. Byte-code is not directly executable on a computer; it can be processed into machine instructions quickly on any given operating system. This means that the compilation process of source code into byte-code can be done once. The errors are caught at that time, and the resultant byte-code can be shared among various operating systems.

Types of Programmers

There are three general categories of programmers: end-users, IT staffs and consultants, and developers. Each type of programmer has different characteristics. You may find yourself in more than one category.

End-Users

End-users write macros and scripts to automate their tasks. Typically, this programming has been personal and idiosyncratic. You may have formalized routines on your own computer quite different from a colleague's routines.

End-user programming is usually oriented toward specific objectives of the user's interests. Domain knowledge, the knowledge of how a law firm, school, or trucking company operates, predominates. The problems of end-user programming tend to arise from inefficiencies in the programming and from logical gaps: certain possibilities that are not covered in the code. Furthermore, end-user programs may be poorly tested, documented, and maintained. They work for the person who wrote them—and that's the objective.

Many end-user programmers write excellent, well-tested, and well-maintained programs. Sometimes, in fact, they are among the most sophisticated programs available. It is not uncommon for an end-user to decide that the sideline of programming is more rewarding than the basic job at hand. The programming tools of Mac OS X can help to forestall such conflicts. Their power and sophistication mean that a sophisticated end-user can develop applications much more quickly than heretofore making the choice between programming and "real work" less troublesome.

IT Staffs and Consultants

Information technology (IT) staffs and consultants specialize in helping develop custom-written solutions. These may entail scripts and macros, and they may entail compiled code. IT staffs and consultants bring expertise in the development of software to the table; their domain knowledge is usually less than that of the user who is on the front line. As a result, programs written by these people tend to be better code in that they are well analyzed, tested, documented, and maintained. They may, however, contain grievous flaws due to misunderstandings of the operations that need to be performed. Typically, custom-written solutions have been fairly expensive. They also tend to go over budget and to be delivered late.

Developers

Software developers generally write applications for broad use; they are designed not for individual users or for a department within an organization, but for hundreds (or thousands) of users who need word processing, veterinary record keeping, or other applications of greater or lesser import.

Whereas IT staffs and consultants frequently work on a contract basis, often at an hourly rate, developers typically develop products that are sold on a unit basis. (Large developers have staffs of designers and programmers who are generally paid salaries; the company itself is paid on a unit basis as it sells the product.) There is less customization in such products than there is in software developed by IT staffs and consultants.

Breaking Down Programming Barriers

One of the problems in the world of computers is that each type of program (scripts, compiled code, and byte-code) and each type of programmer (end-users, IT staffs and consultants, and developers) functions well on its own, but making the transition from one type to another is difficult. In other words, if you have written a script (or set of scripts) to do something, it is often hard to expand that script to a larger and more complex scale. Likewise, if IT staffs and consultants have developed a customized solution, it sometimes appears that it would be relatively easy to transform such a solution into a shrink-wrapped product. Unfortunately, that transformation often requires going back and rewriting everything.

The range of programming tools in Mac OS X, ranging from AppleScript to shell commands and to compiled programs, makes these transitions easier. In fact, when it comes to AppleScript, it is an intrinsic part, not only of Carbon, but also of Cocoa and Mac OS 9 and earlier. Applications developed with Cocoa automatically have scripting capabilities.

Aspects of Programming

Finally, consider the aspects of programming—those characteristics that are common to all types of programming:

- Not Interactive
- Designed for multiple uses
- Designed for multiple users
- Self-controlling
- Documented
- Maintained over time
- Tested

Programming Overview

Not Interactive

When you type a memo or draw a diagram, you constantly interact with the software. Many other programs, whether they be scripts or compiled programs, start from a set of inputs (such as a memo's text); then they apply certain logical rules to them; and, finally, they print them, store them, or otherwise end their operations. Interactions with the user usually occur when the program or script stops and waits for user input.

This matters because it means that programs and scripts can run when no user is at the computer. They can run over the Internet on a Web server and place the results on a Web page or send them back via email.

Multiple Uses

Programs are designed to be used repeatedly. There is little point writing a program to do something you need to do only once, although sometimes you may do so in order to perfect a complicated series of mouse clicks and other steps. A consequence of this is that, to some extent, programs are generalized so that they can be reused. (Often the generalization comes in the form of user input, such as the date for which stock quotations are to be obtained.)

Multiple Users

Programs frequently are designed for multiple users. This means that the instructions often are placed in the program so that a variety of users will understand what they should do.

Self-Control

Programs and scripts can contain control logic. They can execute sequences of their instructions repeatedly, and they can dynamically execute one set of instructions or another. This is a critical aspect of programming, and it leads to an important rule: programs with conditional statements are much more difficult to document, maintain, and test than programs that run from start to finish without repetition or interruption.

Documentation

Programs designed for repeated use by multiple users need to be documented. This fact is often ignored for macros and scripts. The authors believe that they are one-time projects that do not need to be documented. In fact, the mere existence of a program or script means that someone might reuse it. How it works and what it does needs to be known.

Maintenance

This leads to the next aspect of programming: programs evolve over time. Sometimes a program needs to be changed because its purpose changes. Other times, it needs to change because the environment changes—it must run on another operating system, for example. This all ties in together: without documentation, maintenance is harder.

Testing

Few scripts and macros are ever tested. Even with custom solutions from IT staffs and consultants, testing is often not performed. As a result, users do not know what to expect from their software, and they often do not even know if it is working correctly.

Introducing AppleScript

AppleScript addresses many of the issues raised in the previous sections. Scripts can be stored in run-only (compiled) versions, as well as in raw form. AppleScript can be used not only by end-users, but also by IT staffs and consultants and by developers producing shrink-wrapped products. (AppleScript is the user interface to Apple events, which are the domain of programmers.) Finally, AppleScript is closely integrated with other programming tools on Mac OS X so that the transition from small-scale scripts and macros to large-scale solutions and programs is made easier.

This section provides an introduction to AppleScript focusing on the following:

- AppleScript's purposes

- Apple events

- Dictionaries

- Script Editor application

- The interrelationship between AppleScript and application programs

- The basic structure of AppleScript

Purposes of AppleScript

AppleScript has three primary purposes:

- Automation

- Integration

- Customization

Automation

Automation is the process of automating keystrokes and mouse commands. It is close to the macros that you can record with many tools.

Integration

Integration, also known as *workflow management*, lets you share data among programs either in whole or in part. You can run a program or script to generate output and then use it as input to another program or script.

Integration of this sort is used extensively in the production of print and online media. In one very common use, television listings and catalog databases are retrieved and then passed into desktop publishing software, where they are manipulated automatically into a format for printing or posting on the Web.

Customization

Customization allows you to create new commands, such as dialogs that an AppleScript script can post, that in turn run an application's native commands. This allows you to substitute more meaningful language for the command; it also allows you to create a command such as "Prepare Daily Absence Report," which queries a database, imports the data into a spreadsheet, and then prints it automatically.

Apple Events

Apple events are the programmatic commands that are executed by AppleScript, scripts. Each event carries out one action: it may print a document, close a window, or perform a calculation. An event may have one or more *parameters.* These are references to objects on which the command should act (the file to be printed, the window to be closed, and so on), or they specify how the command should be carried out (saving before closing, for example).

Dictionaries

Each application that supports scripting has a dictionary that you can view. A particularly interesting aspect of AppleScript's design is that the dictionary must be present. The dictionary that you can view for an application is the same set of syntactical rules that are invoked when Apple events are sent to an application. It is impossible to have one (such as the user-viewable dictionary) without the other (such as the program-viewable dictionary).

This is important because historically, many scripting methodologies have fallen into disuse because their syntax became forgotten. Integrating the documentation with the functionality is a good way to prevent that from happening. Not all scripting languages in use today have this type of foolproof integrated dictionary.

Script Editor

Script Editor is an application program that ships as part of the Macintosh operating system. On Mac OS 9 and earlier, it is installed in the AppleScript folder inside the Apple Extras folder. On Mac OS X, it is found in the AppleScript folder inside Applications. (Script Runner and Example scripts are also there.)

You can use Script Editor to view dictionaries of supported Apple events in various applications; you can use it to type new scripts, check them for syntax, and save them; and you can use it to record scripts.

AppleScript and Applications

AppleScript and Apple events provide an architecture to support automation, integration, and customization of applications. Remember, however, that it takes two to tango. In order to use AppleScript and Apple events, you need to have both a script and an application that supports Apple events.

Not all applications support Apple events. There are several categories of applications that typically do support Apple events (and thus, AppleScript). Among these categories are the following:

- Application programs that are designed to be part of a workflow process are often scriptable. This allows them to function.

- Application programs that are involved in desktop publishing and prepress are often scriptable (for the same reason).

- Application programs that are developed using an application framework (such as MacApp or Cocoa on Mac OS X) are often scriptable—that is part of the framework's general functionality.

Support for Apple events is often not provided in other types of applications:

- Applications initially developed before scripting was developed by Apple (that is, before System 7) might not have been retrofitted.

- Cross-platform applications might not support features unique to one platform. (However, some applications, such as those in Microsoft Office, often support AppleScript, as well as a native scripting interface such as Visual Basic. You can write an AppleScript command that sends a Visual Basic command to Microsoft Word, for example.)

Support for scripting is most easily achieved when an application is *factored*: that is, the basic functionality of the application is implemented separately from the interface.

Scriptability

Applications are said to be *scriptable* if they have a dictionary and can receive Apple events and respond to them. All applications should respond to the four required Apple events (Open Application, Open Document, Print Document, and Quit). Other Apple events are implemented as needed (and subject to the considerations in the previous section).

If an application is scriptable, you can use Script Editor to open its dictionary and see the Apple events that it supports and the syntax for them. (See the section "Using Script Editor," later in this chapter, for more details.)

Introducing AppleScript

Recordability

Some applications are *recordable*: that is, you can perform operations using the standard point-and-click interface and have Script Editor build a script that records your actions. You can then play that script back or modify it to repeat your actions. Not all scriptable applications are recordable, but all recordable applications are scriptable.

Send-Only Applications

Some applications can send Apple events to other applications, but they are neither scriptable nor recordable. They are usually custom-written applications used for very specific purposes.

AppleScript Structure

The AppleScript programming language is described later in this chapter. For now, it is useful to understand a little bit about its structure.

AppleScript Statements

AppleScript commands can be written as single, English-like sentences such as the following:

```
set the name of window 1 to "AppleScript Demo"
```

Tell Blocks

They may be directed to a specific application, as in the following:

```
tell application "TextEdit" to set the name of window 1 to
"AppleScript Demo"
```

Compound Statements

They may also consist of more than one command; in such a case, the commands are enclosed in a block. That block can be a tell block, as in the following:

```
tell application "TextEdit"
  activate
  set the name of window 4 to "test"
end tell
```

As you can see from these snippets, it is very important to be able to identify the objects you want to manage, since you cannot just point and click. This will be described later in this chapter in the section "AppleScript Language Components."

Handlers and Subroutines

You can also create a block that is called a *handler* or a *subroutine*. That block consists of statements that are executed whether the handler or subroutine is called. Here is a subroutine:

```
on setuppages()
  set the title to "Heading for Report"
  set the footer to "Page Footer"
end setuppages
```

It is executed if you execute the following AppleScript command:

```
setuppages()
```

Handlers are subroutines with predefined names. If the name of the handler is one of several predefined AppleScript words (such as `run`, `idle`, or `error`), it is automatically invoked when certain conditions occur. Handlers are described later in this chapter.

In programming terminology, handlers and subroutines are declarations. They specify actions that should be taken if a certain condition occurs or if that section of code is invoked. The code does not automatically execute by itself.

Using Script Editor

As noted previously, Script Editor is part of the Mac OS—both Mac OS 9 and earlier, and Mac OS X. You can use it to write scripts, as well as to record them. You can run scripts from Script Editor, but it is not necessary to do so. Scripts can be run simply by clicking them if they have been saved in a runtime format.

In order to write scripts from scratch, you need a basic understanding of AppleScript's syntax. That is provided in the remaining sections of this chapter. However, to write and edit scripts, you can frequently use Script Editor and your own instincts, without having a full understanding of the language.

Use the Record button in Script Editor to record a script that does what you want, or something close to it. It's very easy to modify the script that has been generated. You can change the names of files or folders, rearrange the sequence of commands, and so forth. If the application for which you want to write a script is not recordable, you can even record a similar operation in an application that is recordable. All AppleScript commands are comparable in format. You can get the basic outline of your script from another application's record feature and then customize it for another application.

Using the Script Editor Window

When you launch Script Editor or when you choose New Script from the File menu, the window shown in Figure 20-1 opens. You can and should type a description of your script in the box at the top of the window. At a minimum, your name and the date, as well as the purpose of the script, should be there.

If you incorporate code from another script, you should indicate this, not just for copyright reasons, but also so that if errors are found in either script, the other can be corrected. In the center of the window are four buttons; they control Script Editor's major functions.

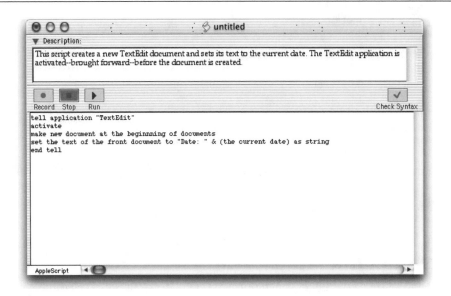

FIGURE 20-1   Script Editor window showing code, buttons, and annotated description

Record

Record is used to record scripts. If you are running a recordable application, you can click this button, and your actions will be recorded in this window as AppleScript commands. As you switch from one application to another, the commands to activate each application will be generated.

Not all actions in recordable applications are recorded. Typically, actions that involve changes to documents are recordable; actions such as resizing windows frequently are not recorded. Also, you should be aware that in some applications, actions that are not recorded are scriptable. So, if you are recording your actions and some do not appear in the Script Editor window, those are the reasons. You can check in the dictionary to see whether the unrecorded actions can be entered manually. Fortunately, in most cases these are rare occurrences.

Stop

The Stop button terminates recording.

Run

When you have a script in the Script Editor window, clicking the Run button will run the script—that is, perform its actions. (You can also run a script by saving it and then double-clicking the script icon in a Finder window.)

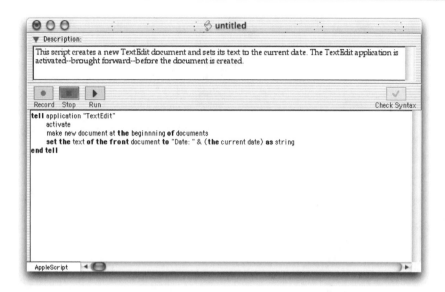

FIGURE 20-2 AppleScript formatted by syntax checking

Check Syntax

Playing a script involves first checking its syntax to make certain that the AppleScript commands you have entered are valid. This is done automatically when you click the Play button. You can also click the Check Syntax button to check the syntax of a script without playing it.

Syntax checking not only checks the syntax of a script, it also reformats it in a distinctive style to make the script easier to read. Figure 20-2 shows a script that has been formatted by checking its syntax (either with the Check Syntax or Run button).

You can set the formatting for AppleScripts. Use the AppleScript Formatting command from the Edit menu of Script Editor to open the window shown in Figure 20-3.

Comments, Formatting, and Multiple Line Issues

When AppleScript is formatted, you will notice not only that keywords are highlighted, but also that statements are indented to make it easier to read the script. In general, a statement is a single line in the Script Editor window. Sometimes, a statement needs to span more than one line; if so, you can continue it on the next line with a ¬ character—OPTION-L on the keyboard.

As you write a script, make certain to include comments to others and to yourself. It's very easy to forget exactly what you were trying to do or why you wrote something one way rather than another. A double hyphen (--) causes text on the remainder of a line to be ignored. You can

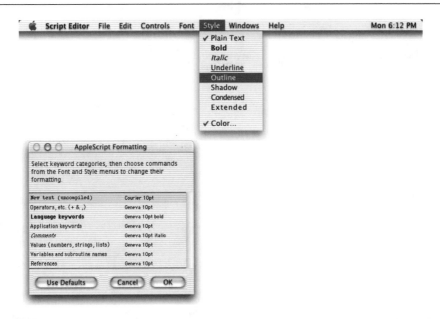

AppleScript Formatting window assigning styles to keyword categories

also use the double characters (* and *) to bracket comments that extend over several lines, as in the following:

```
(* this comment extends over
several lines
*)
```

Using Dictionaries

Dictionaries for scriptable applications provide you with the syntax to use in scripting them. This section shows you how to open dictionaries, and it describes the major items you will see in them: suites, optional parameters, and classes.

Opening a Dictionary

You can easily create scripts by recording your actions; but that only works for scriptable applications, and it does not release the full power of AppleScript. To do that, you need to know the basics of AppleScript, as well as each scriptable application's AppleScript syntax. You do that by opening a dictionary. Choose Open Dictionary from the File menu and select the application you want to view, as shown in Figure 20-4.

The dictionary contains both the commands and the object descriptors available in that application. Figure 20-5 shows part of the dictionary for FileMaker Pro.

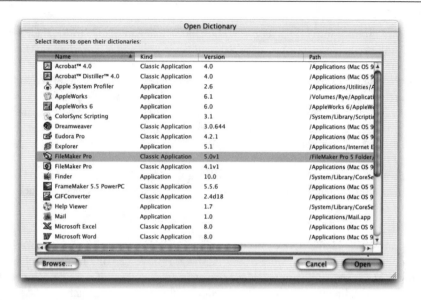

FIGURE 20-4   Opening AppleScript dictionaries

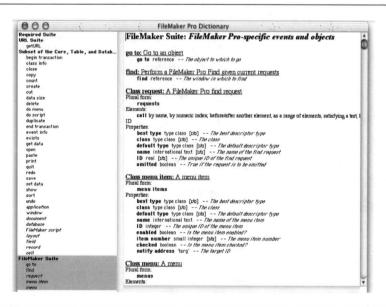

FIGURE 20-5   FileMaker Pro dictionary

Suites

Commands are grouped into suites. You can click individual commands to see their syntax, or you can click the suite name to show all of its commands. In Figure 20-5, the FileMaker Pro suite is selected, and all of its commands and classes are shown at the right.

Suites are listed in order of increasing specificity for the application. In this case, the required suite is listed first (it includes open and quit application commands, open and print document commands, and a variety of classes). The URL suite with its single command, getURL, is implemented in virtually every scriptable application that accesses the Internet. In this case, a subset of several other suites (Core, Table, and Database) is shown next. Finally, the FileMaker suite is shown.

Suites defined by Apple, such as Core, Required, Table, and Database, can be used for any application that supports their functionality. You do not have to learn new syntax for each application.

Commands

Commands are shown on the right of the dictionary window in boldface type. Figure 20-6 shows the commands in the third suite from FileMaker Pro. Some commands—such as begin transaction (a two-word command), copy, and cut—consist of a single command. You type them alone on a line in a Script Editor window. Other commands, such as close, require a parameter. The parameter is shown in italics. Finally, some commands, such as create, have optional parameters. These optional parameters are enclosed in square brackets.

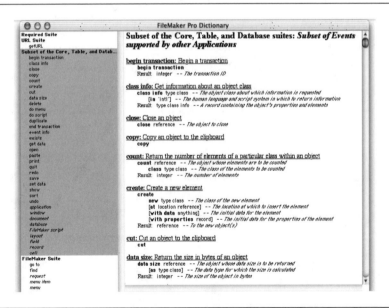

FIGURE 20-6   FileMaker subset of Core, Table, and Database suites

Classes

In the dictionary entries shown in this chapter, you will notice that some of the entries are class definitions, definitions of object types. These are the nouns to the verbs of commands; they are how you describe references that so many commands use. In the first script shown in this chapter, you can see a reference at work. The `close` command is used with a reference in this line of code:

```
close front window
```

Integrating AppleScript with Other Scripting Systems

AppleScript can interface with other scripting systems. For example, Figure 20-7 shows FileMaker's scripting capability. It is used in this case to define a script called Remember. When the script is run, the message box shown in Figure 20-8 is displayed. Figure 20-9 shows an AppleScript script that runs the Remember script in FileMaker.

Most of the Microsoft Office products use Visual Basic for their scripting language. Word and Excel support a `do Visual Basic` AppleScript command that you can use to script those applications (and others) from AppleScript.

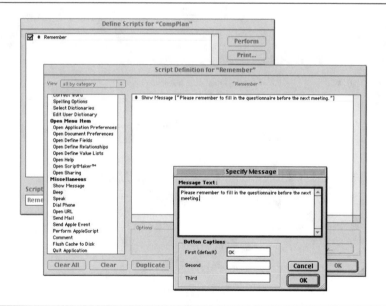

FIGURE 20-7   Creating the Remember script in FileMaker

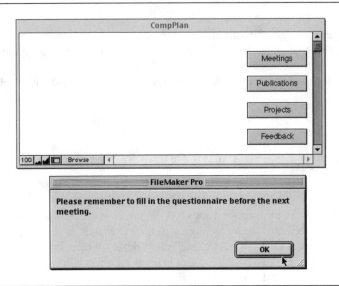

FIGURE 20-8 Remember script running

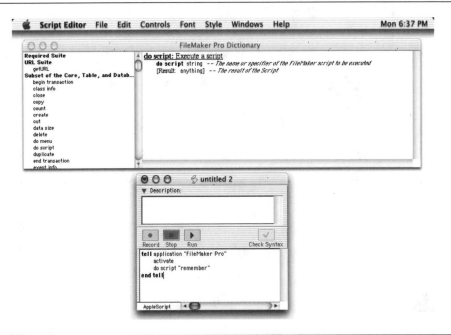

FIGURE 20-9 Running a FileMaker script with AppleScript

AppleScript Language Components

AppleScript's language components are similar to those in other programming languages. They consist of the following:

- **Commands**   The verbs of AppleScript.
- **Objects**   Items that can respond to commands.
- **Values**   Numeric or alphabetic values that can be stored in.
- **Variables**   Named items that contain values. (For example, Width may have the value 2.9 meters.)
- **Operators**   The standard arithmetic operators (and a few more) that combine values and variables to produce results.
- **Expressions**   Combinations of values, variables, and operators that yield a value as a result.
- **Control statements**   Programming statements that let you execute commands repeatedly or only under certain circumstances.

AppleScript is the scripting language that lets you use Apple events, the underlying implementation of the functionality. This section deals with the components of the AppleScript language. The following section deals with the underlying Apple Events.

Commands

Commands are the verbs of AppleScript. There are four types of commands, each command with the same basic structure. Commands fall into four categories: application, AppleScript, scripting additions, and user-defined commands.

Application Commands

These are commands that are sent to applications. They are the commands you usually think of when you are scripting. Examples of these commands are those shown in the dictionaries earlier in this chapter: `open`, `close`, `delete`, `connect`, and so forth.

AppleScript Commands

A small set of commands are processed by AppleScript itself rather than by an application. These commands help in processing scripts:

- `copy`   This command copies a value from one AppleScript variable to another. It is not the same as the application `copy` command, which copies a file or other application element.
- `count`   This command counts classes within an element.

- ■ **display**   This command displays a dialog and lets you find out what button (such as OK or Cancel) was used to dismiss it. (See "Variables," later in this chapter, for an example.)

- ■ **error**   This command lets you access the error result of the last executed AppleScript command.

- ■ **get**   This command lets you get an expression within a script. An application `get` command can be used to get a reference to an application object.

- ■ **run**   This command runs a script.

- ■ **set**   This command sets an AppleScript variable's value.

Scripting Additions

Scripting additions are placed in files that are located in the Scripting Additions folder in the Library for both the system as a whole and for each user. (In other words, individual users can add scripting additions that only they can use.) They frequently are installed automatically for you when some applications are installed.

Scripting additions provide extensions to the AppleScript syntax. They provide new commands or new coercions between types. They are useful when such commands or coercions need to be added to the language in order to be used by a variety of scriptable applications. Apple itself provides a number of scripting additions. They frequently are linked to new technologies. (For example, scripting additions for ColorSync are provided by Apple in Mac OS X.)

Over time, some scripting additions move into the AppleScript language itself, making the additions unnecessary. This structure allows for the implementation of new technologies that involve scripting without requiring updates to AppleScript itself.

User-Defined Commands

You can also define your own commands in your own scripts. They were described previously in the section "Handlers and Subroutines."

Objects

Objects receive Apple events. They are the nouns to the AppleScript's verbs (commands). In addition to a general definition of the class and the format for its plural form, you will often find two sets of information about a class in a dictionary: how to identify its objects and what its properties are.

Identification of Class Objects

Elements of a class object can be contained within the class. Items, containers, sharable containers, folders, and files (and more) can be contained within a container. You can identify these contained objects by name and numeric index; you can also identify application files by ID.

This is a very precise (if somewhat complicated) way of saying that you can identify files and folders by their names, provided that you also give the name of·their container, as in the following:

```
folder "Applications" of disk "Rye"
```

Since the Finder also stores numeric indices for elements in containers, you can also write

```
folder 2 of disk 1
```

or

```
folder 2 of disk "Rye"
```

Numeric indices are less useful than names for most purposes; however, AppleScript can manipulate numeric indices directly, and thus you can write

```
the last folder of disk 1
```

and

```
the first file of the last folder of disk "Rye"
```

Properties of Classes

Properties of classes are listed in the dictionary, and you can use them in AppleScript scripts. Properties for the window class are shown in Figure 20-10.

This script, for example, gets the name of the frontmost window on the Desktop.

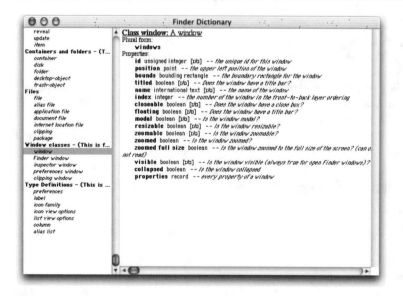

FIGURE 20-10   Window class properties

```
tell application "Finder"  get the name of the front window
end tell
```

Some properties are marked read only [r/o]; others can be read and written [r/w]. The capacity of a disk, for example, cannot be changed with a script: it is the size of the hardware device. Thus, you cannot write the following:

```
set the capacity of disk "Rye" to 40000000
```

Read/write [r/w] access is the default; if no access is listed, then it is r/w.

The position and bounds of windows are writable. You can move a window with the following script:

```
tell application "Finder"
  set the position of window "Applications" to {292, 117}
end tell
```

In many cases, the first property is <Inheritance>. That is a special property that indicates that the object in question also contains all of the properties of the object named in the inheritance statement. Item is the most basic AppleScript object. All objects inherit from it. In addition, objects such as application files inherit from files, and so forth. For example, here is the <Inheritance> property for application files in the Finder suite:

<Inheritance> file [r/o] *-- inherits some of its properties from the file class*

Values

Values are data. They can be the result of expressions, such as 2+2, or they can be the values of properties. Values not only have a data value, they also have a type.

You may have noticed in the previous section that each property has a type, such as point and bounding rectangle for position and bounds in the previous example. A point consists of x and y coordinates enclosed in curly brackets, such as {292, 117}. A bounding rectangle consists of the four corners of a rectangle also enclosed in brackets.

Where values of one type can be transformed into values of another type automatically, rules are built into AppleScript to do so. This is called *coercion*.

Types are defined in Apple event suites, The Required suite defines four of the most basic types for Apple events. AppleScript itself recognizes the following types:

- ■ **boolean**   True or false; sometimes represented with 1 or 0.

- ■ **class**   The identifier of a class. You can use a class type to coerce a value to another type, as in

```
get true as boolean -- This returns true, a Boolean value
get true as string -- This returns "true", a string value (note the ")
```

- **constant**   Reserved words such as yes, no, or ask.

- **data**   Binary data.

- **date**   Date and/or time information.

- **integer**   A whole number.

- **list**   A collection of other values; lists can be of numbers, dates, or references to objects.

- **number**   Either an Integer or a Real.

- **real**   A number with a fractional part, such as 2.5. The fractional part could be 0. 2 can be a Real or an Integer—you cannot tell from looking at it.

- **record**   A collection of properties.

- **reference**   A reference to an object. Although you can use a reference as if it were the object, it is only a reference, somewhat like a file alias.

- **string or text**   A series of characters.

- **styled text**   A string or text with styling features (font, size, and so on.)

Since AppleScript handles coercion for you automatically, you can often ignore the type of the values you are dealing with. You need to know about values so that you can interpret error messages you may encounter, often through typographical errors.

Variables

You deal with objects and their properties for much of your scripting work. For example, in the following code:

```
tell application "Finder"
  set the position of window "Mac OS X" to {192, 117}
end tell
```

position is a property of the window Mac OS X, and {192, 117} is a value.

You can also create a variable to store a value. For example,

```
tell application "Finder"
  set myposition to {192, 117}
  set the position of window "Mac OS X" to myposition
end tell
```

has the same effect as the first script, but it uses a variable, myposition, to store the value.

You use the set command to set the value of a variable. You can write

```
set answer to the text returned of the result
```

AppleScript Language Components

In some programming languages, the = symbol is used to set values. You cannot write *answer = the text returned of the result* in AppleScript. In AppleScript, = is a comparison not a replacement operator.

Variables are created when you use them for the first time. You do not predeclare them. Each variable has a type, and that type is determined by the type of the data to which you set the variable when you first use it. Variables can contain letters and numbers, but they must start with a letter. It is good practice to make them meaningful.

Start variables with my (as in myposition) if they could possibly be mistaken for properties or for AppleScript constructs. Variables are useful in reusing your scripts. One way to use variables is to ask for input from the user and place values into variables as the script runs. Here is the code to post a dialog with two buttons—Choice 1 and Choice 2. You can set a variable—such as myvariable—to the value of the button that is clicked.

```
display dialog "Ask the question" buttons {"Choice 1", "Choice 2"}
default button "Choice 2"
set myvariable to the button returned of the result
```

Experiment with these two lines of code in Script Editor to see how you can create dialogs and use the results.

Operators

Operators act on values of specific types, for example, the addition operator + acts on two numbers. Many of the operators in AppleScript are familiar to you; others have special manipulative functions that are useful in writing scripts. Table 20-1 lists the AppleScript operators and the types of the variables on which they operate.

Most operators act on two values, one before and one after the operator. Some are *unary*—they act on only one value. Unary operators precede their values, as is the case with not.

First Value	Operator	Second Value
number	*	number
number	+	number
date	+	number
number	−	number
date	−	number
number	−	date
number	÷	number
number	/	number
number	^	number

TABLE 20-1   AppleScript Operators and Their Variables

First Value	Operator	Second Value
number	div	number
number	mod	number
Boolean	and	Boolean
	not	Boolean
Boolean	Boolean	
list	starts with begins with	list
string	starts with begins with	string
list	ends with	list
string	ends with	string
list	does not contain doesn't contain	list
record	does not contain doesn't contain	record
string	does not contain doesn't contain	string
list	is in is contained by	list
record	is in is contained by	record
string	is in is contained by	string
list	is not in is not contained by isn't contained by	list
record	is not in is not contained by isn't contained by	record
string	is not in is not contained by isn't contained by	string
expression	= equal equals equal to is is equal to	expression

TABLE 20-1   AppleScript Operators and Their Variables *(continued)*

First Value	Operator	Second Value
expression	? does not equal doesn't equal is not is not equal to isn't isn't equal to	expression
date	< comes before is less than is not greater than or equal to isn't greater than or equal to less than	date
integer	< comes before is less than is not greater than or equal to isn't greater than or equal to less than	integer
real	< comes before is less than is not greater than or equal to isn't greater than or equal to less than	real
string	< comes before is less than is not greater than or equal to isn't greater than or equal to less than	string
date	> comes after greater than is greater than is not less than or equal to isn't less than or equal	date
integer	> comes after greater than is greater than is not less than or equal to isn't less than or equal	integer

TABLE 20-1   AppleScript Operators and Their Variables *(continued)*

First Value	Operator	Second Value
real	> comes after greater than is greater than is not less than or equal to isn't less than or equal	real
string	> comes after greater than is greater than is not less than or equal to isn't less than or equal	string
date	= <= does not come after doesn't come after is less than or equal to is not greater than isn't greater than less than or equal to	date
integer	= <= does not come after doesn't come after is less than or equal to is not greater than isn't greater than less than or equal to	integer
real	= <= does not come after doesn't come after is less than or equal to is not greater than isn't greater than less than or equal to	real
string	= <= does not come after doesn't come after is less than or equal to is not greater than isn't greater than less than or equal to	string

TABLE 20-1   AppleScript Operators and Their Variables *(continued)*

AppleScript Language Components

First Value	Operator	Second Value
date	= >= does not come before doesn't come before greater than or equal to is greater than or equal is not less than isn't less than	date
integer	= >= does not come before doesn't come before greater than or equal to is greater than or equal is not less than isn't less than	integer
real	= >= does not come before doesn't come before greater than or equal to is greater than or equal is not less than isn't less than	real
string	= >= does not come before doesn't come before greater than or equal to is greater than or equal is not less than isn't less than	string
expression	& [concatenation operator]	expression
expression	as	Class name
	a reference to	reference

TABLE 20-1 AppleScript Operators and Their Variables *(continued)*

Expressions

Expressions are combinations of operators, values, and variables that produce a value in AppleScript. Here are several expressions:

```
the name of the first file of disk "Rye"
14
15÷3
```

Control Statements

Control statements let you manage how a script is executed. You can repeat sections of it, execute sections conditionally, and even terminate the script before all of the instructions have been executed. Control statements are almost always necessary in complex scripts. They always have to be written by hand—they cannot be recorded.

Use Script Editor to open the samples in the AppleScript folder inside Applications. Look at how these commands are used. It is often easier to see an example than to try to construct syntax from scratch.

Except for `exit`, control statements apply to one or more AppleScript commands. They start with the keyword listed here and terminate with `end` followed by the keyword. The AppleScript commands to which they apply fall in between. Here are some examples:

```
tell application "Finder"
  activate
  try
  set the position of window "Mac OS X" to {192, 117}
  on error
    display dialog "Could not reposition the window. Is it open?"
  end try
end tell
```

A try block (between `try` and `end try`) is enclosed within a tell block (between `tell` and `end tell`). If the position of the window cannot be set as specified, the code in the `on error` block will execute.

Try blocks are very powerful and important programming structures in many languages. Instead of checking to see whether an error has occurred, simply specify what should happen if an error is encountered and let AppleScript (or another programming language) do the testing.

```
if total > 15 then
set limit to 15
  if mean < 4 then
    set adjustedmean to 4
  end if
end if
```

Checking the syntax not only reformats the style of the text in your scripts, it also aligns ends. One frequent cause of programming errors is mistaking which `end if` corresponds to which `if`. If you have misaligned them in typing, Check Syntax will realign them, and you may notice a problem.

These are the AppleScript control statements:

- ■ **tell**   Used to enclose a set of AppleScript commands to be sent to an individual application such as the Finder, Microsoft Word, Quark Xpress, and so on.

- **if**   Used to create a test. If it succeeds, the statement(s) in the block that follows is executed. You can use a two-part `if` statement—it has an `else` in the middle. Either one section or the other is executed.

- **repeat**   The statements between `repeat` and `end repeat` are executed repeatedly.

- **exit**   Terminates a `repeat` loop. It is a single statement; there is no corresponding end.

- **try**   A statement or series of statements is executed. If an error occurs, one or more statements is executed. This is a very simple yet sophisticated way of implementing error checking.

- **considering/ignoring**   Tests within a considering or ignoring block are executed considering or ignoring the characteristics identified in these statements. For example, you use these to determine whether AppleScript cares about case (capitalization) in string comparisons.

- **with timeout**   Waits for a given amount of time for statements to execute, and then continues. Useful when sending a message with a `tell` command to an application on a network. If no response is received, you can go on your way.

- **with transaction**   Used to interact with transaction-oriented systems such as databases.

The `if` and `repeat` control statements have variants. They are shown in the following section.

if Variants

An `if` statement can have an `else` statement. Without an `else` statement, the statements following the `if` are only executed if the test is true; with an `else`, either of two sets of statements is executed. Here is an `if` statement without an `else`:

```
if username = "Tina" then
  set userpriority to 5
end if
```

Here is one with an `else`:

```
if username = "Tina" then
  set userpriority to 5
else
  set userpriority to 0
end if
```

Here is a perfectly valid if/else block that may confuse you the first time you see it:

```
if username = "Tina" then
else
  set userpriority to 0
end if
```

Nothing executes if the statement is true. The reason for constructing an `if` statement of this sort is that sometimes it is easier to construct the logic in a positive way (that is, to execute a test that fails) rather than to construct a more complicated `if` statement.

Repeat Statements

Repeat statements can be formulated in several ways. You can repeat a statement endlessly as in the following example:

```
repeat
  set x to 7
end repeat
```

This normally is not a good idea (it's called an infinite loop). However, when you add the `exit` statement, it can be meaningful, as in the following sample:

```
repeat
  display dialog "Continue processing?" buttons {"Stop", "OK"} default button "OK"
  if the button of the result is "Stop" then exit repeat
end repeat
```

The `repeat` loop will only terminate if the user clicks the Stop button. Two `repeat` loops use Booleans to terminate:

```
repeat while x < 100
  set x to x + y
end repeat
```

and

```
repeat until x > 100
  set x to x + y
end repeat
```

You can specify a loop to repeat a given number of times:

```
repeat 3 times
  set x to x + y
end repeat
```

You can also use repeat loops as for loops (constructs from other programming languages). For example, in this loop, the loop is executed five times. More important, the variable *i* has values of 2, 4, 6, 8, and 10 that can be accessed within the loop:

```
repeat with i from 2 to 10 by 2
  set x to x + i
end repeat
```

A variant lets you specify the values of the variable:

```
repeat with i in {1, 5, 12, 20}
  set x to x + i
end repeat
```

The AppleScript control statements are similar to those in other scripting and programming languages.

Apple Events

Each Apple event has its own syntax. Apple events are defined by Apple for events affecting the operating system and standard actions that many programs take. Through the use of suites (described later in this section), Apple events can be defined for specific applications. This section is for programmers and for scriptwriters who want to understand a little more about how AppleScript works.

Direct Objects

The object on which the command should act is called the *direct object*. A direct object can be a list of objects (that is, you can print a list of documents with one command). Each command has no more than one direct object.

The syntax of each Apple event defines what the direct object is. Some commands require files as direct objects (examples of these commands are those that print documents). Other commands require strings of text as direct objects (these commands often are used in word processing applications). This structure of a command acting on a direct object is directly parallel to natural language: grammarians also speak of direct objects.

Parameters

One or more parameters can be specified in the Apple event. Parameters are like direct objects in that they have specific meanings and types. They may specify a location at which a file is to be saved (the file to be saved is the direct object—it is what is acted on—and the location is an additional parameter). Some commands have no parameters; other commands have a variety of parameters.

Class and Event IDs

Apple events are identified by two four-character codes. You rarely if ever see these codes when you are creating scripts; programmers, however, use them all the time. For example, you can create a new folder on the desktop with the following AppleScript code:

```
make new folder at desktop
```

The AppleScript command—`make`—is formally identified with the following identifiers:

1. The command itself is identified with the four-character string *crel*. Apple event programming headers identify this as *kAECreateElement*, a constant that programmers can use. It is more meaningful than *crel*. However, you, as an AppleScript author, can use the even more meaningful *make*.

2. In order to ensure that Apple events are unique, they are grouped into suites. The combination of a four-character suite code and a four-character event code is guaranteed to be unique. Apple has defined some suites. Others are defined by application program developers. Thus, you will find Core and Text suites from Apple, custom suites for Quark Xpress (page layout/desktop publishing software), and for email applications such as Eudora. In the case of the `make` AppleScript command, the suite is *core*; the programmer's code for it is *kAECoreSuite*. You can refer to it as the Core suite.

Behind the scenes, Apple events are identified by these pairs of four-character codes. What you see in AppleScript scripts is a dialect of AppleScript. The English word *make* is used as the English dialect of the Apple event Create (kAECreateElement). In other dialects, other words invoke the kAECreateElement Apple event.

Suites

Suites are defined as collections of Apple event syntax that are relevant to a specific application program or a specific type of processing (text, for example). Wherever possible, developers should reuse existing suites so that users are presented with consistent syntax. Custom suites should contain only that syntax that is truly unique to an application.

Suites are self-contained; that is, they do not inherit from one another or rely on one another. As a result, some definitions appear in several suites. A suite can contain any of the following:

- Apple events
- Object classes
- Descriptor types
- Primitive object classes
- Key forms
- Comparison operators
- Constants

Apple events and object classes have been described previously in this chapter. The other elements of suites provide more advanced programming tools. For further details, consult the documentation of AppleScript on Apple's Web site.

Reply Parameters

Each Apple event specifies parameters that are returned to it. In the actual implementation of Apple event support, each Apple event that an application receives causes the application to generate one in return. This data can be sent to and from an application for processing.

Result Codes

In addition to the reply parameters, each Apple event should generate a result code. Result codes can indicate whether an error was encountered; they also sometimes provide a summary of the event's actions: *X* number of files deleted, *Y* occurrences replaced, and so forth.

Suites

There are seven Apple-defined suites of Apple events:

- **Required**   Any application that supports Apple events must implement these.

- **Core**   These Apple events are used by almost all applications. They should be supported wherever possible. It is absolutely wrong to reimplement any core suite functionality using other syntax. Scripters should be able to rely on the syntax being consistent.

- **Text**   These events are used to manipulate text. Word processing applications support them. Frequently, word processing and desktop publishing software implement customized advanced text suites in addition to (not instead of) the text suite.

- **QuickDraw Graphics**   These are the basic drawing events. They are implemented by drawing programs and other programs that perform graphical operations.

- **QuickDraw Graphics Supplemental**   These are more advanced graphics events.

- **Table**   Useful for spreadsheets and databases, these events help users organize data in a two-dimensional way.

- **Finder**   This suite is implemented in the Finder and not in application programs.

The events in the Required and Core suites are listed next.

Required Suite

There are four events in the required suite. They should be implemented in all event-aware applications unless they are illogical (for example, if an application program does not support printing, it cannot support the Print Documents event).

- Open Application
- Open Documents
- Print Documents
- Quit Application

Core Suite

The Core suite is composed of events that are common to many applications. Note that these are the event names; individual applications may have different names for these functions. (For example, Clone may be Duplicate for many users.)

- Clone
- Close
- Count Elements
- Create Element
- Delete
- Do Objects Exist
- Get Class Info
- Get Data
- Get Data Size
- Get Event Info
- Move
- Open
- Print
- Quit Application
- Save
- Set Data

Using Dialogs

You can use dialogs to communicate with users from your scripts. You may want to provide information to them; you may also need input from them. Here is a brief guide to using dialogs from a script.

Presenting Information to the User

If you want to present information to the user in a dialog, you can use the following code:

```
display dialog "Message to user"
```

Insert whatever text you want in the quoted string. Of course, you may not know in advance what message is to be displayed; you can use a variable, as in the following code:

```
set x to "Message to user"
display dialog x
```

A more complicated but useful version of this would be the following:

```
if resultsareOK then
  --various processing steps
  set msg to "Successful completion"
else
  --other processing steps
  set msg to "Problems."
end if
display dialog msg
```

Apple Events

In each of these cases, the message will be displayed in a dialog with OK and Cancel buttons. Clicking either one will dismiss the dialog.

Getting Information from the User with Buttons

Sometimes you want to ask a question and know whether the OK or Cancel button has been clicked. You do that by testing the result of the dialog, as in the following code:

```
display dialog "Do you want to continue?"
if the button returned of the result = "OK" then
  --do your processing
end if
```

You can further customize the dialog by specifying names for buttons, as in the following:

```
display dialog "Run reports for which time period?"
  buttons {"Day", "Week", "Month"}
```

Instead of OK and Cancel buttons, you will have buttons labeled Day, Week, and Month. Avoid using more than three buttons in a dialog. It is confusing to users.

You can further customize the dialog by specifying which button is the default button (the button that is clicked when the user presses the RETURN key).

```
display dialog "Run reports for which time period?" buttons {"Day",
Week", "Month"} default button "Month"
```

To find out which button was clicked, you use the same syntax you did previously:

```
if the button returned of the result = "Month" then
```

Getting Information from the User on the Keyboard

Sometimes in addition to or instead of knowing which button was clicked, you want the user to be able to enter data. You create a dialog with a space for data entry using the following syntax:

```
display dialog "Enter your name" default answer ""
display dialog "Enter your department" default answer "Personnel"
```

If you specify a default answer, that text will be entered into the dialog. In the first case, the text field would be blank; however you need to specify a default answer (even if blank) to get the text field displayed.

You can access the value of the text field with the following code:

```
the text returned of the result
```

You can access both the text returned and the button returned to test whether a user has clicked OK (or the equivalent) and if so, to look at the data entered.

Summary

AppleScript lets you automate, integrate, and customize your work and applications. It is a powerful scripting language that relies on natural language-like syntax, rather than keystrokes and macros.

This chapter has provided an overview of AppleScript Script Editor, the tool you use to create and edit scripts, and Apple events, the programmatic underpinning of it all. You can also automate and integrate your work using shell commands, instructions processed at the very basic level of the operating system. The next chapter shows you how.

Summary

Chapter 21

Using the Command Line

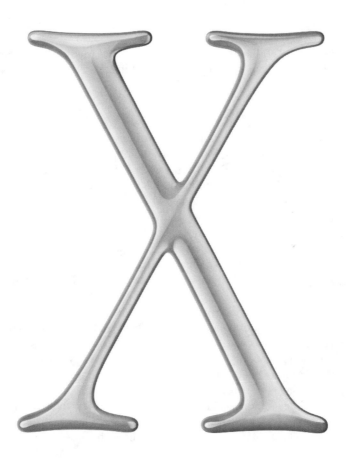

How times have changed! In two decades, graphical user interfaces have become such an integral part of people's lives that a command-line interface is a novelty. In fact, there are a number of times in which you might want to use a command-line interface. The sections of this chapter are

- **Command-Line Concepts**   Everything you know about a graphical user interface is irrelevant when it comes to a command line.

- **When to Use a Command-Line Interface**   One of the powerful features of Mac OS X is its Unix-like underpinning in Darwin; that core is accessible through the command line.

- **Using a Command-Line Interface**   This is how to use the interface in which the mouse is irrelevant.

- **Using the Terminal Application**   Shipped with Mac OS X, Terminal provides you with access to several command-line interfaces.

- **Useful commands**   A variety of Unix and other useful commands are described here.

The command line and Terminal application are features of Mac OS X; they are made possible by its Unix-like Darwin core. They did not exist in Mac OS 9 and earlier.

Command-Line Concepts

In the early 1950s, commands were typed into computers using teletype machines. They also were sometimes fed into computers using paper tape (automating the teletype); in addition, they could be entered using punched cards. Commands on the command line are the direct descendants of these original computer commands. They are entered via the keyboard—no mouse is used—and they are sent to the computer when you press the RETURN key.

Two decades ago, it was the graphical user interface that needed explaining to people. Today, people take for granted the ability to use a mouse to select objects on the screen and then to select commands to act on those objects (for example, to change their color). Also part of the user experience is the ability to manipulate objects directly, to drag items from one place to another, even from one application's window to another. Almost everything is directly manipulatable and interactive.

Less noticed (but nonetheless critical to contemporary software design) is the host of commands and palettes that are present as you work. These commands and palettes come and go, their contents changing as you select text, video clips, and other types of objects. Software designers try to present only the commands and tools that you can use on the currently selected objects. The goal is to avoid letting you try to do something that will fail. In other words, eschew error messages and prevent the possibility of error.

These concepts were revolutionary. The standard command-line interface that had been part and parcel of computers since the early 1950s was precisely the opposite. Command-line commands, text commands typed into a terminal, have these characteristics:

■ They are *textual*. That means no mouse clicks to select objects. Objects to be selected must be defined in text. (Most objects that are selected turn out to be text themselves. There are few commands that manipulate video clips via text.)

■ They provide *indirect manipulation*. Direct manipulation is not part of the command-line experience. No mouse is involved, so you must specify, using text, what is to be done to the (textually specified) objects.

■ Most commands on the command line are *not interactive*. You specify what you want to do and what you want to do it to. Then you sit back (or go home). This is called *batch mode* processing, to distinguish it from *real-time* or *online* processing.

■ You're *on your own*. The command line is a tabula rasa: you can type any command you want on it. If the command is illogical, you can type it. If it is misspelled, that, too, is your option. Rather than selecting from correctly spelled and relevant commands, you type in what you want. If it fails, it fails.

When to Use a Command-Line Interface

There are four primary cases in which you might use a command-line interface:

■ There are a very few commands and functions that cannot be found in the Mac OS X interface or that are not implemented in application programs. If you must issue these commands, you need to use the command line. There are few of these. For an individual user, as opposed to a network administrator, there are incredibly few, none for most people.

■ If you are familiar with a command-line interface (as, for example, in a Unix environment) you may be more comfortable continuing with those commands, rather than learning the Mac OS X interface. However, the graphical user interface is easier to use. You will need to learn it eventually. (You can refer to the frequently used commands later in this chapter for indications of Mac OS X commands that provide the same functionality.)

■ If you have a set of commands developed in a Unix environment, it may be easier for you to execute those commands (possibly in the form of a prepared script), rather than using the Mac OS X interface. If you are integrating legacy applications (possibly involving mainframe computers), you may need to manipulate input and output in ways that more modern applications do not.

■ In addition, there occasionally are cases in which commands on a command line can save you from switching back and forth between keyboard and mouse or some other repetitive and physically complicated operation that may involve several applications. (AppleScript also is very useful in these cases.)

Then there is the most common case: you do not have the access privileges to do what you want to do. Of course, there is usually a reason for this, but there are a few (extremely few!) cases in which you need access to files that you normally cannot and should not touch.

In general, these files are owned by the system and should not be removed. They include the directories for users, as well as a host of software files and support files. When you delete a user, for example, the directory remains on disk. This is no problem in most cases on an individual computer. (For a network file-sharing computer, Mac OS X provides the necessary utilities.)

One case in which you might want to remove a user's directory is if someone (you?) has created a user with a name that is inappropriate. It may be inappropriate because it reflects a bad joke. It may be inappropriate because it is misspelled and you do not want to have to look at it forever and ever. (You may also not want your nearest and dearest to know that you could not remember how to spell their names.)

Another case in which you legitimately might want to remove a file or directory to which you do not have access is in the case of software that was installed by accident. Normally, the Installer application can remove outdated software as part of its normal operations. Occasionally, sometimes in testing software, accidents happen.

Here is an example of how to use the command line to remove a file to which you normally do not have access.

Figure 21-1 shows the problem. In the Finder window at the left, several printer drivers are shown. One is highlighted, and the Info window at the right shows that it is owned by system, a user ID to which you do not have access.

FIGURE 21-1   You cannot remove files owned by system using the Aqua interface.

You can drag it to the Trash, but when you try to empty the Trash, you will get an error message like the one shown here:

You can type a command in the Terminal application to remove the file. First, you type the basic command, as shown in Figure 21-2. Instead of typing the filename (including its directories), you can drag the file to the command line in Terminal. The correct filename will be inserted, as shown in Figure 21-3.

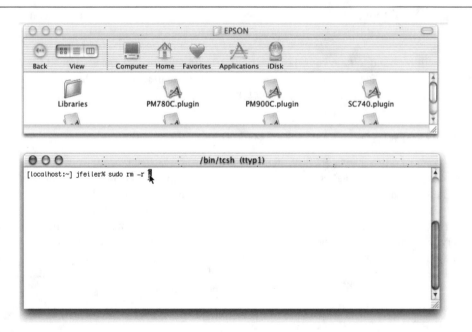

FIGURE 21-2 You can type commands in the Terminal application.

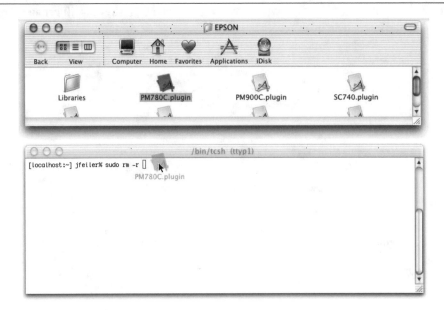

FIGURE 21-3   Terminal responds to drag-and-drop by interpreting filenames of icons.

You will be asked to type your password; when you have done so, the command is executed. When prompted for the password, your typing is not shown on the screen, as shown in Figure 21-4. If the password is wrong, the command is not executed.

Using a Command-Line Interface

Using a command-line interface requires you to understand somewhat how the system's shell operates; you also need to understand the basics of entering commands. Those topics are explored in this section; they apply to all Unix and Unix-like systems. The section that follows this one, "Using the Terminal Application," shows you how to use Mac OS X to enter commands.

Large books have been written on using Unix shell command-line interfaces. Of necessity, this is a very brief overview. If you are brushing up a long-ago knowledge of command-line interfaces or if you want a general familiarization, it will help you. If you need an in-depth, from-scratch tutorial, you will need to augment it. Fortunately, a great deal of command-line interface information is available on the Internet. You may want to start with http://www.FreeBSD.org.

Shells and Terminology

A shell is a command-line interpreter. It accepts commands that you type in and converts them to instructions to the operating system, in the case of Mac OS X, instructions to Darwin. Whether

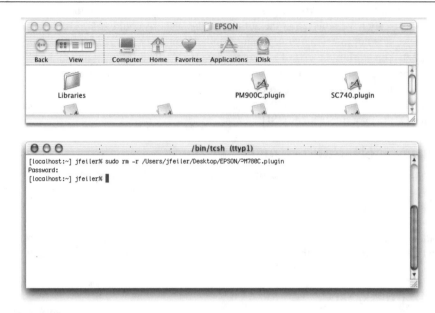

FIGURE 21-4   Critical commands require a password to be executed.

formally or not, a shell defines a language that you can use to communicate with the underlying operating system.

The distinction between a formal programming language and an ad hoc programming language, which is what most shells are, is considered by many to be whether or not an underlying linguistic grammar is created. The great programming languages, Cobol, C and its variants, and Algol, have all been built on very strict grammars that in some ways mimic natural (human) language. Other programming languages, notably Fortran and BASIC, have been built on a formulaic structure, that is to say, an outgrowth of mathematics, rather than natural language. Unix shells fall into the second category. They are readily understood and written by people who are adept at mathematics and codes; they are less readily understood and written by speakers and writers of natural languages. The consistency of these languages lies in their typography, not an inherent system of meaning. For further information on the origin of programming languages, see *History of Programming Languages*, edited by Richard L. Wexelblat, Academic Press, New York, 1981.

A variety of shells have been written for Unix and Unix-like operating systems. They have names such as sh, tcsh (the default shell in Mac OS X), csh, ksh, psh, pdksh, bash, and zsh. When you compare these various shells, you will discover that they implement very similar commands—after all, the underlying operating systems are quite similar. What differentiates one shell from another is the nuances of its commands—the dialect of its language. The original Unix shell, for example, is sh. Some C language programmers preferred a more C-like language. Thus, csh was born. Improvements were made, and the enhanced C shell, tcsh, was born.

From this listing of shells, you can easily see their formulaic origins in their names; you can also detect (as many have noted) that the authors of these shells could not or did not want to type. (In all fairness, it is not just a matter of typing. Memory on early computers was scarce, and the difference between storing the text of a command named "List Files" and one named "ls" was significant. Furthermore, for commands that need to be transmitted over telecommunications links, each additional character is a burden when the links are as slow as early links were.) What may not be immediately apparent from the names of these shells is that capitalization does matter—csh is not the same as CSH.

Programs, Tools, Utilities, and Commands

A shell command causes one or more instructions to be sent to the operating system. Whether that command causes a program to run or a function within the operating system to be carried out normally makes little difference. Shells ship with a variety of tools, programs, and utilities. Distinctions can be made among them, but for the purpose of this book, "program" and "application program" are reserved for software that runs at the user interface level. Programs, tools, and utilities that are run through shell commands are referred to as commands, whether they are shell commands or not.

Command Processing

Commands may affect the computer and its environment. For example, you can set the date and time, as well as how they are displayed. They also can process data, usually in batch mode. Shell commands normally assume three files are in existence (or can be created by the command if needed):

- STDIN is an input file, the standard input. Data can be read from this file.

- STDOUT is an output file, the standard output. Results are written to this file.

- STDERR is an output file for errors and warnings, the standard error. (The separation of STDOUT from STDERR means that errors can go to a computer terminal and output can go to a printer. It also means that errors are separated from output.)

This is all necessary because shell commands are normally not interactive. You need to specify what you want to be done (in the command), what you want to do it to (STDIN), and where to put the results (STDOUT. This paradigm is less applicable to word processing than to the repetitive processing of utility bills, checking account deposits, and other operations of that sort.

The fact that many commands are not interactive means that commands can run in the background on your computer. If you need to process a file of purchase orders (input) in order to generate packing slips and invoices (output), this can be done overnight or while other operations are carried on.

What's Old is New Again

This non-interactive way of working turns out to be extraordinarily relevant to Web pages. The Web's basic communication protocol, HTTP, is not particularly interactive. You ask for a page and then you get it. That completes the transaction. As a Web server is producing the page, it may need to perform some additional processing. That processing is batch-oriented, since there is no user to interact with it (the Web server is the user). Thus, shell commands and batch processing are often used to support dynamic Web pages.

Entering Commands

You enter shell commands at a prompt, press RETURN, and the command is executed. This section provides you with the details of this process. Remember that the shell is text oriented. Think of the window into which you are typing as a teletype. You are dealing only with the last line of text. You should see a blinking cursor where the next key you press will appear. Do not try to click the mouse in a line of text three lines above the bottom of the window; you can do so in order to copy the text, but you cannot type back there. It is over and done with. Only the last line counts.

In strict Unix terminology, the RETURN key generates a *newline* character. To maintain consistency with the more familiar graphical user interface, RETURN is used rather than newline.

The Prompt

Shells display a *prompt* to indicate that they are ready to receive data. That prompt may be $ or %. In addition, the $ or % may be preceded by text generated by the shell, making a prompt that can be fairly lengthy. If you do not see the prompt, the shell is not running or (more likely) is working on a command that it has not completed. (If you want to terminate a command that is running, see "Terminating a Command or Input" later in this section.)

The Command

All shell commands are documented in manual pages, *man pages,* for short. You can use the man command to find out about any shell command. Just type **man**, followed by the command name, as in

```
man date
```

All manual pages have a common format. Each command consists of a single word, usually in the lower case. Examples of shell commands like this are

```
date
pwd
```

Certain basics apply to many commands. They are discussed in this section:

- Arguments
- Options
- Reading command synopses
- Wildcards

- ■ Quoting and escaping texts
- ■ Multiple commands

Arguments   Some commands are self-contained; however, other commands require one or more *arguments* to be given after the command. For example, the chown command lets you change the ownership of a file. Thus, to change the ownership of file filename to user jfeiler, the command could be written

```
chown jfeiler filename
```

If you type

```
chown
```

without a user name or filename, you will get an error. As Figure 21-5 shows, the error consists of a summary of the correct usage of the command. This terse usage message is your invitation to try again.

More than one argument may be required for some commands; if that is the case, the order of the arguments matters. For example, the copy command (cp) lets you copy one file to another. Here is an example of that command:

```
cp original_file duplicate_file
```

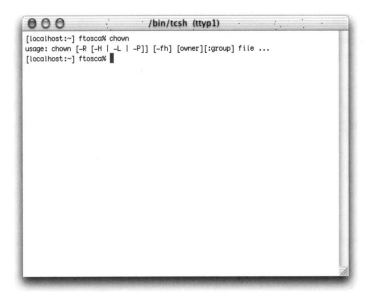

FIGURE 21-5   Incorrectly entered command with usage prompt

This copies orginal_file into duplicate_file. If you want to copy duplicate_file into original_file, you must reverse the arguments.

Options   Many commands allow you to enter options after the command. Options are customarily preceded by –. For example, if you want to prompt the user before overwriting a file in a copy command, you use the –i option:

```
cp -i original_file duplicate_file
```

Reading Command Synopses   A standard format for describing commands is used on manual pages. It is called command *synopses*.

NOTE

Synopses are shown in some of the figures at the end of the section on using Terminal.

Text that is presented without special symbols is to be typed in as shown. Arguments are presented in italics. Options are presented in square brackets. For example, in the cp command, you will find the –i option shown as [-i]. This means that it is optional. Sometimes, you can choose from one or more options; in those cases a vertical bar (|) delineates the choices, as in this section of the synopsis of the cp command:

```
[-H | -L | -P]
```

You can use –H or –L or –P; you need not use any (they are all enclosed in square brackets), but you cannot use two or three.

Brackets can be embedded within other brackets. In the cp command, you will find this combination:

```
[-R [-H | -L | -P]]
```

The whole thing is optional (because of the square brackets). If you choose, you may use the –R option. You may choose to follow it with one of –H, –L, or –P. (Those three are enclosed within brackets which means they are optional.) As a result, -R -H is legal, as is -R. -R -H -L is not legal (you can only choose –H or –L to follow –R).

The full synopsis of the cp command is as follows:

```
cp [-R [-H | -L | -P]] [-f | -i] [-p] source_file target_file
```

TIP

In deciphering commands, match up brackets from the inside out. In other words, in this example, first match up the -H -L -P combination, then its containing bracket which also include -R. The -f -I combination is another set. -p is on its own.

Wildcards   One way in which commands work is to expand abbreviations for files into one or more files The shell executes the command for each file that matches your abbreviation. These abbreviations use *wildcards*, and the process is referred to as *globbing*.

When you type * into a filename, it is interpreted as one or more characters of any sort. Thus, if you enter **file***, it will be interpreted as being filea, fileabc, fileb, and so forth, whichever files are found on disk matching the pattern.

A ? matches a single character. Thus, file? matches filea and fileb, but not fileab. (This mechanism works because neither * nor ? is normally a part of a standard filename. If you need to use them in a filename, you must precede them with an escape character, \, as in thisisafile\?. In practice they are rarely used in filenames.)

You can also define a set of characters to use as a wildcard. Since they are sets, they are enclosed in square brackets [and]. The set of characters consisting of A, B, and C is notated as follows:

```
[ABC]
```

The set of characters consisting of lowercase a, b, and c, is shown in this way:

```
[abc]
```

and the set of uppercase and lowercase a, b, and c is shown as

```
[ABCabc]
```

Thus, the notation

```
file?[ABC]
```

matches filesA, filexB, and file1A, but it does not match filesd or filesdA. The expression requires one character following file and one character from the set A, B, and C following that. Both filesd and filesdA fail that test.

You can use sequences of characters in a set, such as

```
[A-Z]
```

That is the set of uppercase characters from A to Z. To include all characters in both upper and lower-cases, use

```
[A-Za-z]
```

In all of these cases, only those files on disk are searched. You cannot construct an output filename with wildcards.

Quoting and Escaping Text   Sometimes a character that has a special meaning in commands, such as ; or | or > is needed in another role in a command, perhaps as a text string to be searched for. You can use quotation marks to delimit a string of one or more of these characters; if you do, they will be passed to the command and not used for their regular meanings.

Using a Command-Line
Interface

> **NOTE** *Single quotes perform this task absolutely. Double quotes do so except for the characters $ and \ and single and double quotes.*

To let a single character pass through, you can *escape* it: precede it with \. (Escape comes from the phrase *escape sequence* that was used in teletype lingo decades ago, when you used a code sequence to simulate pressing the ESC key or other nonprinting characters.) The escape method using \ works only on the one character immediately following it; for more than one character, you must either intersperse \ before each ambiguous character or use quotes.

Multiple Commands   You can enter more than one command on a command line. If you do so, you terminate the commands (except the last) with a semicolon (;).

Redirecting Input and Output

As noted previously, most commands deal with three files: STDIN, STDOUT, and STDERR. When you run a command from a terminal, all three of those files are set to your computer display (which is a Terminal window). As a result, you may not notice the difference. You can split them apart by redirecting them.

Use > to send output from STDOUT to a file. You type in the name of the file immediately following > as in

```
>myoutputfile
```

If your command is producing a report, this will let you create a disk file, which can then be edited in a word processor or manipulated by still other commands.

Some commands require input from STDIN. You can redirect this to a file from the terminal by using <. Thus, the expression

```
<myinputfile
```

reads the command's inputs from myinputfile. Obviously, the file needs to exist (output files do not need to exist before the command is executed).

You can also redirect STDERR. You do so with the symbols 2> as in

```
2>myerrorfile
```

Finally, you can append STDOUT output to an existing file. Use >> to do so. If you enter

```
>>myoutputfile
```

into your command, output from that command will be placed at the end of myoutputfile (if it exists). If you use

```
>myoutputfile
```

output will replace myoutputfile.

Piping

As you can imagine, you can take the output from one command and send it to another by using redirection. This is helpful when a command generates a report, which you then want to scan automatically for certain information.

You can accomplish this using redirection, as described in the last section. However, a more straightforward method is to use *pipes*. When you specify a pipe between two commands, the output of the first (STDOUT) is send to the second (as STDIN). You do not have to worry about naming files. Use | to create a pipe. Instead of separating the two commands with a ; as you would normally do when you place two commands on one line use |.

Terminating a Command or Input

Sometimes a command will read data from STDIN until it encounters the end of the file. Unfortunately, if it is reading from the terminal (the default), it cannot tell where the end of file is. The standard keyboard sequence of CONTROL-D is used to indicate the end of file. Use it when you have finished typing a command's input. (You can use CONTROL-C to terminate a runaway command.)

A preferable way of terminating a runaway command is to use CONTROL-OPTION-ESCAPE to bring up the Process window. You can then select the errant command and force it to quit.

Return Values

All commands return a value. Typically, this value indicates whether an error has occurred. Most successful commands return zero. If an error has occurred, the value the command returns can indicate what error happened.

Since commands return values, they can be used in expressions. Thus, anywhere you see *expression* in the synopsis of a command, realize that it can be a simple arithmetic expression or the invocation of a command and the use of its return value.

The use of zero as a good result can cause confusion among programmers who are used to returning a true (1) or false (0) indicating success or failure.

TIP   *If there is any possibility of confusion on your part (or on the part of someone who will be maintaining your code), include the value, so that you know if you are testing for 0 as good or 0 as false.*

Using a File for Command Input

Finally, you can create files with commands in them. You can put one or more commands into a text file and then execute the entire file. You simply type in the name of the file. You can combine commands, often using their return values, to create complex workflows.

You must make the file executable using the chmod command with options +rx. You also need to identify the interpreter for the commands. This is done on the first line, with a statement such as #!/bin/tcsh. The simplest way of seeing how to set up a script file is to look at an existing one that works.

Using the Terminal Application

Everything in this chapter up to this point applies to all Unix shells. Now it is time to deal with the Mac OS X Terminal application: your gateway to the land of shells. Terminal is located in the Utilities folder within Applications.

You can use Terminal to run a single shell command or to open a Terminal window into which you can type several commands (and see their results). These topics, along with how to set Terminal preferences, are covered in this section.

Running a Single Shell Command

To simply run a shell command, use Run Command from the Shell menu, as shown next. Input and output will be redirected if you specify them Otherwise, a Terminal window (shown later) will be used.

Using the Terminal Window

Use the Terminal window to interact with Terminal and to execute a variety of commands. If it has not opened automatically when you launch Terminal (this is a preference that you will see later how to set), you can open a Terminal window using the New command from the Shell menu. A Terminal window is shown in Figure 21-6.

At the top of the window, you can see the prompt

```
[localhost:~] jfeiler%
```

Following the prompt, on the same line, a command has been entered. This command is a `gzip` command: it combines and compresses files. You can use `gzip` for a folder by typing the name of the folder into the command. Since that name must include the directories in which the folder is located, it can be a complex string of characters. It is far easier to drag the file or folder into the terminal window and have terminal create the appropriate filename string for you.

In Figure 21-7, another command has been typed into the window:

```
man intro
```

The `man` command takes a single argument: the name of the command to be explained. The shell's response is

```
man: Formatting manual page...
```

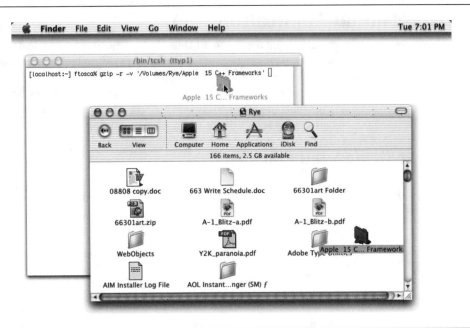

FIGURE 21-6 Using the terminal window

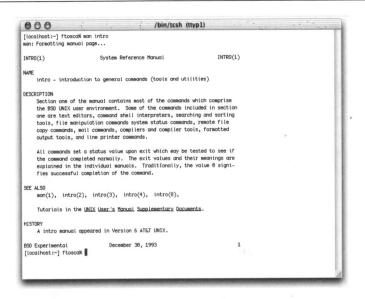

FIGURE 21-7 Use the man command to see information (manuals)

Following that, the output (STDOUT) is shown. When the output has finished, the prompt at the bottom of the window is shown, and a new command can be entered.

If the window is not big enough to display all of the output, it is *paged*—that is, a full window is shown, and an indication of the amount of the output is displayed at the bottom, as in Figure 21-8.

You can then advance line by line (by pressing RETURN), or you can view another page (by pressing SPACE). You can use the scrollbar to look at previous screens' data, but only if you have enabled the Scrollback Buffer in Buffer preferences. Also, you can resize the window to view more of the data, but if you have not checked the Wrap lines option in Buffer preferences, resizing the window will not change the display.

Setting Preferences

The Preferences command lets you set a variety of preferences for your terminal window—the window into which you type commands and view output. Buttons in a scrolling toolbar at the top of the window let you choose the sets of preferences you wish to set. Each set is described in this section. The Preferences window with its first set of preferences, General, selected in shown in Figure 21-9.

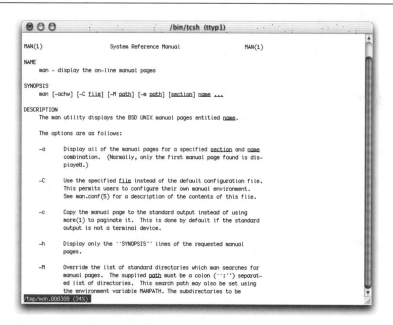

FIGURE 21-8   man page display

FIGURE 21-9   General preferences to control display of Terminal's window

General Preferences

Teletypes typically had lines of 80 characters. You can now use more characters than that. Enabling the wrap option lets the window wrap lines to its width; if it is not enabled, you may have to scroll horizontally to see a full line of text.

This panel also lets you set the default font for the Terminal window, as well as what to do with the window when the shell exits.

Startup Preferences

You have control over how the Terminal application starts up using the Startup preferences in Figure 21-10.

Shell Preferences

The Shell preference, shown in Figure 21-11, lets you select which shell is used. As shown here, the tcsh shell is the default in Mac OS X. A login script can be executed if you want whenever the shell starts up.

Emulation Preferences

Remember that your terminal window is emulating a teletype device. The Display terminal preferences (shown in Figure 21-12) help you set preferences that improve its functionality.

FIGURE 21-10   Startup preferences: setting what Terminal does when it starts and quits

FIGURE 21-11   Shell preferences: choosing which shell

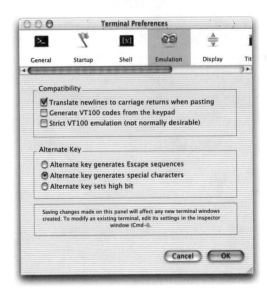

FIGURE 21-12   Emulating various terminal preferences

The VT100 was a DEC teletype replacement Although such devices are rare today, its standard formats and protocols remain widely used. If you are using Telnet to access a legacy application on the Internet, you may need to adjust the settings in this window. If you do not know what these settings mean, do not change them.

Display Preferences

The Scrollback Buffer is the amount of data, both input and output, that is preserved in the window. If you enable it and set its length to Unlimited, everything that has happened from the time you opened that terminal window is visible if you scroll back. If disable it or limit it to a specific number of lines (as shown in Figure 21-13), data disappears (oldest first) when the window is full.

Finally, you can choose the scroll to the bottom option. If you select this, the window is automatically positioned to the bottom (where a new line of text appears). If you want to review data that has scrolled off the window, you may be irritated to have the window jumping to the bottom. You may want to turn this option on and off depending on what you are doing. The Display preferences are shown in Figure 21-13.

Title Bar Preferences

Figure 21-14 shows the Title Bar preferences. You can control how each window is labeled. If you will have multiple Terminal windows open, you might want to clarify what each one is. Note that the embedded title bar changes as you select the elements to be included so that you can see what it will look like.

FIGURE 21-13   Display preferences with scroll, wrap, and buffer options

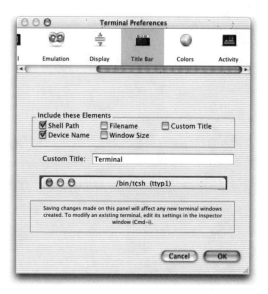

FIGURE 21-14   Title Bar preferences

Colors Preferences

Colors preferences, shown in Figure 21-15, let you set the defaults for windows. Note that the Extra Bold checkbox can help you to distinguish boldface type from normal type In many typefaces it is not readily apparent. Manual pages use boldface type differently than normal type, and so this distinction is important.

Activity Preferences

Activity preferences are shown in Figure 21-16.

Useful Commands

In this section, you will find an introduction to useful commands. As noted previously, using the commands on the command line in Terminal can help you learn the Mac OS X interface. It can also help you port Unix-based shell scripts from other environments.

To get a full description of each of these commands, use the man command. Follow it with the name of the command in which you are interested. (You can use man at the prompt in the Terminal application.) The arguments and parameters for the commands are provided here for reference; their definitions are on the man pages. However, if you are somewhat familiar with the commands, the listings here may be sufficient to remind you of the sequence of arguments. These commands may differ slightly from the commands that you are used to in other Unix variants.

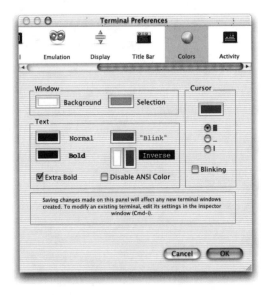

FIGURE 21-15   Colors preferences can make the text easier to read.

FIGURE 21-16   Activity preferences

Using sudo

Many commands that manipulate files and directories require that an administrator execute them. In many user environments, people are used to logging in as a root user in order to do this.

On Mac OS X, you never log in as root or any other such user. You log in with your own ID. As noted previously, that ID is not sufficient to execute many of these privileged commands. In order to do so, you use the sudo command; this replaces root login on Mac OS X.

The command you wish to execute follows sudo on the command line. You will then be asked for your password. The command will then be executed and logged in the system log. Your password is valid for five minutes That means that you can execute additional sudo commands without reentering your password during that time period.

You do not need root access, and you do not need to hack around Mac OS X security. This is the way to gain access to commands that you must use (in the few cases in which you do need to execute a privileged command.)

Regular Expressions

Regular expressions describe a set of strings. The are used in text editors and in some other commands They are normally delimited by characters such as /.Within those delimiters, you can specify individual characters (or sets of characters) that must occur in certain sequences and with certain numbers of repetitions. To those who are unfamiliar with them, regular expressions resemble hieroglyphics, but they can be useful for constructing batch mode edits. They also can serve to help create crude file searching mechanisms (such as may be needed in a low-volume Web site).

Editing

These commands are used to edit text. See "Text Editors" later in this section for more powerful tools that work on entire files. Editing a word processing document from the command line is normally much clumsier than in a graphical word processor; however, for rearranging the formatted data (usually in columns) that is printed out by legacy applications, they can be very useful.

col This command filters reverse line feeds, backspaces, and other characters from a file. It can help fix output from nroff and tbl, as well as from scripts and programs written on other systems.

```
col [-bfx] [-l num]
```

cut Based on character position or delimiters, this removes portions of each line of a text file.

```
cut -b list [-n] [file ...]
cut -c list [file ...]
cut -f list [-d delim] [-s] [file ...]
```

eqn Formats equations for use with troff. Useful in hybrid environments such as universities, where Unix files with mathematical and scientific formulas need to be shared. Word processors and page layout programs often handle equation formatting; however, their formats may not be sharable across platforms and across applications.

```
eqn [ -rvCNR ] [ -dcc ] [ -Tname ] [ -Mdir ] [ -fF ] [ -sn ] [ -pn ]
    [ -mn ] [ files... ]
```

fmt Formats brief text messages as for sending in mail. It is generally not needed today.

```
fmt -c [goal [maximum]] [name ...]
```

hexdump Displays the contents of a file in hexadecimal, octal, or character formats. You use hexdump if you want to examine non-printing characters in a file. Non-printing characters include tabs and other editing symbols in word processing files, as well as binary data and characters from other alphabets than your own.

```
hexdump [-bcCdovx] [-e format_string] [-f format_file]
    [-n length] [-s skip] file ...
hd [-bcdovx] [-e format_string] [-f format_file]
    [-n length] [-s skip] file ...
```

paste This command merges records from two files together. Unlike join, which works on a key field, paste merges records in sequence: file A's first record, file B's first record, file A's second record, and so on.

```
paste [-s] [-d list] file ...
```

sort   Sorts a file based on a specified key or keys. Because of the crudeness of this command, it can sometimes be more useful than sorting within a word processing, spreadsheet, or database application.

```
sort  [-cmus] [-t separator] [-o output-file] [-T tempdir]
  [-bdfiMnr] [+POS1 [-POS2]] [-k POS1[,POS2]] [file...]
sort {--help,--version}
```

tr   Translates strings of characters using specified translations. You can translate to or from uppercase, eliminate non-printing characters, and so on.

```
tr [-csu] string1 string2
tr [-cu] -d string1
tr [-cu] -s string1
tr [-cu] -ds string1 string2
```

uniq   For each line of a text file, eliminates immediately subsequent lines that are identical. This is a very easy way to remove identical lines from a log or other automatically produced file. Because uniq only works on adjacent lines, you may need to sort the file to cause identical lines to be adjacent. You also may need to use one of the other editing routines to remove time stamps, which may be the only data in the files that are not identical.

```
uniq [-c | -d | -u] [-i] [-f fields] [-s chars]
[input_file[output_file]]
```

File Compression and Archiving

Unix supports a variety of file compression mechanisms. You will find files with .z extensions. They use adaptive Lempel-Ziv coding to save space. You will also find .tar files. These are collections of files. By creating a .tar file from several files, you can send the one archive (containing several files) to another user. You can combine compression and archiving by compressing first and then creating an archive of the compressed files.

compress, uncompress, zcat   These commands use adaptive Lempel-Ziv coding to compress and uncompress files. A suffix of .z is added. Compare to tar which adds and subtracts files to an archive. These commands work on individual files.

```
compress [-cfv] [-b bits] [file ...]
uncompress [-cfv] [file ...]
zcat [file ...]
```

tar

This is the tape archiver program. This program creates, adds, or extracts files from a compressed .tar archive.

Useful Commands

```
tar [[-]bundled-options Args] [gnu-style-flags]
  [filenames | -C directory-name] ...
```

gzip, gunzip   This zips and unzips files and folders. Use −r to perform recursively (if a folder is selected, all of the files within it will be zipped). Files are replaced by their zipped versions.

```
gzip [ -acdfhlLnNrtvV19 ] [-S suffix] [ name ... ]
gunzip [ -acfhlLnNrtvV ] [-S suffix] [ name ... ]
```

Files and Directories

The commands in this section are the shell's version of the Finder. Use the Finder or AppleScript to accomplish these commands wherever possible.

cd   Change working directory from the home directory.

chmod   Change file permissions.

```
chmod [-R [-H | -L | -P]] mode file ...
```

chown   Change the owner or group of a file or link. Only an administrator user can change file ownership. On a network, if you need to provide emergency access (such as when someone is out of work), it is usually better to change ownership than to give out someone else's password.

```
chown [-R [-H | -L | -P]] [-f] [-h] owner [:group] file ...
chown [-R [-H | -L | -P]] [-f] [-h] :group file ...
```

cmp   Compares two files, writing out differences. See also diff.

```
cmp [-l | -s] file1 file2 [skip1 [skip2]]
```

comm   Selects or rejects lines common to two files. See also diff and cmp.

```
comm [-123i] file1 file2
```

cp   This command copies a file to another by specifying the new name or to a new directory by specifying only the directory (the name will remain the same).

```
cp [-R [-H | -L | -P]] [-f | -i] [-pv]
  source_file target_file
cp [-R [-H | -L | -P]] [-f | -i] [-pv]
  source_file ... target_directory
```

diff This command finds differences between two files. See also `cmp` and `comm`.

```
diff [options] from-file to-file
```

file Gets information about one or more files. This information includes whether or not it is executable, and so forth. Aqua's Get Info command is usually more complete.

```
file [-vczL] [-f namefile] [-m magicfiles] file ...
```

ls Lists a directory contents or file information. Normally the Finder does this.

```
ls [-ABCFHLPRTWabcdfgikloqrstul] [file ...]
```

mkdir Makes a directory. You use the Finder to do this (New Folder). However if you are writing a script and want to create a directory into which to place files automatically, you may need to use `mkdir`.

```
mkdir [-p] [-m mode] directory_name ...
```

mv Moves files from one place to another. Its companion command, `cp`, copies files. At the end of `cp`, you have two sets of files; at the end of `mv`, you have the same number you started with (but in a different place). Use the Finder for this functionality.

```
mv [-f | -i] [-v] source target
mv [-f | -i] [-v] source ... directory
```

pwd This command returns the name of the present working directory.

```
pwd
```

rcp The remote copy command copies files from one computer to another across a local area network. This can be an efficient way of copying files to computers running other operating systems on your local area network.

```
rcp [-Kpx] [-k realm] file1 file2
rcp [-Kprx] [-k realm] file ... directory
```

rm This removes one or more files (not directories). See `rmdir` to remove directories.

```
rm [-dfiPRrvW] file ...
```

rmdir This removes directories. They must be empty. That is, you must have removed any files with the `rm` command.

```
rmdir [-p] directory ...
```

touch   This command sets file access and modification dates. A common use of touch is to update access dates so that files are not removed in automated cleanups, as well as to force them to be backed up in automated backups for "recently" accessed files.

```
touch [-acfm] [-r file] [-t [[CC]YY]MMDDhhmm[.SS]] file ...
```

umask   This command sets the mask for file creation, This is similar to prespecifying chmod for new files that you create.

```
umask mode
```

Internet

The Internet is built into the shell in the form of standard protocols that are listed in this section. Mail is also available from the shell, but it is discussed in its own chapters.

finger   Taken from '30s gangster jargon, this command provides information on users logged on to a host on the network. It can be used across the Internet (it is an Internet protocol).

```
finger [-lmpshoT] [user ...] [user@host ...]
```

ftp   This command initiates file transfers across a local area network or the Internet. Use Fetch or another application program to do this with a graphical user interface.

```
ftp [-a] [-d] [-e] [-g] [-i] [-n] [-U] [-p] [-P port]
  [-t] [-v] [-V] [host [port]]
ftp ftp://[user:password@]host[:port]/file[/]
ftp http://host[:port]/file
ftp host:[/path/]file[/]
```

ping   Sending ICMP ECHO_REQUEST packets to network hosts, this command checks network status.

```
ping [-QRadfnqrv] [-c count] [-i wait] [-l preload]
  [-p pattern] [-s packetsize] [-S src_addr]
  [host | [-L] [-I interface] [-T ttl] mcast-group]
```

telnet   This initiates a Telnet session in which your terminal functions as a terminal on a remote computer. This is one of the original Internet protocols. You may need to Telnet into legacy applications on mainframes that do not have graphical user interfaces.

```
telnet [-8EFKLacdfrx] [-S tos] [-X authtype] [-e escapechar]
  [-k realm] [-l user] [-n tracefile] [host [port]]
```

tftp   The trivial file transfer protocol is used to transfer publicly available files. Unlike FTP, it has no security built in.

```
tftp [host]
```

Networking

These commands help you manipulate your network environment.

ifconfig   This command sets interface configuration parameters. Use Network Manager instead.

```
ifconfig interface address_family [address [dest_address]]
  [parameters]
ifconfig -a [-d] [-u] [address_family]
ifconfig -l [-d] [-u] [address_family]
```

mesg   This command controls whether messages from other users can appear on your terminal (in the Terminal.app window).

```
mesg [n | y]
```

netstat   Shows network status.

```
netstat [-Aan] [-f address_family] [-M core] [-N system]
netstat [-bdghimnrs] [-f address_family] [-M core] [-N system]
netstat [-bdn] [-I interface] [-M core] [-N system] [-w wait]
netstat [-p protocol] [-M core] [-N system]
```

rlogin   The remote login command starts a terminal session on a remote host. You can also use `telnet`. This is useful on networks running multiple operating systems.

```
rlogin [-8DEKLdx] [-e char] [-k realm] [-l username] host
```

rsh   The remote shell command executes a command on a remote host's shell.

```
rsh [-Kdnx] [-t timeout] [-k realm] [-l username] host [command]
```

ruptime   This command shows status of host computers on the network. This information is broadcast approximately every three minutes, so it may be slightly out of date.

```
ruptime [-alrtu]
```

talk   You can talk to another user on the local network. This is somewhat like instant messaging for the 1960s.

```
talk person [ttyname]
```

telnet   Use to start the Telnet protocol to log into other hosts on the local network or across the Internet. You may also use telnet to log into a router or firewall on your LAN.

```
telnet [-8] [-E] [-F] [-K] [-L] [-S tos] [-X authtype]
  [-a] [-b hostalias] [-c] [-d] [-e escapechar]
  [-f] [-k realm] [-l user] [-n tracefile]
  [-r] [-x] [host [port]]
```

Useful Commands

wall   Sends the contents of the file to all logged-on users. If they have blocked messages with mesg, the message can still get through. This is commonly used on internal networks and only in rare cases. If users are not running Terminal.app, they may not see this message. It can be useful, though, in hybrid networks with Unix terminals.

```
wall [file]
```

write   This sends lines of text that you type until an end-of-file character to another user.

```
write user [ttyname]
```

Printing

Printing from the shell can be useful when manipulating the output of legacy reports, particularly those that have been manipulated by text editors in the shell. These commands refer to printing on a printer. The following section describes commands that print or display data on the screen.

lpc   Use Print Center instead of the line printer control command to mange printers.

```
lpc [command [argument ...]]
```

lpr   Use this commant to print files to the printer.

```
lpr [-Pprinter] [-#num] [-C class] [-J job] [-T title]
  [-U user] [-i numcols] [-1234 font] [-wnum]
  [-cdfghlnmprstv] [name ...]
lp [-c] [-d printer] [-n num] [name ...]
```

Printing and Displays

These commands format data for display on the printer or monitor.

cat   This concatenates files and sends them to STDOUT (for display or printing).

```
cat [-benstuv] [-] [file ...]
```

grep, egrep, fgrep   These commands search files for a pattern of characters and print them out. Patterns can be literals or regular expressions—composite structures of character sets and sequences.

```
grep [-[AB] num] [-HRPS] [-CEFGLVabchilnqsvwx]
  [-e expr] [-f file] files...
```

head   This command displays the first lines or bytes of a file. See also `tail`.

```
head [-n count] [-c bytes] [file ...]
```

more   This commands helps you scroll through text on your terminal. It is based on the `vi` commands. You use them in the Terminal application to view text that cannot appear in the window. The most common commands are space (displays another screenful of data) and return (displays another line of data).

```
more [-ceinsu] [-t tag] [-x tabs] [-/ pattern] [file ...]
```

nroff   This command uses `groff` to emulate the Unix `nroff` command.

```
nroff [ -h ] [ -i ] [ -mname ] [ -nnum ] [ -olist ] [ -p ]
   [ -rcn ] [ -t ] [ -Tname ] [ file... ]
```

pr   This prints text files.

```
pr [+page] [-column] [-adFmrt] [[-e] [char] [gap]]
   [-L locale] [-h header] [[-i] [char] [gap]]
   [-l lines] [-o offset] [[-s] [char]] [[-n] [char]
   [width]] [-w width] [-] [file ...]
```

tail   This command displays the last bytes or lines of a file. See also `head`.

```
tail [-F | -f | -r] [-b number | -c number | -n number] [file ...]
```

troff   This uses `groff` to emulate the Unix `troff` command.

```
troff [ -abivzCER ] [ -wname ] [ -Wname ] [ -dcs ]
   [ -ffam ] [ -mname ] [ -nnum ] [ -olist ] [ -rcn ]
   [ -Tname ] [ -Fdir ] [ -Mdir ] [ files... ]
```

Programming

These commands let you create programs and manipulate files.

cc   This invokes the C, C++, and Objective-C compiler. Invoked from Project Builder, which is normally the tool that you use.

```
cc [ option | filename ]...
```

join   This command lets you specify fields within two files. You determine delimiters in the records that delimit the fields. The files are then joined based on a specific field. If identical values for that field appear in both files, all fields for that value in both files are merged. Thus, given a field such as Name, you can merge address information from one file with account information from another. You can do this easily with database and word processing applications. `join` lets you work with text files generated from dissimilar applications. See also `paste`.

```
join [-a file_number | -v file_number] [-e string]
   [-j file_number field] [-o list] [-t char] [-1 field]
   [-2 field] file1 file2
```

kill   This command send a signal to a process or terminate it. Use CONTROL-OPTION-ESCAPE to display running processes in Mac OS X and kill them from there.

```
kill [-s signal_name] pid ...
kill -l [exit_status]
kill -signal_name pid ...
kill -signal_number pid ...
```

make   make compiles programs as needed based on dependencies. Use Project Builder for Cocoa applications or an integrated development environment such as Code Warrior.

```
make [-Beiknqrstv] [-D variable] [-d flags] [-f makefile]
  [-I directory] [-j max_jobs] [-m directory] [-V variable]
  [variable=value] [target ...]
```

yacc   From a set of grammar specifications, this command produces a set of LALR parsing tables and a C routine to run them. It is very useful in computer science courses.

```
yacc [-dlrtv] [-b file_prefix] [-o output_filename] [-p
symbol_prefix]filename
```

Scripting/Shell Programming

These are the frequently used commands for scripts that you create in the shell. See also the commands in the previous section, "Programming."

bc   This is an arbitrary precision calculator language, which allows access to a C-style math library.

```
bc [ -lwsqv ] [long-options] [  file ... ]
```

cal   This displays a calendar for the current month or year. ncal provides the date of western and/or Russian and Orthodox Easter, as well as additional formatting options.

```
cal [-jy] [[month] year]
ncal [-jJpwy] [-s country_code] [[month] year]
ncal [-Jeo] [year]
```

calendar   This displays a customized calendar. The command can incorporate additional files (with the -f option). This lets you merge your own calendar with a calendar from your employer, school, and so forth.

```
calendar [-a] [-A num] [-B num] [-t dd[.mm[.year]]]
  [-f calendarfile]
```

csh   If you like the C programming language, this shell lets you use C-like commands.

```
csh [-bcefimnstvVxX] [arg ...]
csh [-l]
```

dc   This is a reverse-Polish notation calculator, designed for mathematicians and compiler writers.

```
dc
```

echo   This echoes the string to STDOUT. Use echo in scripts to display status messages.

```
echo [-n] [string ...]
```

find   This finds files in a directory hierarchy that match certain characteristics of name, type, access date, and so on. You can cause a specific program or script to be executed on all found files.

```
find [-H | -L | -P] [-Xdsx] [-f pathname]
  [pathname ...] expression
```

ln   This creates links (aliases) to files. Use the Finder for this.

```
ln [-fs] source_file [target_file]
ln [-fs] source_file ... [target_dir]
```

man   This formats and displays online manual pages. (See the section on man pages previously in this chapter.)

```
man [-adfhktw] [-m system] [-p string] [-M path]
  [-P pager] [-S list] [section] name ...
```

script   This command saves a log of your typed input and output. In some ways it is similar to the Record button in AppleScript's ScriptEditor. It does not record input and output of the graphical user interface, such as mouse movement, outside the terminal window.

```
script [-a] [-k] [-q] [-t time] [file] [command ...]
```

sh   This command starts the shell; you normally do not execute it. For a complete introduction to the shell, use the man shell page.

```
sh [-/+abCEefIimnpsTuVvx] [-/+o longname] [-c string] [arg ...]
```

stty   This command shows and allows you to set options for the terminal. The Terminal application's preferences let you set many of these as well.

```
stty [-a | -e | -g] [-f file] [operands]
```

tee   Using a metaphor from the world of plumbing and pipe fittings, this command copies input from STDIN to STDOUT and also sends it to one or more files. Use it to trace your input (as opposed to `script` which copies input and output).

```
tee [-ai] [file ...]
```

units   This little utility lets you convert measurements from one system to another, provided that the conversion is a matter of multiplication (for example feet to meters). If the conversion is more complex (such as Farenheit to Centigrade), this will not work.

```
units [-f filename] [-qv] [to-unit from-unit]
```

wc   This counts words, lines and bytes in files.

```
wc [-clw] [file ...]
```

System Administration

These commands often require you to be logged in as an administrator user. If you are familiar with other Unix variants, you may be familiar with these commands.

at, batch, atq, atrm   These commands manage queues of jobs for execution in the future.

```
at [-V] [-q queue] [-f file] [-mldbv] time
at [-V] -c job [job ...]
atq [-V] [-q queue] [-v]
atrm [-V] job [job ...]

batch [-V] [-q queue] [-f file] [-mv] [time]
```

atrun   This runs jobs that have been queued.

```
atrun [-l load_avg] [-d]
```

cron   `cron` is a daemon that, once a minute, checks to see if jobs should be run. Output is mailed to users, thus it does not require the terminal window to be open.

```
cron [-x debugflag[,...]]
```

date   This displays the date and/or time in a user-specified format. For the super-user, it allows setting of the date and time.

```
date [-nu] [-d dst] [-r seconds] [-t minutes_west]
  [-v[+|-]val[ymwdHMS]] ... [-f fmt date |
  [[[[[cc]yy]mm]dd]HH]MM[.ss]] [+format]
```

df   This displays the number of blocks free on a given file system (or for all). It can be used in maintenance and backup scripts.

```
df [-ikn] [-t type] [file | filesystem ...]
```

du   This provides disk usage information. The Finder's Get Info command provides some of this information; AppleScript scripts can also do so.

```
du [-P | -H | -L] [-a | -s | -d depth] [-c] [-k] [-x] [file ...]
```

env   This command displays environmental variables, each of which is identified by a name such as the home directory, the user, and so forth. You can set selected environment variables with the `env` command.

```
printenv [name]
env [-] [name=value ...] [command]
```

init   This is the last step in the boot process. If it fails, it creates a single-user process that you can use to attempt to debug problems. In practical use on Mac OS X, only for extreme cases, such as to confirm that hardware has failed (you can't even run `init`).

```
init
init [0 | 1 | 6 | c | q]
```

login   This lets you log into the computer. You normally quit from Mac OS X and choose Login or Restart. This command is presented for compatibility with other operating systems. Logging in without going through the Mac OS X login process may cause problems.

```
login [-fp] [-h hostname] [user]
```

nice   This sets a command to a new priority (generally low).

```
nice [-number] command [arguments]
```

nohup   A command invoked by `nohup` cannot be hung up or quit while it is executing. This command is often used to start up servers that need to continue running after the terminal window that launched them is closed. Modern servers do this inside their code, but you may have old servers or old procedures that still use `nohup` (necessarily or not).

```
nohup command [arg ...]
```

passwd   Use this to change your password. You need to enter the original password and the new one twice. Use Aqua's preferences for passwords to do this

```
passwd [-l] [user]
yppasswd [-l] [-y] [-d domain] [-h host] [-o]
```

printenv   See env.

ps   This displays process status about selected (or all) processes. Use the Mac OS X utility Processes.app instead.

```
ps [-aCcefhjlmrSTuvwx] [-M core] [-N system]
  [-O fmt] [-o fmt] [-p pid] [-t tty] [-U username]
  [-W swap]ps [-L]
```

quota   For a given user, this shows disk usage and quota.

```
quota [-g] [-u] [-v | -q]
quota [-u] [-v | -q] user
quota [-g] [-v | -q] group
```

rwho   This provides a list of who is logged onto computers on the network. Use network management tools such as NetInfo instead.

```
rwho [-a]
```

shutdown   This shuts down the system at a given time, with a warning message. Use Network Administrator for this.

```
shutdown [-] [-hknpr] time [warning-message ...]
```

su   Use this to substitute user identity. You may need to supply a password. This lets you temporarily run a command with another user's privileges and identity.

```
su [-Kflm] [-c class] [login [args]]
```

uname   This writes operating system name, hardware platform, and so on, to STDOUT.

```
uname [-amnprsv]
```

users   Lists login IDs of current users. The who command lists more information about them.

```
users
```

vacation   This sends an automated reponse to incoming mail. The response is sent once to each person sending you mail. Note that this functionality is normally implemented and used in mail applications such as Microsoft Outlook Express, Eudora, or the Mail application provided with Mac OS X.

```
vacation -i [-r interval]
vacation -l
vacation [-a alias] login
```

who   Use this to display your real name (not the login name), as well as users who are logged onto the system.

```
who am I
who [file]
```

Text Editors

These are the shell's text editors. They are driven by the command line and are useful at formatting reports. They are not particularly easy to use to write a memo.

grep, sed, awk   These text editors provide interactive editing in a command-line world. That is, you cannot select text with a mouse to edit it. You describe it and the operations that you want to perform on it with text and symbols.

ed   This is a line-oriented text editor.

```
ed [-] [-sx] [-p string] [file]
```

ex, vi, view   These are text editors. ex is line-oriented; vi is full-screen-oriented (but still text-based, not a graphical user interface); and view is a vi that allows only viewing.

```
ex [-eFGRrSsv] [-c cmd] [-t tag] [-w size] [file ...]
vi [-eFGlRrSv] [-c cmd] [-t tag] [-w size] [file ...]
view [-eFGRrSv] [-c cmd] [-t tag] [-w size] [file ...]
```

Summary

This chapter has provided an introduction to shell commands and to the Terminal application. Shell commands can be an easy way to use Mac OS X if you are coming from another environment. They also can be useful in converting existing shell scripts from other platforms to Mac OS X. In general, though, learning to use the graphical user interface of Mac OS X is preferable to using the command line.

Chapter 22

Programming Mac OS

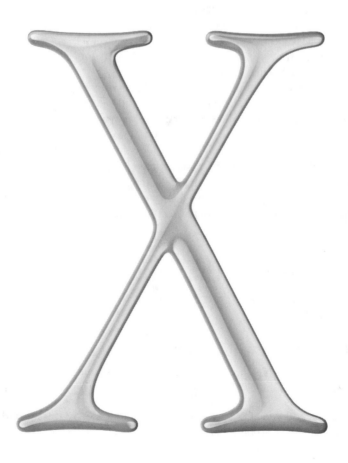

This part of the book shows you how to program Mac OS X. Chapter 20, "Automating Your Work with Applescript," provided an introduction to AppleScript, a language designed to let people automate, integrate, and customize their applications and workflow. The previous chapter focused on the Terminal application and shell commands. These are instructions you can issue and collect into scripts to program the underlying shell and some of the Unix applications that are provided as part of Mac OS X.

But, what if there is no application to script? What if there is no Unix tool to use for your task? More critically, what if there is a program, but it needs to be changed?

In this chapter, you will find an overview of programming for the Mac OS—both for the Mac OS 9 and earlier, and for Mac OS X. In the next chapter, you will find a detailed introduction to Classic Mac programming, including the use of MacApp, Apple's object-oriented application framework, and to the Classic environment that is part of Mac OS X.

Carbon is the set of technologies that lets you have it both ways; you can use it to write programs that run both on Mac OS 9 and earlier, and on Mac OS X. It is the subject of Chapter 24. Finally, Cocoa, the preferred programming environment of Mac OS X, is described in Chapter 25.

Programming for Mac OS X—and only Mac OS X—is easiest using Cocoa, Project Builder, and Interface Builder. Start by deciding whether your project is for Mac OS X only or whether you need to support Mac OS 9 and earlier as well.

But before delving into these topics, the chapter begins with a checklist for programmers and follows with a very basic technique: how to read—not write—a program.

Apple's Web site has a section for developers; you can reach it by clicking the Developer tab on the home page at http://www.apple.com. You will find extensive up-to-date documentation on that site, including white papers, specifications, samples, and bug reports (as well as fixes). For more information on the topics discussed in this chapter, look to that site first for more recent and detailed information. Much of the information is freely available both in HTML and PDF formats. Apple's developer programs are also described on those pages. Becoming an Apple developer entitles you to a variety of additional services, including evaluation copies of prerelease software.

Mac OS X Programmer's Checklist

Here's a very quick way to help you orient yourself. The details behind the checklist are described later in this chapter.

Are You Writing a New Program?

If you are starting from scratch (or totally rewriting an old program), you need to answer the following questions:

- Must it run on both Mac OS 9 and earlier and on Mac OS X? If so, use MacApp or PowerPlant and the Carbon libraries.

- Must it run only on Mac OS 9 and earlier? (Possible for an in-house application in special circumstances.) If so, use MacApp or PowerPlant with either Carbon or older libraries.

- Must it run only on Mac OS X? If so, use Cocoa, MacApp, or PowerPlant together with Project Builder and Interface Builder, the Code Warrior IDE.

Are You Modifying an Existing Program?

In this case, you need to do the following:

1. Recompile the program without touching it. Do not assume that your code works or that your development environment is up to date. If you can't compile it untouched, you're not going to be able to modify it. (Mac OS X has many features; automatically fixing compiler syntax errors is not one of them.) If you cannot recompile the program and the error list is large, you may want to consider rewriting it from scratch.

2. Once it compiles, make a copy of the sources. (You know this already, but strange things sometimes happen . . .)

3. Recompile it for Carbon. If it is a MacApp program, recompile it against the latest MacApp; if it is not, use the latest Carbon libraries. If the compile succeeds, start testing.

4. If it fails, *don't fix a single error*. Look at them and decide which category you are in:

   - Do you have the same error many times over? If so, a single fix—perhaps a different interface call—may fix all of them. Alternatively, a single replacement of an offending line of code throughout the application may fix them all.

   - Do you have the same type of error many times? If so, you can modify the previous steps to automate your work.

   - If you have many errors of many kinds with no apparent patterns, you have a lot of work to do. Consider using the Classic environment only. If the program runs without recompilation, you can use it—but you will not be able to modify it or maintain it. This may at least buy you some time. However, you probably will have to rewrite the program from scratch or undertake a major revision to get much more usage out of it.

   - If none of these applies, fix the few remaining bugs.

If the program you are converting is very old—that is, it is 68K code, not PowerPC code—convert it to PowerPC code first.

Test, Test, Test

Testing is boring. Being awakened at 2:00 A.M. by a hysterical user is exciting. Which do you want in your life?

Programming 101: How to Read a Program

In most programming courses, the first thing students learn how to do is write a simple program; one that prints out "Hello World" is a common instance. If you think about it for a moment, this is very odd. English majors don't start with a blank sheet of paper; their first assignment is to read *Hamlet* or *Pickwick Papers*. Chemists don't start with beakers and Bunsen burners, they start with the periodic table of the elements. And astronomers don't start by scanning the skies for newly discovered stars. They start by learning what their predecessors have learned and identifying the known stars.

Although the authors of millions of Hello World programs might be disappointed to hear it, most programmers do not write programs from scratch. In fact, most programmers do not write programs: they write specifications, they fix bugs, and they maintain programs by incorporating new features and adapting to new requirements. All of these require as a starting point an understanding of the existing program. And that means knowing how to read a program (unless you happened to write the original).

When it comes to Classic and Carbon, two of the programming technologies described in this section, reading programs is more important than ever. Mac OS 9 and earlier programs are those written for operating systems before Mac OS X; they run in the Classic environment. It is a fair bet that few such programs will be written from scratch in the future. New programs will be written to run directly on Mac OS X—and on Mac OS 9 and earlier if they need to run on legacy computer systems.

Carbon is a technology that lets programmers write for both Mac OS 9 and earlier, and Mac OS X. However, its programs do not take advantage of all of the Mac OS X features. Those are only available with Cocoa or with Carbon applications compiled with Project Builder.

In practical terms, the distinction often boils down to whether the object code that is generated is based on code fragments (the Classic paradigm) or Mach-O (the native Mac OS X paradigm).

What this means is that maintenance of existing programs can be done in the Classic or Carbon environments, but that it is almost always unwise to develop a brand new application from scratch in either Classic or Carbon unless it needs to run on Mac OS 9 or earlier. Thus, much of your work in Classic or Carbon will be bug fixing and maintenance, not writing code from scratch. And that, in turn, means that when it comes to Classic and Carbon, you need to hone your skills at reading code—code that may be old and that may not adhere to standards and designs you are familiar with.

The following are some basic rules and tips for reading programs. They will save you a lot of grief if you use them in your work.

What Does the Program Do?

Make sure you know what the program is intended to do. When a user says, "This program prints test scores by students," make certain you know if it also happens to calculate those scores, and if not, where it gets those scores from. Documentation often is incomplete on old programs.

Talk to the users until you understand what the program does and what they need it to do. If you are looking at an old program, make certain that all of it is still needed. (There are endless stories of programmers fixing reports that haven't been run in years when they do routine maintenance.)

Does the Program Work?

Make sure the program works; or, if you are fixing a bug, make sure you know what parts of the program (if any) work properly. One interesting finding in the work surrounding the Y2K computer problem was that a large number—perhaps a third—of the bugs found were not only not related to Y2K but had actually been there for years.

Can You Run the Program?

Get your hands on the program and make certain that you understand how to use it. Do what the users do, and try it your own way, too. One of the major causes of time and cost overruns in maintenance programming is programmers jumping in and reinventing wheels that already exist in the software.

Your Predecessors Weren't Nuts

The people who worked on the program you are working on probably weren't nuts. There was a reason they did what they did. Sometimes, you may find comments in the program that help you understand why it is written the way it is. "Fix later, after the deadline" is a frequent comment on many pages of source code. It is not uncommon to come across code that is well over a decade old. A program written in Fortran to run on a VAX computer may have been converted to Fortran on a Macintosh and then later to C++. Variables' names may retain their ancient conventions; logic structures (including Fortran's famous three-way If statements) may have persisted. Understand as much as possible about the program before you touch it.

Talk to the Furniture

Before you start to work, make certain that your ideas make sense. Explain the problem and what you are doing about it to someone or something that is not going to be bamboozled by your expertise. Borrow a child who says "Why?" or explain your thoughts to a sleeping dog. Be sure it makes sense.

TIP

You may find this advice laughable; unfortunately, it is not. A manager of programming projects identified this as the single biggest mistake programmers make. They identify a solution that could not possibly fix the problem. Yes, there may be a logic flaw in the code that computes withholding taxes; but if the problem that needs urgent attention is the fact that the program crashes consistently if it is left running with no input for more than two hours, the logic problem is (for those purposes) irrelevant.

Programming for Mac OS X

Mac OS X is a major leap forward for all personal computing. It sets new standards in usability, program integration, and maturity for the personal computing platform in general. For Macintosh users, it promises increased stability, improved use of resources (particularly memory and multiple processors), and a new era of user-created applications based on scripting and on Project Builder and Interface Builder.

But this comes at a price. Almost all existing Macintosh applications will run in one way or another on Mac OS X, and newly written applications will be able to take advantage of a host of new features. During the years-long transition to Mac OS X, there will be a variety of applications around that use the old (Mac OS 9 and earlier) technologies, as well as those using the new Mac OS X technologies. Not "breaking" old applications is important to Apple; doing so requires a carefully thought-out conversion process.

Apple Has Done This Before

Fortunately, Apple has done this before. The original Macintosh computer was built around a Motorola 68000 processor. Over the years, later versions of that processor (68020, 68030, and 68040) served as the heart of many Macintosh computers. However, by the late 1980s, it was clear that the major step forward in processing power that would be required for technologies such as video would be very hard to achieve using the 680x0 architecture.

A new chip, with a new architecture (reduced instruction set chip or RISC) was designed by Apple, IBM, and Motorola. Based on IBM's existing RISC chip, the new chips became the core of a new line of processors. The operating system of any computer is tied closely to its processor. Thus, the Mac OS and application programs needed to be revised to take advantage of the new chips. Unchanged, neither operating system nor application programs would run on the PowerPC. The reason for this is that the chip processes the computer instructions that are in the applications and the operating systems. If those instructions change (as they did) and if the architecture of the chip changes (as it did) new instructions in a new format must be presented to the chip.

Apple's approach to this conversion is a textbook example of how such a major technological transformation can be accomplished. Indeed, it is used in some business schools as a case study. The PowerPC conversion was successful, and the conversion to Mac OS X is being handled in the same way. There are three elements of the process:

- ■ **Don't break existing applications.** This is accomplished by providing software that emulates the previous hardware or, in the case of Mac OS X, that runs the Mac OS 9 operating system.

- ■ **Provide transitional development tools.** New programs will be written for the old technologies during the transition for a variety of reasons, including maintenance and repairs. Developers don't wake up one day with the ability to start afresh.

■ **Take your time.**   The PowerPC conversion process had no "drop dead" date at the start. Only when the market showed that most of their customers had PowerPC equipment did software manufacturers phase out their support for 68K applications.

Apple has actually done this twice before. In 1984, all the software and initial applications for the Macintosh were written on the Lisa either in Pascal or in assembly language.

Don't Break Existing Applications

Not breaking existing applications is accomplished through conversion, emulation, and information.

Conversion   In an ideal world, you could wave a magic wand and everything would be converted to a new technology at once: hardware, operating system, application programs, and data. Unfortunately, that is usually not possible.

In the PowerPC transition, key sections of code in the operating system and in applications were converted to native PowerPC code. They were rewritten to take advantage of the power of the new processor. Apple scanned many of the most popular applications and discovered that most of their processing involved a relatively few operations. Those sections were converted; moreover, the scanning techniques and information were widely disseminated to developers so that they could perform similar analyses and conversions.

Emulation   Before Apple approached the PowerPC transition process, emulation had a bad name among computer professionals. The term refers to software (and sometimes hardware) that is designed to mimic another computer's hardware or software. For example, you can buy products such as Virtual PC that uses software to run the Windows operating system on the Macintosh or on Unix. Terminal emulation software lets you use a personal computer as if it were a dumb terminal or a special-purpose terminal.

Emulation's bad reputation comes from the fact that it typically is slow. Each command has to be handled twice, once in the native environment and then again in the emulated environment. Clearly, it has to be slower than doing everything once.

Apple's achievement with the PowerPC transition involved making emulation work. Combined with shrewd conversions of key sections of the operating system and programs to native code, emulated programs wowed developers when they first saw them displayed at Apple's World Wide Developers Conference in 1993.

The Classic environment (described in detail later in this chapter) is the environment that runs old Mac OS applications. It benefits from everything that Apple has learned about emulation; it is fast and as stable as possible.

Mac OS 9 runs on Mac OS X very much as it runs when it runs directly on a computer's hardware. For that reason, you might say that it actually is not emulated. However, the process—running one operating system on another—is so much like emulation that you can consider it so for most purposes.

Information   Another strategy that Apple uses to ease the transition is to work closely with developers to catch at an early stage programs that do break in the new environment. Both with

PowerPC and with Mac OS X, it has been possible to predict what programs will break: old programs and programs that skirt programming guidelines and rules. These programs are disproportionately found in three categories: device-related software (for printers and scanners, for example), games, and poorly written code.

Although Apple is corporately tactful, there is no getting around the fact that there are well-written programs and poorly written programs. Every release of an operating system— whether from Apple or another vendor—typically breaks some widely used program. An urgent investigation is undertaken by the operating system developer and the application developer. Very often it turns out that the developer misunderstood (polite term) the programming rules. And, equally often, the operating system vendor modifies the operating system to make the noncompliant but widely used program run.

Since it is known in advance that some programs will break, and since it is also not a secret what types of programs may break, Apple can focus its attention on outreach, and it has done so. Developers have been barraged with warnings and compatibility concerns. The breakage rate is very low.

TIP
If you use custom-written software, you may be vulnerable to having it break. If it was custom written by a current member of Apple's developer community, the developer should be up to date on what works and what doesn't. And, if that person works for you, all is well. If he or she is a consultant who is not on a retainer or otherwise employed by you now, you may not get the information you need. If the software was written by a consultant or employee who is no longer around, you need to evaluate your level of risk. If it is mission-critical software, you need to confirm that it will continue to function. This is really not a Mac OS X issue: if you use custom-written software that is important to you, you should have a plan for its maintenance.

Transitional Tools

Apple's transitional tools for the PowerPC conversion involved a variety of diagnostic tools, as well as revised compilers and linkers. For the first pioneers, two-computer debugging environments were devised, with the application running on the new processor and the debugging software running on the old processor. This was necessary because native PowerPC debuggers did not exist at the beginning.

Similar tools are available for the Mac OS X conversion. However, there is one very important difference: the PowerPC chip, although based on the PowerPC chip used in the IBM RS600 workstation, was new to the Macintosh and the personal computing environment. Mac OS X has its roots both in the Macintosh operating systems and in NeXTSTEP, as well as in Unix. As a result, there are existing tools and applications for developers to use on Mac OS X. In addition, Mac OS X Server, a product derived from NeXTSTEP, was marketed by Apple starting in early 1999. As a result, there are more transitional tools available for the Mac OS X conversion than there were for the PowerPC conversion.

An essential part of the transition is smoothing the way for users. Some of the new interface features of Mac OS X (the Windows menu, for example) were included in Mac OS 9.1 so that the users' transition would be more gradual. Multiple users were introduced in Mac OS 9.0; optional there, the concept nevertheless helped prepared users for the functionality in Mac OS X that is not optional.

Taking Your Time

Converting to Mac OS X—whether by installing an upgrade or through buying a new computer—is a decision that can be made independent of the software running on the computer (with the limited exceptions noted previously). With PowerPC, Apple did not pull the plug on the 680x0 architecture. Over time, more and more of the operating system was converted from emulated 680x0 code to native PowerPC code. Not until Mac OS 8.6 was the conversion complete. Overall, it took nearly a decade to complete the transition.

When it comes to upgrades and conversions, the statement by an Apple executive still holds: People who don't upgrade their hardware usually don't upgrade their software.

Programming for Mac OS X involves object-oriented programming as well as key environments, languages, frameworks, and tools. They are introduced in the remainder of this section.

Object-Oriented Programming

Object-oriented programming was developed as an attempt to deal with the fact that traditional programming architecture did not scale well. After completing a program of 50,000 lines of code, a programming staff was often requested to add another feature or two—and soon the code base was up to 500,000 lines of code. A year or so later, several million lines of code could exist. Design, testing, and maintenance soared astronomically because as the lines of code increased arithmetically, the possible sequences in which they could be executed rose exponentially.

Smalltalk is considered the original object-oriented programming language. It was developed in the early 1970s at the Xerox Palo Alto Research Center Learning Group as an attempt to make it easy for ordinary people to use computers. (The Palo Alto Research Center—PARC—also developed the notion of the graphical user interface.) Together with later dynamic languages such as Lisp and Dylan, it had an influence on programming that is out of proportion to its use in commercial products.

Objects

Object-oriented programming uses as its model objects that can send and receive messages. These small and reusable objects can be combined to make applications that work. Objects often have parallels in real life and in the work that application programs do; however, they do not always do so.

For example, you can define an object that corresponds to a building. Such an object might have an address, certain types of dimensions, and so forth. You can also define functionality for an object. A building object might be able to heat or cool itself, to open or close its windows, and to report the amount of fuel in its fuel tank.

Objects contain *methods*. Methods carry out the tasks that an object does. In general, the processes by which these tasks are performed are private to the object. As a programmer, you can ask an object to draw itself, write itself, or present some of its data. How that is done is not your concern—just as exactly how pushing on the accelerator causes a car to move is not a concern to most people (unless it does not move).

Objects are said to have been *instantiated* when they are created while a program runs. You can refer to instantiated objects as *instances* if you want to.

Classes

The abstract definition of an object is a *class*; you instantiate the class to make an object at runtime. You can also say that you instantiate the class to make an instance.

Since the word "object" is sometimes used as a synonym for class and sometimes as a synonym for a runtime instance, there is the potential for confusion. Fortunately, the context usually makes the meaning clear.

Inheritance

One of the essential features of objects is inheritance: they can descend from one another. A descendant object inherits data elements and functionality from its ancestor, just as in life.

Polymorphism

Polymorphism refers to the ability of descendants of a common ancestor to respond differently to the same request. For example, you might create a room object that inherits from the building object described previously. By default, it would have an address—this time, a room number, not a street number—its own dimensions, and other characteristics. When asked for its dimensions, the building, as well as its room descendant, would do the same thing: multiply length by width by height.

However, when asked to heat or cool itself, a room would not do anything at all. It would ask its ancestor, the building, to do the job. In a reverse case, rooms might be able to open their own windows, but the building would only be able to ask each of its rooms to open its windows.

How you define objects and what matters about them greatly influences the design of inheritance. For example, a room and a building may be very different concepts in the problem you are dealing with. In other situations, they are quite similar: they have boundaries and doorways, they contain furniture, and people can live in them. To a city apartment dweller, an apartment—even a single room—is a "house." The key to successful object-oriented design is determining what the underlying class (or concept) is. For a municipal accounting system, the base class might be "taxable real estate." Its descendants could be buildings, condos, vacant land, and easements. Each such descendant could respond to the request "display your tax assessment."

Data Hiding

Objects can contain data. Although it is possible to evade these standards, most object-oriented programming today hides object data. In other words, although in some cases you could access the temperature of a room object directly, you normally call a room object's "GetTemperature" method to return the data value. This allows polymorphic methods to compute the data differently. Such methods are called *accessors*.

No **If** Statements

A variety of consequences of the use of object-oriented programming ensue. One of the most interesting is that the use of objects tends to make an application program consist of a large number of objects, each with its own short methods. Just as the complexity of programs increases astronomically as the lines of code increase arithmetically, the reverse also applies. As methods get shorter and shorter, they become more straightforward. Typically, they are either executed from start to finish or they are not executed at all. Eliminating If statements in object-oriented programming is comparable to eliminating GoTo statements in structured programming.

The Environments

Three environments are provided on Mac OS X for programs to run in: Cocoa, Classic, and Carbon. (Carbon and Cocoa actually run in the same environment, but in different ways.)

Cocoa

Cocoa is the environment users think of when they think of Mac OS X. It has the distinctive Aqua interface, and it includes technologies such as services, as well as the standard menu layout. Programs written for Cocoa can provide the full range of functionality users expect from Mac OS X.

In early development at Apple, a box diagram illustrated the various components of the operating system. What is now Cocoa was called the Yellow Box because of its distinctive coloring in that diagram. The phrase is sometimes still heard and found in documentation. Cocoa is derived from NeXTSTEP, which is an older name for OpenStep.

Classic

The Classic environment is Mac OS 9. Programs written for operating systems that predate Mac OS X run in that environment. What actually happens is that the entire Mac OS 9 operating system (with very minor modifications) runs as a Mac OS X application. That application can run programs just as the Mac OS 9 operating system does.

Classic environment is sometimes referred to as the Blue Box, since that was its color on the famous diagram. It is also sometimes referred to as a boxless Blue Box. The original design of the emulation made it abundantly clear to the user that two operating systems were running on the same computer; the "box" was quite visible to users.

TIP

Classic environment runs Mac OS 9. If you have an application that runs under a previous version of the operating system and that will not run under Mac OS 9, it will not run in the Classic environment and, therefore, will not run on Mac OS X.

Carbon

Carbon is a transitional environment; however, as noted with the PowerPC transition, that period of time is likely to be very long. A programmer can modify a Mac OS 9 and earlier application to Carbon standards. When that is done, the application runs on Mac OS X directly. As a result, Carbon applications run a bit faster than Classic applications. They also are somewhat more stable since they can take advantage of some of Cocoa's underpinnings.

Carbon applications have most of the Aqua look and feel, but they do not have all of it. Carbon applications also have Mac OS 9 and earlier Save dialogs rather than the window-based Save dialogs that roll down from the title bar.

The Languages

Nothing gets programmers more hot and bothered than "religious wars" about programming languages. On mainframes, the original programming languages were Fortran (for engineering and scientific purposes) and Cobol (for business purposes). On personal computers, the original programming language was Basic—neither Fortran nor Cobol would fit on a personal computer in 1980.

Today, a variety of languages are available. On the Macintosh, Pascal, Java, and several C variants predominate.

Pascal

Pascal was developed by Niklaus Wirth in 1971. Its primary goal was as a teaching language, and it succeeded very well in that regard. By the 1980s, people who hired Cobol programmers looked for Pascal experience. Cobol programmers with a Pascal background were better Cobol programmers.

Pascal is small and highly structured. It was implemented on personal computers very early. Compared to Basic—the other commonly used language—Pascal was much easier to use and modify since it was a well-designed language. Basic, however, was much easier to learn to use quickly, since you didn't have to adhere to strict rules of type and syntax.

When the Macintosh was developed, Pascal was adopted as its primary programming language. The examples in the early Macintosh documentation are in Pascal. The intrinsic functions (the Macintosh Toolbox) are defined in Pascal. While many of them were implemented in assembly language for speed, over time, many of them were converted to Pascal.

Older Macintosh programs are still around that use Pascal. If you are converting or modifying an old program, you may need to be able to read (if not compile) Pascal.

C

C's origins are on Unix, specifically on a DEC PDP-11. It followed on the heels of the language B, written in 1970 on a PDP-7 for the first Unix system. The first version of C was written by Dennis M. Ritchie. C was used to write Unix, the C compiler, and many Unix applications.

Compared to Pascal, C is a much less structured language. In the early 1980s, C was abhorrent to many programmers and managers because it seemed to be involved with many incidents of undecipherable spaghetti code.

However, like Wagner's Ring Cycle, which while of dubious merit itself inspired such works of genius as Anna Russell's famed monologue, C spawned two very important languages: Objective-C and C++. (Whether Objective-C and C++ are languages or dialects is a subject for debate; it is not relevant to this discussion, however.)

You can program in C on Mac OS X and compile those programs with the GNU C compiler. Those programs will run without the benefit of a user interface; you execute them from Terminal.app.

C++

C++ is perhaps the most widely used variant of C today. It is object oriented, and it tightens up all of the C features that some people find too loose.

C++ is highly typed, and that typing occurs at compile time. This means that when you write code that uses an object, you must specify when you write the code what type of object that will be. If you do not specify the right type of object, your program will not compile. This makes the compilation process very strict, and it makes the runtime process very efficient.

Today, C++ programs often create a plethora of tiny objects. These are often stack-based objects—objects that are created right on the program's stack rather than in memory somewhere. There is little overhead to creating such stack-based objects, and they can be very useful. They can, for example, override operators such as + so as to make it easy to combine strings and complex data structures.

One of the consequences of compile-time typing is the fragile base class problem. This problem occurs when you refer to an object's method in your code. The compiler must be able to verify that the method exists. If the object to which you refer is modified (or if one of its ancestors is modified), your code will break. In large collaborative projects, the fragile base class problem is severe. Several ways of getting around it exist, but each has its disadvantages.

C++ supports multiple inheritance—that is, an object can inherit from more than one ancestor. For example, a room object might inherit from a building object, as well as from a shape object and a shelter object. The building object might define things such as address. The shape object, which might have as descendants objects such as desks and cars, might define three-dimensional shapes. The shelter object might define anything that can protect you from the weather: a tree, an awning, or a room.

In this scenario, some of these classes might be abstract superclasses. A shape might never be instantiated; only its descendants such as cars, rooms, and desks would be instantiated.

Most object-oriented programs on Mac OS 9 and earlier are written in C++.

Objective-C

Objective-C represents a different approach to adding objects to C. Rather than relying totally on compile-time checking, it dynamically creates objects at runtime, performing the error-checking at that time. It avoids most of the fragile base class problem.

Programming for Mac OS X

Although Objective-C does not support multiple inheritance directly, a language construct called *protocols* can simulate it.

Because the design of Objective-C doesn't lend itself to the small C++ objects that are around today, Objective-C classes tend to be larger than C++ classes. However, since Objective-C can communicate with objects without having known their class information at compile time, it is very convenient to use with dynamic authoring systems, such as the combination of Project Builder and Interface Builder.

Objective-C looks different from programming languages such as C, C++, and Java, but it is not at all hard to grasp. The background of Objective-C includes some of the terminology from Smalltalk. As a result, instead of talking about invoking methods of an object or calling functions of a class, Objective-C talks of sending messages to receivers. A message expression consists of a receiver and a message, all enclosed in square brackets. Thus, you can write

```
[myImage reDraw];
```

to send the reDraw message to the myImage object (or to call the myImage's reDraw method, to use other terminology).

Sometimes, messages take parameters, as in the following:

```
[userInputs objectAtIndex:i]
```

Arguments to a message are preceded by a colon (:) and they may be preceded by their names. Here, the variable i is the argument of the objectAtIndex message that is sent to the userInputs object.

Message expressions can return a value. As a result, messages can be part of Objective-C expressions, as in the following:

```
unsigned i = [userInputs count];
```

Message expressions can also be part of other message expressions (that is, their result can be passed as a message to another receiver), as in the following:

```
[[userInputs  objectAtIndex:i] reDraw];
```

Here, the i-th object in the userInputs array is the receiver of the reDraw message. (The userInputs array's objectAIndex message is called with the value i—and that returns the i-th object. The reDraw message is then sent to that object.)

The benefits of dynamic languages are increasingly being recognized. Java, perhaps the most widely discussed language of recent years, is one such.

Java

Java was designed as a platform-neutral language. It is object oriented throughout, and it supports many of the dynamic aspects demonstrated in Objective-C.

Java can be used on Mac OS X as a programming language for the Cocoa framework. Here is the equivalent Java syntax of the code from the previous section. You call myImage's reDraw method as follows:

```
myImage.reDraw();
```

Sometimes, Java method calls take parameters, as in the following:

```
userInputs.objectAtIndex(i);
```

Message expressions can return a value. As a result, messages can be part of Java expressions, as in the following:

```
int i = userInputs.count();
```

Message expressions can also be part of other message expressions (that is, their result can be passed as a message to another receiver), as in the following:

```
userInputs.objectAtIndex(i).reDraw;
```

The Frameworks

Frameworks are object-oriented libraries that are designed to be extended by programmers for specific applications. The framework implements basic functionality—mouse movement, window controls, and so forth—and the application programmer implements descendants of the framework classes that provide unique features.

Cocoa

Cocoa is based on OpenStep (and NeXTSTEP before that). It is the set of frameworks you use to develop Mac OS X applications. Applications developed with Cocoa run on Mac OS X, and not on Mac OS 9 and earlier.

MacApp

MacApp is Apple's primary object-oriented framework. Developed over more than a decade, it has served as the basis for commercial projects (such as the first version of Photoshop), for many custom applications, and for a host of other purposes. MacApp applications can be run either under the Classic environment or as Carbon applications (depending on how they are written). This means you can use MacApp to develop for Mac OS X and Mac OS 9 and earlier.

MacApp is discussed in detail in Chapter 23, "Classic."

PowerPlant

PowerPlant is a cross-platform application framework that is developed by Metrowerks, the developers of CodeWarrior. It is appropriate for use in a cross-platform environment. On Mac OS X, it produces Classic or Carbon code.

The Tools

You need compilers and other tools to develop software. Here are some of the key components of Macintosh software development.

GNU Compiler

On Mac OS X, the GNU C compiler incorporates C, C++, and Objective-C. It is part of the Mac OS X package. You use it to compile code to run under Mac OS X (not under Mac OS 9 and earlier).

NOTE   *The GNU project dates from 1984. Now promoted by the Free Software Foundation, its initial goal was to provide a free Unix-like operating system, together with associated utilities, such as compilers. At the time, Unix was a proprietary product of AT&T. The Free Software Foundation makes a distinction between free software and the open source movement; however, the two are quite closely intertwined. GNU stands for Gnu's Not Unix.*

CodeWarrior

CodeWarrior is an integrated development environment (IDE) that supports development on Mac OS 9 and earlier, Windows, handheld devices, and other platforms. It is widely used, very powerful, and very stable. It can be obtained from Metrowerks (http://www.metrowerks.com).

MPW

The Macintosh Programmer's Workshop (MPW) is the original development tool for Macintosh programmers. An Apple product, its text-oriented command-line interface makes some programmers feel more at home than CodeWarrior's IDE.

Although MPW is not widely used today, if you are modifying old programs, you may discover ancient Make files in MPW format.

Project Builder and Interface Builder

Project Builder and Interface Builder are Mac OS X tools with graphical user interfaces that let you develop and modify applications.

Summary

This chapter has provided an overview of the Classic, Carbon, and Cocoa technologies. Together, they enable you to write for Mac OS 9 and earlier, Mac OS X, or both.

Much programming work involves rewriting and modifying existing code. The chapter started with a guide to reading code, as well as a checklist to help you determine whether you should be looking at Classic, Carbon, or Cocoa for your work.

An overview of Mac OS 9 and earlier programming introduces the technology you need to know to read older programs. Much of the development work on Mac OS 9 and earlier has been done with the MacApp application framework. You have seen an overview of that framework's architecture and an introduction to its concepts.

The Classic environment lets programs run on Mac OS X without changes. The features and limitations of that environment have been found in this chapter. See Chapter 23 for more information.

Carbon—the transitional tool that lets programs run under Mac OS 9 and earlier, as well as Mac OS X—has many important features, not least of which are the Core Foundation objects. See Chapter 24 for more information on Carbon.

Finally, the Cocoa framework's basic concepts have been presented. Cocoa is presented in more detail in the next chapter, along with information about using Project Builder and Interface Builder. See Chapter 25 for more information on Cocoa.

Summary

Chapter 23

Classic

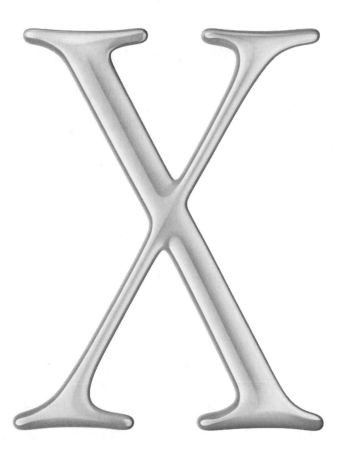

T his chapter examines the Classic Compatibility Environment, which developers have used since 1984, to program some of the most innovative software that exists today.

The sections of this chapter provide

- An overview of Classic Mac OS Macintosh programming.

- An introduction to CodeWarrior, a very important third-party tool from Metrowerks that is essential to much of the Mac OS 9 and earlier development. (Native Mac OS X tools include Project Builder and Interface Builder; they are discussed in Chapter 26, "Creating a Nothing Program with Cocoa.")

- An introduction to MacApp, Apple's C++ framework for application development, which is used for many legacy applications, as well as for new applications that need to run both on Mac OS 9 or earlier, and on Mac OS X using Classic Mac OS or Carbon.

- Finally, you will find programming information about the Classic Mac OS Environment.

Introduction to Classic Macintosh Programming

One of the reasons for the rise of application frameworks (such as Cocoa and MacApp) is that they can handle the nitty-gritty of interacting with the operating system and with users so that application programmers don't have to worry about those issues and start fom scratch each time.

That is all well and good, but not all programming consists of starting from scratch. Unfortunately, you may find yourself reading, modifying, and converting ancient programs in which you do need to be aware of what goes on in the background. This section provides a brief guide to the fundamental concepts behind every Classic Macintosh program.

These are the topics that are described in this section:

- The Toolbox and the managers
- Events and the event loop
- Traps
- The stack
- Memory management
- QuickDraw

- Resources
- Program formats
- Windows and dialogs
- Menus
- Interfaces
- Gestalt

The Toolbox and the Managers

The Macintosh provided programmers with a wide variety of routines to manage the interface. Together with printed guidelines, these routines helped developers give users the powerful and intuitive interface that made the Macintosh a success. These routines were referred to as the

Macintosh Toolbox. They were divided into managers—the Window manager, the Printing manager, and so forth.

The basic documentation for the toolbox was provided in a series of books called *Inside Macintosh*—often abbreviated IM. Over time, the Inside Macintosh/IM terminology fell into disuse, along with toolbox and manager. You may, however, encounter these terms in program documentation and in comments within source code.

Events and the Event Loop

Traditional programs started and stopped without user intervention. A calculation was done, or an input file was processed, and that was the end.

User-driven software has a different structure. After some initialization, the program goes into a neutral state, called an *event loop*. It does nothing except interrogate the operating system for an event that is directed to it. Events include mouse, keyboard, and window activation events.

The GetNextEvent routine retrieves events that are relevant to an application. When the GetNextEvent routine is called, the operating system checks to see which events the application wants (as well as which events should be directed to it). It also performs other operating system functions at this time, such as checking for mouse clicks in other applications' windows.

> **CAUTION** *If you do not call GetNextEvent frequently, you have seized control of the computer's event loop. You may experience this when you sort a file or click on a menu item that causes a lengthy process to begin. You cannot activate another application or get back to the Finder's menus in such a case. You just have to wait until the processing stops and GetNextEvent is called again. This behavior cannot happen in Mac OS X applications (those running in Cocoa or Carbon environments).*

Event loops should contain no extraneous code; they must operate as swiftly as they can so as not to tie up the computer. The user should be able to get a response from the computer at all times, and this means calling GetNextEvent as frequently as possible. In addition to keeping the event loop as tight as you can, resist the temptation to create additional event loops, such as within lengthy processes. There should be only one place in a program where GetNextEvent is called.

This architecture is the basis of cooperative multitasking: a program must allow itself to be interrupted for the operating system to perform other tasks. Mac OS X implements preemptive multitasking. You cannot seize control of an event loop and thereby lock out other users. However, if your application runs on Mac OS 9 or earlier or in the Classic Environment, you can seize control of the event loop and lock up the machine (on Mac OS 9 or earlier) or the Classic Environment. In the latter case, you prevent other Classic applications from being serviced, although the entire Classic Environment can be preemptively multitasked so that other applications under Mac OS X receive processor time.

Traps

Traps were a terrific approach to the problem of extending the processor's capabilities and customizing its operations. In a simplified overview, here is what happened. The 680x0 processor had a number of operations—many of them hardware related—that could be accessed directly from programs. These were called *traps*. In this way, it was no different from other processors.

When a program needed to call a trap, the system called a trap handler to get the address of the trap's instructions. Control was then passed to that address. Most toolbox routines were implemented as traps.

Programmers could patch the trap table; this meant that when a program called the trap that managed a certain function—perhaps some window behavior—the patched trap table would return a different address. This meant that all programs calling that trap would exhibit the different behavior (until the trap table was repatched). This was terrific in 1984, but it started causing trouble very quickly. Patched traps meant that application programmers couldn't really rely on what traps did. Sometimes a patched trap exhibited slightly different behavior from the original trap and programs misbehaved.

Furthermore, this architecture was highly tied to the Motorola 680x0 chip. In the transition to the PowerPC architecture, programmers were asked repeatedly to stop patching traps because there were problems in doing so on the PowerPC architecture. Many did.

However, there still are programs that patch traps. In each case, there's a perfectly valid reason for doing so, at least in the programmer's eyes, and in each case, those trap patches will fail on Mac OS X. If you are modifying a program that patches traps, you must implement the functionality differently if it ever is to run on Mac OS X.

The Stack

The 1984 Macintosh was a stack-based machine. This means the data for a subroutine was placed in a *stack*—a series of memory locations—that could be accessed quickly. Since Pascal supported the concept of scope for variables, it was easy to determine which variables were declared within a subroutine. On exit from the subroutine, the stack was *cut back*—that is, all the space for those variables was returned to the system.

Memory

Any stack-based computer has a fundamental problem: how to place very large memory structures on the stack. If a subroutine declares an array that is 5,000 elements long, placing 5,000 elements on the stack can be an expensive operation (the expense comes from the shifting around of memory); and if a 5,000-element array is troublesome, imagine the difficulty in moving a QuickTime movie around.

On mainframes, the solution was frequently to place such large memory structures off in the computer's memory and place an indirect reference word on the stack. Thus, the stack would contain a single address for the movie or the large array. When the operating system retrieved the value from the stack, it notes that it was a reference to a large block of disk data, and it handles the data as if it were on the stack.

This implementation was not feasible on the original personal computers. Consequently, an alternative way of managing large data objects was devised: programmers were allowed to manipulate memory directly. (On mainframes, particularly timesharing mainframes, this was absolutely forbidden because of the instability it engendered.)

The Stack and the Heap

On the Macintosh, each program was assigned a section of memory for its use. At one end of this chunk of memory, the stack grew and then retreated as it was cut back. At the other end, a *heap* (unstructured memory subject to the programmer's control) grew and retreated. Managing the stack was the responsibility of the operating system and the compiler. Managing the heap was the programmer's responsibility. If the combined usage of the stack and the heap exceeded the amount of memory allocated, the error message Stack Hit Heap was generated, and the program crashed.

Pointers

These chunks of memory that programmers could control were manipulated using *pointers*. Pointers serve exactly the same function as indirect reference words on mainframes. Instead of being manipulated by the operating system, however, they are manipulated by programmers.

That's where the problems set in. Programmers must allocate and deallocate memory space. There is no automatic deallocation when the stack is cut back. A pointer is a local variable—that is, a variable that can be placed on the stack. The pointer disappears when the stack is cut back, but the memory to which it points is still marked as in use unless the programmer explicitly deallocates it.

Many Macintosh programs, particularly in the early days, were plagued with *memory leaks*. These were chunks of memory that were allocated and never deallocated. In the most serious—and mysterious—of these, memory would be allocated during idle time as the result of some processing in the main event loop. As a result, a program that was left unattended with no input or output could eventually crash the computer.

Handles

The original Mac OS (before PowerPC) supported *handles*—pointers to pointers. Handles provide a level of indirection that makes memory management easier. If the fundamental memory structure needs to be moved, it can appear to be moved by changing the value of the indirect pointer. You may find handles in old, pre-PowerPC code. They should be removed.

Pointers point directly to memory chunks. Consequently, the memory is not relocatable. Handles point to relocatable memory structures; the operating system can—and does—move the memory structures and fix up the intermediate pointer. One common problem in old Macintosh programs occurred when application programs stored the value of the memory location—the intermediate pointer—and then used it to refer to memory after memory had been moved.

QuickDraw

The graphics environment on Mac OS 9 or earlier is built around QuickDraw, a series of toolbox calls that manipulates graphical objects quickly and efficiently. Programs use QuickDraw routines to do most of the graphics work.

NOTE   *High-end graphics programs often reimplement QuickDraw routines for their own purposes.*

QuickDraw is built around the concept of *ports*, complete graphic environments with their own settings for colors, transfer patterns, and so forth. An application program can create a port and draw into it; it can then quickly move the port into a window. These ports are called *grafports*.

Some programs manipulate memory directly. A screen buffer that contains the screen image is located in memory, and if you know where it is and how it is organized, you can change its contents and thus the screen display. This means that one application can manipulate windows belonging to another application. You cannot do this on Mac OS X, but there are programs out there that still do it on Mac OS 9 or earlier.

Manipulating the screen buffer was normally done for two reasons. High-performance applications—such as games—sometimes could not perform fast enough on slow computers to go through the regular QuickDraw calls. More recently, the implementations of drag-and-drop in the late 1980s sometimes involved kludges. Drag-and-drop is now implemented directly and less dangerously; however, old code is still out there.

Resources

Macintosh files have two sections, called forks. The *data fork* contains the data in whatever format the program wishes to store it. (In the case of executable programs, the data format is determined by the program that runs the program—the operating system.)

The *resource fork* contains structured data called resources. Each resource is identified by a type and by an ID number. Resources can consist of text strings, graphics, and icons. Application programs can create their own types of resources that they alone read.

This is a very elegant structure, and it permits easy customization of applications because the logic is in the code and the variable information—strings that might change by language—is in the resource fork. Resource forks are created by special software; they are not compiled as languages are.

A problem rises with regard to this use of resources. It comes about due to a use of resources that was not dangerous at the beginning but is so now. Some application programs modify their resource forks while they are running. Games, for example, may contain resources identifying high scores. This means that the program file's resource fork is continually updated. Good programming practice today eschews self-modifying code; the code of a program should not be modified while it is running. This use of resource forks breaks that rule.

Program Formats

In old (pre-PowerPC) applications, you will see resources used in yet another way. Code segments are stored in their resource fork, and they are loaded by the operating system as needed. On PowerPC, the native code is located in the data fork of a file. For these pre-PowerPC applications, it was quite a science to distribute procedures and subroutines to the appropriate code segments so that routines used together would be loaded and kept in memory together. You may find segmentation directives in code that you are modifying. Those directives do not matter on PowerPC or on Mac OS X.

On PowerPC computers running Mac OS 9 or earlier, the executable code is stored in *code fragments*. The Code Fragment Manager loads the code as necessary and takes any needed initialization actions. The code fragments are stored in the data fork of program files; they also may be in libraries—that is, in other files.

Windows and Dialogs

The heart of any graphical user interface is its windows and dialogs. In one way or another, every application uses some reusable code to implement its windows and dialogs. There just are not that many ways to write the code to respond to a mouse click in a Close box.

Menus

Along with windows and dialogs, menus and their commands define the interface. On Mac OS 9 or earlier, menus are identified by number, and each command within a menu is identified with its own number. Together, the two numbers uniquely identify a menu command.

Unfortunately, this structure means that the menu identification changes when menu commands are moved from one menu to another. It also poses problems when a menu is of variable length. MacApp handles these problems by assigning unique ID numbers to menu commands, no matter where they appear.

Interfaces

Interface files contain the definitions of all of the toolbox routines. You will find the interfaces inside the Universal folder in the CodeWarrior environment; that folder is located inside the MacOS Support folder (CodeWarrior is discussed later in this chapter.)

 The locations and names of these folders are subject to change. Use Sherlock to find the file adsp.h (one of the header files). This should help you locate the enclosing folder. As shipped, CodeWarrior normally has the files set up correctly. You may need to identify the locations of the files if you are modifying an old program that has old file paths installed.

There is a complete set of interfaces for assembly language, one for Pascal, and one for C. Additional interfaces for resources and for QuickTime components are also located in the Interfaces folder. Together with the contents of the Libraries folder (the executable code for these routines), these files let you include the toolbox routines in your programs.

Use the interfaces in the Universal folder for development of Classic Mac OS applications. For Carbon, you use the Universal Interfaces located inside the CarbonSupport folder. You will note that the only interfaces are RIncludes and CIncludes; Pascal and assembler are not supported.

Gestalt

Interfaces change over time, and features are added to the operating system. In addition, different computers support different hardware and software features. To manage all of this, the Gestalt Manager helps you interrogate the runtime environment to know what it looks like.

Calls to the Gestalt Manager return a specified word for the type of information you want—hardware, operating system version, and so on. Bits within each word are defined for specific aspects of the operating system. You typically use the Gestalt Manager with a code snippet such as the following:

```
long response;
if (Gestalt(gestaltContextualMenuAttr, &response) ==
  noErr &&
  (response >> gestaltContextualMenuTrapAvailable) & 1)
    {
    … do something
    }
```

This checks to see whether contextual menus are available. The bit, `gestaltContextualMenuTrapAvailable`, is checked inside the Gestalt selector `gestaltContextualMenuAttr`, which is temporarily stored in the long response.

Of course, instead of writing this code each time, if you use MacApp you can call `MAGestaltAttribute` (from which the code shown above was adapted):

```
hasContextMenus = MAGestaltAttribute

(gestaltContextualMenuAttr, gestaltContextualMenuTrapAvailable);
```

Using CodeWarrior

CodeWarrior is an integrated development environment (IDE) that includes an editor, compilers, linkers, debuggers, and a variety of helpful tools. It is available from Metrowerks (http://www. metrowerks.com) in a variety of editions aimed all the way from students to professional developers.

CodeWarrior comes with extensive documentation and tutorials. This section provides a brief overview of some of the features that are useful in developing applications. You can use it to build MacApp applications, and you can also use it to build C, C++, and Java applications. It can generate code for the original 68K Macintosh computers, for PowerPC computers running Mac OS 9 or earlier (or for the Mac OS X Classic Environment), and it can generate code for Intel processors. On Macintosh, it can generate code using both the CFM format (for Mac OS 9 or earlier) and using Mach-O (for Mac OS X).

Installing CodeWarrior

CodeWarrior is a mature development environment. Like the Project Builder/Interface Builder pair of applications in Mac OS X, many professional developers swear by it. Installing CodeWarrior is usually as simple as popping a CD-ROM into your computer's drive and following the directions. Here are a few additional tips.

Immediately after your installation, attempt to build a known program. If you are using MacApp, immediately build the Nothing sample. If this does not work right out of the box, fix it. It is unlikely (in fact, almost impossible) that future compilations and fiddlings will make things better.

New Installations

You can download MacApp from Apple's Web site (see the section on MacApp that follows). To make your installation as smooth as possible, install CodeWarrior and then download the MacApp installer and install it.

> **TIP**
>
> *Keep the compressed installer on disk (or on a removable cartridge) until you have completed your installation. That way you can reinstall without redownloading the files in case something goes wrong.*

With CodeWarrior and MacApp installed, open the Nothing project and try to build it. Figure 23-1 shows the location of the Nothing project. In CodeWarrior, you use projects to organize your files. The MacApp Nothing sample is encased in the CodeWarrior Nothing project.

The MacApp installation will create a folder called Apple C++ Frameworks; within it, you will see folders providing support for CodeWarrior, in this case for versions 5 and 6. Within that folder, you will find a MacApp folder, then an Examples folder, and then the Nothing folder. Within that folder are one or more projects to compile Nothing. In this case, both Carbon and traditional versions exist.

> **TIP**
>
> *Be careful to follow this route. A MacApp folder is located within the Apple C++ Frameworks folder, but it does not contain the CodeWarrior files. Make certain you open the CWP6 Support (or whatever version you need), rather than the MacApp folder at the top level of the Apple C++ Frameworks folder.*

Updating Installations

If you have an existing Apple C++ Frameworks folder, you can continue to use it with a new version of CodeWarrior. However, follow exactly the same procedure: after you have installed CodeWarrior, make certain that you can recompile Nothing. (For this reason, do not remove Nothing from your disk after installation.)

If this fails, the simplest way to troubleshoot the problem is to download the newest MacApp and create a new Apple C++ Frameworks folder. You should always be able to compile the latest MacApp with the latest CodeWarrior. If you cannot, a notice will be displayed on the MacApp site. Sometimes, there are brief periods in which the latest version of one requires the other to be updated. However, in these cases, which are rare, the previous version of MacApp will work and is available for download. Remember that many, many MacApp users are using CodeWarrior. The combination works.

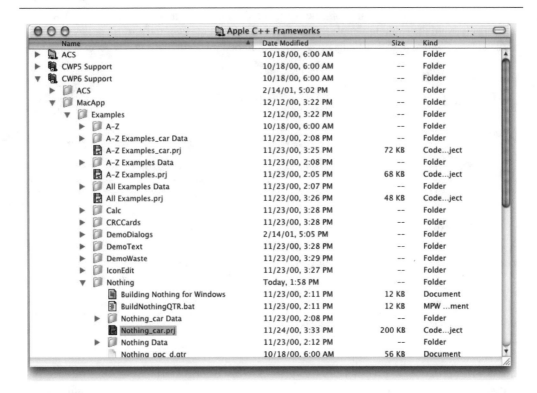

FIGURE 23-1   Nothing project location

If you cannot build Nothing with newly downloaded files, repeat the installation process carefully. If you can't build Nothing, you need to find out systematically what the difference is between your current set of MacApp files and the newly downloaded set.

Projects and Targets

CodeWarrior organizes files into *projects*. Each project contains one or more targets, which can be an application, a library, or a code resource. Each target has a name. Frequently you create a project that contains two targets, a debug and a nondebug version. The MacApp samples contain even more.

The basic IDE window is shown next. Three tabs let you switch among listings of files, their link order, and the targets. In this case, the Nothing project's Carbon targets are shown. Disclosure triangles let you look at the files within projects, and projects within projects. In this case, Nothing Carbon Debug contains two projects: the Apple Class Suites project and MacApp itself.

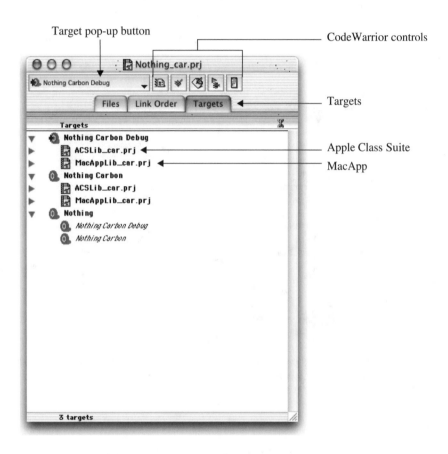

The next illustration shows the files for Nothing. You add files to the project window by dragging them or by using the Add Files command from the Project menu. Files from a variety of different locations on disk can be combined into groups. This helps you create a logical program structure that may differ from the actual layout of files on disk. (Remember, though, that all of a project's files must be accessible. It is a good idea to locate all of them in a single folder.)

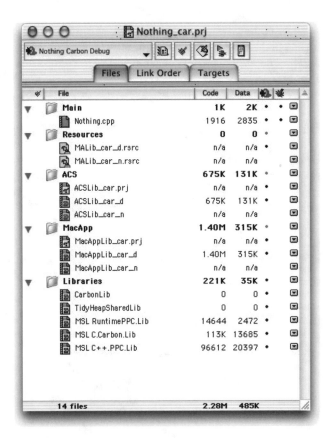

File	Code	Data			
Main	**1K**	**2K**	•	•	⊡
Nothing.cpp	1916	2835	•	•	⊡
Resources	**0**	**0**	•		⊡
MALib_car_d.rsrc	n/a	n/a	•		⊡
MALib_car_n.rsrc	n/a	n/a	•		⊡
ACS	**675K**	**131K**	•		⊡
ACSLib_car.prj	n/a	n/a	•		⊡
ACSLib_car_d	675K	131K	•		⊡
ACSLib_car_n	n/a	n/a	•		⊡
MacApp	**1.40M**	**315K**	•		⊡
MacAppLib_car.prj	n/a	n/a	•		⊡
MacAppLib_car_d	1.40M	315K	•		⊡
MacAppLib_car_n	n/a	n/a	•		⊡
Libraries	**221K**	**35K**	•		⊡
CarbonLib	0	0	•		⊡
TidyHeapSharedLib	0	0	•		⊡
MSL RuntimePPC.Lib	14644	2472	•		⊡
MSL C.Carbon.Lib	113K	13685	•		⊡
MSL C++.PPC.Lib	96612	20397	•		⊡

14 files   2.28M   485K

> **TIP** *MacApp uses CodeWarrior's project structure environment very well. Look at the examples in the project window and on disk to see one way to manage a very large development project.*

IDE Controls

You can use the tabs at the top of the window to view the files by link order and to create or modify targets. A pop-up button lets you select quickly from among the targets in the project. At the right of the top section of the IDE window, five buttons let you control CodeWarrior.

Settings

The Settings button opens a window that lets you specify every detail for the project and its components. Settings are described in the next section.

Synchronize Modification Dates

The Synchronize Dates button updates the project's tables indicating what needs to be recompiled. This is useful if you are using files edited in other applications with CodeWarrior.

Make

The Make button makes the project, compiling and linking everything that needs to be compiled and linked. When you make a project, you can follow its progress in the window that is shown here:

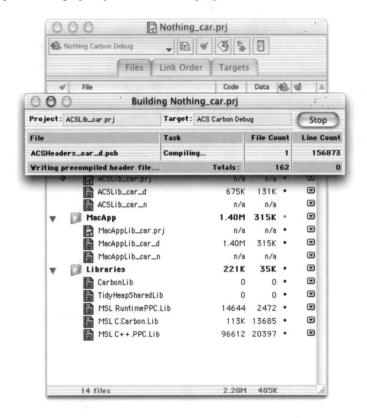

Run

Use the Run button to make the project (if necessary) and then to run it. You can use the CodeWarrior debugging environment to monitor the program as it runs and to move between a display of the program's source code and the executing program itself.

Using CodeWarrior

Project Inspector

Finally, the Project Inspector button lets you view information about the project or about the file(s) selected in the project window.

CodeWarrior Settings

The Settings button opens the window shown next. As you can see from the list of panes on the left, there are many settings ranging from the use of debuggers to which compilers to use.

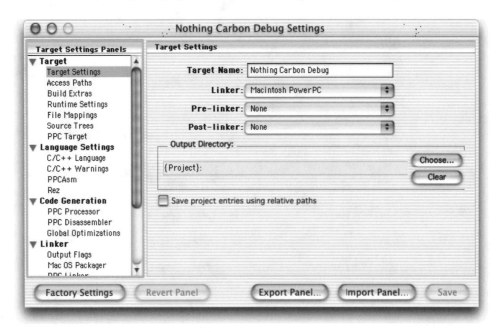

TIP *When you first get CodeWarrior, compile one of the examples without modifying any settings. Make certain that you have successfully installed the product before experimenting with settings.*

Working with Object-Oriented Programs

CodeWarrior has a host of tools to support object-oriented programming. If you activate the browser, you can maneuver through the source code in an object-oriented way. In order to activate the browser, you need to use the Settings button to open the window shown next. In the Build Extras pane, you will see the option to activate the browser.

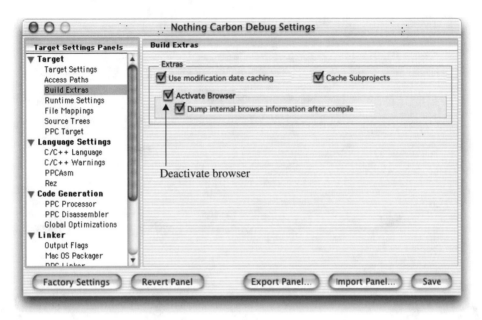

Deactivate browser

On slower processors or on projects where the source code is on a slow network, you can save time by leaving the browser deactivated. You activate it in these cases when you need it. Maintaining the browser can be expensive in these environments. If CodeWarrior seems sluggish, check to see if the browser is activated: if so, deactivate it and see if performance improves. If the browser is activated, you can view a class hierarchy, as shown in Figure 23-2.

The arrow at the right of each class's name lets you expand or contract its subclasses to make the size of the display more manageable. In the case of multiple inheritance, a small arrow to the left of the class name appears. Clicking this lets you select which hierarchy you want to display in the window; thus, you can view the class in the context of any of its base classes. This is shown in Figure 23-3.

A class browser is shown next. There are separate displays for classes, functions, data members, and the source. You can create new classes, functions, and data members from this window. You can also expand the functions, data members, and source panes to their own windows. `TApplication::ChooseApplication` is a virtual function.

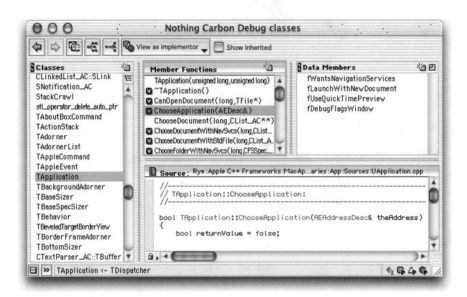

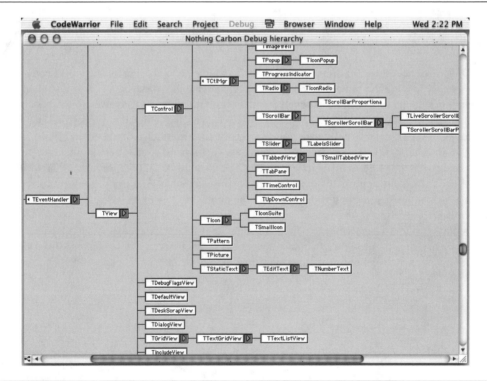

FIGURE 23-2   Class hierarchy

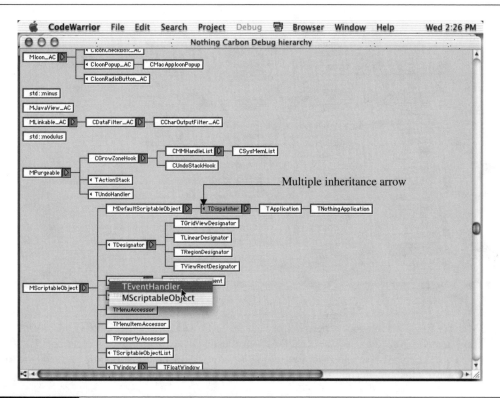

FIGURE 23-3   Class Hierarchy with multiple inheritance

TIP

Many programmers work totally in the Browser window.

The browser can display a class on its own or with its inherited functions and members. The checkbox at the top of the window controls this. Compare the previous illustration with the one the following, which shows inherited classes.

Inherited classes shown

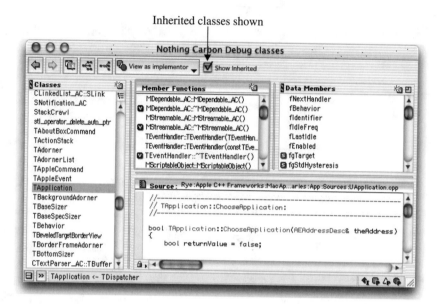

Member functions may be marked V (for virtual), S (for static), or P (for pure virtual). Virtual functions may be overridden; pure virtual functions must be overridden. `TApplication::ChooseApplication` in an earlier illustration is a virtual function. The pop-up button at the top of the browser window lets you further refine what you see in the window, as shown here:

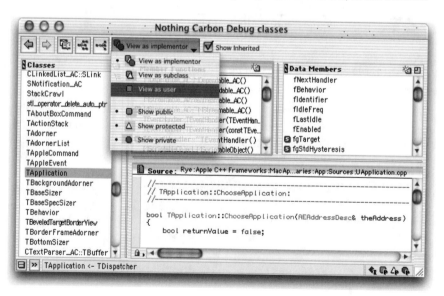

MacApp

MacApp is Apple's first object-oriented application framework. Just as the toolbox provides programmers with the basic tools to implement the graphical user interface, MacApp provides programmers with the next level of abstraction—tools to implement the functionality of applications.

MacApp was one of the first object-oriented frameworks to support application programs with a graphical user interface to be commercially viable. Smalltalk preceded MacApp, but few commercially successful mass-market applications have been developed in Smalltalk. Since then, other object-oriented application frameworks have appeared.

The Cocoa application framework (originally OpenStep and NeXTSTEP) was developed shortly after MacApp was first developed. It was able to benefit from the advantage of 20/20 hindsight in some cases; in other cases, it closely matched some of MacApp's architecture. This is scarcely surprising, since there aren't too many ways to construct an object-oriented framework to support applications programs with a graphical user interface. (The first version of Microsoft Foundation Classes was almost eerily familiar to MacApp programmers.)

Because of this inherent similarity, you can use any application framework to learn more about all application frameworks. If you are not familiar with application frameworks or if you are not comfortable with the concepts of object-oriented design, studying MacApp can be very helpful. The fact that it may be more extensively documented than most other application frameworks can be useful in this regard.

When to Use MacApp

MacApp is the framework you normally use if you are starting to develop an application that needs to run on Mac OS 9 or earlier. You can compile it as a Carbon MacApp application and it will run on Mac OS X as well. MacApp also is likely to be the framework you need to deal with if you are modifying existing programs or studying them in order to convert them to Cocoa.

Finding Out More About MacApp

There is a great deal of documentation on MacApp, much of it on Apple's Web site. In addition, there are books and magazine articles, as well as many applications written in MacApp.

TIP   *Look at http://developer.apple.com/tools/macapp/ for further information on MacApp.*

History of MacApp

MacApp started very early in the development of the Macintosh. Object-oriented programming was not the standard that it is today. In fact, there was a lot of discussion about whether it was feasible. True, it appeared to offer a way to avoid rewriting the same code repeatedly. It also was clear, however, that object-oriented programs contained more code and ran slower than programs written from scratch. Fortunately, the advent of faster and cheaper processors made this concern a moot point.

MacApp

There were qualms about whether advanced programming techniques would be feasible in the real world—it's an issue that repeatedly arises in the computer world. When databases first came on the scene in the 1960s, they were not used for mission-critical systems because programmers were afraid they would be too slow. Custom-written sort routines were used instead of standard packages for the same reason. In each case, the fears of inefficiency were overblown, and the steady increase in processor speed quickly made up for any performance degradation that the improved programming techniques may have engendered.

MacApp and Pascal

The first versions of MacApp were written in Pascal, the usual programming language on the Macintosh. It provided the functionality for an application program, but that functionality was far less than what users expect today. Over time, MacApp was expanded to include more and more features. MacApp programmers who moved their work to later releases of MacApp often found that converting to a new release meant removing their own code, since MacApp now supported their custom-written functionality. Features such as floating windows and palettes, drag-and-drop, and Apple event support moved into the framework and out of custom-written applications.

MacApp and C++

With the increasing popularity of C++, the decision was made to convert MacApp to that language. For a period of time, two versions of MacApp were maintained—one in Pascal and the other in C++. One of the consequences of this was that MacApp was constrained to use a common subset of code that was supported in both languages. An example of this was the use of initialization routines. C++ supports constructors and destructors—routines that are automatically called when objects are created and destroyed. Pascal does not do so. Consequently, MacApp implemented methods such as `IWindow` to initialize window objects. `IWindow` and other routines of its ilk needed to be called explicitly by programmers; not doing so caused problems and was the source of many bugs.

Eventually, the decision was made to drop support for Pascal and to adopt all of the C++ programming techniques that would be useful. Templates, constructors and destructors, C++ exception handling, and other techniques were incorporated into a drastically rewritten MacApp. One of the changes that occurred at this time was the incorporation of stack-based objects into MacApp and the use of multiple inheritance.

Objects in Memory

Whatever the programming language, most MacApp objects live off in memory and are manipulated by the use of pointers (and in Object Pascal, by handles). They must be explicitly allocated and deallocated by the programmer using the `new` and `free` functions. All the problems involving memory manipulation that were previously described apply to objects. A great deal of code in MacApp and compiler diagnostics is devoted to mitigating these problems.

Stack-Based Objects

Small, stack-based objects were devised; they often were bitwise compatible with toolbox objects. Thus, the object CRect_AC is a wrapper for the toolbox Rect object. Stack-based objects start with the letter *C*.

Whereas other objects are created with the `new` function and destroyed with the `free` function, stack-based objects are declared just as any other types would be declared. They are used—without explicit programmer allocation—exactly as are other stack-based objects (reals, integers, and characters, for example). Thus, for the stack-based object CRect_AC, here is how it can be used (in UWindow.cpp):

```
CRect_AC screenRect;
```

The variable `screenRect` is declared like any other variable; its type is CRect_AC.

```
GetMaxIntersectedDevice(screenRect);
```

In the next line of code, `screenRect` is used as the argument to `GetMaxIntersected Device`. There is no explicit creation or destruction of the object. `screenRect` is passed into the function by name (or by reference), not by value. In the declaration of `GetMaxIntersected Device`, you will see the argument declared as `CRect_AC& screenRect`. The `&` indicates that the variable might be modified and a value is to be returned from that function in `screenRect`.

Object Naming Conventions

In Pascal, objects were implemented as types. By convention, object names started with *T*, as in TDocument, TWindow, and so forth. When stack-based objects were implemented, their names were determined to start with *C*, as in CRect, which is described in more detail later. Objects with multiple inheritance have an *M* as their first letter.

Apple Class Suites

One of the criticisms of MacApp was its degree of integration. It was very useful for building large applications (the first version of Photoshop was built with MacApp). However, if you wanted to use a little piece of MacApp in an application—the case when you were not starting from scratch—it was hard to do so.

One of the more recent changes to MacApp was its split into two parts. The Apple Class Suites (ACS) is a set of classes that are usable on their own. They tend to be basic interface elements that you may want to use outside of MacApp. (MacApp uses them extensively itself, too.) There are 16 suites explained in Table 23-1.

MacApp

Appearance	Interface elements such as checkboxes, progress indicators, and text boxes
Containers	Arrays, lists, iterators, and maps
Core	Memory management (see also the Memory suite), pointers and handles, and exception handling
Files	Files, streams, resources, and file type handling
Help	Support for help and assistance
Imaging	Graphics objects such as points, rects, patterns and regions; grafports, basic text handling
Java	Support for the Java programming language
Memory	Memory management
Patterns	Events, properties, and tasks
QuickTime	Media management
Streams	Sinks and streams provide input and output management for a variety of types of data
Text	Parser
TextEditor	Styled text support
Threads	Thread management
TidyHeap	Debugging
Toolbox	Windows, date and time utilities, resources, menus, Apple events, and Clipboard support

TABLE 23-1   Apple Class Suites

Inside an Object

Here is part of the header file for CRect_AC. The code is annotated to show you how to read it. (This matters if you have to read a header file to find out exactly what it does. It also helps you learn how to construct your own class definitions.) CRect_AC is a small stack-based object; a detailed annotation of a larger object is beyond the scope of this book. However, this annotation should give you a basic idea of what to look for when reading header files.

The Header

Refer to the next code string to see that the class definition starts with the reserved word class. EXPORT_AC is a compiler directive defined in the Apple Class Suite headers. It indicates that the class is to be exported (made visible to programmers). The name of the class is CRect_AC. In keeping with the conventions, it starts with *C* (as a stack-based object). Being part of the Apple Class Suite, it ends with _*AC*.

```
class EXPORT_AC CRect_AC : public Rect
```

The base class of this object (Rect) is identified after the required colon (:), as is the access that this class has to that class's members. Here, all public members are made public to the new class.

Methods (or functions) and members (or elements) of a class can be identified as public, private, or protected. When public, any other class can access them. When private, no other class can access them. When protected, descendants of the class (and the class itself) can access them.

Often you will find the members of a class made private or protected with accessor methods made public. This forces programmers to use the accessor methods. The body of the declaration is enclosed in { and }.

```
{
public:
```

The methods in this section are public(available to all).

TIP *A common source of compiler errors is a missing { or }. If you get error messages indicating that methods are being compiled into the wrong class, look for a missing or extra bracket.*

Constructors

Constructors are called automatically in C++. In the following code listing, you see three different constructors; each takes a different set of arguments. The first takes none, and it creates an empty rectangle. (That is, a valid rectangle with all points set to zero.) The next constructor creates a rectangle from four values: the left, top, right, and bottom coordinates. The third constructor creates a rectangle from two points: the top left and the bottom right coordinates.

```
CRect_AC() { Clear(); }
CRect_AC(short iLeft, short iTop, short iRight, short iBottom)
  { top = iTop; left = iLeft; bottom = iBottom; right = iRight; }
CRect_AC(const CPoint_AC& topLeftPt, const CPoint_AC& botRightPt)
  {
    *(CPoint_AC*)&top = topLeftPt;
    *(CPoint_AC*)&bottom = botRightPt;
  }
```

Some code, including additional constructors, has been omitted for reasons of space.

Geometry

There are several small utility routines that let you access the width, height, and middle of a rectangle. In these (and in many other routines in this header file) the complete definition of the method is provided. This means that the complete source code (one statement) is written out. For lengthier methods, the code is specified in a definition that occurs later. Typically, declarations—without the code definitions—are in header files, with a suffix of .h, and definitions are in definition files, with a suffix of .cpp.

```
short Width() const { return right - left; }
short Height() const { return bottom - top; }
CPoint_AC Middle()
    const { return CPoint_AC((left + right) / 2, (top + bottom) / 2); }
```

Operators

Operators can be overridden in a class declaration. Here the + operator is overridden. In the first case, a rectangle (rt) is added to the object; in the second a point (rt) is added. These are declarations; the definitions—the code, enclosed in brackets—are located in another file named CRect_AC.cpp.

```
CRect_AC& operator+=(const CRect_AC& rt);

CRect_AC& operator+=(const CPoint_AC& pt);
```

Here is the code for the first method:

```
CRect_AC& CRect_AC::operator+=(const CRect_AC& rt)
{
  top += rt.top;
  left += rt.left;
  bottom += rt.bottom;
  right += rt.right;

  return *this;
}
```

This is the code for the second method:

```
CRect_AC& CRect_AC::operator+=(const CPoint_AC& pt)
{
  top += pt.v;
  bottom += pt.v;
  left += pt.h;
  right += pt.h;

  return *this;
}
```

Other Routines

The `Clear` method is used in the first constructor of the class; here it is defined. You can see that it sets all values to 0:

```
void Clear() { *(long*)&top = *(long*)&bottom = 0; }
```

Accessors let you retrieve or set data values. These routines complement the constructors; you use them to set values in an existing rectangle:

```
void Set(short iLeft, short iTop, short iRight, short iBottom)
  {top = iTop; left = iLeft; bottom = iBottom; right = iRight;}

void Set(const CPoint_AC& topLeftPt, short width, short height);

void Set(const CPoint_AC& topLeftPt, const CPoint_AC& botRightPt)
  {*(CPoint_AC*)&top = topLeftPt; *(CPoint_AC*)&bottom = botRightPt;}
```

Constants

You can add constants to a class declaration. Here is one:

```
public: static const CRect_AC kZeroRect;
};
```

The combination of the CRect object's routines creates a valuable and reusable utility object. If you are not familiar with this type of programming, you may run to your programming documentation to find out what this object is and look in vain for a discussion of how the += operator applies to rectangles. Remember to look at type names and use your development environment's search tools to find the declarations of objects and operators that confuse you. Furthermore, use all the documentation and search tools available to find these objects so that you can reuse them. Most modern frameworks today have a host of small objects of this sort. Certainly MacApp (via the Apple Class Suites) and Cocoa (through the Core Framework) have objects that can make your life much, much easier.

The Target Chain

Control in a MacApp program is managed from an event loop deep in the heart of the framework. Each major type of MacApp object—windows, documents, buttons, and so forth—is an *event handler*. Event handlers do just that: they handle events passed to them from the main event loop. Each event handler is linked to the next one, and that chain—called the target chain—extends to the frontmost active window.

MacApp

Processing Commands

Consider the case of an application that has one document and one window open. When you choose a command, such as Close, that command is sent first to the window (the head of the target chain). The window can respond to Close, and it does so. If you had chosen the command Save or Quit, the window would be unable to respond. It would pass the command on to the next event handler, the document.

The document can respond to Save, so it would do so. If the command were Quit, it would pass that command on to the next handler, the application itself. The application can respond to Quit, and it would do so.

After handling a command, an event handler can signify that it is finished, and it also can pass the command on. In this case, after the document processes the Save command, there would be nothing left to do. After the window processed the Close command, it would pass it on so that the document could be closed.

> **NOTE**
> *In many cases, a distinction between* Close [window] *and* Close [document] *needs to be made. Often, documents close all of their windows as part of their closing routines. In such designs, windows associated with documents simply pass the Close command on to the document that does all the work. It all depends on how your application is structured.*

Target chains can grow quite complex. Objects much smaller than windows can be event handlers (scrollbars, for example). MacApp's target chain structure is very robust; it is managed almost entirely by the framework itself.

Managing Menus

The target chain is also used to manage menus. When it is time to set up menus, the target chain is traversed in the reverse direction from command handling. That is, the application (usually at the end of the target chain) enables the commands it handles, such as Quit. The document enables its commands, the window its commands, the active button its commands, and so forth. In the course of this traversal, commands may be enabled and disabled. Since the menus are not redrawn until the entire process is complete, it is seamless from the user's point of view.

Division of Labor

Using a framework such as MacApp means that you have a basic set of objects that can be used to construct an application. Some of those objects you override to create customized versions of your own. Objects such as the application and document objects fall into this category. Other objects are part of the MacApp framework and you use them—call their methods—but do not override them. This section provides a very brief overview of the division of labor between MacApp and your application. Broadly speaking, the functions that MacApp performs are done by non-overridden objects. The functions your application performs involve overrides of MacApp objects.

NOTE

Not only can you override MacApp objects, but also you can change them by modifying the source code. Many years ago, this sometimes was necessary to add functionality. Today, however, MacApp is so powerful and so stable that doing so is almost always an invitation to disaster. If you can't make MacApp work the way you want it to, investigate whether you are trying to break the interface guidelines or to do something that doesn't make sense.

The Major Classes

There are literally hundreds of classes in MacApp. Rather than start by studying them all, start by studying the examples that ship with MacApp. Look at whatever example is closest to the work you need to do. You will see which objects are overridden and which are used. Here are a few salient features of some of the major classes in MacApp.

TApplication

This is the major object in your application: the application itself. You always override this object. It is an event handler, so it automatically participates in the target chain. You don't have to do anything special for this. You also write (or copy) a very brief program that initializes MacApp, creates the application object, and then sends it the run message. Here is the `main` function of the Nothing sample:

```
void main()
{
  try
  {
    InitUMacApp(3);
    TNothingApplication aNothingApplication;
    aNothingApplication.Run();
  }
```

That is all the code that is needed. Other initializations may be called—`InitUDialog`, `InitUPrinting`, and so on—to prepare various MacApp modules. The balance of this function is exception handling:

```
  catch(CException_AC& theException)
  {
    DoCatchMessageAndStop_AC(theException);
    ::BailOutAlert(theException);
  }
  catch(exception& ex)
  {
```

MacApp

```
      DoCatchISOMessageAndStop_AC(ex);
      ::BailOutAlert(ex);
    }
    catch(...)
    {
      DoCatchForeignMessageAndStop_AC();
      ::BailOutAlert();
    }
  }
```

In your override of the application object, you must create a document, or a window, if your application has no document. You do whatever else is necessary to do at the application level. (In general, if you examine the TApplication object thoroughly, you will discover there is very little you have to do that hasn't been thought of before.

> **TIP**   *Add functionality; don't implement changed functionality. Those changes are likely deviations from interface standards and will confuse users.*

TCommand

Command objects are frequently created when users choose commands. These objects frequently have references to documents and data that must be used in carrying out the command. Descendants of the command object have built-in undo and redo capabilities; you just need to enable them.

When designing your application, you need to decide which commands will be carried out inline—that is, by code without a command object—and which will use command objects. Typically, if a command can be undone, it should be a command object. If a command can be invoked from AppleScript, it, too should be a command object. A very common way of handling commands is a two-step process:

1. Collect data, perhaps with a dialog, so that everything needed for the command is ready.

2. Create a command object using that data and cause it to be executed.

The reason for this process is that if commands are launched via AppleScript, the scripter will need to collect the supporting data and package it off in an Apple event. The same command can ultimately do the processing whether it's interactive or not. (This is an example of factoring the interface: keeping the functionality separate from the dialogs, and so on.)

TView

TViews are drawable parts of windows. They can be assembled into complex structures (scrolling views containing text views, for example). They may also be very simple objects, such as buttons. Views can be nested within one another. MacApp provides default behavior for drawing and printing views.

Old MacApp programs often contain overrides of the view object. You will find that by using newer features of MacApp (such as adorners and behaviors), you can avoid these overrides.

TWindow

The window object contains all of the views that make up a window. You don't need to override this object very often. If you do, you are likely to break the user interface.

TDocument

Like TApplication, TDocument is overridden in MacApp applications. Its range of methods to manipulate its default window, to save and restore itself, and to do other document-type things rarely needs overriding. However, you do need to override its data structures and methods that are unique to your application.

TDocument is a major MacApp class; similar classes exist in other major frameworks, including Cocoa. The commands for both classes are presented in this chapter. Here are the MacApp document object commands listed by category. Eighteen percent of them have analogs in Cocoa (the Cocoa analogs are listed in parentheses, just as the MacApp analogs are listed in the Cocoa tables later). The analogs are not exact—they are in different languages and in different framework structures—still, the comparison can be helpful.

> TIP
>
> *If you are familiar with either framework, you can use these tables to help you find direct analogs in the other framework. You will also find a variety of near-analogs— after all, there are only so many things a document can do in an application program!*

Command Handling   As an event handler (and member of the target chain), TDocument needs to handle menu commands.

    DoMenuCommand

This section provides a listing of the MacApp TDocument methods. Other methods— including event handling—are declared in the event handler objects and are inherited by TDocument. Most important of those is DoSetupMenus, the counterpart to DoMenuCommand.

Opening and Reading   When a document is created, these methods need to be called.

    DoInitialState

    DoReadData

    OpenAgain

    ReadDocument

    ReadStationery

    TDocument (init)

Document Titles   Documents need to be created with names such as Untitled 17, Untitled 18. If they have names, those titles have to be inserted into the appropriate window title bars. These are those methods.

```
GetTitle (displayName)

SetTitle

UntitledName
```

Editing   Although editing is handled by edit commands, the document needs to maintain the user selection. These commands do that.

```
GetUserSelection

RevealSelection

SetUserSelection

UserSelectionChanged
```

Change Management   A critical aspect of a document is managing change, including undo/redo and indicating whether the document is dirty—that is, whether a save needs to be done. Here are the MacApp change management methods.

```
Changed (isDocumentEdited)

DoRevert

GetChangeCount

GetUndoHandler (undoManager)

IsChanged

MarkChanged

RevealUndoRedo

RevertDocument (revertToSavedFromFile, revertToSavedFromURL)

SetChangeCount

ShowReverted
```

Scripting   MacApp's support for scripting is extensive. It supports not only Apple events (the verbs), but also the object model (the nouns, descriptors of objects).

```
DoAEClose

DoAERevert
```

```
DoAESave

DoAESetData

DoScriptCommand

GetContainedObject

GetObjectProperty

GetSetPropertyInfo

SetObjectProperty
```

Printing   The document object manages printing.

```
AttachPrintHandler

DetachPrintHandler

GetPrintInfo

GetSavePrintInfo
```

Views   The document's data is displayed in one or more views. Here are the view management methods in MacApp.

```
AddView

DeleteView

DoMakeViews

DoPostMakeViews

GetViewList
```

Windows   The document is displayed in one or more windows; the windows contain the views. These are the window methods.

```
AddWindow

CloseWindow

DeleteWindow

GetWindowList

OpenWindowCount

ShowWindows (showWindows)
```

MacApp

Closing and Writing   A lot of processing needs to happen when documents are closed. Here are the close methods.

```
Close (close)

CloseAndFree

DoClose

DoSave

DoWriteData (writeToFile, writeToURL)

FreeData

FreeFromClipboard

GetAskOnClose

GetCommitOnSave

GetSaveLocation

MakeCloseCommand

MakeSaveCommand

PoseSaveDialog (runModalSavePanel)

SaveAgain

SaveDocument (saveDocument)

SetAskOnClose
```

MacApp-Specific   The concept of a ghost document is used to interact with an iterator. For completeness, these methods are shown here. Documents used to support the Clipboard and documents that are not scriptable are ghost documents.

```
GetIsGhostDocument

SetIsGhostDocument
```

To Be Overridden   MacApp provides these TDocument classes; they are empty and can be overridden if you need to do so. They are called at the appropriate times by MacApp.

```
Abandon
```

```
FindDocument

RegainControl
```

The Minor Classes

A number of minor classes in MacApp make your life easier. Some of them are described in this section.

Adorners

Adorners are small routines that are called in the process of drawing a view. They can provide highlighting, framing, and other such features. Any number of adorners can be attached to a view. They can be given varying priorities so that they are drawn before or after the main view and with a great deal of ordering among themselves. Adorners are particularly important because they can frequently customize your view drawing to the extent that you do not need to override TView (a very large and bulky object).

NOTE   *If you are looking at an old MacApp program, you may not find adorners. If you find overrides of TView and no adorners, it's an old program.*

Behaviors

Like adorners, behaviors are small objects that can be attached to larger ones—in this case to event handlers. They have parallel methods to those in event handlers: they can receive idle time, they can set up menus, and they can process commands.

Use behaviors and adorners to avoid customizing standard objects. You can also use them to change the behavior of objects as the program is executing. For example, if you have a drawing program in which a double-click sometimes opens a graphic object and sometimes performs a scripted action, adding or removing behaviors can help you toggle between layout and run modes.

Lists and Iterators

A wide variety of stack-based iterators are available in MacApp. Together with lists, they help you store and manipulate ordered (and unordered) sets of objects. There is probably no need ever to write a for-loop of objects in MacApp. Specialized iterators loop through windows, behaviors, adorners, and other classes.

Failure Handling

Failure handling in MacApp has been well written, several times. Today, it uses the catch/exception mechanism in C++. This is the fastest and most robust form of exception handling available.

MacApp

> TIP
>
> *Most programmers understand that they should write code that can withstand any failure. Few realize that every failure must be tested. Some of the most horrendous failures arise from incorrectly functioning error messages and failure handlers that have never been tested.*

MacApp on Mac OS X

If you need to write or modify a program that must run on Mac OS X and Mac OS 9 or earlier, MacApp is the framework of choice for most people. Recent versions of MacApp support Carbon, discussed in the next chapter. By using MacApp's Carbon version, you may be able to produce a Carbonized application without changing a line of your source code.

Classic Environment

Classic applications, written in MacApp or otherwise, run on Mac OS X. The Classic Environment (formerly known as the Blue Box) is a Mac OS X application that runs Mac OS 9.1. Within that application, Classic applications run just as they would—almost. Memory and file management are two areas where some changes are made. This is explored from the programmer's perspective in Chapter 3, "How It Works."

Memory

The virtual memory management system of Mac OS X is not a feature that can be turned on or off. It is on and available to all processes running on the computer, including the Classic Environment. For that reason, the Virtual Memory option within Mac OS 9, or earlier version, running in the Classic Environment is turned off. It appears to be running with one gigabyte of memory and no virtual memory. Applications that deal with Mac OS 9 or earlier virtual memory may display nondeterminative and innovative behaviors when running in Classic.

File Systems

The Classic Environment supports two access modes for disks: shared and exclusive. Disks mounted in Mac OS X when the Classic Environment is launched will be mounted in the Classic Environment as well. They will be shared—both environments will be able to access them.

This sharing is actually accomplished by not sharing their access. The Classic File Manager routines call Mac OS X file system routines; they are the only ones that actually access the disks. As a result, disks mounted in shared access mode cannot be accessed by low-level Classic routines (that is, routines below the level of the File Manager). Disk utilities, ancient programs, and poorly written code may attempt to make these calls and may fail under the Classic Environment.

Summary

An overview of Mac OS 9 or earlier programming introduced you to the technology you need to know to read older programs. CodeWarrior, a development tool from Metrowerks is used extensively in programming Mac OS 9 and earlier projects; MacApp development frequently has relied on CodeWarrior. A brief introduction to the CodeWarrior IDE should have whetted your appetite.

Much of the development work on Mac OS 9 or earlier has been done with the MacApp application framework. You have seen an overview of that framework's architecture and an introduction to its concepts. The Classic Compatibility Environment lets programs run on Mac OS X without changes. The features and limitations of that environment have concluded this chapter. If you want your application to run both on Mac OS 9 and earlier and on Mac OS X, the Carbon environment is for you. It is covered in the next chapter.

Chapter 24

Carbon

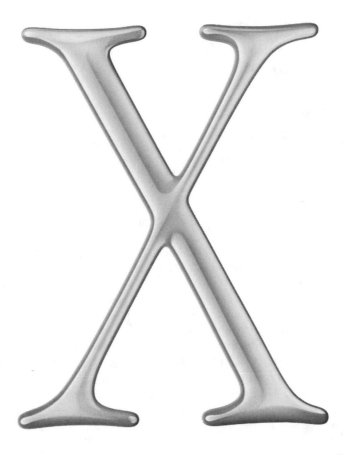

C arbon is the set of interfaces you use to build applications that run on Mac OS 9 and Mac OS X. You can write and compile your code just once and have it run in both environments. This chapter provides a high-level view of Carbon. For programmers, it offers a roadmap to its use; for others, it helps put the technology in perspective so you can decide among Classic Mac OS, Carbon, and Cocoa versions of applications.

Specifically, this chapter focuses on the following topics:

- **Carbon Overview**
- **File Formats**
- **MacApp Is Carbon**
- **Carbon Event Model**
- **Core Foundation**
- **Installing the Carbon Development Environment**
- **Porting to Carbon**
- **What's Missing in Carbon**

Carbon Overview

Carbon is a set of transitional technologies that helps developers move from Classic Mac OS to Mac OS X. It is much easier for a programmer to move existing code from Classic Mac OS to Carbon than to move it to Cocoa in most cases. In addition, it is easier for a Classic Mac OS programmer to learn Carbon than Cocoa.

For users, Carbon provides many of the features of Mac OS X in applications that can run both on Classic Mac OS and on Mac OS X. When Carbonized applications run on Mac OS X, these features include the Aqua user interface, increased stability, and overall greater responsiveness for all applications on Mac OS X. On Mac OS 8 and Mac OS 9, Carbon applications cannot take advantage of these features; however, they can take advantage of a number of new features.

The issue of transition is critically important both for developers and for users. The transition from the original 68K chip architecture to the PowerPC chip architecture took many years. The first PowerPC computers were shipped by Apple in 1994. In 1997, Apple shipped its last 68K-powered computers (the PowerBook 3400c/240). Although it was generally considered that Apple took too long to bring the PowerPC chip to its PowerBook line, moving its entire product line from one hardware architecture to another in three years was fairly remarkable. (One year would have been a miracle, and two would have been what most people would have wanted.)

Software transitions on a smaller scale than the move from Classic Mac OS to Mac OS X have occurred as well. While moving somewhat faster than hardware transitions, they nevertheless take years to make.

What this means for Carbon is that while it is a transitional technology, it is one that can be expected to have a lifetime of a number of years. Computers have a useful life of from three to five years. This means that for someone buying a Macintosh computer the day before Apple has installed Mac OS X on its new products, three to five years may pass before Cocoa products (that is, Mac OS X-only products) can be run. Vendors of productivity software, games, accounting software, and the like must provide either a Classic or Carbon version of their software unless they want to write off such customers.

Thus, while the word "transition" clearly suggests that Carbon will not be a permanent item on the Macintosh landscape, it is important enough and will be for long enough for developers to pay attention.

There are two ways of looking at Carbon; each is described in this section, and then the balance of this chapter deals with the technical issues involved.

The Minimalist Approach

For developers, Carbon can be minimally different from the libraries they currently use to create Classic Mac OS applications. Seventy percent of the application program interfaces (APIs) in those libraries exist in Carbon; they account for almost 95 percent of the functionality used by most programs. Some obscure or outdated APIs have been removed. Programs that use these need to be rewritten in those areas to use new Carbon APIs.

Thus, there is little reason (or so the theory goes) not to convert an application to Carbon. In practical terms, however, there can be extenuating circumstances. The most serious is that poorly written applications in general—and older application in particular—are most likely to use the deprecated APIs. These applications are also most likely to have minimal documentation or even documentation that is incorrect. (It is a sad fact that documentation is frequently not updated when software is, and as a result it does not match the software.)

Perhaps the most extenuating circumstance involved in not Carbonizing an application is the loss of the source code or of someone who knows how to compile it. Many ad hoc custom-written applications exist in this world. (This is true on all platforms: the Y2K problem sounded somewhat of a wakeup call to many organizations that had lost track of their source code.)

Before the release of the first public beta of Mac OS X, a number of developers included Carbon support in their planned revisions to products (AppleWorks and Quicken are two such products that provided Carbon support very early). Carbon support can be included in routine maintenance if it is planned for in advance, since getting an application to compile and run under Carbon is usually not particularly difficult.

The Maximalist Approach

The other view, however, is that Carbon support is a big deal. Both perspectives are right, since there are varying degrees of Carbon support. You can, for example, remove deprecated API calls and make the minimal changes to make an application run under Carbon. You also can adopt new features in Carbon—such as the Carbon event model—to take advantage of powerful new technologies. Obviously, such changes require more work.

Carbon Overview

Remember that Carbon is a transitional tool not only for users but also for developers. Many of the larger architectural changes in Carbon, such as the Carbon event model or its help mechanism, help you make the transition to the new architectural structure of Cocoa.

You can thus use Carbon to prepare yourself for using the Cocoa application framework at a later date. Since Cocoa applications run only on Mac OS X, if you must support Mac OS 8 or 9, you cannot yet move totally to Cocoa.

File Formats

On Classic Mac OS, object code is stored in code fragments. The file format is referred to as CFM (for the Code Fragment Manager, the software that loads the fragments). On Mac OS X, the file format is Mach-O. Mac OS X can read and execute CFM files, but the native debuggers and tools such as Project Builder only work on Mach-O files. If you compile a program using Carbon on Classic Mac OS, your default output will normally be code fragments. That program will run—without recompilation—on Classic Mac OS and Mac OS X.

MacApp Is Carbon

Starting with Release 14, MacApp supports the Carbon libraries. Both Carbon and non-Carbon versions of the MacApp libraries and examples are part of the shipping product. You should move to the Carbonized versions as quickly as possible; normally that work is fairly insignificant.

Carbon Event Model

The Carbon event model implements *direct dispatching* of events. As you saw in the previous chapter, the event loop is the heart of Classic Mac OS programs. In Apple's SimpleApp sample program, here is the main function:

```
void main(void)
{
   Initialize();
   MakeWindow();
   MakeMenu();
   EventLoop();
}
```

As you can see, after initialization it calls the EventLoop function, which is shown here:

```
void EventLoop()
{
  Boolean      gotEvent;
  EventRecord  event;

  gQuitFlag = false;

  do
  {
    gotEvent = WaitNextEvent(everyEvent,&event,0,nil);
    if (gotEvent)
      DoEvent(&event);
  } while (!gQuitFlag);

  ExitToShell();
}
```

The do-while loop in this function is the program's main event loop. As you can see, it repeats continuously until the gQuitFlag is set. If it encounters an event, it calls DoEvent, the beginning of which is shown here:

```
void DoEvent(EventRecord *event)
{
  short      part;
  Boolean    hit;
  char       key;
  Rect       tempRect;
  WindowPtr  myWindow;

  switch (event->what)
  {
    case mouseDown:
      part = FindWindow(event->where, &myWindow);
      switch (part)
      {
        case inMenuBar: // process a moused menu command
          DoMenuCommand(MenuSelect(event->where));
        break;
```

This structure is found—usually very much in this format—in all Classic Mac OS programs. The event loop continuously calls WaitNextEvent, and if an event is found it is dispatched to an enormous case statement which sorts it out to the appropriate recipient.

Direct dispatching moves the event loop and the dispatching process into the Carbon libraries. This is more efficient, both for the programmer and for the user. For the programmer, it requires far less code. The BasicCarbEvents sample uses this line of code to create a new window:

```
err = CreateNewWindow(kDocumentWindowClass,
  kWindowStandardDocumentAttributes |

  kWindowStandardHandlerAttribute,
  &bounds, &window);
```

It subsequently installs a window event handler onto that window with this line of code:

```
    InstallWindowEventHandler(window, NewEventHandlerUPP(MyWindowEventHandler),
3, list, 0, &ref);
```

If an event is directed to the window, the Carbon library then calls MyWindowEventHandler:

```
static pascal OSStatus
MyWindowEventHandler(EventHandlerCallRef myHandler, EventRef event, void* userData)
{
  WindowRef   window;
  Rect        bounds;
  OSStatus    result = eventNotHandledErr;

  GetEventParameter(event, kEventParamDirectObject,

    typeWindowRef, NULL, sizeof(window), NULL, &window);

  if (GetEventKind(event) == kEventWindowDrawContent)
    {
      HandleWindowUpdate(window);
      result = noErr;
    }
      else if (GetEventKind(event) == kEventWindowSizeChanged)
    {
      InvalWindowRect(window, GetWindowPortBounds(window, &bounds));
      result = noErr;
    }

  else if (GetEventKind(event) == kEventWindowClose)
    {
      DisposeWindow(window);
      QuitApplicationEventLoop();
      result = noErr;
    }

    return result;
}
```

There is no need to code an event loop or to create a large case statement to sort out keyboard, mouse, and menu events. The relevant events are sent to the appropriate handlers automatically.

This is also a very significant saving for the user. Although today's processors are fast, those endless event loops churning away in all of the running applications can eat up a lot of resources. When you consider that most repetitions of the event loop turn up nothing, this is a great waste of power.

Core Foundation

Core Foundation is a library that is derived from the concepts of the Foundation framework in Cocoa. You can (but need not) use it in your Carbonized applications. The components of Core Foundation are very small objects that bring the benefits of code reuse and object-oriented programming to your application.

Core Foundation components include strings and arrays, as well as date and time utility objects. More sophisticated—but still simple—objects include dictionaries and sets, property lists, plug-ins and preferences.

Core Foundation objects provide object-programming-like objects to manage basic operations and data types. They are written in C as types. They are not classes as defined in an object-oriented programming language such as Objective-C, C++, or Java, but as the saying goes (more or less), if it walks like a duck and quacks like a duck—it's an object.

Why Use Core Foundation?

There are several reasons to use Core Foundation. Very simply, this is code that handles many of the routine tasks you need to do, and it has been written and debugged. It may be challenging to write your own version, but the debugging part is usually not fun.

Some programmers do not like to use code written by others. In some cases, this is a matter of pride; in other cases, it is because they cannot understand the code—they know how to write but not read programs. Refusing to use code written by other people limits the sophistication and complexity of your work. You will keep on writing and rewriting the basics over and over. This lack of trust in others' code can exist at an organizational level, not just at a personal level. Some companies have a "Not Invented Here" (NIH) phobia. They want to write and control all of their code.

In addition to the gift of code that is written and debugged, Core Foundation gives you support for Unicode. This is important for internationalization and a degree of operating system independence, which is important for moving from Mac OS 9 or earlier to Mac OS X, but the major reason to use Core Foundation is data sharing.

Data Sharing with Core Foundation

Core Foundation objects are designed from the beginning to be shared among different processes. This sharing means that a data element can be passed as a parameter from one program to another. That's all very well and good, but it wouldn't make Core Foundation so important on its own.

Don't think of the data sharing that goes on when you copy text from a word processor and paste it into a spreadsheet. Think instead of the data sharing that is necessary in a multithreaded application. Mac OS X supports preemptive multitasking. You can break an application down into a variety of threads so that each thread can operate independently. In some cases, it's easy to do this: you can have a printing thread communicating with a (slow) printer while an indexing thread indexes another document.

But how do you split apart processing of a single data set? Is it possible to let two threads operate on the same data? If you can do that, you can start to produce very, very efficient and fast applications. Using sharable objects, you can let two or more threads manipulate common data without getting in one another's way.

NOTE *Core Foundation is not totally thread-safe. Shared objects that are changed (mutated) while being shared need to be locked explicitly by programmers.*

Using Core Foundation

Three concepts of Core Foundation are important to using it properly: opaque types, accessors, and reference counts.

Opaque Types

Core Foundation objects are implemented as opaque types. They are objects (of a sort) into whose innards you cannot peer. Consider a typical class definition of a "true" object (in C++):

```
class myClass : public myBaseClass
{
public:
  void myClass (); //constructor
  short GetA(); //accessor (out)
  void SetA(short valueA); //accessor (in)
private:
  short A;
};
```

You can create an instance of this class and call one of its methods with the following code:

```
myClass * myinstantiation = new (myClass);
myClass.SetA (14);
```

Here is the same declaration and code in Java:

```
public class myClass extends myBaseClass
{
  public myClass (); //constructor
```

```
public short GetA(); //accessor (out)
  public void SetA(short valueA); //accessor (in)
  private short A;
};
myClass myinstantiation = new myClass;
myClass.SetA (14);
```

Core Foundation data is hidden within the interfaces to Core Foundation calls. Each Core Foundation object has a reference object (which is the name of the type, followed by Ref). That pointer is passed in and out of each call.

In Core Foundation, the SetA method shown previously would appear like this:

```
short CFmyClassSetA (CFmyClassRef inst, short A);
```

The constructor would appear like this:

```
CF_EXPORT CFmyClassRef CfmyClassCreate ();
```

You would use it like this:

```
CFmyClassRef myInstantiation = CfmyClassCreate ();
CfmyClassSetA (myInstantiation, 14);
```

All the naming conventions implied here are used throughout Core Foundation. In short, what you do is convert

```
anobject.amethod
```

to

```
amethod (anobject)
```

In the first example, anobject.amethod, anobject is an instantiated instance of a class. In the second example, amethod(anobject), anobject is a variable of type anobjectref. In practice, it is easier to do this than worry about it.

> NOTE *Objects in object-oriented programming languages are declared in a class declaration. Objects in the architecture used in Core Foundation are implied in the use of common routines and parameters—in this case, the reference pointer that is the first argument to most Core Foundation routines. The first architecture is enforced by compilers; the second is enforced by usage.*

Accessors

The opacity of Core Foundation objects comes from the fact that you simply cannot see the data within the object. It's always located within an objectref structure that you cannot see. This forces you to use accessors—Get and Set routines.

If you are used to accessing data members directly, this may seem awkward and a nuisance. In fact, it is good programming style, and your fingers will soon get used to typing `Get` and `Set`.

Reference Counts

Since Core Foundation objects are designed to be shared, there needs to be a way to manage their persistence. They need to remain in memory as long as needed, and they need to be purged when no longer needed.

Core Foundation objects manage this with an internal reference count. This simple mechanism consists of a counter that is incremented every time an object is used and decremented every time it is discarded. In the case of shared objects, one object may use another object that already is in use by a third object. The reference count in this case would be 2. If either object indicates it is finished with the object, the reference count would be decremented to 1. (If another came along, the reference count would be bumped up to 2.)

When the reference count reaches 0, the object's memory is deallocated automatically by the Core Foundation routines. This mechanism works, but you need to participate in it explicitly. Fortunately, this is very easy.

If you call a `CFCreate`... routine, the reference count is automatically incremented to indicate that you are using the object. You must explicitly call `CFRelease` when you are finished with the object. This may free its memory, depending on whether you are the last user, but it will definitely indicate that from your point of view the object can be deleted.

In addition to `CFCreate`... routines, `CFCopy`... routines also increment the reference count. You can use the objects returned without fear of their disappearing under your feet.

Of course, you need to do your part so that objects can be removed when necessary. Do not directly delete or free an object when you are finished with it. Call `CFRelease` when you are finished.

If you do not call `CFRelease`, the reference count will be too high. You will have finished using an object, but it will not be able to be deleted. If you accidentally call `CFRelease` an extra time, you will decrement the reference count too much, and the object will be deleted before it should be.

> TIP   *Be careful when you call* `CFRelease` *in* `if`/`else` *statements. It is very easy to accidentally call too often or not enough in these structures. Conditional code is always tricky to debug.*

Accessors—`Get` methods—return weak references to objects. That is, they return an object (strictly speaking, a reference to an object) that may be controlled by another user, task, or process. You should immediately call `CFRetain` to increment the reference count and to indicate that you are using the object. `CFRetain` must be balanced by a call to `CFRelease` when you are finished with an object.

In short, there should be one—and only one—call to `CFRelease` to balance each call to `CFCreate`..., `CFCopy`..., and `CFRetain`. That `CFRelease` call must be made unconditionally in the logic of your program (that may mean calling it both in the if and else clauses of a conditional statement).

Getting the Object

Sharing objects can be very efficient not only in the use of memory, but also in the creation of thread-aware programs that can run very fast. However, there is always a problem that arises with sharing objects: how do you get them in the first place? If process A creates an object and process B creates an object, they are two separate objects—they are not shared. There are only two ways to share objects.

In the first scenario, a third party creates and shares the object. A main program or process can create an object and then pass it to threads or processes that it creates. In this scenario, the main program may release the object as soon as it has passed it on. In some cases, the main program does not release the object until it completes its processing.

The second structure requires that threads or processes know something about each other's internals. A thread can be queried for an object that will be shared, but the inquiring process or thread needs to know what objects that might be.

In short, data sharing is not automatic. It relies on your use of Core Foundation objects, as well as on structuring your code so that sharing can take place.

Making the Transition

You can write to the Carbon API or move an application to Carbon without explicitly using Core Foundation. The transition consists of two parts: think in terms of Core Foundation and remember to use it in new code, and convert code to Core Foundation as possible.

The transition is worth it not only because it will enable your applications to take advantage of multithreading, but also because the concepts behind Core Foundation are found in Cocoa. You'll have to learn this someday, so why not now?

If you think you won't have to learn this technology, consider that the use of shared objects is increasingly essential to most application development. Some of the techniques embodied in Core Foundation (such as reference counting) go back to IBM's System Object Model (SOM) in the 1980s.

Installing the Carbon Development Environment

Because Carbon is a transitional tool, it is subject to changes over time. When you are ready to start using it, begin by downloading the Carbon SDK from Apple's Web site (it is located in the Developer section). If you have an Apple CD through the developer program, check that the Carbon SDK on that CD has the same version number as that of the SDK on the Web site.

Follow the instructions in the SDK. Typically, the installation process involves moving a folder named Carbon Support into your CodeWarrior folder. On Mac OS 9, a system extension needs to be installed. It will be either CarbonLib or DebuggingCarbonLib, depending on the work you are doing. CarbonLib will likely be installed already; check the version numbers to make certain that you have the latest version. An additional extension, LiteCarbonLib, may be included in the SDK. Because Carbon runs on both Mac OS 9 and Mac OS X, its routines need to be implemented on both systems. During the transition, it is typically the case that the Mac OS X implementations lag slightly behind those on Mac OS 9. LiteCarbonLib contains only those routines implemented in both environments; use it to test against if you are writing an application that needs to run on both environments.

Carbon support may also be distributed with CodeWarrior. Check the versions in all places—CodeWarrior distribution, Apple's Web site, and developer CDs—to ensure you have the latest.

Porting to Carbon

Porting to Carbon is easiest for well-written programs and for programs that use MacApp. For those programs, porting to Carbon frequently means no more than recompiling. If you run into problems or if you know in advance that you are dealing with a program that may have hidden complexities, here is a quick summary of issues that Apple has identified for you to consider.

Apple has a tool called CarbonDater that you can download from the developer section of http://www.apple.com. It will scan your code and help you identify areas that need to be looked at in your Carbon porting process.

Preemptive Scheduling

Carbon applications are scheduled preemptively on Mac OS X. (This means the operating system can suspend them at will in order to improve the computer's throughput.)

Not all toolbox routines will be converted to this model at the start. As a result, you may need to create cooperatively scheduled threads for them—that is, threads that can only be suspended at points specified by the programmer.

Over time, preemptive scheduling will become the norm. You should write for it now.

Protected Addressing

Application programs on Mac OS 9 or earlier are not supposed to manipulate memory that does not belong to them (but they sometimes do so). On Mac OS X, it is impossible to do so. The accidental manipulation of another application's memory structures is a common cause of catastrophic system failures (crashes).

Programs that have been manipulating memory directly will need to be modified.

Printing

Printing is implemented differently on Mac OS X than on Mac OS 9 or earlier. As a result, different Print Manager calls need to be invoked.

If you use MacApp, these changes have already been made for you in the framework.

Data Access

To help implement preemptive threads and more stable programs, more and more operating system data structures are being made opaque. You can use accessors now, and you should get in the habit of doing so. The data structure that you can access directly today is likely to be invisible to you tomorrow.

Memory

Virtual memory always appears enabled to Carbon applications on Mac OS X. In addition, the Mac OS X memory management model provides each application with apparently unlimited memory. As a result, routines that check memory levels (`StackSpace` or `MaxMem`) have little meaning. Likewise, `FreeMem` and `PurgeMem` function as they have in the past on Mac OS 9, but have no purpose on Mac OS X.

Remove Non-PowerPC Code

If there is any 68K code left around, remove it or rewrite it. It will not run on Mac OS X.

Remove Trap Calls

These are a legacy of 68K code. You cannot patch traps or use the Trap Manager or the Patch Manager.

Adjust the Menus

Since the structure of menus on Mac OS X differs from that on Classic Mac OS, you need to set up menus differently depending on the system on which your program is running. The gestalt selector (`gestaltMenuMgrAttr`) has a bit—`gestaltMenuMgrAquaLayoutBit`—that will help you test.

What's Missing in Carbon

Certain features of Mac OS 9 and earlier are not available in Carbon, just as certain features of Mac OS X are not available. There are two types of reasons for this:

- ■ Carbon is one of the transition tools that Apple provides for developers. The features you are looking for may not yet be in, but will be there in the future.

- ■ Certain routines in each operating system will never be available in Carbon.

Mac OS X routines that are not available in Carbon include the APIs in Quartz and the Posix file system. Classic Mac OS routines that are not available in Carbon include those that directly access the operating system. The main routines in the File Manager, Window Manager, and other toolbox managers are implemented.

Summary

This chapter has provided an overview of Carbon, the transitional tool that lets programs run under Mac OS 8 and 9, as well as Mac OS X. Carbon has many important features, not least of which are the Core Foundation objects.

You have also explored how to install the ever-changing Carbon libraries and how to port your Mac OS 9 or earlier application to Carbon.

If you want to go all the way to Mac OS X (and produce an application that will run only on Mac OS X), Cocoa is your best bet. It is described in the next chapter.

Chapter 25

Cocoa

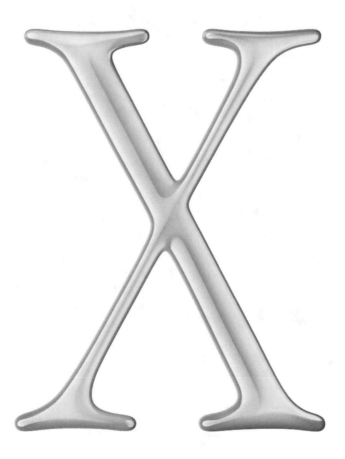

C ocoa is the application development framework (formerly known as Yellow Box) in Mac OS X. As with MacApp, you can use it to develop powerful applications quickly and easily.

Cocoa is written in Objective-C, and it has Java interfaces as well. You can use either language in writing your code. One of the consequences of its being based in dynamic languages such as Objective-C and Java is that the compile-time type checking used in MacApp's C++ code does not occur. This makes it easier for you to create applications dynamically.

Project Builder and Interface Builder let you create, modify, test, and debug programs. In particular, Interface Builder lets you dynamically experiment with connecting menu commands and interface elements to sections of code. You can create and modify an application's interface more easily and completely than with other authoring tools.

Project Builder and Interface Builder are discussed at length in the next chapter. In this chapter, you will find a brief overview of Cocoa, its concepts, and the basic structure of the framework.

You can program Cocoa using either Objective-C or Java. The code in this chapter (there's not much of it) is Objective-C. In the next chapter, all of the code is duplicated in both languages.

This chapter provides an overview of Cocoa that can help you to get started. Its five sections are

■ **Cocoa History**   Cocoa has a long history that extends back well over a decade. Its multiple framework structure has stood the test of time—and of enhancement.

■ **Cocoa Concepts**   The basic terms and classes are described here.

■ **Using Cocoa Documents**   This very high level overview of the NSDocument class lets you compare its functionality to that of MacApp's TDocument described previously in Chapter 23, "Classic Mac OS." The purpose is to show you that despite their very significant differences, both frameworks allow you to do the very similar things.

■ **Writing for Users**   Here are some tips on the issues you need to consider before you start writing code.

■ **Writing for User Developers**   Cocoa makes it possible for users to enhance applications easily. Interface Builder allows sophisticated users to build on the code that you write: this section points out some of the ideas to consider in making your user developers lives' easier.

Cocoa History

Cocoa was known as the Yellow Box in the Rhapsody project, the direct precursor of Mac OS X at Apple. The technology was developed by NeXT as the NeXTSTEP framework, later known as the OpenStep framework. This is not just of historical interest; you can find documentation and discussions about the technology under any of these names.

Variables in the framework are usually preceded by NS, for NeXTSTEP, as in NSWindow and NSArray.

Cocoa was originally the name of a programming toolkit for young children developed at Apple. The technology was later pursued by another company, but Apple retained title to the name.

There are two major frameworks within Cocoa today. More may be added over time.

AppKit

The AppKit framework contains the bulk of the classes used in developing applications. Windows, documents, and views are all found here.

Foundation

The Foundation framework provides support for low-level objects such as dates, arrays, and numbers of all kinds. In fact, the Core Foundation was created largely from the Foundation Cocoa framework.

Cocoa Concepts

Cocoa's concepts and terminology are heavily influenced by Smalltalk-80. The major ones are listed here.

Some of these concepts are actually part of the Cocoa set of frameworks; other concepts are part of Interface Builder. The distinctions are not critical for most purposes. They're all concepts you use in programming for Mac OS X with Cocoa.

Classes

Classes are definitions of objects. In Objective-C, they are also actual runtime objects, instantiations of the class Class. The Class object is capable of creating instantiations of its class definition.

Consider the Foundation class NSArray. At runtime, an instantiation of the Class object with the name NSArray exists. The NSArray `Class` object can create an instance of the NSArray class—`myArray`, for example.

This issue—the "first cause" of objects—is always tricky. It's very easy to conceptualize the process of objects communicating with one another, and few people have trouble drawing nice diagrams with arrows on a chart. However, the actual nitty-gritty of creating an object—or of locating and somehow forging a link to an object that exists in the address space of a running application—is very, very tricky. Every object-oriented system has different ways of dealing with these issues. To be robust, they need to work not only within a single process on a single computer, but also among different processes and across networks.

Objects

Objects are runtime instantiations of class definitions. They have whatever names you assign to them.

NSObject

NSObject is the base object for the Cocoa framework. It contains a great number of basic methods that all its descendants can access and override. Following this section of basic Cocoa concepts, NSObject's main classes are listed. You will see how its structure reflects and implements the architecture of Cocoa.

Messages

Objects send messages to one another. In other environments, you may be familiar with objects calling one another's functions. These are comparable (but not identical) processes. A *selector* is the name of the method invoked in a message.

Actions

When you send a message to an object, a method in the receiving object is invoked. *Action* refers both to the message that is sent as well as to the method that is invoked.

Actions have the following syntax:

```
(void*) actionName: (id) sender [Objective-C]
void actionName (Object sender) [Java]
```

If they do not, they are not visible to Interface Builder.

Outlets

Objects frequently have references to other objects stored in variables of their own. These are collectively known as *outlets*—the references to other objects that one object contains.

Outlets have the type `id` (Objective-C) or Object (Java). Assigning other, more specifics, types to them will hide them from Interface Builder effectively.

Connections

Connections are made in Interface Builder between actions and outlets and your interface elements.

Events

Events in Cocoa are like MacApp's event objects, rather than events in Classic Mac OS. In Classic Mac OS, events are a data type; in MacApp, events are TEvent objects. By transforming simple data structures into objects, you can add functionality to the data.

The trend in programming over the last decade has been toward encapsulating functionality in objects in this way.

Responders

Events and actions can be handled by descendants of NSResponder. Referred to generally as responders, these are similar to MacApp's TEventHandler class.

Responder Chain

The Responder chain is similar to MacApp's target chain. It is a linked list of responders, each of which is given an opportunity to respond to an event or action. The actual implementation of the responder chain is different from the target chain. In MacApp's target chain, each object in the chain is given the event. It decides if it can respond to it at that time.

In Cocoa, responders have a method that can be called by the framework to determine if the object is capable of responding to the event or action in question. Thus, the decision of whether a particular event or action will be handled by one object or another in the responder chain is actually made by the framework (not the object), although it is based on information from the object.

Delegates

This object can be inserted at the end of the responder chain to pass unprocessed events or actions to other objects.

Protocols

Protocols are collections of methods that you can mix into classes. For example, the NSCopying protocol supports copying of objects. An object is said to *adopt* protocols if it implements the protocol's methods. An object *conforms* to a protocol if it or a superclass adopts them.

Protocols provide an architectural element that has some commonalities with multiple inheritance in C++ and with interfaces in Java.

NSObject's Interface

These are the methods of NSObject. Since NSObject is the base object of all objects in Cocoa, it is useful to know what it looks like.

Methods of Objective-C classes can be class or instance objects. Class methods—similar to C++ static methods—are actually members of the NSObject instance of the class Class. Class methods are preceded with +; instance methods are preceded with –.

The interface is presented in a different order than in NSObject.h, the header file. Methods are grouped slightly differently as well.

Object Creation and Destruction Methods

```
+ (id)alloc;
- (id)init;
```

Cocoa Concepts

```
+ (id)new;
+ (void)load;
- (void)dealloc;
```

There is a distinction between allocating an object and initializing it. The first operation is performed by the class object; it creates an instance. Initialization is performed by an instance method. The class method new calls both of them, saving a few keystrokes and making the code easier to read.

```
+ (id)allocWithZone:(NSZone *)zone;
```

You can specify where in memory you want to allocate an object.

```
+ (void)initialize;
```

This is the initialization method for the class object. You rarely call it yourself—it is called automatically just before the first time the class is used in a program. (The instance method's initialization method is init, not initialize.)

Copying Methods

```
- (id)copy;
- (id)mutableCopy;
+ (id)copyWithZone:(NSZone *)zone;
+ (id)mutableCopyWithZone:(NSZone *)zone;
```

These methods allow objects to copy themselves. The NSCopying protocol is invoked. In order to use these methods, the subclass of an NSObject must support the protocol.

What's important to note is that objects can copy themselves.

Class Management and Introspection Methods

```
+ (Class)superclass;
+ (Class)class;
+ (void)poseAsClass:(Class)aClass;
- (BOOL)isKindOfClass:(Class)aClass;
- (BOOL)isMemberOfClass:(Class)aClass;
- (BOOL)conformsToProtocol:(Protocol *)aProtocol;
+ (NSString *)description;
```

These methods return the class's class or superclass object. With poseAsClass, you can have a class behave as one of its superclasses.

Coder Methods

```
- (Class)classForCoder;
- (id)replacementObjectForCoder:(NSCoder *)aCoder;
- (id)awakeAfterUsingCoder:(NSCoder *)aDecoder;
```

These methods let you manipulate the coding and decoding of objects supported in the NSCoding protoçol. What matters here is that NSObjects can read and write themselves.

Memory Management

```
- (id)retain;
- (oneway void)release;
- (id)autorelease;
- (unsigned)retainCount;
```

These methods implement Cocoa's memory management with reference counts for objects. What's important to note is that NSObjects contain reference counts, which means they can be safely shared.

Responders and Selectors

```
- (BOOL)respondsToSelector:(SEL)aSelector;
- (void)forwardInvocation:(NSInvocation *)anInvocation;
- (NSMethodSignature *)methodSignatureForSelector:(SEL)aSelector;
+ (NSMethodSignature *)instanceMethodSignatureForSelector:(SEL)aSelector;
- (id)performSelector:(SEL)aSelector;
- (id)performSelector:(SEL)aSelector withObject:(id)object;
- (id)performSelector:(SEL)aSelector withObject:(id)object1 withObject:(id)object2;
+ (BOOL)instancesRespondToSelector:(SEL)aSelector;
- (IMP)methodForSelector:(SEL)aSelector;
+ (IMP)instanceMethodForSelector:(SEL)aSelector;
- (void)doesNotRecognizeSelector:(SEL)aSelector;
```

These are the methods involved in managing selectors, messages, and responders. The are at the heart of Cocoa's responder chain. From an architectural point of view, the most important may be `respondsToSelector`. This is the method that the framework calls to query an object to see if it can respond to a message. For each object in the responder chain, this method is called to find the object to process an event or action.

This is called direct dispatch; MacApp's architecture actually presents the event to each object in turn. The choice and the processing are done together.

The second method, `forwardInvocation`, is used in conjunction with `methodSignatureForSelector` to implement delegation. If a message is presented to an object that does not recognize it, the object's `forwardInvocation` method can be called.

That method can locate another object, check to see if it responds to the selector, and then send the message on. You set this up in `methodSignatureForSelector`.

What's important is that objects can appear to handle events for which they are not prepared. In addition, the delegation structure means that the object that ultimately responds to a message may not be in the responder chain.

Archiving

These methods are used for writing objects out.

```
- (Class)classForCoder;
+ (void)setVersion:(int)aVersion;
+ (int)version;
- (void)encodeWithCoder:(NSCoder *)aCoder;
- (id)initWithCoder:(NSCoder *)aDecoder;
```

Using Cocoa Documents

In Chapter 23, "Classic Mac OS," you saw how MacApp's TDocument class lets you manage documents easily without writing very much repetitive code: the common code is all in the framework. So it is, too, with Cocoa.

The document class in Cocoa is called NSDocument. The methods of NSDocument differ from those of MacApp's TDocument, but there is a degree of similarity because both do very similar things. Here, the methods of NSDocument are categorized in the same way in which the methods of TDocument were in Chapter 23. Comparable methods in TDocument are listed in parentheses.

Opening and Reading

These are the methods to create, open, and read documents.

```
fileType

init (TDocument)

initWithContentsOfFile

initWithContentsOfURL

loadDataRepresentation

loadFileWrapperRepresentation

readableTypes
```

```
readFromFile (ReadDocument)

readFromURL
```

Document Titles

These documents generate titles for new, unsaved documents and also set and retrieve the file name for the title bar.

```
displayName (UGetName)

fileName

setFileName
```

Change Management

To support undo and redo, as well as to keep track of whether a document needs to be saved when it is closed, these methods keep track of changes.

```
hasUndoManager

isDocumentEdited (IsChanged)

revertToSavedFromFile (DoRevert)

revertToSavedFromURL (DoRevert)

revertDocumentToSaved (RevertDocument)

undoManager (GetUndoHandler)

setHasUndoManager

setUndoManager
```

Printing

Comparing the methods of TDocument in MacApp with NSDocument in Cocoa, you can see something of the differences in the two frameworks' structure. In TDocument, there are far fewer printing methods; you will note that there are accessors for a print handler object. That object handles the printing, and if you look in its documentation, you will find analogs of the methods shown here.

```
printDocument

printInfo
```

```
printShowingPrintPanel

runModalPageLayoutWithPrintInfo

runPageLayout

setPrintInfo

shouldChangePrintInfo
```

Windows

Note here the accessors for window controllers. Just as MacApp uses print handlers to assist in printing, Cocoa uses window controllers to do comparable work with windows. While the overall architectures have many similarities, they diverge at the detail level. However, the techniques (handlers and controllers being added to extend generic objects' functionalities) are very similar.

```
addWindowController

makeWindowControllers

removeWindowController

showWindows (ShowWindows)

windowControllers
```

Closing and Writing

Finally, these are the methods involved in closing documents and writing them to disk.

```
canCloseDocumentWithDelegate

close (Close)

dataRepresentationOfType

(PoseSaveDialog)

saveDocument

saveDocumentAs

saveDocumentTo

setFileType
```

```
writeToFile (DoWriteData)

writeToFile (DoWriteData)

writeToURL (DoWriteData)

writeWithBackupToFile
```

Writing for Users

You always write for users: they are the people who use (and pay for!) your software. Cocoa is no different from any other programmer productivity tools and development environments in supporting this.

But Cocoa goes further in its Interface Builder and Program Builder applications. You may need to train yourself—and users—to look at unfinished software in a different way. When something looks finished (as many Cocoa prototypes do), it's very easy to avoid looking at it critically. Users may hesitate to ask questions or make comments because they are afraid too much work has already been done. Developers may be seduced into thinking that things are working because they appear to work.

The ease of development should in no way deter or inhibit testing. In fact, knowing that your early drafts of projects are likely to look far more finished than they ever have before, you must guard against your users and yourself relaxing.

Application frameworks make developing software easier than ever; you really can reuse objects in a way that was only dreamed of two decades ago. However, that means that every object you use and reuse must be tested repeatedly. The objects you create today may be used next year in a very different way. Every aspect of an object's functionality must be tested. The fact that a feature isn't used now doesn't mean it won't be used in the future, and chances are it won't be specifically tested then, because no one will know that one particular feature wasn't tested.

Writing for User Developers

You can create frameworks for people to use in putting new applications together. You may be the integrator, but it may also be users. As you name methods and classes, as you define outlets and actions, consider how they will appear to user developers—sophisticated users who will be making connections in Interface Builder. For example, `DoIt` may be a good name for a method to be used by a programmer with several CDs full of documentation. For a user developer, `Alphabetize` might be a better choice of method name.

Don't hide your outlets and actions. You can do so if you do not follow Interface Builder's standards. Allowing user developers to put the pieces of your application code together with other applications isn't going to put you out of a job, it's going to increase your value.

Finally, remember to support all of the user developer tools. That means including scripting wherever possible. Make your actions scriptable, but also implement the object model. Make it possible for users to easily identify objects on which they want to perform work.

And definitely make your application recordable!

Summary

This part of the book has shown you how to automate your work and to program using AppleScript, the command line, MacApp (for Classic Mac OS and Carbon applications), and Cocoa (for Mac OS X applications). Cocoa is the most advanced programming framework yet; you can use it with Objective-C or with Java, and you can take advantage of its Mac OS X Aqua interface elements that make users' experiences excellent.

In the next and final chapter of the book, you will see how to use Project Builder and Interface Builder to create and modify Cocoa applications. If you are a programmer, you have extremely powerful tools waiting for your imagination. If you are a user, the arcane mysteries of programming are made less so with the graphical interface and simple architectural design of the Mac OS X development tools.

Chapter 26

Creating a Nothing Program for Cocoa

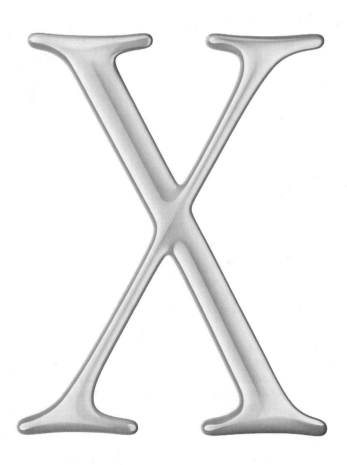

This chapter is devoted to Cocoa and its Project Builder and Interface Builder development tools, the primary tools you use to develop Mac OS X applications. In it you will find a step-by-step guide to creating a basic Mac OS X application. Although basic, the application, together with the Mac OS X frameworks, displays windows, uses buttons and menus as interface elements, and lets you write some basic code to interact with user input. The application you will build here is called Nothing. Based on the ideas behind the MacApp Nothing application, it is just about the smallest application you can create with Cocoa.

The sections of this chapter are

- When to Use Project Builder and Interface Builder

- Getting Started

- Creating a New Application

- Building the Nothing Application

- Troubleshooting

- Running Nothing

- Exploring Project Builder

- Exploring Interface Builder

- Changing a Menu Command

- Adding Functionality to Nothing

- Adding Interface and Data Elements to Nothing.

Note that you can use the last two sections as an all-purpose template for incorporating existing C or Java code into the rich Cocoa graphical user interface. You can find an excellent example of this in the Mac OS X Server tools, as well as in Mac OS X applications such as Network Utility: they add Cocoa interfaces to ancient Unix tools.

When to Use Project Builder and Interface Builder

Project Builder and Interface Builder are the tools you use to develop Cocoa applications, applications using the frameworks that are derived from the OpenStep and NeXTSTEP frameworks. You can use Java or Objective-C (or a combination) to develop these applications. (In some cases, you can implement an application without writing any code at all.)

Applications built in this environment can run on Mac OS X, and they do so very efficiently, with great stability, and quickly. They do not run on Classic Mac OS. As a result, if you need to develop an application for both Classic Mac OS and for Mas OS X, you should explore Carbon (ideally, Carbonized MacApp or PowerPlant, as described in Chapter 24, "Carbon").

Project Builder provides an integrated development environment with editor, online assistance, compilers, and a debugger. From Project Builder you can automatically launch Interface Builder, the tool that lets you create and modify your application program's interface.

This chapter provides a step-by-step guide to creating a small Cocoa application with Project Builder and Interface Builder. Try it once without embellishments: just make certain that everything is installed correctly and that it all works. Thereafter, you can go back and experiment with modifications.

Getting Started

The Mac OS X Developer Tools are available to members of the Apple Developer Connection. Several levels of membership are available—including a free Internet membership. You can order the Developer Tools or download them from Apple's site. They also are distributed with Mac OS X in many cases. Start by launching Project Builder. Once you have installed the Developer Tools, you will find it in the Applications folder inside the Developer folder

Creating a New Application

Launch Project Builder and select New Project from the File menu. You will be able to choose from among a wide variety of projects. They are grouped into seven categories:

- WebObjects
- Application
- Bundle
- Framework
- Java Applet
- Kernel Extension
- Tool

Within each category, a number of project shells are found. In this example, you want to create an application, so click the disclosure triangle next to Application to see its choices:

- Carbon Application
- Carbon Application (nib-based)
- Cocoa Application

- Cocoa Document-based Application

- Cocoa-Java Application

- Cocoa-Java Document-based Application

- Java Application

Select Cocoa Application and click Next. Name the project on the next screen and select a location for its files. This project will be called Nothing. Take a moment to look at the range of projects you can create with Project Builder. You can create Nothing projects for many of them: the default functionalities produce runnable, and nearly usable, programs.

When you have clicked Finish, the project's files will be created as you have specified. The file you are most concerned with has the suffix pbproj; that is the project file, and from it you can open all of the other files. Henceforth, you can open the project by clicking the .pbproj file.

The Project Builder main window opens. This window contains a variety of resizable panes and tabs as you will see in the figures throughout this chapter. Your Project Builder window will almost certainly differ from those shown here.

Building the Nothing Application

At the upper left of the window, four buttons let you build the project, remove object code, run it, and launch the debugger. For now, click the Build button, as shown in Figure 26-1. (Yes, after having done nothing but create a new project, the next thing you do is build it.)

This will cause Project Builder to compile the files that need compiling and to make the project from the compiled files. The Build icon will change to a stop sign, and messages will appear in the Project Build window.

Troubleshooting

What you will have compiled at this point is the most basic application possible. After all, you haven't written a single line of code or implemented a single interface element. If you do not successfully complete these steps, something is wrong with your installation. If you can, fix it or reinstall the software. If necessary, have someone else, a system administrator or the vendor from whom you purchased the equipment, solve the problem. If you cannot build Nothing, you can't build anything.

CAUTION *If you have a minor problem, you may be tempted to work around it or continue. Don't. Problems in basic installations do not go away or get better.*

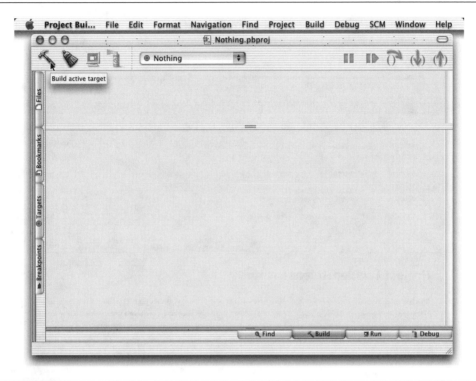

FIGURE 26-1   Building the project: the Build button is a hammer.

Running Nothing

The Nothing application now exists on disk. You can run it from the Finder. You can also run it from Project Builder. Click Run, the computer screen button that is third from the left of the row of buttons at the top of the window. This will launch Nothing, as shown in Figure 26-2.

Exploring Nothing

Exactly what does Nothing do, or, to put it another way, what basic functionality do you start with in a Cocoa application from Project Builder?

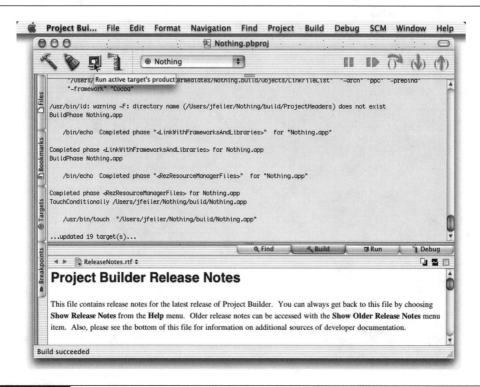

FIGURE 26-2   Running Nothing

The Nothing Window

When you run Nothing, a window titled simply Window will open. Note that while the program is running, the Run button changes to a Stop button. Clicking it stops the program. The window is movable, resizable, and the control buttons all work—without your having written a single line of code.

The Nothing Menus

The basic Mac OS X menus appear in the menu bar. Some of the commands are grayed out because they are not implemented, but others are available even in Nothing.

Application

The Application menu is automatically managed for you. About, Services, Hide/Show, and Quit are available. These are supported by Mac OS X, so all applications, even Nothing, automatically have them.

File

In the File menu, Open Recent, Close, Page Setup, and Print are enabled. Cocoa supports these implementations, and Nothing uses the default implementations. In fact, for these commands, the default implementations will probably be sufficient for all of your programs.

Edit

The Edit menu is created; however, none of its commands is enabled. They require programming on your part.

Window

The Window menu is also built automatically by Cocoa. Although only one window is open when you first run Nothing, as more windows are opened (or closed), the Window menu will be updated appropriately.

Help

Finally, the Help menu is created. If you choose the Help command in the menu, a default Help error message appears.

Exploring Project Builder

Choose Quit from the Nothing Application menu, and you will return Project Builder. Figure 26-3 shows the Files tab in Project Builder. You can click the disclosure triangles to the left of any of the items in the left-hand scrolling list to see the components of that type in the project. If you click Classes, you will see that there are none.

Other Sources

When you expand Other Sources, you will be able to see `main`—the function that actually runs the program. The `main` function is the heart of all programs written in C and languages or dialects derived from it.

The `main` function is generated automatically for you when you create a project in Project Builder. It happens to be generated in Objective-C; but that scarcely matters, even if you are programming in Java. You do not modify `main` in most cases. The `main` function is placed in a file called main.m, which is also created for you.

Resources

Within a project, resources are organized by language. Within each language, several nib files may exist. When the application is launched, the main nib file is loaded into memory. It contains the user interface—menus and windows, for example—along with the application itself. In short, everything needed to launch the program and to start it running is contained in the main nib file. This is a slight oversimplification; however, it is sufficient for most purposes.

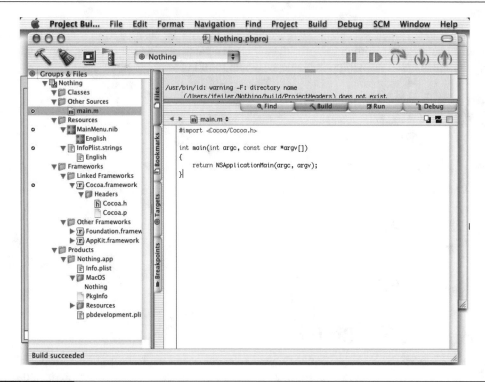

Examine project files and organization in Project Builder.

Frameworks

Still further down, you will find frameworks—both the Foundation and AppKit frameworks are included.

Exploring Interface Builder

Go back to Resources and open MainMenu.nib by double-clicking it. Project Builder will automatically launch Interface Builder. You will see the interface elements and nib file contents, as shown in Figure 26-4.

Four windows appear, as shown in the figure. Clockwise from upper left, they are

- Nib file window
- Cocoa windows palette

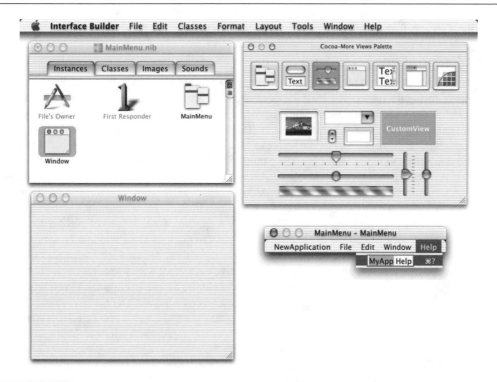

Exploring Interface Builder

FIGURE 26-4   Interface Builder lets you create and modify your user interface using graphical tools.

- Nothing main menu
- Nothing window

Nib File Window

This file contains the application's objects. It starts with the four shown in Figure 26-4. Other objects are found under the Sounds and Images tabs. The Classes tab contains a list of the objects defined in the project. These will be explored later. For now, concentrate on the Instances tab (the default when you open it).

Each icon in the Instances panel represents an object that is instantiated. (The objects are defined under the Classes tab.) You must instantiate an object in order to manipulate it.

File's Owner

The File's Owner object in the main nib file window represents the application object: an object of type NSApplication. You can think of this as your application itself. Complex applications may have several nib files. The main nib file has an owner that is the application. Other nib files may have owners that are other objects, such as documents.

First Responder

The First Responder object represents the object at the head of the responder chain. For MacApp developers, this is the target. The First Responder can be a window, a button or other control within a window, a view within a window, or the application itself. It is always a subclass of NSResponder, but most interface elements are. The First Responder changes as users click different interface elements, just as the target in MacApp changes in the same way.

You don't have to worry about changing the First Responder in response to user actions (if you try to do so, except in very special cases, you will probably break the user interface guidelines and confuse your users). There are cases in which an object will resign First Responder status in order to pass an event on to another object, such as when implementing tabbing.

The First Responder object in the nib file window represents whatever object may be the First Responder at any time during the program's execution. Do not look for a window or button in Interface Builder that is the First Responder. You specify actions for the First Responder in order to allow interface elements, typically menu commands, to interact with whatever object happens to be the First Responder at any given moment. For example, the menu command Preferences almost always should be sent to the application's preferences window. The menu command Close should be sent to whichever window is active. Thus, the Close menu command is connected to the First Responder and, at run time, it will be sent to the appropriate window. You can link Preferences directly to the preferences window.

In the case of windows, an action normally goes to the active view. If the action is not handled, it goes to that view's next responder, and from there to that view's next responder, all the way up to the window. If it has not yet been handled, it goes to the window's delegate, to the window controller, and then to the document. If the action is still unprocessed, it goes to the application's main window (if it is not the window containing the active view). From there, the process is repeated. If there is still no responder to the action, the application itself is given a chance to respond. This is the responder chain, and the First Responder is whatever the start of it happens to be. As you can see, depending on the active view, window, or document, that chain—and the First Responder—will change. Each object just worries about responding or not (or sometimes delegating) the action it receives. The interaction of the responders is what creates the responder chain.

MainMenu

The MainMenu object is the application's menu bar. You can double-click it to open the menu bar (the Nothing menu, beneath the Nib File window). The Nothing menu may already have been opened for you.

MyWindow

Finally, the MyWindow object in the nib file window is the default window that opened when you launched Nothing. You may see a window titled Window; if you do not, double-click the MyWindow object in the nib file to open it.

Cocoa Windows Palette

The Cocoa Windows Palette may be opened for you when you launch Interface Builder. If it is not, you can open it from the Tools menu's Palettes submenu. It is shown at the upper right of Figure 26-4.

This palette contains interface elements that you can use in building your interface. You can drag buttons, text fields, and menus from the palette to your own interface elements. You will see how to do so shortly.

Nothing Menu

The Nothing menu appears in its own window. If it does not, double-click the MainMenu object in the nib file window.

Nothing Window

The Window window appears in Interface Builder at the lower left. This is the window that will open when your application is launched. If it is not visible, double-click the Window object in the nib file window.

Changing a Menu Command

As a first step to seeing how Interface Builder works, change the Help menu.

Changing the Menu Text

If you click the Help menu command in the MainMenu window, the menu will drop down as shown in Figure 26-4. The single command is named MyApp Help. Double-click the command name; you will be able to edit it. Rename it, perhaps to Nothing Help.

Testing the Interface

From the File menu, choose Test Interface (COMMAND-R). Interface Builder will run the revised interface. You can choose your retitled command from the Help menu.

Rebuilding the Program

Return to Project Builder, either by clicking its icon in the Dock or by clicking the project browser window if it is visible on your screen. Rebuild the program by clicking the Build button, and you will be prompted to save MainMenu.nib unless you already did so in Interface Builder.

Project Builder tracks the changes that you make in Interface Builder. You can now run your application, either using the Run button in Project Builder or by running the application by double-clicking it in the Finder.

Adding Functionality to Nothing

Next, add functionality to Nothing. This will not be particularly flashy functionality—it will be a beep. The reason that beeps are often used is because you can debug them very easily. If you do something sophisticated, such as displaying "Hello World," your code may fail, either in processing the command or in displaying the output. There is not much you can screw up with a simple beep.

Overview of the Process

Adding functionality to an application normally involves the following steps:

1. You *declare* an object that will be able to carry out the action or respond to the message specifying the action. (Responding to a message is the way most message-oriented systems such as Cocoa and Smalltalk describe this.) This declaration must include the names of the variables that it will need in its operations. It also includes the object's name. You can do this graphically in Interface Builder. You can also write code in Project Builder to do so, but it is not nearly so easy.

2. You *instantiate* this object. The instantiation is the actual object that will exist at runtime.

3. You create an *interface element* that will request the action, for example, a menu command or a button. This is also easiest to do in Interface Builder, although if you are a determined code-based programmer, you can do it in Project Builder.

4. You *define* the class. That is, you write the actual code that is executed. This step must be done in Project Builder. You cannot use Interface Builder to write code.

5. You *link* the interface element to the declaration. This linking associates the object's variables with data values in the interface. This step, too, can be done in either Interface Builder or Project Builder.

6. Finally, you *test, test, test*. You test that it works as it should; you test that it fails elegantly; and you test that when it is used incorrectly (passed bad data, for example), it doesn't cause harm to other elements in your application. You test the interface in either Interface Builder or Project Builder. You test the full application using Project Builder's debugging facilities.

In short, you can declare objects, create interface elements, link, and test them in either Interface Builder or Project Builder. By far, Interface Builder is the easier tool to use. It is the only one discussed in this chapter. Defining the object and linking its interface to the declaration can be done in either order. On large development projects, different people frequently do these tasks.

Declaring the Object

You create a class declaration for the object you want to create. The new class is always a descendant of an existing class. The class you will create here, a class to beep, is a class that needs only the minimal ancestry. As a result, it is a descendant of NSObject or of java.lang.Object. If you will be writing the code in Objective-C, it should be a subclass of NSObject. If you will be writing the code in Java, it should be a subclass of java.lang.Object. You can combine Java and Objective-C classes in the same project.

Subclassing an Object

Now, you need to decide whether you will be writing your code in Java or Objective-C. Both cases are shown here. To start, click the Classes tab in the nib file window. The display will change to a listing of classes.

Scroll to the top of the list. You will see java.lang.Object and NSObject toward the top. (Initially, they are the first two items.) Select one of them by clicking it once; then choose Subclass from the Classes menu. A subclass called `MyObject` will be created. It will be indented to indicate that it is a subclass. To work in Java, select java.lang.Object and subclass it. To work in Objective-C, subclass NSObject. The two processes will then continue identically until it comes time to write the code.

Figure 26-5 shows `MyObject` created as a subclass of java.lang.Object as you would do if you want to write its code in Java. (Note that Figure 26-5 shows the Subclass command and its result in the same image. You highlight java.lang.Object, choose Subclass, and `MyObject` is then created and selected for you.) If you want to write in Objective-C, create `MyObject` as a subclass of NSObject

Naming the Subclass

Double-click the name of the class (`MyObject`) and type a new name, `Beeper`. When you click elsewhere or press RETURN, the class will be moved to its appropriate place in the alphabetical class listing in the window.

Adding an Action to Beeper

With the name of the class still selected, choose Add Action from the Classes menu. The class `Beeper` will be opened. Two subsections, outlets and actions, will appear. These exist for all classes. Figure 26-6 shows the result of adding an action.

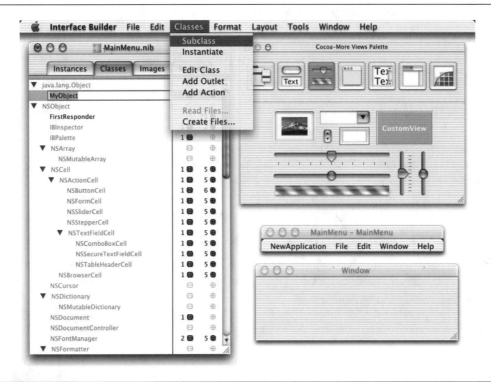

FIGURE 26-5 Adding a Java subclass

Outlets Outlets are instance variables in a class. They contain references to other objects. Instance variables that contain other types of data, integers or strings, for example, are not outlets. Outlets are always typed in Objective-C as type id. In Java, they are of type `Object`.

Actions Actions are methods of a class. In languages derived from Smalltalk, methods are invoked in response to messages sent to an object. The word *action* can be used for the object's method, as well as for the message sent to it. In this context, it is the method of a class.

Under the Actions heading, you will see an action named `myAction`. That is the action that was created by the Add Action command. To open a class to view its outlets and actions, you can select the class and choose Edit Class from the Classes menu. You can also click either of the small icons in the column at the right. The icon on the right is for actions; the one on the left is for outlets. You will note a 1 next to the actions outlet icon for your class. That indicates that you have one action, the one you just created. Click the name of the new action; type in a new (and meaningful) name, such as `beep`. Remember to leave the () at the end for Java. In Objective-C, you need a colon (:).

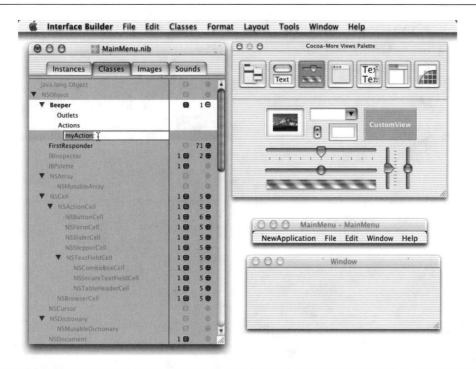

FIGURE 26-6 Add actions to classes to link to code that you write.

Instantiating the Object

Next, create an instance of the Beeper object in your nib file. From the Classes pane, make certain that the Beeper class is selected; then, choose Instantiate from the Classes menu. An instantiation will appear in the Instances panel, as shown in Figure 26-7.

Creating the Interface Element

You need a way to invoke the beep method of the Beeper object. One way of doing this is to place a command in the menu bar. Make certain that the MainMenu window is visible, as well as the Cocoa Palette. If MainMenu is not visible, double-click the MainMenu object in the nib file window. If the palette is not visible, open it with the command from the Palettes submenu of the Tools palette.

The Cocoa palette contains a panel at its top that lets you select the interface elements it displays. A menu icon (the same one as the MainMenu icon in the nib file window) displays menu elements. Select it, and you will see the menu interface elements shown in the palette at

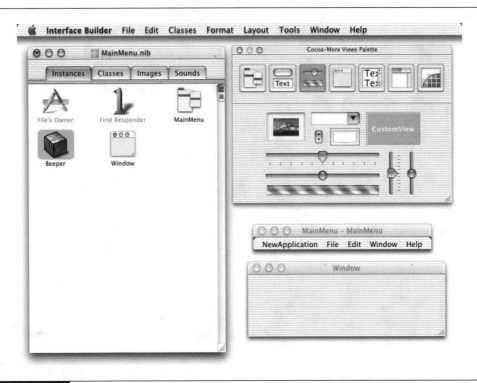

FIGURE 26-7   Instantiation of the Beeper

the upper right of Figure 26-8. If you don't see the menu icon in the palette, scroll the icons at the top to the right or left until it appears.

Drag the Submenu element to the MainMenu window's toolbar. Place it between the Edit and Window menus (they will move aside when you release the mouse button). If you put the submenu in the wrong place, you can slide the menus in the menu bar around to reorder them.

Rename the menu and menu command to Sounds and Beep, respectively. Just as you did in the first example in this chapter, simply click the command or menu name to select it and type the new name. (To place additional commands in the menu, you drag the Item icon from the menus palette to the appropriate menu.)

Defining the Object (Writing Code)

Next, you write the code that defines the class you just created in Interface Builder.

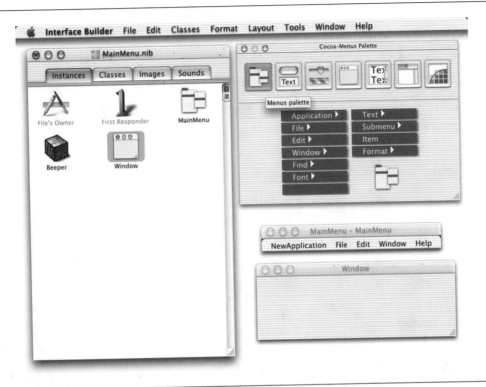

FIGURE 26-8   The menus pane of the palette

Creating the Files in Interface Builder

Make sure that the class (Beeper) is selected in the Classes tab of the nib file window. Then choose the Create Files command from the Classes menu. You can choose where to locate the files.

Writing the Code in Project Builder

Interface Builder will normally open the class in Project Builder at this point. If it does not, return to Project Builder by clicking on the project browser window (if it is visible) or by clicking its icon in the Dock.

Viewing the Header Created for You   If you are writing in Java, you will see the window shown in Figure 26-9. If you are working in Objective-C, you will see the window shown in Figure 26-10.

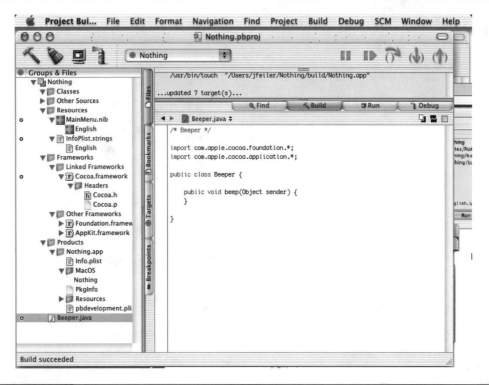

FIGURE 26-9   Project Builder header in Java

Adding a Line of Code   At this point, you need to know that there is a method of the NSApplication class object called beep. It does what you want. Since it is a method of the class, not of an instantiation of that class, you can call it using the class name. For methods of instantiations of classes, you need to use the reference variable containing the instantiation. In MacApp, for example, you always have an instantiation of a descendant of TApplication in gApplication.

Compare the code snippets with which you are familiar with ones you may not be familiar with. That way, you can learn how to convert the programming style you are familiar with to

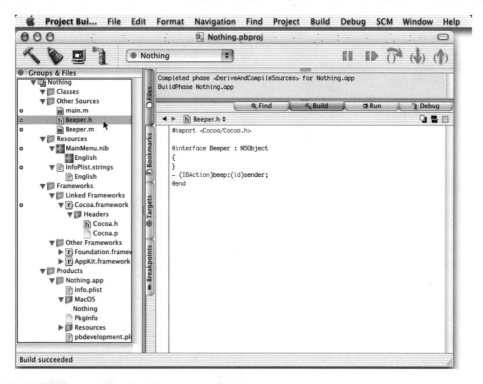

FIGURE 26-10   Project Builder header in Objective-C

a new one if necessary. For Java, add a call to the NSApplication `beep` method. The added line is bolded here:

```
/* Beeper */
import com.apple.cocoa.foundation.*;
import com.apple.cocoa.application.*;

public class Beeper {
```

```
public void beep (Object sender) {
  NSApplication.beep ();
}

}
```

For Objective-C, add a call to the NSBeep function. The added line is bolded here:

```
#import "Beeper.h"

@implementation Beeper
-  (IBAction)beep:(ID)sender
{
NSBeep ();
}
@end
```

Recompiling Use the Build button to open the Build window and build the application. If you have errors, check for extraneous semicolons, brackets, and so forth. You can run the application if you want, but nothing new will happen: you have written the Beeper code, but it is never called. That's the next step: linking the interface to the object you have created.

Linking the Interface to the Object

Return to Interface Builder by clicking one of its windows, clicking Interface Builder in the Dock, or selecting your nib file from the Interfaces in the project window.

As noted earlier in this chapter, the word *action* can refer to the method of an object that responds to a message. It can also refer to the message itself. Thus, the Beeper object has a method named beep. That method is an action. It will respond to a message named beep. That message, too, can be called an action. Linking the interface to the object requires dealing with the beep action in both senses of its meaning. This is all quite simple in practice. Just go through the following steps and you will see how it works. These steps become habitual as you develop objects and link them to the interface.

Linking the Menu to the Beeper Object

In the nib file window, make certain that the Beeper object is visible. Open the Main Menu object so that the menu bar is visible in its own window. Click the Sounds menu to open it. Then, holding down the CONTROL key, drag a line from the Beep menu command to the Beeper object, as shown in Figure 26-11.

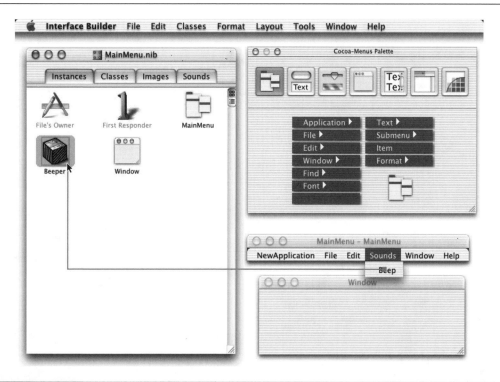

FIGURE 26-11   Connecting the menu to the Beeper object

Depending on where the objects are on your screen, the line may take different shapes. Don't worry about making it look like this line; just make certain that it runs from the menu command to the Beeper object.

Specifying the Connection

The Info window will open. It is shown in Figure 26-12. The target (which is the Beeper object) has only one action available—beep(). If you had declared other actions, they would appear here. Select beep() with a single click and click the Connect button at the bottom of the window. You will see the connection at the bottom of the window.

Testing

Test, test, test! Run the application from disk or use the Run button in Project Builder. In this case, there isn't much to test, and if this is your first Cocoa application, you'll probably make

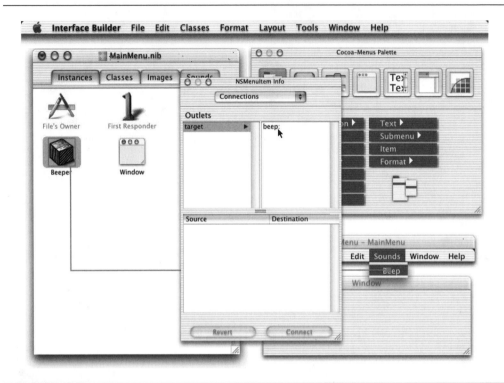

FIGURE 26-12   Info window for connections

yourself thoroughly unpopular by causing everyone within a wide radius to look and listen repeatedly at the program and its beep. (To be perfectly honest, a beeping computer is not considered by many people to be a great achievement; but creating a sophisticated user interface and application by writing only one line of code is.)

When you have your Nothing application complete, quit Project Builder and copy it to somewhere safe. Using the copy, experiment some more. Change the menu name; move the command around. Experiment. Test. Get comfortable with it all.

Adding Interface and Data Entry Elements to Nothing

Beeping is all very well and good, but a somewhat more sophisticated step-by-step process may help you develop more usable skills in using Project Builder and Interface Builder. This section shows you how to create a new window and add data entry fields to it. Specifically, you will create a window that performs one arithmetic calculation—division. There will be three fields: the numerator, the denominator, and the result. A button will perform the division.

When you have finished, you can modify this window to venture into the mysterious realms of addition, subtraction, multiplication, and other operations. In practical terms, this step-by-step guide shows you how to create a window that will allow users to enter any sort of data, will also allow them to process it with some kind of button, and will let you display dynamic data. You will write a single method, `divide`, to perform the calculation. However, you can insert any C or Java code into that method (and add any other necessary methods). This is the basic recipe.

As in the previous step-by-step example (as well as in all cases in which you add functionality to an application), these are the steps that you go through:

- You *declare* an object that will be able to carry out the action (Interface Builder).

- You *instantiate* that object (Interface Builder).

- You create an *interface element* that will request the action (Interface Builder).

- You *define* the class (Project Builder, using Objective-C or Java).

- You *link* the interface element to the declaration (Interface Builder).

- Finally, you *test, test, test* (Interface Builder and Project Builder).

The object that you will create will be called Calculator. It will have one method—divide. Remember that these steps can be done in many sequences. You must declare the Class in Interface Builder before defining its code in Project Builder, and you must create the interface elements before you link them. However, you can use any combination that appeals to you—declare, define, interface, link, test, for example. The sequence outlined here is identical to that shown in the previous section.

You can start by creating a new Cocoa project, or you can continue with the Nothing project that you have already created. In either case, open InterfaceBuilder by clicking MainMenu.nib.

Declaring the Object

In the nib file window, click the Classes tab and scroll to the top. Subclass either java.lang. Object or NSObject, depending on whether you want to write in Java or in Objective-C. (Select the appropriate object by clicking it once to select it, and then choose Subclass from the Classes menu.) Name this new class `Calculator`. (This is the same sequence of steps you used to create the Beeper class.) You need to add one action, `divide`, to this object. Repeating the steps from the first example, do so. (That is, with the new object still selected in the Classes list, choose Add Action from the Classes menu.)

In this case, you need three variables: `numerator`, `denominator`, and `result`. These three variables are used by the object, and they are also used in the interface (that is, they will appear in the Calculator window). They are called *outlets*. Create three outlets by choosing Create Outlet from the Classes menu three times. Rename the outlets and the action. Click each name and then type a new name: `denominator`, `numerator`, and `result`.

Remember, you can move on to Defining the Object now, if you want. You can come back to create the interface elements.

Creating the Interface Elements

You need to create a window, and then place data entry and results fields into it.

Creating the Window

Although you could use the window that was created automatically for you (Window), you can create a new window for the calculator. Do so by opening the palette and dragging the window icon into the nib file window Instances display, as shown in Figure 26-13. (Note that the window created for you still remains: either delete it by selecting it in the nib file and choosing Delete from the Edit menu or use it for some other purpose.)

If the Info window is not open, open it by using the Show Info command in the Tools window. With the window selected, the Info window will show its data. If necessary, use the pop-up menu at the top of the Info window to select the Attributes pane. If the Info window is not titled Window

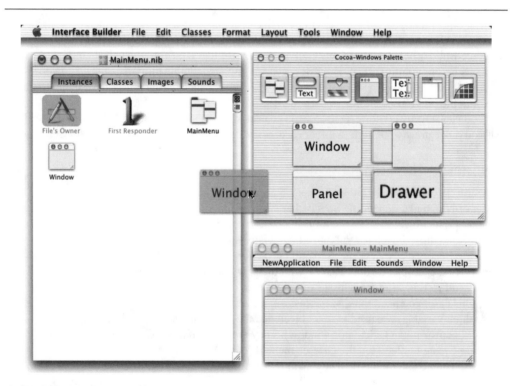

FIGURE 26-13   Creating a new window

Info, the wrong object is selected in the nib file window. Click the window that you just created. Change the window's name to Calculator by typing into the Title field. You can set other window attributes at this time using the Info window. You can also resize the window itself in Interface Builder; its size will be set automatically.

If you enter coordinates in the Info window, remember that the coordinate system for Cocoa windows has its origin, 0,0, at the lower left of the screen. On Classic Mac OS, the origin is at the upper left.

Creating the Fields

Next, you need to place the text fields into the window. Using the Cocoa palette, scroll the icons at the top until the view icons are visible. Drag the form, the group of two labeled fields, into the window you have created, as in Figure 26-14.

Similarly, drag the Informational Text field and the Button into the window as shown in Figure 26-15. As you can see in the figure, dotted guide lines appear when objects are placed appropriately according to Aqua guide lines.

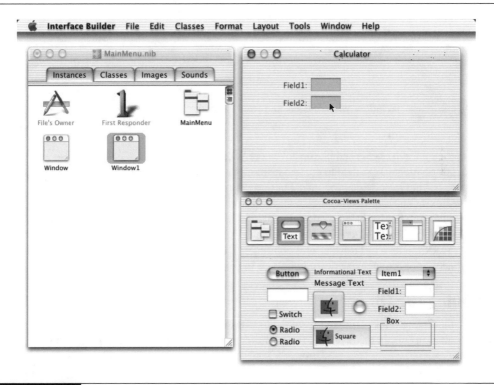

FIGURE 26-14   View icons in the Cocoa palette

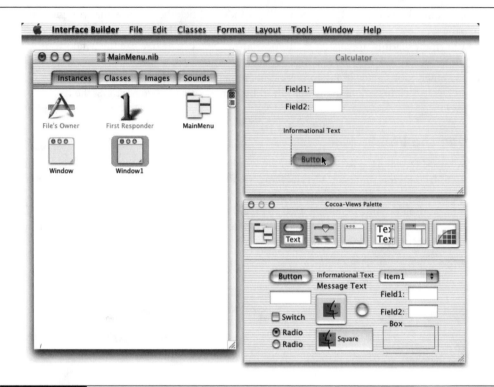

FIGURE 26-15   Window with buttons and fields added

You can place the fields and button anywhere you want in the window. You can also add another Informational Text field to contain instructions. Interface Builder contains the usual layout tools that you find in drawing programs. For that reason, you don't have to be too careful how you place the fields. You can use the Align command from the Layout menu to center the fields.

Rename each field or label by double-clicking it and typing a new name, as in Figure 26-16. Note that the field that will contain the result has had its name removed—you select the text and press RETURN to erase it ("Result" will be implied). Its font has been enlarged and changed to bold, which will become clear when you see it in action.

Defining the Object

Choose the Create Files command from the Classes menu to create the interface and implementation files in the project. Project Builder will open with the class definition shell

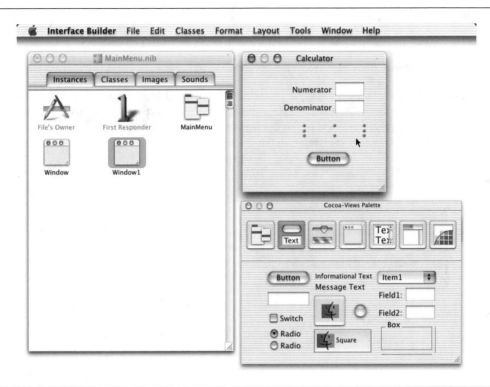

FIGURE 26-16 Renamed fields and button

selected. If not, switch to Project Builder by clicking the project browser or clicking its icon in the Dock.

Working in Java

The shell of the divide method of the Calculator class will look like this in Java:

```
public class divide {  Object numerator;
  Object denominator;
  Object result;
  public void divide (Object sender) {}
}
```

Make the following modifications:

■ Type the variables. Change Object to NSFormCell and NSTextField.

■ Add the line of code to perform the division.

For now, just make these changes. If you want to know what type to use for each data entry field, use the Info window. Click the interface element that you have moved from the palette to your interface; in the title bar at the top of the Info window, you will see its type.

The result is as follows (the changes in the code are bolded).

```
public class divide {
NSFormCell numerator;
NSFormCell denominator;
NSTextField result;
  public void divide (Object sender) {
  result.setFloatValue (numerator.floatValue()_
      / denominator.floatValue());}
}
```

Working in Objective-C

In Objective-C, the stubbed code written by Project Builder will look like this:

```
@implementation Calculator

- (void)divide: (id)sender
(id)numerator;
(id)denominator;
(id)result;
{
}
```

As before, type the variables and add the line of code to perform the division. The changes are bolded in the following code:

```
- (void)divide: (id)sender
(NSFormCell)numerator;
(NSFormCell)denominator;
(NSTextField)result;
{
  [result setFloatValue [numerator floatValue]_
      / [denominator floatValue]];
}
@end
```

Linking the Interface to the Object

Next, you link the interface elements to the instantiated object. There are three steps:

1. You need to create a Calculator object in the Instances display of the nib file window.

2. You need to open the window you have created with a menu command.

3. You need to link the window's button and fields to the object's action and outlets.

Creating the Calculator Object

Start by selecting the Calculator class in the Classes tab of the nib file window. Instantiate it with the Instantiate command in the Classes window and return to the Instances tab. (This is the identical procedure you followed with Beeper.)

Opening the Window with a Menu Command

Add a menu, Calculator, and a menu command, Show Calculator Window, to the application. This is exactly the same process you followed to add the Sounds menu with its Beep command.

You then connect the menu command to the window object that you have created. You want the window to be opened by the menu command. (In the Beeper example, you connected the menu command to the Beeper object. In both cases, the object to which you connect the menu command carries it out. The window opens, and the Beeper beeps.) You can connect the menu command to the window object in the nib file window, as in Figure 26-17.

If you prefer, you can connect the menu command to the window object itself. Drag the connection to the window's title bar. In either case, the Info will open (if it is not open already), and you will be able to select an action in the target, the window, for the menu item to perform. Choose `orderFront`.

You open windows with `orderFront`. You close them with `performClose`. The reason for doing so has to do with how windows are created and layered in the interface. You normally don't need to worry about it.

Connecting the Button and the Fields to an Action and Outlets

There are four connections to make here. The button needs to be connected to the Calculator's divide action, and the fields need to be connected to the Calculator's outlets. Once those connections are made, the interface (window, fields, and button) will be linked to the code in the object.

Connecting the Action   In the previous example, you connected a menu command to an object. You follow the same procedure here, except that you draw a connection (holding down the CONTROL key while moving the mouse) from the Divide button you placed in your window to the object.

Once again, you will need to select the action to perform. Choose `divide()` from the list at the right of the Info window. Remember to start drawing *from* the Divide button *to* the Calculator object. This process is shown in Figure 26-18.

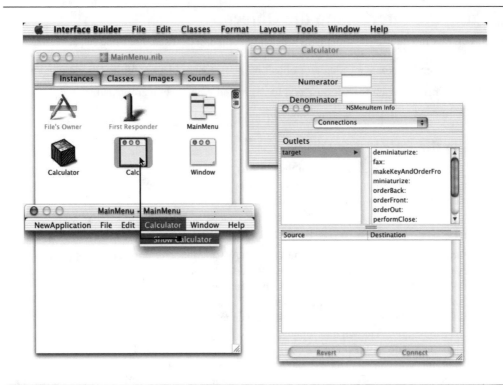

FIGURE 26-17   Connecting a menu command to an object

Connecting the Outlets   Finally, you connect the text fields to the outlets in the class declaration: the variables in the code that you have written. These connections are drawn in the reverse direction from actions. While holding down the CONTROL key, draw a connection from the Calculator object to one of the fields in the window. When you release the mouse button, you will see something like Figure 26-19. Remember to draw *from* the object *to* the fields in the interface.

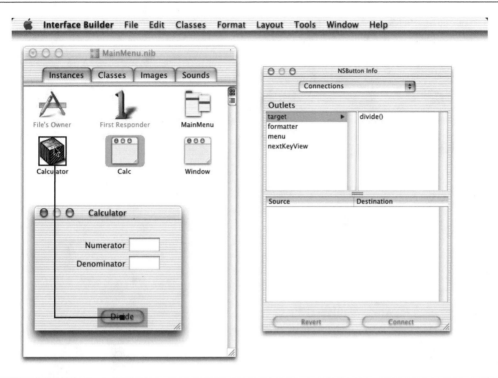

FIGURE 26-18   Connect the Divide button to the `divide` action.

Depending on which field you have chosen to release the mouse button in, you will need to select one or another of the outlets in the Info window. Click the Connect button to proceed. Next, connect the other outlets.

Testing

At this point, you have connected the interface fields to the outlets declared in the Calculator class. You have also connected the button in the interface to the Calculator's divide method.

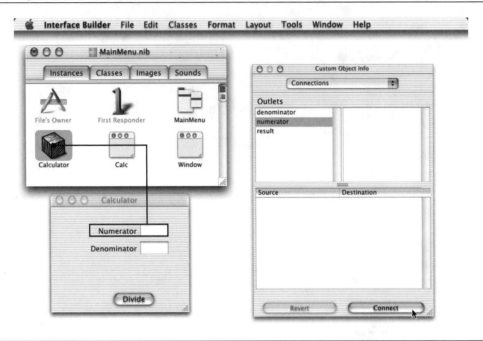

FIGURE 26-19 Connecting an outlet

Build the application and test it. You can test the interface from Interface Builder. However, if it does not work the way you think it should, return to Project Builder and rebuild the project. Some types of connections need to be built in Project Builder before they work in Interface Builder. Rather than worry about whether or not that is the case, just rebuild the application in Project Builder. The Calculator program in action is shown here:

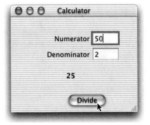

Continue to explore this little application. You can add another button to perform addition or multiplication. Instead, you can add a pop-up menu to select the operation to perform. In such a case, the button would be labeled Calculate.

This paradigm is the way in which you implement any existing functionality written in C or Java that performs calculations of any sort. You can use this shell to write any number of small Cocoa applications using existing code.

Don't try to learn all of the methods of all of the classes in the framework. Get a feel for how things work; then proceed to the next chapter and a more formal introduction to the frameworks and how to find out more about them.

Summary

This chapter has provided a high-level overview of how Project Builder and Interface Builder work. In the two walk-throughs of very simplistic projects, you have repeated the six basic steps of developing for Cocoa:

1. You *declare* an object that will be able to carry out the action (Interface Builder).

2. You *instantiate* an instance of the object (Interface Builder).

3. You create an *interface element* that will request the action (Interface Builder).

4. You *define* the class (Project Builder, using Objective-C or Java).

5. You *link* the interface element to the declaration (Interface Builder).

6. Finally, you *test, test, test* (Interface Builder and Project Builder).

You have a basic introduction to the important terminology of actions (which can refer to methods or messages), outlets (variables linked to the interface), and objects (instantiations of class declarations).

This only scratches the surface of Cocoa. However, this is enough to get started building some applications that can be very useful to you. The basics of using menus, entering and displaying data, and creating buttons in interface elements have been presented.

Part VI

Appendixes

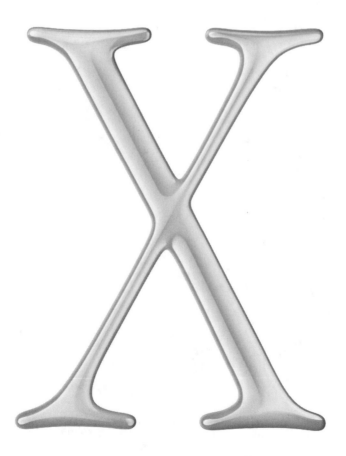

Appendix A

Installing Mac OS X

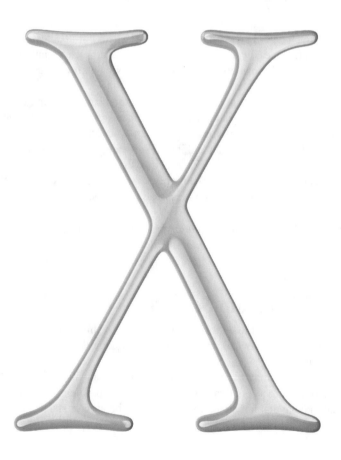

The easiest way to have Mac OS X installed on your computer is to buy a Macintosh computer: since mid-2001, all Macintosh computers have shipped with Mac OS X installed. There are four circumstances in which you may need to install Mac OS X: this appendix describes each of them:

- You may need to upgrade your already-installed Mac OS X software.

- You may need to install Mac OS X from scratch on a new disk or a reformatted disk.

- You may need to re-install Mac OS X if the software has become corrupted for some reason.

- You may want to upgrade a Mac OS 9 computer to Mac OS X.

Upgrading Mac OS X

This is the simplest case. If you have Mac OS X installed on your computer and you want to update it, use Software Updater in System Preferences to check for updates. As described in Chapter 6, "Setting Preferences," you can set Software Updater to check automatically for updates on a regular basis. You can also click the Update Now button to run it whenever you choose.

Software Updater uses an Internet connection to communicate with Apple's file servers; you need to be connected to the Internet to run it. Note that Software Updater may be used behind the scenes as part of Apple's routine upgrades to Mac OS X: when you run an updater, it will actually link to Apple to download and install software. This allows updates to your software to be distributed in very small packages, since the actual update software that you run merely initiates the connection to Apple. The highly modular structure of Mac OS X allows updates to be made easily without causing widespread problems.

NOTE   *In general, updates are relatively minor revisions and bug fixes. Upgrades are more substantial changes. For most vendors, updates to software are downloadable without charges; upgrades may involve a fee.*

Installing Mac OS X from Scratch

The only case in which you need to do this is if you have a freshly formatted hard disk. This is not the case when you buy a new computer: each new Macintosh is ready to run, with the operating system preinstalled.

A freshly formatted disk may be the result of installing a new disk (either internally or externally) or of reformatting a disk that has had very serious problems. (Reformatting a disk erases all of its data.) Note that not all external drives can be used as startup disks.

You need a Mac OS X installation CD-ROM to perform this task. First, restart from the installation CD-ROM. Do this by inserting the CD-ROM into the computer and restarting while holding down the C key. If you have only a freshly formatted hard disk, the only possible disk from which the computer can start up will be the CD-ROM. If you have other disks connected to your computer, they may contain operating systems, and the computer may start up from them unless you hold down the C key during startup.

When the computer has started up, you will see a variety of icons. Two or more will open documents with important information for you to read before installing the software. They may have names such as "Read Before You Install" and "Welcome to Mac OS X." It is a good idea to open these documents and read them. They are deliberately kept brief so that you will not have to spend a lot of time before you get to Mac OS X.

Other folders in this window have the names of various languages on them. If you want to install an English, Italian, Japanese or other version of Mac OS X, do not use these folders: the installation process will let you choose later on.

Double-click the Install Mac OS X icon to start the installation process. The first screen lets you choose the language of installation. Proceed through the process, answering each question. You will need to accept the software license agreement by clicking on it.

If you want to partition your hard disk, you can do so at this point. From the Installer menu, choose Open Disk Utility before continuing with the installation process. When Disk Utility opens, you can use it to partition your hard disk as described in Chapter 8, "Managing Your Computer Environment." (A common strategy is to partition the disk into one relatively small partition that can be used for emergency restarts: 1 gigabyte is sufficient. The rest of the disk is a single large partition.)

You will be prompted to select the disk or partition onto which you want to install Mac OS X. You will be notified if there is not enough room. In the case of a freshly formatted disk, this should not be the case. However, you may need to use Disk Utility to repartition the disk if you have not created a large enough partition.

Continue through the installation process as prompted. You will need to enter your name, your time zone, and other setup information. If you do not have any of this information, you can enter it later using the appropriate preferences as described in Chapter 6, "Setting Preferences." However, it is much better to set everything up at the beginning. If you do so, everything will be ready to run once the installation is complete.

If you use a DHCP router (either on a local area network or at your Internet service provider via a DSL or cable connection), you do not need any IP addresses. Otherwise, you will need the addresses of your DNS servers, as well as of your Internet service provider.

Under all circumstances, you will need the names of your incoming and outgoing e-mail servers; you also will need your account ID and password. If you do not have these accounts, the installation process will walk you through the process of opening an iTools email account with Apple. Thus, you may not need to collect any information whatsoever if you want to use a mac.com email address.

Although it is not necessary for your computer to be connected to the Internet during installation, if you will be using a local area network, it is a good idea for you to be connected to that network during installation: that way, the Installer can locate shared devices such as printers.

Installing Mac OS X from Scratch

Allow 30–60 minutes for a complete installation. It will not take that long, but you will not be rushed if you have the time set aside.

Reinstalling Mac OS X

If you have Mac OS X installed, you can reinstall it at any time. Restart from the installation CD-ROM by holding down the C key while you restart. Proceed as in the previous section; the Installer will skip over any items that do not need reinstallation.

If you are having problems with your computer, back up all of your files; be particularly careful about backing up the contents of your Applications, Library, and Users folders of your hard disk. This is where your data files, applications, and preferences will be stored.

After your reinstallation, if your computer is still behaving strangely, you may need to reformat your hard disk. With everything backed up, you should not have qualms about doing so. Reformat the hard disk and install from scratch as in the previous section. Then, copy the entire contents of your Users folder back. Copy those files in Applications and Library that have not been installed automatically. (In general, these will be the third-party products that you have installed. New versions of Apple software such as Disk Utility or Preview may have been installed; you should leave them there.)

Some people are eager to reformat their hard disk at the slightest sign of trouble. This usually does solve problems, but it is an extreme solution. Almost always a less drastic remedy is available. Service providers can typically back up data, reformat a hard disk, and reinstall the latest software for $100–$200. When you factor in the value of your own time and of the data that you may accidentally lose or corrupt, this is often a good investment.

Of course, an even better investment is a good preventive maintenance process involving automated backups such as Retrospect from Dantz (http://www.dantz.com). Once you know that everything is regularly backed up to an external FireWire drive or to tape cartridges or CD or DVD discs, you will sleep much more soundly.

Upgrading from Mac OS 9

The final situation involving an installation of Mac OS X is that in which you have a relatively recent Macintosh computer that is able to run Mac OS X but that has Mac OS 9 installed.

First, make certain that everything is backed up. The installation process normally runs smoothly, but you must assume that it could corrupt all of your files. An operating system upgrade is a good time to do a serious backup. Although you can do both yourself, many people couple the backup and the upgrade together and have an Apple Authorized Service Center do them both at the same time. According to Mark Bogossian of Castle Computers in Latham, NY, "We can back up the data on your hard drive and burn it to a CD-ROM (or multiple CDs if necessary). This will leave you with a permanent backup of the data that can be used during the installation process and again later if ever necessary. This will cost $100–$200, depending upon the amount of data on your drive." (The cost of Mac OS X itself is separate.)

Next, check that your computer will run Mac OS X. If it is running Mac OS 7, it will not. If it is running a version of Mac OS 8, it may. The Apple Mac OS X site will show you which computers can run Mac OS X.

If you want to continue running your Mac OS 9 applications in the Mac OS X Classic environment, you will need to upgrade to Mac OS 9.1 or later if you have not already done so. Perform this upgrade first.

Remember that you need not run the Classic Mac OS environment under Mac OS X. You can set the startup disk to your version of Mac OS 9 and restart under it; you can then change your startup disk to Mac OS X and restart again as needed. You will need to do this if you have to access a serial port, since Mac OS X does not support serial ports in any manner (even in the Classic Mac OS environment).

If you are planning to use the Classic Mac OS environment under Mac OS X, make certain that your critical software runs properly before you start to install Mac OS X. There is no magic in the Mac OS X installation process that will fix preexisting problems with Mac OS 9 installations.

Next, you must decide how to install Mac OS X. You have two choices:

- ■ You can install Mac OS X on the same disk or disk partition as Mac OS 9.1.

- ■ You can install Mac OS X on a separate disk or partition.

Once you have installed Mac OS X, you can use the ClassicMac OS preferences to set the version of Mac OS 9 that you use; thus, you can set your preference to use either a Mac OS 9 System Folder on the same or a different disk.

The argument in favor of installing Mac OS X and Mac OS 9 on separate disks and partitions is that you will keep everything separate. When they are installed on the same partition, you will see your Mac OS X folders (such as Applications) next to your old Mac OS 9 folders. In general, installing Mac OS X adjacent to Mac OS 9 on the same disk or partition seems to work well for many people.

Once you have decided where to install Mac OS X, run the Installer as described in the first section.

Upgrading from Mac OS 9

Appendix B

Glossary of Terms

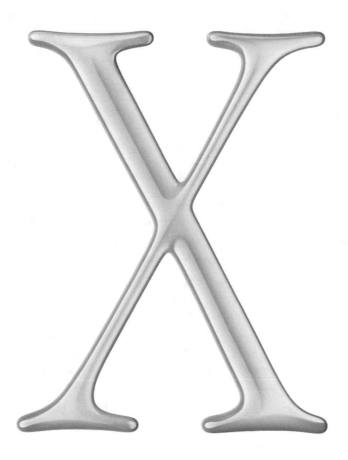

This glossary provides brief definitions of some common terms used in this book. Use the index to find references to major topics in Mac OS X. This glossary relies extensively on *Apple Publications Style Guide* and on "Mac OS X Terminology Guidelines" (Appendix B) of *Aqua Human Interface Guidelines*. Both are available for download from http://www.apple.com/. Search for their titles.

administrator   The user who has privileges to administer the computer. There can be more than one user with these privileges. Administrator users can create new users. Administrators can also set privileges for documents and folders.

always-on Internet   Connections such as DSL or cable that do not require dial-up access and that are available whenever the computer is turned on.

Apple Desktop Bus (ADB)   No longer manufactured, this was the mechanism for connecting the keyboard and mouse to the computer. It has been replaced by USB.

Apple key   Located next to the space bar on most keyboards, this key has the Apple logo and a cloverleaf or propeller image. It is the COMMAND key.

application   A program you use, such as Preview, Disk Copy, or AppleWorks. Note that in mainframe environments, "application" frequently refers to a process such as payroll that is carried out by a variety of programs and databases.

bit   A single on/off value. Bits are used to measure communication speeds (as in bps—bits per second). A kilobit (Kbit) is 1,000 bits; a gigabit (Gbit) is 1,000,000.

boot   The process of starting or restarting your computer. During the boot process, operating system software is initiated and network connections are established. Startup and restart are more commonly used.

byte   Eight bits, which is the amount of storage needed to store a single character in the Roman alphabet. Memory is measured in bytes (as in MB or GB—megabytes and gigabytes).

cable modem   An always-on modem, frequently provided by a cable company, to which you connect a router or your computer using an RJ-45 connector.

CD-ROM   Discs that are used to distribute software. CD-R discs can be written to once; CD-RW discs can be written to repeatedly. CD-ROM drives normally read these discs; you need CD-RW drives to write (or "burn") discs.

Chooser   A component of Mac OS 9 and earlier that let you choose printers and networked computers to use. When running the Classic Mac OS environment under Mac OS X, you may need to use the Chooser from the Apple menu in the Classic Mac OS environment to select a printer.

Classic   Applications written for Mac OS 9 and earlier. The Classic Mac OS environment runs on Mac OS X, and these applications run within it.

Clipboard   When you copy or cut material from a document, it is placed in the Clipboard. You can show the Clipboard from the Edit menu of the Finder, thus viewing material that is in transit from one application to another into which you will paste it.

COMMAND key   The key next to the SPACEBAR with the Apple logo and a propeller/cloverleaf pattern on it. It is a modifier key.

control panel   Small applications on Mac OS 9 or earlier that let you control volume, display resolution, and the like. Control panels are located in the Control Panel folder of the Classic Mac OS Apple menu. Most are not used on Mac OS X, although in the ClassicMac OS environment you may still need to use some of them. In particular, the Startup Disk control panel is used when you have started up from Mac OS 9 and then reset your startup disk to start up from Mac OS X. Settings such as these are set using System Preferences on Mac OS X.

dialog   A small window that provides information or asks for information (or both). On Mac OS 9 and earlier, dialogs often required action before you could continue with an application. On Mac OS X, sheets perform this task; they immobilize a single window.

directory   A subdivision of a disk or partition in which other directories and files are placed. Directories help you organize your hard disk. Macintosh usage prefers "folder" as a synonym to "directory."

document   An individual file that is not an application. Documents contain your data and information; they may also contain operating system and application preferences.

drag   When you select an item, you can hold the mouse button down and drag the item to another location. This can be a folder or document in the Finder, an object in a drawing application, or some selected text in a word processor. Note that dragging only starts after an item is selected. Thus, you must first click or otherwise select the item.

DSL   Digital subscriber line. An always-on, high-speed Internet connection that can be used over existing telephone cabling in many cases.

DVD   Similar to CD-ROM discs, DVD discs have much higher storage capacities; they are used for data, music, and video.

extensions   Small software components on Mac OS 9 and earlier that are loaded at startup to enhance or modify basic operating system features. They are loaded during startup of the Classic Mac OS environment, but they are not used in Mac OS X. (Extensions contributed to a lack of stability in Mac OS 9 and earlier in many cases.)

Extensions Manager   A Classic Mac OS application you can use to select sets of extensions to be loaded at startup. If you have problems launching the Classic Mac OS environment, use the Classic Mac OS preferences to turn off all extensions. Thereafter, use Extensions Manager to gradually reenable extensions until you find those that have caused problems.

Glossary of Terms

file   Any file that exists on your computer. Directories are a special kind of file. On the Macintosh computer, "document" is preferred to "file."

folder   A folder can contain documents or subfolders. "Folder" is preferred to "directory."

Gbit   Gigabit. 1,000,000 bits. Often a measurement of communication speed.

GB   Gigabyte. 1,000,000 bytes. Often a measurement of memory or disk space.

insertion point   A blinking vertical bar that indicates where the next text character you type will appear. You control the insertion point by typing, as well as by moving the mouse and clicking where you want it to appear. As you move the mouse, the pointer (not "cursor") moves on the screen.

Internet service provider (ISP)   A vendor who provides any Internet services. Typically an ISP provides you with access to the Internet; most ISPs also provide you with email. You may have additional vendors who provide you with Web site hosting, other email, and services including e-commerce and remote backups. Corporate and campus networks may serve as their own ISPs.

Mbit   Megabit. 1,000 bits. Often a measurement of communication speed.

MB   Megabyte. 1,000,000 bytes. Often a measurement of memory or disk space.

modifier key   You hold down a modifier key while you depress one or more other keys. Examples are the SHIFT, COMMAND, OPTION, and CONTROL keys. These modifier keys change the actions of the other keys that you press. (For example COMMAND-P chooses the Print command rather than typing a letter p.) Modifier keys can also be used with the mouse; for example, the COMMAND key allows you to click on a variety of objects and have them included in one selection.

mouse   The pointing device you use to control the pointer on the display. Trackpads and trackballs can also be used.

NeXT   A company founded by Steve Jobs which was bought by Apple in 1996. Originally a computer manufacturer, its operating system and object-oriented development environment became the basis of Mac OS X.

NeXTSTEP   The object-oriented framework that was created for NeXT computers.

OpenStep   When NeXT went out of the hardware business, NeXTSTEP was implemented on other hardware (including Intel-based processors). It was renamed OpenStep.

owner   The owner of a computer has administrator privileges and an administrator password. "Administrator" is preferred to "owner."

pane   A view within a window that may be controlled by tabs or a pop-up menu. Frequently a single window will have many panes that can be displayed within it. System Preferences illustrates the use of panes.

pasteboard   In NeXTSTEP and OpenStep, "pasteboard" was used to refer to the Clipboard.

PDA   Prima donna assoluta. Also, personal digital assistant (such as a Palm handheld device).

permissions   Controls over how individual users and groups of users can access documents and folders. Controlled from the Info window, permissions are applied to the owner, a group, and everyone else. They let people read and write, read only, write only, or have no access. Note that write-only is applicable only to folders, not documents; also, write access is needed to delete documents or folders. The term "privileges" is preferred to "permissions" in Mac OS X.

pointer   You use the mouse (or a trackball or trackpad) to move the pointer around the display.

privileges   Controls over how individual users and groups of users can access documents and folders. Controlled from the Info window, privileges are applied to the owner, a group, and everyone else. They let people read and write, read only, write only, or have no access. Note that write-only is applicable only to folders, not documents; also, write access is needed to delete documents or folders. On some other operating systems, "privileges" are referred to as "permissions."

propeller key   Located next to the space bar, the COMMAND key has an Apple icon and a propeller/cloverleaf on it. It is a modifier key.

scrap   Programmers refer to the Clipboard as the scrap for historical reasons dating back to the original Macintosh operating system. The correct terminology for users is "Clipboard."

Unix   An operating system originally developed in 1969 at AT&T's Bell Laboratories. The Darwin core of Mac OS X is Unix-like. (See Part I, "Welcome to Mac OS X," for more about Unix and the Darwin core.)

Glossary of Terms

Appendix C

Glossary of Visual Objects

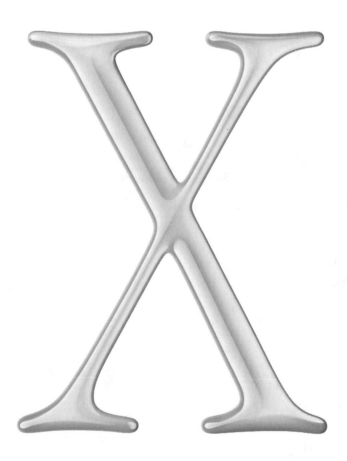

Note that some icons, particularly from third-party vendors, may not look exactly like these and may not adhere to the standards. A digital camera icon, for example, may appear as a removable disk (which it is, from the computer's point of view).

Disk Icons

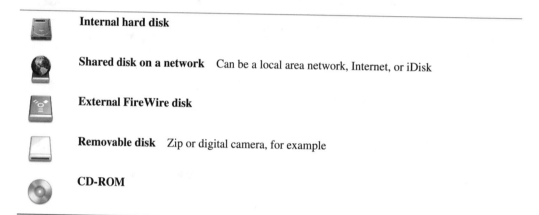

Internal hard disk

Shared disk on a network   Can be a local area network, Internet, or iDisk

External FireWire disk

Removable disk   Zip or digital camera, for example

CD-ROM

Network Icon

 Network icon   Through this icon, you can reach network services and other computers. Use the Finder's Go menu to mount networked disks such as those shown in the previous section; use this icon to access computers themselves.

Folder Icons

 Folder

Folders Within Your Home Directory

 Documents   Use this for your work. By default, most Mac OS X applications look for documents in this folder.

 Public folder   By default, this folder allows access to other users. Place documents you wish to share over the network here, and ask people to place documents for you here.

 Sites   Place your Web site HTML files in this folder.

 Library   Contains fonts, printers, and preferences for your applications

 Desktop   Contains the items on your desktop. (Yes, this is a folder, although it does not have a tab on it like a file folder.)

 Movies   Use this for Movie clips. iMovie looks here for movies.

 Music   Place music here. iTunes uses this folder.

 Pictures   Use this folder for still images. Image Capture works with this folder.

System Folders

 Mac OS X System folder   *Stay out of here.*

 Mac OS 9 System Folder   To install fonts or extensions for the Classic environment, drag them to this folder. They will be placed in the appropriate subfolders.

Folder Icons

Folder Privileges

 No access   You cannot read or write to this folder; you cannot examine its contents.

 Write-only access   You can place items into this folder, but you cannot open it. A Drop Box folder within your Public folder is created for you. People can drop documents into it, but they cannot look at its other contents.

Application Icons

User Applications

User application icons typically reflect both the media they let you manipulate and the tools you use. They are diamond shaped, with the media tilting toward the left and the tool toward the right. Here are three examples:

 TextEdit   This word processing application is part of Mac OS X. The medium (paper) is represented tilted toward the left; the tool (a pencil) is represented tilted toward the right.

 Internet Connect   Manages dial-up connections to the Web. The medium (the Web) is represented by a telephone directory; the tool is represented by a telephone.

 Mail   Here, there is only a medium—email.

 Preview   The medium is graphic images; the tool is a magnifying glass. In both cases (the medium and the tool), the icon is suggestive rather than complete: you can use preview to do far more than look at photos through a magnifier.

Utilities

Utilities use very little color; they are normally grayscale icons. They simply represent the task they perform.

 Disk Copy

 Image Capture

 System Preferences

Assistants

Interactive assistants walk you through setup tasks. They all have a variation on a butler icon. Only one is shown here.

 Display Calibrator

Document Icons

 RTF (text and graphics) document

 TIF (image) document

Menu Keyboard Equivalents

Note the symbols at the right of each menu command that represent the COMMAND, OPTION, and SHIFT keys.

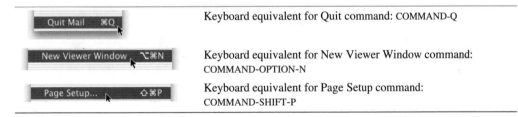

Keyboard equivalent for Quit command: COMMAND-Q

Keyboard equivalent for New Viewer Window command: COMMAND-OPTION-N

Keyboard equivalent for Page Setup command: COMMAND-SHIFT-P

Aliases

 Alias to a folder

 Alias to a document

Window Parts

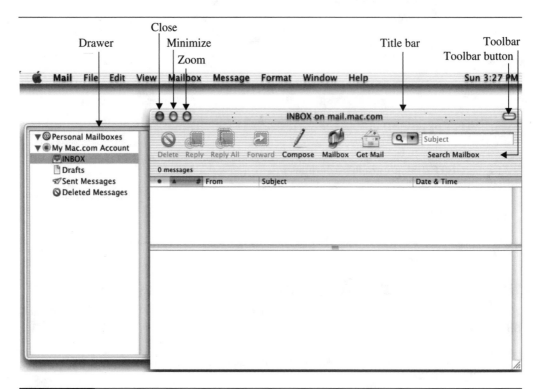

FIGURE C-1   Aqua windows and their controls are discussed in Chapter 2.

Index

M

INTERNATIONAL CONTACT INFORMATION

AUSTRALIA
McGraw-Hill Book Company Australia Pty.
Ltd.
TEL +61-2-9417-9899
FAX +61-2-9417-5687
http://www.mcgraw-hill.com.au
books-it_sydney@mcgraw-hill.com

CANADA
McGraw-Hill Ryerson Ltd.
TEL +905-430-5000
FAX +905-430-5020
http://www.mcgrawhill.ca

**GREECE, MIDDLE EAST,
NORTHERN AFRICA**
McGraw-Hill Hellas
TEL +30-1-656-0990-3-4
FAX +30-1-654-5525

MEXICO (Also serving Latin America)
McGraw-Hill Interamericana Editores S.A. de
C.V.
TEL +525-117-1583
FAX +525-117-1589
http://www.mcgraw-hill.com.mx
fernando_castellanos@mcgraw-hill.com

SINGAPORE (Serving Asia)
McGraw-Hill Book Company
TEL +65-863-1580
FAX +65-862-3354
http://www.mcgraw-hill.com.sg
mghasia@mcgraw-hill.com

SOUTH AFRICA
McGraw-Hill South Africa
TEL +27-11-622-7512
FAX +27-11-622-9045
robyn_swanepoel@mcgraw-hill.com

**UNITED KINGDOM & EUROPE
(Excluding Southern Europe)**
McGraw-Hill Education Europe
TEL +44-1-628-502500
FAX +44-1-628-770224
http://www.mcgraw-hill.co.uk
computing_neurope@mcgraw-hill.com

ALL OTHER INQUIRIES Contact:
Osborne/McGraw-Hill
TEL +1-510-549-6600
FAX +1-510-883-7600
http://www.osborne.com
omg_international@mcgraw-hill.com